Wei Gao
School of ECE
Peking University
Shenzhen, China

Ge Li
School of ECE
Peking University
Shenzhen, China

ISBN 978-981-97-9569-7 ISBN 978-981-97-9570-3 (eBook)
https://doi.org/10.1007/978-981-97-9570-3

This Springer imprint is published by the registered company Springer Nature Singapore Pte Ltd.
The registered company address is: 152 Beach Road, #21-01/04 Gateway East, Singapore 189721, Singapore

Wei Gao • Ge Li

Deep Learning for 3D Point Clouds

Springer

Deep Learning for 3D Point Clouds

Preface

The last decade has witnessed the great success of deep learning theories, methods, and applications in almost all science and engineering fields. As is implied by the name, deep learning leverages the powerful capability of deep neural networks as machine learning models to fulfill complex prediction, understanding, and decision problems, as long as there are large-scale datasets and sufficient computing power. For computer vision tasks, people are now not satisfied with 2D images any more, and in these circumstances, 3D modeling capability from 3D point clouds becomes much more important and popular. For 3D human and machine perception, 3D point clouds can provide the immersive visual experience and the high-precision 3D modeling for 3D objects, indoor and outdoor scenes. Moreover, recently large language model (LLM) and Multi-modal LLM have been extensively investigated, and 3D pre-trained models and 3D large models are expected to bring new opportunities to reshape the world, especially by the means of embodied AI.

Consisting of 11 chapters, this book focuses on the deep learning-based point cloud technologies, and seeks to provide readers with an in-depth understanding of point cloud processing methods in a textbook manner, including enhancement, analysis, pre-trained models and large models, multi-modal large models, open source projects, and engineering applications, etc. This book puts an emphasis on the perspectives of deep learning, 3D human and machine perception, and large models. The detailed chapters are organized as follows:

Chapter 1 presents an overview of the 3D world representation with point clouds, including representative datasets, processing tasks, and applications.

Chapter 2 introduces the fundamental background knowledge of deep learning, and several basic deep neural networks for point cloud tasks.

Chapters 3 and 4 demonstrate the deep learning-based point cloud enhancement principles and methods, including upsampling, downsampling, frame interpolation, completion, and denoising.

Chapters 5 and 6 delve into the deep learning-based point cloud analysis principles and methods, including classification and segmentation, object detection, tracking, retrieval, registration, and multimodal analysis.

Chapter 7 illustrates the point cloud pre-trained models and large models, including the fundamental principles, and point cloud-based pre-trained models and large models.

Chapter 8 presents the point cloud-language multi-modal learning methods, including large language modeling in natural language processing, 2D vision-language models, 2D vision-language multi-modal large language models, 3D point cloud multi-modal large language models, and 3D embodied intelligence.

Chapter 9 outlines the point cloud open source projects. This chapter starts with an introduction to the open source culture and community, and then presents the open source works in two aspects, including point cloud processing and analysis algorithms.

Chapter 10 discusses the typical engineering applications of point cloud technologies, which introduces and analyzes the application status quo of point cloud technologies in autonomous driving, reverse engineering, robotics, topographic mapping, digital twin cities, medical analysis, digital museum, etc.

Chapter 11 concludes the future works for various point cloud technologies, including deep learning-based enhancement, deep learning-based analysis, large models, open source projects, and the point cloud applications.

This book presents the fundamental knowledge and recent advances in deep learning-based point cloud technologies. As a textbook on 3D point cloud compression technologies, this book comprises the above selected chapters. Through the progressive presentation, readers can comprehensively understand and master the basic knowledge, the main techniques, and the development trends in deep learning-based point cloud processing tasks. We hope you enjoy this book and join the growing community of point cloud learning enthusiasts.

Shenzhen, China

Wei Gao
Ge Li

Acknowledgments

We are very fortunate to have worked with many colleagues, collaborators, and graduate students, and are very grateful for their collaborations and efforts to complete this book. Without their significant technical contributions, this book would have not evolved into its current form.

The technical chapters and some of the research works presented in this book were developed in collaboration with our students and colleagues at Peking University. Particularly, we would like to thank Shunzhou Wang, Songlin Fan, Wang Liu, Bowen Qu, Xijing Lu, Wenxu Gao, Shuqing Luo, Xiaoyu Liang, Ruonan Zhang, Zhuangzi Li, and Zhiyi Pan for their considerable efforts. Our postdocs and graduate students also helped edit this book, and spent much time in proofreading and figure drawing, including Shunzhou Wang, Jingxuan Su, Zhaojian Yao, Jilong Wang, Hang Yuan, Songlin Fan, Wenxu Gao, Wang Liu, Shangkun Sun, Huiming Zheng, Liang Xie, Xingming Mu, Yuan Li, Bowen Qu, Zhuozhen Yu, Haohui Liu, Kaiyu Zheng, Chenhao Zhang, Shuqing Luo, Yao Li, Haoruo Liu, Xiaoyu Liang, Yuqi Ye, Kangli Wang, Changhao Peng, and Shihao Li.

We would like to express our special thanks to Prof. Wen Gao (Peking University) for his advice, support, and help to our work, and the first-class academic environment and working conditions he provided, making us better focus on the research of point cloud technologies and achieve progress.

We also would like to thank many colleagues for working together to promote the point cloud research and its standardization efforts in the Audio Video coding Standard (AVS) Workgroup of China, including Dr. Huifang Sun, Dr. Shan Liu (Tencent), Dr. Xiaozhen Zheng (Dajiang Innovation Technology), Dr. Lu Yu (Zhejiang University), Dr. Wen Gao (Tencent), Dr. Xiaozhong Xu (Tencent), Dr. Fan Liang (Sun Yat-sen University), Dr. Yiling Xu (Shanghai Jiao Tong University), Dr. Siwei Ma (Peking University), Dr. Ronggang Wang (Peking University), Dr. Tiejun Huang (Peking University), Dr. Yun He (Tsinghua University), Dr. Feng Wu (University of Science and Technology of China), Dr. Sam Kwong (Lingnan University, Hong Kong), Dr. Weisi Lin (Nanyang Technological University, Singapore), and Dr. Zhu Li (University of Missouri, Kansas City, USA).

We are also very grateful to the Springer Nature team for helping us create this book.

Contents

Acronyms

3D	Three-Dimensional
3DCNN	Three-Dimensional Convolutional Neural Network
AI	Artificial Intelligence
AIGC	Artificial Intelligence Generated Content
BCE	Binary Cross-Entropy
BERT	Bidirectional Encoder Representations from Transformers
BLIP	Bootstrapping Language-Image Pre-training
CAD	Computer-Aided Design
CD	Chamfer Distance
CLIP	Contrastive Vision-Language Pre-training
CNN	Convolutional Neural Network
CUDA	Compute Unified Device Architecture
DGCNN	Dynamic Graph Convolutional Neural Network
EMD	Earth Mover's Distance
EdgeConv	Edge Convolution
FD	FiDelity
FN	False Negative
FP	False Positive
FPS	Farthest Point Sampling
GAN	Generative Adversarial Network
GDN	Generalized Divisive Normalization
GNN	Graph Neural Network
GPT	Generative Pre-training Transformer
GeM	Generalized-Mean pooling
HD	Hausdorff Distance
HVS	Human Visual System
IDIS	Inverse Density Importance Sampling
ITC	Image-Text Contrastive Loss
ITM	Image-Text Matching Loss
InfoNCE	Information Noise-Contrastive Estimation
IoU	Intersection over Union

KITTI	Karlsruhe Institute of Technology and Toyota Technological Institute Dataset
KL	Kullback-Leibler
KNN	K-Nearest Neighbors
LiDAR	Light Laser Detection and Ranging
LLM	Large Language Models
MAE	Masked Autoencoders
MLLM	Multi-Modal Large Language Models
MLP	Multi-layer Perception
MMD	Minimal Matching Distance
MSE	Mean Square Error
NLP	Natural Language Processing
OA	Open Access
PDS	Poisson Disk Sampling
PE	Position Embedding
PSNR	Peak Signal-to-Noise Ratio
RDP	Relative Direction Prompts
RE	Rotation Error
RLHF	Reinforcement Learning via Human Feedback
RNN	Recurrent Neural Networks
RPN	Region Proposal Network
RS	Random Sampling
RSS	Random Seed Sampling
rmseP	Root Mean Square Error of Projection
rmseT	Root Mean Square Error of Transformation
S3DIS	Stanford 3D Indoor Scene Dataset
SFT	Supervised Fine-Tuning
SGD	Stochastic Gradient Descent
SPU	Semantic Point Cloud Upsampling
STN	Spatial Transform Network
TE	Translation Error
TN	True Negative
TOF	Time of Flight
TP	True Positive
UAV	Unmanned Aerial Vehicles
VLP	Vision-and-Language Pre-training
VQA	Visual Question Answering
ViT	Vision Transformer

Chapter 1
Introduction to 3D Point Clouds: Datasets and Perception

Abstract Point cloud is a highly sought-after form of 3D data representation that has ignited a surge in multimedia research over the years. Given its ability to accurately capture the geometry of the real world, point clouds have become indispensable for various applications such as immersive media and 3D reconstruction. As such, it is imperative to develop advanced point cloud processing algorithms that can meet the ever-growing demands of these applications. This chapter provides a comprehensive overview of deep learning-based point cloud processing technologies. This chapter begins with an introduction to 3D world representation, then turns to the 3D reconstruction based on point clouds, covering the definition, properties, categorization, and different acquisition techniques. Subsequently, the discussion delves into the benchmark datasets commonly employed by the research community to enhance the processing and understanding of point cloud data. The discussion then shifts the focus toward various 3D perception tasks involved in point cloud processing and their application fields. This chapter equips readers with the necessary foundations to delve deeper into the subsequent chapters of the book.

Keywords Point cloud properties · Point cloud datasets · Point cloud processing · 3D visual representation · 3D perception · Deep learning

1.1 Representation of 3D Visual Data

Unlike 2D images and videos [1–3], 3D visual data are usually considered as a data presentation type beyond 2D, which uses different types of acquisition devices to capture 3D information, e.g., Light Detection and Ranging (LiDAR) and light field cameras. These devices differ from traditional pinhole cameras. Meanwhile, 3D data generally do not always refer to the data described in 3D space but to the data implicitly or explicitly from the extra information, e.g., the geometrical information or the depth map. Therefore, this section reviews the most frequently used categories of implicit and explicit 3D data representations, including multi-view images, RGB-D images, light fields, voxels, point clouds, and meshes, as shown in Fig. 1.1.

W. Gao, G. Li, *Deep Learning for 3D Point Clouds*,
https://doi.org/10.1007/978-981-97-9570-3_1

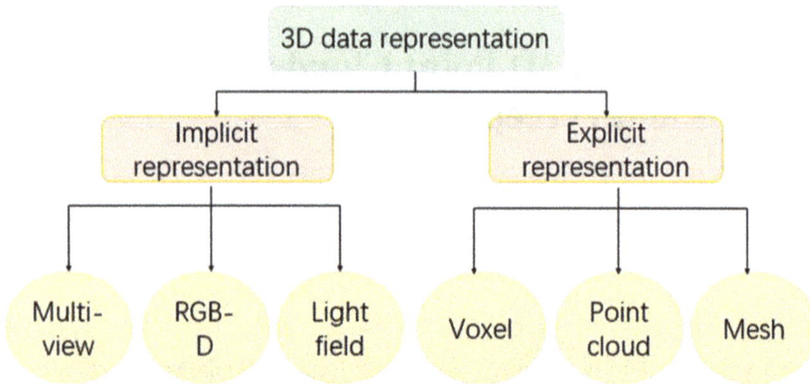

Fig. 1.1 Different 3D data representations (Source: Author)

Multi-view Images Multi-view images represent 3D scenes by capturing images from multiple viewpoints [4]. These viewpoints can be either real scenes from camera capturing simultaneously or virtual views generated through computer graphics techniques. By combining the images from different viewpoints, a more comprehensive representation of the 3D scene can be obtained.

RGB-D Images RGB-D images consist of an RGB image and a depth map [5–7]. The RGB image provides color information, while the depth map gives distance information. RGB-D images are typically captured using depth-sensing devices, such as structured light cameras or time-of-flight cameras. They can associate the depth values with the corresponding color information.

Light Fields Light fields describe the amount of light flowing in every direction through every point. The light ray can be given by a five-dimensional plenoptic function (x, y, z, θ, ϕ), where x, y, z represent the spatial coordinates of the human eye in 3D space, and θ, ϕ represent the horizontal and vertical angles of the incoming light [8–16].

Voxels: Voxels represent a 3D space as a grid of 3D pixels. Each voxel can store various attributes such as color, transparency, or material properties. They are often used in volumetric imaging and rendering.

Point Clouds Point clouds refer to a collection of 3D points in space, where each point represents a specific location and potentially additional attributes such as color, reflectance or intensity [17–76]. They are often obtained through laser scanners or depth cameras.

Meshes Meshes represent 3D surfaces as a collection of interconnected vertices, edges, and faces. Each vertex defines a point in 3D space, while edges and faces define the shape and topology of the surface.

1.2 Data Format and Acquisition of Point Clouds

1.2.1 *Definition of Point Clouds*

3D reconstruction of the physical world is a critical research topic in computer vision, playing an indispensable role in real-world application scenarios such as autonomous driving and topographic mapping. More and more researchers have carried out in-depth research on 3D data representation, and point cloud data are the most concerned one. The future prospects for 3D world reconstruction based on point clouds are highly promising.

Point clouds refer to a set of discrete sample points that represent surfaces within a 3D space. These points are obtained through data acquisition equipment and contain geometric information, such as the coordinates (x, y, and z) in 3D space. Additionally, point clouds may include optional attributes like normal vectors, intensity, color, and reflectance. Point clouds serve as digital representations of the 3D world, enabling the depiction of object surfaces and the accurate representation of their properties. Processing point cloud data to fulfill diverse practical needs is a fundamental aspect of point cloud technologies.

1.2.2 *Properties of Point Clouds*

Point cloud is a common representation format of 3D objects. Other representations include point, voxel, and mesh. A comparison among them is shown in Fig. 1.2. Compared with the traditional 2D image data, the information capacity of 3D point cloud is richer, and its depiction of spatial structure is closer to actual human perception. However, the disordered and irregular properties of point clouds bring great challenges for developing point cloud processing technologies.

Fig. 1.2 Comparison among common 3D object representations, including point cloud, mesh and voxel (From left to right). Public domain open access image (https://tianchi.aliyun.com/forum/post/77470)

Disorder Point cloud is a data collection and should be insensitive to the order of the data. This means that the model that processes point cloud data needs to be invariant to different data arrangements. This property makes the processing of point clouds very different from images. For the spatially distributed point cloud data, there is no regular unit similar to the image pixel, and the spatial correlation of point cloud is difficult to exploit, which leads to directly applying traditional CNNs on it in a fix. Among all solutions for the disordering of point clouds, symmetric functions based on max pooling operations are widely used in common point cloud processing networks.

Spatial Relationship Among Points An object usually consists of a certain number of point clouds in a specific space, which means there is a spatial relationship among these point clouds. Usually, point cloud processing networks use local features and global feature aggregation methods to process spatial relationships. It suggests that the information about the position of a point in 3D space and its surrounding points are meaningful.

Immutability The objects represented by point cloud data should be invariant to certain spatial transformations, such as rotation and translation. It means that the object represented by the point cloud does not change with rigid transformation (including translation and rotation). For object-level point cloud data, the coordinate value normalization method is usually used to solve the translation invariance, and the data enhancement method is used to improve the rotation robustness.

1.2.3 Different Types of Point Clouds

Point clouds can be categorized into two types based on point density: sparse point clouds and dense point clouds. Generally, dense point clouds have a higher concentration of points per unit of measurement, while sparse point clouds have a lower density with a smaller number of points. For instance, The 3D models from Computer Aided Design (CAD), such as ModelNet40 [77], often consist of dense point clouds containing approximately 2,000 points per frame due to their limited bit width. These point clouds are typically generated rather than acquired through scanning or sensing techniques.

Point cloud data can also be classified based on their composition characteristics as organized point clouds and unorganized point clouds. Organized point clouds correspond to depth maps, where the order of points and the structure of their neighbors can be easily inferred from the depth information. On the other hand, unorganized point clouds are more commonly encountered and consist of a single stream of coordinates. The points in unorganized point clouds are spatially distributed and lack the structured grid characteristics found in organized point clouds.

Another way to categorize point clouds is based on their temporal aspect. Point clouds can be static or dynamic. Similar to 2D images and videos, a static point cloud represents a single frame of point cloud data. In contrast, a dynamic point cloud is a sequence of multiple point cloud frames, capturing changes or motions over time.

1.2.4 Acquisition of Point Clouds

There are generally two categories of the existing mainstream point cloud data acquisition devices, including laser scanners and depth cameras. This section begins with describing their working principles and representative devices and then performs parameter comparison and analysis of these solutions.

- **Laser Scanner**

A laser scanner works by using laser range for 3D visual reconstruction. A point can be modeled in 3D space by recording distance and orientation information. Specifically, a point cloud is acquired by sending out thousands of lasers simultaneously to collect thousands of points on the surface of an object. Therefore, the laser scanner can quickly obtain the 3D information of the object to be measured and complete the 3D visual reconstruction of the object. Laser scanners utilize laser ranging technology to reconstruct 3D visual models by capturing distance and orientation information of individual points. By simultaneously emitting thousands of lasers, a point cloud is generated from the surface of an object, allowing for rapid acquisition of its 3D data and completing visualization.

Laser scanners are widely used in reverse engineering and other practical applications [78, 79]. Depending on the deployment environment, laser scanners can be classified into satellite, terrestrial, airborne, mobile, and backpack laser scanners. There are some of the current representative laser scanning solutions: satellite platform like ICESat/GLAS of National Aeronautics and Space Administration (NASA),[1] Resource 3 No. 02 from China's earth observation satellites (ZY3-02);[2] terrestrial platform such as Surestar UT - 5000,[3] Leica ScanStation P50,[4] FARO Focus^{S} 70;[5] airborne platform like Riegl VUX-240[6] and Leica Chiroptera-5;[7] mobile platform including Velodyne Alpha Prime[8] and Hesai Pandar128E3X;[9] backpack platform, e.g., Kaarta STENCIL 2-16[10] and Beijing Green Valley Tech-

[1] icesat.gsfc.nasa.gov/icesat/glas.php

[2] data.tpdc.ac.cn/en/data/425297e3-6f99-40b6-b026-33c85b5b11ec

[3] www.isurestar.com/arm-101.html

[4] leica-geosystems.com/products/laser-scanners/scanners/leica-scanstation-p50

[5] www.faro.com/en/Products/Hardware/Focus-Laser-Scanners

[6] www.riegl.com/products/unmanned-scanning/riegl-vux-240

[7] leica-geosystems.com/products/airborne-systems/bathymetric-lidar-sensors/leica-chiroptera-5

[8] velodynelidar.com/products/alpha-prime

[9] www.hesaitech.com/zh/Pandar128

[10] www.kaarta.com/products/stencil-2-for-rapid-long-range-mobile-mapping

nology LiBackpack C50.[11] Table 1.1 compares the laser scanners, where the main parameters of these devices, including wavelength, maximum range, scan frequency, field angle, precision, and weight, are listed.

The application scenarios of different types of laser scanners are very different. For example, ZY3-02 is commonly used in ground control point measurement and satellite mapping. Surestar (UT-5000) can be used for topographic survey, engineering survey, deformation monitoring, and vegetation survey. Velodyne (Alpha Prime) is applied in autonomous driving, robot location and navigation, security monitoring, and other fields. These various laser scanners meet the needs of different applications in daily life.

- **Depth Camera**

Depth cameras play an important role in the field of 3D visual reconstruction. The depth cameras are capable of accurately depicting the 3D coordinates of the object through the additional depth information and the original 2D image information. The 3D modeling of the object can be carried out, and the point cloud data are acquired. According to the working principles, depth cameras are divided into structured light, Time of Flight (TOF), and binocular stereo depth cameras.

Structured Light Depth Camera A structured light depth camera consists of a camera and a projector. The projector projects structured light onto the object to be measured and then uses one or more infrared cameras to obtain the depth information of the object. There are two variants of structured light depth cameras, i.e., monocular IR + projected infrared dot matrix and binocular IR + projected infrared dot array. Both of them have their pros and cons. Binocular IR utilizes the principle of binocular stereo vision, which makes the measurement accuracy of depth information better than monocular. However, due to the complexity of the hardware system, the volume of the binocular IR device will be larger. Monocular IR is the other way around.

Representative products of structured light depth camera include Intel RealSense D415,[12] Orbbec Astra +,[13] Percipio.XYZ FM830-RI,[14] ASUS Xtion2,[15] MANTIS VISION F6 SMART,[16] Optonic Ensneso N35-606-16-BL,[17] PrimeSense Carmine 1.09,[18] Revopoint POP 2,[19] etc. At present, the mainstream structured light depth cameras on the market and their performance comparison are shown in Table 1.2.

---

[11] www.lidar360.com/archives/portfolio/libackpack-c50

[12] www.intelrealsense.com/depth-camera-d415/

[13] orbbec3d.com/index/Product/info.html?cate=38&id=9

[14] en.percipio.xyz/product-list

[15] www.asus.com/ch-en/networking-iot-servers/smart-home/security-camera/xtion-2

[16] mantis-vision.com/handheld-3d-scanners

[17] www.optonic.com/en/support/selector/model/?id=N35-606-16-BL

[18] xtionprolive.com/primesense-carmine-1.09

[19] www.revopoint3d.com/pop-3d-scanner-2/

Table 1.1 Parameters of various types of 3D laser scanning equipment. "-" means that the parameter is unknown, "@" means the measuring error at the specific distance, and "a + b" indicates the precision is a + b × D where D is the distance. The table shown is modified and updated with MPEG open access (OA) work under CC BY Licence (Copyright © 1988–2024, www.mpeg.org) [80]

Manufacturer and model	Wave length (/nm)	Maximum range (/km)	Maximum scan frequency (/Hz)	Field angle	Precision	Weight (/kg)
NASA ICESat/GLAS	532/1,064	600	40	0.5 mrad/0.16 mrad	-	300
ZY3-02	1,064	520	2	-	1 m	40
SureStar UT-5000	1,064	5	-	360° × 100°	5 mm @ 100 m	15.5
Leica ScanStation P50	1,550/658	>1	-	360° × 290°	3 mm + 10 ppm (>1 km mode) Angle measurement accuracy 8″	12.25
FARO Focus^S 70	1,550	0.07	97	360° × 300°	±1 mm	4.2
Riegl VUX-240	Near-infrared	1.2	-	75°	20 mm	4.1
Leica Chiroptera-5	515/1,064	-	140	53.8° × 41.8°	<1 cm	48
Velodyne Alpha Prime	905	0.3	20	360° × 40°	±3 cm	3.5
Hesai Pandar128E3X	905	0.2	20	360° × 40°	±2 cm	1.63
Kaarta STENCIL 2-16	-	0.1	10	360° × 30°	±30 mm	1.73
GreenValleyLiBackpack C50	-	0.1	-	360° × 30°	3 cm	7.1

Table 1.2 The specific parameters of various structured light depth cameras. "-" stands for unknown. "@" means the measuring error at the specific distance in the parameter Depth Accuracy, as well as the frame rate with video resolution in the parameter Depth Resolution and RGB Resolution (Source: Author)

Structured light	Depth field of view (FoV)	Depth range (/m)	Depth resolution	RGB resolution	Depth accuracy	Operating system and connection
Intel RealSense D415	65°(H) × 40°(V)	0.5–3	(1,280 × 720)@90 fps	(1,920 × 1,080)@30 fps	<2%@2 m	-
Orbbec Astra +	57°(H) × 45.2°(V) × 68.76°(D)	0.6–8	(640 × 480)@30 fps	(1,920 × 1,080)@30 fps	-	Android Linux Windows USB3.0 Type-C
Percipio.XYZ FM830-RI	56°(H) × 46°(V)	0.5–6	(1,280 × 9,60)@13 fps (640 × 480)@23 fps (320 × 240)@23 fps	(1,280 × 9,60)@12 fps (640 × 480)@24 fps (320 × 240)@24 fps	0.2–1% z: 2 mm@ 1 m x, y: 4 mm@ 1 m	Windows Linux Android ROS USB2.0
ASUS Xtion2	74°(H) × 52°(V) × 90°(D)	0.8–3.5	(640 × 480)@30 fps (320 × 240)@30 fps	(2,592 × 1,944)@30 fps	-	Windows 8/10 Linux Ubuntu 14.04 USB3.0
MANTIS VISION F6	20"(H) × 26"(V) (closest) 15"(H) × 20"(V) (farthest)	0.5–4.5	1/25"@8 fps	1.3 MPix@8 fps	500 micron	-
Optonic Ensneso N35-606-16-BL	58°(H) × 52°(V)	0.25–0.5	1,280 × 1,024@10 fps	1,280 × 1,024@10 fps	<0.2 mm@0.4 m	Gigabit ethernet
PrimeSense Carmine 1.09	54°(H) × 45°(V)	0.35–3	640 × 480)@60 fps	1,280× 960)@60 fps	<1 mm@0.5 m	USB2.0 USB3.0
Revopoint POP 2	-	0.15–0.4	(1,920 × 1,080)@10 fps	-	0.05 mm	Windows 8/10 iOS Android MAC Harmony Micro USB

Although there are many mature solutions for structured light depth cameras, the common basic working principle is to obtain depth value based on feature matching, which is easy to be interfered with by ambient light. As a result, the accuracy decreases quickly with the increase of ranging distance.

TOF Depth Camera TOF depth cameras acquire point cloud data based on the time of flight. Depending on the carrier type, TOF can be divided into two modulation modes, i.e., pulse modulation and continuous wave modulation. The carrier of pulse modulation is a rectangular pulse signal, while the carrier of continuous wave modulation is a continuous wave.

At present, the common TOF depth camera products of the mainstream manufacturers include MESA Swiss Ranger 4000,[20] PMD CamCube3.0,[21] SoftKinect DS311,[22] Azure Kinect DK,[23] LIPS LIPSedge™ DL,[24] VZense DCAM710,[25] Orbbec Femto,[26] and Basler blaze-101.[27] See Table 1.3 for detailed parameters and performance of TOF cameras.

Binocular Stereo Depth Camera The working principle of binocular stereo depth cameras is binocular stereo vision. That is, two cameras are used at different positions to obtain the image information of the object and calculate the corresponding parallax. According to the geometric relationship between depth and parallax in the 3D system, the depth information of the object can be calculated.

Representative products of binocular stereo depth cameras are Stereolabs ZED Mini/2/2i,[28] FLIR Bumblebee® 2/XB3,[29] Humanplus AI PSP010-800,[30] Rubedos VIPER0,[31] etc. See Table 1.4 for the configuration parameters of typical binocular stereo-depth cameras in the market.

In addition to structured light, TOF, and binocular stereo depth cameras, light field camera is also a kind of depth camera. Lytro Illum[32] is one of the representative light field camera products.

---

[20] www.mesa-imaging.ch

[21] www.pmdtec.com

[22] www.sony-depthsensing.com

[23] azure.microsoft.com/en-us/products/kinect-dk/

[24] www.lips-hci.com/lipsedge-dl-series

[25] www.vzense.com/RGBDToFProducts.html

[26] www.orbbec.com.cn/index/Product/info.html?cate=38&id=18

[27] www.baslerweb.com/cn/products/cameras/3d-cameras/basler-blaze/#cameras

[28] www.stereolabs.com/products

[29] www.flir.com/support/browse/camera-cores-amp-components/stereo-imaging-systems

[30] humanplustech.com/?list=51

[31] www.rubedos.com/solutions/viper

[32] raytrix.de

Table 1.3 The parameters of various TOF cameras. "-" represents unknown. "@" means the measuring error at the specific distance in the parameter Depth Accuracy, as well as the frame rate with video resolution in the parameter Depth Resolution and RGB Resolution (Source: Author)

TOF	Depth field of view (FoV)	Depth range (/m)	Depth resolution	RGB resolution	Depth accuracy	Operating system and connection
MESA swiss ranger 4000	43°(H) × 34°(V) (Standard) 69°(H) × 56°(V) (Wide)	0.1–5/0.1–10	(176 × 144)@50 fps	None	±10 mm/±15 mm	Windows XP/7 Vista Linux USB or fast ethernet
PMD CamCube3.0	40°(H) × 40°(V)	0.3–7	(200 × 200)@40 fps (176 × 144)@60 fps (160 × 120)@80 fps	None	<3 mm@4 m	-
SoftKinetic DS311	57.3°(H) × 42°(V) × 73.8°(D)	0.15–1/1.5–4.5	(160 × 120)@60 fps	(640 × 480)@60 fps	<3 cm@3 m	-
Azure Kinect DK	120°(H) × 120°(V) (Wide) 75°(H) × 65°(V) (Narrow)	0.25–2.21/0.5–3.86	(1,024 × 1,024)@15 fps (512 × 512)@30 fps (640 × 576)@30 fps	(3,840 × 2,160)@30 fps	-	Windows 10 USB3
LIPS LIPSedge DL	74.2°(H) × 58.1°(V)	0.2–1.2 (Near) 1–4 (Normal)	(320 × 240)@30 fps (640 × 480)@30 fps	(1,920 × 1,080)@30 fps	≤3	Windows 10 Ubuntu 16.04/18.04 LTS USB3.0 Micro-B
VZense DCAM710	69°(H) × 51°(V)	0.35–4.4	(640 × 480)@30 fps	(1,920 × 1,080)@30 fps	1%	Windows Linux Arm Linux ROS USB2.0
Orbbec Femto	64.6°(H) × 50.8°(V) × 78°(D)	0.2–5	(640 × 576)@5/10/15/30 fps	None	0.2%@1 m, 0.2%@5 m	Windows10 Ubuntu Android USB3.0 Tpye-C
Basler blaze-101	67°(H) × 51°(V)	0–10	(640 × 480)@30 fps	None	±5 mm	-

Table 1.4 The parameters of various binocular stereo depth cameras. "-" represents unknown. "@" means the measuring error at the specific distance in the parameter Depth Accuracy, as well as the frame rate with video resolution in the parameter Video Resolution (Source: Author)

Binocular stereo	Depth field of view (FoV)	Baseline (/cm)	Depth range (/m)	Video resolution	Depth accuracy	Operating system and connection
FLIR Bumblebee® 2	97°(H), 66°(H), or 43°(H)	12	-	Side by side 2× (648 × 488)@48 fps (1,032 × 776)@20 fps	-	-
FLIR Bumblebee® XB3	66°(H) or 43°(H)	12, 24	-	Side by side 2× (1,280 × 960)@16 fps	-	-
Stereolabs ZED Mini	90°(H) × 60°(V) × 110°(D)	6.3	0.10–15	Side by side 2× (2,208 × 1,242)@15 fps (1,920 × 1,080)@30 fps (1,280 × 720)@60 fps (672 × 376)@100 fps	<1.5% up to 3 m, <7% up to 15 m	
Stereolabs ZED 2/2i 2.1 mm	110°(H) × 70°(V) × 120°(D)	12	0.3–20	Side by side 2× (2,208 × 1,242)@15 fps (1,920 × 1,080)@30 fps (1,280 × 720)@60 fps (672 × 376)@100 fps	< 1% up to 3 m, <5% up to 15 m	Windows 10 Ubuntu 16.04/18.04 Debian, CentOS Jetson L4T USB 3.0/2.0
Humanplus AI PSP010-800	70°(H) × 50°(V)	16	1–30	Side by side 2× (1,280 × 8,00)@25 fps	<2% up to 10 m, <6% up to 30 m	Windows Linux USB3.0
Rubedos VIPER	70°(H) × 43°(V) × 82°(D)	20	<50	(1,280 × 720)@40 fps	-	Windows 10 Linux ROS Ethernet/TCP

1.3 Representative Datasets of Point Clouds

Point cloud datasets serve as the fundamental basis for further exploration of point cloud processing algorithms. To enhance the understanding of point cloud data, this section provides an overview of benchmark datasets in the field of point cloud processing, which are presented in Table 1.5. These highly representative datasets have been extensively studied by the research community.

1.3.1 ShapeNet

ShapeNet Core [81] is a synthetic dataset manually drawn with computer-aided design (CAD), which contains 55 common subjects in daily life. Each subject corresponds to a kind of object point cloud. The annotated models of "chair," "sofa," "car," and "vessel" are shown in Fig. 1.3. ShapeNet Core is a large-scale dataset with a total of 51,300 point cloud models. The ShapeNetPart [83] dataset is a subset of ShapeNet Core, containing only 16 unbalanced categories with semantic annotations. As for ShapeNetPart, the training/validation/test set contains 12,137, 1,870, and 2,874 samples, respectively. Since ShapeNetPart contains semantic information about point cloud parts, it is often used for visual tasks such as semantic segmentation.

Table 1.5 A brief summary of various point cloud datasets (Source: Author)

Dataset	Data source	Attributes	Category	Applications
ShapeNet	CAD models	RGB	Objects	Classification, segmentation
ModelNet40	CAD models	None	Objects	Classification, shape retrieval, compression
S3DIS	Depth cameras	RGB, surface Normals, semantic annotations	Indoor scenes	Semantic segmentation
KITTI	Laser scanner	Intensity	Outdoor scenes	3D object detection and tracking, compression
3DMatch	Depth cameras	RGB	Indoor scenes	3D registration
PCSOD	Depth cameras	RGB	Objects	Salient object detection

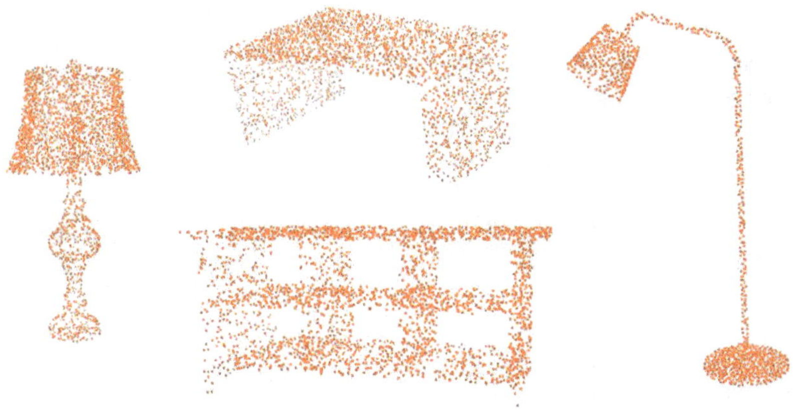

Fig. 1.3 Instances of ShapeNet dataset. The image shown is introduced with MPEG open access (OA) work under CC BY Licence (Copyright © 1988–2024, www.mpeg.org) [82]

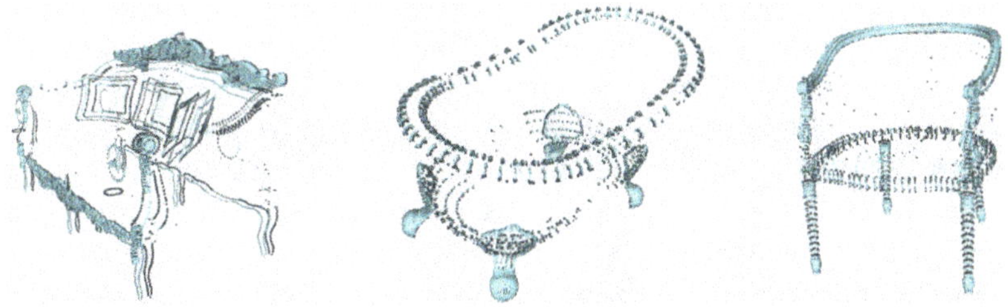

Fig. 1.4 Instances of ModelNet40 dataset. The image shown is introduced with MPEG open access (OA) work under CC BY Licence (Copyright © 1988–2024, www.mpeg.org) [84]

1.3.2 ModelNet40

Princeton University provided ModelNet40 [77], which is a set of 3D models generated by CAD, including 40 subjects, such as "airplane," "bookshelf," "curtain," and "range_hood". ModelNet40 consists of 12,311 samples, of which 9,843 are training data, and 2,468 are test data. The raw data format is mesh, and the 3D point cloud data can be acquired by point sampling of surface elements. ModelNet40 is one of the most common datasets in the field of point cloud processing, which is widely used in various analysis tasks such as point cloud classification. Figure 1.4 shows three models of ModelNet40, i.e., "sofa," "bathtub," and "chair."

Fig. 1.5 Instances of S3DIS dataset. The image shown is introduced with MPEG open access (OA) work under CC BY Licence (Copyright © 1988–2024, www.mpeg.org) [85]

1.3.3 S3DIS

As a typical dataset for semantic segmentation of point cloud data, Stanford 3D Indoor Segmentation (S3DIS) [85] comes from the Stanford 2D-3D Semantic dataset and is a subset of it. There are 13 categories in S3DIS, including "wall," "table," "bookshelf," "ceiling," etc. Each point of the point cloud has a semantic label, as shown in Fig. 1.5. The point clouds are scanned from 271 rooms in six different indoor environments. Each point in the resulting point cloud contains geometric information (3D geometric coordinates x, y, and z) and attribute information (RGB and normalized x, y, z). When using S3DIS, preprocessing is usually performed, where the point cloud is partitioned into square blocks with a side length of 1 meter, and then 4,096 points are sampled from each block for training.

1.3.4 KITTI

The KITTI dataset [86], currently the most important benchmark dataset in the field of autonomous driving, was created by the Karlsruhe Institute of Technology (KIT) in Germany and Toyota Technological Institute at Chicago (TTIC). KITTI provides multiple data types, such as 3D point clouds and depth images. Figure 1.6 shows some point cloud samples of KITTI. The dataset includes a large number of real-world driving scenarios, such as urban, rural, and highway. Moreover, it provides a variety of benchmarks for different visual tasks, including depth estimation, visual odometer, object detection, object tracking, road segmentation, and more. For example, KITTI provides 22 sequences for the visual odometer, half for training and the remaining half for testing. For the object detection task, KITTI provides 3,712 training samples, 3,769 validation samples, and 7,518 test samples, with a total of 80,256 annotations.

Fig. 1.6 Instances of KITTI dataset. The image shown is introduced with MPEG open access (OA) work under CC BY Licence (Copyright © 1988–2024, www.mpeg.org) [87]

Fig. 1.7 Instances of 3DMatch dataset. The image shown is introduced with MPEG open access (OA) work under CC BY Licence (Copyright © 1988–2024, www.mpeg.org) [88]

1.3.5 3DMatch

3DMatch [88] is an indoor scene dataset. Two instances are presented in Fig. 1.7. It is often used for point cloud geometry registration, key point matching, and other processing tasks. 3DMatch includes scene samples of datasets such as 7-scenes [89] and SUN3D [90]. The raw data of 3DMatch includes RGBD images, as well as data files of camera pose and intrinsic parameters. By fusing the RGB and depth images, the generated point cloud fragments are generally used in 3D point cloud processing tasks. There are 62 scenarios in the dataset, 54 for training and 8 for testing. These indoor scenes contain "stairs," "redkitchen," "study room," "pumpkin," etc. The 54 scenes of the training set preprocessed by FCGF [91] provide 7,960 point cloud pairs.

1.3.6 PCSOD

PCSOD is the first dataset for point cloud salient object detection (SOD) [48], which contains 2,872 object samples. These samples are indoor or outdoor 3D objects in daily life, belonging to 12 superclasses (such as "furniture," "public utilities," "artifact," "building," etc.), which can be further subdivided into 138 subclasses (such as "table," "bridge," "doll," "playground," etc.), as depicted in Fig. 1.8. The annotations of the dataset are hierarchical, with each view corresponding to hierarchical annotations, including category, segmentation map, and bounding box, as shown in Fig. 1.9. In practice, PCSOD can be randomly divided into 2,000 samples as the training set and the rest as the test set, according to a rough split ratio of 7:3.

Fig. 1.8 Categories of PCSOD dataset [48] (Source: Author)

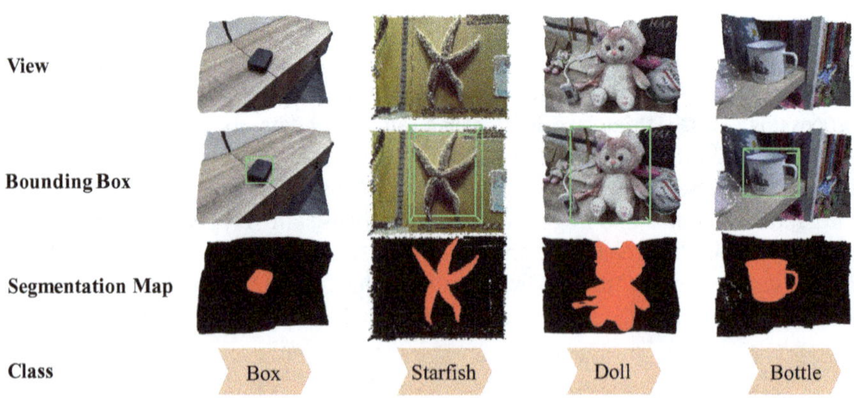

Fig. 1.9 Samples in the PCSOD dataset labeled with hierarchical annotations, such as superclass/subclass, bounding boxes, and segmentation maps [48] (Source: Author)

1.4 Deep Learning-Based 3D Perception with Point Clouds

During the past years, non-learning and learning techniques have been broadly developed for different types of computer vision and image processing tasks and have obtained fruitful achievements [1–3, 5, 6, 9–12, 14, 15, 92–136]. Point clouds can provide more powerful modeling capability for 3D objects and scenes to elevate the 3D perception of both human and machine. We can witness the increasing applications of point cloud technologies, such as autonomous driving [137], 3D medical imaging [138], and reverse engineering [139]. Therefore, there is a great demand for technical research efforts for the corresponding point cloud tasks in these applications, such as upsampling, completion, object detection (shown in Fig. 1.10), semantic segmentation, object tracking, and classification, to improve the visual experience and the machine analysis performances. Thanks to the fast growth of deep learning theories and methods, data-driven multimedia computing technologies have achieved a big success during the past decade and have brought new challenges and opportunities to further enhance 3D perception capabilities powered with point clouds. Hence, researchers have leveraged deep learning to generate new efficient solutions for 3D point cloud data processing.

Due to the increased available computing power, deep neural networks are becoming more and more capable of processing complicated tasks, which have shown superior performances than human brain and traditional algorithms. Point

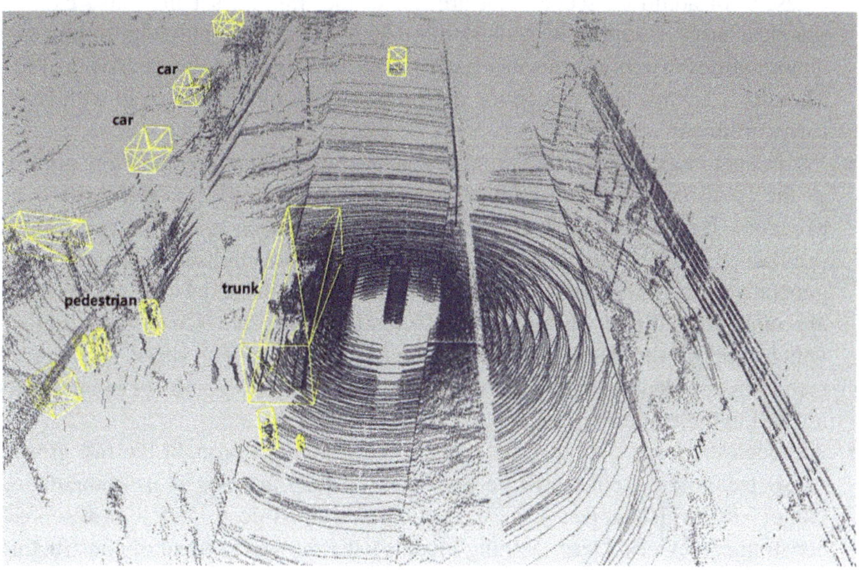

Fig. 1.10 Object detection based on LiDAR point cloud in autonomous driving. The image shown is introduced with MPEG open access (OA) work under CC BY Licence (Copyright © 1988–2024, www.mpeg.org) [148]

cloud enhancement tasks, including denoising, upsampling, completion, etc., are also benefited from the adoption of deep learning methods, as well as diverse point cloud analysis tasks, including segmentation, detection, classification, etc. For example, the advanced algorithms include REAL [140] and Box2Mask [141] for point cloud semantic segmentation, SFD [142], CMT [143] and VirConv [144] for point cloud object detection, and Pointaugment [145] and ScanObjectNN [146] for point cloud shape classification.

In order to support and validate point cloud related tasks, different point cloud datasets and benchmarks have been developed and accessible for use in the past few years. For example, KITTI [147] is a large-scale autonomous driving dataset for optical flow estimation, visual odometry, object detection, and tracking. nuScenes [148] is a large-scale autonomous driving dataset for detection, segmentation, and tracking. SemanticKITTI [86] is a semantic segmentation dataset. S3DIS [85] is a dataset for semantic segmentation of indoor scene point clouds. These public datasets provide training data for the research of point cloud algorithms and also provide test data for performance comparison of different algorithms. Although the point cloud technologies have achieved remarkable progress, some challenges still exist in practical application scenarios:

- The most advanced algorithms in classification [149], segmentation [150], and detection [151] have been proved to be effective on public datasets. However, in practical applications, due to the complexity and diversity of real scenes, the properties of point cloud data are often inconsistent with those of the public datasets. In addition, scenes that are not in the training set may also exist in practical cases, resulting in the loss of efficacy of deep learning algorithms, and abnormalities in applications involving safety, such as autonomous driving [152]. Therefore, 3D machine perception performances should be improved with better trustworthiness.
- Pre-trained models and foundation models are becoming more and more popular as the solutions for more intelligent tasks in the new AI era, and there is no exception for point clouds. Increased efforts have been made for point cloud pre-trained models and foundation models, as well as multi-modal models and generative models. As a type of 3D visual data, these models for point clouds are more difficult to train, but point cloud datasets are scanty and limited, which hinders the developments of point cloud-based 3D visual intelligence technologies. Hence, model establishments and data collections for point clouds are still in the beginning stage.
- Although the introduction of deep neural networks has brought the fast growth of 3D technologies, the intrinsic drawback of deep learning is its computation complexity, which impedes the utilization of trained deep models in resource-constrained devices. Deep learning models have shown the trend of constructing large models to make the computing machine more intelligent, as the foundation model research has emerged as a more and more popular direction. In view of these, model compression and acceleration become important for deep learning model software and hardware implementations. Additionally, different

programming frameworks, including Pytorch, Tensorflow, MindSpore, etc., have made the implementations too diverse to ensure the easy reproductions. As a consequence, building open source projects for 3D point cloud technologies is critical for better academic and technical communications, since it can provide more solutions to facilitate further research and developments.

To sum up, point cloud technologies have been widely used in many industries and have a bright future. It is foreseeable that with the fast developments of deep learning and artificial intelligence, the problems in point cloud tasks will be solved much more efficiently and elegantly. Deep-learning-based point cloud enhancement and analysis will generate more powerful capabilities of 3D human and machine perceptions, especially with the advent of large foundation models.

1.5 Summary

This chapter presents an introduction to 3D world representation with point clouds, including the definition, properties, types, and data acquisition of point clouds. Then, we enumerate representative point cloud datasets, based on which the research works for related point cloud tasks have been carried out. Following that, the deep-learning-based 3D perception technologies with point clouds are briefly illustrated, as well as the key problems in the current AI era from traditional deep learning models to large models. Finally, we provide the organization structure of this book.

Exercises

1. How does point cloud differ from image data?
2. What requirements does the disorder of point cloud data put forward for deep learning network structures?
3. What are the application scenarios of sparse and dense point clouds, respectively? Please give some examples.
4. What are the application scenarios of organized and unorganized point clouds, respectively? Please give some examples.
5. What are the advantages and disadvantages of structured light, Time of Flight (TOF), and binocular stereo depth cameras, respectively?
6. What do you think the differences are between point cloud acquisition and image acquisition?
7. What are the typical point cloud tasks? Please list the corresponding representative datasets for each task.
8. What challenges do we encounter during processing point clouds in actual application scenarios?

9. Can you list some typical point cloud applications for human perception and machine perception, respectively?
10. What do you think the new emerging technologies in aritificial intelligence will bring to point cloud enhancement and analysis research?

References

1. Y. Guo, W. Gao, S. Ma, G. Li, Accelerating transform algorithm implementation for efficient intra coding of 8k uhd videos. ACM Trans. Multimedia Comput. Commun. Appl. **18**(4), 1–20 (2022)
2. H. Yuan, W. Gao, S. Ma, Y. Yan, Divide-and-conquer-based RDO-free CU partitioning for 8k video compression. ACM Trans. Multimedia Comput. Commun. Appl. **20**(4), 1–20 (2024)
3. W. Gao, H. Yuan, G. Liao, Z. Guo, J. Chen, Pp8k: a new dataset for 8k UHD video compression and processing. IEEE MultiMedia **30**(3), 100–109 (2023)
4. H. Yuan, S. Kwong, X. Wang, W. Gao, Y. Zhang, Rate distortion optimized inter-view frame level bit allocation method for mv-hevc. IEEE Trans. Multimedia **17**(12), 2134–2146 (2015)
5. H. Zheng, W. Gao, End-to-end RGB-D image compression via exploiting channel-modality redundancy. Proc. AAAI Confer. Artif. Intell. **38**(7), 7562–7570 (2024)
6. W. Gao, G. Liao, S. Ma, G. Li, Y. Liang, W. Lin, Unified information fusion network for multi-modal RGB-D and RGB-T salient object detection. IEEE Trans. Circ. Syst. Video Technol. **32**(4), 2091–2106 (2021)
7. G. Liao, W. Gao, Q. Jiang, R. Wang, G. Li, MMNeT: Multi-stage and multi-scale fusion network for RGB-D salient object detection, in *Proceedings of the 28th ACM International Conference on Multimedia* (2020), pp. 2436–2444
8. E.H. Adelson, J.R. Bergen et al., The plenoptic function and the elements of early vision. Comput. Models Visual Process. **1**(2), 3–20 (1991)
9. L. Zhou, W. Gao, G. Li, H. Yuan, T. Zhao, G. Yue, Disentangled feature distillation for light field super-resolution with degradations, in *IEEE International Conference on Multimedia and Expo Workshops* (2023), pp. 116–121
10. W. Gao, S. Fan, G. Li, W. Lin, A thorough benchmark and a new model for light field saliency detection. IEEE Trans. Pattern Analy. Mach. Intell. **45**(7), 8003–8019 (2023)
11. L. Zhou, W. Gao, G. Li, End-to-end spatial-angular light field super-resolution using parallax structure preservation strategy, in *IEEE International Conference on Image Processing* (2022), pp. 3396–3400
12. Y. Sun, Z. Li, L. Li, S. Wang, W. Gao, Optimization of compressive light field display in dual-guided learning, in *IEEE International Conference on Acoustics, Speech and Signal Processing* (2022), pp. 2075–2079
13. Z. Guo, W. Gao, H. Wang, J. Wang, S. Fan, No-reference deep quality assessment of compressed light field images, in *IEEE International Conference on Multimedia and Expo* (2021), pp. 1–6
14. W. Gao, L. Zhou, L. Tao, A fast view synthesis implementation method for light field applications. ACM Trans. Multimedia Comput. Commun. Appl. **17**(4), 1–20 (2021)
15. Y. Sun, Z. Li, S. Wang, W. Gao, Depth-assisted calibration on learning-based factorization for a compressive light field display. Opt. Express **31**(4), 5399–5413 (2023)
16. G. Liao, W. Gao, Rethinking feature mining for light field salient object detection, in *ACM Transactions on Multimedia Computing, Communications, and Applications* (2024)
17. W. Gao, G. Li, H. Yuan, R. Hamzaoui, Z. Li, S. Liu, Apccpa'22: 1st international workshop on advances in point cloud compression, processing and analysis, in *Proceedings of the 30th ACM International Conference on Multimedia* (2022), pp. 7392–7393

18. T. Qin, G. Li, W. Gao, S. Liu, Multi-grained point cloud geometry compression via dual-model prediction with extended octree, in *ACM Transactions on Multimedia Computing, Communications, and Applications* (2024)
19. Y. Shao, W. Gao, S. Liu, G. Li, Advanced patch-based affine motion estimation for dynamic point cloud geometry compression. Sensors **24**(10), 3142 (2024)
20. Y. Shao, F. Song, W. Gao, S. Liu, G. Li, Texture-guided graph transform optimization for point cloud attribute compression. Appl. Sci. **14**(10), 4094 (2024)
21. Y. Shao, X. Yang, W. Gao, S. Liu, G. Li, 3D point cloud attribute compression using diffusion-based texture-aware intra prediction, in *IEEE Transactions on Circuits and Systems for Video Technology* (2024), pp. 1–1
22. J. Zhang, Y. Chen, G. Liu, W. Gao, G. Li, Efficient point cloud attribute compression framework using attribute-guided graph fourier transform, in *IEEE International Conference on Acoustics, Speech and Signal Processing* (2024), pp. 8426–8430
23. W. Gao, H. Yuan, G. Li, Z. Li, H. Yuan, Low complexity coding unit decision for video-based point cloud compression. IEEE Trans. Image Process. **33**, 149–162 (2023)
24. Y. Shao, G. Li, Q. Zhang, W. Gao, S. Liu, Non-rigid registration-based progressive motion compensation for point cloud geometry compression. IEEE Trans. Geosci. Remote Sens. **61**, 1–14 (2023)
25. F. Song, G. Li, X. Yang, W. Gao, S. Liu, Block-adaptive point cloud attribute coding with region-aware optimized transform. IEEE Trans. Circ. Syst. Video Technol. **33**(8), 4294–4308 (2023)
26. Y. An, Y. Shao, G. Li, W. Gao, S. Liu, A fast motion estimation method with hamming distance for lidar point cloud compression, in *IEEE International Conference on Visual Communications and Image Processing* (2022), pp. 1–5
27. H. Yuan, W. Gao, G. Li, Z. Li, Rate-distortion-guided learning approach with cross-projection information for V-PCC fast CU decision, in *Proceedings of the 30th ACM International Conference on Multimedia* (2022), pp. 3085–3093
28. F. Song, G. Li, W. Gao, T.H. Li, Rate-distortion optimized graph for point cloud attribute coding. IEEE Signal Process. Lett. **29**, 922–926 (2022)
29. F. Song, G. Li, X. Yang, W. Gao, T.H. Li, Fine-grained correlation representation for graph-based point cloud attribute compression, in *IEEE International Conference on Multimedia and Expo* (2022), pp. 1–6
30. F. Shen, W. Gao, A rate control algorithm for video-based point cloud compression, in *International Conference on Visual Communications and Image Processing* (2021), pp. 1–5
31. F. Song, Y. Shao, W. Gao, H. Wang, T. Li, Layer-wise geometry aggregation framework for lossless lidar point cloud compression. IEEE Trans. Circ. Syst. Video Technol. **31**(12), 4603–4616 (2021)
32. L. Xie, W. Gao, H. Zheng, G. Li, SPCGC: Scalable point cloud geometry compression for machine vision, in *Proceedings of IEEE International Conference on Robotics and Automation* (2024)
33. L. Xie, W. Gao, H. Zheng, H. Ye, Semantic-aware visual decomposition for point cloud geometry compression, in *Data Compression Conference* (2024), pp. 595–595
34. Z. Qi, W. Gao, Variable-rate point cloud geometry compression based on feature adjustment and interpolation, in *Data Compression Conference* (2024), pp. 63–72
35. Z. Yu, W. Gao, When dynamic neural network meets point cloud compression: Computation-aware variable rate and checkerboard context, in *Data Compression Conference* (2024), pp. 600–600
36. L. Xie, W. Gao, S. Fan, Z. Yao, PDNeT: Parallel dual-branch network for point cloud geometry compression and analysis, in *Data Compression Conference* (2024), pp. 596–596
37. L. Xie, W. Gao, H. Zheng, End-to-end point cloud geometry compression and analysis with sparse tensor, in *Proceedings of the 1st International Workshop on Advances in Point Cloud Compression, Processing and Analysis* (2022), pp. 27–32

38. C. Fu, G. Li, R. Song, W. Gao, S. Liu, Octattention: Octree-based large-scale contexts model for point cloud compression. Proc. AAAI Confer. Artif. Intell. **36**(1), 625–633 (2022)
39. W. Liu, W. Gao, X. Mu, Fast inter-frame motion prediction for compressed dynamic point cloud attribute enhancement. Proc. AAAI Confer. Artif. Intell. **38**(4), 3720–3728 (2024)
40. Z. Yang, W. Gao, X. Lu, Danet: Density-adaptive network for geometry-based point cloud compression artifacts removal, in *IEEE International Conference on Visual Communications and Image Processing* (2023), pp. 1–5
41. X. Fan, G. Li, D. Li, Y. Ren, W. Gao, T.H. Li, Deep geometry post-processing for decompressed point clouds, in *IEEE International Conference on Multimedia and Expo* (2022), pp. 1–6
42. X. Zhang, G. Liao, W. Gao, G. Li, TDRNeT: Transformer-based dual-branch restoration network for geometry based point cloud compression artifacts, in *IEEE International Conference on Multimedia and Expo* (2022), pp. 1–6
43. Z. Li, G. Li, T.H. Li, S. Liu, W. Gao, Semantic point cloud upsampling. IEEE Trans. Multimedia **25**, 3432–3442 (2023)
44. R. Zhang, W. Gao, G. Li, T.H. Li, QINeT: decision surface learning and adversarial enhancement for quasi-immune completion of diverse corrupted point clouds. IEEE Trans. Geosci. Remote Sens. **60**, 1–14 (2022)
45. R. Bao, Y. Ren, G. Li, W. Gao, S. Liu, Flow-based point cloud completion network with adversarial refinement, in *ICASSP 2022-2022 IEEE International Conference on Acoustics, Speech and Signal Processing (ICASSP)* (IEEE, Piscataway, 2022), pp. 2559–2563
46. J. Chen, G. Li, R. Zhang, T.H. Li, W. Gao, Pointivae: Invertible variational autoencoder framework for 3D point cloud generation, in *2022 IEEE International Conference on Image Processing (ICIP)* (IEEE, Piscataway, 2022), pp. 3216–3220
47. R. Zhang, J. Chen, W. Gao, G. Li, T.H. Li, Pointot: interpretable geometry-inspired point cloud generative model via optimal transport. IEEE Trans. Circ. Syst. Video Technol. **32**(10), 6792–6806 (2022)
48. S. Fan, W. Gao, G. Li, Salient object detection for point clouds, in *European Conference on Computer Vision* (2022), pp. 1–19
49. S. Luo, W. Gao, A general framework for rotation invariant point cloud analysis, in *IEEE International Conference on Acoustics, Speech and Signal Processing* (2024), pp. 3665–3669
50. X. Lu, W. Gao, Attentivenet: Detecting small objects for lidar point clouds by attending to important points, in *IEEE International Conference on Visual Communications and Image Processing* (IEEE, Piscataway, 2023), pp. 1–5
51. Z. Pan, N. Zhang, W. Gao, S. Liu, G. Li, Less is more: label recommendation for weakly supervised point cloud semantic segmentation. Proc. AAAI Confer. Artif. Intell. **38**(5), 4397–4405 (2024)
52. Z. Pan, G. Liu, W. Gao, T. Li, Epcontrast: Effective point-level contrastive learning for large-scale point cloud understanding, in *IEEE International Conference on Multimedia and Expo* (2024)
53. N. Zhang, Z. Pan, T.H. Li, W. Gao, G. Li, Improving graph representation for point cloud segmentation via attentive filtering, in *Proceedings of the IEEE/CVF Conference on Computer Vision and Pattern Recognition* (2023), pp. 1244–1254
54. K. Wen, N. Zhang, G. Li, W. Gao, MPVNN: Multi-resolution point-voxel non-parametric network for 3D point cloud processing, in *IEEE International Conference on Multimedia and Expo* (2024)
55. S. Fan, W. Gao, Screen-based 3D subjective experiment software, in *Proceedings of the 31st ACM International Conference on Multimedia* (2023), pp. 9672–9675
56. J. Wang, W. Gao, G. Li, Zoom to perceive better: No-reference point cloud quality assessment via exploring effective multiscale feature, *IEEE Transactions on Circuits and Systems for Video Technology* (2024), pp. 1–1
57. J. Wang, W. Gao, G. Li, Applying collaborative adversarial learning to blind point cloud quality measurement. IEEE Trans. Instrument. Measur. **72**, 1–15 (2023)

58. W. Gao, H. Ye, G. Li, H. Zheng, Y. Wu, L. Xie, Openpointcloud: An open-source algorithm library of deep learning based point cloud compression, in *Proceedings of the 30th ACM international conference on multimedia* (2022), pp. 7347–7350
59. Y. Zhang, W. Gao, G. Li, Openpointcloud-v2: A deep learning based open-source algorithm library of point cloud processing, in *Proceedings of the 1st International Workshop on Advances in Point Cloud Compression, Processing and Analysis* (2022), pp. 51–55
60. H. Zheng, W. Gao, Z. Yu, T. Zhao, G. Li, ViewPCGC: View-guided learned point cloud geometry compression, in *Proceedings of the 32nd ACM International Conference on Multimedia* (2024)
61. L. Xie, W. Gao, H. Zheng, G. Li, Roi-guided point cloud geometry compression towards human and machine vision, in *Proceedings of the 32nd ACM International Conference on Multimedia* (2024)
62. C. Peng, W. Gao, Laplacian matrix learning for point cloud attribute compression with ternary search-based adaptive block partition, in *Proceedings of the 32nd ACM International Conference on Multimedia* (2024)
63. S. Luo, B. Qu, W. Gao, Learning robust 3D representation from clip via dual denoising (2024). arXiv preprint arXiv:2407.00905
64. G. Li, G. Wei, W. Gao, *Point Cloud Compression: Technologies and Standardization* (Springer Nature, Berlin, 2024)
65. G. Li, W. Gao, W. Gao, Introduction, in *Point Cloud Compression: Technologies and Standardization* (Springer, Berlin, 2024), pp. 1–28
66. G. Li, W. Gao, W. Gao, Background knowledge, in *Point Cloud Compression: Technologies and Standardization* (Springer, Berlin, 2024), pp. 29–51
67. G. Li, W. Gao, W. Gao, Predictive coding, in *Point Cloud Compression: Technologies and Standardization* (Springer, Berlin, 2024), pp. 53–70
68. G. Li, W. Gao, W. Gao, Transform coding, in *Point Cloud Compression: Technologies and Standardization* (Springer, Berlin, 2024), pp. 71–96
69. G. Li, W. Gao, W. Gao, Quantization techniques, in *Point Cloud Compression: Technologies and Standardization* (Springer, Berlin, 2024), pp. 97–112
70. G. Li, W. Gao, W. Gao, Entropy coding, in *Point Cloud Compression: Technologies and Standardization* (Springer, Berlin, 2024), pp. 113–133
71. G. Li, W. Gao, W. Gao, MPEG geometry-based point cloud compression (G-PCC) standard, in *Point Cloud Compression: Technologies and Standardization* (Springer, Berlin, 2024), pp. 135–165
72. G. Li, W. Gao, W. Gao, AVS point cloud compression standard, in *Point Cloud Compression: Technologies and Standardization* (Springer, Berlin, 2024), pp. 167–197
73. G. Li, W. Gao, W. Gao, MPEG video-based point cloud compression (V-PCC) standard, in *Point Cloud Compression: Technologies and Standardization* (Springer, Berlin, 2024), pp. 199–218
74. G. Li, W. Gao, W. Gao, MPEG AI-based 3D graphics coding standard, in *Point Cloud Compression: Technologies and Standardization* (Springer, Berlin, 2024), pp. 219–241
75. G. Li, W. Gao, W. Gao, Future work, in *Point Cloud Compression: Technologies and Standardization* (Springer, Berlin, 2024), pp. 243–250
76. D. Yang, W. Gao, G. Li, H. Yuan, J. Hou, S. Kwong, Exploiting manifold feature representation for efficient classification of 3D point clouds. ACM Trans. Multimedia Comput. Commun. Appl. **19**(1s), 1–21 (2023)
77. Z. Wu, S. Song, A. Khosla, F. Yu, L. Zhang, X. Tang, J. Xiao, 3D ShapeNets: A deep representation for volumetric shapes, in *IEEE Conference on Computer Vision and Pattern Recognition* (2015), pp. 1912–1920
78. A.M. Eslami, Integrating reverse engineering and 3D printing for the manufacturing process, in *ASEE Annual Conference and Exposition* (2017), pp. 1–10
79. R. Li, T. Luo, H. Zha, 3D digitization and its applications in cultural heritage, in *Euro-Mediterranean Conference* (2010), pp. 381–388

80. B. Yang, F. Liang, H. Ronggang, Progress, challenges and perspectives of 3D LiDAR point cloud processing. Acta Geodaetica et Cartographica Sinica **46**(10), 1509–1516 (2017)
81. A.X. Chang, T. Funkhouser, L. Guibas, P. Hanrahan, Q. Huang, Z. Li, S. Savarese, M. Savva, S. Song, H. Su, J. Xiao, L. Yi, F. Yu, ShapeNet: An information-rich 3D model repository, Stanford University—Princeton University—Toyota Technological Institute at Chicago, Technical Report (2015)
82. X. Yu, Y. Rao, Z. Wang, Z. Liu, J. Lu, J. Zhou, Pointr: Diverse point cloud completion with geometry-aware transformers, in *Proceedings of the IEEE/CVF International Conference on Computer Vision* (2021), pp. 12478–12487
83. L. Yi, V.G. Kim, D. Ceylan, I.-C. Shen, M. Yan, H. Su, C. Lu, Q. Huang, A. Sheffer, L. Guibas, A scalable active framework for region annotation in 3D shape collections. ACM Trans. Graph. **35**(6), 1–12 (2016)
84. Z. Wu, S. Song, A. Khosla, F. Yu, L. Zhang, X. Tang, J. Xiao, 3D ShapeNets: A deep representation for volumetric shapes, in *Proceedings of the IEEE Conference on Computer Vision and Pattern Recognition* (2015), pp. 1912–1920
85. I. Armeni, O. Sener, A.R. Zamir, H. Jiang, I. Brilakis, M. Fischer, S. Savarese, 3D semantic parsing of large-scale indoor spaces, in *IEEE Conference on Computer Vision and Pattern Recognition* (2016), pp. 1534–1543
86. J. Behley, M. Garbade, A. Milioto, J. Quenzel, S. Behnke, C. Stachniss, J. Gall, SemanticKITTI: A dataset for semantic scene understanding of LiDAR sequences, in *IEEE/CVF International Conference on Computer Vision* (2019), pp. 9296–9306
87. A. Geiger, P. Lenz, C. Stiller, R. Urtasun, Vision meets robotics: the KITTI dataset. Int. J. Rob. Res. **32**(11), 1231–1237 (2013)
88. A. Zeng, S. Song, M. Nießner, M. Fisher, J. Xiao, T. Funkhouser, 3DMatch: Learning local geometric descriptors from RGB-D reconstructions, in *IEEE Conference on Computer Vision and Pattern Recognition* (2017), pp. 199–208
89. B. Glocker, S. Izadi, J. Shotton, A. Criminisi, Real-time RGB-D camera relocalization, in *IEEE International Symposium on Mixed and Augmented Reality* (2013), pp. 173–179
90. J. Xiao, A. Owens, A. Torralba, SUN3D: A database of big spaces reconstructed using SfM and object labels, in *IEEE International Conference on Computer Vision* (2013), pp. 1625–1632
91. C. Choy, J. Park, V. Koltun, Fully convolutional geometric features, in *Proceedings of the IEEE/CVF International Conference on Computer Vision* (2019), pp. 8958–8966
92. B. Qu, X. Liang, S. Sun, W. Gao, Exploring aigc video quality: A focus on visual harmony, video-text consistency and domain distribution gap, in *Proceedings of the IEEE/CVF Conference on Computer Vision and Pattern Recognition Workshops* (2024)
93. B. Qu, H. Li, W. Gao, Bringing textual prompt to ai-generated image quality assessment, in *2024 IEEE International Conference on Multimedia and Expo (ICME)* (IEEE, Piscataway, 2024)
94. Y. Wu, L. Xie, S. Sun, W. Gao, Y. Yan, Adaptive intra period size for deep learning-based screen content video coding, in *2024 IEEE International Conference on Multimedia and Expo Workshops (ICMEW)* (IEEE, Piscataway, 2024)
95. L. Tao, W. Gao, G. Li, C. Zhang, Adanic: Towards practical neural image compression via dynamic transform routing, in *Proceedings of the IEEE/CVF International Conference on Computer Vision* (2023), pp. 16879–16888
96. Y. Wu, W. Gao, End-to-end lossless compression of high precision depth maps guided by pseudo-residual (2022). arXiv preprint arXiv:2201.03195
97. Y. Wu, Z. Qi, H. Zheng, L. Tao, W. Gao, Deep image compression with latent optimization and piece-wise quantization approximation, in *Proceedings of the IEEE/CVF Conference on Computer Vision and Pattern Recognition* (2021), pp. 1926–1930
98. W. Gao, L. Tao, L. Zhou, D. Yang, X. Zhang, Z. Guo, Low-rate image compression with super-resolution learning, in *Proceedings of the IEEE/CVF Conference on Computer Vision and Pattern Recognition Workshops* (2020), pp. 154–155

99. W. Gao, S. Sun, H. Zheng, Y. Wu, H. Ye, Y. Zhang, Opendmc: An open-source library and performance evaluation for deep-learning-based multi-frame compression, in *Proceedings of the 31st ACM International Conference on Multimedia* (2023), pp. 9685–9688
100. Y. Guo, W. Gao, G. Li, Interpretable task-inspired adaptive filter pruning for neural networks under multiple constraints. Int. J. Comput. Vision **132** , 1–17 (2024)
101. W. Gao, Y. Guo, S. Ma, G. Li, S. Kwong, Efficient neural network compression inspired by compressive sensing. IEEE Trans. Neural Netw. Learn. Syst. **35**, 1965–1979 (2022)
102. Y. Guo, W. Gao, Semantic-driven automatic filter pruning for neural networks, in *2022 IEEE International Conference on Multimedia and Expo (ICME)* (IEEE, Piscataway, 2022), pp. 1–6
103. L. Tao, W. Gao, Efficient channel pruning based on architecture alignment and probability model bypassing, in *2021 IEEE International Conference on Systems, Man, and Cybernetics (SMC)* (IEEE, Piscataway, 2021), pp. 3232–3237
104. Z. Yang, W. Gao, G. Li, Y. Yan, Sur-driven video coding rate control for jointly optimizing perceptual quality and buffer control, in *IEEE Transactions on Image Processing* (2023)
105. F. Shen, Z. Cai, W. Gao, An efficient rate control algorithm for intra frame coding in AVS3, in *2021 IEEE International Conference on Systems, Man, and Cybernetics (SMC)* (IEEE, Piscataway, 2021), pp. 3164–3169
106. H. Yuan, W. Gao, J. Wang, Dynamic computational resource allocation for fast inter frame coding in video conferencing applications, in *2021 IEEE International Conference on Multimedia and Expo (ICME)* (IEEE, Piscataway, 2021), pp. 1–6
107. W. Gao, Q. Jiang, R. Wang, S. Ma, G. Li, S. Kwong, Consistent quality oriented rate control in HEVC via balancing intra and inter frame coding. IEEE Trans. Ind. Inf. **18**(3), 1594–1604 (2021)
108. H. Yuan, W. Gao, A new coding unit partitioning mode for screen content video coding, in *Proceedings of the 2021 5th International Conference on Digital Signal Processing* (2021), pp. 66–72
109. W. Gao, On the performance evaluation of state-of-the-art rate control algorithms for practical video coding and transmission systems, in *Proceedings of the 2020 4th International Conference on Video and Image Processing* (2020), pp. 179–185
110. W. Gao, S. Kwong, Q. Jiang, C.-K. Fong, P.H. Wong, W.Y. Yuen, Data-driven rate control for rate-distortion optimization in hevc based on simplified effective initial qp learning. IEEE Trans. Broadcast. **65**(1), 94–108 (2018)
111. W. Gao, A multi-objective optimization perspective for joint consideration of video coding quality, in *2019 Asia-Pacific Signal and Information Processing Association Annual Summit and Conference (APSIPA ASC)* (IEEE, Piscataway, 2019), pp. 986–991
112. W. Gao, S. Kwong, Y. Jia, Joint machine learning and game theory for rate control in high efficiency video coding. IEEE Trans. Image Process. **26**(12), 6074–6089 (2017)
113. W. Gao, S. Kwong, Y. Zhou, H. Yuan, Ssim-based game theory approach for rate-distortion optimized intra frame ctu-level bit allocation. IEEE Trans. Multimedia **18**(6), 988–999 (2016)
114. W. Gao, S. Kwong, H. Yuan, X. Wang, Dct coefficient distribution modeling and quality dependency analysis based frame-level bit allocation for hevc. IEEE Trans. Circ. Syst. Video Technol. **26**(1), 139–153 (2015)
115. W. Gao, S. Kwong, Phase congruency based edge saliency detection and rate control for perceptual image and video coding, in *2016 IEEE International Conference on Systems, Man, and Cybernetics (SMC)* (IEEE, Piscataway, 2016), pp. 000264–000269
116. H. Yuan, W. Gao, Openfastvc: An open source library for video coding fast algorithm implementation, in *Proceedings of the 31st ACM International Conference on Multimedia* (2023), pp. 9660–9663
117. L. Tao, W. Gao, A hardware implementation of entropy encoder for 8k video coding, in *2022 IEEE International Conference on Multimedia and Expo (ICME)* (IEEE, Piscataway, 2022), pp. 1–6
118. Z. Cai, W. Gao, Efficient fast algorithm and parallel hardware architecture for intra prediction of AVS3, in *2021 IEEE International Symposium on Circuits and Systems (ISCAS)* (IEEE, Piscataway, 2021), pp. 1–5

119. W. Gao, H. Yuan, Y. Guo, L. Tao, Z. Cai, G. Li, Openhardwarevc: An open source library for 8k uhd video coding hardware implementation, in *Proceedings of the 30th ACM International Conference on Multimedia* (2022), pp. 7339–7342
120. W. Liu, W. Gao, G. Li, S. Ma, T. Zhao, H. Yuan, Enlarged motion-aware and frequency-aware network for compressed video artifact reduction. IEEE Trans. Circ. Syst. Video Technol. **34**, 10339–10352 (2024)
121. X. Zang, W. Gao, G. Li, H. Fang, C. Ban, Z. He, H. Sun, A baseline investigation: Transformer-based cross-view baseline for text-based person search, in *Proceedings of the 31st ACM International Conference on Multimedia* (2023), pp. 7737–7746
122. G. Liao, W. Gao, G. Li, J. Wang, S. Kwong, Cross-collaborative fusion-encoder network for robust RGB-thermal salient object detection. IEEE Trans. Circ. Syst. Video Technol. **32**(11), 7646–7661 (2022)
123. Y. Chen, S. Sun, G. Li, W. Gao, T.H. Li, Closing the gap between theory and practice during alternating optimization for gans. IEEE Trans. Neural Netw. Learn. Syst. **35**, 14005–14017 (2023)
124. Y. Chen, C. Jin, G. Li, T.H. Li, W. Gao, Mitigating label noise in gans via enhanced spectral normalization. IEEE Trans. Circ. Syst. Video Technol. **33**, 3924–3934 (2023)
125. X. Zang, G. Li, W. Gao, Multidirection and multiscale pyramid in transformer for video-based pedestrian retrieval. IEEE Trans. Ind. Inf. **18**(12), 8776–8785 (2022)
126. X. Zang, G. Li, W. Gao, X. Shu, Learning to disentangle scenes for person re-identification. Image Vision Comput. **116**, 104330 (2021)
127. X. Zang, G. Li, W. Gao, X. Shu, Exploiting robust unsupervised video person re-identification. IET Image Process. **16**(3), 729–741 (2022)
128. Z. Yue, G. Li, W. Gao, Cross-level guided attention for human-object interaction detection, in *2023 IEEE International Conference on Multimedia and Expo Workshops (ICMEW)* (IEEE, Piscataway, 2023), pp. 284–289
129. Z. Yao, W. Gao, Iterative saliency aggregation and assignment network for efficient salient object detection in optical remote sensing images. IEEE Trans. Geosci. Remote Sens. **62**, 5633213 (2024)
130. Z. Li, G. Li, T. Li, S. Liu, W. Gao, Information-growth attention network for image super-resolution, in *Proceedings of the 29th ACM International Conference on Multimedia* (2021), pp. 544–552
131. X. Zhang, W. Gao, G. Li, Q. Jiang, R. Cong, Image quality assessment-driven reinforcement learning for mixed distorted image restoration. ACM Trans. Multimedia Comput. Commun. Appl. **19**(1s), 1–23 (2023)
132. X. Zhang, W. Gao, H. Yuan, G. Li, Je 2 net: Joint exploitation and exploration in reinforcement learning based image restoration, in *ICASSP 2022-2022 IEEE International Conference on Acoustics, Speech and Signal Processing (ICASSP)* (IEEE, Piscataway, 2022), pp. 2090–2094
133. X. Zhang, W. Gao, Hirl: Hybrid image restoration based on hierarchical deep reinforcement learning via two-step analysis, in *ICASSP 2022-2022 IEEE International Conference on Acoustics, Speech and Signal Processing (ICASSP)* (IEEE, Piscataway, 2022), pp. 2445–2449
134. C. Zhang, W. Gao, Learned rate control for frame-level adaptive neural video compression via dynamic neural network, in *European conference on computer vision* (Springer, Berlin, 2024)
135. S. Sun, J. Liu, T.H. Li, H. Li, G. Liu, W. Gao, Streamflow: Streamlined multi-frame optical flow estimation for video sequences (2023). arXiv preprint arXiv:2311.17099
136. R. Liu, J. Huang, W. Gao, T.H. Li, G. Li, Mug-stan: Adapting image-language pretrained models for general video understanding (2023). arXiv preprint arXiv:2311.15075
137. Y. Li, L. Ma, Z. Zhong, F. Liu, M.A. Chapman, D. Cao, J. Li, Deep learning for lidar point clouds in autonomous driving: a review. IEEE Trans. Neural Netw. Learn. Syst. **32**(8), 3412–3432 (2020)

138. Q. Cheng, P. Sun, C. Yang, Y. Yang, P.X. Liu, A morphing-based 3D point cloud reconstruction framework for medical image processing. Comput. Methods Progr. Biomed. **193**, 105495 (2020)
139. J. Huang, C.-H. Menq, Automatic cad model reconstruction from multiple point clouds for reverse engineering. J. Comput. Inf. Sci. Eng. **2**(3), 160–170 (2002)
140. J. Cen, P. Yun, S. Zhang, J. Cai, D. Luan, M. Tang, M. Liu, M. Yu Wang, Open-world semantic segmentation for LIDAR point clouds, in *European Conference on Computer Vision* (2022), pp. 318–334
141. J. Chibane, F. Engelmann, T. Anh Tran, G. Pons-Moll, Box2Mask: Weakly supervised 3D semantic instance segmentation using bounding boxes, in *European Conference on Computer Vision* (2022), pp. 681–699
142. X. Wu, L. Peng, H. Yang, L. Xie, C. Huang, C. Deng, H. Liu, D. Cai, Sparse fuse dense: Towards high quality 3D detection with depth completion, in *Proceedings of the IEEE/CVF Conference on Computer Vision and Pattern Recognition* (2022), pp. 5408–5417
143. J. Yan, Y. Liu, J. Sun, F. Jia, S. Li, T. Wang, X. Zhang, Cross modal transformer: Towards fast and robust 3D object detection, in *Proceedings of the IEEE/CVF International Conference on Computer Vision* (2023), pp. 18268–18278
144. H. Wu, C. Wen, S. Shi, X. Li, C. Wang, Virtual sparse convolution for multimodal 3D object detection, in *Proceedings of the IEEE/CVF Conference on Computer Vision and Pattern Recognition* (2023), pp. 21653–21662
145. R. Li, X. Li, P.-A. Heng, C.-W. Fu, Pointaugment: An auto-augmentation framework for point cloud classification, in *Proceedings of the IEEE/CVF Conference on Computer Vision and Pattern Recognition* (2020), pp. 6378–6387
146. M.A. Uy, Q.-H. Pham, B.-S. Hua, T. Nguyen, S.-K. Yeung, Revisiting point cloud classification: A new benchmark dataset and classification model on real-world data, in *Proceedings of the IEEE/CVF International Conference on Computer Vision* (2019), pp. 1588–1597
147. A. Geiger, P. Lenz, R. Urtasun, Are we ready for autonomous driving? the KITTI vision benchmark suite, in *IEEE Conference on Computer Vision and Pattern Recognition* (2012), pp. 3354–3361
148. H. Caesar, V. Bankiti, A.H. Lang, S. Vora, V.E. Liong, Q. Xu, A. Krishnan, Y. Pan, G. Baldan, O. Beijbom, nuscenes: A multimodal dataset for autonomous driving, in *Proceedings of the IEEE/CVF Conference on Computer Vision and Pattern Recognition* (2020), pp. 11621–11631
149. E. Grilli, F. Menna, F. Remondino, A review of point clouds segmentation and classification algorithms. Int. Arch. Photogramm. Remote Sens. Spat. Inf. Sci. **42**, 339–344 (2017)
150. J. Zhang, X. Zhao, Z. Chen, Z. Lu, A review of deep learning-based semantic segmentation for point cloud. IEEE Access **7**, 179118–179133 (2019)
151. X. Wang, J. Lin, L. Yang, S. Wang, A review of point cloud 3D object detection methods based on deep learning, in *CCF National Conference of Computer Applications* (2023), pp. 30–39
152. D. Fernandes, A. Silva, R. Névoa, C. Simões, D. Gonzalez, M. Guevara, P. Novais, J. Monteiro, P. Melo-Pinto, Point-cloud based 3D object detection and classification methods for self-driving applications: A survey and taxonomy. Inf. Fusion **68**, 161–191 (2021)

Chapter 2
Learning Basics for 3D Point Clouds

Abstract This chapter presents the principles of point cloud learning, including the foundations of deep learning and classical neural networks applied to point clouds. The first part covers the basic concepts of deep learning and provides a taxonomy of neural networks, including convolutional neural networks (CNNs), recurrent neural networks (RNNs), and graph neural networks (GNNs), among others. The second part focuses on the design of common point cloud learning networks, such as the PointNet series, point cloud transformers, and an efficient algorithm called Point Voxel CNN.

Keywords Principles of deep learning · Taxonomy of neural networks · Point cloud learning · Convolution neural network · Transformer

2.1 Deep Learning Foundations

Deep learning as a part of machine learning enables computers to learn from data in artificial intelligence [1–62]. It has become a powerful technique to support underpinning and almost all algorithm development, such as computer vision (CV), natural language processing (NLP), audio and speech recognition, and deep reinforcement learning. This section introduces basic concepts about deep learning.

2.1.1 Introduction to Deep Learning

Deep learning aims to learn the data distribution of a dataset $\mathcal{D}$ by training a carefully designed neural network model in an end-to-end manner. The model comprises numerous neurons, each containing weights and biases. These are processed through activation functions to introduce nonlinearity. An illustration of a neural network is shown in Fig. 2.1. Training deep learning models involves multiple layers of abstraction, enabling the network to learn complex patterns in the data. Training a neural network involves optimizing a loss function to update its

W. Gao, G. Li, *Deep Learning for 3D Point Clouds*,
https://doi.org/10.1007/978-981-97-9570-3_2

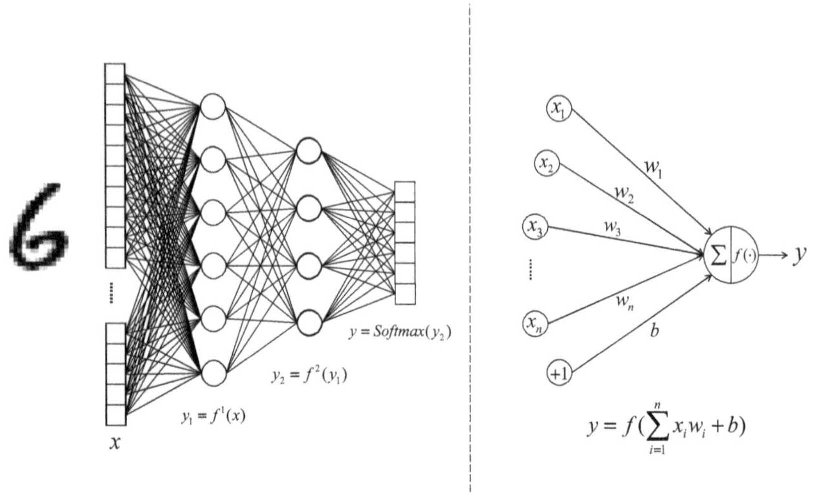

Fig. 2.1 An illustration of the neural network model. Left is an intuitive figure for the neural model taking image recognition as an example. The raw input figure is first flattened into a vector x. Then it is processed hierarchically as $y_1 = f^1(x)$ and $y_2 = f^2(y_1)$. The output is finally processed as $y = \text{Softmax}(y_2)$ to normalize each element into range 0~1. Right is the details of a neural. It takes the output of n neurals from the previous level as input, adds it with b, and finally, processes the sum with an activation function. The output y can be computed as $f(\sum_{i=1}^{n} x_i w_i + b)$ (Source: Author)

parameters. This loss function is specifically designed to quantify the discrepancy between the model's predictions and the ground truth. We can take a macro view of deep learning from the following aspects:

- **Data Representation:** Deep learning depends on massive data operation. The basic data units usually contain many dimensions. To uniformly represent the data operation, we introduce a tensor, which can represent multidimensional arrays conveniently.
- **Model:** For different applications, we usually need to develop different deep neural network (DNN) models for specialized areas, including convolutional neural networks, recurrent neural networks, transformers, graph neural networks, and so on.
- **Optimization:** As deep learning models usually contain lots of parameters, we need to compute the optimal values using optimization techniques. This process is also called training, which will be described in Sect. 2.1.2.
- **Software:** Deep learning models are essentially a form of software. The rapid developments of deep learning theory and algorithms have promoted the emergence and improvement of deep learning frameworks such as Caffe [63], TensorFlow [64], PyTorch [65], and MXNet [66]. These frameworks significantly facilitate the research and implementation of deep learning models through unified interfaces of basic modules and highly efficient parallel implementations.

- **Hardware and Architecture:** The basic operation for deep learning is matrix multiplication, which is suitable for parallel computing. GPU is the most widely used hardware for training and inference. The compute unified device architecture [67] (CUDA) developed by NVIDIA provides convenient interaction between hardware and software frameworks.

Moreover, there are also some basic concepts for deep learning, which we will denote in the following sections.

- **Training Dataset, Evaluation Dataset, and Test Dataset:** These three components are split from the integral dataset, which is used to update model parameters, test the performance during training, and test the performance after training.
- **Generalization:** The goal of deep learning is to obtain a model that can perform well even for unseen data. This is measured within the test dataset, which is inaccessible during training.
- **Overfitting and Underfitting:** When a deep learning model is trained and evaluated on separate datasets to ensure generalization, it may exhibit high performance on the training dataset while performing poorly on the test dataset, a phenomenon known as overfitting. Conversely, if the model is insufficiently trained and demonstrates poor performance on the training dataset, this condition is referred to as underfitting.
- **Parameters and Hyper-Parameters:** Parameters are learnable in deep learning models and hyper-parameters are the configurations of parameters, depth of the architecture, and so on.

2.1.2 *Training Deep Learning Models*

In most deep learning contexts, we focus on a performance metric P that is assessed using the test dataset. Directly optimizing P can be impractical, so we instead optimize a surrogate loss function $J(\theta)$ with the aim of indirectly improving P. The primary objective in training a deep learning model revolves around minimizing an objective function. The expected value of this function is calculated with respect to the underlying data distribution p_{data}, and it is denoted as:

$$J(\boldsymbol{\theta}) = \mathbb{E}_{(\boldsymbol{x},y)\sim p_{\text{data}}} L(f(\boldsymbol{x};\boldsymbol{\theta}), y). \tag{2.1}$$

where L is the loss function for each example, $f(\boldsymbol{x};\boldsymbol{\theta})$ denotes the predicted output when the input is $\boldsymbol{x}$ and parameter $\boldsymbol{\theta}$, and $\mathbb{E}$ means mathematical expectation. In supervised learning, y is the target output. The objective of a deep learning algorithm is to minimize the expected generalization error as expressed Eq. (2.1). This expected value, referred to as the *risk*, is computed over the true underlying data distribution p_{data}. Since $p_{\text{data}}(\boldsymbol{x}, y)$ is not directly accessible, we work with a finite sample training dataset. One of the most direct approaches to converting a machine learning problem into an optimization problem is to formulate it as a minimization task, where the goal is to reduce the average loss or error on the training dataset. This approach essentially involves substituting the true distribution of the data, $p(x, y)$, with the empirical distribution, $\hat{p}(x, y)$, which is estimated from the available training data. Therefore, we minimize the empirical risk as:

$$\mathbb{E}_{(\boldsymbol{x},y)\sim\hat{p}_{\text{data}}} L(f(\boldsymbol{x};\boldsymbol{\theta}), y) = \frac{1}{m}\sum_{i=1}^{m} L(f(\boldsymbol{x}^{(i)};\theta), y^{(i)}), \tag{2.2}$$

where m is the number of training examples, and $\hat{p}_{\text{data}}$ is the empirical distribution based on the training dataset.

In deep learning, the objective function can usually be broken down into a sum of individual losses, each corresponding to a single training example. To optimize this objective, machine learning algorithms typically calculate parameter updates based on an estimated expected loss, which is computed using a random subset of the total training data, rather than the entire dataset. There are two main categories of optimization methods in machine learning: batch methods and stochastic methods. Batch methods, also known as deterministic gradient methods, process the entire training dataset simultaneously, using all examples to compute a single update. In contrast, stochastic methods, also referred to as online methods, update the parameters using one example at a time, processing the training data in a sequential manner. The term "online" often refers to situations where examples are continuously created rather than being drawn from a fixed-size training set processed over multiple passes.

Most deep learning algorithms use minibatch methods, which process a small batch of training examples to compute each update. This approach is often referred to as stochastic optimization, with stochastic gradient descent (SGD) being a well-known example. Deep learning models are optimized using the gradient descent algorithm. Figure 2.2 illustrates a simple case. Consider a naive scenario where the loss is represented as a function of model parameters θ. We need to search the solution space according to certain rules to reach the global optimal point θ_0. Typically, we start from a random initial point and update θ in the direction of gradient descent. The learning rate determines the update step size, controlling how far the model moves in the direction of the gradient during each iteration. Deep learning training can be implemented end-to-end using the chain rule from calculus.

The chain rule allows us to compute the derivatives of composed functions using known derivatives. Backpropagation is an algorithm that leverages the chain rule to efficiently compute gradients by carefully ordering its computations, recursively propagating error gradients through the network. Let x be a real number and consider $y = g(x)$ and $z = f(g(x)) = f(y)$. The chain rule is then expressed as:

$$\frac{dz}{dx} = \frac{dz}{dy}\frac{dy}{dx}. \tag{2.3}$$

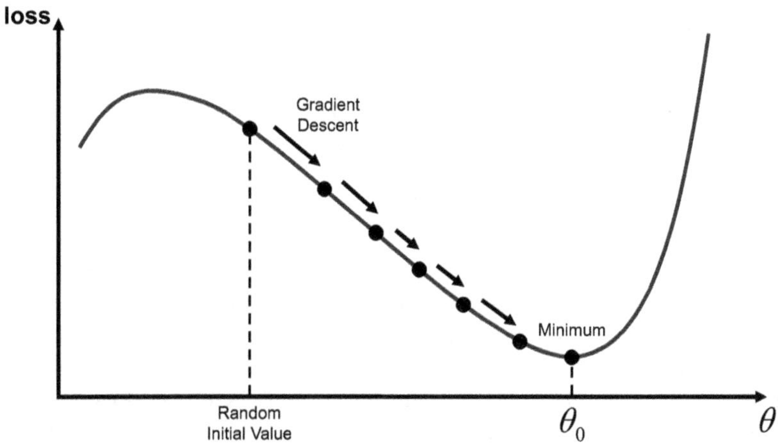

Fig. 2.2 An illustration of how the gradient descent works to optimize a model to reach global minimum value (Source: Author)

In a more generalized scenario, let $\boldsymbol{x} \in \mathbb{R}^m$, $\boldsymbol{y} \in \mathbb{R}^n$, g maps from $\mathbb{R}^m$ to $\mathbb{R}^n$, and f maps from $\mathbb{R}^n$ to $\mathbb{R}$. If $\boldsymbol{y} = g(\boldsymbol{x})$ and $z = f(\boldsymbol{y})$, then:

$$\frac{\partial z}{\partial x_i} = \sum_j \frac{\partial z}{\partial y_j} \frac{\partial y_j}{\partial x_i}. \tag{2.4}$$

This principle underpins the operation of deep learning models, where gradients are computed from back to front, leading to the updating of learnable parameters through a process known as backpropagation. Stochastic gradient descent and its variants are the dominant optimization algorithms in deep learning [68]. An unbiased gradient estimate can be obtained by averaging the gradients from a minibatch of m independently and identically distributed (i.i.d.) examples, ensuring a representative sample of the true gradient. The specifics of this algorithm are outlined in Algorithm 1.

Algorithm 1 SGD algorithm

Require: Learning rate ϵ
Require: Initial parameter $\boldsymbol{\theta}$
while stopping criterion not meet **do**
Sample a minibatch of m examples from the training set $\{\boldsymbol{x}^{(1)}, \ldots, \boldsymbol{x}^{(m)}\}$ with corresponding targets $\boldsymbol{y}^{(i)}$
Compute gradient estimate: $\hat{\boldsymbol{g}} \leftarrow \frac{1}{m} \nabla_\theta \sum_{i=1}^{m} L(f(\boldsymbol{x}^{(i)}; \boldsymbol{\theta}), \boldsymbol{y}^{(i)})$
Update $\boldsymbol{\theta} \leftarrow \boldsymbol{\theta} - \epsilon \hat{\boldsymbol{g}}$
end while

Although stochastic gradient descent enjoys widespread popularity as an optimization approach, it can exhibit sluggishness at times. To tackle this, the momentum method has been devised to expedite the learning process, particularly when dealing with scenarios such as high curvature, small yet consistent gradients, or gradients afflicted with noise. This momentum-based algorithm functions by accumulating a moving average of past gradients that decays exponentially, thereby enabling it to maintain momentum and continue moving in the direction indicated by these gradients.

To put it in a different manner, the momentum algorithm incorporates a variable v, which serves as a momentum indicator, signifying both the direction and the rate of movement of parameters in the parameter space. This momentum is calculated as an exponentially decaying average of the negative gradient. This concept finds its roots in a physical comparison, where the negative gradient is analogous to a force propelling a particle through the parameter space, adhering to Newton's principles of motion. In physics, momentum is defined as the product of mass and velocity, but in the context of the momentum learning algorithm, assuming a unit mass, the velocity vector v can be viewed as a force vector. A hyperparameter α, ranging from 0 to 1 (excluding 1), governs the exponential decay rate of the contributions from previous gradients. The update formula is as:

$$\boldsymbol{v} \leftarrow \alpha \boldsymbol{v} - \epsilon \nabla_{\theta} \left(\frac{1}{m} \sum_{i=1}^{m} L(\boldsymbol{f}(\boldsymbol{x}^{(i)}; \boldsymbol{\theta}), \boldsymbol{y}^{(i)}) \right), \tag{2.5}$$

$$\boldsymbol{\theta} \leftarrow \boldsymbol{\theta} + \boldsymbol{v}. \tag{2.6}$$

The velocity vector, denoted as $\boldsymbol{v}$, integrates the gradient elements. As the parameter α increases relative to learning rate ϵ, the influence of previous gradients on the current update direction becomes more pronounced. The momentum-enhanced version of the Stochastic Gradient Descent (SGD) algorithm is outlined in Algorithm 2, providing a refined approach to optimization.

Algorithm 2 SGD algorithm with momentum

Require: Learning rate ϵ and momentum parameter α.
Require: Initial parameter $\boldsymbol{\theta}$ and initial velocity $\boldsymbol{v}$.
  while stopping criterion not meet **do**
    Sample a minibatch of m examples from the training set $\{\boldsymbol{x}^{(1)}, \ldots, \boldsymbol{x}^{(m)}\}$ with corresponding targets $\boldsymbol{y}^{(i)}$
    Compute gradient estimate: $\hat{\boldsymbol{g}} \leftarrow \frac{1}{m} \nabla_{\theta} \sum_{i=1}^{m} L(f(\boldsymbol{x}^{(i)}; \boldsymbol{\theta}), \boldsymbol{y}^{(i)})$
    Compute velocity update: $\boldsymbol{v} \leftarrow \alpha \boldsymbol{v} - \epsilon \hat{\boldsymbol{g}}$
    Apply update: $\boldsymbol{\theta} \leftarrow \boldsymbol{\theta} + \boldsymbol{v}$
  end while

2.1.3 Multilayer Perception

Multilayer Perceptron (MLP), also called a deep feedforward network or feedforward neural network, is a foundational neural network model, widely used in contemporary deep learning systems [69]. An MLP can be expressed as a mapping $y = f(x, \theta)$, where θ represents the learnable parameters. The MLP approximates a certain distribution function $f^{\star}$. For instance, in image classification, x and y represent the input image and the classification output, respectively. $f^{\star}$ and f denote the ground truth mapping and the predicted mapping, respectively. The term feedforward signifies the absence of feedback loops, meaning the model's outputs are not fed back into the network. If feedback connections are added to feedforward neural networks, they transform into recurrent neural networks (Sect. 2.1.5).

MLPs are often referred to as networks because they integrate multiple functions, represented as nodes in a directed acyclic graph. For instance, in a network with three sequential functions f^1, f^2, and f^3, the composite function can be expressed as $f(x, \theta) = f^3(f^2(f^1(x; \theta_1); \theta_2); \theta_3)$. The total number of layers in the sequence is described as the depth of the model, which underpins the concept of deep learning. The final layer of a feedforward network is trained to approximate the ground truth. This layer plays a critical role in mapping input data to predicted outcomes, thereby enabling accurate predictions based on the learned model.

Now we consider a simple classification task using MLP. Given that the training dataset contains N classes, the output consists of N neurons. The ground truth label is represented as a one-hot vector, meaning that one digit is 1 and the other $N - 1$ digits are 0. The position of the 1 indicates the category label. The model's output is trained to approximate this distribution. The output y is normalized such that the sum of the N digits equals 1. This normalization is achieved using the Softmax function as:

$$\text{Softmax}(y)_i = \frac{\exp(y_i)}{\sum_{j=1}^{N} \exp(y_j)}, \tag{2.7}$$

where y_i is the i-th digit of y. For classification tasks, the cross-entropy loss function J is adopted. Cross-entropy is derived from information theory, where it quantifies the uncertainty of the probability distribution with the Shannon entropy:

$$H(x) = -\mathbb{E}_{x \sim P}[\log P(x)], \tag{2.8}$$

where P is a probability distribution. This equation is also referred to as $H(P)$. For classification tasks, we have two probability distributions P and Q, representing the ground truth and the model prediction, respectively. The difference between these distributions can be estimated using the Kullback–Leibler (KL) divergence:

$$D_{\text{KL}}(P \| Q) = \mathbb{E}_{x \sim P} \log \frac{P(x)}{Q(x)}. \tag{2.9}$$

The smaller the KL divergence value, the higher the similarity of the distribution. In information theory, KL divergence is closely related to cross-entropy:

$$H(P, Q) = H(P) + D_{\mathrm{KL}}(P \| Q), \tag{2.10}$$

where P denotes the ground truth distribution, and Q is the model prediction. We need to optimize Q, then $H(P)$ is constant. In this scenario, cross-entropy is equivalent to KL divergence. Assuming $y = [y_0, y_1, \ldots, y_{N-1}]$ is the one-hot label and $p = [p_0, p_1, \ldots, p_{N-1}]$ is the normalized model prediction, cross-entropy loss is formulated by:

$$\text{Loss} = -\sum_{i=0}^{N-1} y_i \log(p_i). \tag{2.11}$$

Mean Squared Error (MSE) loss is another common loss function that calculates the difference between the predicted values and ground truth values. MSE is generally oriented to regression tasks, whereas the cross-entropy loss is adopted by classification tasks.

2.1.4 Convolution Neural Network

Convolutional Neural Networks (CNNs) are designed for structured data with fixed and grid-like topology [70, 71]. Such as time-series data and images are suitable for CNNs, which can be viewed as 1D grids with time points and 2D grids with pixels, respectively. CNN is typical feedforward neural network. Consider an image recognition task as an example. If we use MLPs to process it, the first layer of the network takes numerous values as input, significantly increasing the computational burden. As shown in Fig. 2.3, CNNs mitigate this by incorporating three key refinements:

- **Sparse Connectivity:** As illustrated in Fig. 2.3, each element corresponds to a local area rather than the entire input.
- **Parameter Sharing:** The convolution operation is performed between the kernel and a section of the input, where the parameters in the kernel are shared across one output channel. To extract more features in parallel, the output usually comprises several channels, each sharing the same kernel parameters.
- **Equivariant Representation:** The parameter sharing design ensures neural network equivariance to translation. Consider a case where input pixels are translated in a specific pattern, but the output values of the first layer change only in a permuted order. Thus, the feature vector and recognition result remain unchanged.

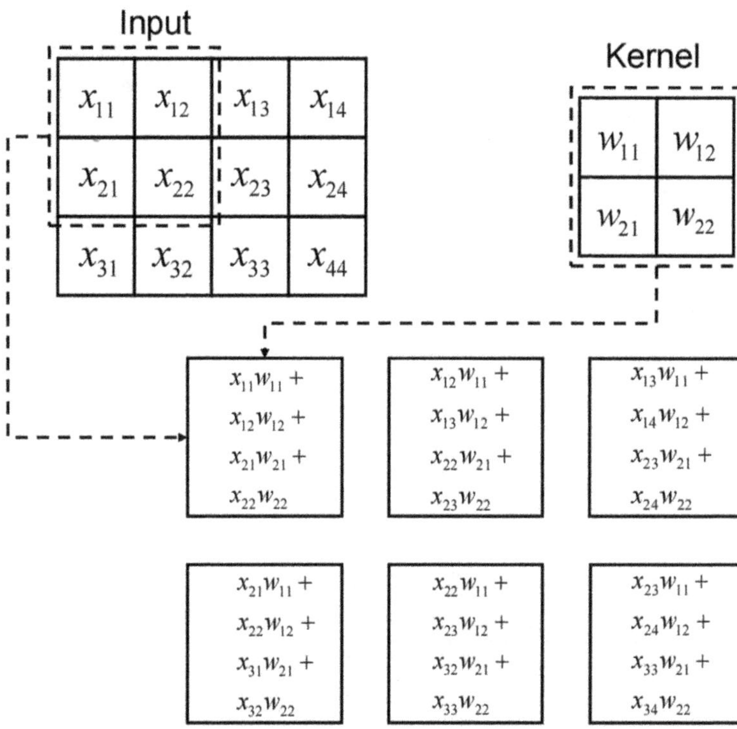

Fig. 2.3 An illustration for Convolution Neural Network. Assuming that the input is a [3, 4] tensor. Convolution is conducted with only one kernel, a [2, 2] tensor. Padding is set to 0, and stride is set to 1. The convolution result is a [2, 3] tensor, derived from dot production. Starting from the top left corner of the input, the kernel processes input in the same manner, sliding in spatial order. In a practical convolution neural network such as ResNet, convolution is hierarchically conducted. During this process, the number of channels for the output increases, while the number of values in a channel decreases. In the end, we take a max-pooling operation to pick out the maximum value for a channel in the output feature map (Source: Author)

Convolutional neural networks are well-suited for parallel computing. With convolution layers, different channels in the output and various regions in the input are processed independently.

For 3D computer vision, convolutional neural networks are also effective. To process structured data, the point cloud is first converted into a structured form called voxelization. As 3D voxels are often sparse, directly applying standard convolutional neural networks can be inefficient. We describe the calculation principle of sparse convolution in detail, with an intuitive sketch shown in Fig. 2.4. Since many voxels are empty, directly using convolution can cause redundancy in computation.

To simplify, we use a 2D image to explain sparse convolution [72]. The image is defined in Fig. 2.5, where points P_1 and $P_2$are nonzero, and other points are zero. These nonzero points are active input sites, with coordinates (1, 2) and (2, 3),

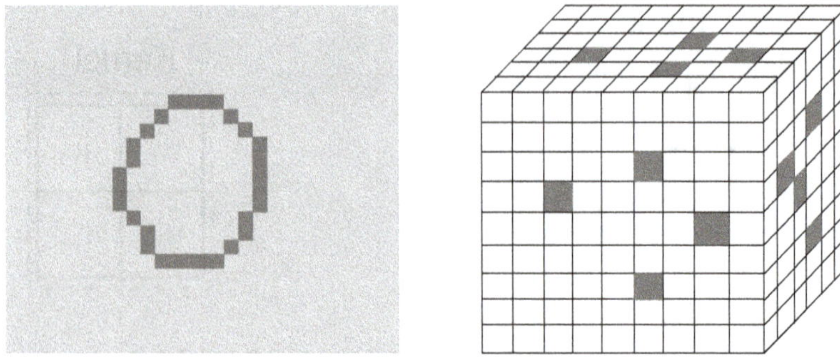

Fig. 2.4 An intuitive sight of sparse convolution on 2D image and 3D voxel (Source: Author)

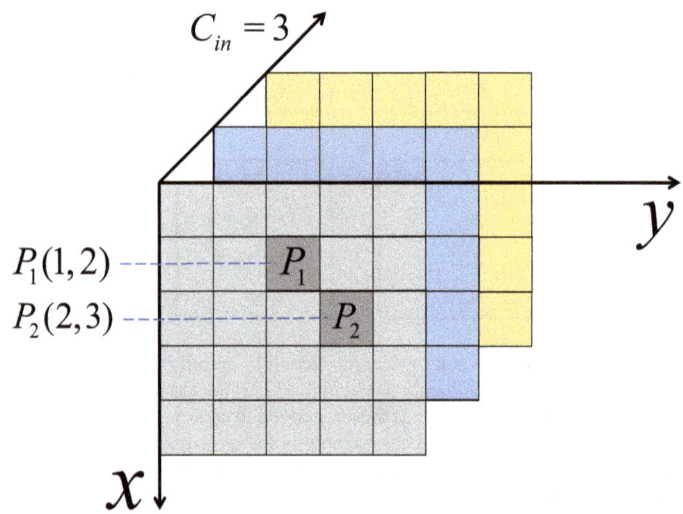

Fig. 2.5 An illustration of sparse convolution on image data (Source: Author)

respectively. The convolution kernel is defined as $[C_{in}, C_{out}, 3, 3]$ with stride=1 and padding=0. In this setting, $C_{in} = 3$ and $C_{out} = 2$. There are two kinds of output modes for sparse convolution, shown in Fig. 2.6. The first mode is the same as general convolution, where an active input site is considered if it falls within the convolution scope. The second mode differs in that only the active output site centered in the kernel is considered. To align with traditional convolution, we only explain the former. The first step for sparse convolution is to build a hash table. This process is illustrated in Fig. 2.7. In the first convolution layer, the input consists of only two elements. It is recorded in a key-value (K-V) structure as Hash_{in}, where key_{in} stores the coordinates for the input. The output sites for key=0 are shown in the upper branch, while key=1 is shown in the lower branch.

For the image, the input size is 5×5, while the output size is 3×3. The coordinates for the output active sites are shown in P_{out}. Then we merge the

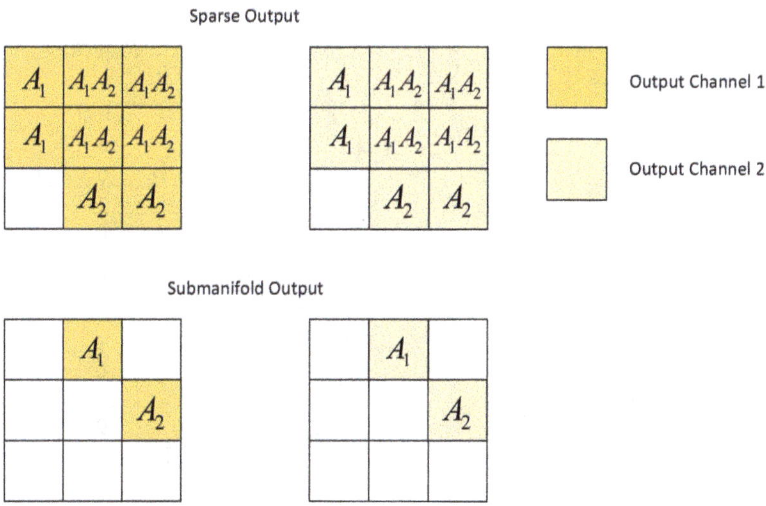

Fig. 2.6 Two output modes for sparse convolution (Source: Author)

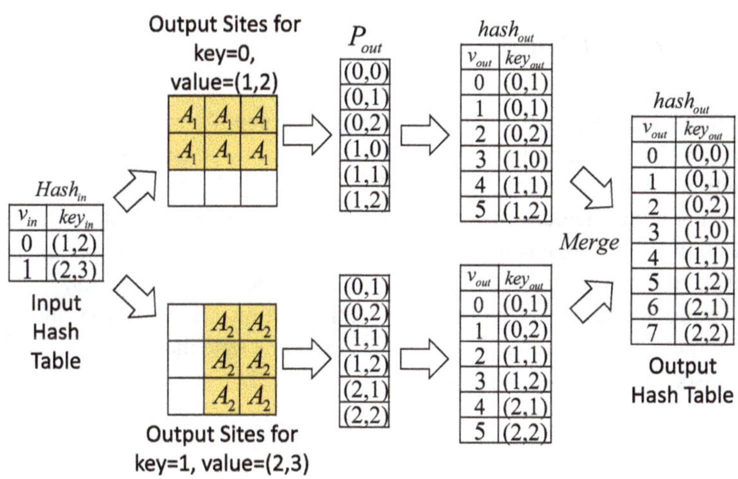

Fig. 2.7 Construction of hash table for sparse convolution (Source: Author)

subtables for each input site and obtain the output hash table, denoted as $hash_{out}$. In this example, there are eight active sites within a total of nine output sites. The second step involves constructing a rulebook for sparse convolution, as shown in Fig. 2.8. After obtaining P_{out} in the first step, we need to determine the position of each input active site in the kernel. This is achieved using the function GetOffset, which queries the kernel to get the kernel parameter for each output active site. Next, we construct the rulebook by aggregating all the items from the previous steps. The rulebook includes columns for the kernel element, count, v_{in} and v_{out}, listed from left to right. Finally, we sum up the items with the same v_{out} to compute the output feature map.

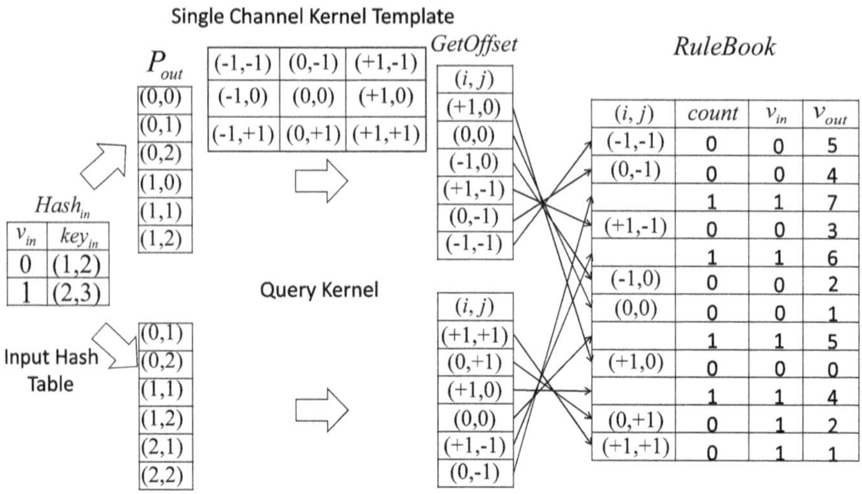

Fig. 2.8 Construction of rulebook for sparse convolution (Source: Author)

2.1.5 Recurrent Neural Networks

In response to the sequential data, another typical neural network recurrent neural network (RNN) is designed. The fundamental concept of RNNs is similar to convolutional neural networks (CNNs). In CNNs, different areas of the same image (and the computed feature maps) use the same kernel for one output dimension. Similarly, in RNNs, tokens at different time points share the same parameters. An example of the computational graph for an RNN is depicted in Fig. 2.9.

Assuming we use the hyperbolic tangent function for activation and that the model outputs discrete items such as words or characters, the update equations can be expressed as:

$$\boldsymbol{a}^{(t)} = \boldsymbol{b} + \boldsymbol{W}\boldsymbol{h}^{(t-1)} + \boldsymbol{U}\boldsymbol{x}^{(t)}, \tag{2.12}$$

$$\boldsymbol{h}^{(t)} = \tanh(\boldsymbol{a}^{(t)}), \tag{2.13}$$

$$\boldsymbol{o}^{(t)} = \boldsymbol{c} + \boldsymbol{V}\boldsymbol{h}^{(t)}, \tag{2.14}$$

$$\hat{\boldsymbol{y}}^{(t)} = \text{Softmax}(\boldsymbol{o}^{(t)}), \tag{2.15}$$

where the parameters include bias vectors $\boldsymbol{b}$ and $\boldsymbol{c}$, along with weight matrices $\boldsymbol{U}$, $\boldsymbol{V}$, and $\boldsymbol{W}$, corresponding to input-to-hidden, hidden-to-output, and hidden-to-hidden connections, respectively. The model is designed to map an input sequence to an output sequence with the same length, effectively mirroring the sequence's structure. A given sequence of $\boldsymbol{x}$ values paired with corresponding $\boldsymbol{y}$ values results in the total loss being calculated as the cumulative sum of the losses at each time step.

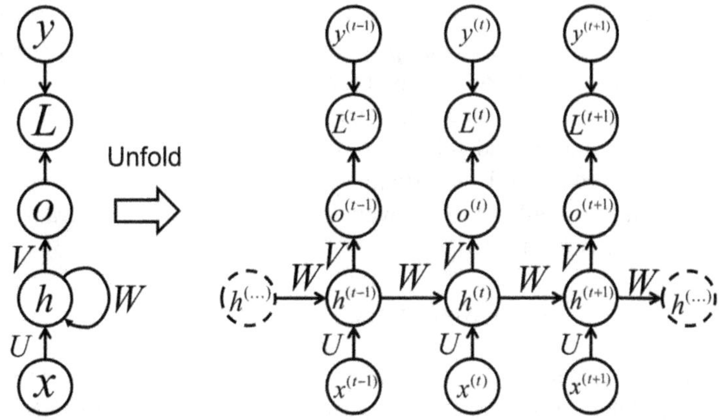

Fig. 2.9 The computational graph for the recurrent neural network. Left is the overall illustration of the nets that map an input sequence of x values to a corresponding sequence of output o values. A loss L measures how far each o is from the corresponding training target $\boldsymbol{y}$. When using *softmax* outputs, we assume $\boldsymbol{o}$ is the unnormalized log probabilities. The loss L internally computes $\hat{y} = \text{softmax}(\boldsymbol{o})$ and compares this to the target $\boldsymbol{y}$. The RNN has input to hidden connections parametrized by a weight matrix U, hidden-to-hidden recurrent connections parametrized by a weight matrix W, and hidden-to-output connections parametrized by a weight matrix V (Source: Author)

2.1.6 *Transformer*

RNNs have been widely used in sequence prediction tasks. Nevertheless, they handle data in a sequential manner rather than in parallel, which limits their efficiency in terms of time and memory usage. The Transformer was initially developed for language translation [73]. Due to its strong representational capabilities, it has been extended to other domains such as computer vision [74, 75] and multimodal research [76]. In the sections that follow, we will explore the fundamental concepts of the vanilla Transformer model within the context of natural language processing (NLP).

We introduce Transformer for machine translation task in NLP as an example [73]. The inputs and outputs are the input sentence from source language and the output sentence from target language, which are tokenized separately. The embedding module transforms the discrete tokens into tensors with consistent dimension. For the transformer encoder, the input embeddings are processed with the self-attention module to establish correlations among the input tokens. For the decoder, the output tokens are processed through masked self-attention and cross-attention modules. Transformer model works in autoregression manner, i.e., it predicts the next token in the output space sequentially, conditioned on the previously predicted tokens. The output of the decoder is processed by *Softmax* to predict the probability distribution over the vocabulary.

Transformer model adopts a typical encoder-decoder framework. Given an input sequence $(x_1, \ldots, x_n)$, the encoder part maps it to a continuous features $\mathbf{z} = (z_1, \ldots, z_n)$. Utilizing $\mathbf{z}$, the decoder part sequentially produces an output sequence $(y_1, ..., y_m)$ one-by-one. The encoder consists of $N = 6$ uniform layers, each of which comprises a multi-head self-attention sub-layer followed by a positionally oriented feed-forward network. The framework integrates a residual connection past each sublayer before implementing layer normalization [77]. The transformation after each sublayer is formalized as:

$$y = \text{LayerNorm}(x + \text{Sublayer}(x)), \tag{2.16}$$

where Sublayer(x) signifies the operation specific to the sublayer. For the summation $y = x + \text{Sublayer}(x)$ in a certain layer of the model, $\bar{y} = \text{LayerNorm}(y)$ is implemented as:

$$y_i = \frac{g_i}{\sigma}(y_i - \mu), \quad \mu = \frac{1}{H}\sum_{i=1}^{H} y_i, \quad \sigma = \sqrt{\frac{1}{H}\sum_{i=1}^{H}(y_i - \mu)^2}, \tag{2.17}$$

where H is the count of hidden units, y_i is the normalized ith hidden unit of y and g_i is a gain parameter scaling the normalized y_i. All layers, including the embedding layers, are designed to output vectors of size $d_{\text{model}} = 512$ to accommodate the residual connections. The decoder mirrors the encoder's structure but adds an another sublayer for multi-head attention over the encoder's outputs. Additionally, the decoder's self-attention mechanism is modified to block forward position attendance, and output embeddings are shifted by one position to ensure that the prediction at any position i relies solely on the previously established outputs.

An attention mechanism involves transforming a query alongside a collection of key-value pairs into a resultant vector. In this process, both the query and each key-value pair are represented as vectors. The resultant vector is generated by taking a weighted average of the values, with weights determined through a compatibility function that assesses how well each key matches the query.

Scaled Dot-Product Attention The attention operation used in the transformer architecture is termed Scaled Dot-Product Attention [73]. This method involves queries and keys of dimension d_k, and values of dimension d_v. The process entails calculating the dot products of the query with all keys, scaling each by $\frac{1}{\sqrt{d_k}}$, and applying a Softmax function to derive the weights for the values. Typically, the attention operation is executed on multiple queries at once, aggregated into a matrix Q. Similarly, keys and values are compiled into matrices K and V respectively. The resultant output matrix is formulated as:

$$\text{Attention}(Q, K, V) = \text{Softmax}\left(\frac{QK^T}{\sqrt{d_k}}\right)V. \tag{2.18}$$

This scaling is critical as, for larger values of d_k, the magnitudes of the dot products increase, which can push the Softmax function into zones with very low gradients, potentially impacting the efficiency and effectiveness of the attention mechanism.

Multi-head Attention Instead of employing a standard approach where all queries, keys, and values are projected into a singular d_{model}-dimensional space for a conventional attention mechanism, an enhanced technique is to employ a series of unique, specialized projections. These projections specifically tailor queries, keys, and values into distinct, reduced dimensions—d_k for queries and keys, and d_v for values—across h different and independently optimized linear transformations. Each distinct projection then independently processes its set of queries, keys, and values through its own attention mechanism, all running concurrently. The outputs, each in d_v dimensions, are subsequently combined and undergo a final transformation. This process, known as Multi-Head Attention, allows the model to simultaneously process diverse segments of information across multiple spatial and representational domains, circumventing the blending effect inherent in single-head attention models. This is mathematically articulated as:

$$\begin{aligned} \text{MultiHead}(Q, K, V) &= \text{Concat}(\text{head}1, \ldots, \text{head}h)W^O \\ \text{where head}i &= \text{Attention}(QW_i^Q, KW_i^K, VW_i^V), \end{aligned} \tag{2.19}$$

where the projection matrices W_i^Q, W_i^K, and W_i^V adapt dimensions from $d$model to d_k or d_v, and W^O is a final projection matrix that adjusts the combined output back to d_{model} dimensions.

Moreover, each layer within the encoder and decoder frameworks incorporates a bespoke fully connected feed-forward network. This network functions through a sequence of two linear transformations, interspaced by a ReLU activation phase, effectively resembling the mechanics of one-dimensional convolutions. The configuration of this network is specified as:

$$\text{FFN}(x) = \max(0, xW_1 + b_1)W_2 + b_2, \tag{2.20}$$

where W_1 and W_2 denote the weight matrices, and b_1 and b_2 are bias elements integral to the transformations.

The attention mechanism inherently lacks sensitivity to the sequence order of input tokens, meaning that its output remains unchanged when the order of input tokens is altered. To enable the transformer model to interpret and utilize the sequence order, it is essential to incorporate specific information about the positions of tokens within the sequence. This is achieved through the addition of "positional encodings" to the input embeddings at the base levels of both the encoder and decoder stacks within the transformer architecture. These positional encodings match the d_{model} dimension of the embeddings, allowing for a direct summation of the two components. The transformer model employs sinusoidal functions for these encodings, opting for sine and cosine functions oscillating at varying frequencies:

$$PE_{(pos,2i)} = \sin\left(\frac{pos}{10{,}000^{2i/d_{\text{model}}}}\right),$$
$$PE_{(pos,2i+1)} = \cos\left(\frac{pos}{10{,}000^{2i/d_{\text{model}}}}\right), \tag{2.21}$$

where pos indicates the token's position and i represents the dimension index. Each dimension in the positional encoding is linked to a sinusoidal wave, and these waves extend in a geometric progression from 2π to $20{,}000\pi$. This particular choice of positional encoding is strategic, as it hypothesizes that such a design will facilitate the model's ability to learn and leverage relative positions effectively, given that any position offset k allows PE_{pos+k} to be linearly deduced from PE_{pos}.

2.1.7 Graph Neural Network

Graphs offer a robust and adaptable framework for representing information. Indeed, many types of data encountered in daily life can be depicted using graphs, including structured formats such as images and text [78]. Graph neural networks (GNNs) are tailored to tackle challenges at both the node and graph levels [79, 80]. This section elaborates on the fundamentals of graphs and GNNs. A graph is represented as $\mathcal{G}(\mathcal{V}, \mathcal{E})$, where $\mathcal{V} = v_1, \ldots, v_N$ comprises a collection of $N = |\mathcal{V}|$ nodes, and $\mathcal{E} = e_1, \ldots, e_M$ consists of $M = |\mathcal{E}|$ edges. The relationships between nodes in graph $\mathcal{G}$ are typically illustrated using an adjacency matrix, symbolized as $\mathbf{A} \in 0, 1^{N \times N}$. In this matrix, $\mathbf{A}i, j = 1$ signifies that node v_i is connected to node v_j, and $\mathbf{A}i, j = 0$ indicates no adjacency. The degree of a node $v_i \in \mathcal{V}$ is quantified by the tally of nodes directly linked to v_i:

$$d(v_i) = \sum_{v_j \in \mathcal{V}} \mathbb{1}_{\mathcal{E}}(\{v_i, v_j\}), \tag{2.22}$$

where $\mathbb{1}$ is an indicator function:

$$\mathbb{1} = \begin{cases} 1 & \text{if } (v_i, v_j) \in \mathcal{E}, \\ 0 & \text{if } (v_i, v_j) \notin \mathcal{E}. \end{cases} \tag{2.23}$$

We can also determine the degree of a node v_i in $\mathcal{G}$ from its adjacency matrix:

$$d(v_i) = \sum_{j=1}^{N} \mathbf{A}_{i,j}. \tag{2.24}$$

For a node v_i, we define its neighborhood as $\mathcal{N}(v_i)$, which consists of all nodes adjacent to v_i. Note that for a node v_i, the number of nodes in $\mathcal{N}(v_i)$ is its degree, i.e., $d(v_i) = |\mathcal{N}(v_i)|$. Next, we consider the attribute of connectivity for a graph. Before discussing connectivity, we introduce some basic concepts such as walks and paths.

A walk on a graph is a sequence of nodes and edges, beginning with a node and ending with a node where each edge is incident with the nodes immediately preceding and following it. A walk starting at node u and ending at node v is called a $u - v$ walk. The length of a walk is the number of edges in this walk. Note that $u - v$ walks are not unique since there exist various $u - v$ walks with different lengths. A trail is defined as a walk whose edges are distinct, and a path is a walk whose nodes are distinct.

A subgraph $\mathcal{G}' = \{\mathcal{V}', \mathcal{E}'\}$ of a given graph $\mathcal{G} = \{\mathcal{V}, \mathcal{E}\}$ is defined as a graph formed with a subset of nodes $\mathcal{V}' \subset \mathcal{V}$ and a subset of edges $\mathcal{E}' \subset \mathcal{E}$. Furthermore, the subset $\mathcal{V}'$ must include all the nodes involved in the edges in the subset $\mathcal{E}'$. A connected component is defined as a subgraph $\mathcal{G}' = \{\mathcal{V}', \mathcal{E}'\}$ if there is at least one path between any pair of nodes in the graph and the nodes in $\mathcal{V}'$ are not adjacent to any vertices in $\mathcal{V}/\mathcal{V}'$.

- **Spectral Graph Theory and Graph Fourier Transform**

Spectral graph theory examines the properties of a graph by analyzing the eigenvalues and eigenvectors of its Laplacian matrix [81]. In this section, we introduce the Laplacian matrix of a graph and discuss its key properties, eigenvalues, and eigenvectors. Next, we introduce the Graph Fourier Transform (GFT), essential for GNNs.

Laplacian Matrix The Laplacian matrix $\mathbf{L}$ can be viewed as another matrix representation for graphs in addition to the adjacency matrix. For graph $\mathcal{G} = (\mathcal{V}, \mathcal{E})$ with $\mathbf{A}$ as its adjacency matrix, the Laplacian matrix is defined as:

$$\mathbf{L} = \mathbf{D} - \mathbf{A}, \tag{2.25}$$

where $\mathbf{D}$ is a diagonal degree matrix, $\mathbf{D} = \text{diag}(d(v_1), \ldots, d(v_N))$. The Laplacian matrix can also be normalized as:

$$\mathbf{L} = \mathbf{D}^{-\frac{1}{2}}(\mathbf{D} - \mathbf{A})\mathbf{D}^{-\frac{1}{2}} = \mathbf{I} - \mathbf{D}^{-\frac{1}{2}}\mathbf{A}\mathbf{D}^{-\frac{1}{2}}. \tag{2.26}$$

Next, we will focus on the discussion of the unnormalized Laplacian matrix. We define a vector $\mathbf{f}$ with length N, where its i-th element $\mathbf{f}[i]$ is associated with node v_i. We can use it to represent a node-level feature with a single dimension. It can be proved that $\mathbf{f}^T\mathbf{L}\mathbf{f}$ is always positive for any $\mathbf{f}$.

The Eigenvalues and Eigenvectors of the Laplacian Matrix For graph $\mathcal{G}$, the eigenvalues of its Laplacian matrix $\mathbf{L}$ are non-negative. To prove this, we suppose that λ is an eigenvalue of the Laplacian matrix $\mathbf{L}$ and $\mathbf{u}$ is the corresponding normalized eigenvector. According to the definition of eigenvalues and eigenvectors, we have:

$$\lambda \mathbf{u} = \mathbf{L}\mathbf{u}. \tag{2.27}$$

Note that $\mathbf{u}$ is a unit nonzero vector and $\mathbf{u}^T\mathbf{u} = 1$. Then,

$$\lambda = \lambda \mathbf{u}^T\mathbf{u} = \mathbf{u}^T\lambda\mathbf{u} = \mathbf{u}^T\mathbf{L}\mathbf{u} \geq 0. \tag{2.28}$$

For a graph $\mathcal{G}$ that contains N nodes, there are N eigenvalues/eigenvectors, accounting for multiplicity. It has been previously established that all of these eigenvalues are non-negative. Additionally, it is guaranteed that there is at least one eigenvalue equal to zero, denoted as λ_1, which corresponds to eigenvector $\mathbf{u}_1 = \frac{1}{\sqrt{N}}(1, \ldots, 1)$. We sort these eigenvalues in ascending sequence as $0 = \lambda_1 \leq \lambda_2 \leq, \ldots, \leq \lambda_N$. The corresponding normalized eigenvectors are denoted as $\mathbf{u}_1, \ldots, \mathbf{u}_N$. It can be proved that, for a graph $\mathcal{G}$, the number of 0 eigenvalues of its Laplacian matrix $\mathbf{L}$ (the multiplicity of the 0 eigenvalue) equals the number of connected components in the graph. We can construct the corresponding eigenvectors satisfying orthogonality.

Graph Fourier Transform In real-world applications, we frequently need to work with graphs endowed with attributes or features linked with their nodes. This type of graph-structured data can be regarded as graph signals, encapsulating both the structural information (or the relationships among nodes) and data (or attributes at nodes). A graph signal is composed of a graph $\mathcal{G} = \{\mathcal{V}, \mathcal{E}\}$, along with a function f defined in the graph domain, assigning real numbers to each node. In mathematical terms, this function could be formulated as:

$$f : \mathcal{V} \to \mathbb{R}^{N \times d}, \tag{2.29}$$

where d denotes the dimension of the signal vector linked to each node. Initially, we set $d = 1$ and then generalize to multidimensional signals. Like traditional signal processing, which allows signals to be represented in both temporal and frequency domains, graph signals can similarly be depicted in two distinct domains: the spatial domain and the spectral domain. The spectral domain representation of a graph signal is obtained through the application of the Graph Fourier Transform (GFT). Specifically, the GFT of a graph signal $\mathbf{f}$ on a graph $\mathcal{G}$ is defined as follows:

$$\hat{\mathbf{f}}[l] =< \mathbf{f}, \mathbf{u}_l >= \sum_{i=1}^{N} \mathbf{f}[i]\mathbf{u}_l[i], \tag{2.30}$$

where $\mathbf{u}_l$ denotes the l-th eigenvector of the Laplacian matrix $\mathbf{L}$. λ_l is the corresponding eigenvalue, indicating the smoothness or the frequency of the eigenvector $\mathbf{u}_l$. The eigenvectors can be viewed as the graph Fourier basis of $\mathcal{G}$, while $\hat{\mathbf{f}}$ is composed of the Fourier coefficients of the signal **f** with respect to the corresponding to basis functions. The GFT of **f** can also be expressed as:

$$\hat{\mathbf{f}} = \mathbf{U}^T\mathbf{f}, \tag{2.31}$$

where $\mathbf{u}_l$ represents the l-th column of $\mathbf{U}$. Additionally, the Inverse Graph Fourier Transform exists, enabling the conversion of the spectral domain representation $\hat{\mathbf{f}}$ back into the spatial representation **f**, which is expressed as follows:

$$\mathbf{f}[i] = \sum_{l=1}^{N} \hat{\mathbf{f}}[l]\mathbf{u}_l[i]. \tag{2.32}$$

This procedure can alternatively be depicted in matrix notation as:

$$\mathbf{f} = \mathbf{U}\hat{\mathbf{f}}. \tag{2.33}$$

- **The General Graph Neural Network Frameworks**

We present the overarching structure of Graph Neural Networks applicable to graph-centric and node-centric tasks. Given a graph $\mathcal{G} = \{\mathcal{V}, \mathcal{E})\}$ comprising N nodes, **A** denotes the adjacency matrix. The features associated with the nodes are represented by the matrix $\mathbf{F} \in \mathbb{R}^{N \times d}$, where each row of **F** signifies a node, and d indicates the feature dimension.

Illustration for Node-Focused Tasks A typical architecture for node-focused tasks includes non-linear activation layers and graph filtering. As depicted in the left part of Fig. 2.10, the graph filtering operation refines node features without altering the graph structure. Subsequently, a GNN framework that includes L graph filtering layers and $L - 1$ activation layers is shown in the left part of Fig. 2.11. In this framework, $h_i(\cdot)$ and $\alpha_i(\cdot)$ represent the i-th graph filtering and activation layers,

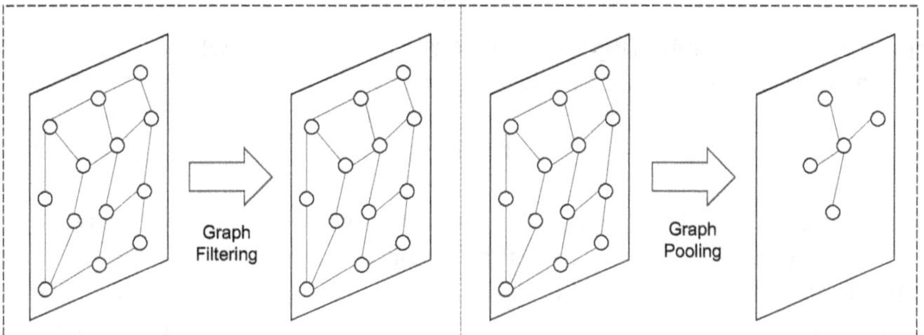

Fig. 2.10 An illustration of Graph filtering operation (left) and Graph pooling operation (right) (Source: Author)

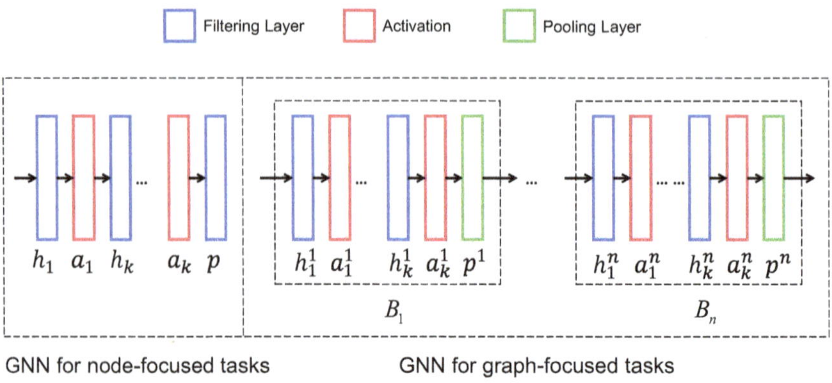

Fig. 2.11 GNN structures for node-focused tasks (left) and graph-focused tasks (right) (Source: Author)

respectively. The output of each graph filtering layer is denoted as $\mathbf{F}^{(i)}$, where $\mathbf{F}^{(0)}$ is initialized with the original features $\mathbf{F}$.

Illustration for Graph-Focused Tasks In general, GNNs aimed at graph-centric tasks can be structured as a series of modular blocks, with each block comprising three main components: the graph filtering layer, the graph pooling layer, and the activation layer. The functionalities of the activation and graph filtering layers are akin to those in node-focused frameworks. However, the graph pooling layer serves as a key component in condensing the node features, generating more abstract information for the entire graph.

- **Graph Filters**

  Graph filters are generally categorized into two types: spectral-based methods and spatial-based methods. In the sections that follow, we will explore how certain spectral-based graph filters can be understood from a spatial viewpoint and will provide specific examples to illustrate these concepts.

Spectral-Based Graph Filters As previously discussed, the GFT of the signal $\mathbf{f} \in \mathbb{R}^N$ on graph $\mathcal{G}$ is defined in the following manner:

$$\hat{\mathbf{f}} = \mathbf{U}^T\mathbf{f}. \tag{2.34}$$

As explained before, $\mathbf{U}$ is composed of N vectors, with each one the eigenvector of Laplacian matrix L for $\mathcal{G}$. $\hat{\mathbf{f}}$ contains the Graph Fourier Coefficients for the signal $\mathbf{f}$. In specific, the i-th entry of $\hat{\mathbf{f}}$ is associated with the i-th component $\mathbf{u}_i$ of Graph Fourier with the associated frequency λ_i. To modulate the spectral representation of $\mathbf{f}$, the Graph Fourier Coefficients could be processed as:

$$\hat{\mathbf{f}}'[i] = \hat{\mathbf{f}}[i] \cdot \gamma(\lambda_i), \quad \text{for} \quad i = 1, 2, \ldots, N. \tag{2.35}$$

It is also be formulated in a matrix form:

$$\hat{\mathbf{f}}' = \gamma(\Lambda) \cdot \hat{\mathbf{f}} = \gamma(\Lambda) \cdot \mathbf{U}^T\mathbf{f}. \tag{2.36}$$

With the filtered coefficients, we can reconstruct **f** using Inverse GFT as:

$$\mathbf{f}' = \mathbf{U}\hat{\mathbf{f}}' = \mathbf{U} \cdot \gamma(\Lambda) \cdot \mathbf{U}^T\mathbf{f}. \tag{2.37}$$

Now we consider how to design graph filters based on Graph Fourier Transform. If we directly take the N diagonal elements as parameters, the computation load would be very high if the graph becomes larger. Therefore, a polynomial filter operator is usually adopted as an alternative for $\gamma(\Lambda)$ [82], which is:

$$\gamma(\Lambda) = \sum_{k=0}^{K} \theta_k \Lambda^k. \tag{2.38}$$

In this way, Eq. (2.37) can be further simplified as:

$$\hat{\mathbf{f}}' = \sum_{k=0}^{K} \theta_k \mathbf{L}^k\mathbf{f}. \tag{2.39}$$

Chebyshev Polynomial and Cheby-Filter Chebyshev Polynomial is used as an alternative for $\gamma(\Lambda)$. The Chebyshev polynomials $T_k(y)$ can be generated recursively:

$$T_k(y) = 2yT_{k-1}(y) - T_{k-2}(y), \tag{2.40}$$

with $T_0(y) = 1$ and $T_1(y) = y$. For $y \in [-1, 1]$, Chebyshev Polynomials can be formulated as:

$$T_k(y) = \cos(k\arccos(y)), \tag{2.41}$$

which means that each $T_k(y)$ is bounded in $[-1, 1]$. To exploit this property, we adjust the eigenvalues of the Laplacian matrix by rescaling and shifting them in the following manner:

$$\tilde{\mathbf{\Lambda}} = \frac{2\mathbf{\Lambda}}{\lambda_{\max}} - \mathbf{I}, \tag{2.42}$$

where **I** denotes the identity matrix. Thus, the Cheby Filter, parametarized by the truncated Chebyshev polynomials, can be expressed as:

$$\gamma(\mathbf{\Lambda}) = \sum_{k=0}^{K} \theta_k T_k(\tilde{\mathbf{\Lambda}}). \tag{2.43}$$

The application of a Cheby Filter to a graph signal **f** is formulated as:

$$\begin{aligned}\mathbf{f}' &= \mathbf{U} \cdot \Big(\sum_{k=0}^{K} \theta_k T_k(\tilde{\boldsymbol{\Lambda}})\Big) \cdot \mathbf{U}^T \mathbf{f} \\ &= \sum_{k=0}^{K} \theta_k \mathbf{U} T_k(\tilde{\boldsymbol{\Lambda}}) \mathbf{U}^T \mathbf{f},\end{aligned} \tag{2.44}$$

This can also be further simplified as:

$$\mathbf{f}' = \sum_{k=0}^{K} \theta_k T_k(\tilde{\mathbf{L}})\mathbf{f}, \tag{2.45}$$

where

$$\tilde{\mathbf{L}} = \frac{2\mathbf{L}}{\lambda_{\max}} - \mathbf{I}. \tag{2.46}$$

GCN-Filter The Polynomial Filter and Chebyshev Filter, with a maximum power of K, utilize the K-hop neighborhood of a node to compute its updated features. GCN Filter is a typical design in GNN [83], which can be considered as a Cheby Filter special case, where K=1 and $\lambda_{\max} \approx 2$. Under this assumption, $\gamma(\Lambda)$ can be transformed as:

$$\begin{aligned}\gamma(\Lambda) &= \theta_0 T_0(\tilde{\boldsymbol{\Lambda}}) + \theta_1 T_1(\tilde{\boldsymbol{\Lambda}}) \\ &= \theta_0 \mathbf{I} + \theta_1 \tilde{\boldsymbol{\Lambda}} \\ &= \theta_0 \mathbf{I} + \theta_1 (\boldsymbol{\Lambda} - \mathbf{I}).\end{aligned} \tag{2.47}$$

We can compute the output signal $\mathbf{f}'$ as:

$$\mathbf{f}' = \theta_0 \mathbf{f} - \theta_1 (\mathbf{D}^{-\frac{1}{2}} \mathbf{A} \mathbf{D}^{-\frac{1}{2}})\mathbf{f}. \tag{2.48}$$

In this equation, we adopt the definition of normalized Laplacian matrix, i.e., $\mathbf{L} = \mathbf{I} - \mathbf{D}^{-\frac{1}{2}} \mathbf{A} \mathbf{D}^{-\frac{1}{2}}$. An additional simplification can be implemented by setting $\theta = \theta_0 = -\theta_1$, leading to:

$$\mathbf{f}' = \theta(\mathbf{I} + \mathbf{D}^{-\frac{1}{2}} \mathbf{A} \mathbf{D}^{-\frac{1}{2}})\mathbf{f}. \tag{2.49}$$

To address numerical instability caused by the eigenvalue range of $\mathbf{I} + \mathbf{D}^{-\frac{1}{2}} \mathbf{A} \mathbf{D}^{-\frac{1}{2}}$, which spans from 0 to 2, we employ re-normalization. This is done by substituting the original matrix with $\tilde{\mathbf{D}}^{-\frac{1}{2}}\tilde{\mathbf{A}}\tilde{\mathbf{D}}^{-\frac{1}{2}}$, where $\tilde{\mathbf{A}} = \mathbf{A} + \mathbf{I}$ and the diagonal elements of $\tilde{\mathbf{D}}$ are updated to $\tilde{\mathbf{D}}_{ii} = \sum_j \tilde{\mathbf{A}}_{ij}$. The final GCN Filter is then defined as:

$$\mathbf{f}' = \theta\tilde{\mathbf{D}}^{-\frac{1}{2}}\tilde{\mathbf{A}}\tilde{\mathbf{D}}^{-\frac{1}{2}}\mathbf{f}. \tag{2.50}$$

The GCN Filter, utilizing only the 0th and 1st powers of $\mathbf{\Lambda}$, essentially aggregates information from a node's immediate 1-hop neighbors within the graph $\mathcal{G}$, considering the node itself as one of its 1-hop neighbors. Therefore, the GCN Filter can be characterized as a filter based on spatial information, focusing on updating node features by incorporating data from directly connected neighbors.

Graph Filters for Multichannel Graph Signals In the previous sections, we only consider graphs where each node correlates to a single signal value. However, in general, the signal combined with one node is usually a vector, i.e., the graph signals are multichannel. In this case, the input signal for graph $\mathcal{G}$ can be denoted as $\mathbf{F} \in \mathbb{R}^{N \times d_{in}}$. We apply signals from every input channel to produce a single-channel output signal:

$$\mathbf{f}_{out} = \sum_{d=1}^{d_{in}} \mathbf{U} \cdot \gamma_d(\Lambda) \cdot \mathbf{U}^T \mathbf{F}_{:,d}, \tag{2.51}$$

where $\mathbf{f}_{out} \in \mathbb{R}^N$ signifies the single-channel output signal, and $\mathbf{F}_{:,d} \in \mathbb{R}^N$ represents the d-th channel of the input signal. The procedure entails applying a graph filter to each channel of the input signal and aggregating the results from all d_{in} channels into the final output. Generally speaking, the output signal could also be multichannel. Suppose that we use d_{out} filters for each input channel, then the procedure for generating the output signal with d_{out} channels can be formulated as:

$$\mathbf{F}'_{:,j} = \sum_{d=1}^{d_{in}} \mathbf{U} \cdot \gamma_{j,d}(\Lambda) \cdot \mathbf{U}^T \mathbf{F}_{:,d}, \quad \text{for } j = 1, \ldots, d_{out}. \tag{2.52}$$

In the case of GCN Filter, this procedure can be summarized as:

$$\mathbf{F}'_{:,j} = \sum_{d=1}^{d_{in}} \theta_{j,d}\tilde{\mathbf{D}}^{-\frac{1}{2}}\tilde{\mathbf{A}}\tilde{\mathbf{D}}^{-\frac{1}{2}}\mathbf{F}_{:,d}, \quad \text{for } j = 1, \ldots, d_{out}. \tag{2.53}$$

Furthermore, it is can be expressed in matrix notation:

$$\mathbf{F}' = \tilde{\mathbf{D}}^{-\frac{1}{2}}\tilde{\mathbf{A}}\tilde{\mathbf{D}}^{-\frac{1}{2}}\mathbf{F}\mathbf{\Theta}, \tag{2.54}$$

where $\boldsymbol{\Theta} \in \mathbb{R}^{d_{in} \times d_{out}}$ denotes the matrix of parameters. Each element $\boldsymbol{\Theta}_{d,j} = \theta_{j,d}$ corresponds to the parameter for the j-th output channel and the d-th input channel.

- **GraphSAGE-Filter**

The GraphSAGE Filter, a spatial-based filter, aggregates information from adjacent nodes [84]. The method used to derive new features for a specific node v_i is described as:

$$\begin{aligned} \mathcal{N}_s(v_i) &= \text{SAMPLE}(\mathcal{N}(v_i), S), \\ \mathbf{f}'_{\mathcal{N}_s(v_i)} &= \text{AGGREGATE}(\{\mathbf{F}_j, \forall v_j \in \mathcal{N}_s(v_i)\}), \\ \mathbf{F}'_i &= \sigma([\mathbf{F}_i, \mathbf{f}'_{\mathcal{N}_s(v_i)}]\boldsymbol{\Theta}). \end{aligned} \tag{2.55}$$

The computation process can be described as follows. Firstly, we sample S nodes from $\mathcal{N}(v_i)$, denoted as the whole set of neighbors for node v_i, using function SAMPLE. The result is denoted as $\mathcal{N}_s(v_i)$. Secondly, the AGGREGATE function is employed to amalgamate information from the neighboring S nodes. Finally, we concatenate the feature of node v_i with the result of aggregation, denoted as $[\mathbf{F}_i, \mathbf{f}'_{\mathcal{N}_s(v_i)}]$, and multiply it with $\boldsymbol{\Theta}$ as well as activate it with $\sigma(\cdot)$ to update the feature of node v_i, denoted as $\mathbf{F}'_i$. Various AGGREGATE functions have been designed in the original paper of GraphSAGE.

- **Mean Aggregator:** This entails computing the element-wise average of the vectors in the set $\{\mathbf{F}_j \mid \forall v_j \in \mathcal{N}_s(v_i)\}$.
- **LSTM Aggregator:** In this method, the collection of sampled neighboring nodes $\mathcal{N}_S(v_i)$ of node v_i is considered as a sequence and is processed using an LSTM network. We denote the output from the final unit of the LSTM as $\mathbf{f}'_{\mathcal{N}_S(v_i)}$. As the order of $\mathcal{N}_S(v_i)$ is uncertain, GraphSAGE adopts a random order to solve it.
- **Pooling Operator:** A max pooling operator is employed to aggregate the neighboring node information. Notice that pooling is permutation invariant, thus it is a reasonable alternative for the AGGREGATE function.

GraphSAGE is well-suited for scaling in large graphs due to its random sampling mechanism. The GraphSAGE Filter maintains a spatially localized approach, always incorporating only 1-hop neighbors, irrespective of the selected aggregator. Additionally, the same aggregator is utilized across all nodes.

- **Graph Pooling**

With graph filters, we could only update features for each node without changing the graph structure. To get the graph level features, we need to introduce graph pooling, similar to the pooling layer in CNNs. There are two ways to implement it as follows:

Hierarchical Graph Pooling This is generating a coarsened graph with fewer nodes step by step to finally obtain a global representation. There are two ways to achieve it, which are sub-sampling based and super-nodes based. The main difference is that the former keeps nodes from the original graph while the latter generates new nodes for the coarsened graph.

Flat Graph Pooling The flat pooling layer constructs a graph-level representation directly from the representations of individual nodes, which is formulated as:

$$\mathbf{f}_{\mathcal{G}} = \text{pool}(\mathbf{A}^{(ip)}, \mathbf{F}^{(ip)}), \tag{2.56}$$

where $\mathbf{f}_{\mathcal{G}} \in \mathbb{R}^{1\times d_{op}}$ denotes the graph representation. One method is max-pooling, which is applying max operation to each channel. This is described as:

$$\mathbf{f}_{\mathcal{G}} = \max(\mathbf{F}^{(ip)}), \text{ where } \mathbf{f}_{\mathcal{G}}[i] = \max(\mathbf{F}^{(ip)}_{:,i}). \tag{2.57}$$

Similarly, the graph average pooling operation performs average pooling across channels as:

$$\mathbf{f}_{\mathcal{G}} = \text{avg}(\mathbf{F}^{(ip)}). \tag{2.58}$$

Additionally, an attention-based flat pooling technique, referred to as gated global pooling [85], computes an attention score for each node to derive a global representation. For each node v_i, the attention score is computed as:

$$s_i = \frac{\exp(h(\mathbf{F}_i^{(ip)}))}{\sum\limits_{v_j\in\mathcal{V}} \exp(h(\mathbf{F}_j^{(ip)}))}, \tag{2.59}$$

where h is a feedforward network that maps $\mathbf{F}_i^{(ip)}$ to a scalar. The graph representation can be summarized as:

$$\mathbf{f}_{\mathcal{G}} = \sum_{v_i\in\mathcal{V}} s_i \cdot \tanh(\mathbf{F}_i^{(ip)}\mathbf{\Theta}_{ip}), \tag{2.60}$$

where $\mathbf{\Theta}_{ip}$ denotes the learned parameters. Moreover, the identity function can substitute the $\tanh(\cdot)$ activation.

Subsampling-Based Hierarchical Graph Pooling The gPool layer introduced the use of a downsampling strategy to facilitate graph pooling, as detailed in [86]. Within the gPool framework, the initial step involves learning the importance scores $\mathbf{y}$ for the input nodes as:

$$\mathbf{y} = \frac{\mathbf{F}^{(ip)}\mathbf{p}}{\|\mathbf{p}\|}, \tag{2.61}$$

where $\mathbf{F}^{(ip)} \in \mathbb{R}^{N_{ip} \times d_{ip}}$ denotes the matrix that represents the features of input nodes, and $\mathbf{p} \in \mathbb{R}^{d_{ip}}$ denotes a learnable vector that projects the input features into importance scores. Following this, nodes can be ranked based on $\mathbf{y}$, and the N_{op} key ones are selected like:

$$\mathrm{idx} = \mathrm{rank}(\mathbf{y}, N_{op}), \tag{2.62}$$

where N_{op} denotes the node count in the coarsened graph. We then use idx to get the adjacent matrix $\mathbf{A}^{(op)}$:

$$\mathbf{A}^{(op)} = \mathbf{A}^{(ip)}(\mathrm{idx}, \mathrm{idx}). \tag{2.63}$$

Similarly, we can obtain the corresponding node features for the coarsened graph:

$$\begin{aligned}
\tilde{\mathbf{y}} &= \sigma(\mathbf{y}(\mathrm{idx})), \\
\tilde{\mathbf{F}} &= \mathbf{F}^{(ip)}(\mathrm{idx}, :), \\
\mathbf{F}_p &= \tilde{\mathbf{F}} \odot (\tilde{\mathbf{y}} \mathbf{1}_{d_{ip}}^T),
\end{aligned} \tag{2.64}$$

where $\sigma(\cdot)$ represents the sigmoid function, which scales the importance scores to the range (0, 1), and $\mathbf{1}_{d_{ip}} \in \mathbb{R}^{d_{ip}}$ is an all-ones vector. However, in gPool the importance score $\mathbf{y}$ is only obtained from the input features. It ignores the graph structure information. To overcome it, we can utilize GCN Filter to calculate $\mathbf{y}$ [87]:

$$\mathbf{y} = \alpha\Big(\text{GCN-Filter}(\mathbf{A}^{(ip)}, \mathbf{F}^{(ip)})\Big), \tag{2.65}$$

where α is an activation function such as tanh.

Supernode-Based Hierarchical Graph Pooling We present DiffPool, a method for generating supernodes in a differentiable manner [88]. Specifically, we first learn an assignment matrix $\mathbf{S}$ with a GCN-Filter:

$$\mathbf{S} = \mathrm{Softmax}\Big(\text{GCN-Filter}(\mathbf{A}^{(ip)}, \mathbf{F}^{(ip)})\Big). \tag{2.66}$$

Let $\mathbf{S} \in \mathbb{R}^{N_{ip} \times N_{op}}$ denote the learned assignment matrix. Each column in $\mathbf{S}$ is a supernode. The Softmax function is applied to each row, ensuring that the elements in every row sum to 1. The new graph structure can then be generated like:

$$\begin{aligned}
\mathbf{A}^{(op)} &= \mathbf{S}^T \mathbf{A}^{(ip)} \mathbf{S}, \\
\mathbf{F}^{(op)} &= \mathbf{S}^T \mathbf{F}^{(inter)}, \\
\mathbf{F}^{(inter)} &= \text{GCN-Filter}(\mathbf{A}^{(ip)}, \mathbf{F}^{(ip)}),
\end{aligned} \tag{2.67}$$

where $\mathbf{A}^{(ip)}$, $\mathbf{F}^{(ip)}$, $\mathbf{A}^{(op)}$, and $\mathbf{F}^{(op)}$ denote the input graph's adjacency matrix, the input graph's features, the output graph's adjacency matrix, and the output graph's features, respectively.

- **Parameter Learning for Graph Neural Network**

In this section, we provide the node and the graph classification tasks to demonstrate how GNNs learn parameters.

Parameter Learning for Node Classification Task In this task, The node set $\mathcal{V}$ of a graph can be partitioned into two non-overlapping subsets: $\mathcal{V}_l$ containing labeled nodes, and $\mathcal{V}_u$ containing unlabeled nodes. GNN is designed to train on $\mathcal{V}_l$ so that it can generalize on $\mathcal{V}_u$, which can be described as:

$$\begin{aligned} \mathbf{F}^{(out)} &= \mathrm{GNN}_{node}(\mathbf{A}, \mathbf{F}; \boldsymbol{\Theta}_1), \\ \mathbf{Z} &= \mathrm{Softmax}(\mathbf{F}^{(out)}\boldsymbol{\Theta}_2), \end{aligned} \tag{2.68}$$

where $\boldsymbol{\Theta}_1, \boldsymbol{\Theta}_2$ are the model parameters and $\mathbf{Z} \in \mathbb{R}^{N \times C}$ is the output logits for the N input nodes. We can summarize the entire forward propagation as:

$$\mathbf{Z} = f_{GNN}(\mathbf{A}, \mathbf{F}; \boldsymbol{\Theta}). \tag{2.69}$$

The total parameters $\boldsymbol{\Theta}$ are learned by minimizing:

$$\mathcal{L}_{\text{train}} = \sum_{v_i \in \mathcal{V}_l} \ell(f_{GNN}(\mathbf{A}, \mathbf{F}; \boldsymbol{\Theta})_i, y_i), \tag{2.70}$$

where $\ell(\cdot, \cdot)$ is the cross-entropy loss.

Parameter Learning for Graph Classification Task In the task of graph classification, we organize the training dataset as $\mathcal{D}(\{\mathcal{G}_i, y_i\})$, where y_i is the label correlated to the graph $\mathcal{G}_i$. GNN is designed to train on $\mathcal{D}$ so that it can generalize on unlabeled graphs, which can be described as:

$$\begin{aligned} \mathbf{f}_{\mathcal{G}} &= \mathrm{GNN}_{\text{graph}}(\mathcal{G}; \boldsymbol{\Theta}_1) \\ \mathbf{z}_{\mathcal{G}} &= \mathrm{Softmax}(\mathbf{f}_{\mathcal{G}}\boldsymbol{\Theta}_2). \end{aligned} \tag{2.71}$$

This can be summarized as:

$$\mathbf{z}_{\mathcal{G}} = f_{GNN}(\mathcal{G}; \boldsymbol{\Theta}). \tag{2.72}$$

The parameter $\mathbf{\Theta}$ is optimized by minimizing:

$$\mathcal{L}_{\text{train}} = \sum_{\mathcal{G}_i \in \mathcal{D}} \ell(f_{GNN}(\mathcal{G}_i; \mathbf{\Theta}), y_i), \tag{2.73}$$

where y_i is the label correlated to $\mathcal{G}_i$ and $\ell(\cdot, \cdot)$ is the loss function for classification.

2.2 Deep Learning on Point Cloud

2.2.1 *PointNet Series*

A set of unordered data requires that point-based neural networks satisfy permutation invariance. PointNet and its variances are designed directly with point cloud as input. This section provides a brief overview of PointNet, PointNet++, and Dynamic Graph Convolutional Neural Network (DGCNN).

PointNet Figure 2.12 shows the pipeline of PointNet. The processing of a raw input point cloud starts with its initial shape $n \times 3$, indicating n points. The first step involves an input transform module, which computes a 3×3 transformation matrix that is applied to coarsely align the point cloud to a viewpoint suitable for downstream tasks. Subsequently, each point in the aligned dataset is processed through a shared multilayer perceptron (MLP), transforming the features from $n \times 3$ to $n \times 64$. This is followed by a feature transform module that, similar to the input transform module, predicts and applies a 64×64 matrix to the $n \times 64$ feature map to enhance the features. The process continues with the point features being

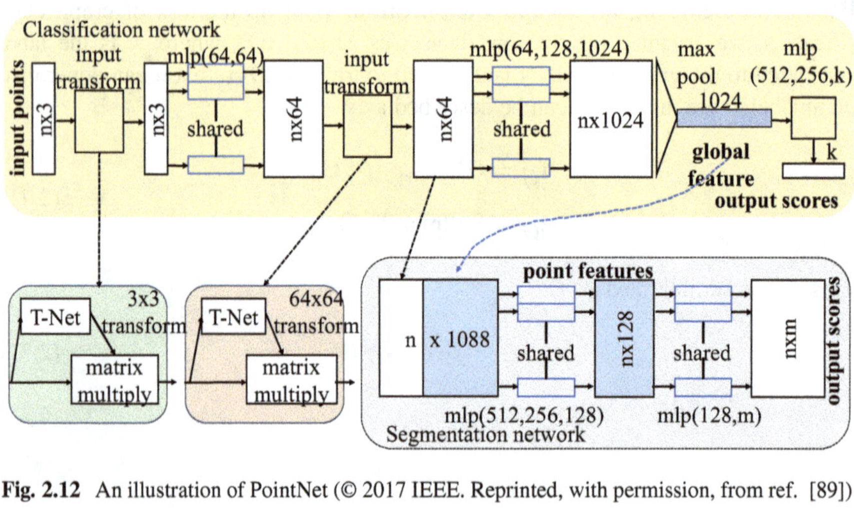

Fig. 2.12 An illustration of PointNet (© 2017 IEEE. Reprinted, with permission, from ref. [89])

further refined through additional shared MLPs that increase the feature dimensions successively to 128 and then to 1024, resulting in a final feature map of $n \times 1024$. This feature map then undergoes a symmetric pooling function on each channel, extracting global features suitable for classification tasks. For segmentation tasks, these global features are concatenated with local features and processed through additional shared MLPs to obtain high-level semantic information for each point.

PointNet, with its straightforward architecture, achieves relatively high performance and has significantly influenced research in 3D computer vision [89]. However, PointNet does not fully utilize geometric information. Subsequent works have primarily aimed to enhance performance by addressing this limitation.

PointNet++ As illustrated in Fig. 2.13, the architecture of PointNet++ is described in [90] as follows. Unlike its predecessor, PointNet++, omits the input transform and feature transform modules and adopts a hierarchical structure inspired by classical CNNs used in image processing. The feature learning network is organized into several stages, each acting as a set abstraction layer. In these stages, points are first processed by downsampling and grouping using farthest point sampling (FPS) and the k nearest neighbor algorithm (kNN). FPS reduces the point count, and kNN allows feature aggregation from its neighbors. Each central point and its neighbors are then processed through a shared pointnet, which learns local feature vectors similar to how convolution layers operate in image processing networks. After all the set abstraction modules have processed the points, a small set of points with learned features remains. For classification tasks, these features are transformed into a global feature vector using another pointnet model. For segmentation tasks, the process is reversed by interpolating the sparse point set at each stage to restore the point count to its original in the corresponding previous stage. This interpolation employs a method that assigns weights inversely proportional to distance, utilizing

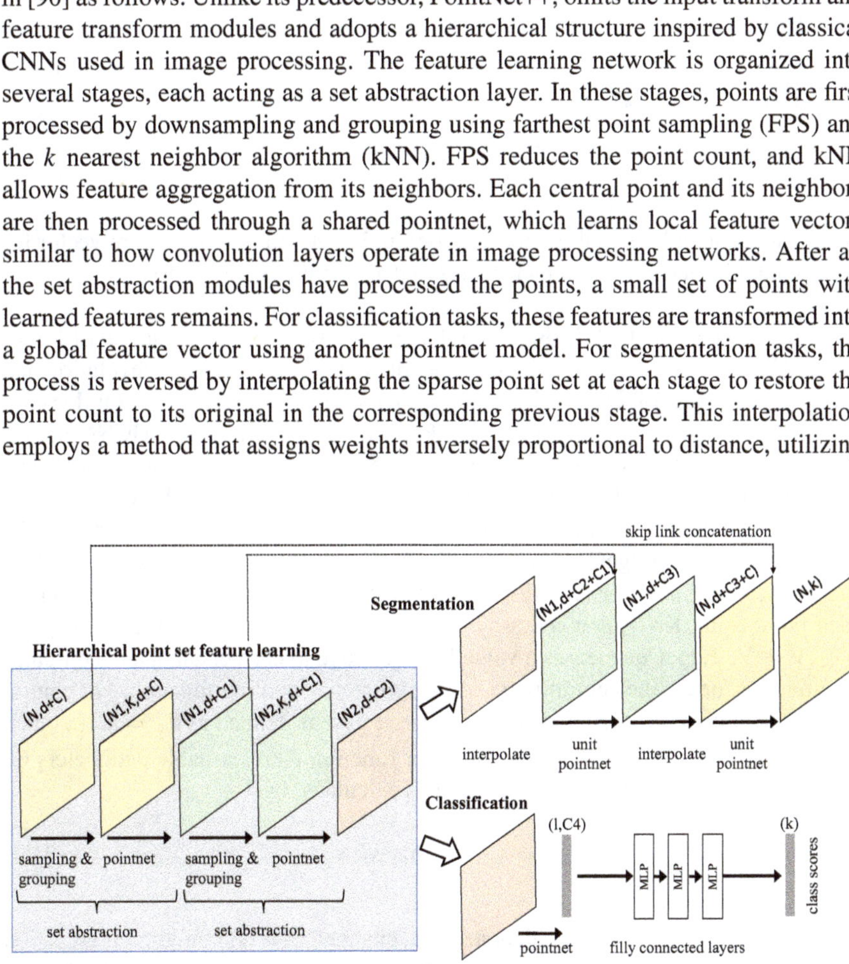

Fig. 2.13 An illustration of PointNet++ [90] (Source: Author)

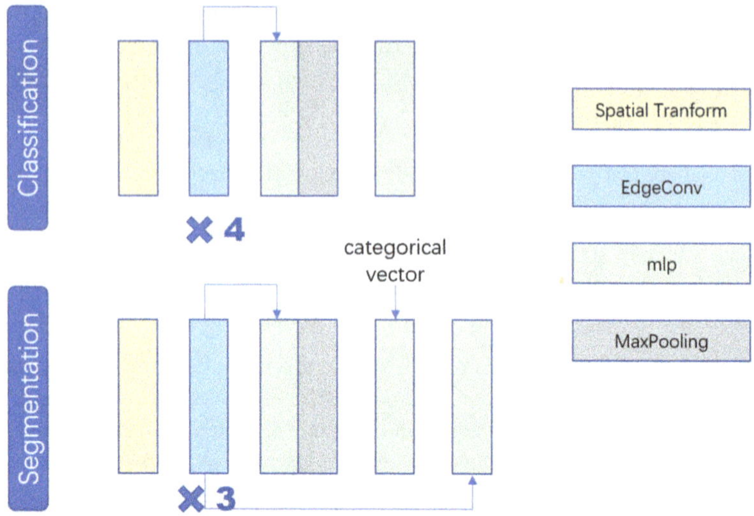

Fig. 2.14 An illustration of DGCNN [91] (Source: Author)

the k nearest neighbors. Subsequently, a unit pointnet updates the feature vector for each point, ultimately restoring all points and assigning semantics to each.

DGCNN To some extent, DGCNN [91] can be viewed as a combination of PointNet and PointNet++, while the feature is learned by dynamic graph convolution net. As shown in Fig. 2.14, DGCNN also adopts a hierarchical structure, but it does not conduct downsampling on the point set. For the raw input points, DGCNN adopts the input transformation module in PointNet, as it is a per-point process model. The basic operation in DGCNN is EdgeConv (shown in Fig. 2.15), which can be roughly regarded as aggregating the features of surrounding neighbors for one point. We denote the input of EdgeConv as a set $X = \{x_1, x_2, \ldots, x_n\} \subset \mathbb{R}^F$, where $\{x_i\}_{i=1}^n$ can be the coordinates or features of the points. We construct a directed graph for each point using KNN, denoted as $\mathcal{G} = (\mathcal{V}, \mathcal{E})$, where $\mathcal{V} = \{x_1, x_2, \ldots, x_n\}$ and $\mathcal{E} \subset \mathcal{V} \times \mathcal{V}$. EdgeConv learns a value for each edge in each channel and computes a feature vector for the central point using symmetric pooling function. For central point i and one of its neighbor points j, edge feature is defined as $\mathbf{e}_{ij} = h_\Theta(x_i, x_j)$, where $h_\Theta : \mathbb{R}^F \times \mathbb{R}^F \rightarrow \mathbb{R}^{F'}$ is a nonlinear function with learnable parameters Θ. The output of EdgeConv at the i-th vertex is calculated by:

$$\mathbf{x}_i' = \mathop{\square}_{j:(i,j)\in\mathcal{E}} h_\Theta(\mathbf{x}_i, \mathbf{x}_j), \tag{2.74}$$

where $\square$ (e.g., $\sum$ or max) denotes the channel-wise symmetric aggregation operation. Specifically, $h_\Theta(\mathbf{x}_i, \mathbf{x}_j)$ is computed through $\bar{h}_\Theta(\mathbf{x}_i, \mathbf{x}_j - \mathbf{x}_i)$. Θ encodes

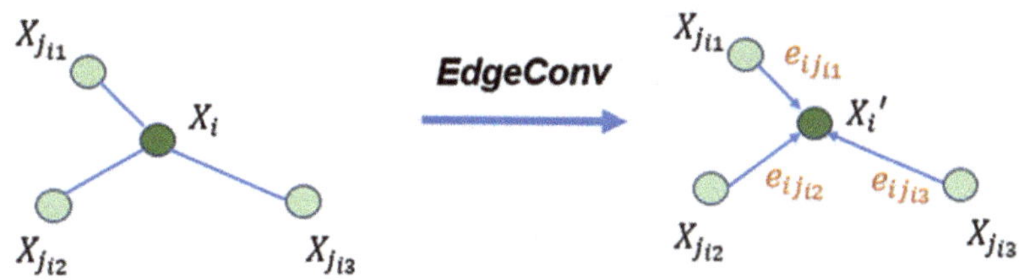

Fig. 2.15 An illustration for EdgeConv in DGCNN [91] (Source: Author)

the weights of M different filters. Each filter computes a partition of the output edge feature, i.e.,

$$e'_{ijm} = \mathrm{ReLU}(\boldsymbol{\theta}_m \cdot (\mathbf{x}_j - \mathbf{x}_i) + \boldsymbol{\phi}_m \cdot \mathbf{x}_i), \tag{2.75}$$

and the corresponding part of $\mathbf{x}'_i$ is computed as:

$$\mathbf{x}'_{im} = \max_{j:(i,j)\in\mathcal{E}} e'_{ijm}, \tag{2.76}$$

where $\Theta = (\theta_1, \theta_2, \ldots, \theta_M, \phi_1, \phi_2, \ldots, \phi_M)$. The graph structure is updated along with the forward propagation, i.e., the graph $\mathcal{G}$ varies at each stage as the feature for each point changes.

For classification task, the features for each point at each stage are concatenated together and projected to 1024 dimension with a shared MLP, followed by a max pooling to derive the overall representation. For segmentation, we also need to get the global feature similarly, but after that we need to concatenate it with a category vector, repeating it and concatenate with the previous feature maps, similar to PointNet. Then it is processed by a shared MLP to obtain the per-point semantics.

2.2.2 *Point Voxel CNN*

Apart from the point-based methods like the pointnet series, another typical method is the voxel-based methods. The basic idea of it is dividing the 3D space into regular voxels and developing 3D learning method on it. The points that fall into the same voxel would be treated equally. This can lead to a dilemma. On the one hand, only with higher resolution of 3D voxels can we obtain an accurate description of the 3D object or 3D scene. On the other hand, there is massive redundancy within the voxels and the learning algorithm cannot scale up with higher resolution, as the complexity of it is cubic. As for point-based methods, if we want to better utilize the local geometric information, we need to search for the k nearest neighbors for one point. This is computationally inefficient. Therefore, it is necessary to combine

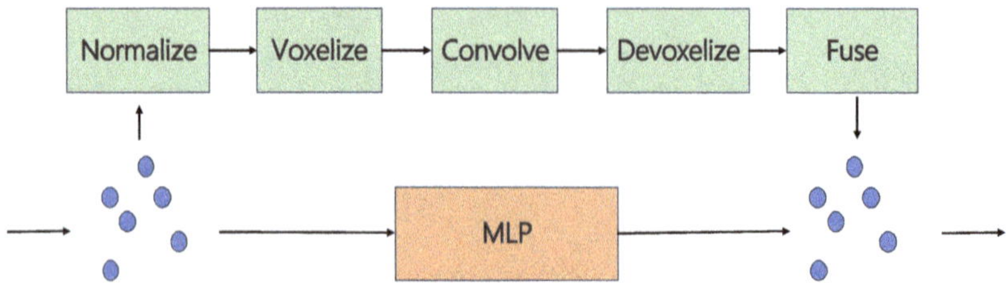

Fig. 2.16 Pipeline for Point Voxel CNN [92] (Source: Author)

the voxel-based and point-based methods to implement an efficient scheme for 3D learning. Then it comes to the Point Voxel CNN (PVCNN).

PVCNN is proposed as an efficient algorithm for 3D deep learning, which is a combination of point-based and voxel-based methods [92]. PVCNN is composed of two branches, as illustrated in Fig. 2.16. In the upper branch, the input points are normalized and voxelized to utilize 3D convolution and extract coarse-grained features. Then devoxelization is adopted to transform the voxel-level features into point-level. To ensure that the features for the devoxelized points are distinct with each other, PVCNN takes trilinear interpolation. In the lower branch, each point is processed through a shared multilayer perception (MLP) module. In this way, PVCNN can not only calculate the fine-grained feature similar to PointNet but can also utilize the local geometric structure efficiently.

2.2.3 Transformer on Point Cloud

As mentioned before, Transformer performs as a powerful model in natural language process area. Recently, it also shows potential in other modalities such as vision and audio. This greatly accelerates the research on multi-modal learning. While numerous studies have explored the application of the Transformer architecture to point clouds, this section adopts a multi-modal learning perspective. We begin by discussing the Vision Transformer (ViT) [74], which pioneered the use of the Transformer framework for vision tasks. Subsequently, we introduce a model that applies a similar design to point clouds.

Vision Transformer Transformer takes a sequence as input for downstream tasks. To transform image into sequence, ViT splits the image with size 224×224 into patches with size 16×16. Each patch is treated as a token in the sequence. Transformer model is permutation invariant, i.e., the output would not change if we randomly change the arrangement of the input tokens. To encode position information, ViT introduces position embedding for each patch. In detail, the 16×16 image patch is first projected to a vector, then it is concatenated with the position embedding vector. These position aware tokens are subsequently fed into the Transformer encoder. For the image, we take self-attention mechanism for the

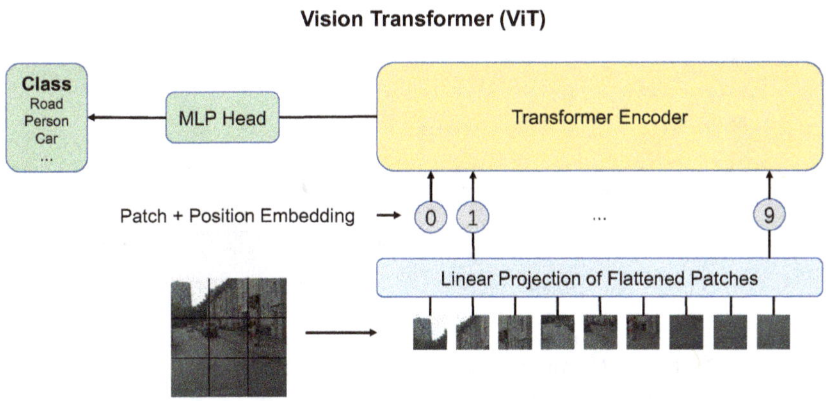

Fig. 2.17 An illustration of vision transformer (Public domain open access image [74])

encoder. The pipeline for ViT is shown in Fig. 2.17. Notice that an initial token is provided additionally. We take the output token corresponding to it as the global feature for downstream tasks. Compared to conventional models on images, ViT is less dependent on locality, an important property with 2D images. This leads to less inductive bias, making it more difficult to train ViT. However, if trained sufficiently, ViT performs more powerful than classical CNNs like ResNet. Besides, ViT performs significantly better than CNNs in transfer learning.

Point Vision Transformer To generalize the idea of Transformer on point cloud and also adapt to the specific point cloud tasks, a similar architecture is designed, named as Point Vision Transformer (PViT) [93]. The first step is also tokenization, i.e., transforming the input point cloud into local patches, also named as tokens. Different from image, point cloud is unstructured. Hence, tokenization is implemented through farthest point sampling (FPS). PViT adopts two stage FPS to ease the optimization and improve generalization. The tokens are then processed by a standard transformer, which is the same as ViT. The pipeline for PViT is shown in Fig. 2.18.

2.3 Summary

Point cloud technologies have made a lot of advances based on different kinds of solutions [94–119], especially using deep learning as an effective tool [120–149]. This chapter delivers an in-depth exploration of the foundational principles of 3D point cloud learning within the deep learning domain. It begins with a foundational overview of deep learning techniques before advancing into a nuanced classification of various neural network architectures including CNNs, RNNs, and GNNs. Particular attention is paid to the development of network models specifically

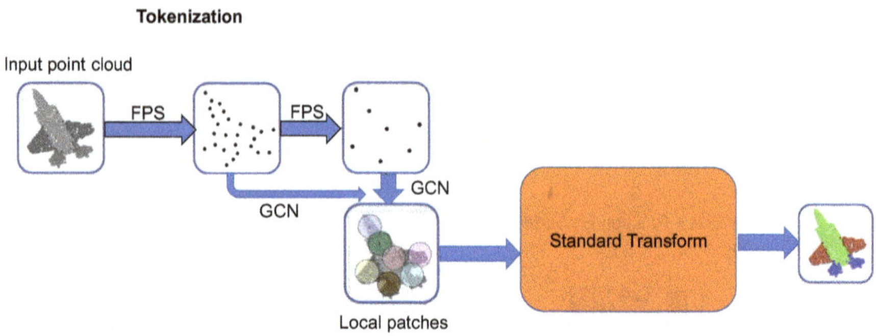

Fig. 2.18 An illustration of transformer on point cloud (© 2024 IEEE. Reprinted, with permission, from ref. [93])

designed for handling point cloud data, with a focus on innovative models like the PointNet series, point cloud transformers, and Point Voxel CNN. These models are particularly adept at navigating the challenges presented by the disorganized and unstructured characteristics of point cloud data. The content extends into detailed methodologies for training deep learning models, emphasizing the strategic use of loss functions, optimization techniques, and the backpropagation algorithm. Innovations in the PointNet architecture are explored through the introduction of PointNet++ and DGCNN, which enhance the model's ability to harness spatial and geometric data effectively. This chapter introduces the PVCNN, which is an innovative approach combining point-based and voxel-based techniques, optimizing efficiency in 3D learning. Additionally, this chapter delves into the integration of Transformer models into point cloud processing, reflecting their significant impact in fields like Natural Language Processing (NLP). It highlights adaptations such as the Vision Transformer and Point Vision Transformer, demonstrating their proficiency in point cloud applications. It concludes with a series of exercises designed to reinforce the reader's understanding of deep learning principles, clarify the distinctions between conventional and sparse convolution, and assess the benefits of Transformer models over RNNs, enhancing both theoretical knowledge and practical application skills in 3D point cloud learning.

Exercises

1. What are the basic elements of deep learning?
2. What are the differences between common convolution and sparse convolution?
3. Why can PointNet work with such simple neural network architecture?
4. Please explain GCN Filter from the perspective of both spectral-based and spatial-based theory.
5. What are the improvements of PointNet++ compared with PointNet?

6. What are the improvements of DGCNN compared with PointNet?
7. How to generalize the architecture of Vision Transformer to point clouds?
8. Why is PVCNN an efficient method for 3D learning?
9. Why can GraphSAGE scale up to large-scale graphs?
10. What are the advantages of Transformer models compared to RNNs?

References

1. B. Qu, X. Liang, S. Sun, W. Gao, Exploring aigc video quality: A focus on visual harmony, video-text consistency and domain distribution gap, in *Proceedings of the IEEE/CVF Conference on Computer Vision and Pattern Recognition Workshops* (2024)
2. B. Qu, H. Li, W. Gao, Bringing textual prompt to ai-generated image quality assessment, in *2024 IEEE International Conference on Multimedia and Expo (ICME)* (IEEE, Piscataway, 2024)
3. Y. Wu, L. Xie, S. Sun, W. Gao, Y. Yan, Adaptive intra period size for deep learning-based screen content video coding, in *2024 IEEE International Conference on Multimedia and Expo Workshops (ICMEW)* (IEEE, Piscataway, 2024)
4. H. Zheng, W. Gao, End-to-end RGB-D image compression via exploiting channel-modality redundancy. Proc. AAAI Confer. Artif. Intell. **38**(7), 7562–7570 (2024)
5. L. Tao, W. Gao, G. Li, C. Zhang, Adanic: Towards practical neural image compression via dynamic transform routing, in *Proceedings of the IEEE/CVF International Conference on Computer Vision* (2023), pp. 16879–16888
6. Y. Wu, W. Gao, End-to-end lossless compression of high precision depth maps guided by pseudo-residual (2022). arXiv preprint arXiv:2201.03195
7. Y. Wu, Z. Qi, H. Zheng, L. Tao, W. Gao, Deep image compression with latent optimization and piece-wise quantization approximation, in *Proceedings of the IEEE/CVF Conference on Computer Vision and Pattern Recognition* (2021), pp. 1926–1930
8. W. Gao, L. Tao, L. Zhou, D. Yang, X. Zhang, Z. Guo, Low-rate image compression with super-resolution learning, in *Proceedings of the IEEE/CVF Conference on Computer Vision and Pattern Recognition Workshops* (2020), pp. 154–155
9. W. Gao, S. Sun, H. Zheng, Y. Wu, H. Ye, Y. Zhang, Opendmc: An open-source library and performance evaluation for deep-learning-based multi-frame compression, in *Proceedings of the 31st ACM International Conference on Multimedia* (2023), pp. 9685–9688
10. Y. Guo, W. Gao, G. Li, Interpretable task-inspired adaptive filter pruning for neural networks under multiple constraints. Int. J. Comput. Vision **132**, 1–17 (2024)
11. W. Gao, Y. Guo, S. Ma, G. Li, S. Kwong, Efficient neural network compression inspired by compressive sensing. IEEE Trans. Neural Netw. Learn. Syst. **35**, 1965–1979 (2022)
12. Y. Guo, W. Gao, Semantic-driven automatic filter pruning for neural networks, in *2022 IEEE International Conference on Multimedia and Expo (ICME)* (IEEE, Piscataway, 2022), pp. 1–6
13. L. Tao, W. Gao, Efficient channel pruning based on architecture alignment and probability model bypassing, in *2021 IEEE International Conference on Systems, Man, and Cybernetics (SMC)* (IEEE, Piscataway, 2021), pp. 3232–3237
14. Z. Yang, W. Gao, G. Li, Y. Yan, SUR-driven video coding rate control for jointly optimizing perceptual quality and buffer control. IEEE Trans. Image Process. **32**, 5451–5464 (2023)
15. F. Shen, Z. Cai, W. Gao, An efficient rate control algorithm for intra frame coding in AVS3, in *2021 IEEE International Conference on Systems, Man, and Cybernetics (SMC)* (IEEE, Piscataway, 2021), pp. 3164–3169
16. H. Yuan, W. Gao, J. Wang, Dynamic computational resource allocation for fast inter frame coding in video conferencing applications, in *2021 IEEE International Conference on Multimedia and Expo (ICME)* (IEEE, Piscataway, 2021), pp. 1–6

17. W. Gao, Q. Jiang, R. Wang, S. Ma, G. Li, S. Kwong, Consistent quality oriented rate control in HEVC via balancing intra and inter frame coding. IEEE Trans. Ind. Inf. **18**(3), 1594–1604 (2021)
18. H. Yuan, W. Gao, A new coding unit partitioning mode for screen content video coding, in *Proceedings of the 2021 5th International Conference on Digital Signal Processing* (2021), pp. 66–72
19. W. Gao, On the performance evaluation of state-of-the-art rate control algorithms for practical video coding and transmission systems, in *Proceedings of the 2020 4th International Conference on Video and Image Processing* (2020), pp. 179–185
20. W. Gao, S. Kwong, Q. Jiang, C.-K. Fong, P.H. Wong, W.Y. Yuen, Data-driven rate control for rate-distortion optimization in hevc based on simplified effective initial QP learning. IEEE Trans. Broadcast. **65**(1), 94–108 (2018)
21. W. Gao, A multi-objective optimization perspective for joint consideration of video coding quality, in *2019 Asia-Pacific Signal and Information Processing Association Annual Summit and Conference (APSIPA ASC)* (IEEE, Piscataway, 2019), pp. 986–991
22. W. Gao, S. Kwong, Y. Jia, Joint machine learning and game theory for rate control in high efficiency video coding. IEEE Trans. Image Process. **26**(12), 6074–6089 (2017)
23. W. Gao, S. Kwong, Y. Zhou, H. Yuan, Ssim-based game theory approach for rate-distortion optimized intra frame CTU-level bit allocation. IEEE Trans. Multimedia **18**(6), 988–999 (2016)
24. W. Gao, S. Kwong, H. Yuan, X. Wang, Dct coefficient distribution modeling and quality dependency analysis based frame-level bit allocation for hevc. IEEE Trans. Circ. Syst. Video Technol. **26**(1), 139–153 (2015)
25. W. Gao, S. Kwong, Phase congruency based edge saliency detection and rate control for perceptual image and video coding, in *2016 IEEE International Conference on Systems, Man, and Cybernetics (SMC)* (IEEE, Piscataway, 2016), pp. 000264–000269
26. H. Yuan, W. Gao, Openfastvc: An open source library for video coding fast algorithm implementation, in *Proceedings of the 31st ACM International Conference on Multimedia* (2023), pp. 9660–9663
27. H. Yuan, W. Gao, S. Ma, Y. Yan, Divide-and-conquer-based RDO-free CU partitioning for 8k video compression. ACM Trans. Multimedia Comput. Commun. Appl. **20**(4), 1–20 (2024)
28. L. Tao, W. Gao, A hardware implementation of entropy encoder for 8k video coding, in *2022 IEEE International Conference on Multimedia and Expo (ICME)* (IEEE, Piscataway, 2022), pp. 1–6
29. Y. Guo, W. Gao, S. Ma, G. Li, Accelerating transform algorithm implementation for efficient intra coding of 8k UHD videos. ACM Trans. Multimedia Comput. Commun. Appl. **18**(4), 1–20 (2022)
30. Z. Cai, W. Gao, Efficient fast algorithm and parallel hardware architecture for intra prediction of AVS3, in *2021 IEEE International Symposium on Circuits and Systems (ISCAS)* (IEEE, Piscataway, 2021), pp. 1–5
31. W. Gao, H. Yuan, Y. Guo, L. Tao, Z. Cai, G. Li, Openhardwarevc: An open source library for 8k UHD video coding hardware implementation, in *Proceedings of the 30th ACM International Conference on Multimedia* (2022), pp. 7339–7342
32. W. Gao, H. Yuan, G. Liao, Z. Guo, J. Chen, PP8K: A new dataset for 8k UHD video compression and processing. IEEE MultiMedia **30**, 100–109 (2023)
33. W. Liu, W. Gao, G. Li, S. Ma, T. Zhao, H. Yuan, Enlarged motion-aware and frequency-aware network for compressed video artifact reduction. IEEE Trans. Circ. Syst. Video Technol. **34**, 10339–10352 (2024)
34. X. Zang, W. Gao, G. Li, H. Fang, C. Ban, Z. He, H. Sun, A baseline investigation: Transformer-based cross-view baseline for text-based person search, in *Proceedings of the 31st ACM International Conference on Multimedia* (2023), pp. 7737–7746
35. G. Liao, W. Gao, G. Li, J. Wang, S. Kwong, Cross-collaborative fusion-encoder network for robust RGB-thermal salient object detection. IEEE Trans. Circ. Syst. Video Technol. **32**(11), 7646–7661 (2022)

36. W. Gao, G. Liao, S. Ma, G. Li, Y. Liang, W. Lin, Unified information fusion network for multimodal RGB-D and RGB-T salient object detection. IEEE Trans. Circ. Syst. Video Technol. **32**(4), 2091–2106 (2021)
37. Y. Chen, S. Sun, G. Li, W. Gao, T.H. Li, Closing the gap between theory and practice during alternating optimization for gans. IEEE Trans. Neural Netw. Learn. Syst. **35**, 14005–14017 (2023)
38. Y. Chen, C. Jin, G. Li, T. H. Li, W. Gao, Mitigating label noise in gans via enhanced spectral normalization. IEEE Trans. Circ. Syst. Video Technol. **33**, 3924–3934 (2023)
39. X. Zang, G. Li, W. Gao, Multidirection and multiscale pyramid in transformer for video-based pedestrian retrieval. IEEE Trans. Ind. Inf. **18**(12), 8776–8785 (2022)
40. X. Zang, G. Li, W. Gao, X. Shu, Learning to disentangle scenes for person re-identification. Image Vision Comput. **116**, 104330 (2021)
41. X. Zang, G. Li, W. Gao, X. Shu, Exploiting robust unsupervised video person re-identification. IET Image Process. **16**(3), 729–741 (2022)
42. Z. Yue, G. Li, W. Gao, Cross-level guided attention for human-object interaction detection, in *2023 IEEE International Conference on Multimedia and Expo Workshops (ICMEW)* (IEEE, Piscataway, 2023), pp. 284–289
43. Z. Yao, W. Gao, Iterative saliency aggregation and assignment network for efficient salient object detection in optical remote sensing images. IEEE Trans. Geosci. Remote Sens. **62**, 5633213 (2024)
44. Y. Sun, Z. Li, S. Wang, W. Gao, Depth-assisted calibration on learning-based factorization for a compressive light field display. Opt. Express **31**(4), 5399–5413 (2023)
45. Y. Sun, Z. Li, L. Li, S. Wang, W. Gao, Optimization of compressive light field display in dual-guided learning, in *ICASSP 2022-2022 IEEE International Conference on Acoustics, Speech and Signal Processing (ICASSP)* (IEEE, Piscataway, 2022), pp. 2075–2079
46. W. Gao, S. Fan, G. Li, W. Lin, A thorough benchmark and a new model for light field saliency detection. IEEE Trans. Pattern Analy. Mach. Intell. **45**, 8003–8019 (2023)
47. Z. Li, G. Li, T. Li, S. Liu, W. Gao, Information-growth attention network for image super-resolution, in *Proceedings of the 29th ACM International Conference on Multimedia* (2021), pp. 544–552
48. L. Zhou, W. Gao, G. Li, H. Yuan, T. Zhao, G. Yue, Disentangled feature distillation for light field super-resolution with degradations, in *2023 IEEE International Conference on Multimedia and Expo Workshops (ICMEW)* (IEEE, Piscataway, 2023), pp. 116–121
49. L. Zhou, W. Gao, G. Li, End-to-end spatial-angular light field super-resolution using parallax structure preservation strategy, in *2022 IEEE International Conference on Image Processing (ICIP)* (IEEE, Piscataway, 2022), pp. 3396–3400
50. W. Gao, L. Zhou, L. Tao, A fast view synthesis implementation method for light field applications. ACM Trans. Multimedia Comput. Commun. Appl. **17**(4), 1–20 (2021)
51. X. Zhang, W. Gao, G. Li, Q. Jiang, R. Cong, Image quality assessment-driven reinforcement learning for mixed distorted image restoration. ACM Trans. Multimedia Comput. Commun. Appl. **19**(1s), 1–23 (2023)
52. X. Zhang, W. Gao, H. Yuan, G. Li, Je 2 net: Joint exploitation and exploration in reinforcement learning based image restoration, in *ICASSP 2022-2022 IEEE International Conference on Acoustics, Speech and Signal Processing (ICASSP)* (IEEE, Piscataway, 2022), pp. 2090–2094
53. X. Zhang, W. Gao, Hirl: Hybrid image restoration based on hierarchical deep reinforcement learning via two-step analysis, in *ICASSP 2022-2022 IEEE International Conference on Acoustics, Speech and Signal Processing (ICASSP)* (IEEE, Piscataway, 2022), pp. 2445–2449
54. Z. Guo, W. Gao, H. Wang, J. Wang, S. Fan, No-reference deep quality assessment of compressed light field images, in *2021 IEEE International Conference on Multimedia and Expo (ICME)* (IEEE, Piscataway, 2021), pp. 1–6
55. G. Liao, W. Gao, Rethinking feature mining for light field salient object detection, in *ACM Transactions on Multimedia Computing, Communications, and Applications* (2024)

56. C. Zhang, W. Gao, Learned rate control for frame-level adaptive neural video compression via dynamic neural network, in *European Conference on Computer Vision* (Springer, Berlin, 2024)
57. H. Zheng, W. Gao, Z. Yu, T. Zhao, G. Li, ViewPCGC: View-guided learned point cloud geometry compression, in *Proceedings of the 32nd ACM International Conference on Multimedia* (2024)
58. L. Xie, W. Gao, H. Zheng, G. Li, Roi-guided point cloud geometry compression towards human and machine vision, in *Proceedings of the 32nd ACM International Conference on Multimedia* (2024)
59. C. Peng, W. Gao, Laplacian matrix learning for point cloud attribute compression with ternary search-based adaptive block partition, in *Proceedings of the 32nd ACM International Conference on Multimedia* (2024)
60. S. Luo, B. Qu, W. Gao, Learning robust 3D representation from clip via dual denoising (2024). arXiv preprint arXiv:2407.00905
61. S. Sun, J. Liu, T.H. Li, H. Li, G. Liu, W. Gao, Streamflow: Streamlined multi-frame optical flow estimation for video sequences (2023). arXiv preprint arXiv:2311.17099
62. R. Liu, J. Huang, W. Gao, T.H. Li, G. Li, Mug-stan: Adapting image-language pretrained models for general video understanding (2023). arXiv preprint arXiv:2311.15075
63. Y. Jia, E. Shelhamer, J. Donahue, S. Karayev, J. Long, R.B. Girshick, S. Guadarrama, T. Darrell, Caffe: Convolutional architecture for fast feature embedding, in *Proceedings of the 22nd ACM International Conference on Multimedia* (2014), pp. 675–678. [Online]. Available: https://api.semanticscholar.org/CorpusID:1799558
64. M. Abadi, P. Barham, J. Chen, Z. Chen, A. Davis, J. Dean, M. Devin, S. Ghemawat, G. Irving, M. Isard, M. Kudlur, J. Levenberg, R. Monga, S. Moore, D.G. Murray, B. Steiner, P.A. Tucker, V. Vasudevan, P. Warden, M. Wicke, Y. Yu, X. Zhang, Tensorflow: A system for large-scale machine learning, in *USENIX Symposium on Operating Systems Design and Implementation* (2016). [Online]. Available: https://api.semanticscholar.org/CorpusID:6287870
65. A. Paszke, S. Gross, F. Massa, A. Lerer, J. Bradbury, G. Chanan, T. Killeen, Z. Lin, N. Gimelshein, L. Antiga, A. Desmaison, A. Köpf, E. Yang, Z. DeVito, M. Raison, A. Tejani, S. Chilamkurthy, B. Steiner, L. Fang, J. Bai, S. Chintala, Pytorch: An imperative style, high-performance deep learning library, in *Neural Information Processing Systems*, vol. 32 (2019), pp. 8026–8037
66. T. Chen, M. Li, Y. Li, M. Lin, N. Wang, M. Wang, T. Xiao, B. Xu, C. Zhang, Z. Zhang, Mxnet: A flexible and efficient machine learning library for heterogeneous distributed systems. CoRR **abs/1512.01274** (2015). [Online]. Available: http://arxiv.org/abs/1512.01274
67. J.R. Nickolls, I. Buck, M. Garland, K. Skadron, Scalable parallel programming with cuda, in *2008 IEEE Hot Chips 20 Symposium* (2008), pp. 1–2
68. L. Bottou, F.E. Curtis, J. Nocedal, Optimization methods for large-scale machine learning. SIAM Rev. **60**(2), 223–311 (2018)
69. D.E. Rumelhart, G.E. Hinton, R.J. Williams, Learning representations by back-propagating errors. Nature **323**(6088), 533–536 (1986)
70. A. Krizhevsky, I. Sutskever, G.E. Hinton, Imagenet classification with deep convolutional neural networks. Adv. Neural Inf. Process. Syst. **25**, 84–90 (2012)
71. K. He, X. Zhang, S. Ren, J. Sun, Deep residual learning for image recognition, in *Proceedings of the IEEE Conference on Computer Vision and Pattern Recognition* (2016), pp. 770–778
72. B. Graham, M. Engelcke, L. Van Der Maaten, 3D semantic segmentation with submanifold sparse convolutional networks, in *Proceedings of the IEEE Conference on Computer Vision and Pattern Recognition* (2018), pp. 9224–9232
73. A. Vaswani, N. Shazeer, N. Parmar, J. Uszkoreit, L. Jones, A.N. Gomez, Ł. Kaiser, I. Polosukhin, Attention is all you need. Adv. Neural Inf. Process. Syst. **30**, 6000–6010 (2017)
74. A. Dosovitskiy, L. Beyer, A. Kolesnikov, D. Weissenborn, X. Zhai, T. Unterthiner, M. Dehghani, M. Minderer, G. Heigold, S. Gelly, et al., An image is worth 16x16 words: Transformers for image recognition at scale (2020). arXiv preprint arXiv:2010.11929

75. Z. Liu, Y. Lin, Y. Cao, H. Hu, Y. Wei, Z. Zhang, S. Lin, B. Guo, Swin transformer: Hierarchical vision transformer using shifted windows, in *IEEE/CVF International Conference on Computer Vision* (2021), pp. 9992–10002
76. Y. Zhang, K. Gong, K. Zhang, H. Li, Y. Qiao, W. Ouyang, X. Yue, Meta-transformer: A unified framework for multimodal learning (2023). arXiv preprint arXiv:2307.10802
77. J.L. Ba, J.R. Kiros, G.E. Hinton, Layer normalization (2016). arXiv preprint arXiv:1607.06450
78. B. Sanchez-Lengeling, E. Reif, A. Pearce, A.B. Wiltschko, A gentle introduction to graph neural networks. Distill (2021). https://distill.pub/2021/gnn-intro
79. F. Scarselli, S.L. Yong, M. Gori, M. Hagenbuchner, A.C. Tsoi, M. Maggini, Graph neural networks for ranking web pages, in *IEEE/WIC/ACM International Conference on Web Intelligence* (2005), pp. 666–672
80. F. Scarselli, M. Gori, A.C. Tsoi, M. Hagenbuchner, G. Monfardini, The graph neural network model. IEEE Trans. Neural Netw. **20**(1), 61–80 (2008)
81. F.R. Chung, *Spectral Graph Theory*, vol. 92 (American Mathematical Society, Providence, 1997)
82. M. Defferrard, X. Bresson, P. Vandergheynst, Convolutional neural networks on graphs with fast localized spectral filtering. Adv. Neural Inf. Process. Syst. **29**, 3844–3852 (2016)
83. T.N. Kipf, M. Welling, Semi-supervised classification with graph convolutional networks (2016). arXiv preprint arXiv:1609.02907
84. W. Hamilton, Z. Ying, J. Leskovec, Inductive representation learning on large graphs. Adv. Neural Inf. Process. Syst. **30**, 1025–1035 (2017)
85. L. Ruiz, F. Gama, A. Ribeiro, Gated graph recurrent neural networks. IEEE Trans. Signal Process. **68**, 6303–6318 (2020)
86. H. Gao, S. Ji, Graph U-nets. IEEE Trans. Pattern Analy. Mach. Intell. **44**(9), 4948–4960 (2022)
87. J. Lee, I. Lee, J. Kang, Self-attention graph pooling, in *Proceedings of the 36th International Conference on Machine Learning*. Proceedings of Machine Learning Research, ed. by K. Chaudhuri, R. Salakhutdinov, vol. 97 (PMLR, New York City, 2019), pp. 3734–3743
88. R. Ying, J. You, C. Morris, X. Ren, W.L. Hamilton, J. Leskovec, Hierarchical graph representation learning with differentiable pooling, in *Proceedings of the International Conference on Neural Information Processing Systems*, ser. NIPS'18 (2018), pp. 4805–4815
89. C. Qi, H. Su, K. Mo, L.J. Guibas, Pointnet: Deep learning on point sets for 3D classification and segmentation, in *IEEE Conference on Computer Vision and Pattern Recognition* (2016), pp. 77–85
90. C.R. Qi, L. Yi, H. Su, L.J. Guibas, Pointnet++: deep hierarchical feature learning on point sets in a metric space. Adv. Neural Inf. Process. Syst. **30**, 5105–5114 (2017)
91. Y. Wang, Y. Sun, Z. Liu, S.E. Sarma, M.M. Bronstein, J.M. Solomon, Dynamic graph CNN for learning on point clouds. ACM Trans. Graph. **38**, 1–12 (2018)
92. Z. Liu, H. Tang, Y. Lin, S. Han, Point-voxel cnn for efficient 3D deep learning, in *Proceedings of the International Conference on Neural Information Processing Systems* (2019), pp. 963–973
93. G. Qian, A. Hamdi, X. Zhang, B. Ghanem, Pix4point: Image pretrained standard transformers for 3D point cloud understanding, in *International Conference on 3D Vision* (2024), pp. 1280–1290
94. T. Qin, G. Li, W. Gao, S. Liu, Multi-grained point cloud geometry compression via dual-model prediction with extended octree, in *ACM Transactions on Multimedia Computing, Communications, and Applications* (2024)
95. Y. Shao, W. Gao, S. Liu, G. Li, Advanced patch-based affine motion estimation for dynamic point cloud geometry compression. Sensors **24**(10), 3142 (2024)
96. Y. Shao, F. Song, W. Gao, S. Liu, G. Li, Texture-guided graph transform optimization for point cloud attribute compression. Appl. Sci. **14**(10), 4094 (2024)

97. Y. Shao, X. Yang, W. Gao, S. Liu, G. Li, 3D point cloud attribute compression using diffusion-based texture-aware intra prediction. IEEE Trans. Circ. Syst. Video Technol. **34**, 9633–9646 (2024)
98. J. Zhang, Y. Chen, G. Liu, W. Gao, G. Li, Efficient point cloud attribute compression framework using attribute-guided graph fourier transform, in *ICASSP 2024-2024 IEEE International Conference on Acoustics, Speech and Signal Processing (ICASSP)* (IEEE, Piscataway, 2024), pp. 8426–8430
99. W. Gao, H. Yuan, G. Li, Z. Li, H. Yuan, Low complexity coding unit decision for video-based point cloud compression. IEEE Trans. Image Process. **33**, 149–162 (2023)
100. Y. Shao, G. Li, Q. Zhang, W. Gao, S. Liu, Non-rigid registration-based progressive motion compensation for point cloud geometry compression. IEEE Trans. Geosci. Remote Sens. **61**, 4705414 (2023)
101. F. Song, G. Li, X. Yang, W. Gao, S. Liu, Block-adaptive point cloud attribute coding with region-aware optimized transform. IEEE Trans. Circ. Syst. Video Technol. **33**, 4294–4308 (2023)
102. Y. An, Y. Shao, G. Li, W. Gao, S. Liu, A fast motion estimation method with hamming distance for lidar point cloud compression, in *2022 IEEE International Conference on Visual Communications and Image Processing (VCIP)* (IEEE, Piscataway, 2022), pp. 1–5
103. H. Yuan, W. Gao, G. Li, Z. Li, Rate-distortion-guided learning approach with cross-projection information for V-PCC fast CU decision, in *Proceedings of the 30th ACM international conference on multimedia* (2022), pp. 3085–3093
104. F. Song, G. Li, W. Gao, T.H. Li, Rate-distortion optimized graph for point cloud attribute coding. IEEE Signal Process. Lett. **29**, 922–926 (2022)
105. F. Song, G. Li, X. Yang, W. Gao, T.H. Li, Fine-grained correlation representation for graph-based point cloud attribute compression, in *2022 IEEE International Conference on Multimedia and Expo (ICME)* (IEEE, Piscataway, 2022), pp. 1–6
106. F. Shen, W. Gao, A rate control algorithm for video-based point cloud compression, in *2021 International Conference on Visual Communications and Image Processing (VCIP)* (IEEE, Piscataway, 2021), pp. 1–5
107. F. Song, Y. Shao, W. Gao, H. Wang, T. Li, Layer-wise geometry aggregation framework for lossless lidar point cloud compression. IEEE Trans. Circ. Syst. Video Technol. **31**(12), 4603–4616 (2021)
108. G. Li, G. Wei, W. Gao, *Point Cloud Compression: Technologies and Standardization* (Springer Nature, Berlin, 2024)
109. G. Li, W. Gao, W. Gao, Introduction, in *Point Cloud Compression: Technologies and Standardization* (Springer, Berlin, 2024), pp. 1–28
110. G. Li, W. Gao, W. Gao, Background knowledge, in *Point Cloud Compression: Technologies and Standardization* (Springer, Berlin, 2024), pp. 29–51
111. G. Li, W. Gao, W. Gao, Predictive coding, in *Point Cloud Compression: Technologies and Standardization* (Springer, Berlin, 2024), pp. 53–70
112. G. Li, W. Gao, W. Gao, Transform coding, in *Point Cloud Compression: Technologies and Standardization* (Springer, Berlin, 2024), pp. 71–96
113. G. Li, W. Gao, W. Gao, Quantization techniques, in *Point Cloud Compression: Technologies and Standardization* (Springer, Berlin, 2024), pp. 97–112
114. G. Li, W. Gao, W. Gao, Entropy coding, in *Point Cloud Compression: Technologies and Standardization* (Springer, Berlin, 2024), pp. 113–133
115. G. Li, W. Gao, W. Gao, MPEG geometry-based point cloud compression (G-PCC) standard, in *Point Cloud Compression: Technologies and Standardization* (Springer, Berlin, 2024), pp. 135–165
116. G. Li, W. Gao, W. Gao, AVS point cloud compression standard, in *Point Cloud Compression: Technologies and Standardization* (Springer, Berlin, 2024), pp. 167–197
117. G. Li, W. Gao, W. Gao, MPEG video-based point cloud compression (V-PCC) standard, in *Point Cloud Compression: Technologies and Standardization* (Springer, Berlin, 2024), pp. 199–218

118. G. Li, W. Gao, W. Gao, MPEG AI-based 3D graphics coding standard, in *Point Cloud Compression: Technologies and Standardization* (Springer, Berlin, 2024), pp. 219–241
119. G. Li, W. Gao, W. Gao, Future work, in *Point Cloud Compression: Technologies and Standardization* (Springer, Berlin, 2024), pp. 243–250
120. L. Xie, W. Gao, H. Zheng, G. Li, SPCGC: Scalable point cloud geometry compression for machine vision, in *Proceedings of IEEE International Conference on Robotics and Automation* (2024)
121. L. Xie, W. Gao, H. Zheng, H. Ye, Semantic-aware visual decomposition for point cloud geometry compression, in *2024 Data Compression Conference (DCC)* (IEEE, Piscataway, 2024), pp. 595–595
122. Z. Qi, W. Gao, Variable-rate point cloud geometry compression based on feature adjustment and interpolation, in *2024 Data Compression Conference (DCC)* (IEEE, Piscataway, 2024), pp. 63–72
123. Z. Yu, W. Gao, When dynamic neural network meets point cloud compression: Computation-aware variable rate and checkerboard context, in *2024 Data Compression Conference (DCC)* (IEEE, Piscataway, 2024), pp. 600–600
124. L. Xie, W. Gao, S. Fan, Z. Yao, PDNeT: Parallel dual-branch network for point cloud geometry compression and analysis, in *2024 Data Compression Conference (DCC)* (IEEE, Piscataway, 2024), pp. , 596–596
125. L. Xie, W. Gao, H. Zheng, End-to-end point cloud geometry compression and analysis with sparse tensor, in *Proceedings of the 1st International Workshop on Advances in Point Cloud Compression, Processing and Analysis* (2022), pp. 27–32
126. C. Fu, G. Li, R. Song, W. Gao, S. Liu, Octattention: Octree-based large-scale contexts model for point cloud compression. Proc. AAAI Confer. Artif. Intell. **36**(1), 625–633 (2022)
127. W. Liu, W. Gao, X. Mu, Fast inter-frame motion prediction for compressed dynamic point cloud attribute enhancement. Proc. AAAI Confer. Artif. Intell. **38**(4), 3720–3728 (2024)
128. Z. Yang, W. Gao, X. Lu, Danet: Density-adaptive network for geometry-based point cloud compression artifacts removal, in *2023 IEEE International Conference on Visual Communications and Image Processing (VCIP)* (IEEE, Piscataway, 2023), pp. 1–5
129. X. Fan, G. Li, D. Li, Y. Ren, W. Gao, T.H. Li, Deep geometry post-processing for decompressed point clouds, in *2022 IEEE International Conference on Multimedia and Expo (ICME)* (IEEE, Piscataway, 2022), pp. 1–6
130. X. Zhang, G. Liao, W. Gao, G. Li, TDRNeT: Transformer-based dual-branch restoration network for geometry based point cloud compression artifacts, in *2022 IEEE International Conference on Multimedia and Expo (ICME)* (IEEE, Piscataway, 2022), pp. 1–6
131. Z. Li, G. Li, T.H. Li, S. Liu, W. Gao, Semantic point cloud upsampling. IEEE Trans. Multimedia **25**, 3432–3442 (2022)
132. R. Zhang, W. Gao, G. Li, T.H. Li, QINeT: Decision surface learning and adversarial enhancement for quasi-immune completion of diverse corrupted point clouds. IEEE Trans. Geosci. Remote Sens. **60**, 1–14 (2022)
133. R. Bao, Y. Ren, G. Li, W. Gao, S. Liu, Flow-based point cloud completion network with adversarial refinement, in *ICASSP 2022-2022 IEEE International Conference on Acoustics, Speech and Signal Processing (ICASSP)* (IEEE, Piscataway, 2022), pp. 2559–2563
134. J. Chen, G. Li, R. Zhang, T.H. Li, W. Gao, Pointivae: Invertible variational autoencoder framework for 3D point cloud generation, in *2022 IEEE International Conference on Image Processing (ICIP)* (IEEE, Piscataway, 2022), pp. 3216–3220
135. R. Zhang, J. Chen, W. Gao, G. Li, T.H. Li, Pointot: interpretable geometry-inspired point cloud generative model via optimal transport. IEEE Trans. Circ. Syst. Video Technol. **32**(10), 6792–6806 (2022)
136. S. Fan, W. Gao, G. Li, Salient object detection for point clouds, in *European Conference on Computer Vision* (Springer, Berlin, 2022), pp. 1–19
137. S. Luo, W. Gao, A general framework for rotation invariant point cloud analysis, in *ICASSP 2024-2024 IEEE International Conference on Acoustics, Speech and Signal Processing (ICASSP)* (IEEE, Piscataway, 2024), pp. 3665–3669

138. X. Lu, W. Gao, Attentivenet: Detecting small objects for lidar point clouds by attending to important points, in *2023 IEEE International Conference on Visual Communications and Image Processing (VCIP)* (IEEE, Piscataway, 2023), pp. 1–5
139. Z. Pan, N. Zhang, W. Gao, S. Liu, G. Li, Less is more: label recommendation for weakly supervised point cloud semantic segmentation. Proc. AAAI Confer. Artif. Intell. **38**(5), 4397–4405 (2024)
140. Z. Pan, G. Liu, W. Gao, T. Li, Epcontrast: Effective point-level contrastive learning for large-scale point cloud understanding, in *2024 IEEE International Conference on Multimedia and Expo (ICME)* (IEEE, Piscataway, 2024)
141. N. Zhang, Z. Pan, T.H. Li, W. Gao, G. Li, Improving graph representation for point cloud segmentation via attentive filtering, in *Proceedings of the IEEE/CVF Conference on Computer Vision and Pattern Recognition* (2023), pp. 1244–1254
142. K. Wen, N. Zhang, G. Li, W. Gao, MPVNN: Multi-resolution point-voxel non-parametric network for 3D point cloud processing, in *2024 IEEE International Conference on Multimedia and Expo (ICME)* (IEEE, Piscataway, 2024)
143. S. Fan, W. Gao, Screen-based 3D subjective experiment software, in *Proceedings of the 31st ACM International Conference on Multimedia* (2023), pp. 9672–9675
144. J. Wang, W. Gao, G. Li, Zoom to perceive better: No-reference point cloud quality assessment via exploring effective multiscale feature. IEEE Trans. Circ. Syst. Video Technol. **34**, 6334–6346 (2024)
145. J. Wang, W. Gao, G. Li, Applying collaborative adversarial learning to blind point cloud quality measurement. IEEE Trans. Instrument. Measur. **72**, 5029215 (2023)
146. W. Gao, H. Ye, G. Li, H. Zheng, Y. Wu, L. Xie, Openpointcloud: An open-source algorithm library of deep learning based point cloud compression, in *Proceedings of the 30th ACM International Conference on Multimedia* (2022), pp. 7347–7350
147. Y. Zhang, W. Gao, G. Li, Openpointcloud-v2: A deep learning based open-source algorithm library of point cloud processing, in *Proceedings of the 1st International Workshop on Advances in Point Cloud Compression, Processing and Analysis* (2022), pp. 51–55
148. D. Yang, W. Gao, G. Li, H. Yuan, J. Hou, S. Kwong, Exploiting manifold feature representation for efficient classification of 3D point clouds. ACM Trans. Multimedia Comput. Commun. Appl. **19**(1s), 1–21 (2023)
149. W. Gao, G. Li, H. Yuan, R. Hamzaoui, Z. Li, S. Liu, Apccpa'22: 1st international workshop on advances in point cloud compression, processing and analysis, in *Proceedings of the 30th ACM International Conference on Multimedia* (2022), pp. 7392–7393

Chapter 3
Deep-Learning-based Point Cloud Enhancement I

Abstract As a pivotal component in modern technological domains such as autonomous driving and virtual reality, point cloud data necessitate enhancement to ensure that the quality meets the demands of downstream tasks. Point cloud enhancement methods delve into postprocessing techniques, including upsampling, frame interpolation, completion, and the removal of compression artifacts, addressing prevalent issues in traditional point cloud intelligent systems. This chapter highlights several deep-learning-based point cloud upsampling methods, such as the pioneering PUNet, the progressive point cloud upsampling network, the GAN-based upsampling method PUGAN, and Semantic Point Cloud Upsampling (SPU). These methods leverage the power of deep neural networks to restore geometric information and generate dense point clouds from sparse data. The SPU method, in particular, emphasizes alignment with downstream tasks by using classification networks to supervise the learning process. Additionally, this chapter explores point cloud frame interpolation techniques, which are crucial for generating intermediate point cloud frames along the temporal dimension, thereby enhancing the frame rate of LiDAR point clouds for applications like autonomous vehicles. Finally, a discussion on the challenges and future directions of point cloud upsampling and point cloud frame interpolation is provided.

Keywords Point cloud enhancement · Point cloud upsampling · Point cloud frame interpolation · Generative adversarial network · Deep learning

3.1 Introduction

As an important component of the point cloud intelligent system, point cloud enhancement [1–12] connects point cloud coding [13–51] and point cloud analysis tasks [52–59]. The research works for image and video enhancement [60–68] can also be good references for the corresponding point cloud enhancement works, as well as the other related ones [69–118]. Figure 3.1 exhibits a flow diagram of a point cloud intelligent system. Firstly, the collected point cloud needs to be cleaned and sampled. The cleaning and sampling are called as preprocessing for point

W. Gao, G. Li, *Deep Learning for 3D Point Clouds*,
https://doi.org/10.1007/978-981-97-9570-3_3

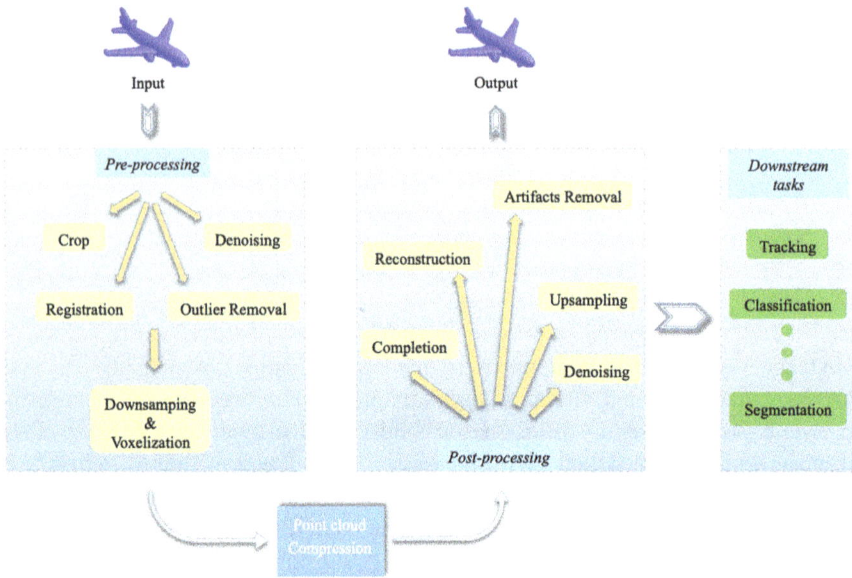

Fig. 3.1 The flow diagram of the intelligent point cloud system, showing the relation of point cloud compression, point cloud enhancement, and downstream tasks. Source: Author

cloud compression. This operation is necessary, because much of the raw point data contain noise and outliers. Here, point cloud denoising and point cloud downsamling technologies are important components in the preprocessing. The preprocessing will influence compression performance because the partitioning of point cloud usually depends on point cloud sparsity and distribution. After point cloud compression and transmission, point clouds need to be further processed again according to corresponding downstream tasks [11, 12, 52, 54, 55, 57]. We call it as postprocessing for point cloud compression. Postprocessing is also necessary because it can solve two problems in the classical point cloud intelligent system. The first problem is that existing compression methods cannot directly face to downstream tasks, they cannot know which points are really critical. The second problem is some geometrical information and attribute information after decoding are easily lost and distorted, which may be caused by quantization and data transmission. The two problems are all not well solved at present, hence the postprocessing is a reasonable solution to bridge compression to downstream tasks. The postprocessing mainly includes upsampling, frame interpolation, completion, compression artifacts removal, and so on.

The concrete technologies utilized by preprocessing and postprocessing are point cloud enhancement. Therefore, this chapter will introduce some point cloud enhancement technologies, which cultivate stronger relations with many point cloud tasks. In Sect. 3.2, we mainly introduce point cloud upsampling method that is expected to recover dense point clouds from sparse point clouds. Further, sparse point clouds can be viewed as a downsampled version of dense point clouds. As a result, point cloud upsampling needs to restore geometric information as a whole. In Sect. 3.3, temporal point cloud upsampling, namely point cloud frame interpolation, is introduced for dynamic point cloud, which considers insert frames between point clouds. We will summarize this chapter in Sect. 3.4.

3.2 Point Cloud Upsampling

3.2.1 Introduction

In the real world, a point cloud is usually captured by LIDAR, which may contain a large number of points (more than 10K or 100K points). But for some point cloud processing tasks, point clouds need to be downsampled to achieve real time and high efficiency. However, a downsampled point may lose some local detailed information, which is adverse for surface reconstruction and point cloud analysis. Point cloud upsampling has the same characteristics with image super-resolution as shown in Fig. 3.2. We can notice that point cloud upsampling focuses on enriching coordinate information by supplementing points for the downsampled point cloud. Given a sparse point cloud $\mathbf{P}_S = \{p_i \in \mathbb{R}^3 | 0 \leq i < n\}$, point cloud upsampling aims at recovering a dense point cloud $\mathbf{P}_D = \{p_i \in \mathbb{R}^3 | 0 \leq i < rn\}$ from $\mathbf{P}_S$, where n is the number of points, and r is the upscaling factor [119]. It is also an

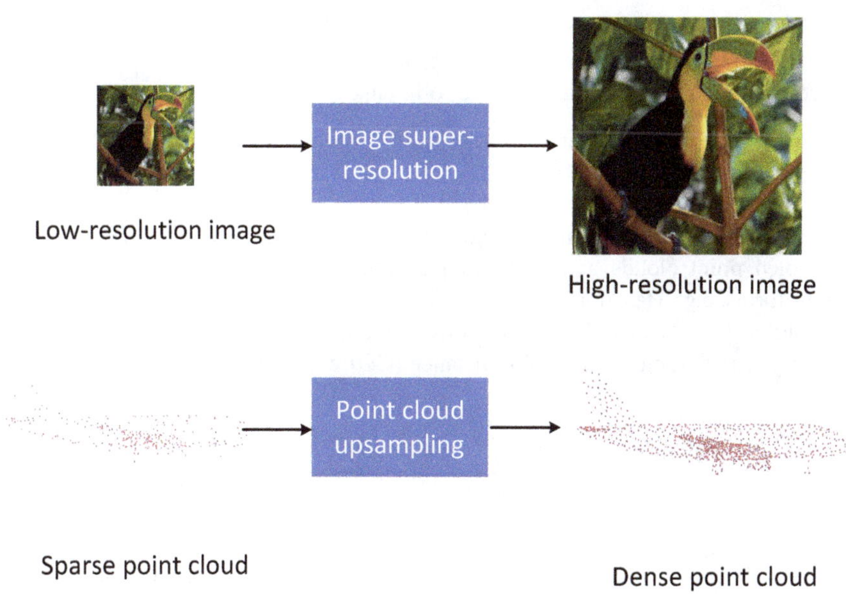

Fig. 3.2 The comparison of image super-resolution and point cloud upsampling. Source: Author

ill-posed problem. In other words, given a dense point cloud, many downsampled sparse point clouds can be generated, and vice versa.

Some early point cloud upsampling methods [120–122] mainly estimate 3D surface according to existing limited point clouds. Optimization methods are good at approximating local geometry, and they have become a popular strategy in previous works. Nevertheless, prior information dominates the mathematical modeling, which brings information bottleneck. In other works, lacking external knowledge is likely to be far from real-world applications. With the development of machine learning and deep learning, recent learning-based upsampling methods consider utilizing a trainable model to directly recover dense point clouds from input sparse point clouds. Especially deep learning has shown amazing potential. The most outstanding characteristic of deep neural networks is the ability to sufficiently utilize external data. To effectively utilize these data, it is essential to address two key aspects in the context of deep model learning. The first aspect concerns the methodology of learning. In accordance with the principles of deep supervised learning, a deep network is trained using input data and corresponding labels through gradient descent. It is assumed that readers are familiar with the fundamental concepts of deep learning. The second aspect pertains to the characteristics of the training data. In the context of point cloud upsampling, the training of a deep network necessitates a large dataset comprising sparse point clouds and their corresponding dense counterparts. Given a dense point cloud $\mathbf{P}_D$, the sparse point cloud is generated by a downsampling function $f_\downarrow$ as:

$$\mathbf{P}_S = f_\downarrow(\mathbf{P}_D). \tag{3.1}$$

The downsampling function $f_\downarrow$ will be illustrated. Therefore, given $\mathbf{P}_S$ and an upsampling network U_θ, where θ is the trainable network parameters, the learning procedure is regarded as optimizing the following formula:

$$\theta^* = \arg\min_\theta L(U_\theta(\mathbf{P}_S), \mathbf{P}_D), \tag{3.2}$$

where L is a loss function in training. It is used to measure the distance between upsampled point clouds and target dense point clouds. The distance may have various forms, e.g., Hausdorff distance, Chamfer distance, point-to-surface distance, and Earth Mover's Distance. Here, this book mainly introduces two common distances. The first one is Chamfer Distance (CD) written by:

$$d_{CD}(S_1, S_2) = \sum_{S_a, S_b \in S_1, S_2}^{2} \frac{1}{2|S_a|} \sum_{x \in S_a} \min_{y \in S_b} ||x - y||_2^2, \tag{3.3}$$

where S_1 and S_2 denote two point sets. To be specific, x and y are corresponding in S_1 and S_2, respectively. CD has wide range of application with different number of point sets. The second one is Earth Mover's Distance (EMD). This metric tries to compute a bijection $\phi : S_1 \rightarrow S_2$ to minimize the average distance between upsampled point clouds and objective dense point clouds. And S_1 and S_2 should be the same size. It can be written by:

$$d_{EMD}(S_1, S_2) = \min_{\phi:S_1 \rightarrow S_2} \frac{1}{S_1} \sum_{x \in S_1} ||s - \phi(x)||_2, \tag{3.4}$$

where s represents a point within the target dense point clouds. It should be noted that these evaluation metrics are not always possible to measure the upsampling quality of a point cloud completely, but they provide a strong guidance. To achieve satisfying upsampling quality, designing an appropriate upsampling model G_θ is necessary in the previous works. Several related studies focus on the development of effective loss functions, while others address practical solutions for real-world applications. These representative works will be introduced in the following subsections.

3.2.2 *The Pioneer Point Cloud Upsampling Network*

PUNet [123] is the pioneer deep learning method for upsampling because it provides an infrastructural scheme for training and testing an upsampling model. This method needs to divide an integrated point cloud into many patches in training and designs a multilevel feature learning network. The training of PUNet contains four stages. As shown in Fig. 3.3, first, an integrated point cloud can be divided into many local patches and each patch contains 4096 points. As described earlier in this article, if the upsampling rate is 4, they randomly sample 1024 points from these 4096 points as sparse points, and the original 4096 points are treated as the ground truth. In the point feature embedding, they refer to PointNet++ [124] and design a hierarchical feature learning network. This kind of design has been proven effective for extracting global and local information. After obtaining the hierarchical

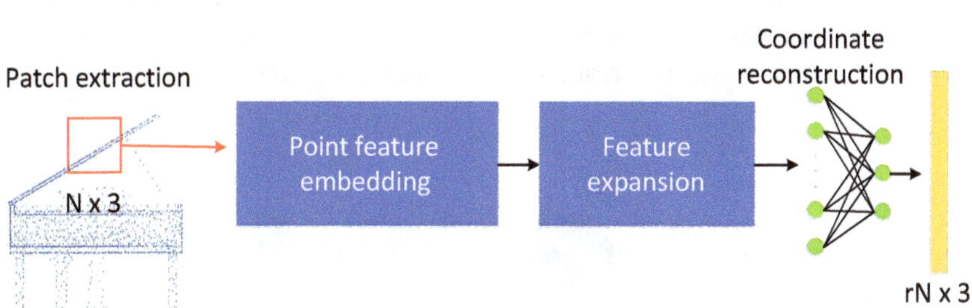

Fig. 3.3 The framework of PUNet. The input point number is N, and the output point number is rN, where r indicates the upsampling rate (© 2018 IEEE. Reprinted, with permission, from ref. [123])

features, a multilevel feature aggregation approach is adopted to fuse the global and local features. Following the embedding process, the feature expansion component involves employing subpixel convolution, akin to techniques utilized in image super-resolution. Let us denote the feature dimension output by feature extraction is $N \times \tilde{C}$. The feature expansion component largely increases feature dimension. The $N \times \tilde{C}$ features are converted to a $N \times r\tilde{C}$ feature by a 1×1 convolution. Then the $N \times r\tilde{C}$ feature is reshaped to a $rN \times \tilde{C}$ feature. Here, r denotes the upsampling ratio. In the coordinate reconstruction, the $rN \times \tilde{C_2}$ are reconstructed to the 3D coordinates with size $rN \times 3$.

This work takes two kinds of loss functions to optimize their network, i.e., EMD loss and repulsion loss. EMD loss tries to approximate the reconstructed points to the targeted dense point clouds, which have been mentioned in Eq. (3.4). The repulsion loss L_{rep} is also designed to make sure the output points have uniform distribution. The experiments conducted on PUNet demonstrate promising outcomes in contrast to previous upsampling methodologies, showcasing notable superiority in upsampling compared to both PointNet and PointNet++.

3.2.3 Progressive Point Cloud Upsampling

Patch-based progressive point cloud upsampling network is an innovative architecture [125] as shown in Fig. 3.4. The authors think that point cloud upsampling should adaptively enlarge receptive fields, so as to effectively reconstruct local information. For example, to achieve 16× upsampling, the network needs to contain four upsampling stages, and each stage is an upsampling network unit. The main characteristics of upsampling network unit are threefold, i.e., feature extraction by intra-level dense connections, feature expansion by code assignment, and inter-level skip connection by bilateral interpolation. The feature extraction by intra-level dense connections adopts features from all previous layers, which makes sure the network can learn global and local information, simultaneously. The feature expansion by code assignment is the same as the idea of PUNet, but PUNet needs to copy the features and handle each feature independently using an individual set of 1×1 convolutions. So this work introduces a 1D code and assign the code for each duplicate features. Next, they reshape the duplicate features to enlarge the feature

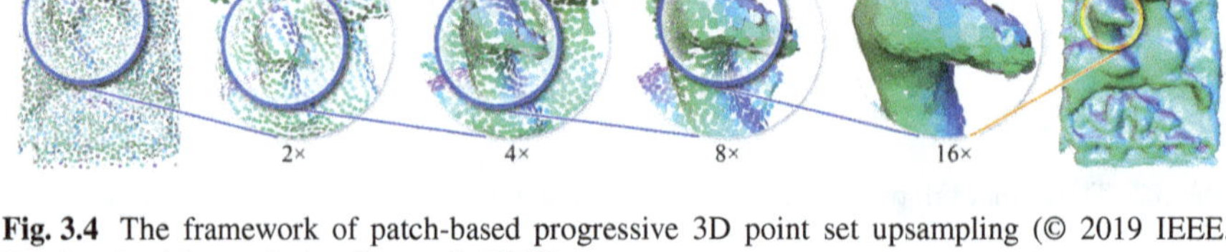

Fig. 3.4 The framework of patch-based progressive 3D point set upsampling (© 2019 IEEE. Reprinted, with permission, from ref. [125])

spatial dimension. The inter-level skip connection by bilateral feature interpolation aims to build a relation with different upsampling levels. In order to maintain the consistency of different levels of feature size, the authors utilize a bilateral interpolation approach to upscale previous features. During the testing phase, to upsample an aggregated point cloud, patches are subdivided using the furthest point sampling strategy from PointNet++ and then nearest neighbor points are grouped.

All the upsampled results are synthesized, and they use furthest point sampling again to collect the specific number of points. In order to optimize parameters, they also propose a modified Chamfer distance loss to prevent misalignment problems on borders.

3.2.4 GAN-Based Point Cloud Upsampling

In previous sections, we have demonstrated some classical loss functions, but it does not mean these loss functions are optimal. The investigation of loss functions is also crucial, because inappropriate loss may limit and determine the distribution pattern of output point clouds. Previous studies have primarily focused on approximating upsampled results to dense point clouds, overlooking the realistic distribution of the upsampled results. Generative Adversarial Network (GAN) is an ingenious idea to improve the output distributions, so it is also introduced in point cloud upsampling [126, 127]. The representative work is PUGAN [126]. It contains two parts, including a generator and a discriminator. As shown in Fig. 3.5, the generator

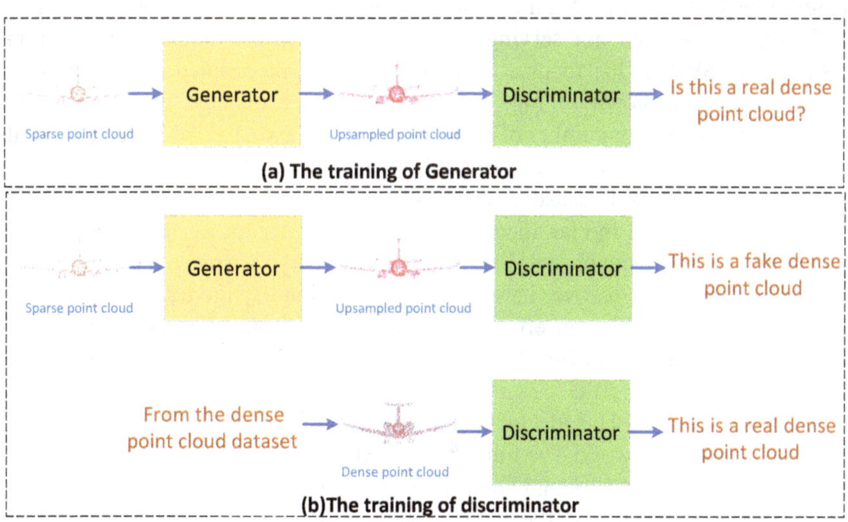

Fig. 3.5 The training of generator and discriminator. Source: Author

can be viewed as the point cloud upsampling network, and it receives sparse point clouds and produces upsampled point clouds.

The discriminator receives the upsampled point clouds to determine whether the upsampled point clouds are real dense point clouds. As a result, the discriminator can provide a supervision for the generator, which compels the generator to produce more realistic upsampled point clouds. In the training phases, the output results of generator are scored by the discriminator so that generator is optimized by an adversarial loss. Same as previous works, PUGAN also uses Earth Mover's distance loss and uniform loss to optimize their generator. The nature of discriminator is a binary classifier, so it needs to be optimized by adversarial loss, in order to accurately learn what is the real dense point cloud. In the testing phases, sparse point clouds are directly fed into the generator (the upsampling network), so the upsampled results are obtained. Furthermore, the feature extraction component of the point upsampling network adopts a dense dynamic graph convolution to embed hierarchical features. Besides, they adopt an up-down-up expansion unit to enhance the feature diversity, avoiding the generator to generate poor point distributions. Finally, they use a set of multilayer perceptrons to reconstruct features to $3D$ coordinate space. The experiments show the excellent performance of PUGAN compared with previous point cloud upsampling approaches.

3.2.5 Semantic Point Cloud Upsampling

Previous point cloud upsampling networks are optimized by surface reconstruction losses, like CD and EMD. Although these losses can achieve good visualizing performance, they are not serving for downstream tasks. Semantic point cloud upsampling (SPU) [119] focuses on conforming the upsampled results to downstream tasks. As shown in Fig. 3.6, the green lines indicate the classification accuracy on decreasing number of points of PointNet and DGCNN. It can be easily found that a small number of downsampled sparse points lead to bad classification performance. This is because downsampled sparse points lose much semantic information, resulting in classification networks that cannot identify key features. As a result, designing an upsampling network to densify the sparse point cloud is an instinctive thinking to recover its semantic information. By the framework of SPU, upsampled point clouds can effectively maintain their accuracy on PointNet and DGCNN. The red lines in Fig. 3.6 show the classification performance of different classification adopting SPU.

The main idea of SPU is to adopt classification networks to supervise the learning of the upsampling network. The framework of SPU is shown in Fig. 3.7, which has a point classification network and an upsampling network. First of all, given a sparse point cloud, they feed it into the point classification network. Thus, they can obtain a key position attention vector. Then, graph aggregation convolution-based (GAC) feature extraction extracts the sparse point cloud's feature. Next, the extracted feature multiplies the attention vector to extrude the key positions of the extracted

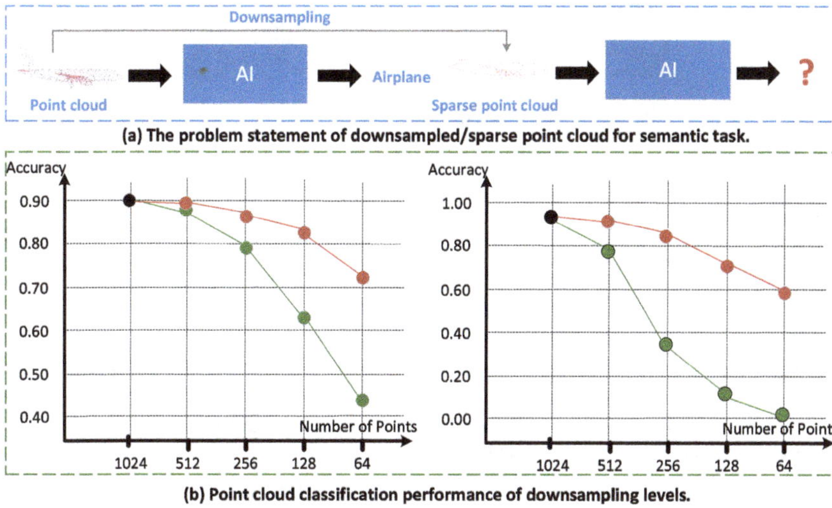

Fig. 3.6 (**a**). When a point cloud becomes sparse, it will influence classification performance. (**b**) Decreasing point numbers on ModelNet40 classification. The green lines indicate the accuracy of the sparse point clouds (left: PointNet [128], right: DGCNN [129]). The red lines denote the classification accuracy upsampled to 1024 points by the proposed SPU (© 2022 IEEE. Reprinted, with permission, from ref. [119])

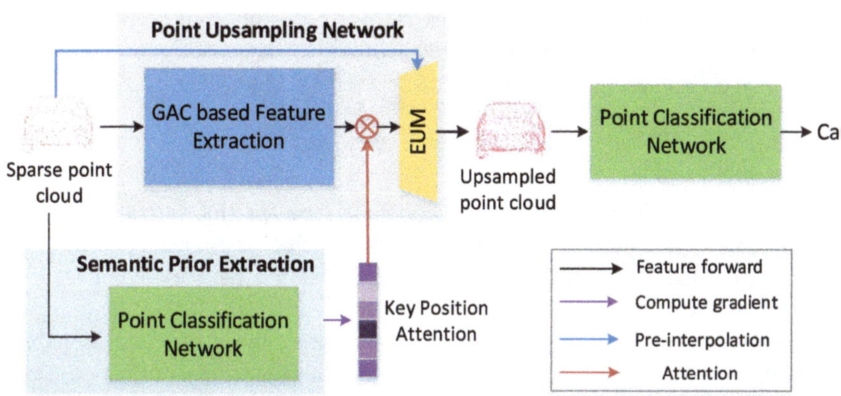

Fig. 3.7 Architecture of semantic point cloud upsampling (SPU) (© 2022 IEEE. Reprinted, with permission, from ref. [119])

feature. After that, the extracted feature is put into the enhanced upsampling module (EUM) to generate an upsampled point cloud. Simultaneously, pre-interpretation is employed for EUM to expedite convergence and stabilize training. During training, the upsampling network should be supervised by the classification network on feature and semantic levels. According to the authors' investigation, a well-trained upsampling network can effectively promote the degradation problem (Fig. 3.6) caused by sparse point clouds. Note that the parameters of classification network

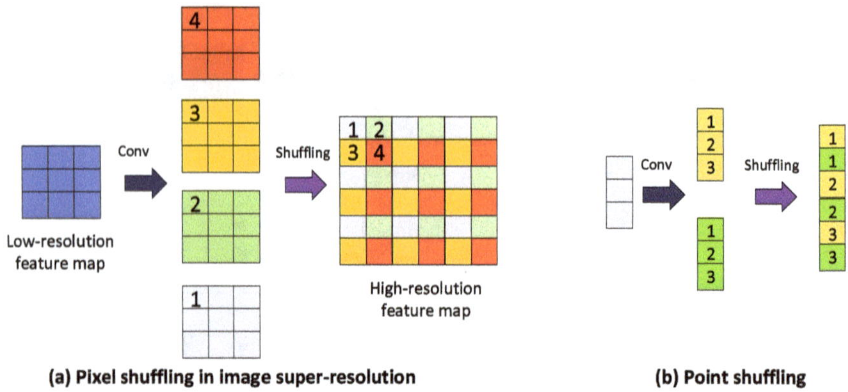

Fig. 3.8 Comparison between (**a**) pixel shuffling and (**b**) point shuffling in SPU (© 2022 IEEE. Reprinted, with permission, from ref. [119])

need to be pretrained and invariable in training, because the classification network needs to provide a stable loss for guiding the learning process.

The main body of the point upsampling network inherits the generator of PUGAN. Note that SPU also refers to the design of pixel shuffling as shown in Fig. 3.8 (a). In EUM, they design point shuffling for extracted feature $\mathbf{F}_c$. Specifically, a 1×1 convolution $\mathbf{W}_u \in \mathbb{R}^{256\times512}$ is employed to extend feature dimension, and then they reorganize the point-wise features. As a result, given $\mathbf{W}_u^{(1)}, ..., \mathbf{W}_u^{(p)}$ an upsampled feature $\mathbf{F}_u \in \mathbb{R}^{rN\times256}$ is obtained by:

$$\mathbf{F}_u = f_s(f_s(\mathbf{F}_c \cdot \mathbf{W}_u^1)...\mathbf{W}_u^p), \tag{3.5}$$

where f_s : is a reshape function. Consequently, they are able to realize $2\times$, $4\times$, $8\times$, and $16\times$ upsampling. Experiments show SPU achieves promising performance on classical ModelNet40 dataset. For the classification network PointNet, SPU outperforms PUGAN by 1% and 5% overall accuracy on $4\times$ upsampling and $8\times$ upsampling, respectively. Besides, SPU provides a novel structural possibility for promoting segmentation task and shows that the semantic information can be upsampled or clarified by this technology.

3.2.6 *Other Methods*

There are some other point cloud upsampling methods [131, 132], and they have different concerns and understandings for upsampling, which guides the development of this area. Qian et al. [133] consider geometry theory and propose a geometry-centric point cloud upsampling network. They are inspired by parameterization-based surface resampling that utilizes the normal vector information, and they

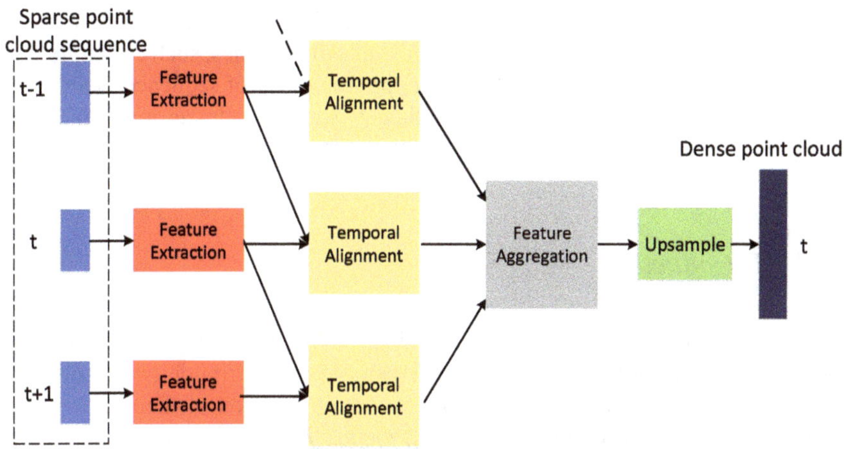

Fig. 3.9 The sketch map of sequential point cloud upsampling (© 2022 IEEE. Reprinted, with permission, from ref. [130])

skillfully combine this complex process with deep networks. Qian et al. [134] propose a lightweight point cloud upsampling using graph convolutional networks. Here, they design an inception dense GCN-based feature extraction to obtain multi-scale features. Hence, Ye et al. [135] present an arbitrary-scale point cloud network using meta-learning technology. Same as video super-resolution, there are also sequential point cloud upsampling methods. Akhtar et al. [136] propose PUDense for upsampling, they employ encoder–decoder architecture and adopt sparse convolution based on Minkowski Engine. Luo et al. [137] propose a flexible-scale point cloud upsampling method that uses edge vectors to approximate the points to insert. Different from single point cloud upsampling, sequential or video point cloud upsampling [130] needs to consider how to utilize temporal information. As shown in Fig. 3.9, their architectures mainly contain feature extraction, feature alignment, feature aggregation, and upsampling. How to design the feature alignment module and feature aggregation module is crucial for high-quality upsampling based on temporal dependency.

3.3 Point Cloud Frame Interpolation

Point cloud frame interpolation is the generation and prediction of point clouds from the temporal dimension. Given two consecutive point clouds and a time step, point cloud frame interpolation focuses on predicting the intermediate frame by forming spatially and temporal coherent point cloud streams. Point cloud frame interpolation plays a vital role in both point cloud processing and applications, which achieves data augmentation in a sense. LiDAR point cloud is a widely used point cloud format scanned and produced by the radar sensor. However, the low frame rate of mechanical LiDAR sensors restricts a lot of application scenes, such as autonomous vehicles and intelligent robots. To increase the frame rate of sequence, point cloud frame interpolation is regarded as an efficient way and attracts more and more attention and research.

3.3.1 Introduction

According to the specific task and application, the frame rate of point cloud interpolation can be set arbitrarily. For the convenience of description, we assume that two consecutive frames provide reference for the prediction of their intermediate frame [138]. Given two consecutive point clouds $P_0 \in \mathbb{R}^{N\times 3}$ and $P_1 \in \mathbb{R}^{N\times 3}$ with an arbitrary time step $t \in (0, 1)$, point cloud frame interpolation task aims to accurately predict the intermediate frame $\hat{P}_t$ at time step t. Suppose f is a real-valued function defined at time step t, the intermediate prediction frame $\hat{P}_t$can be expressed as:

$$\hat{P}_t = f(P_0, P_1, t), t \in (0, 1). \tag{3.6}$$

To vividly describe the process of point cloud frame interpolation, we choose the KITTI odometry datasets [139] for visualization. As shown in Fig. 3.10, the input two consecutive frames of point clouds are marked in blue and green, respectively, and the red point clouds represent predicted intermediate frame. Only the geometric coordinate information in the point cloud sequence is considered, that is, the spatial position of the point in the intermediate frame is predicted. Due to the regularity and consistency of pixel position distribution in 2D images, video frame interpolation mainly concentrates on predicting the color information of pixels. Compared with the color information prediction of video frame interpolation, the simultaneous prediction of geometric coordinates and attribute information will be another more complicated generation task.

3.3.2 FlowNet3D

Different from the 2D video frame interpolation process, the 3D point cloud interpolation task needs to estimate the temporal motion information between adjacent frames as accurately as possible. Recently, optical flow estimation techniques have been widely used in video super-resolution and video frame interpolation. The motion relationship between video frames is explicitly modeled by optical flow estimation. In order to describe the motion displacement of points in a 3D scene,

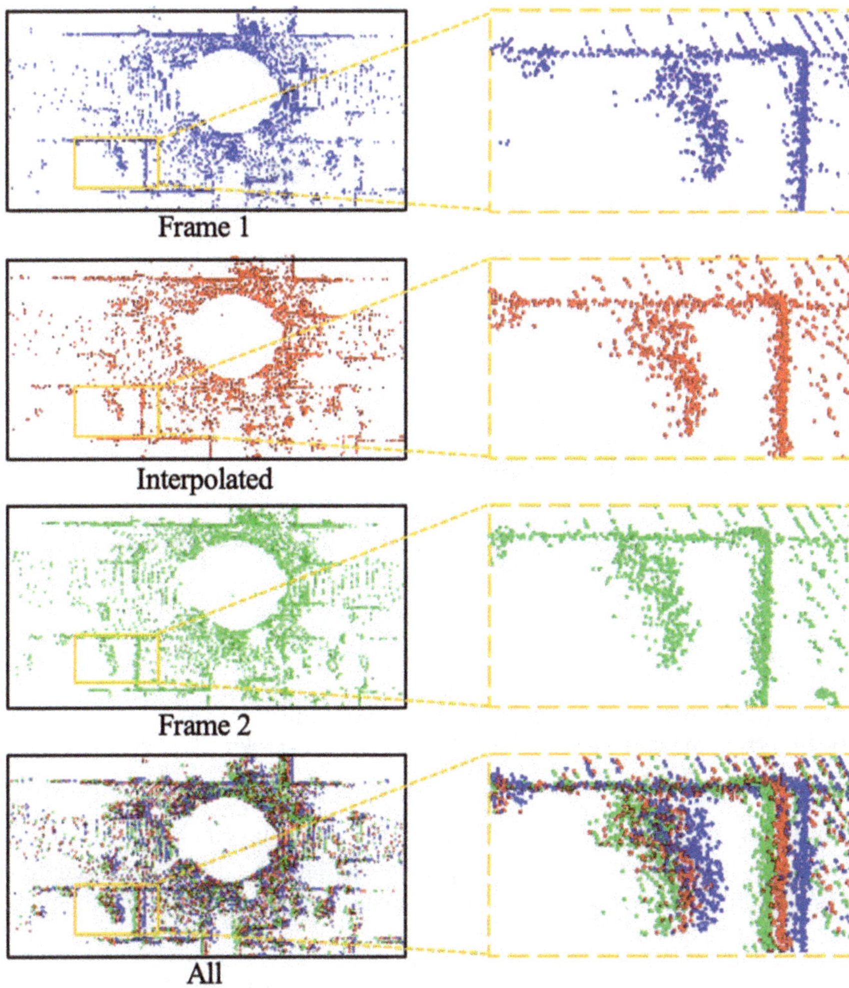

Fig. 3.10 Illustration of point cloud frame interpolation [138]. Source: Author

FlowNet3D is proposed to learn 3D scene flow between point cloud frames in an end-to-end manner.

As shown in Fig. 3.11, given two consecutive frames, FlowNet3D predicts a 3D vector between each point in the first frame and corresponding point in the second frame to represent motion displacement [140]. FlowNet3D consists of three key steps: point cloud feature extraction, point integration, and flow refinement. Inspired by PointNet++ architecture, the set conv layer is designed to extract features for prediction of scene flow. Given an input point cloud with n points, $p_i = \{x_i, f_i\}$ with coordinates $x_i \in \mathbb{R}^3$ and feature $f_i \in \mathbb{R}^c$. The output of the set convolution layer is a sub-sampled point cloud, which has n' points, $p'_j = \left\{x'_j, f'_j\right\}$ with existing

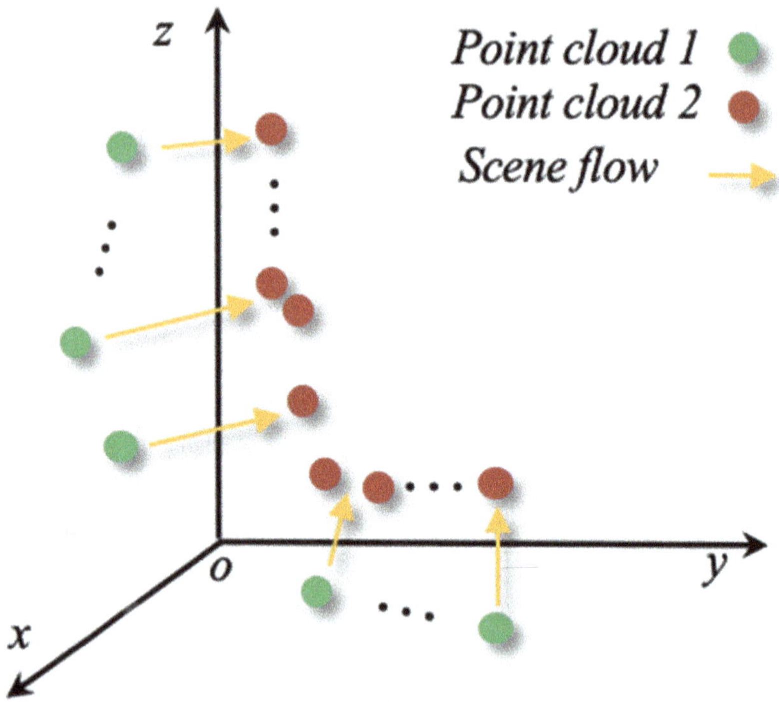

Fig. 3.11 Scene flow estimation (© 2019 IEEE. Reprinted, with permission, from ref. [140])

coordinates $x'_j \in R^3$ and updated feature $f'_j \in R^{c'}$. In detail, the layer firstly downsamples n' points from the input point cloud through farthest point sampling. Then, the local features of each sampling point are extracted with the following symmetric function:

$$f'_j = \underset{\left\{i \mid \left\| x_i - x'_j \right\| \le r\right\}}{\text{MAX}} \left\{ h\left(f_i, x_i - x'_j\right) \right\}, \tag{3.7}$$

where h and MAX denote a nonlinear function and element-wise max pooling, respectively. After obtaining the hierarchical features of two consecutive point cloud frames $\{p_i = (x, f_i)\}_{i=1}^{n_1}$ and $\{q_i = (y, g_i)\}_{j=1}^{n_2}$, FlowNet3D performs point integration by designing a flow embedding layer for all points in the first frame $\{e_i\}_{i=1}^{n_1}$, which is voted by:

$$e_i = \underset{\{j \mid \|y_j - x_i\| \le r\}}{\text{MAX}} \left\{ h\left(f_i, g_j, y_j - x_i\right) \right\}. \tag{3.8}$$

Finally, FlowNet3D upsamples the flow embeddings on downsampled point cloud to original point cloud. The flow obtained in the previous step is refined and

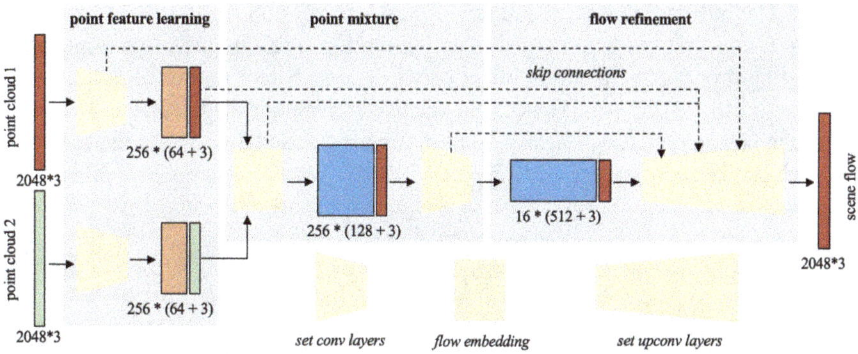

Fig. 3.12 Overall architecture of FlowNet3D (© 2019 IEEE. Reprinted, with permission, from ref. [140])

predicted in the last layer. The upsampling step consists of a upconv layer, which can propagate and refine the embeddings. The architecture of FlowNet3D is displayed in Fig. 3.12.

Given two consecutive frames of point cloud $P_1 = \{x_i\}_{i=1}^{n_1}$ and $P_2 = \left\{y_j\right\}_{j=1}^{n_2}$, FlowNet3D predicts scene flow as $S = \{s_i\}_{i=1}^{n_1}$ under the supervision of ground truth $S^* = \left\{s_i^*\right\}_{i=1}^{n_1}$. In addition, the cycle-consistency between the forward flow $\{s_i\}_{i=1}^{n_1}$ and the backward flow $\left\{s_i'\right\}_{i=1}^{n_1}$ is also considered in loss function. Here, the backward flow $\left\{s_i'\right\}_{i=1}^{n_1}$ is estimated from the shift point cloud $P' = \{x_i + s_i\}_{i=1}^{n_1}$ to the first point cloud P_1 by the same network and parameters. The joint loss function L is described as follows:

$$L\left(P_1, P_2, S^*, \Theta\right) = \frac{1}{n_1}\sum_{i=1}^{n_1}\left\{\left\|s_i - s_i^*\right\| + \lambda\left\|s_i' + s_i\right\|\right\}, \tag{3.9}$$

where Θ is the trainable parameters for FlowNet3D, and λ is the weight parameter.

3.3.3 PointINet

Given two consecutive point clouds $P_0 \in \mathbb{R}^{N\times 3}$ and $P_1 \in \mathbb{R}^{N\times 3}$ with an arbitrary time step $t \in (0, 1)$, the target of PointINet is to predict the intermediate point cloud frame $\hat{P}_t$ as accurate as possible [138]. PointINet mainly includes two key parts: point cloud warping module to warp the input point cloud and points fusion module to fuse the warped point cloud. Given two consecutive frames of point clouds P_0 and P_1, point cloud warping module is responsible for predicting the position of each point of P_0 in $\hat{P}_{0,t}$, where $\hat{P}_{0,t}$ is the corresponding point cloud of P_0 at time step t. The key point is to accurately estimate motion information between consecutive frames. The bidirectional 3D scene flow $F_{0\to1} \in \mathbb{R}^{N\times3}$ and $F_{1\to0} \in \mathbb{R}^{N\times3}$ between P_0 and P_1 are first predicted to estimate the motion of each point. To simplify the forecasting process, the position offset between consecutive frames of point clouds is supposed to be uniform. Hence, the relative movement displacement $S_{0\to t}$ and $S_{1\to t}$ can be calculated by linearly interpolating $F_{0\to1}$ and $F_{1\to0}$ with the time step t, which can be represented as:

$$\begin{aligned} S_{0\to t} &= t \times F_{0\to1}, \\ S_{1\to t} &= (1-t) \times F_{1\to0}. \end{aligned} \tag{3.10}$$

After obtaining the relative motion displacement $S_{0\to t}$ and $S_{1\to t}$, the intermediate point cloud frame $\hat{P_{0,t}}$ and $\hat{P_{1,t}}$ is roughly warped by adding the adjacent frames P_0 and P_1,

$$\begin{aligned} \hat{P}_{0,t} &= P_0 + F_{0\to1}, \\ \hat{P}_{1,t} &= P_1 + F_{1\to0}. \end{aligned} \tag{3.11}$$

To generate an intermediate point cloud frame and maintain motion smoothness between adjacent point cloud frames, PointNet designs an adaptive sampling and a fusion module to combine $\hat{P_{0,t}} \in \mathbb{R}^{N\times3}$ and $\hat{P_{1,t}} \in \mathbb{R}^{N\times3}$ effectively. Given two warped point clouds $\hat{P_{0,t}}$ and $\hat{P_{1,t}}$, the fused intermediate point cloud frame $\hat{P_t} \in \mathbb{R}^{N\times3}$ is predicted by the following three steps: adaptive sampling, adaptive k-NN cluster, and attention points fusion. According to the time interval with adjacent frames, PointNet randomly selects a certain number of points N_0 and N_1 from $\hat{P_{0,t}}$ and $\hat{P_{1,t}}$. Here, $N_0 = (1-t)\times N$, $N_1 = t\times N$. Then, all selected points are integrated as a new point clouds $\tilde{P_t} \in \mathbb{R}^{N\times3}$. For each point x^i in $\tilde{P_t}$, k-NN cluster algorithm is chosen to search for K nearest neighbor points from warped point cloud $\hat{P_{0,t}}$ and $\hat{P_{1,t}}$. Similar to process of adaptive sampling, PointNet selects K_0 and K_1 nearest points from $\hat{P_{0,t}}$ and $\hat{P_{1,t}}$. Here, $K_0 = (1-t) \times K$, $K_1 = t \times K$. Furthermore, the coordinates of the K nearest neighbors and the Euclidean distance from the center point x^i are concatenated to obtain the feature of the point x^i, which is denoted as $F^i \in \mathbb{R}^{K\times4}$. Finally, the proposed attentive points fusion module learns a set of weight parameters $W^i \in \mathbb{R}^{K\times1}$ to fuse all K neighbor points. For each point x^i in $\tilde{P_t}$, the parameters of fusion module are shared.

3.3.4 IDEA-Net

PointINet is a flow-based interpolation method that limited by the assumption of linear motion. Therefore, it is not suitable for large non-rigid deformation. Unlike existing works, IDEA-Net seeks to build an explainable interpolation

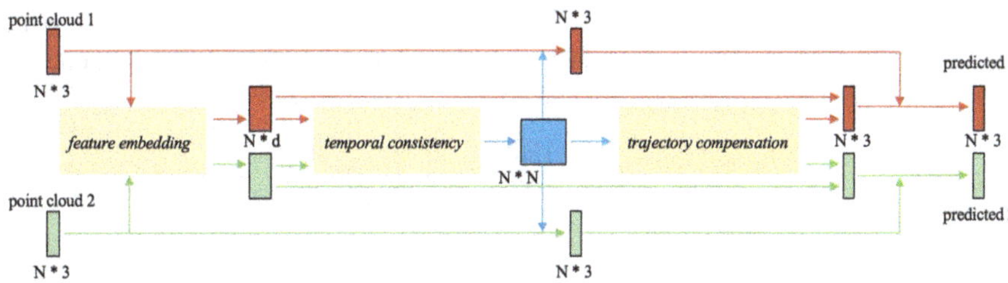

Fig. 3.13 Overall architecture of IDEA-Net (© 2022 IEEE. Reprinted, with permission, from ref. [141])

framework for the point cloud with dynamic non-rigid motion [141]. IDEA-Net formulated the point cloud frame interpolation task as a prediction problem of point-wise trajectories and disentangled the problem into a two-stage process: coarse linear interpolation and trajectory compensation. The architecture of IDEA-Net is displayed in Fig. 3.13. Without loss of generality, let $P_0 \in \mathbb{R}^{N\times 3}$ and $P_1 \in \mathbb{R}^{N\times 3}$ be any two consecutive point cloud frames with N points, p_0^i and p_1^j are the $i-$th and $j-$th point of P_0 and P_1, respectively. Assume that the matrix $A \in \mathbb{R}^{N\times N}$ constructs an explicit temporal consistency from P_0 to P_1, i.e., if p_0^i corresponds to p_1^j, $a_{i,j} = 1$. IDEA-Net first uniformly performs trajectory estimation point by point through linear curve fitting, and the two coarse intermediate frame $P_{0\to t} \in \mathbb{R}^{N\times 3}$ and $P_{1\to t} \in \mathbb{R}^{N\times 3}$ at time $t \in (0, 1)$ can be calculated as:

$$\begin{aligned} P_{0\to t} &= (1-t) \times P_0 + tAP_1, \\ P_{1\to t} &= (1-t) \times A^\top P_0 + tP_1. \end{aligned} \tag{3.12}$$

The aforementioned linear interpolation is able to provide a rough interpolated frame. Then, a trajectory compensation process is proposed to further predict the high-order nonlinear trajectories. In detail, the input is mapped into a high-dimensional vector space by a typical nonlinear function $\phi(\cdot) : R^3 \to R^d$. After that, the aligned features are fused by estimating a function $f(\cdot) : R^d \to R^d$. Finally, the fused features are finally mapped into the point cloud space by a new nonlinear function $\psi(\cdot) : R^d \to R^3$ to obtain the increments $\Delta_{0\to t} \in R^{N\times 3}$ and $\Delta_{1\to t} \in R^{N\times 3}$ for trajectory compensation:

$$\begin{aligned} \Delta_{0\to t} &= \psi\left(f\left(\phi(P_0), \phi(P_1)\right), A, t\right), \\ \Delta_{1\to t} &= \psi\left(f\left(\phi(P_0), \phi(P_1)\right), A^\top, 1-t\right). \end{aligned} \tag{3.13}$$

The two predicted in-intermediate frames are finally obtained as:

$$\begin{aligned} O_{0\to t} &= P_{0\to t} + \Delta_{0\to t}, \\ O_{1\to t} &= P_{1\to t} + \Delta_{1\to t}. \end{aligned} \tag{3.14}$$

IDEA-Net is trained by minimizing the earth mover's distance (EMD) among the two predicted point cloud $O_{0\to t}$ and $O_{1\to t}$ and the ground truth O_{gt}^{t} simultaneously:

$$\mathcal{L} = \frac{1}{2}\left(L_{emd}\left(O_{0\to t}, O_{gt}^{t}\right) + L_{emd}\left(O_{1\to t}, O_{gt}^{t}\right)\right). \tag{3.15}$$

3.3.5 *NeuralPCI*

Existing methods explicitly construct the inter-frame motion relationship of point clouds, which has a certain gap with the complex motion in the real world. In contrast, the neural field offers a more sophisticated means of implicitly parameterizing the continuous point cloud sequence. NeuralPCI [142], drawing inspiration from NeRF's view synthesis for images, is introduced to leverage spatial and temporal information. The 4D neural spatiotemporal field predicts the intermediate point cloud at the specified time based on point cloud sequence and independent interpolation time. The architecture of NeuralPCI is depicted in Fig. 3.14, organized into three main sections for detailed explanation. As shown in Fig. 3.14, the architecture of NeuralPCI includes three parts. In the training stage, the formation of the 4D neural field involves encoding the spatiotemporal coordinates of the multi-frame input point cloud utilizing a coordinate-based Multi-Layer Perceptron (MLP) network. The neural field is trained in a self-supervised manner. Given an inference moment and a continuous sequence of reference point clouds, the corresponding intermediate frames are generated in the trained neural field. To better deal with local rigid motions, the smoothness loss is designed and denoted as:

$$\mathcal{L}_S = \sum_{p_i \in P} \frac{1}{|N(p_i)|} \sum_{p_j \in N(p_i)} \left\| \Delta \mathbf{x}_j - \Delta \mathbf{x}_i \right\|_2^2, \tag{3.16}$$

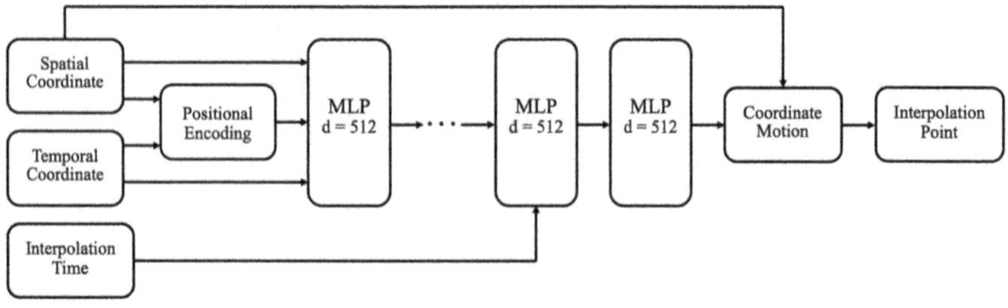

Fig. 3.14 The framework of NeuralPCI (© 2023 IEEE. Reprinted, with permission, from ref. [142])

where $N(p_i)$ and $|\cdot|$ denotes the set of neighborhood points of the i-th point p_i and the number of points in the set, respectively. The total loss function is obtained by adding CD loss and EMD loss.

3.4 Summary

This chapter introduces the point cloud enhancement methods like point cloud upsampling and frame interpolation. Upsampling techniques restore detailed geometric information, similar to image super-resolution, with notable methods including PUNet and PUGAN, which use GAN-based approaches to produce realistic point clouds. Frame interpolation, exemplified by FlowNet3D, generates intermediate frames essential for high frame rate applications. Future research in point cloud upsampling and frame interpolation could focus on enhancing the efficiency and accuracy of these processes using more advanced machine learning models. Exploring unsupervised and semi-supervised learning methods could improve performance in scenarios lacking labeled data. Additionally, integrating spatial-temporal coherence in dynamic environments could refine frame interpolation, particularly for applications involving rapid movements, thereby enhancing the realism and utility of 3D models in real-time systems.

Exercises

1. What are the relations and differences between point cloud upsampling and point cloud completion?
2. The shuffling approach has been widely used in recent upsampling tasks. Please implement the point shuffling algorithm in code.
3. In this chapter, we have introduced some deep-learning-based point cloud upsampling methods. Can you select a network and implement its structure using PyTorch or Tensorflow.
4. Point cloud upsampling and point cloud frame interpolation are performed in the spatial dimension and temporal dimension, respectively. How to deal with a new point cloud enhancement task such as spatiotemporal upsampling of dynamic point clouds?
5. In the video interpolation task, the position and number of interpolation points are fixed on a 2D grid. How to choose the number of points for the intermediate predicted point cloud frame and estimate nonlinear motion trajectories between point cloud frames?
6. Existing point cloud upsampling and point cloud frame interpolation methods mainly focus on the geometric information of point clouds. What challenges will be encountered when point cloud attribute information is introduced?

7. Farthest point sampling (FPS) is expected to reduce storage overhead and preserve valid point cloud features as much as possible. Therefore, FPS is regarded as a special point cloud compression manner. What are the differences between existing point cloud compression methods and downsampling methods?
8. Most existing point cloud interpolation methods predict intermediate frames at fixed temporal locations in a supervised manner. How to predict intermediate frames at arbitrary time positions or point cloud frames that exceed the range of the reference frame?
9. Existing point cloud upsampling methods upsample the entire point cloud, which ignores the inconsistency of point cloud distribution. For example, in practical application scenarios such as LiDAR point clouds, the density of non-ground objects is expected to be increased. How to upsample local areas of point clouds in the form of human–computer interaction?
10. Point cloud frame interpolation improves the frame rate of dynamic point clouds, such as Lidar point clouds in autonomous driving scenarios. However, the performance of the generated point clouds with high frame rates on downstream tasks such as object detection is rarely considered by existing methods. Can existing point cloud frame interpolation methods be optimized to adapt to downstream machine perception tasks?

References

1. W. Liu, W. Gao, X. Mu, Fast inter-frame motion prediction for compressed dynamic point cloud attribute enhancement, in *Proceedings of the AAAI Conference on Artificial Intelligence*, vol. 38(4) (2024), pp. 3720–3728
2. Z. Yang, W. Gao, X. Lu, Danet: Density-adaptive network for geometry-based point cloud compression artifacts removal, in *2023 IEEE International Conference on Visual Communications and Image Processing (VCIP)* (IEEE, New York, 2023), pp. 1–5.
3. X. Fan, G. Li, D. Li, Y. Ren, W. Gao, T. H. Li, Deep geometry post-processing for decompressed point clouds, in *IEEE International Conference on Multimedia and Expo* (IEEE, New York, 2022), pp. 1–6
4. X. Zhang, G. Liao, W. Gao, G. Li, Tdrnet: Transformer-based dual-branch restoration network for geometry based point cloud compression artifacts, in *2022 IEEE International Conference on Multimedia and Expo (ICME)* (IEEE, New York, 2022), pp. 1–6
5. Z. Li, G. Li, T. H. Li, S. Liu, W. Gao, Semantic point cloud upsampling. IEEE Trans. Multimedia **25**, 3432–3442 (2022)
6. R. Zhang, W. Gao, G. Li, T. H. Li, Qinet: Decision surface learning and adversarial enhancement for quasi-immune completion of diverse corrupted point clouds. IEEE Trans. Geosci. Remote Sens. **60**, 1–14 (2022)
7. R. Bao, Y. Ren, G. Li, W. Gao, S. Liu, Flow-based point cloud completion network with adversarial refinement, in *ICASSP 2022-2022 IEEE International Conference on Acoustics, Speech and Signal Processing (ICASSP)* (IEEE, New York, 2022), pp. 2559–2563
8. J. Chen, G. Li, R. Zhang, T.H. Li, W. Gao, Pointivae: Invertible variational autoencoder framework for 3d point cloud generation, in *2022 IEEE International Conference on Image Processing (ICIP)* (IEEE, New York, 2022), pp. 3216–3220

9. R. Zhang, J. Chen, W. Gao, G. Li, T. H. Li, Pointot: Interpretable geometry-inspired point cloud generative model via optimal transport. IEEE Trans. Circuits Syst. Video Technol. **32**(10), 6792–6806 (2022)
10. S. Fan W. Gao, Screen-based 3d subjective experiment software, in *Proceedings of the 31st ACM International Conference on Multimedia* (2023), pp. 9672–9675
11. J. Wang, W. Gao, G. Li, Zoom to perceive better: no-reference point cloud quality assessment via exploring effective multiscale feature, in *IEEE Transactions on Circuits and Systems for Video Technology* (2024), pp. 1–1
12. J. Wang, W. Gao, G. Li, Applying collaborative adversarial learning to blind point cloud quality measurement. IEEE Trans. Instrum. Meas. **72**, 1–15 (2023)
13. W. Gao, G. Li, H. Yuan, R. Hamzaoui, Z. Li, S. Liu, Apccpa'22: 1st international workshop on advances in point cloud compression, processing and analysis, in *Proceedings of the 30th ACM International Conference on Multimedia* (2022), pp. 7392–7393
14. T. Qin, G. Li, W. Gao, S. Liu, Multi-grained point cloud geometry compression via dual-model prediction with extended octree. ACM Trans. Multimed. Comput. Commun. Appl. **20**(9), 1–30 (2024)
15. Y. Shao, W. Gao, S. Liu, G. Li, Advanced patch-based affine motion estimation for dynamic point cloud geometry compression. Sensors **24**(10), 3142 (2024)
16. Y. Shao, F. Song, W. Gao, S. Liu, G. Li, Texture-guided graph transform optimization for point cloud attribute compression. Appl. Sci. **14**(10), 4094 (2024)
17. Y. Shao, X. Yang, W. Gao, S. Liu, G. Li, 3d point cloud attribute compression using diffusion-based texture-aware intra prediction. *IEEE Transactions on Circuits and Systems for Video Technology* (2024)
18. J. Zhang, Y. Chen, G. Liu, W. Gao, G. Li, Efficient point cloud attribute compression framework using attribute-guided graph fourier transform, in *IEEE International Conference on Acoustics, Speech and Signal Processing* (2024), pp. 8426–8430
19. W. Gao, H. Yuan, G. Li, Z. Li, H. Yuan, Low complexity coding unit decision for video-based point cloud compression. IEEE Trans. Image Process. **33**, 149–162 (2023)
20. Y. Shao, G. Li, Q. Zhang, W. Gao, S. Liu, Non-rigid registration-based progressive motion compensation for point cloud geometry compression. *IEEE Transactions on Geoscience and Remote Sensing* (2023)
21. F. Song, G. Li, X. Yang, W. Gao, S. Liu, Block-adaptive point cloud attribute coding with region-aware optimized transform. IEEE Trans. Circuits Syst. Video Technol. **33**(8), 4294–4308 (2023)
22. Y. An, Y. Shao, G. Li, W. Gao, S. Liu, A fast motion estimation method with hamming distance for lidar point cloud compression, in *2022 IEEE International Conference on Visual Communications and Image Processing (VCIP)* (IEEE, New York, 2022), pp. 1–5
23. H. Yuan, W. Gao, G. Li, Z. Li, Rate-distortion-guided learning approach with cross-projection information for v-pcc fast cu decision, in *Proceedings of the 30th ACM International Conference on Multimedia* (2022), pp. 3085–3093
24. F. Song, G. Li, W. Gao, T. H. Li, Rate-distortion optimized graph for point cloud attribute coding. IEEE Signal Process Lett. **29**, 922–926 (2022)
25. F. Song, G. Li, X. Yang, W. Gao, T. H. Li, Fine-grained correlation representation for graph-based point cloud attribute compression, in *IEEE International Conference on Multimedia and Expo* (IEEE, New York, 2022), pp. 1–6
26. F. Shen W. Gao, A rate control algorithm for video-based point cloud compression, in *2021 International Conference on Visual Communications and Image Processing (VCIP)* (IEEE, New York, 2021), pp. 1–5
27. F. Song, Y. Shao, W. Gao, H. Wang, T. Li, Layer-wise geometry aggregation framework for lossless lidar point cloud compression. IEEE Trans. Circuits Syst. Video Technol. **31**(12), 4603–4616 (2021)
28. L. Xie, W. Gao, H. Zheng, G. Li, SPCGC: Scalable point cloud geometry compression for machine vision, in *Proceedings of IEEE International Conference on Robotics and Automation* (2024)

29. L. Xie, W. Gao, H. Zheng, H. Ye, Semantic-aware visual decomposition for point cloud geometry compression, in *2024 Data Compression Conference (DCC)* (IEEE, New York, 2024), pp. 595–595
30. Z. Qi W. Gao, Variable-rate point cloud geometry compression based on feature adjustment and interpolation, in *2024 Data Compression Conference (DCC)* (IEEE, New York, 2024), pp. 63–72
31. Z. Yu W. Gao, When dynamic neural network meets point cloud compression: computation-aware variable rate and checkerboard context, in *2024 Data Compression Conference (DCC)* (IEEE, New York, 2024), pp. 600–600
32. L. Xie, W. Gao, S. Fan, Z. Yao, Pdnet: Parallel dual-branch network for point cloud geometry compression and analysis, in *2024 Data Compression Conference (DCC)* (IEEE, New York, 2024), pp. 596–596
33. L. Xie, W. Gao, H. Zheng, End-to-end point cloud geometry compression and analysis with sparse tensor, in *Proceedings of the 1st International Workshop on Advances in Point Cloud Compression, Processing and Analysis* (2022), pp. 27–32
34. C. Fu, G. Li, R. Song, W. Gao, S. Liu, OctAttention: Octree-based large-scale contexts model for point cloud compression, in *AAAI Conference on Artificial Intelligence* (2022), pp. 625–633
35. W. Gao, H. Ye, G. Li, H. Zheng, Y. Wu, L. Xie, OpenPointCloud: an open-source algorithm library of deep learning based point cloud compression, in *ACM International Conference on Multimedia* (2022), pp. 7347–7350
36. H. Zheng, W. Gao, Z. Yu, T. Zhao, G. Li, ViewPCGC: View-guided learned point cloud geometry compression, in *Proceedings of the 32nd ACM International Conference on Multimedia* (2024)
37. L. Xie, W. Gao, H. Zheng, G. Li, Roi-guided point cloud geometry compression towards human and machine vision, in *Proceedings of the 32nd ACM International Conference on Multimedia* (2024)
38. C. Peng W. Gao, Laplacian matrix learning for point cloud attribute compression with ternary search-based adaptive block partition, in *Proceedings of the 32nd ACM International Conference on Multimedia* (2024)
39. S. Luo, B. Qu, W. Gao, Learning robust 3d representation from clip via dual denoising. arXiv preprint arXiv:2407.00905 (2024)
40. G. Li, G. Wei, W. Gao, *Point Cloud Compression: Technologies and Standardization* (Springer Nature, Berlin, 2024)
41. G. Li, W. Gao, W. Gao, Introduction, in *Point Cloud Compression: Technologies and Standardization* (Springer, Berlin, 2024), pp. 1–28
42. G. Li, W. Gao, W. Gao, Background knowledge, in *Point Cloud Compression: Technologies and Standardization* (Springer, Berlin, 2024), pp. 29–51
43. G. Li, W. Gao, W. Gao, Predictive coding, in *Point Cloud Compression: Technologies and Standardization* (Springer, Berlin, 2024), pp. 53–70
44. G. Li, W. Gao, W. Gao, Transform coding, in *Point Cloud Compression: Technologies and Standardization* (Springer, Berlin, 2024), pp. 71–96
45. G. Li, W. Gao, W. Gao, Quantization techniques, in *Point Cloud Compression: Technologies and Standardization* (Springer, Berlin, 2024), pp. 97–112
46. G. Li, W. Gao, W. Gao, Entropy coding, in *Point Cloud Compression: Technologies and Standardization* (Springer, Berlin, 2024), pp. 113–133
47. G. Li, W. Gao, W. Gao, MPEG geometry-based point cloud compression (G-PCC) standard, in *Point Cloud Compression: Technologies and Standardization* (Springer, Berlin, 2024), pp. 135–165
48. G. Li, W. Gao, W. Gao, AVS point cloud compression standard, in *Point Cloud Compression: Technologies and Standardization* (Springer, Berlin, 2024), pp. 167–197
49. G. Li, W. Gao, W. Gao, MPEG video-based point cloud compression (V-PCC) standard, in *Point Cloud Compression: Technologies and Standardization* (Springer, Berlin, 2024), pp. 199–218.

50. G. Li, W. Gao, W. Gao, MPEG AI-based 3d graphics coding standard, in *Point Cloud Compression: Technologies and Standardization*. (Springer, Berlin, 2024), pp. 219–241
51. G. Li, W. Gao, W. Gao, Future work, in *Point Cloud Compression: Technologies and Standardization* (Springer, Berlin, 2024), pp. 243–250
52. S. Fan, W. Gao, G. Li, Salient object detection for point clouds, in *European Conference on Computer Vision* (2022), pp. 1–19
53. S. Luo W. Gao, A general framework for rotation invariant point cloud analysis, in *IEEE International Conference on Acoustics, Speech and Signal Processing* (2024), pp. 3665–3669
54. X. Lu W. Gao, Attentivenet: Detecting small objects for lidar point clouds by attending to important points, in *IEEE International Conference on Visual Communications and Image Processing* (2023), pp. 1–5.
55. Z. Pan, N. Zhang, W. Gao, S. Liu, G. Li, Less is more: label recommendation for weakly supervised point cloud semantic segmentation, in *Proceedings of the AAAI Conference on Artificial Intelligence*, vol. 38(5) (2024), pp. 4397–4405
56. Z. Pan, G. Liu, W. Gao, T. Li, Epcontrast: effective point-level contrastive learning for large-scale point cloud understanding, in *IEEE International Conference on Multimedia and Expo* (2024)
57. N. Zhang, Z. Pan, T.H. Li, W. Gao, G. Li, Improving graph representation for point cloud segmentation via attentive filtering, in *Proceedings of the IEEE/CVF Conference on Computer Vision and Pattern Recognition* (2023), pp. 1244–1254
58. K. Wen, N. Zhang, G. Li, W. Gao, MPVNN: Multi-resolution point-voxel non-parametric network for 3d point cloud processing, in *IEEE International Conference on Multimedia and Expo* (2024)
59. D. Yang, W. Gao, G. Li, H. Yuan, J. Hou, S. Kwong, Exploiting manifold feature representation for efficient classification of 3d point clouds. ACM Trans. Multimed. Comput. Commun. Appl. **19**(1s), 1–21 (2023)
60. W. Liu, W. Gao, G. Li, S. Ma, T. Zhao, H. Yuan, Enlarged motion-aware and frequency-aware network for compressed video artifact reduction, in *IEEE Transactions on Circuits and Systems for Video Technology* (2024)
61. Z. Li, G. Li, T. Li, S. Liu, W. Gao, Information-growth attention network for image super-resolution, in *Proceedings of the 29th ACM International Conference on Multimedia* (2021), pp. 544–552
62. L. Zhou, W. Gao, G. Li, H. Yuan, T. Zhao, G. Yue, Disentangled feature distillation for light field super-resolution with degradations, in *2023 IEEE International Conference on Multimedia and Expo Workshops (ICMEW)* (IEEE, New York, 2023), pp. 116–121
63. L. Zhou, W. Gao, G. Li, End-to-end spatial-angular light field super-resolution using parallax structure preservation strategy, in *2022 IEEE International Conference on Image Processing (ICIP)* (IEEE, New York, 2022), pp. 3396–3400
64. W. Gao, L. Zhou, L. Tao, A fast view synthesis implementation method for light field applications. ACM Trans. Multimed. Comput. Commun. Appl. (TOMM) **17**(4), 1–20 (2021)
65. X. Zhang, W. Gao, G. Li, Q. Jiang, R. Cong, Image quality assessment–driven reinforcement learning for mixed distorted image restoration. ACM Trans. Multimed. Comput. Commun. Appl. **19**(1s), 1–23 (2023)
66. X. Zhang, W. Gao, H. Yuan, G. Li, Je 2 net: Joint exploitation and exploration in reinforcement learning based image restoration, in *ICASSP 2022-2022 IEEE International Conference on Acoustics, Speech and Signal Processing (ICASSP)* (IEEE, New York, 2022), pp. 2090–2094
67. X. Zhang W. Gao, Hirl: Hybrid image restoration based on hierarchical deep reinforcement learning via two-step analysis, in *ICASSP 2022-2022 IEEE International Conference on Acoustics, Speech and Signal Processing (ICASSP)* (IEEE, New York, 2022), pp. 2445–2449
68. Y. Zhang, W. Gao, G. Li, Openpointcloud-v2: A deep learning based open-source algorithm library of point cloud processing, in *Proceedings of the 1st International Workshop on Advances in Point Cloud Compression, Processing and Analysis* (2022), pp. 51–55

69. B. Qu, X. Liang, S. Sun, W. Gao, Exploring aigc video quality: A focus on visual harmony, video-text consistency and domain distribution gap, in *Proceedings of the IEEE/CVF conference on computer vision and pattern recognition workshops* (2024)
70. B. Qu, H. Li, W. Gao, Bringing textual prompt to ai-generated image quality assessment, in *2024 IEEE International Conference on Multimedia and Expo (ICME)* (IEEE, New York, 2024)
71. Y. Wu, L. Xie, S. Sun, W. Gao, Y. Yan, Adaptive intra period size for deep learning-based screen content video coding, in *2024 IEEE International Conference on Multimedia and Expo Workshops (ICMEW)* (IEEE, New York, 2024)
72. H. Zheng W. Gao, End-to-end rgb-d image compression via exploiting channel-modality redundancy, in *Proceedings of the AAAI Conference on Artificial Intelligence*, vol. 38(7) (2024), pp. 7562–7570
73. L. Tao, W. Gao, G. Li, and C. Zhang, Adanic: towards practical neural image compression via dynamic transform routing, in *Proceedings of the IEEE/CVF International Conference on Computer Vision* (2023), pp. 16879–16888
74. Y. Wu, W. Gao, End-to-end lossless compression of high precision depth maps guided by pseudo-residual. arXiv preprint arXiv:2201.03195 (2022)
75. Y. Wu, Z. Qi, H. Zheng, L. Tao, W. Gao, Deep image compression with latent optimization and piece-wise quantization approximation, in *Proceedings of the IEEE/CVF Conference on Computer Vision and Pattern Recognition* (2021), pp. 1926–1930
76. W. Gao, L. Tao, L. Zhou, D. Yang, X. Zhang, Z. Guo, Low-rate image compression with super-resolution learning, in *Proceedings of the IEEE/CVF Conference on Computer Vision and Pattern Recognition Workshops* (2020), pp. 154–155
77. W. Gao, S. Sun, H. Zheng, Y. Wu, H. Ye, Y. Zhang, OpenDMC: An open-source library and performance evaluation for deep-learning-based multi-frame compression, in *Proceedings of the 31st ACM International Conference on Multimedia* (2023), pp. 9685–9688
78. Y. Guo, W. Gao, G. Li, Interpretable task-inspired adaptive filter pruning for neural networks under multiple constraints. Int. J. Comput. Vis. **132**(6), 1–17 (2024)
79. W. Gao, Y. Guo, S. Ma, G. Li, S. Kwong, Efficient neural network compression inspired by compressive sensing. IEEE Trans. Neural Networks Learn. Syst. **35**(2), 1965–1979 (2022)
80. Y. Guo, W. Gao, Semantic-driven automatic filter pruning for neural networks, in *2022 IEEE International Conference on Multimedia and Expo (ICME)* (IEEE, New York, 2022), pp. 1–6
81. L. Tao, W. Gao, Efficient channel pruning based on architecture alignment and probability model bypassing, in *2021 IEEE International Conference on Systems, Man, and Cybernetics (SMC)* (IEEE, New York, 2021), pp. 3232–3237
82. Z. Yang, W. Gao, G. Li, Y. Yan, SUR-driven video coding rate control for jointly optimizing perceptual quality and buffer control. IEEE Trans. Image Process. **32**, 5451–5464 (2023)
83. F. Shen, Z. Cai, W. Gao, An efficient rate control algorithm for intra frame coding in avs3, in *2021 IEEE International Conference on Systems, Man, and Cybernetics (SMC)* (IEEE, New York, 2021), pp. 3164–3169
84. H. Yuan, W. Gao, J. Wang, Dynamic computational resource allocation for fast inter frame coding in video conferencing applications, in *2021 IEEE International Conference on Multimedia and Expo (ICME)* (IEEE, New York, 2021), pp. 1–6
85. W. Gao, Q. Jiang, R. Wang, S. Ma, G. Li, S. Kwong, Consistent quality oriented rate control in hevc via balancing intra and inter frame coding. IEEE Trans. Industr. Inform. **18**(3), 1594–1604 (2021)
86. H. Yuan, W. Gao, A new coding unit partitioning mode for screen content video coding, in *Proceedings of the 2021 5th International Conference on Digital Signal Processing* (2021), pp. 66–72
87. W. Gao, On the performance evaluation of state-of-the-art rate control algorithms for practical video coding and transmission systems, in *Proceedings of the 2020 4th International Conference on Video and Image Processing* (2020), pp. 179–185

88. W. Gao, S. Kwong, Q. Jiang, C.-K. Fong, P.H. Wong, W.Y. Yuen, Data-driven rate control for rate-distortion optimization in hevc based on simplified effective initial qp learning. IEEE Trans. Broadcast. **65**(1), 94–108 (2018)
89. W. Gao, A multi-objective optimization perspective for joint consideration of video coding quality, in *2019 Asia-Pacific Signal and Information Processing Association Annual Summit and Conference (APSIPA ASC)* (IEEE, New York, 2019), pp. 986–991
90. W. Gao, S. Kwong, Y. Jia, Joint machine learning and game theory for rate control in high efficiency video coding. IEEE Trans. Image Process. **26**(12), 6074–6089 (2017)
91. W. Gao, S. Kwong, Y. Zhou, H. Yuan, SSIM-based game theory approach for rate-distortion optimized intra frame ctu-level bit allocation. IEEE Trans. Multimedia **18**(6), 988–999 (2016)
92. W. Gao, S. Kwong, H. Yuan, X. Wang, DCT coefficient distribution modeling and quality dependency analysis based frame-level bit allocation for HEVC. IEEE Trans. Circuits Syst. Video Technol. **26**(1), 139–153 (2015)
93. W. Gao, S. Kwong, Phase congruency based edge saliency detection and rate control for perceptual image and video coding, in *2016 IEEE International Conference on Systems, Man, and Cybernetics (SMC)* (IEEE, New York, 2016), pp. 000264–000269
94. H. Yuan, W. Gao, OpenFastVC: An open source library for video coding fast algorithm implementation, in *Proceedings of the 31st ACM International Conference on Multimedia* (2023), pp. 9660–9663
95. H. Yuan, W. Gao, S. Ma, Y. Yan, Divide-and-conquer-based RDO-free CU partitioning for 8K video compression. ACM Trans. Multimedia Comput. Commun. Appl. **20**(4), 1–20 (2024)
96. L. Tao, W. Gao, A hardware implementation of entropy encoder for 8K video coding, in *2022 IEEE International Conference on Multimedia and Expo (ICME)* (IEEE, New York, 2022), pp. 1–6
97. Y. Guo, W. Gao, S. Ma, G. Li, Accelerating transform algorithm implementation for efficient intra coding of 8K uhd videos. ACM Trans. Multimed. Comput. Commun. Appl. (TOMM) **18**(4), 1–20 (2022)
98. Z. Cai W. Gao, Efficient fast algorithm and parallel hardware architecture for intra prediction of AVS3, in *2021 IEEE International Symposium on Circuits and Systems (ISCAS)* (IEEE, New York, 2021), pp. 1–5
99. W. Gao, H. Yuan, Y. Guo, L. Tao, Z. Cai, G. Li, Openhardwarevc: an open source library for 8K UHD video coding hardware implementation, in *Proceedings of the 30th ACM International Conference on Multimedia* (2022), pp. 7339–7342
100. W. Gao, H. Yuan, G. Liao, Z. Guo, J. Chen, PP8K: A new dataset for 8K UHD video compression and processing. IEEE MultiMedia **30**(3), 100–109 (2023)
101. X. Zang, W. Gao, G. Li, H. Fang, C. Ban, Z. He, H. Sun, A baseline investigation: transformer-based cross-view baseline for text-based person search, in *Proceedings of the 31st ACM International Conference on Multimedia* (2023), pp. 7737–7746
102. G. Liao, W. Gao, G. Li, J. Wang, S. Kwong, Cross-collaborative fusion-encoder network for robust rgb-thermal salient object detection. IEEE Trans. Circuits Syst. Video Technol. **32**(11), 7646–7661 (2022)
103. W. Gao, G. Liao, S. Ma, G. Li, Y. Liang, W. Lin, Unified information fusion network for multi-modal RGB-D and RGB-T salient object detection. IEEE Trans. Circuits Syst. Video Technol. **32**(4), 2091–2106 (2021)
104. Y. Chen, S. Sun, G. Li, W. Gao, T. H. Li, Closing the gap between theory and practice during alternating optimization for GANs, in *IEEE Transactions on Neural Networks and Learning Systems* (2023)
105. Y. Chen, C. Jin, G. Li, T. H. Li, W. Gao, Mitigating label noise in GANs via enhanced spectral normalization, in *IEEE Transactions on Circuits and Systems for Video Technology* (2023)
106. X. Zang, G. Li, W. Gao, Multidirection and multiscale pyramid in transformer for video-based pedestrian retrieval. IEEE Trans. Industr. Inform. **18**(12), 8776–8785 (2022)
107. X. Zang, G. Li, W. Gao, X. Shu, Learning to disentangle scenes for person re-identification. Image Vis. Comput. **116**, 104330 (2021)

108. X. Zang, G. Li, W. Gao, X. Shu, Exploiting robust unsupervised video person re-identification. IET Image Process. **16**(3), 729–741 (2022)
109. Z. Yue, G. Li, W. Gao, Cross-level guided attention for human-object interaction detection, in *2023 IEEE International Conference on Multimedia and Expo Workshops (ICMEW)* (IEEE, New York, 2023), pp. 284–289
110. Z. Yao, W. Gao, Iterative saliency aggregation and assignment network for efficient salient object detection in optical remote sensing images, in *IEEE Transactions on Geoscience and Remote Sensing* (2024)
111. Y. Sun, Z. Li, S. Wang, W. Gao, Depth-assisted calibration on learning-based factorization for a compressive light field display. Opt. Express **31**(4), 5399–5413 (2023)
112. Y. Sun, Z. Li, L. Li, S. Wang, W. Gao, Optimization of compressive light field display in dual-guided learning, in *ICASSP 2022-2022 IEEE International Conference on Acoustics, Speech and Signal Processing (ICASSP)* (IEEE, New York, 2022), pp. 2075–2079
113. W. Gao, S. Fan, G. Li, W. Lin, A thorough benchmark and a new model for light field saliency detection. IEEE Trans. Pattern Anal. Mach. Intell. **45**(7), 8003–8019 (2023)
114. Z. Guo, W. Gao, H. Wang, J. Wang, S. Fan, No-reference deep quality assessment of compressed light field images, in *2021 IEEE International Conference on Multimedia and Expo (ICME)* (IEEE, New York, 2021), pp. 1–6
115. G. Liao, W. Gao, Rethinking feature mining for light field salient object detection, in *ACM Transactions on Multimedia Computing, Communications, and Applications* (2024)
116. S. Sun, J. Liu, T. H. Li, H. Li, G. Liu, W. Gao, Streamflow: streamlined multi-frame optical flow estimation for video sequences. arXiv preprint arXiv:2311.17099 (2023)
117. R. Liu, J. Huang, W. Gao, T.H. Li, G. Li, Mug-STAN: Adapting image-language pretrained models for general video understanding. arXiv preprint arXiv:2311.15075 (2023)
118. C. Zhang, W. Gao, Learned rate control for frame-level adaptive neural video compression via dynamic neural network, in *European Conference on Computer Vision* (Springer, Berlin, 2024)
119. Z. Li, G. Li, T.H. Li, S. Liu, W. Gao, Semantic point cloud upsampling. IEEE Trans. Multimedia **25**, 3432–3442 (2023)
120. M. Alexa, J. Behr, D. Cohen-Or, S. Fleishman, D. Levin, C.T. Silva, Computing and rendering point set surfaces. IEEE Trans. Vis. Comput. Graph. **9**(1), 3–15 (2003)
121. H. Huang, S. Wu, M. Gong, D. Cohen-Or, U.M. Ascher, H.R. Zhang, Edge-aware point set resampling. ACM Trans. Graph. **32**(1), 9:1–9:12 (2013)
122. S. Wu, H. Huang, M. Gong, M. Zwicker, D. Cohen-Or, Deep points consolidation. ACM Trans. Graph. **34**(6), 176:1–176:13 (2015)
123. L. Yu, X. Li, C. Fu, D. Cohen-Or, P. Heng, Pu-net: Point cloud upsampling network, in *Proceedings of the IEEE/CVF Conference on Computer Vision and Pattern Recognition* (2018), pp. 2790–2799
124. C.R. Qi, L. Yi, H. Su, L.J. Guibas, PointNet++: Deep hierarchical feature learning on point sets in a metric space, in *Advances in Neural Information Processing Systems* (2017), pp. 5099–5108
125. Y. Wang, S. Wu, H. Huang, D. Cohen-Or, O. Sorkine-Hornung, Patch-based progressive 3d point set upsampling, in *Proceedings of the IEEE/CVF Conference on Computer Vision and Pattern Recognition* (2019), pp. 5958–5967
126. R. Li, X. Li, C. Fu, D. Cohen-Or, P. Heng, PU-GAN: A point cloud upsampling adversarial network, in *Proceedings of the IEEE/CVF International Conference on Computer Vision* (2019), pp. 7202–7211
127. H. Liu, H. Yuan, J. Hou, R. Hamzaoui, W. Gao, Pufa-gan: A frequency-aware generative adversarial network for 3d point cloud upsampling. IEEE Trans. Image Process. **31**, 7389–7402 (2022)
128. C.R. Qi, H. Su, K. Mo, L.J. Guibas, PointNet: deep learning on point sets for 3D classification and segmentation, in *Proceedings of the IEEE/CVF Conference on Computer Vision and Pattern Recognition* (2017), pp. 652–660

129. Y. Wang, Y. Sun, Z. Liu, S.E. Sarma, M.M. Bronstein, J.M. Solomon, Dynamic graph CNN for learning on point clouds. ACM Trans. Graph. **38**(5), 1–12 (2019)
130. K. Wang, L. Sheng, S. Gu, D. Xu, VPU: a video-based point cloud upsampling framework. IEEE Trans. Image Process. **31**, 4062–4075 (2022)
131. W. Zhao, X. Liu, Z. Zhong, J. Jiang, W. Gao, G. Li, X. Ji, Self-supervised arbitrary-scale point clouds upsampling via implicit neural representation, in *Proceedings of the IEEE/CVF Conference on Computer Vision and Pattern Recognition* (2022), pp. 1999–2007
132. H. Liu, H. Yuan, R. Hamzaoui, W. Gao, S. Li, Pu-refiner: a geometry refiner with adversarial learning for point cloud upsampling, in *IEEE International Conference on Acoustics, Speech and Signal Processing* (2022), pp. 2270–2274
133. Y. Qian, J. Hou, S. Kwong, Y. He, PUGeo-Net: a geometry-centric network for 3d point cloud upsampling, in *European Conference on Computer Vision*, vol. 12364 (2020), pp. 752–769
134. G. Qian, A. Abualshour, G. Li, A.K. Thabet, B. Ghanem, PU-GCN: point cloud upsampling using graph convolutional networks, in *Proceedings of the IEEE/CVF Conference on Computer Vision and Pattern Recognition* (2021), pp. 11683–11692
135. S. Ye, D. Chen, S. Han, Z. Wan, J. Liao, Meta-PU: an arbitrary-scale upsampling network for point cloud. IEEE Trans. Vis. Comput. Graph. **28**(9), 3206–3218 (2022)
136. A. Akhtar, Z. Li, G.V. d. Auwera, L. Li, J. Chen, Pu-dense: sparse tensor-based point cloud geometry upsampling. IEEE Trans. Image Process. **31**, 4133–4148 (2022)
137. L. Luo, L. Tang, W. Zhou, S. Wang, Z. Yang, PU-EVA: an edge-vector based approximation solution for flexible-scale point cloud upsampling, in *Proceedings of the IEEE/CVF International Conference on Computer Vision* (2021), pp. 16188–16197
138. F. Lu, G. Chen, S. Qu, Z. Li, Y. Liu, A. Knoll, PointINet: point cloud frame interpolation network, in *AAAI Conference on Artificial Intelligence* (2021), pp. 2251–2259
139. A. Geiger, P. Lenz, R. Urtasun, Are we ready for autonomous driving? the KITTI vision benchmark suite, in *Proceedings of the IEEE/CVF Conference on Computer Vision and Pattern Recognition* (2012), pp. 3354–3361
140. X. Liu, C.R. Qi, L.J. Guibas, Flownet3d: learning scene flow in 3d point clouds, in *Proceedings of the IEEE/CVF Conference on Computer Vision and Pattern Recognition* (2019), pp. 529–537
141. Y. Zeng, Y. Qian, Q. Zhang, J. Hou, Y. Yuan, Y. He, IDEA-Net: dynamic 3D point cloud interpolation via deep embedding alignment, in *Proceedings of the IEEE/CVF Conference on Computer Vision and Pattern Recognition* (2022), pp. 6338–6347
142. Z. Zheng, D. Wu, R. Lu, F. Lu, G. Chen, C. Jiang, Neuralpci: spatio-temporal neural field for 3d point cloud multi-frame non-linear interpolation, in *Proceedings of the IEEE/CVF Conference on Computer Vision and Pattern Recognition* (2023), pp. 909–918

Chapter 4
Deep-Learning-Based Point Cloud Enhancement II

Abstract This chapter delves into advanced methods and technologies for point cloud enhancement, primarily focusing on processing challenges such as downsampling, completion, and denoising. It outlines various approaches, including heuristic sampling, learning-based sampling, and key point sampling, to optimize point cloud processing for applications like autonomous driving and virtual reality. Each section not only explains the technical processes involved but also discusses the implications for real-world applications, emphasizing the integration of these technologies into larger intelligent systems. This chapter aims to address the limitations of current technologies and suggests future directions for more robust, efficient, and accurate point cloud processing methods.

Keywords Point cloud downsampling · Point cloud completion · Point cloud denoising · Heuristic sampling · Learning-based sampling · Robustness and efficiency

4.1 Introduction

As mentioned in the previous chapter, point cloud enhancement [1–13] connects point cloud coding [14–52] and point cloud analysis tasks [53–60]. Similar to the important role of image and video enhancement [61–68] in the whole image and video processing systems [69–118], point cloud enhancement also plays a critical role in point cloud processing systems.

An inverse technology of the geometrical point cloud upsampling is named as point cloud downsampling. It largely promotes the point cloud processing efficiency. Due to incomplete point clouds comes from many aspects, e.g., specular reflection, signal adsorption, self-occlusion of objects, occlusion of external objects, and blind spots. Some point clouds completion approaches are introduced. Different with upsampling, point cloud completion aims at the lack of local structure. Some point cloud denoising methods for overcoming the distortion caused by data transmission are introduced. Next, this chapter focuses particularly on the unique challenges associated with processing point clouds, specifically downsampling, completion,

W. Gao, G. Li, *Deep Learning for 3D Point Clouds*,
https://doi.org/10.1007/978-981-97-9570-3_4

and denoising. These processes are crucial for various real-world applications such as autonomous driving, virtual reality, and extensive 3D modeling efforts where precise and reliable data are paramount.

A comprehensive discussion on various deep learning approaches tailored for point cloud data is introduced. Techniques such as heuristic sampling, learning-based sampling, and key point sampling are outlined as strategies to optimize point cloud processing. Each technique is dissected to reveal how it contributes to reducing computational load, enhancing data fidelity, or both.

Moreover, the practical implications of these technologies are considered in depth, emphasizing how their integration into larger intelligent systems can lead to more efficient and accurate applications. By addressing the limitations of current technologies and proposing future directions, this chapter aims to equip readers with the knowledge to push the boundaries of point cloud processing further. This includes exploring how these techniques can be adapted and extended to accommodate the growing demands of industries reliant on 3D data.

4.2 Point Cloud Downsampling

4.2.1 Introduction

Point cloud downsampling is an inverse operation of upsampling, and it aims to sample some sparse representative points from relatively dense point clouds. Although downsampling inevitably loses information, it plays a vital role in preprocessing real-world point clouds because downsampling drastically reduces subsequent computational costs. This task focuses on two key challenges. The primary challenge pertains to efficiently downsampling, while the secondary concern involves sampling valuable points. The two challenges are contradictory, because sample valuable points must know which points may be valuable. However, different downsampling methods can adapt to different application tasks, there is no the absolute optimal downsampling method. In the following sections, we will illustrate three kinds of downsampling methods including heuristic sampling, learning-based sampling, and key point sampling.

4.2.2 Heuristic Sampling

The heuristic sampling approach is based on one's subjective experience. This approach usually has a clear purpose and can be easily generalized to various point clouds. The heuristic sampling approaches include Farthest Point Sampling (FPS), Inverse Density Importance Sampling (IDIS), Poisson Disk Sampling (PDS), and Random Sampling (RS).

Random Sampling Random sampling is intuitive thinking in downsampling, which samples points according to a particular distribution. The advantage of random sampling is its fast running speed, and this sampling strategy is often utilized to handle large-scale point clouds. For example, it can achieve fast segmentation for large-scale point cloud through random sampling in [119].

Farthest Point Sampling Farthest point sampling considers sampling the points with the farthest distance. Given a point set $\{p_1, p_2, ...p_N\}$, farthest point sampling needs to find a subset $\{p_{i1}, p_{i2}, ...p_{iM}\}$ to guarantee p_{ij} is the most distant point from the set $\{p_{i1}, p_{i2}, ...p_{ij-1}\}$. Compared with random sampling, it can cover the entire point cloud more quickly for a given number of points. The farthest point sampling method is usually adopted by methods [120] involving the point cloud downsampling process. As a result, the algorithm is exhibited in Algorithm 3 for readers to implement. However, the running complexity of FPS is very high.

Inverse Density Importance Sampling Another downsampling method considers sampling points according to density. More points are sampled for regions with high density and fewer points are sampled for areas with low density. The inverse density importance sampling is utilized in [121], and this method needs to define an inverse density function for each point that adds up all distances from one point its k-neighbors by $\phi(p) = \sum_{p' \in \mathcal{N}_k(p)} ||p - p'||$, where $\mathcal{N}_k(p)$ is the k-neighbors with respect to p. Then IDIS selects the top M points based on the density of the point cloud. Although this method is reasonable for conventional point clouds, it is adverse to handling outliers and noises.

Poisson Disk Sampling In some conditions, humans prefer the sampling points to be as evenly distributed as possible. As shown in Fig. 4.1, the left image shows points using random sampling. We can see some points are very close to others. These sampling results are usually harmful to reflecting the overall shape or some local regions of one object. Hence, the Poisson disk sampling [122] can solve the problem, and it aims to sample points uniformly to make sure each sampled point

---

Algorithm 3 Farthest point sampling algorithm

Input: An input point set containing N points, which is denoted as $P = \{p_1, p_2, ...p_N\}$, and an empty set S used to save sampled points.

Randomly select a point from P and put it into S; Here, P contains $N-1$ points and S contains 1 points.
Through all points in P and compute their distances to the one point in S.
Select the point in P with the farthest distance and put it into S; Here, P contains $N-2$ points and S contains 2 points.
for t = 2 to M **do**
    Through all points in P, and calculate the distances to the points in S.
    Select the minimum distances as the final distances from P to S.
    For each point in P, obtain their distance to S, select the point with the minimum distance, and put it into S.
end for

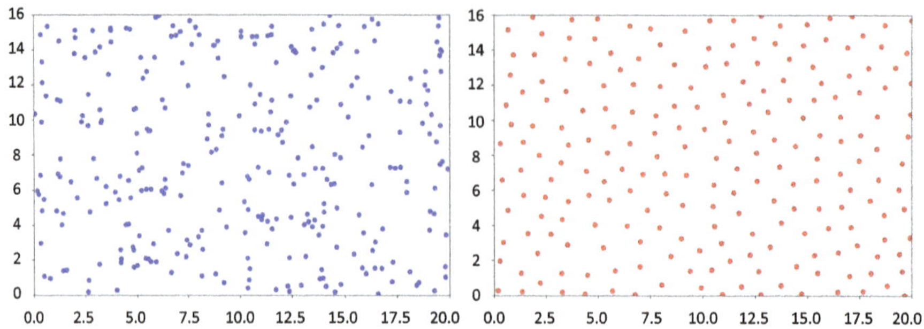

Fig. 4.1 Comparisons random sampling (left) and Poisson disk sampling (right). Source: Author

should not be close to other sampled points with a predefined minimum distance. Let us define an n-dimensional space and define the minimum distance between sampled points as r. This sampling approach contains three steps.

In the first step, a background grid is constructed to save sampled points and accelerate spatial searches. Each cell size is set to $r/\sqrt{n}$ to ensure each cell only contains one point. As a result, this grid can be easily achieved by a n-dimensional array of integers, i.e., the default -1 denotes no point in the cell, and a non-negative integer denotes the location index in a cell. An "active list" (a list used for searching sampled points) and a "sample list" (a list used for saving sampled points) are also constructed. In the second step, randomly sample a point in the background grid, and choose uniformly from the domain. At the same time, the sample list and the active list have added the point. In the third step, the loop stops when the activation list is empty. A random point is chosen from the active list denoted as A. Based on the chosen point A, k points are uniformly generated from the spherical annulus between radius r and $2r$, as shown in Fig. 4.2. The generated k points are checked if it is within distance r of existing samples. Note that the checking is not global, it only needs to check the nearest several background grid cells of nearby samples. A point becomes a new sample point when it is far enough away from the existing sample set. New sampling point is subsequently added to both the active list and the sampled list. If after k attempts no such point is found, instead remove A from the active list. Table 4.1 shows the time complexity of these downsampling methods. We can notice the random sampling is the fastest sampling method compared with others.

4.2.3 Learning-Based Sampling

The learning-based sampling can utilize the knowledge from internal and external data. Therefore, this method is easier to access, and it can easily obtain the representative points compared to the heuristic sampling strategies. This subsection will introduce some learning-based sampling methods, including generator-based

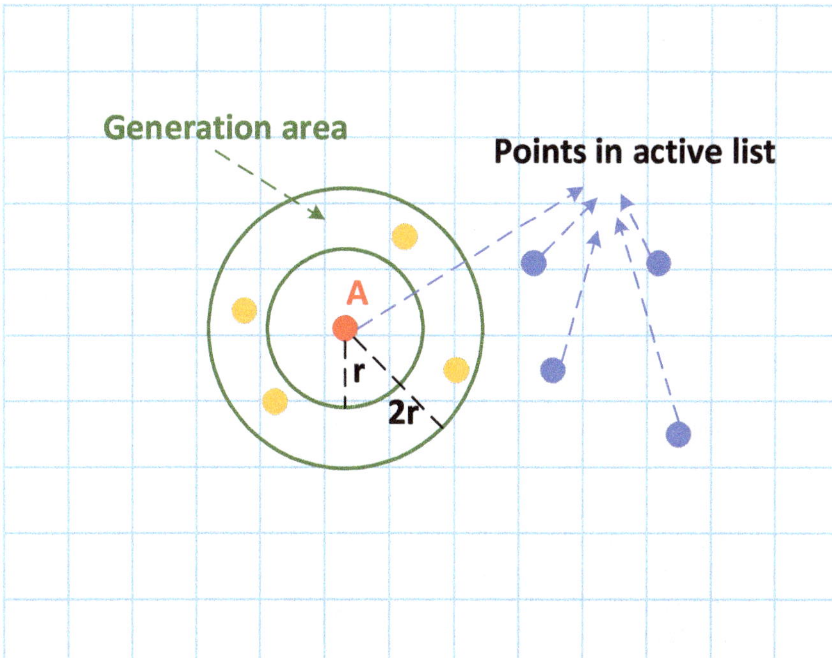

Fig. 4.2 An example sketch map of Poisson disk sampling. Source: Author

sampling, continuous relaxation-based sampling, and key point sampling. Although they can achieve very excellent sampling performance, the training procedure will bring more time cost to learn from data, and they are also easy to involve in overfitting.

Table 4.1 Complexity of different downsampling methods (©2021 IEEE. Reprinted, with permission, from ref. [119])

Method	RS	FPS	IDIS	PDS
Complexity	O(M)	O(M^2N)	O($(K+N)logN$)	O(MN)
Time	0.004	200	10	8

Generator-Based Sampling This method aims to produce a set of points that approach the corresponding raw point cloud as close as possible. "Learning to sample" [123] is a representative deep learning-based downsampling approach for point clouds. As shown in Fig. 4.3, in their framework, there is a correlation between downsampling and other tasks. Conventional sampling methods do not serve downstream tasks, and thus, the performance of downstream tasks is often greatly affected by missing key points. However, their sampling method can keep performance for downstream tasks with sampled point clouds to a certain extent.

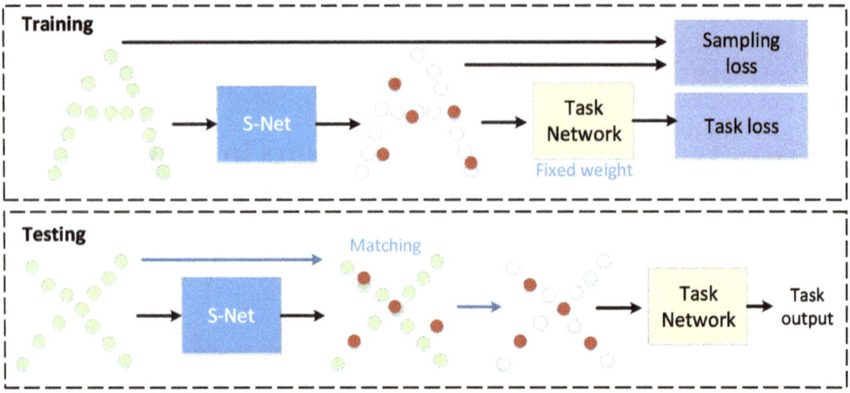

Fig. 4.3 The framework of generator-based sampling (©2019 IEEE. Reprinted, with permission, from ref. [123])

In the training phase, it produces points and then puts them into a task network in [123]. Note that the weights of the task network should be fixed because the task network needs to provide stable supervisory information. The loss function includes task-driven loss and sampling loss. The latter emphasizes geometry signal fidelity between the input and sampled point clouds. Furthermore, this approach needs to consider three aspects of the framework. The first one is the design of sampling loss. Given the input point cloud P and the sampled point cloud G, the sampling loss is composed of three terms:

$$L_f(G, P) = \frac{1}{|G|} \sum_{g \in G} \min_{p \in P} \|g - p\|_2, \tag{4.1}$$

$$L_m(G, P) = \min_{g \in G} \min_{p \in P} \|g_i - p_i\|_2, \tag{4.2}$$

$$L_f(G, P) = \frac{1}{|P|} \sum_{p \in P} \min_{g \in G} \|p - g\|_2. \tag{4.3}$$

These losses limit the downsampled points that need to have the same distribution as the input point. The second one is the matching problem between input points and downsampled points. Because the output of a network cannot completely cover a point, accurately matching the sampled points with input points is important. As a result, they adopt the nearest-neighbor matching strategy. The sampled points are computed as their closest points in input points, and these closest points are viewed as the sampled points from input points. The last one is adjusting the number of points with different downsampling ratios. To achieve it, they propose a ProgressiveNet [123]. During the training stage, the input and output point clouds of ProgressiveNet should be same. Hence, the output point can be adaptively selected according to corresponding requirements. They also show their advanced performance compared to traditional farthest point sampling in downstream tasks.

Continuous Relaxation-Based Sampling We know that conventional sampling is not differentiable for networks, but how are they embedded into a neural network as a module? To solve this problem, continuous relaxation-based sampling methods use a re-parameterization trick, which relaxes the discrete sampling to a continuous matrix multiplication. Hence, these methods inevitably introduce extra parameters, so they usually bring unaffordable memory cost. In [124], they relax one-hot vectors. A temperature parameter controls the range to which the one-hot vector is relaxed. They define two parameters, i.e., $\alpha \in \mathbb{R}^d$ and T to sample a concrete random variable in d dimensions. The d-dimensional vector is independently and identically distributed and sampled from a Gumbel distribution. Then each element of the sample m from the concrete distribution is defined as:

$$m_j = \frac{exp((log_{\alpha} + g_i)/T)}{\sum_{k=1}^{d} exp((log_{\alpha} + g_i)/T)}, \tag{4.4}$$

where m_j is the j-th element in the sample vector. By this way, this formulation adopts a continuous representation to approximate the discrete distribution. They can produce a one-hot vector with $m_j = 1$ with probability $\alpha_j / \sum_p \alpha_p$. Concrete random variable should keep its differentiation with respect to its parameters α via the re-parametrization trick. As a result, based on the derivable sampling weight m_j, the sampling process can be trained with the network end-to-end. In the testing stage, the concrete selector layer is substituted to a discrete arg max layer. The output of the i-th neuron is written as $\boldsymbol{x}_{\arg\max_j \boldsymbol{\alpha}_j^{(i)}}$.

Key Point Sampling Nezhadarya et al. [125] propose an adaptive downsampling strategy for point cloud classification, which aims at finding key points in point cloud learning. They think points with maximum responses are critical points that should be retained and sampled. To extract these critical points, they propose a critical point layer (CPL) and its improved version weighted critical points layer (WCPL). Here, we mainly introduce the CPL as shown in Fig. 4.4. Given a point feature with $\mathbf{F} \in \mathbb{R}^{N \times d}$, where N is the number of point clouds and d is the feature dimension. First, CPL selects the maximum location along the feature dimension, thereby resulting in a $d \times 1$ vector. At the same time, the corresponding location indexes are also saved. Due to the $d \times 1$ vector having some repeat points, they remove these redundancies by the "set" operation. Next, they sort these critical points in ascending order, the index list is also adjusted according to the sort operation. Then CPL can be handled by the batch operation, they use the nearest neighbor upsampling to resize the sorted index vector to $N \times 1$. Finally, owing to the $N \times 1$ vector containing the index of these critical points, they can gather the point from the original point feature. Hence, the downsampling process can be achieved by the CPL.

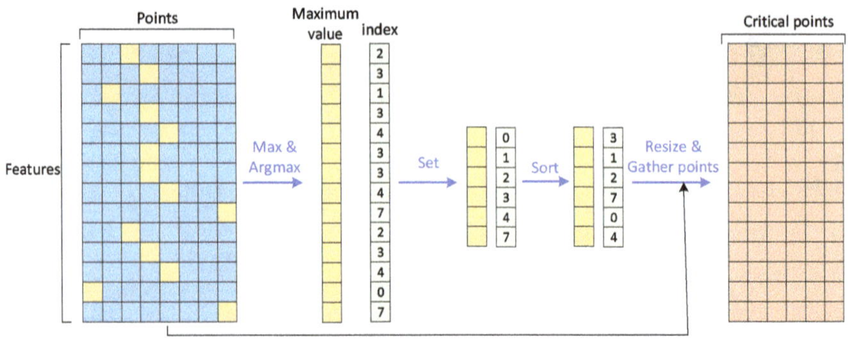

Fig. 4.4 The structure of critical points layer (CPL) (©2020 IEEE. Reprinted, with permission, from ref. [125])

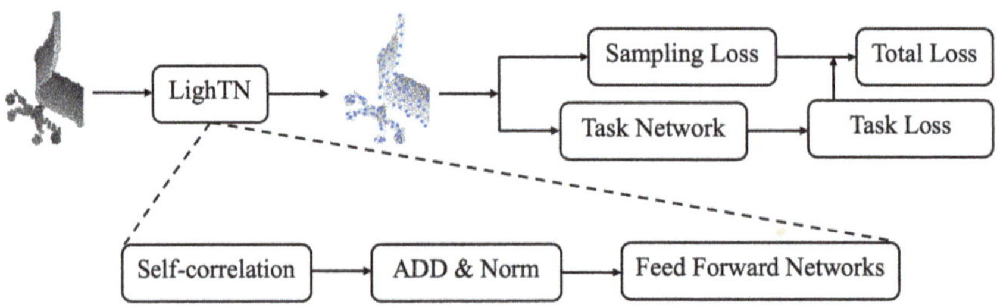

Fig. 4.5 The framework of Transformer-based sampling (©2023 IEEE. Reprinted, with permission, from ref. [126])

Transformer-Based Sampling Wang et al. [126] propose an innovative and lightweight Transformer network called LighTN, designed for task-specific point cloud downsampling. Compared to the existing complex Transformer networks, LighTN is more streamlined and resource-efficient, demonstrating exceptional task-oriented downsampling capabilities. Figure 4.5 shows the overall architecture in LighTN. The backbone of LighTN is built upon the Transformer network, primarily composed of a single Transformer block and a single-head self-correlation attention mechanism. For the self-correlation attention, we eliminate the matrices projection of Query (Q), Key (K), and Value (V). This omission potentially enhances the extraction of refined global geometric features of points due to the permutation invariance of its internal symmetry matrix. To address the reduction in learnable parameters caused by the lightweight framework, we implement an expand-reduce strategy to adjust the depth and width of the FFN layer, referred to as scalable FFN. Consequently, LighTN can effectively learn geometric information, with the overhead increase in downsampling being significantly lower than the resource savings from the simplified point set. Lastly, we develop a novel sampling loss to maximize the distance between generated points, ensuring that they cover more significant regions.

The total loss function comes from two parts, i.e., the loss of geometry sampling L_S between the downsampled point cloud B and the raw point cloud P, and the loss of downstream tasks L_T. The sampling L_S is constructed from the following three perspectives. First, the sampled point cloud B is required to have a geometry position that is closed to the raw point cloud P as a whole, which is usually supervised by the CD distance loss function L_{CD}. Second, to ensure the differentiability of the generated point cloud and downstream tasks during the connection process, a nonlinear soft projection method is proposed for achieving differentiable sampling. We utilize the average weight of the k nearest neighbors of point b_j in P as the soft projected point z to represent b_j. Thus, the soft projected point z is defined as:

$$z = \sum_{i \in \mathcal{N}_P(b_j)} w_i \cdot p_i, \tag{4.5}$$

$$w_i = \frac{e^{-dist_i^2/t}}{\sum_{l \in \mathcal{N}_P(b_j)} e^{-dist_l^2/t}}, \tag{4.6}$$

where $dist_i$ represents the point distance, t is a learnable temperature coefficient that controls the distribution shape of the weight w_i. Hence, the soft projection L_{sp} is denoted as:

$$L_{sp} = T(t), t \in [0, +\infty). \tag{4.7}$$

Thirdly, a primary limitation of LCD is its disregard for the uniform distribution of points, complicating the simplified point sets' ability to represent the global surface effectively. To address this issue, the repulsion loss L_r is defined as follows:

$$L_r(B) = \frac{1}{M \cdot k} \sum_{1 \le j \le M} \sum_{j' \in \mathcal{N}_k(j)} \eta\left(\|b_{j'} - b_j\|_2\right), \tag{4.8}$$

where $\eta(r) = \max\left(0, h^2 - r^2\right)$ is a function ensuring that b_i maintains a minimum distance from other points in B, h represents the average separation distance between the generated points, and $N_k(j)$ denotes the set of indices for the K-nearest neighbors of b_j. Based on the discussion earlier, the total sampling loss is defined as follows:

$$L_S = L_{CD} + \alpha L_r + \beta L_{sp}. \tag{4.9}$$

4.3 Point Cloud Completion

Point cloud completion task refers to generate and predict complete points from partial point clouds, which shows an important role in 3D computer vision applications. Recently, deep-learning-based methods have shown better performance in terms of robustness and capabilities. However, the completed point cloud struggles with matching downstream analysis tasks due to incomplete point clouds coming from many aspects, e.g., spectral reflection, signal adsorption, self-occlusion of objects, external-occlusion objects, and blind spots. In this part, we introduce the pint cloud completion formulation and then review several typical methods of point cloud completion.

4.3.1 Introduction

Point cloud completion targets reconstructing the corrupted input point clouds with complete 3D shapes, which can be seen in Fig. 4.6. The reconstruction should be as natural as the visual consistencies of human perception. Given the completion function $C(.)$, the corrupted input $\mathbf{P}_{in}$, and the complete output $\mathbf{P}_{out}$, the completion process is defined as follows:

$$\mathbf{P}_{out} = C(\mathbf{P}_{in}). \tag{4.10}$$

Here, for point cloud completion, we introduce three metrics, including Cov, F-score, and CD. Cov measures how complete the enhanced point cloud $\mathbf{S}_{eval}$ is compared to the raw point cloud $\mathbf{S}_{GT}$:

$$Cov(S_{eval}, S_{GT}) = \frac{\left|\left\{ \arg\min_{y \in S_{GT}} d(x, y) | x \in S_{eval} \right\}\right|}{|S_{GT}|}, \tag{4.11}$$

Fig. 4.6 Point cloud completion. Source: Author

where $d(\cdot, \cdot)$ is L_2 norm. First, computer each x's nearest neighbor y in S_{GT}. Next, form all y as the numerator. This formulation records the coverage of S_{eval} versus S_{GT}. However, Cov is commonly computed by dense points in 3D space for optimization. Then F-score is proposed as:

$$F(\mathbf{S}_{eval}, \mathbf{S}_{GT}) = \frac{2Cov(\mathbf{S}_{eval}, \mathbf{S}_{GT})Cov(\mathbf{S}_{GT}, \mathbf{S}_{eval})}{Cov(\mathbf{S}_{eval}, \mathbf{S}_{GT}) + Cov(\mathbf{S}_{GT}, \mathbf{S}_{eval})}, \tag{4.12}$$

where F-score guarantees that if either $Cov(\mathbf{S}_{eval}, \mathbf{S}_{GT}) \rightarrow 0$ or $Cov(S_{GT}, S_{eval}) \rightarrow 0$, $F(\mathbf{S}_{eval}, \mathbf{S}_{GT}) \rightarrow 0$. F-score can measure completeness, while CD only gauges the distance of two sets.

Furthermore, more evaluation metrics, e.g., Consistency, Fidelity (FD), and Minimal Matching Distance (MMD) can be referred to [127]. Consistency can evaluate the changes in output against disturbances on theinput point cloud. FD evaluates the degree of the preservation of the input, and MMD measures the degree of reconstruction of the model's outputs.

When dating back to point cloud completion literature, we can find that traditional approaches commonly draw lessons from diffusion-based or patch-based image completion approaches. These approaches concentrate on the current local-area information without taking their global relationships into account. Benefitting from deep-learning-based frameworks, various approaches [127–130] have presented remarkable performances for point cloud completion. Here, we mainly introduce deep-learning-based methods and their basic process. The whole pipeline is shown in Fig. 4.7, which involves the model design process and model optimization process. The classic network architecture mainly includes two parts: encoder and decoder. The former is designed to extract global features or local features, while the latter is used to generate and refine rough completion point cloud. Model optimization process is performed by minimizing the loss function. Different methods may use various enhancement models as additional parts to further improve the results.

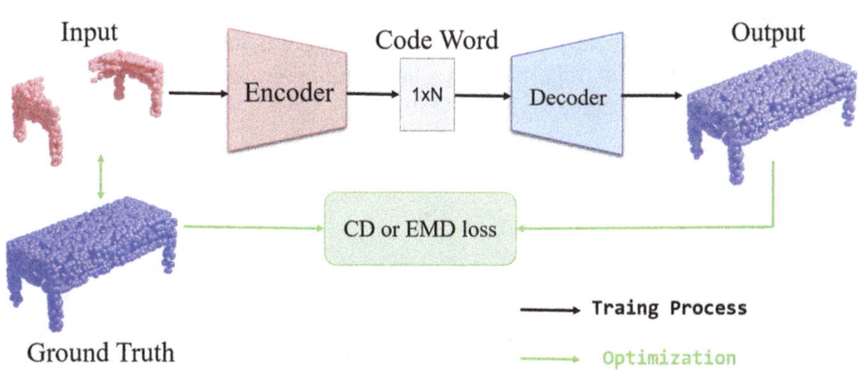

Fig. 4.7 Basic paradigm of existing point cloud completion methods based on deep learning. N records the dimension of the latent feature vector. Source: Author

Table 4.2 Comparison of representative completion methods. Source: Author

Methods	Structure	Feature	Form	Stage	Loss
Han et al. [131]	voxel	3DCNN	generation	full	BCE
Yuan et al. [127]	point	MLP	generation	full	CD
Yang et al. [128]	point	MLP	generation	full	CD
Tchapmi et al. [129]	point	MLP	generation	coarse-fine	CD
Xie et al. [132]	point & voxel	MLP & 3DCNN	generation	coarse-fine	CD
Huang et al. [133]	point	MLP	generation	coarse-fine	CD & GAN
Wen et al. [134]	point	MLP	offset & generation	coarse-fine	CD & EMD
Xiang et al. [135]	point	transformer	generation	coarse-fine	CD
Wang et al. [136]	point	transformer	generation	full	EMD
Zhou et al. [137]	point	MLP	generation	coarse-fine	CD
Yu et al. [138]	point	transformer	offset & generation	coarse-fine	CD

To summarize the generality and specialty of existing representative methods more clearly, we analyze and classify these methods according to the following aspects: data structure, feature extractor, inference form, inference stage and loss function. Related content is displayed in Table 4.2. According to the data organization structure used in the point cloud feature extraction process, existing methods are classified into three branches: point-based, voxel-based, and sparse convolution-based. Considering the paradigm of feature extraction, it includes 3D convolutional neural network (3DCNN), multilayer perceptron (MLP), self-attention mechanism (transformer). When it comes to the generation form of unknown points, it includes the direct generation of new points and the learning of coordinate offsets between the new points and existing points. The generation stage of new points can be divided into single-step (full) output and multi-step output from coarse to fine. The loss functions used in point cloud completion under supervised learning mainly refer to CD loss, EMD loss, binary cross-entropy (BCE) loss, and adversarial generation (GAN) loss.

Next, we will elaborately describe three existing architectures, a point-based method TopNet [129], a graph-based method FoldingNet [128], and a generative model-based method Vaccine-style-net [130].

4.3.2 *TopNet*

TopNet [129] builds a decoder similar to a tree structure to generate a series of random candidate points, which at the same time illustrates the decoder via showing a node of the tree as presented in Figs. 4.8 and 4.9.

The pipeline is made up of a two-stage encoder and a tree-structured decoder. Both the encoder and decoder are composed of multilayer perceptron (MLP).

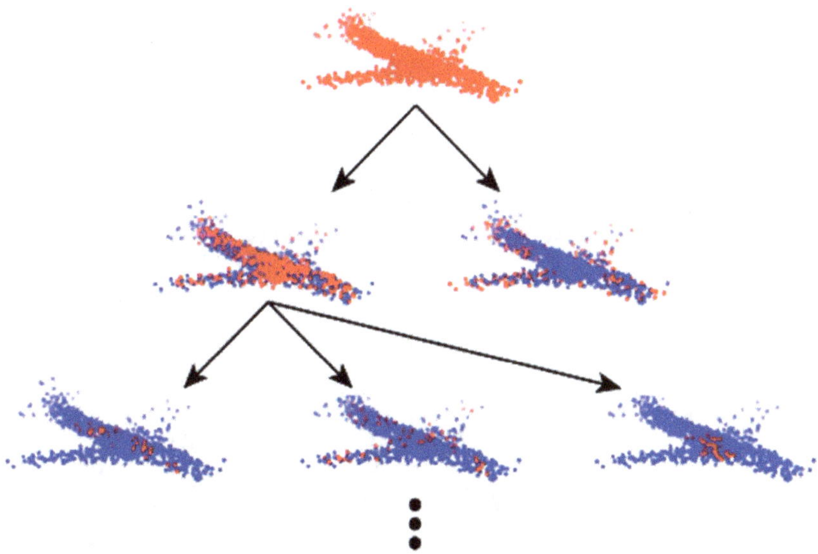

Fig. 4.8 TopNet. The decoder generates a point cloud according to a tree-structured architecture in which each node denotes a point-cloud subset (©2019 IEEE. Reprinted, with permission, from ref. [129])

Similar colored MLPs have the same parameters. The point cloud loss still uses CD distance. Their decoder produces point clouds via a tree structure in which each node denotes a point cloud subset (Fig. 4.8). The decoder is optimized by CD loss within an architecture that includes an encoder as a first stage. The decoder is shown in Fig. 4.9. The decoder takes a root node that gets the feature vector from the encoder and applies M_1 MLPs to produce M_1 feature vectors of C dimension related to M_1 children node at tree level 1. Next, for each node, the feature vector at tree level $i \geq 1$ is connected by global feature from the encoder and then, processed by M_{i+1} MLPs to produce M_{i+1} children features for the next tree level $i + 1$. Every node with known tree level i is handled by the same shared M_i MLPs. As for the last tree level, the feature vectors produced for each leaf have three dimensions.

4.3.3 FoldingNet

Until now, FoldingNet [128], in the existing point cloud completion architecture, is the most widely applied decoding part. The intuition comes from elastic paper folding. Observing that 3D point clouds are often obtained from object surfaces and 3D object surfaces intrinsically 2D-manifolds. The former can be understood by the point clouds that are discretized from CAD-model and are able to sampled from line-of-sight sensors. The latter can be seen as the 2D-3D mapping known as

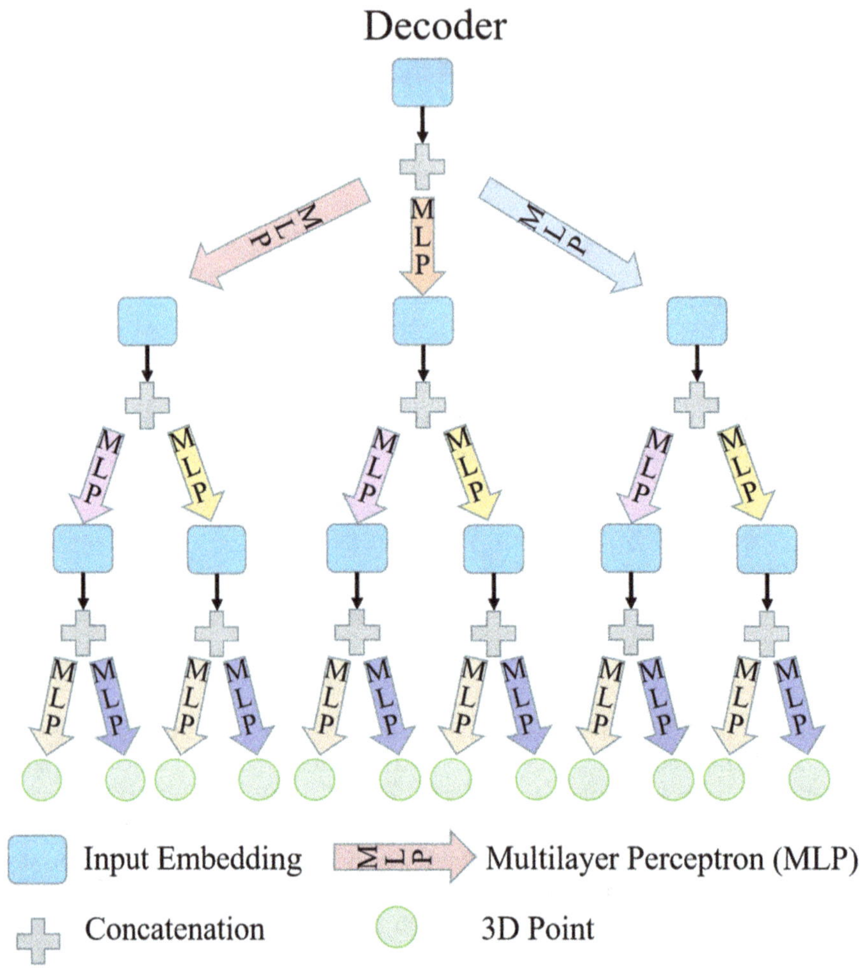

Fig. 4.9 The architecture of TopNet (©2019 IEEE. Reprinted, with permission, from ref. [129])

the parameterization process. Then they construct the whole pipeline as shown in Fig. 4.10.

The encoder uses PointNet [139], which can be seen as a projection into a codeword. In total, the FoldingNet deforms/stretches/cuts a 2D grid onto a 2D latent surface, where the deforming force is modulated or affected by the adjacent meshes' interconnections. Because the reconstructed points could represent the intermediate steps in the folding and training processes, the gradual changes of the deforming force can be visualized intuitively. In detail, the architecture can be divided into two parts:

Encoder Architecture The encoder connects MLP and graph-based layers. First of all, calculate every point v's local covariance matrix (3-by-3) and make it vectorized

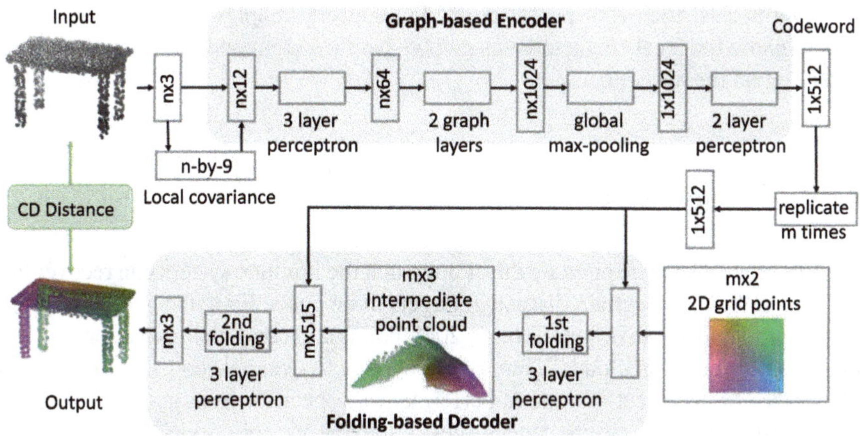

Fig. 4.10 The architecture of FoldingNet (©2019 IEEE. Reprinted, with permission, from ref. [128])

to 1-by-9. Next, connect the matrix of point positions and the local covariances of all points and feed them to a perceptron with three layers. The obtained output is then passed through two consecutive graph convolutional layers containing max pooling operations. In specific, given adjacency matrix $\mathbf{A}$ on graph and the input signal $\mathbf{X}$, the output can be defined as:

$$\mathbf{Y} = \mathbf{A}_{max}(\mathbf{X})\mathbf{K}, \tag{4.13}$$

where K denotes the mapping matrix, and (i, j)-th elements of $\mathbf{A}_{max}(\mathbf{X})$ can be formulated by:

$$(\mathbf{A}_{max}(\mathbf{X}))_{ij} = ReLU(max_{k \in \mathcal{N}(i)} x_{kj}), \tag{4.14}$$

where $max_{k \in \mathcal{N}(i)} x_{kj}$ denotes the local max pool operation. It calculates a local feature based on graph structure. This feature is able to hold the topology information of the local-area neighborhoods, which promotes the network to propagate the topology into larger areas.

Decoder Architecture The designed decoder applies two tandem perceptrons with three layers to warp a 2D fixed grid into the partial point cloud. The obtained codeword is replicated m times and concatenated by the square matrix (m-by-2). This matrix is then operated row-wisely by an MLP layer with three layers, and the output is m-by-3. Next, the replicated codeword is concatenated with the above m-by-3 matrix. This combination is then fed to an MLP layer with three layers to predict the enhanced point cloud. n denotes the number of the input point cloud, which is set to 2048, and m is the grid point size set as 2025.

Nevertheless, for every parent point, FoldingNet samples the same 2D grids, which ignore the local characteristics involved in the parent ones. This needs further exploring on the decoder.

4.3.4 *Vaccine-Style-Net*

Vaccine-Style-Net is inspired by the biology that the immune system can recover the infected cells from a certain disease. It targets three goals: First, the generated point clouds are in sparse distribution (e.g., 2048 points). Second, the resolution is fixed in the generated point clouds. Third, these approaches cannot represent the smooth 3D surface of an object with good performance, especially in large-area corrupted scenes. To deal with these challenges, they design the Vaccine-Style-Net as shown in Fig. 4.11. This architecture comprises three components, including mask generation, the continuous representation (CR) module, and the completion of the point cloud module. In the following subsections, each module is described in detail.

Mask Generation Diverse masks are given to evaluate the adaptability and robustness of the model. As shown in Fig. 4.12, an onion peeling mask (OPM) is designed. The existing random seed sampling (RSS) chooses a seed as the missing ratio to erode only one region, while OPM adopts the saliency score to generate several regions applying like "onion-peeling." The score in OPM reveals the important degree of each point to the 3D shape. The intuition holds that the edge points influence more than the inner points to the 3D shape because they encode the edge of the shape.

Continuous Representation (CR) They use the continuous 3D geometry representation to generate complete 3D shapes with high resolution and smooth surfaces. In particular, they represent the 3D surface as a continuous decision boundary that assigns each possible location $p \in \mathbb{R}^3$ a probability within [0,1]. This process can be

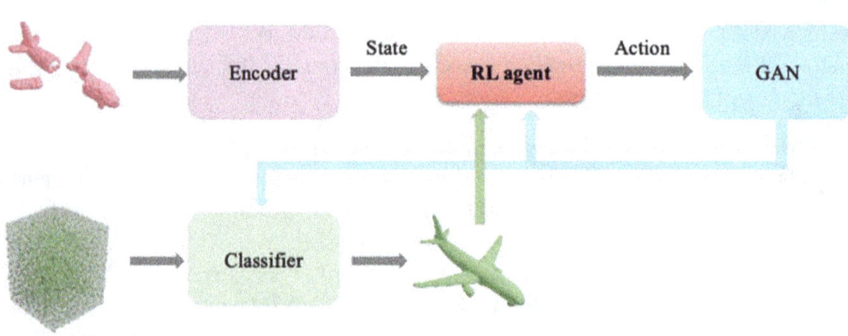

Fig. 4.11 Overview of Vaccine-style-net (©2022 IEEE. Reprinted, with permission, from ref. [140])

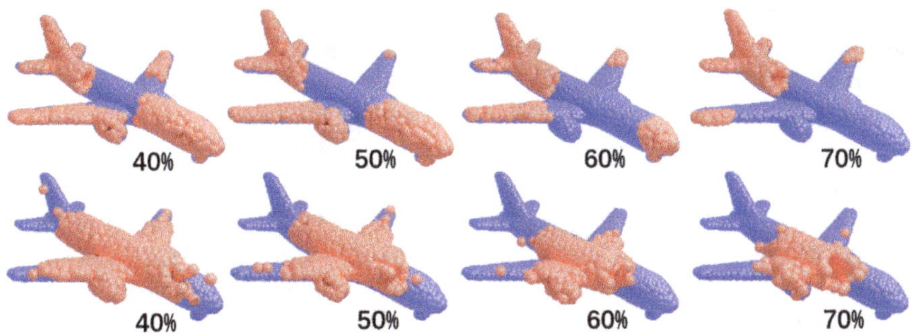

Fig. 4.12 Mask generation methods. Row 1: random seed sampling. Row 2: onion-peeling-mask generation. Remaining points and discarded points are marked in red and blue, respectively [130]. Source: Author

approximated by a binary classification neural network, considering the 3D shape X and its one point $p \in \mathbb{R}^3$. Overall, the whole decision boundary can be defined as:

$$y = f_\theta(p, X) = f_c(p, f_a(X)), y \in [0, 1], \tag{4.15}$$

where y predicts the possible probability of $p \in \mathbb{R}^3$ on X. f_a and f_c represent the analysis network and the classifier, respectively. θ denotes the model parameters. During the training process of f_θ, for each complete X in the training dataset, N number of locations ($p_i \in \mathbb{R}^3, i = 1, ..., N$) in X are sampled. The loss of this binary classification is measured by:

$$\mathcal{L}(\theta) = \sum_i^N \mathcal{L}_c(f_\theta(p_i, X), g_{p_i}), \tag{4.16}$$

where $\mathcal{L}_c$ is the recognition loss based on cross-entropy. g_{p_i} denotes the true label of p_i. Once the cR network is trained, the residence of each point can be evaluated. Next, the Multiresolution IsoSurface Extraction algorithm is used to obtain the isosurface. Then, a mesh surface can finally be recovered by the common Marching Cube algorithm.

Point Cloud Completion by Latent Representation Recovery Considering that if we can recover the incomplete latent representation to the complete one, the complete 3D shape can be acquired by feeding the complete latent representation to f_c. Therefore, in this step, the goal to achieve point cloud completion can be reduced as the recovery of latent representation. Based on this assumption, they adopt two stages. First, learn the manifold of complete latent representation via a GAN. Second, learn the action z by the RL to trigger the incomplete latent representation as a microbe for the GAN to finally obtain a complete latent representation.

First, train a latent-space GAN (L-GAN) on complete latent representation obtained from the pre-trained CR network in Step 2. Fed with a noise z, the generator G of L-GAN generates a new complete latent representation $G(z)$. $G(z)$ is then guide the classifier f_c to generate a complete 3D shape.

Then, an RL agent then is used to estimate a CLR from an ICLR. They follow the assumption in [141]: x_t denotes the most observation recently, which is enough to define the observed state s_t. s_t is actually the incomplete latent representation produced from f_a in Step 2. a_t denotes the action, which is the true guidance for the input of L-GAN. The CR network and L-GAN make up the environment. For getting the right policy denoted as π, the RL agent should receive reasonable rewards from the environment. In this method, two rewards are applied, which are formulated as:

$$r_{rec} = IoU(M_{pred}, M_{GT}) = \frac{|M_{pred} \cap M_{GT}|}{|M_{pred} \cup M_{GT}|}, \tag{4.17}$$

$$r_{latent} = -||G(z) - f_a(P_{in})||_2^2, \tag{4.18}$$

$$r = \alpha \cdot r_{rec} + \beta \cdot r_{latent}, \tag{4.19}$$

where r_{rec} and r_{latent} represent the shape reconstruction reward (volumetric IoU) and the latent reconstruction reward, respectively. M_{pred} is the set of points on predicted mesh, while M_{GT} is the set of points on the ground truth mesh. r_{rec} guarantees the predicted 3D shape close to GT. r_{latent} is the l_2 distance between $G(z)$ and $f_a(P_{in})$ to ensure them similar. α and β in r are the weights for each reward, respectively. Because the action is in continuous space, they use the deep deterministic policy gradient algorithm. As for training RL, the environment is made up by the pretrained CR network and L-GAN with their parameters fixed.

4.4 Point Cloud Denoising

4.4.1 Introduction

According to the previous description, point cloud denoising is very important in research communities, and it attempts to reconstruct the original point cloud by removing noise points. We know that noisy data tend to have large entropy, so it has the same property as point cloud compression. They can be viewed as an entropy reduction process. A noisy point cloud $\mathbf{P}_N = \{p_i \in \mathbb{R}^3 | 0 \le i < n\}$ is generated by:

$$p_i = q_i + n_i, \tag{4.20}$$

where $q_i, n_i \in \mathbb{R}^3$. q_i is a clean point and n_i is noise in location i. So, point cloud denoising aims to reconstruct the appropriate point q_i from the noisy point by a function G:

$$q_i = G(q_i + n_i). \tag{4.21}$$

Most existing point cloud denoising methods concentrate on handling synthetic noises, such as Gaussian noise. However, real-world noises are different from synthetic noises because real-world noises may be produced by different data distributions. Therefore, recent studies tend to an accurate and robust denoising strategy, mainly including filter-based, optimization-based, and deep-learning-based. Filter-based method is more general and hardly relies on the information about external data, but it could be better at some specific complex scenarios. Optimization-based method tries to use mathematical optimization methods to model the small amount of data available. Deep-learning-based method can be viewed as a unique optimization-based method, which needs lots of data samples. Due to its excellent performance, the deep-learning-based method is gradually becoming a popular solution.

4.4.2 *Filter-Based Methods*

Filter-based denoising methods refer to concepts of image area. It assumes noise pixels are high frequency. So in point cloud area, these filters are designed to handle point positions or point normals. Here we mainly introduce bilateral filtering for point cloud denoising. Bilateral filtering is applied on point cloud geometry, normal vectors, and attribute information in [142]

Due to the high-frequency nature of noisy points, this method considers utilizing neighbor points to generate a weighted average offset. The classical bilateral filtering for point clouds is introduced in this section by considering both spatial and normal distances. Given the denoised position $p_i^{'}$, p_i is updated by:

$$p_i^{'} = p_i + \lambda_i N_i, \tag{4.22}$$

where N_i is the normal vector of p_i, and λ_i is a weight coefficient defined by:

$$\lambda_i = \frac{\sum_{p_{ij} \in N(p_i)} w_d(\|v_{ij}\|) w_n(| < n_i, v_{ij} > |) < n_i, v_{ij} >}{\sum_{p_{ij} \in N(p_i)} w_d(\|v_{ij}\|) w_n(| < n_i, v_{ij} > |)}, \tag{4.23}$$

where $v_{ij} = p_{ij} - p_i$ and $N(p_i)$ denotes the neighbors of p_i. $w_d(x) = e^{-x^2/2\sigma_d^2}$ and $w_n(x) = e^{-x^2/2\sigma_n^2}$ are Gaussian functions with variance σ_d and σ_n, respectively. $<, >$ represents the vector inner product. For the flat area, the difference between point normals and adjacent points is small, and the corresponding value weight is close to 1. Here, the spatial weight is important because it is the same as Gaussian blurring in this area directly. In the margin area, the normal difference between point and adjacent points is large, so the corresponding value weight approaches to 0, leading to the decrease of the kernel function.

4.4.3 Optimization-Based Methods

Optimization-based methods try to find a denoised point cloud by defining a series of constraints on the geometry prior. The parameters of optimization-based methods are usually large, and they need to careful parameter tuning to achieve satisfying results.

Optimization-based methods are generally classified into the following categories, including methods based on Moving Least Squares (MLS), methods based on Locally Optimal Projection (LOP), sparsity-based methods, and methods based on non-local aggregation. This section will mainly introduce the sparsity-based methods because this approach is very close to some of the ideas in the transformation part of compression. There is no doubt that these methods often require the assumption of piece-wise smooth underlying surfaces. The core idea of this method is to adopt a linear combination of dictionary elements to represent a new point cloud, as shown in Fig. 4.13. It is the same as the Fourier transform and tries to use a group of basis vectors to reconstruct a new signal vector. But for sparse representation, most dictionary elements not be used to represent the new point clouds. Just like many roots and letters in a dictionary, not all roots and letters are used to represent a word. The matrix form of sparse representation is shown in Fig. 4.14, and thus, a reconstructed matrix can be written as a matrix multiplication of dictionary and sparse coefficients.

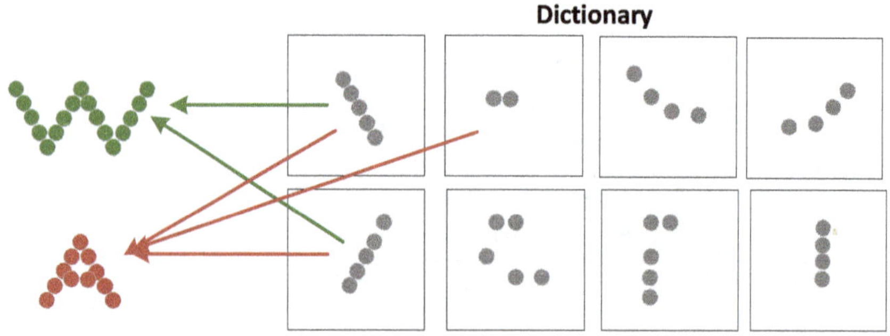

Fig. 4.13 The point cloud is assumed to be decomposed into a linear combination of a set of dictionary bases. Source: Author

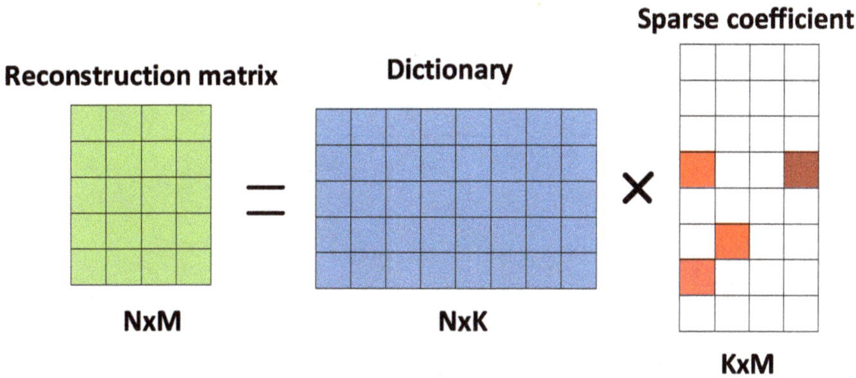

Fig. 4.14 The matrix forms of sparse representation. Source: Author

At this point, the reader may have two questions. The first one is how to get the dictionary. To answer the question, we need to define an optimization function as:

$$\min \frac{1}{2}\|\mathbf{X} - \mathbf{DC}\|_F^2 + \lambda\|C\|_p, \tag{4.24}$$

where $\mathbf{X} \in \mathbb{R}^{N \times M}$ denotes the element matrix generated from the input point cloud and each column represents the geometry signal of a certain point cloud. $\mathbf{D} \in \mathbb{R}^{N \times K}$ and $\mathbf{C} \in \mathbb{R}^{K \times M}$ represent the dictionary matrix and sparse coefficient matrix, respectively. λ is preset to control the weight between the objective functions and $0 \leq p \leq 1$. As a result, the dictionary and sparse coefficients can be learned by some existing iterative algorithms like Matching Pursuits (MP) and Orthogonal Matching Pursuit (OMP). The second one is why the sparse representation can achieve denoising? Equation (4.24) tries to let **DC** approximate the noisy points **X**, but there is a limited term $\|C\|_p$ can control the values of C will be not too large, leading to many 0 values. Therefore, the coefficients can only use a small number of elements in the dictionary. Since the dictionary is a description of the basic components of the point cloud, a small number of these elements can be combined to approximate the noisy point cloud with a noiseless representation.

4.4.4 Deep-Learning-Based Methods

Recently, point cloud denoising methods based on deep learning have come into people's sight. The mapping between noisy point clouds and high-quality original point clouds is obtained in a learning manner. The trained model can denoise new samples with similar geometry distribution and noise characteristics. Here, this section mainly discusses three kinds of deep denoising methods with different architectures, including PCPNet [143], PointProNet [144], and Pointfilter [145].

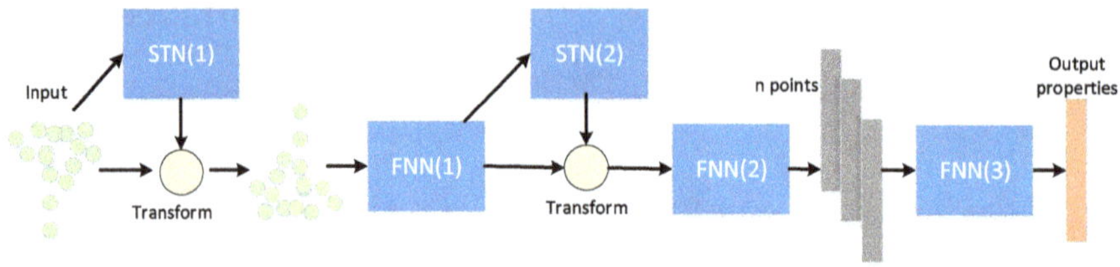

Fig. 4.15 The framework of PCPNet [143]. Source: Author

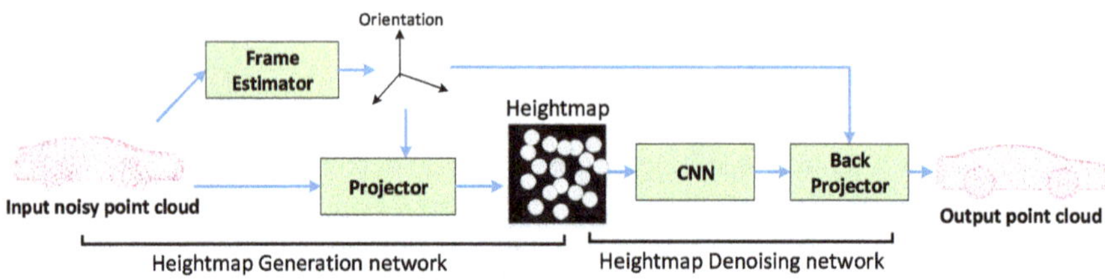

Fig. 4.16 The framework of PointProNet [144]. Source: Author

As shown in Fig. 4.15, PCPNet [143] is a simple architecture for point cloud denoising that can estimate local 3D shape. The backbone of PCPNet is PointNet. The PointNet can extract the local feature from the individual point and does not utilize the information of neighbor points. The input is a local patch, centered at points with a fixed radius r proportional to the point cloud's bounding box extent. Given an input patch, the spatial transform network (STN) firstly rotates point and adopts fully connected networks (FNN) to generate their features. Then the second STN adjusts features to obtain a robust representation. After the second FNN, they adopt the max symmetric operation with a sum to get a global feature vector. After the last FNN, PCPNet learns a set of k nonlinear functions in the local patch neighborhoods and gives a k-dimensional feature vector per patch that can then be used to regress various local features.

Previous networks consider to handle point-wise relations, but PointProNet [144] designs a CNN-based architecture to handle 2D images. As shown in Fig. 4.16, PointProNet contains two components, including a heightmap generation network and a heightmap denoising network. In the first component, a noisy point cloud is fed into frame estimator and projects the points onto to a noisy heightmap. Then in the second component, a CNN is utilized to denoise the heightmap to a new representation. Then they use a back projector to recover the clean heightmap to 3D geometry space. The biggest characteristic of PointProNet is converting a 3D problem to a 2D problem. This way largely simplifies the denoising process on 3D space.

Pointfilter [145] is the representative auto-encoder framework for point cloud denoising as shown in Fig. 4.17. Same as PCPNet, Pointfilter also filters noisy points in a local way, i.e., the filtered point is dependent on its neighbors. Hence, Pointfilter needs to preprocess the input patches and use Principle Component Analysis (PCA)

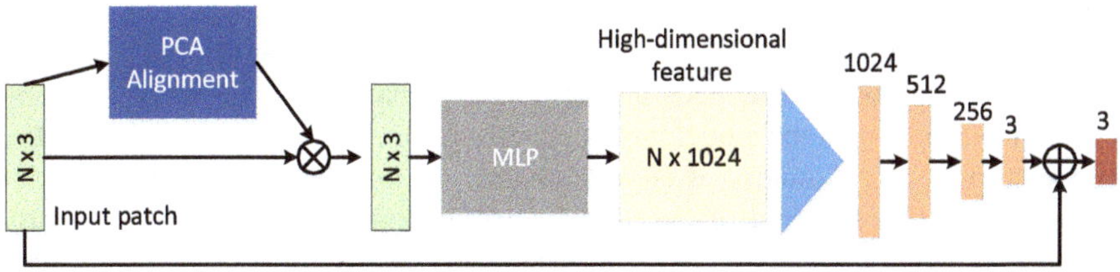

Fig. 4.17 The framework of Pointfilter (©2020 IEEE. Reprinted, with permission, from ref. [145])

to get the principle axes of the input patches and align them with the Cartesian space. In the encoder module, patches after aligned are fed into MLPs to obtain different scales of features. The obtained high-dimension feature vector is embedded into a latent feature vector with 1024 dimension. For the decoder, a regressor estimates the offset vector using latent vectors. At last, the inverse operation of PCA alignment is adopted to multiply the predicted displacement vector to obtain the refined offset vector. To retain more complete point cloud surface information, they design a projection loss so as to lead to less sharp feature results. Another repulsion loss is used for keeping filtered points have a uniform distribution. By their ingenious design, Pointfilter shows outstanding performance compared with previous methods.

4.5 Summary

This chapter extensively covers the advancements in point cloud processing technologies, focusing on enhancing the quality and usability of 3D point cloud data. It discusses three main areas: downsampling, completion, and denoising, each critical for improving the application of point clouds in fields like autonomous driving, virtual reality, and 3D modeling. Downsampling is optimized for reducing computational load without significant loss of detail. The completion section addresses the reconstruction of complete point clouds from partial data, crucial for robust 3D object reconstruction. Denoising techniques are explored to clean point cloud data from noise, enhancing the accuracy of the resultant models. The integration of deep learning methods across these processes highlights the shift toward more automated, accurate, and efficient point cloud processing systems, promising improvements in both speed and performance.

Point cloud enhancement will undertake processing tasks in various point cloud-based systems, digital retina, and the construction of smart cities. According to its application, there are two trends in point cloud enhancement. The first one is how to improve the robustness. Because noise and distortion inevitably exist in data collection and data transmission in the real world, so preprocessing and postprocessing have to process a certain number of "unseen" point clouds. However, due to the limited training samples, existing learning-based methods tend to overfit some specific distributions. If a model is trained in an online manner that constantly updates parameters according to the new data, it can easily cause catastrophic forgetting problem that the model may achieve declining performance in the original data. An appropriate thinking is combining deep learning model and optimization method, making the output of the model depend on the current data distribution. The second one is how to build connections with compression tasks. As emphasized many times throughout this book, point cloud enhancement is a preprocessing or postprocessing for compression. The processing is only unilaterally serving the compression, but compression does not give feedback to the processing tasks or provide guidance with prior knowledge. For example, if the downsampling algorithm knows what point clouds are suitable for compression, it will indirectly improve compression efficiency. For the point cloud upsampling, it also needs to learn the distributions of compressed point clouds or make sure the frequency information after the transformation in the compression is used to guide which areas to focus. Hence, the training of compression, upsampling, and other downstream tasks should be joint, and the loss functions with its optimizing strategy should also be combined end-to-end. In the future, these challenges are expected to be solved with highly integrated hardware devices, digital retinas, and cloud computing.

Exercises

1. Farthest point sampling is a classical downsampling algorithm. Please implement the farthest point cloud sampling algorithm in code.
2. According to the organization manner of point cloud data, existing point cloud processing methods based on deep learning can be roughly divided into three categories: point-based, voxel-based, and sparse convolution-based. Is there a more efficient point cloud organization manner that takes into account both memory consumption and task performance?
3. What is the difference between graph convolution and sparse convolution in extracting point cloud attribute features?
4. Assume that the 1D Gaussian functions with chosen variance is set to 1, and given a point $\mathbf{p}$ with a coordinate $(1, 1, 1)$ with its three neighbors $(1, 2, 0)$, $(0, 2, 0)$ and $(0, 0, 1)$, can you figure out the result of the updated point $\mathbf{p}'$ using bilateral filtering-based methods?
5. What is the difference between those point cloud completion methods?
6. Chamfer distance is an important evaluation metric for a point set. Given two point sets $S_1 = \{(2, 3, 1), (-1, 0, 1), (1, 0, 2)\}$ and $S_2 = \{(1, 2, 1), (0, -1, 1), (2, 0, 1)\}$, can you calculate the Chamfer distance between S_1 and S_2?
7. Please briefly summarize the relationship between the tasks in this chapter and point cloud compression.

8. Point cloud geometry compression distortion occurs during the coordinate quantization process, while the point cloud noise appears as outliers in the acquisition process. How does the point cloud denoising method perform in the compression distortion removal task?
9. What is the relationship between point cloud geometry sampling methods and point cloud geometry compression algorithms in terms of bit overhead and impact on downstream tasks?
10. Point cloud completion task is benefiting from the generative large model of point cloud. How to develop corresponding point cloud quality evaluation metrics in the future?

References

1. W. Liu, W. Gao, X. Mu, Fast inter-frame motion prediction for compressed dynamic point cloud attribute enhancement, in *Proceedings of the AAAI Conference on Artificial Intelligence*, vol. 38(4) (2024), pp. 3720–3728
2. Z. Yang, W. Gao, X. Lu, Danet: Density-adaptive network for geometry-based point cloud compression artifacts removal, in *2023 IEEE International Conference on Visual Communications and Image Processing (VCIP)* (IEEE, New York, 2023), pp. 1–5
3. X. Fan, G. Li, D. Li, Y. Ren, W. Gao, T. H. Li, Deep geometry post-processing for decompressed point clouds, in *2022 IEEE International Conference on Multimedia and Expo (ICME)* (IEEE, New York, 2022), pp. 1–6
4. X. Zhang, G. Liao, W. Gao, G. Li, TDRnet: transformer-based dual-branch restoration network for geometry based point cloud compression artifacts, in *2022 IEEE International Conference on Multimedia and Expo (ICME)* (IEEE, New York, 2022), pp. 1–6
5. Z. Li, G. Li, T. H. Li, S. Liu, W. Gao, Semantic point cloud upsampling. IEEE Trans. Multimedia **25**, 3432–3442 (2022)
6. R. Zhang, W. Gao, G. Li, T. H. Li, Qinet: decision surface learning and adversarial enhancement for quasi-immune completion of diverse corrupted point clouds. IEEE Trans. Geosci. Remote Sens. **60**, 1–14 (2022)
7. R. Bao, Y. Ren, G. Li, W. Gao, S. Liu, Flow-based point cloud completion network with adversarial refinement, in *ICASSP 2022-2022 IEEE International Conference on Acoustics, Speech and Signal Processing (ICASSP)* (IEEE, New York, 2022), pp. 2559–2563
8. J. Chen, G. Li, R. Zhang, T. H. Li, W. Gao, Pointivae: invertible variational autoencoder framework for 3d point cloud generation, in *2022 IEEE International Conference on Image Processing (ICIP)* (IEEE, New York, 2022), pp. 3216–3220
9. R. Zhang, J. Chen, W. Gao, G. Li, T. H. Li, Pointot: interpretable geometry-inspired point cloud generative model via optimal transport. IEEE Trans. Circuits Syst. Video Technol. **32**(10), 6792–6806 (2022)
10. S. Fan, W. Gao, Screen-based 3d subjective experiment software, in *Proceedings of the 31st ACM International Conference on Multimedia* (2023), pp. 9672–9675
11. X. Mao, H. Yuan, X. Lu, R. Hamzaoui, W. Gao, PCAC-GAN: A sparse-tensor-based generative adversarial network for 3d point cloud attribute compression, in *Computational Visual Media* (2024)
12. J. Wang, W. Gao, G. Li, Applying collaborative adversarial learning to blind point cloud quality measurement, in *IEEE Transactions on Instrumentation and Measurement* (2023)
13. Y. Zhang, W. Gao, G. Li, Openpointcloud-v2: a deep learning based open-source algorithm library of point cloud processing, in *Proceedings of the 1st International Workshop on Advances in Point Cloud Compression, Processing and Analysis* (2022), pp. 51–55

14. W. Gao, G. Li, H. Yuan, R. Hamzaoui, Z. Li, S. Liu, Apccpa'22: 1st international workshop on advances in point cloud compression, processing and analysis, in *Proceedings of the 30th ACM International Conference on Multimedia* (2022), pp. 7392–7393
15. T. Qin, G. Li, W. Gao, S. Liu, Multi-grained point cloud geometry compression via dual-model prediction with extended octree, in *ACM Transactions on Multimedia Computing, Communications, and Applications* (2024)
16. Y. Shao, W. Gao, S. Liu, G. Li, Advanced patch-based affine motion estimation for dynamic point cloud geometry compression. Sensors **24**(10), 3142 (2024)
17. Y. Shao, F. Song, W. Gao, S. Liu, G. Li, Texture-guided graph transform optimization for point cloud attribute compression. Appl. Sci. **14**(10), 4094 (2024)
18. Y. Shao, X. Yang, W. Gao, S. Liu, G. Li, 3d point cloud attribute compression using diffusion-based texture-aware intra prediction, in *IEEE Transactions on Circuits and Systems for Video Technology* (2024)
19. J. Zhang, Y. Chen, G. Liu, W. Gao, G. Li, Efficient point cloud attribute compression framework using attribute-guided graph fourier transform, in *ICASSP 2024-2024 IEEE International Conference on Acoustics, Speech and Signal Processing (ICASSP)* (IEEE, New York, 2024), pp. 8426–8430
20. W. Gao, H. Yuan, G. Li, Z. Li, H. Yuan, Low complexity coding unit decision for video-based point cloud compression. IEEE Trans. Image Process. **33**, 149–162 (2023)
21. Y. Shao, G. Li, Q. Zhang, W. Gao, S. Liu, Non-rigid registration-based progressive motion compensation for point cloud geometry compression, *IEEE Transactions on Geoscience and Remote Sensing* (2023)
22. F. Song, G. Li, X. Yang, W. Gao, S. Liu, Block-adaptive point cloud attribute coding with region-aware optimized transform. IEEE Trans. Circuits Syst. Video Technol. **33**(8), 4294–4308 (2023)
23. Y. An, Y. Shao, G. Li, W. Gao, S. Liu, A fast motion estimation method with hamming distance for lidar point cloud compression, in *2022 IEEE International Conference on Visual Communications and Image Processing (VCIP)* (IEEE, New York, 2022), pp. 1–5
24. H. Yuan, W. Gao, G. Li, Z. Li, Rate-distortion-guided learning approach with cross-projection information for v-pcc fast cu decision, in *Proceedings of the 30th ACM International Conference on Multimedia* (2022), pp. 3085–3093
25. F. Song, G. Li, W. Gao, T. H. Li, Rate-distortion optimized graph for point cloud attribute coding. IEEE Signal Process Lett. **29**, 922–926 (2022)
26. F. Song, G. Li, X. Yang, W. Gao, T.H. Li, Fine-grained correlation representation for graph-based point cloud attribute compression, in *2022 IEEE International Conference on Multimedia and Expo (ICME)* (IEEE, New York, 2022), pp. 1–6
27. F. Shen, W. Gao, A rate control algorithm for video-based point cloud compression, in *2021 International Conference on Visual Communications and Image Processing (VCIP)* (IEEE, New York, 2021), pp. 1–5
28. F. Song, Y. Shao, W. Gao, H. Wang, T. Li, Layer-wise geometry aggregation framework for lossless lidar point cloud compression. IEEE Trans. Circuits Syst. Video Technol. **31**(12), 4603–4616 (2021)
29. L. Xie, W. Gao, H. Zheng, , G. Li, SPCGC: scalable point cloud geometry compression for machine vision, in *Proceedings of IEEE International Conference on Robotics and Automation* (2024)
30. L. Xie, W. Gao, H. Zheng, H. Ye, Semantic-aware visual decomposition for point cloud geometry compression, in *2024 Data Compression Conference (DCC)* (IEEE, New York, 2024), pp. 595–595
31. Z. Qi, W. Gao, Variable-rate point cloud geometry compression based on feature adjustment and interpolation, in *2024 Data Compression Conference (DCC)* (IEEE, New York, 2024), pp. 63–72
32. Z. Yu, W. Gao, When dynamic neural network meets point cloud compression: computation-aware variable rate and checkerboard context, in *2024 Data Compression Conference (DCC)* (IEEE, New York, 2024), pp. 600–600

33. L. Xie, W. Gao, S. Fan, Z. Yao, Pdnet: Parallel dual-branch network for point cloud geometry compression and analysis, in *2024 Data Compression Conference (DCC)* (IEEE, New York, 2024), pp. 596–596
34. L. Xie, W. Gao, H. Zheng, End-to-end point cloud geometry compression and analysis with sparse tensor, in *Proceedings of the 1st International Workshop on Advances in Point Cloud Compression, Processing and Analysis* (2022), pp. 27–32
35. C. Fu, G. Li, R. Song, W. Gao, S. Liu, OctAttention: Octree-based large-scale contexts model for point cloud compression, in *AAAI Conference on Artificial Intelligence* (2022), pp. 625–633
36. W. Gao, H. Ye, G. Li, H. Zheng, Y. Wu, L. Xie, OpenPointCloud: an open-source algorithm library of deep learning based point cloud compression, in *ACM International Conference on Multimedia* (2022), pp. 7347–7350
37. H. Zheng, W. Gao, Z. Yu, T. Zhao, G. Li, Viewpcgc: view-guided learned point cloud geometry compression, in *Proceedings of the 32nd ACM International Conference on Multimedia* (2024)
38. L. Xie, W. Gao, H. Zheng, G. Li, Roi-guided point cloud geometry compression towards human and machine vision, in *Proceedings of the 32nd ACM International Conference on Multimedia* (2024)
39. C. Peng, W. Gao, Laplacian matrix learning for point cloud attribute compression with ternary search-based adaptive block partition, in *Proceedings of the 32nd ACM International Conference on Multimedia* (2024)
40. S. Luo, B. Qu, W. Gao, Learning robust 3d representation from clip via dual denoising. arXiv preprint arXiv:2407.00905 (2024)
41. G. Li, G. Wei, W. Gao, *Point Cloud Compression: Technologies and Standardization* (Berlin, Springer Nature, 2024)
42. G. Li, W. Gao, W. Gao, Introduction, in *Point Cloud Compression: Technologies and Standardization* (Springer, Berlin, 2024), pp. 1–28
43. G. Li, W. Gao, W. Gao, Background knowledge, in *Point Cloud Compression: Technologies and Standardization* (Springer, Berlin, 2024), pp. 29–51
44. G. Li, W. Gao, W. Gao, Predictive coding, in *Point Cloud Compression: Technologies and Standardization* (Springer, Berlin, 2024), pp. 53–70
45. G. Li, W. Gao, W. Gao, Transform coding, in *Point Cloud Compression: Technologies and Standardization* (Springer, Berlin, 2024), pp. 71–96
46. G. Li, W. Gao, W. Gao, Quantization techniques, in *Point Cloud Compression: Technologies and Standardization* (Springer, Berlin, 2024), pp. 97–112
47. G. Li, W. Gao, W. Gao, Entropy coding, in *Point Cloud Compression: Technologies and Standardization* (Springer, Berlin, 2024), pp. 113–133
48. G. Li, W. Gao, W. Gao, MPEG geometry-based point cloud compression (G-PCC) standard, in *Point Cloud Compression: Technologies and Standardization* (Springer, Berlin, 2024), pp. 135–165
49. G. Li, W. Gao, W. Gao, AVS point cloud compression standard, in *Point Cloud Compression: Technologies and Standardization* (Springer, Berlin, 2024), pp. 167–197
50. G. Li, W. Gao, W. Gao, MPEG video-based point cloud compression (V-PCC) standard, in *Point Cloud Compression: Technologies and Standardization* (Springer, Berlin, 2024), pp. 199–218
51. G. Li, W. Gao, W. Gao, MPEG AI-based 3D graphics coding standard, in *Point Cloud Compression: Technologies and Standardization* (Springer, Berlin, 2024), pp. 219–241
52. G. Li, W. Gao, W. Gao, Future work, in *Point Cloud Compression: Technologies and Standardization* (Springer, Berlin, 2024), pp. 243–250
53. S. Fan, W. Gao, G. Li, Salient object detection for point clouds, in *European Conference on Computer Vision* (2022), pp. 1–19
54. S. Luo, W. Gao, A general framework for rotation invariant point cloud analysis, in *ICASSP 2024-2024 IEEE International Conference on Acoustics, Speech and Signal Processing (ICASSP)* (IEEE, New York, 2024), pp. 3665–3669

55. X. Lu, W. Gao, Attentivenet: Detecting small objects for lidar point clouds by attending to important points, in *2023 IEEE International Conference on Visual Communications and Image Processing (VCIP)* (IEEE, New York, 2023), pp. 1–5
56. Z. Pan, N. Zhang, W. Gao, S. Liu, G. Li, Less is more: label recommendation for weakly supervised point cloud semantic segmentation, in *Proceedings of the AAAI Conference on Artificial Intelligence*, vol. 38(5) (2024), pp. 4397–4405
57. Z. Pan, G. Liu, W. Gao, T. Li, Epcontrast: effective point-level contrastive learning for large-scale point cloud understanding, in *2024 IEEE International Conference on Multimedia and Expo (ICME)* (IEEE, New York, 2024)
58. N. Zhang, Z. Pan, T.H. Li, W. Gao, G. Li, Improving graph representation for point cloud segmentation via attentive filtering, in *Proceedings of the IEEE/CVF Conference on Computer Vision and Pattern Recognition* (2023), pp. 1244–1254
59. D. Yang, W. Gao, G. Li, H. Yuan, J. Hou, S. Kwong, Exploiting manifold feature representation for efficient classification of 3d point clouds. ACM Trans. Multimed. Comput. Commun. Appl. **19**(1s), 1–21 (2023)
60. K. Wen, N. Zhang, G. Li, W. Gao, MPVNN: Multi-resolution point-voxel non-parametric network for 3d point cloud processing, in *2024 IEEE International Conference on Multimedia and Expo (ICME)* (IEEE, New York, 2024)
61. W. Liu, W. Gao, G. Li, S. Ma, T. Zhao, H. Yuan, Enlarged motion-aware and frequency-aware network for compressed video artifact reduction, in *IEEE Transactions on Circuits and Systems for Video Technology* (2024)
62. Z. Li, G. Li, T. Li, S. Liu, W. Gao, Information-growth attention network for image super-resolution, in *Proceedings of the 29th ACM International Conference on Multimedia* (2021), pp. 544–552
63. L. Zhou, W. Gao, G. Li, H. Yuan, T. Zhao, G. Yue, Disentangled feature distillation for light field super-resolution with degradations, in *2023 IEEE International Conference on Multimedia and Expo Workshops (ICMEW)* (IEEE, New York, 2023), pp. 116–121
64. L. Zhou, W. Gao, G. Li, End-to-end spatial-angular light field super-resolution using parallax structure preservation strategy, in *2022 IEEE International Conference on Image Processing (ICIP)* (IEEE, New York, 2022), pp. 3396–3400
65. W. Gao, L. Zhou, L. Tao, A fast view synthesis implementation method for light field applications. ACM Trans. Multimed. Comput. Commun. Appl. (TOMM) **17**(4), 1–20 (2021)
66. X. Zhang, W. Gao, G. Li, Q. Jiang, R. Cong, Image quality assessment–driven reinforcement learning for mixed distorted image restoration. ACM Trans. Multimed. Comput. Commun. Appl. **19**(1s), 1–23 (2023)
67. X. Zhang, W. Gao, H. Yuan, G. Li, Je 2 net: joint exploitation and exploration in reinforcement learning based image restoration, in *ICASSP 2022-2022 IEEE International Conference on Acoustics, Speech and Signal Processing (ICASSP)* (IEEE, New York, 2022), pp. 2090–2094
68. X. Zhang, W. Gao, HIRL: Hybrid image restoration based on hierarchical deep reinforcement learning via two-step analysis, in *ICASSP 2022-2022 IEEE International Conference on Acoustics, Speech and Signal Processing (ICASSP)* (IEEE, New York, 2022), pp. 2445–2449
69. B. Qu, X. Liang, S. Sun, W. Gao, Exploring aigc video quality: a focus on visual harmony, video-text consistency and domain distribution gap, in *Proceedings of the IEEE/CVF Conference on Computer Vision and Pattern Recognition Workshops* (2024)
70. B. Qu, H. Li, W. Gao, Bringing textual prompt to AI-generated image quality assessment, in *2024 IEEE International Conference on Multimedia and Expo (ICME)* (IEEE, New York, 2024)
71. Y. Wu, L. Xie, S. Sun, W. Gao, Y. Yan, Adaptive intra period size for deep learning-based screen content video coding, in *2024 IEEE International Conference on Multimedia and Expo Workshops (ICMEW)* (IEEE, New York, 2024)
72. H. Zheng, W. Gao, End-to-end rgb-d image compression via exploiting channel-modality redundancy, in *Proceedings of the AAAI Conference on Artificial Intelligence* **38**(7), 7562–7570 (2024)

73. L. Tao, W. Gao, G. Li, C. Zhang, Adanic: Towards practical neural image compression via dynamic transform routing, in *Proceedings of the IEEE/CVF International Conference on Computer Vision* (2023), pp. 16879–16888
74. Y. Wu, W. Gao, End-to-end lossless compression of high precision depth maps guided by pseudo-residual. arXiv preprint arXiv:2201.03195 (2022)
75. Y. Wu, Z. Qi, H. Zheng, L. Tao, W. Gao, Deep image compression with latent optimization and piece-wise quantization approximation, in *Proceedings of the IEEE/CVF Conference on Computer Vision and Pattern Recognition* (2021), pp. 1926–1930
76. W. Gao, L. Tao, L. Zhou, D. Yang, X. Zhang, Z. Guo, Low-rate image compression with super-resolution learning, in *Proceedings of the IEEE/CVF Conference on Computer Vision and Pattern Recognition Workshops* (2020), pp. 154–155
77. W. Gao, S. Sun, H. Zheng, Y. Wu, H. Ye, Y. Zhang, OpenDMC: An open-source library and performance evaluation for deep-learning-based multi-frame compression, in *Proceedings of the 31st ACM International Conference on Multimedia* (2023), pp. 9685–9688
78. Y. Guo, W. Gao, G. Li, Interpretable task-inspired adaptive filter pruning for neural networks under multiple constraints. Int. J. Comput. Vis. **132**(6), 2060–2076 (2024)
79. W. Gao, Y. Guo, S. Ma, G. Li, S. Kwong, Efficient neural network compression inspired by compressive sensing. IEEE Trans. Neural Networks Learn. Syst. **35**(2), 1965–1979 (2022)
80. Y. Guo, W. Gao, Semantic-driven automatic filter pruning for neural networks, in *2022 IEEE International Conference on Multimedia and Expo (ICME)* (IEEE, New York, 2022), pp. 1–6
81. L. Tao, W. Gao, Efficient channel pruning based on architecture alignment and probability model bypassing, in *2021 IEEE International Conference on Systems, Man, Cybernetics (SMC)* (IEEE, New York, 2021), pp. 3232–3237
82. Z. Yang, W. Gao, G. Li, Y. Yan, Sur-driven video coding rate control for jointly optimizing perceptual quality and buffer control, in *IEEE Transactions on Image Processing* (2023)
83. F. Shen, Z. Cai, W. Gao, An efficient rate control algorithm for intra frame coding in avs3, in *2021 IEEE International Conference on Systems, Man, and Cybernetics (SMC)* (IEEE, New York, 2021), pp. 3164–3169
84. H. Yuan, W. Gao, J. Wang, Dynamic computational resource allocation for fast inter frame coding in video conferencing applications, in *2021 IEEE International Conference on Multimedia and Expo (ICME)* (IEEE, New York, 2021), pp. 1–6
85. W. Gao, Q. Jiang, R. Wang, S. Ma, G. Li, S. Kwong, Consistent quality oriented rate control in hevc via balancing intra and inter frame coding. IEEE Trans. Industr. Inform. **18**(3), 1594–1604 (2021)
86. H. Yuan, W. Gao, A new coding unit partitioning mode for screen content video coding, in *Proceedings of the 2021 5th International Conference on Digital Signal Processing* (2021), pp. 66–72
87. W. Gao, On the performance evaluation of state-of-the-art rate control algorithms for practical video coding and transmission systems, in *Proceedings of the 2020 4th International Conference on Video and Image Processing* (2020), pp. 179–185
88. W. Gao, S. Kwong, Q. Jiang, C.-K. Fong, P.H. Wong, W.Y. Yuen, Data-driven rate control for rate-distortion optimization in hevc based on simplified effective initial qp learning. IEEE Trans. Broadcast. **65**(1), 94–108 (2018)
89. W. Gao, A multi-objective optimization perspective for joint consideration of video coding quality, in *2019 Asia-Pacific Signal and Information Processing Association Annual Summit and Conference (APSIPA ASC)* (IEEE, New York, 2019), pp. 986–991
90. W. Gao, S. Kwong, Y. Jia, Joint machine learning and game theory for rate control in high efficiency video coding. IEEE Trans. Image Process. **26**(12), 6074–6089 (2017)
91. W. Gao, S. Kwong, Y. Zhou, H. Yuan, SSIM-based game theory approach for rate-distortion optimized intra frame CTU-level bit allocation. IEEE Trans. Multimedia **18**(6), 988–999 (2016)
92. W. Gao, S. Kwong, H. Yuan, X. Wang, DCT coefficient distribution modeling and quality dependency analysis based frame-level bit allocation for HEVC. IEEE Trans. Circuits Syst. Video Technol. **26**(1), 139–153 (2015)

93. W. Gao, S. Kwong, Phase congruency based edge saliency detection and rate control for perceptual image and video coding, in *2016 IEEE International Conference on Systems, Man, and Cybernetics (SMC)* (IEEE, New York, 2016), pp. 000264–000269
94. H. Yuan, W. Gao, Openfastvc: an open source library for video coding fast algorithm implementation, in *Proceedings of the 31st ACM International Conference on Multimedia* (2023), pp. 9660–9663
95. H. Yuan, W. Gao, S. Ma, Y. Yan, Divide-and-conquer-based RDO-free CU partitioning for 8K video compression. ACM Trans. Multimed. Comput. Commun. Appl. **20**(4), 1–20 (2024)
96. L. Tao, W. Gao, A hardware implementation of entropy encoder for 8K video coding, in *2022 IEEE International Conference on Multimedia and Expo (ICME)* (IEEE, New York, 2022), pp. 1–6
97. Y. Guo, W. Gao, S. Ma, G. Li, Accelerating transform algorithm implementation for efficient intra coding of 8K UHD videos. ACM Trans. Multimed. Comput. Commun. Appl. (TOMM) **18**(4), 1–20 (2022)
98. Z. Cai, W. Gao, Efficient fast algorithm and parallel hardware architecture for intra prediction of AVS3, in *2021 IEEE International Symposium on Circuits and Systems (ISCAS)* (IEEE, New York, 2021), pp. 1–5
99. W. Gao, H. Yuan, Y. Guo, L. Tao, Z. Cai, G. Li, OpenHardwareVC: an open source library for 8K UHD video coding hardware implementation, in *Proceedings of the 30th ACM International Conference on Multimedia* (2022), pp. 7339–7342
100. W. Gao, H. Yuan, G. Liao, Z. Guo, J. Chen, PP8K: A new dataset for 8K UHD video compression and processing. IEEE MultiMedia **30**(3), 100–109 (2023)
101. X. Zang, W. Gao, G. Li, H. Fang, C. Ban, Z. He, H. Sun, A baseline investigation: transformer-based cross-view baseline for text-based person search, in *Proceedings of the 31st ACM International Conference on Multimedia* (2023), pp. 7737–7746
102. G. Liao, W. Gao, G. Li, J. Wang, S. Kwong, Cross-collaborative fusion-encoder network for robust RGB-thermal salient object detection. IEEE Trans. Circuits Syst. Video Technol. **32**(11), 7646–7661 (2022)
103. W. Gao, G. Liao, S. Ma, G. Li, Y. Liang, W. Lin, Unified information fusion network for multi-modal RGB-D and RGB-T salient object detection. IEEE Trans. Circuits Syst. Video Technol. **32**(4), 2091–2106 (2021)
104. Y. Chen, S. Sun, G. Li, W. Gao, T.H. Li, Closing the gap between theory and practice during alternating optimization for GANs, in *IEEE Transactions on Neural Networks and Learning Systems* (2023)
105. Y. Chen, C. Jin, G. Li, T. H. Li, W. Gao, Mitigating label noise in gans via enhanced spectral normalization. IEEE Trans. Circuits Syst. Video Technol. **33**(8), 3924–3934 (2023)
106. X. Zang, G. Li, W. Gao, Multidirection and multiscale pyramid in transformer for video-based pedestrian retrieval. IEEE Trans. Industr. Inform. **18**(12), 8776–8785 (2022)
107. X. Zang, G. Li, W. Gao, X. Shu, Learning to disentangle scenes for person re-identification. Image Vis. Comput. **116**, 104330 (2021)
108. X. Zang, G. Li, W. Gao, X. Shu, Exploiting robust unsupervised video person re-identification. IET Image Process. **16**(3), 729–741 (2022)
109. Z. Yue, G. Li, W. Gao, Cross-level guided attention for human-object interaction detection, in *2023 IEEE International Conference on Multimedia and Expo Workshops (ICMEW)* (IEEE, New York, 2023), pp. 284–289
110. Z. Yao, W. Gao, Iterative saliency aggregation and assignment network for efficient salient object detection in optical remote sensing images. *IEEE Transactions on Geoscience and Remote Sensing* (2024)
111. Y. Sun, Z. Li, S. Wang, W. Gao, Depth-assisted calibration on learning-based factorization for a compressive light field display. Opt. Express **31**(4), 5399–5413 (2023)
112. Y. Sun, Z. Li, L. Li, S. Wang, W. Gao, Optimization of compressive light field display in dual-guided learning, in *ICASSP 2022-2022 IEEE International Conference on Acoustics, Speech and Signal Processing (ICASSP)* (IEEE, New York, 2022), pp. 2075–2079

113. W. Gao, S. Fan, G. Li, W. Lin, A thorough benchmark and a new model for light field saliency detection. IEEE Trans. Pattern Anal. Mach. Intell. **45**(7), 8003–8019 (2023)
114. Z. Guo, W. Gao, H. Wang, J. Wang, S. Fan, No-reference deep quality assessment of compressed light field images, in *2021 IEEE International Conference on Multimedia and Expo (ICME)* (IEEE, New York, 2021), pp. 1–6
115. G. Liao, W. Gao, Rethinking feature mining for light field salient object detection, *ACM Transactions on Multimedia Computing, Communications, and Applications* (2024)
116. S. Sun, J. Liu, T. H. Li, H. Li, G. Liu, W. Gao, Streamflow: streamlined multi-frame optical flow estimation for video sequences. arXiv preprint arXiv:2311.17099 (2023)
117. R. Liu, J. Huang, W. Gao, T.H. Li, G. Li, Mug-STAN: adapting image-language pretrained models for general video understanding. arXiv preprint arXiv:2311.15075 (2023)
118. C. Zhang, W. Gao, Learned rate control for frame-level adaptive neural video compression via dynamic neural network, in *European Conference on Computer Vision* (Springer, Berlin, 2024)
119. Q. Hu, B. Yang, L. Xie, S. Rosa, Y. Guo, Z. Wang, N. Trigoni, A. Markham, Learning semantic segmentation of large-scale point clouds with random sampling. IEEE Trans. Pattern Anal. Mach. Intell. **44**(11), 8338–8354 (2022)
120. C.R. Qi, L. Yi, H. Su, L.J. Guibas, PointNet++: Deep hierarchical feature learning on point sets in a metric space. Adv. Neural Inf. Proces. Syst. **30**, 5099–5108 (2017)
121. F. Groh, P. Wieschollek, H.P.A. Lensch, Flex-convolution—million-scale point-cloud learning beyond grid-worlds, in *Asian Conference on Computer Vision*, vol. 11361 (2018), pp. 105–122
122. R. Bridson, Fast poisson disk sampling in arbitrary dimensions, in *International Conference on Computer Graphics and Interactive Techniques*, ed. by M. Alexa, A. Finkelstein (2007), p. 22
123. O. Dovrat, I. Lang, S. Avidan, Learning to sample, in *Proceedings of the IEEE Conference on Computer Vision and Pattern Recognition* (2019), pp. 2760–2769
124. M. F. Balın, A. Abid, J. Zou, Concrete autoencoders: differentiable feature selection and reconstruction, in *International Conference on Machine Learning* (2019), pp. 444–453
125. E. Nezhadarya, E. Taghavi, R. Razani, B. Liu, J. Luo, Adaptive hierarchical down-sampling for point cloud classification, in *Proceedings of the IEEE/CVF Conference on Computer Vision and Pattern Recognition* (2020), pp. 12953–12961
126. X. Wang, Y. Jin, Y. Cen, T. Wang, B. Tang, Y. Li, Lightn: light-weight transformer network for performance-overhead tradeoff in point cloud downsampling, in *IEEE Transactions on Multimedia* (2023), pp. 1–16
127. W. Yuan, T. Khot, D. Held, C. Mertz, M. Hebert, PCN: Point completion network, in *International Conference on 3D Vision* (2018), pp. 728–737
128. Y. Yang, C. Feng, Y. Shen, D. Tian, FoldingNet: point cloud auto-encoder via deep grid deformation, in *IEEE Conference on Computer Vision and Pattern Recognition* (2018), pp. 206–215
129. L.P. Tchapmi, V. Kosaraju, H. Rezatofighi, I.D. Reid, S. Savarese, TopNet: structural point cloud decoder, in *Proceedings of the IEEE/CVF Conference on Computer Vision and Pattern Recognition* (2019), pp. 383–392
130. W. Yan, R. Zhang, J. Wang, S. Liu, T.H. Li, G. Li, Vaccine-style-net: point cloud completion in implicit continuous function space, in *ACM International Conference on Multimedia* (2020), pp. 2067–2075
131. X. Han, Z. Li, H. Huang, E. Kalogerakis, Y. Yu, High-resolution shape completion using deep neural networks for global structure and local geometry inference, in *Proceedings of the IEEE International Conference on Computer Vision* (2017), pp. 85–93
132. H. Xie, H. Yao, S. Zhou, J. Mao, S. Zhang, W. Sun, Grnet: Gridding residual network for dense point cloud completion, in *European Conference on Computer Vision* (2020), pp. 365–381

133. Z. Huang, Y. Yu, J. Xu, F. Ni, X. Le, Pf-net: Point fractal network for 3d point cloud completion, in *Proceedings of the IEEE/CVF Conference on Computer Vision and Pattern Recognition* (2020), pp. 7662–7670
134. X. Wen, P. Xiang, Z. Han, Y.-P. Cao, P. Wan, W. Zheng, Y.-S. Liu, Pmp-net: Point cloud completion by learning multi-step point moving paths, in *Proceedings of the IEEE/CVF Conference on Computer Vision and Pattern Recognition* (2021), pp. 7443–7452
135. P. Xiang, X. Wen, Y.-S. Liu, Y.-P. Cao, P. Wan, W. Zheng, Z. Han, Snowflakenet: point cloud completion by snowflake point deconvolution with skip-transformer, in *Proceedings of the IEEE/CVF International Conference on Computer Vision* (2021), pp. 5499–5509
136. Y. Wang, D.J. Tan, N. Navab, F. Tombari, Learning local displacements for point cloud completion, in *Proceedings of the IEEE/CVF Conference on Computer Vision and Pattern Recognition* (2022), pp. 1568–1577
137. H. Zhou, Y. Cao, W. Chu, J. Zhu, T. Lu, Y. Tai, C. Wang, Seedformer: patch seeds based point cloud completion with upsample transformer, in *European Conference on Computer Vision* (2022), pp. 416–432
138. X. Yu, Y. Rao, Z. Wang, J. Lu, J. Zhou, Adapointr: diverse point cloud completion with adaptive geometry-aware transformers. IEEE Trans. Pattern Anal. Mach. Intell. **45**(12), 14114–14130 (2023)
139. C.R. Qi, H. Su, K. Mo, L.J. Guibas, PointNet: deep learning on point sets for 3D classification and segmentation, in *Proceedings of the IEEE Conference on Computer Vision and Pattern Recognition* (2017), pp. 652–660
140. R. Zhang, W. Gao, G. Li, T.H. Li, Qinet: decision surface learning and adversarial enhancement for quasi-immune completion of diverse corrupted point clouds. IEEE Trans. Geosci. Remote Sens. **60**, 1–14 (2022)
141. M. Sarmad, H.J. Lee, Y.M. Kim, RL-GAN-Net: a reinforcement learning agent controlled GAN network for real-time point cloud shape completion, in *Proceedings of the IEEE/CVF Conference on Computer Vision and Pattern Recognition* (2019), pp. 5891–5900
142. S. Fleishman, I. Drori, D. Cohen-Or, Bilateral mesh denoising. ACM Trans. Graph. **22**(3), 950–953 (2003)
143. P. Guerrero, Y. Kleiman, M. Ovsjanikov, N.J. Mitra, Pcpnet learning local shape properties from raw point clouds. Comput. Graphics Forum **37**(2), 75–85 (2018)
144. R. Roveri, A.C. Öztireli, I. Pandele, M.H. Gross, Pointpronets: consolidation of point clouds with convolutional neural networks. Comput. Graphics Forum **37**(2), 87–99 (2018)
145. D. Zhang, X. Lu, H. Qin, Y. He, Pointfilter: point cloud filtering via encoder-decoder modeling. IEEE Trans. Vis. Comput. Graph. **27**(3), 2015–2027 (2021)

Chapter 5
Deep-Learning-Based Point Cloud Analysis I

Abstract Point clouds serve not only as a type of spatiotemporal data but also as a 3D representation model, providing a fundamental method for 3D digitization and semantic expression. With the advancement of 3D equipment, such as LiDAR, the volume of point cloud data has been rapidly increasing, necessitating the use of deep-learning-based analytics to manage these data effectively. Consequently, point cloud machine vision analysis has garnered significant attention in the field of computer vision and various applications, including smart cities, digital preservation of cultural heritage, autonomous driving, film and television entertainment, and infrastructure security monitoring. In this chapter, we present a comprehensive overview of foundational methods for deep-learning-based point cloud analysis. We commence with an examination of traditional techniques for point cloud classification and semantic segmentation. This is followed by an exploration of methodologies for point cloud object detection and tracking. Each method is detailed starting with a problem statement, followed by an exposition of the general solution processes, representative works, and prevailing trends. Collectively, this chapter aims to elucidate the core methods underpinning deep-learning-based point cloud analysis.

Keywords Point cloud · Deep learning · Point cloud analysis · Point cloud tracking · Point cloud object detection · Point cloud segmentation · Feature extraction · Point cloud classification · Foundational tasks · Data understanding

5.1 Introduction

The advent of advanced 3D sensing technologies, such as LiDAR, has ushered in a deluge of point cloud data, necessitating robust analytics powered by deep learning. Point clouds, as a comprehensive spatiotemporal data structure, are crucial for a myriad of applications, demanding a transformative approach to their interpretation and utilization. The amalgamation of geometric intricacy and semantic information

W. Gao, G. Li, *Deep Learning for 3D Point Clouds*,
https://doi.org/10.1007/978-981-97-9570-3_5

within these datasets is a substantial asset across diverse fields, from autonomous driving to cultural heritage preservation.

In response to this burgeoning data landscape, there are concerted efforts within the research community to develop deep learning techniques adept at processing [1–8] and analyzing point clouds [9–13], which is similar to the successful efforts to image processing and analysis technologies [14–63]. These methodologies are pivotal for parsing the intricate nature of point cloud data, facilitating a transition from mere data collection to actionable insights. This chapter focuses on the confluence of deep learning and point cloud analytics [9, 10, 12, 64–69], addressing foundational tasks such as point cloud classification and semantic segmentation, which are essential for initial data understanding. We extend our discussion to encompass object detection and tracking, highlighting their significance in dynamic environment interpretation. Note that the low-level vision point cloud processing technologies, such as compression [7, 70–105] and enhancement [1, 2, 4, 13, 106–113], are the basics for the middle-level and high-level analysis technologies and may have mutual influences in the whole point cloud systems.

Throughout the chapter, each topic is systematically unpacked, beginning with a concise problem statement, followed by a discussion of general solution strategies, seminal contributions, and emerging trends. Our aim is to encapsulate the state-of-the-art in deep-learning-based point cloud analytics, setting the stage for future advancements in the field.

5.2 Point Cloud Classification and Segmentation

Point cloud classification aims to recognize the 3D point cloud object model into a specific class, which is the basis of the 3D vision task. Referring to image classification tasks for higher-level 2D image vision tasks (i.e., segmentation, detection, and tracking), point cloud classification dedicates to extracting the feature vectors of the point cloud, from which to identify the categories [69, 114, 115]. Furthermore, the classification method can be used as a feature extractor to serve higher-level 3D vision tasks.

Different from point cloud classification, which takes the whole object as the unit, the point cloud segmentation task is a point-level classification task, i.e., each point is categorized into related class, which mainly includes two subtasks: (1) part segmentation: the classification of different points of a single object [65]; (2) semantic segmentation: the classification of points in a scene [67, 68].

This section introduces these tasks in five parts, including definition of point cloud classification and segmentation, processing procedure, representative methods, evaluation metrics, datasets, and results.

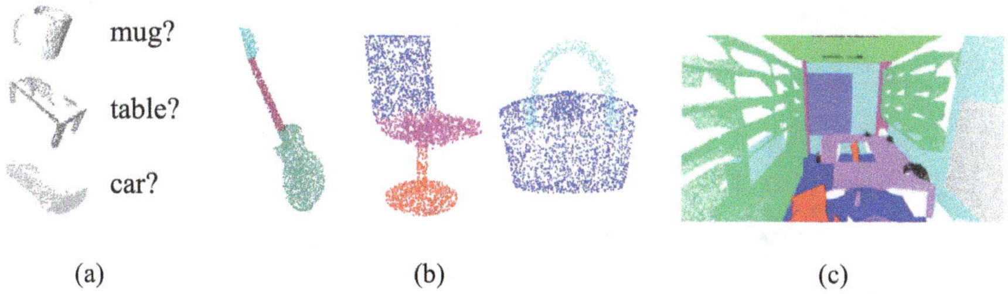

Fig. 5.1 Examples of point cloud classification and segmentation (©2017 IEEE. Reprinted, with permission, from ref. [116]). (**a**) Classification. (**b**) Part Segmentation. (**c**) Semantic Segmentation

5.2.1 Problem Formulation

Let $P = \{p_1, ..., p_n\}$ denote a set of n points, and we formulate the point cloud classification and segmentation tasks as follows:

- Suppose P is a point set of an object model (e.g., Fig. 5.1a), point cloud classification dedicates to assign one class label c to P.
- Suppose P is a point set of an object model (e.g., Fig. 5.1b) or a scene (e.g., Fig. 5.1c), point cloud segmentation dedicates to assign a class set $C = \{c_1, ..., c_n\}$ to P, i.e., each point p_i is categorized to predefined c_i. This task is defined as part segmentation for the object model case, while for the scene case, this task is defined as semantic segmentation.

5.2.2 Process Description

Generally, the processing pipeline of point cloud classification and segmentation consists of two parts: (1) extracting handcrafted or learned feature vectors from the point cloud; (2) using traditional machine learning or deep learning classifier to categorize points in terms of these feature vectors. As shown in Fig. 5.2, the classification branch directly adopts the downsampled global feature after symmetric feature aggregation, while the segmentation branch further conducts feature fusion by upsampling to acquire more precise feature information for point-wise classification.

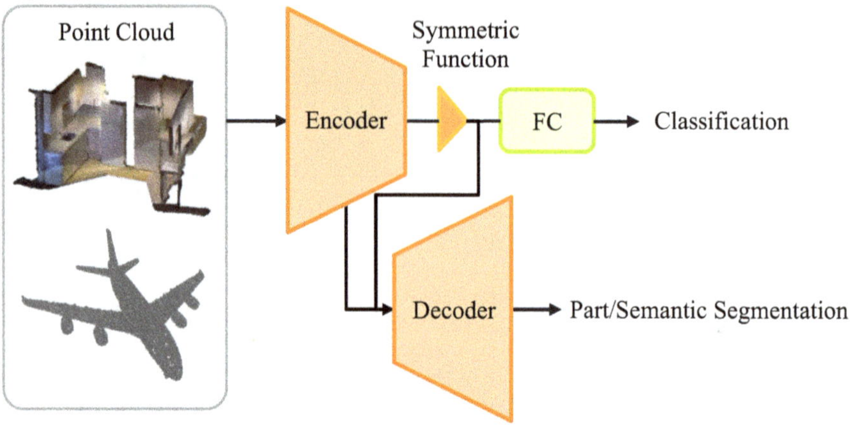

Fig. 5.2 General pipeline of point cloud classification and segmentation. Point cloud is processed by encoder to extract features and then decoded for final segmentation result. Source: Author

5.2.3 Categorization

According to the modeling type of feature extraction and processing, point cloud classification and segmentation methods can be divided into the following three categories:

- **View-based and Voxel-based Methods**

  Early methods directly project 3D point clouds into 2D images, then use 2D convolutional neural networks (CNN) for image classification to conduct point cloud classification [117, 118]. Since voxel can be deemed as the extension of pixel from 2D to 3D, promoting 2D CNN to 3D modality is another solution to deal with point cloud analysis [119]. Nevertheless, 3D CNN for point clouds is sparse and confronted with a large computational quantity. In addition, due to the sparse and uneven density distribution, both projection and dividing points to the voxel are not lossless. Hence, these view-based and voxel-based methods are not sufficiently effective to obtain satisfactory performances.

- **Point-based Methods**

  A pragmatic feature modeling approach for point cloud is adopting the point type directly. Charles R. Qi et al. propose PointNet [114], which employs the multilayer perceptron (MLP) to embed point features to high-dimension space. To solve the permutation invariance problem of the point cloud, PointNet uses max pooling as a readout layer to obtain the representative feature vectors. Compared with previous methods, PointNet alleviates the huge computation cost of 3D CNN and illustrates excellent classification performances. However, the individual treatment of each point in PointNet neglects the local and global relationship among points. To overcome this defect, Charles R. Qi et al. propose PointNet++ [120], which introduces multiscale auto-encoder architecture. Collecting multiscale features can solve the problem of uneven point cloud density. In recent years, these two methods have provided the foundation for deep-learning-based point cloud analysis. With the development of a vision transformer, Point Transformer [121] introduces a local vector attention mechanism on PointNet++, while Point Cloud Transformer [115] uses global attention. Both two transformer-based methods lead to a new type of backbone for point cloud analysis. Next, we will introduce three representative models in detail, including PointNet, PointNet++, and Point Transformer.

PointNet PointNet [114] is the milestone of deep-learning-based point cloud analysis methods and one of the main baselines for the following works. The architecture of PointNet is depicted in Fig. 5.3, which can be summarized into three parts as follows:

- Since point clouds described from different angles should be the same, PointNet set the T-Net structure to learn a transformation matrix to solve the permutation invariance of the point cloud. The matrix is actually 3×3 or 64×64, whose parameters are all learnable.
- The MLP layers are used to gradually increase the point cloud from 3 dimensions to 64 and 1024 dimensions. This step is similar to feature embedding by CNN, which increases the network complexity, learns the potential expression of point cloud features, and avoids the loss of too much information in the subsequent global max pooling operation.
- Use max pooling to reduce the $n \times 1024$ dimension feature to 1×1024, and then conduct classification or segmentation. This step needs to utilize symmetric functions, i.e. summation (Sum), maximum (Max), average (Avg), etc. The symmetric functions can ensure the same result of the point cloud described from different angles; that is, permutation invariance is solved.

To formulate the pipeline of PointNet, suppose the input n points $X = \{x_1, ..., x_n\}$, then the feature embedding is:

$$f(X) = g(h_\Theta(X)), \tag{5.1}$$

where $f(\cdot)$ is the feature embedding function of PointNet, $h_\Theta(\cdot)$ is the nonlinear transformation implemented by MLP, $g(\cdot)$ is the symmetric function. The main optimization object of PointNet is to learn Θ.

PointNet++ PointNet++ [120] is an improvement method based on PointNet. Since PointNet does not consider geometry characteristics and multiscale feature fusion during feature extraction, its performance is limited faced with uneven and disordered situations. Similar to mainstream 2D image classification and segmentation methods, PointNet++ introduces a hierarchical feature embedding autoencoder with a downsampling and an upsampling mechanism, as shown in Fig. 5.4.

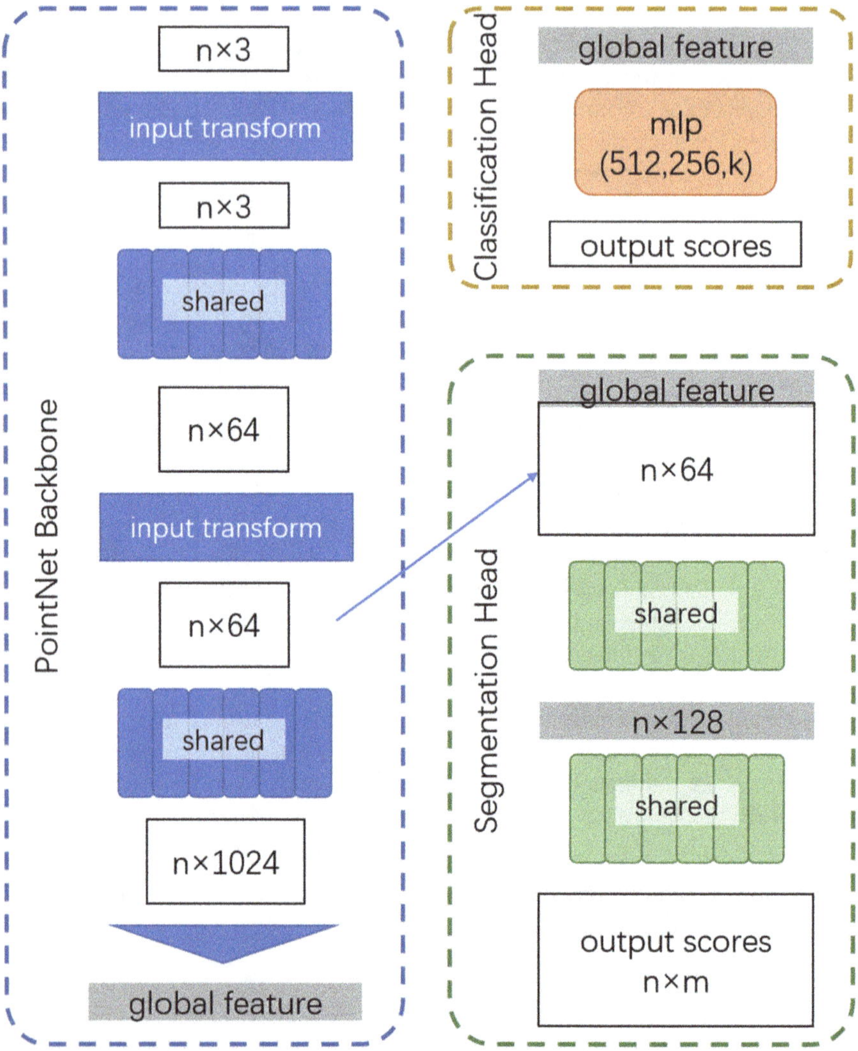

Fig. 5.3 The architecture of PointNet. T-Net structure is proposed to learn the transformetion matrix (©2017 IEEE. Reprinted, with permission, from ref. [114])

The basic feature extraction unit of PointNet++ is the set abstraction (SA) module, which consists of three parts as follows:

- **Sampling:** To acquire the centroid of each local region in a point set, the farthest point sampling (FPS) algorithm is adopted, which is better than random sampling due to the shape representation capability.
- **Grouping:** After the sampling operation, for each centroid, the SA module needs to group its neighboring points and build a local point subset. There are two

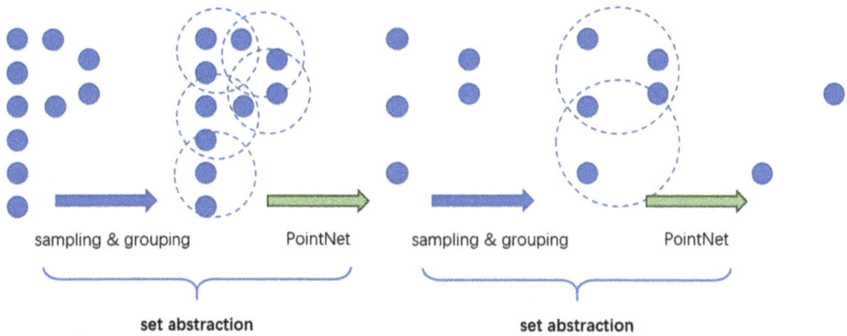

Fig. 5.4 The architecture of PointNet++, which introduces geometry characteristics and multi-scale feature fusion [120]. Source: Author

methods for selecting neighboring points. First, the k-nearest neighbor (kNN) algorithm calculates the k-nearest points to the centroid. Second, the ball query method selects all points with a distance d less than r from the centroids as neighboring points. In the experiment part, PointNet++ adopts the ball query method with better performance.

- **PointNet Feature Extraction:** SA module uses PointNet to extract features of each local region and update the feature of the centroid, then drop the neighboring points for downsampling. In the decoder, PointNet++ reconstructs the neighboring points by inverse distance-weighted average-based interpolation.

The SA module makes PointNet++ have better capability on local-global feature extraction compared with PointNet. Moreover, PointNet cannot solve the density variant of the point cloud. To alleviate this defect, PointNet++ proposes multiscale grouping and multiresolution grouping as follow:

- **Multi-scale Grouping:** For the same centroid, k of different orders of magnitude is used to form multiscale neighborhoods. Feature vectors containing multiscale information are obtained by concatenation after feature extraction by PointNet.
- **Multiresolution Grouping:** PointNet is used first to extract features from multiple point subsets and then used to extract updated features from each subset, and the features before and after are concatenated to obtain final feature vectors with multilevel information.

PointNet++ performs significantly better than PointNet on classification and segmentation tasks, but suffers from its complex hierarchical structure, the training time and testing time are much slower.

Point Transformer There are two types of self-attention operation in transformer: scalar attention [122] and vector attention [123]. Point Transformer [121] introduces the local vector attention to the SA module of PointNet++ architecture, which is suitable for building a local-to-global feature aggregation pipeline, as shown in Fig. 5.5. Let $\mathcal{X}$ be a set of feature vectors, $\mathcal{X}(i) \subseteq \mathcal{X}$ is a set of points in one local

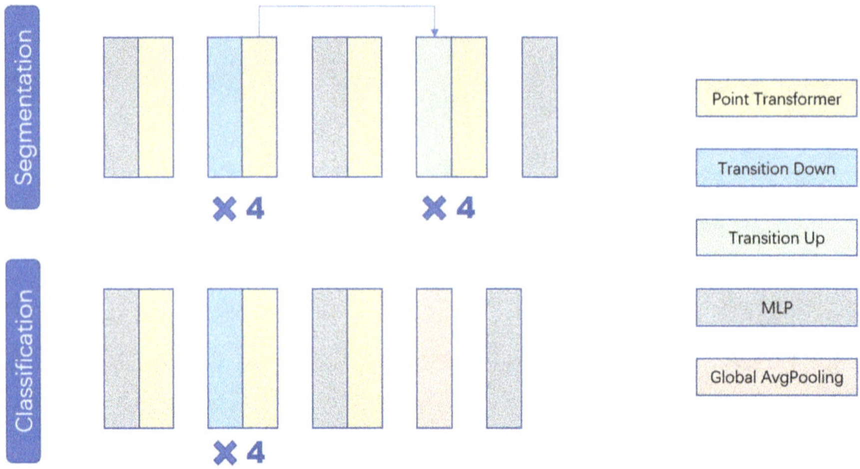

Fig. 5.5 The architecture of Point Transformer, which introduces the local vector attention to the SA module of PointNet++ architecture, which is suitable for building a local-to-global feature aggregation pipeline (©2021 IEEE. Reprinted, with permission, from ref. [121])

region by kNN, and $\mathbf{y}_i$ is the output feature, the self-attention of Point Transformer can be formulated as:

$$\mathbf{y}_i = \sum_{\mathbf{x}_j \in \mathcal{X}(i)} \rho\left(\gamma\left(\varphi\left(\mathbf{x}_i\right) - \psi\left(\mathbf{x}_j\right) + \delta\right)\right) \odot \left(\alpha\left(\mathbf{x}_j\right) + \delta\right) \tag{5.2}$$

where γ, φ and α are point-wise feature transformations implemented by linear projection, ρ is a mapping function implemented by MLP, and δ is the position encoding, which is defined by subtraction similar to EdgeConv in DGCNN [124]. The architecture of the point transformer layer is shown in Fig. 5.6.

The transition down and transition up layer is based on PointNet++. Benefit from better modeling the relationship among points from local to global by the attention mechanism. Point Transformer achieves better performances than PointNet++ in all vision tasks.

- **Graph-based Methods**

Graph is defined with edges and nodes, and thus, it is suitable to depict the permutation invariant point cloud data. To construct an edge on the point cloud, the relationship between point pairs can be established from handcrafted features. With the development of graph neural networks, applying graphs to point cloud analysis has become an emerging research direction. DGCNN [124] proposes EdgeConv, which uses graph and convolution operations to acquire point features. This work makes a summary of the graph-based point cloud analysis method and expresses this framework in the formula. DeepGCN [125] discusses how to make a deep

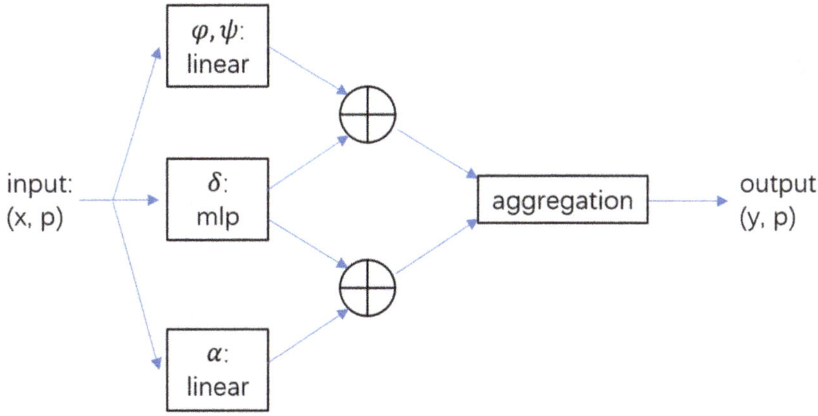

Fig. 5.6 The architecture of point transformer layer, which is defined by subtraction similar to EdgeConv in DGCNN [124] (©2021 IEEE. Reprinted, with permission, from ref. [121])

graph conventional neural network on the point cloud. Next, we will introduce the representative DGCNN [124] model.

DGCNN Based on PointNet as the backbone structure, DGCNN [124] proposes an edge convolution (EdgeConv) module based on graph neural network, which extends traditional convolution to point cloud with graph modeling and uses graph method to conduct feature aggregation of points. Moreover, the results are better than PointNet and PointNet++, and the speed is faster than PointNet++. The architecture of DGCNN is shown in Fig. 5.7.

The EdgeConv module can extract local geometric features with permutation invariance. After the center point i is determined, the kNN algorithm is used to compute the neighboring points, and then the edge feature e_{ij} between the center point and neighboring point j is embedded. The graph G is constructed for convolution operation. Since the neighbors need to be recalculated after each forward propagation stage, it is also called a dynamic graph. The schematic diagram of edge convolution is shown in Fig. 5.7. The convolution operation is represented by $h(\cdot, \cdot)$, which is implemented by MLP. The edge features can be expressed as follows:

$$e_{ij} = h(x_i, x_j - x_i), \tag{5.3}$$

where x_i, x_j denote the feature vector of point i and j, respectively. After constructing all edge features between center point i and its neighboring points, the symmetric function $g(\cdot)$ is utilized to build permutation invariance, and the new feature of point i is represented as:

$$x_i' = g(e_{ij}) = \max_{j:(i,j)\in\mathcal{E}} e_{ij} = \max_{j:(i,j)\in\mathcal{E}} h(x_i, x_j - x_i), \tag{5.4}$$

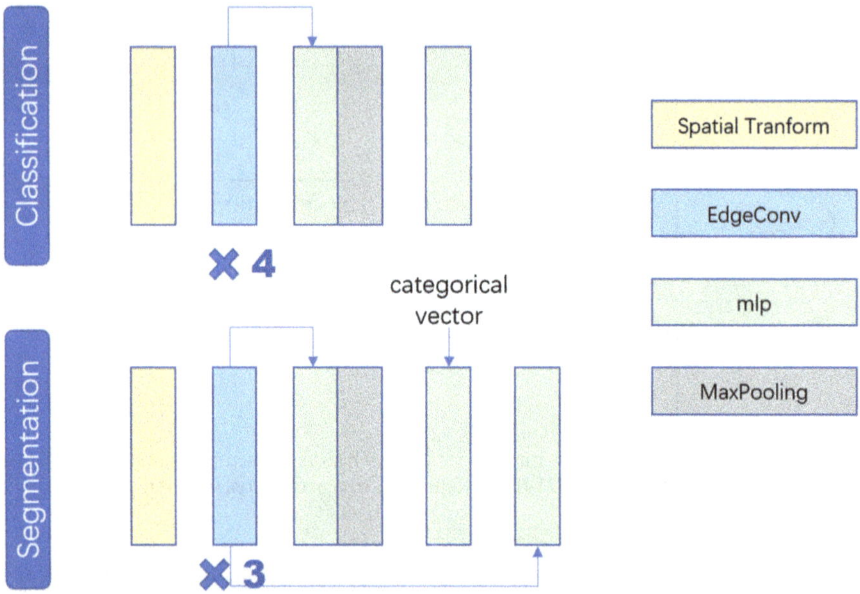

Fig. 5.7 The architecture of DGCNN [124]. Source: Author

Table 5.1 Comparison of some existing methods in graph modeling view. Source: Author

	Symmetric function	Edge function	Learnable parameters
PointNet	–	$h_\Theta(x_i, x_j) = h_\Theta(x_i)$	Θ
PointNet++	Max	$h_\Theta(x_i, x_j) = h_\Theta(x_j)$	Θ
DGCNN	Max	$h_\Theta(x_i, x_j) = h_\Theta(x_i, x_j - x_i)$	Θ

where $x_i^{'}$ is the feature representation of global information, while $x_j - x_i$ is local feature within neighbor. Equation (5.4) is a general type of graph convolution on a point cloud. Furthermore, traditional convolution is one of EgdeConv's specific forms, i.e. $h(\cdot, \cdot)$ is multiplication and $g(\cdot) = \sum$. As shown in Table 5.1, PointNet and PointNet++ can be abstracted as Eq. (5.4).

5.2.4 Evaluation Metrics

- **Point Cloud Classification**

The evaluation metrics of point cloud classification follow the general setting of classification. Classification result evaluation involves four cases: True Positive (TP), True Negative (TN), False Positive (FP), and False Negative (FN). The accuracy is defined as:

$$accuracy = \frac{TP + TN}{TP + TN + FP + FN}. \tag{5.5}$$

Let $C = \{c_1, ..., c_n\}$ denote the set of all classes, s_{ij} denotes the number of points which belong to class i but are predicted to class j, we can get two types of accuracy on point cloud classification:

$$mean\ class\ accuracy\ (mA) = \frac{1}{n+1}\sum_{i=1}^{n}\frac{s_{ii}}{\sum_{j=1}^{n} s_{ij}}, \tag{5.6}$$

$$overall\ accuracy\ (oA) = \frac{\sum_{i=1}^{n} s_{ii}}{\sum_{i=1}^{n}\sum_{j=1}^{n} s_{ij}}. \tag{5.7}$$

- **Point Cloud Segmentation**

The evaluation metrics of point cloud segmentation extend the segmentation metric intersection over union (IoU) to points situation. The IoU of A and B is defined as:

$$IoU(A, B) = \frac{|A \cap B|}{|A \cup B|}. \tag{5.8}$$

Following the symbol hypothesis mentioned in the classification part, we can get the accuracy and mean class intersection over union (mIoU) for the segmentation task:

$$overall\ accuracy\ (oA) = \frac{\sum_{i=1}^{n} s_{ii}}{\sum_{i=1}^{n}\sum_{j=1}^{n} s_{ij}}, \tag{5.9}$$

$$mIoU = \frac{1}{n+1}\sum_{i=1}^{n}\frac{s_{ii}}{\sum_{j=1}^{n} s_{ij} + \sum_{j=1}^{n} s_{ji} - s_{ii}}. \tag{5.10}$$

Notice that the class set is at point level rather than object level compared with the classification task.

5.2.5 Datasets and Results

- **Point Cloud Classification**

In terms of recent point cloud classification works, there are three mainstream benchmarks, namely ModelNet40 [126], ShapeNet [127], and ScanObjectNN [128]. The first two datasets are generated from computer-aided design (CAD) models,

Table 5.2 Comparison of point cloud classification dataset. It includes task categories, data types (DT), Number of Samples (NS), Number of Classes (NC), and Sampling Density (SD). Source: Author

Dataset	DT	NS	NC	SD
ModelNet40 [126]	CAD	12308	40	2048
ShapeNet [127]	CAD	57448	55	2048
ScanObjectNN [128]	Real-world	~15000	15	–

Table 5.3 Comparison of point cloud segmentation dataset. It includes task categories, data types (DT), Number of Samples (NS), Number of Classes (NC), and Sampling Density (SD). Source: Author

Dataset	Task	DT	NS	NC	SD
ShapeNetPart [127]	Part	CAD	16881 (objects)	16	2048
S3DIS [129]	Semantic	CAD	272 (scenes)	55	4096
ScanNet [130]	Semantic	Real-world	1613 (scenes)	21	–

while the last one is scanned indoor scene data. The detailed comparison of the three datasets is demonstrated in Table 5.2.

- **Point Cloud Segmentation**

For the point cloud part segmentation task, the main benchmark is ShapeNet-Part [127], which consists of 16881 CAD models in 16 object categories, and each category is annotated to $2 \sim 6$ parts. For the point cloud semantic segmentation task, there are two mainstream datasets, namely The Stanford 3D Indoor Segmentation (S3DIS) dataset [129] and ScanNet [130]. S3DIS contains 6 indoor areas with 271 rooms, with 13 categories and 9 dimensions information for each point (i.e. XYZ, RGB and normalized XYZ), and the sampling density is 4096 points. ScanNet is an RGB-D image dataset, which can be converted to point cloud type. There are 1513 scenes in ScanNet with 21 categories. The detailed comparison of the three datasets is demonstrated in Table 5.3.

5.2.6 *Summary of Existing Methods*

As shown in Table 5.4, we make a summary and comparison of some existing methods aforementioned, compare their performances on point cloud classification and segmentation, and analyze their merits and demerits with application suggestions.

Table 5.4 Summary of some existing point cloud classification and segmentation methods. Cls, Sem Seg, and Part Seg are the abbreviations for classification, semantic segmentation, and part segmentation, respectively. Classification is evaluated by overall accuracy on ModelNet40. Semantic segmentation is evaluated by sixfold mIoU on S3DIS. Part segmentation is evaluated by instance mIoU on ShapeNetPart. For simplicity, the '%' after each value is omitted, and '-' denotes the results are not available. Source: Author

	Performances					
Methods	Cls	Sem Seg	Part Seg	Advantages	Disadvantages	Applicable Scenarios
VoxNet [119]	83.0	–	–	High efficiency in 3D CNN methods	Not available for segmentation tasks	Voxel-based classification
PointNet [114]	89.2	47.6	83.7	Fast inference speed (6.8ms on Cls)	Limited performances and large model size (40MB)	Computationally constrained situations
PointNet++ [120]	90.7	54.5	85.1	First hierarchical architecture with multi-scale feature aggregation	Slow inference speed (163.2ms on Cls)	Uneven and disordered point cloud situations
PTrans [121]	93.7	73.5	86.6	Best performances	Limited training efficiency and inference speed	Task performances first situations
DGCNN [124]	92.2	56.1	85.1	Nice trade-off in performances (21MB model size with 27.2ms forward time on Cls)	Limited training stability	Task performances and efficiency trade-off situations
PTM [131]	93.1	–	–	Best classification performance in MLP methods	Not available for segmentation tasks	MLP-based classification

5.3 Point Cloud Object Detection

Point cloud object detection is one of the most fundamental and challenging problems in 3D computer vision, aiming to locate object instances from a large number of predefined categories in natural scenes. Point cloud object detection supports a wide range of applications, including robot vision, consumer electronics, security, autonomous driving, human–computer interaction, content-based image retrieval, intelligent video surveillance, and augmented reality [66, 132, 133]. Compared to images, 3D point clouds can provide detailed geometry and capture 3D structure of the scene. On the other hand, point clouds are irregular and cannot be processed by powerful deep-learning models. This poses a big challenge for effective feature learning.

5.3.1 Problem Formulation

Object detection is an essential branch of computer vision. 3D object detection takes the scene's point cloud as input and generates an oriented 3D bounding box around each object being detected. Compared to image-based object detection, LiDAR point clouds provide reliable depth information, which can be utilized for the precise localization and shape description of objects. However, unlike images, LiDAR point clouds are sparse and exhibit nonuniform point density due to factors such as the nonuniform sampling of the 3D space, the limited sensing range of the sensors, occlusions, and relative pose variations.

Given a raw point cloud $P = \{p_i | i = 1, \ldots, N\}$, where each point p_i is represented by its coordinates (x_i, y_i, z_i) and potentially additional features such as intensity or reflectance, the task is to identify a set of objects $O = \{O_j | j = 1, \ldots, M\}$. Each detected object O_j is characterized by a tuple (C_j, B_j), with C_j denoting the class label and B_j describing the parameters of an oriented 3D bounding box.

A 3D bounding box B_j is typically parameterized by its center (c_x, c_y, c_z), dimensions (d_x, d_y, d_z), and orientation θ, the latter of which is often represented by a rotation matrix or a quaternion to mitigate angle representation discontinuities. A typical 3D object detector takes the point cloud of a scene as its input and produces an oriented 3D bounding box, as shown in Fig. 5.8.

5.3.2 Process Description

The 3D point cloud object detection method generally consists of three parts, i.e., data representation, feature extraction, and detection network. The details of each part are illustrated as follows.

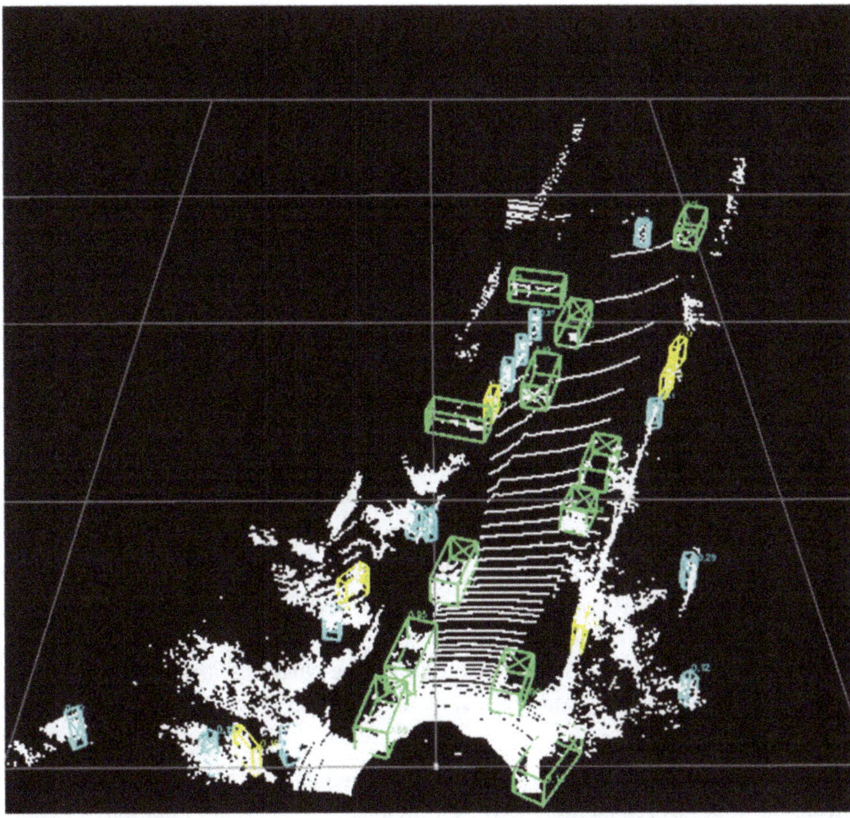

Fig. 5.8 An illustration of 3D object detection. Source: Author

In the data representation phase, raw point cloud data are preprocessed and organized into a format suitable for further processing, such as voxel grids, octrees, or simply maintaining the raw point cloud structure. This stage may also involve normalization, augmentation, and other techniques to enhance data quality and robustness.

Feature extraction follows, where the processed point cloud data are passed through various algorithms or neural network architectures to capture meaningful features. Techniques like PointNet, PointNet++, or graph-based networks are commonly employed to extract local and global features from the point clouds. These features are crucial for accurately identifying and classifying objects within the 3D space.

Finally, in the detection network phase, the extracted features are utilized to detect and classify objects. This involves using region proposal networks, bounding box regression, and classification layers to identify the objects' locations and categories within the point cloud. Advanced models may integrate multiscale feature extraction and hierarchical structures to improve detection accuracy and efficiency. Overall, the synergy of these three components enables effective and precise 3D object detection in various applications, from autonomous driving to robotic navigation.

5.3.3 Categorization

Among point cloud object detection methods, data representation includes voxel-based, point-based, and point-based & voxel-based. Data feature extraction includes point level, object level, classification level, 2D-CNN, 3D-CNN, and other methods. The detection module has two-stage detection based on the recommended area, frameless detection, sliding window, and hybrid methods.

- **Voxel-based Methods**

The voxel-based point cloud object detection framework consists of the following three parts:

- Encoder (feature coding) encodes point clouds into sparse pseudo images.
- The intermediate network (for feature extraction) extract feature of the pseudo image using the backbone network.
- Region Proposal Network (RPN) is used for the classification and regression of 3D frames, which can be an improvement of detection heads such as SSD [134] and FPN [135].

VoxelNet [132] is the earliest proposed method that converts point clouds into voxels for 3D object detection. VoxelNet divides the 3D point cloud into a certain number of voxels, then conducts random sampling and normalization, extracts non-empty voxel features from 3D convolution network to obtain voxel-wise features, and finally uses RPN to classify and detect objects and regress their positions. Its network architecture is shown in Fig. 5.9.

On the basis of VoxelNet [132], SECOND [136] takes into account the sparsity of point cloud features and replaces traditional convolution with 2D sparse convolution, which gives a great hint of speed. PointPillar [137] does not split the vertical

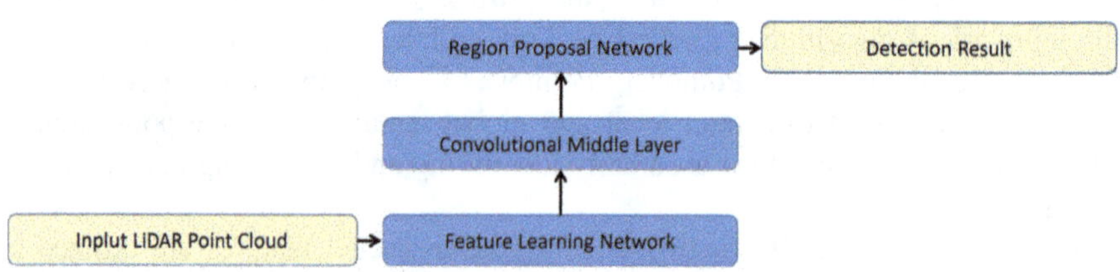

Fig. 5.9 The architecture of VoxelNet (©2018 IEEE. Reprinted, with permission, from ref. [132])

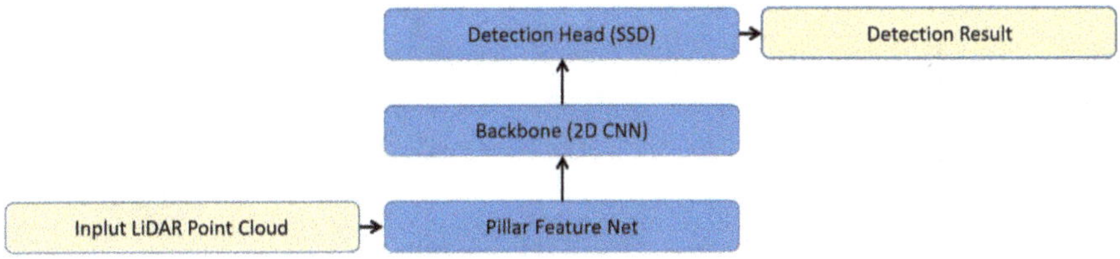

Fig. 5.10 The architecture of PointPillar (©2019 IEEE. Reprinted, with permission, from ref. [137])

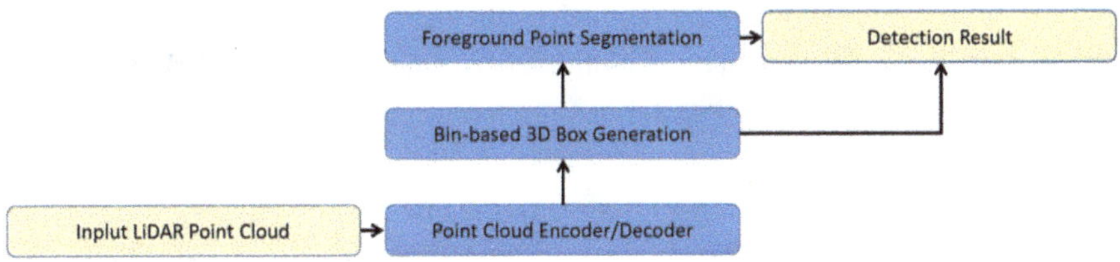

Fig. 5.11 The architecture of PointRCNN (©2023 IEEE. Reprinted, with permission, from ref. [133])

column of voxels and removes the 3D convolution, further improving the detection speed. The network architecture of PointPillar [137] is shown in Fig. 5.10.

- **Point-based Methods**

This kind of method does not voxelize the point cloud data but directly processes the original point cloud data.

PointRCNN [133] is a two-stage object detection network. The Stage-1 network uses PointNet++ [120] to extract features and segment front and rear points and directly generates a 3D proposal from the point cloud in a bottom-up manner. The Stage-2 network combines semantic features with local spatial features and optimizes the proposal in standard coordinates. The network structure of PointRCNN [133] is shown in Fig. 5.11.

- **Point-based & Voxel-based Methods**

PV-RCNN [138] first uses 3D voxel CNNs as the backbone network to generate high-quality proposals. Then, in order to pool point cloud features fully and effectively in each proposal, two new pooling methods are proposed: voxel to key point scene encoding and key point to grid region of interest (ROI) feature abstraction. The two pooling methods can effectively improve the prediction reliability and optimize the object location.

The highlight of PV-RCNN [138] is the acquisition of key points, which can not only optimize the proposal but also save computing and memory resources. In addition, PV-RCNN [138] uses multiscale receiver fields in a key point feature fusion and proposed optimization steps, which can obtain richer context information

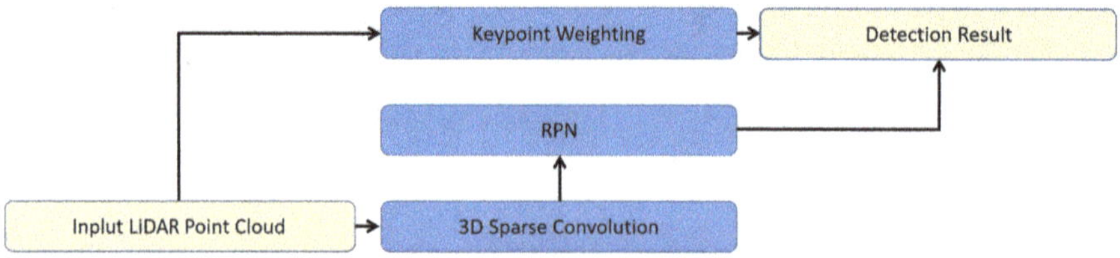

Fig. 5.12 The architecture of PV-RCNN (©2020 IEEE. Reprinted, with permission, from ref. [138])

and promote the improvement of recognition performance. The network structure of PV-RCNN [138] is shown in Fig. 5.12.

5.3.4 Evaluation Metrics

For 3D point cloud detection, Average Precision (AP) is the most frequently used criterion, which is calculated as the area under the precision–recall curve. This metric provides a comprehensive evaluation of the detection model's performance by considering both precision and recall across different thresholds. Higher AP values indicate better performance, reflecting the model's ability to accurately identify and localize objects within the 3D space.

In addition to AP, other metrics such as Mean Average Precision (mAP), Intersection over Union (IoU), and F1 score are often used to provide a more nuanced understanding of a model's capabilities. These metrics help in assessing different aspects of detection performance, such as localization accuracy and robustness to varying object sizes and densities. By leveraging these evaluation criteria, researchers and practitioners can benchmark and improve their 3D point cloud detection models more effectively.

5.3.5 Datasets

According to recent object detection tasks based on LiDAR [133, 137, 138], three large-scale datasets are usually applied as the benchmark, namely KITTI [139], Nuscenes [140], and Waymo [141]. KITTI [139]is proposed in 2012, captured by a standard station wagon equipped with two cameras, a Velodyne laser scanner, and a GPS localization system driving in different outdoor scenes. Nuscenes [140] is proposed in 2019, captured with full sensor suite (1x LiDAR, 5x RADAR, 6x camera, IMU,GPS); 1000 scenes of 20s each. Waymo [141] is captured with 1 midrange LiDAR, 4 short-range LiDARs and 5 cameras (front and sides); 1,950 segments of 20s each, collected at 10 Hz.

Table 5.5 Comparison of point cloud object detection algorithms. The algorithms are evaluated based on object detection accuracy, efficiency, and their applicability in different scenarios. Source: Author

Methods	Performance		Advantages	Disadvantages	Applicable Scenarios
	Accuracy	Efficiency			
VoxelNet [132]	High	Moderate	Effective in dense point clouds	High computational cost	Urban environments
PointPillars [137]	Moderate	High	Fast processing speed Efficient in sparse point clouds	Less effective in dense environments	Highway and open-road scenarios
PointRCNN [133]	High	Moderate	Accurate in 3D object localization and classification	Requires high computational resources	Detailed object detection tasks
PV-RCNN [138]	Very High	Low	Highly accurate Integrates voxel and point features	Very computationally intensive	High-precision detection tasks

5.3.6 *Summary of Existing Methods*

Table 5.5 provides a comparative analysis of various point cloud object detection algorithms, focusing on their accuracy, efficiency, advantages, disadvantages, and applicable scenarios. VoxelNet [132] is highlighted for its high accuracy and moderate efficiency. It is particularly effective in dense point clouds, making it suitable for urban environments. However, it has a high computational cost. PointPillars [137] offers moderate accuracy with high efficiency, making it efficient in sparse point clouds and suitable for highway and open-road scenarios. Its fast processing speed is an advantage, although it is less effective in dense environments. PointRCNN [133] is noted for its high accuracy and moderate efficiency. It excels in 3D object localization and classification, making it ideal for detailed object detection tasks. The downside is its requirement for high computational resources. PV-RCNN [138] achieves very high accuracy but has low efficiency due to its computational intensity. It integrates voxel and point features effectively, making it suitable for high-precision detection tasks.

5.4 Point Cloud Tracking

Point cloud tracking is a critical task in computer vision, focusing on the temporal alignment of point cloud frames to monitor the motion and transformation of objects or the environment over time. This task is pivotal in applications such as autonomous navigation, augmented reality, and robotics, where understanding dynamic changes in 3D space is essential for interaction and decision-making.

Tracking in point clouds involves establishing correspondences between points in consecutive frames, often amidst noise, occlusions, and changing point densities. The primary challenge lies in the high dimensionality of the data and the computational complexity of processing it in real time. The task becomes even more daunting when dealing with unstructured environments where objects have non-rigid deformations or when the viewpoint changes significantly between frames.

5.4.1 Problem Formulation

Given the position of the target in the first frame, the task of target tracking is to estimate its state in subsequent frames. Because 3D target tracking can make use of the rich geometric information in point clouds, it can overcome the shortcomings of image-based target tracking such as occlusion, illumination, and scale change.

Given a temporally ordered sequence of point cloud frames $\mathcal{F} = \{F_1, F_2, \ldots, F_t\}$, where each frame F_t is composed of a set of points $P_t = \{p_i^t \mid i = 1, \ldots, N_t\}$, with each point p_i^t defined by its 3D coordinates (x_i^t, y_i^t, z_i^t).

The challenge is to develop a tracking algorithm $\mathcal{T}$ that aligns the point clouds over time, managing the correspondences between points or sets of points $C_{t-1} \subseteq P_{t-1}$ from the previous frame F_{t-1} to points $C_t \subseteq P_t$ in the current frame F_t, under conditions of noise, varying densities, occlusions, and non-rigid object transformations. The outcome of this tracking process is a set of trajectories $\Theta = \{\theta_j \mid j = 1, \ldots, M\}$, with each trajectory θ_j representing the motion path of an object or point of interest.

The point cloud tracking task demonstrates how the algorithm navigates the point cloud frames in the sequence as shown in Fig. 5.13. The left part red 3D bounding box is the tracking object with its moving trajectory map in the middle. The right part shows the real video.

5.4.2 Process Description

Usually, three steps are involved in the point cloud tracking process. Step 1: Extract the compact representations of the first frames and the candidates. Step 2: Search the location of the tracked object in the next frame. Step 3: Refine the tracking results.

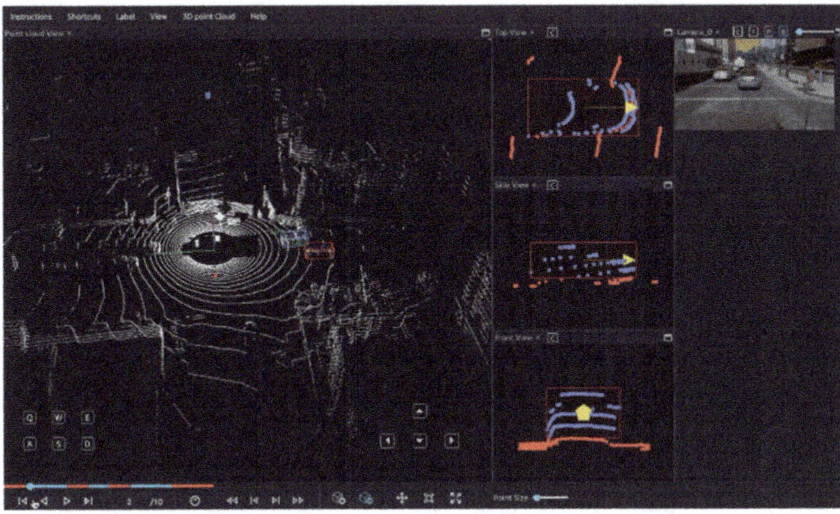

Fig. 5.13 Point cloud tracking. Public domain open access image (https://docs.aws.amazon.com/sagemaker/latest/dg/sms-point-cloud-object-tracking.html)

5.4.3 Categorization

According to the matching method in the tracking algorithm, the point cloud target tracking based on deep learning can be divided into two categories: Detection-based tracking and Tracking-based on the Siamese framework.

- **Detection-based Tracking**

Detection-based methods usually have more than one tracking object. The idea can be summarized as one target detection for each frame to get some boxes, and then the box of the same object in different frames is associated to form a trajectory.

PointTrackNet [142] uses PointNet++ for foreground and background segmentation and uses a detection algorithm to detect objects at foreground points. The consecutive frames are put into the network to predict the motion of objects, and then the object matching and trajectory generation between different frames are realized. Instead of using the traditional Kalman filter and particle filter to predict the trajectory, PointTrackNet [142] puts two frames into the network to predict the displacement at the point level and then predicts the trajectory. The structure of PointTrackNet is shown in Fig. 5.14.

The feature extraction module produces both point-wise mask and object-bounding boxes. The input of this module is $N \times 3$ point cloud data, and the output mask $N \times 2$ and M boxes. The association module has a probability filter to reserve the high-probability foreground points and an association head to fuse the features of the two frames. The refinement module outputs the point-wise tracking association

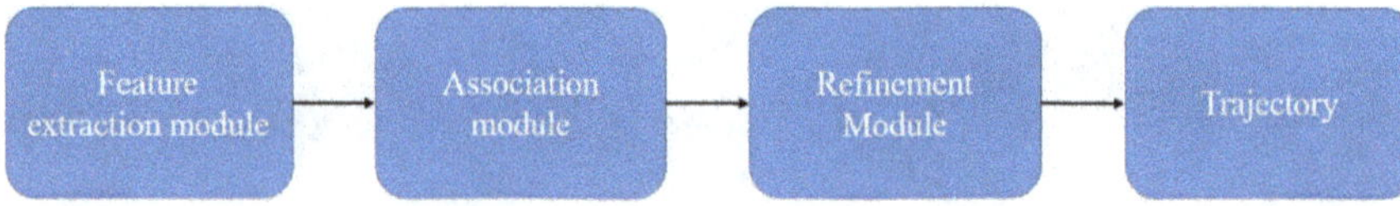

Fig. 5.14 The architecture of PointTrackNet. The pipeline of the network structure consists of four modules: Feature extraction module, association module, refinement Module, and trajectory generator (©2020 IEEE. Reprinted, with permission, from ref. [142])

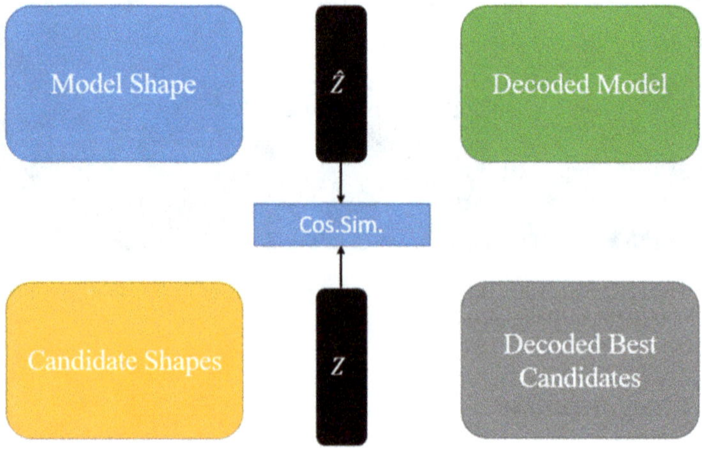

Fig. 5.15 The architecture of SC3D (©2019 IEEE. Reprinted, with permission, from ref. [143])

displacements. Trajectory generator matches the same object and visualizes the bird's-eye-view and 3-D trajectories.

- **Tracking based on The Siamese Framework**

The target tracking method based on the Siamese framework is to transplant the tracking method of Siamese in 2D to 3D point cloud data. The main idea is to calculate the point cloud features of different locations in the search area and the point cloud features of the template area. Then the cross-correlation calculation of the obtained features is carried out to find the place with the largest response value as the target point.

SC3D [143] proposes a completion based on the shape of single object tracking. The geometric features calculated from sparse point clouds are sent into the Siamese network to create a potential representation by using a shape completion network. The cosine similarity is used to match part of the point cloud to the model shape. Then, the coding is regularized through the automatic encoder network to generate a potential representation with geometric significance. It hopes to enrich the potential representation by using the semantic and geometric information from the given object, so as to improve the tracking performance. An overview of SC3D [143] network is shown in Fig. 5.15.

5.4.4 Evaluation Metrics

Precision and success are commonly used to evaluate the overall performance of a 3D single object tracker. Average Multi-Object Tracking Accuracy (AMOTA) and Average Multi-Object Tracking Precision (AMOTP) are the most frequently used criteria for the evaluation of 3D multi-object tracking.

5.4.5 Datasets

Recent advancements in LiDAR-based object tracking have relied on a few extensive datasets to benchmark performance. These datasets are KITTI, NuScenes, and Waymo, each offering unique characteristics and challenges for tracking algorithms. The KITTI dataset [139], introduced in 2012, was recorded using a standard station wagon outfitted with a Velodyne laser scanner, a pair of cameras, and a GPS system to capture outdoor driving scenarios. It provides a rich source of data for the development and testing of tracking systems under various environmental conditions. NuScenes [140], released in 2019, expands on the concept with a comprehensive sensor suite that includes a LiDAR, multiple RADAR units, and cameras, along with inertial measurement units (IMU) and GPS for precise localization. This dataset consists of 1000 diverse urban scenes, each recorded for 20 seconds, offering a substantial amount of data to train and evaluate tracking models. Similarly, the Waymo dataset [141], also introduced in 2019, provides a detailed collection of urban driving scenarios. It is characterized by its use of multiple LiDAR sensors and cameras, which capture data at 10 frames per second. The dataset comprises 1950 segments, each 20 seconds long, providing a large volume of high-quality data for the research community to develop and refine object tracking technologies. Together, these datasets form a cornerstone for the evaluation and comparison of state-of-the-art object tracking methods in the field of autonomous driving and computer vision, emphasizing the importance of diverse and challenging datasets for advancing tracking algorithms.

5.4.6 Summary of Existing Methods

Deep learning has revolutionized point cloud tracking with its ability to learn complex representations directly from data. Deep neural networks can automatically extract high-level features from point clouds, capturing intricate geometric and topological properties. These features are more discriminative than traditional handcrafted features, leading to improved tracking performance. Siamese Networks are trained to learn a similarity metric between two point clouds. They consist of two identical subnetworks sharing weights, which process a pair of point clouds and output a similarity score, useful for tracking by matching points across frames. Treating point clouds as graphs, GCNs can effectively capture the spatial relationships between points. They are particularly powerful for tracking non-rigid deformations and motions in 3D data. PointNet can learn a global feature representation of a point cloud, while PointNet++ enhances it by exploiting local features through a hierarchical structure. Both are capable of encoding point clouds into a feature space conducive to tracking. Recently, attention mechanisms from transformers have been adapted for point cloud processing. They can model the relationships between points in a permutation-invariant manner, which is beneficial for tracking objects without a fixed structure. These deep-learning-based methods are pushing the boundaries of point cloud tracking by providing more accurate, efficient, and robust solutions compared to traditional algorithms. They are particularly effective in handling noisy data, complex motions, and real-time tracking requirements in applications like autonomous driving and robotics.

5.5 Summary

In conclusion, this chapter has provided an extensive exploration of deep-learning-based techniques for point cloud analysis, emphasizing the various methods tailored to different scenarios. We have delved into critical areas such as 3D point cloud classification and segmentation, object detection and tracking. Each section systematically elucidated the significance of these techniques and their specific implementation procedures. By understanding these methodologies' theoretical and practical aspects, readers are equipped with a comprehensive understanding of the diverse approaches in point cloud machine vision analysis. This foundation empowers readers to apply and innovate within this dynamic field, advancing the capabilities of point cloud processing in applications ranging from autonomous driving to robotics. Through this detailed examination, we highlight the pivotal role of deep learning in enhancing the precision and robustness of point cloud interpretations, driving forward the frontier of 3D data analysis.

Exercises

1. What are the primary challenges in applying deep learning to point cloud data?
2. How does deep learning facilitate classification in point clouds?
3. What role does semantic segmentation play in point cloud analytics?
4. What are the key approaches in deep learning for object detection in point clouds?
5. How does PointNet++ enhance the features extracted by PointNet?
6. Please discuss the concept of voxel-based methods for point cloud analysis as mentioned in the chapter. What are their limitations?

7. What is the primary advantage of using graph-based methods for point cloud analysis?
8. Please describe the evaluation metrics used for point cloud classification and segmentation tasks.
9. What datasets are commonly used for benchmark point cloud classification?
10. Please explain the importance of feature extraction in point cloud object detection as outlined in the chapter.

References

1. Z. Li, G. Li, T. H. Li, S. Liu, W. Gao, Semantic point cloud upsampling. IEEE Trans. Multimedia **25**, 3432–3442 (2022)
2. R. Bao, Y. Ren, G. Li, W. Gao, S. Liu, Flow-based point cloud completion network with adversarial refinement, in *ICASSP 2022-2022 IEEE International Conference on Acoustics, Speech and Signal Processing (ICASSP)* (IEEE, New York, 2022), pp. 2559–2563
3. W. Zhao, X. Liu, Z. Zhong, J. Jiang, W. Gao, G. Li, X. Ji, Self-supervised arbitrary-scale point clouds upsampling via implicit neural representation, in *Proceedings of the IEEE/CVF Conference on Computer Vision and Pattern Recognition* (2022), pp. 1999–2007
4. J. Chen, G. Li, R. Zhang, T.H. Li, W. Gao, Pointivae: Invertible variational autoencoder framework for 3d point cloud generation, in *2022 IEEE International Conference on Image Processing (ICIP)* (IEEE, New York, 2022), pp. 3216–3220
5. W. Gao, H. Ye, G. Li, H. Zheng, Y. Wu, L. Xie, OpenPointCloud: An open-source algorithm library of deep learning based point cloud compression, in *ACM International Conference on Multimedia* (2022), pp. 7347–7350
6. Y. Zhang, W. Gao, G. Li, Openpointcloud-v2: A deep learning based open-source algorithm library of point cloud processing, in *Proceedings of the 1st International Workshop on Advances in Point Cloud Compression, Processing and Analysis* (2022), pp. 51–55
7. F. Song, G. Li, X. Yang, W. Gao, S. Liu, Block-adaptive point cloud attribute coding with region-aware optimized transform, in *IEEE Transactions on Circuits and Systems for Video Technology* (2023)
8. Y. Wang, W. Gao, X. Mu, H. Yuan, Rate control optimization for joint geometry and attribute coding of lidar point clouds, in *2023 IEEE International Conference on Visual Communications and Image Processing (VCIP)* (IEEE, New York, 2023), pp. 1–5
9. K. Wen, N. Zhang, G. Li, W. Gao, MPVNN: Multi-resolution point-voxel non-parametric network for 3d point cloud processing, in *2024 IEEE International Conference on Multimedia and Expo (ICME)* (IEEE, New York, 2024).
10. Z. Pan, G. Liu, W. Gao, T. Li, Epcontrast: effective point-level contrastive learning for large-scale point cloud understanding, in *2024 IEEE International Conference on Multimedia and Expo (ICME)* (IEEE, New York, 2024)
11. R. Zhang, G. Li, W. Gao, T.H. Li, Compoint: can complex-valued representation benefit point cloud place recognition? in *IEEE Transactions on Intelligent Transportation Systems* (2024)
12. S. Luo, W. Gao, A general framework for rotation invariant point cloud analysis, in *ICASSP 2024-2024 IEEE International Conference on Acoustics, Speech and Signal Processing (ICASSP)* (IEEE, New York, 2024), pp. 3665–3669
13. J. Wang, W. Gao, G. Li, Applying collaborative adversarial learning to blind point cloud quality measurement, in *IEEE Transactions on Instrumentation and Measurement* (2023)
14. B. Qu, X. Liang, S. Sun, W. Gao, Exploring aigc video quality: a focus on visual harmony, video-text consistency and domain distribution gap, in *Proceedings of the IEEE/CVF Conference on Computer Vision and Pattern Recognition Workshops* (2024)

15. B. Qu, H. Li, W. Gao, Bringing textual prompt to AI-generated image quality assessment, in *2024 IEEE International Conference on Multimedia and Expo (ICME)* (IEEE, 2024)
16. Y. Wu, L. Xie, S. Sun, W. Gao, Y. Yan, Adaptive intra period size for deep learning-based screen content video coding, in *2024 IEEE International Conference on Multimedia and Expo Workshops (ICMEW)* (IEEE, New York, 2024)
17. H. Zheng, W. Gao, End-to-end rgb-d image compression via exploiting channel-modality redundancy, in *Proceedings of the AAAI Conference on Artificial Intelligence*, vol. 38(7) (2024), pp. 7562–7570
18. L. Tao, W. Gao, G. Li, C. Zhang, Adanic: towards practical neural image compression via dynamic transform routing, in *Proceedings of the IEEE/CVF International Conference on Computer Vision* (2023), pp. 16879–16888
19. Y. Wu, W. Gao, End-to-end lossless compression of high precision depth maps guided by pseudo-residual. arXiv preprint arXiv:2201.03195 (2022)
20. Y. Wu, Z. Qi, H. Zheng, L. Tao, W. Gao, Deep image compression with latent optimization and piece-wise quantization approximation, in *Proceedings of the IEEE/CVF Conference on Computer Vision and Pattern Recognition* (2021), pp. 1926–1930
21. W. Gao, L. Tao, L. Zhou, D. Yang, X. Zhang, Z. Guo, Low-rate image compression with super-resolution learning, in *Proceedings of the IEEE/CVF Conference on Computer Vision and Pattern Recognition Workshops* (2020), pp. 154–155
22. W. Gao, S. Sun, H. Zheng, Y. Wu, H. Ye, Y. Zhang, OpenDMC: An open-source library and performance evaluation for deep-learning-based multi-frame compression, in *Proceedings of the 31st ACM International Conference on Multimedia* (2023), pp. 9685–9688
23. Y. Guo, W. Gao, G. Li, Interpretable task-inspired adaptive filter pruning for neural networks under multiple constraints. Int. J. Comput. Vis. **132**(6), 2060–2076 (2024)
24. W. Gao, Y. Guo, S. Ma, G. Li, S. Kwong, Efficient neural network compression inspired by compressive sensing. IEEE Trans. Neural Networks Learn. Syst. **35**(2), 1965–1979 (2022)
25. Y. Guo, W. Gao, Semantic-driven automatic filter pruning for neural networks, in *2022 IEEE International Conference on Multimedia and Expo (ICME)* (IEEE, New York, 2022), pp. 1–6
26. L. Tao, W. Gao, Efficient channel pruning based on architecture alignment and probability model bypassing, in *2021 IEEE International Conference on Systems, Man, and Cybernetics (SMC)* (IEEE, New York, 2021), pp. 3232–3237
27. Z. Yang, W. Gao, G. Li, Y. Yan, Sur-driven video coding rate control for jointly optimizing perceptual quality and buffer control, in *IEEE Transactions on Image Processing* (2023)
28. F. Shen, Z. Cai, W. Gao, An efficient rate control algorithm for intra frame coding in avs3, in *2021 IEEE International Conference on Systems, Man, and Cybernetics (SMC)* (IEEE, New York, 2021), pp. 3164–3169
29. H. Yuan, W. Gao, J. Wang, Dynamic computational resource allocation for fast inter frame coding in video conferencing applications, in *2021 IEEE International Conference on Multimedia and Expo (ICME)* (IEEE, New York, 2021), pp. 1–6
30. W. Gao, Q. Jiang, R. Wang, S. Ma, G. Li, S. Kwong, Consistent quality oriented rate control in hevc via balancing intra and inter frame coding. IEEE Trans. Industr. Inform. **18**(3), 1594–1604 (2021)
31. H. Yuan, W. Gao, A new coding unit partitioning mode for screen content video coding, in *Proceedings of the 2021 5th International Conference on Digital Signal Processing* (2021), pp. 66–72
32. W. Gao, On the performance evaluation of state-of-the-art rate control algorithms for practical video coding and transmission systems, in *Proceedings of the 2020 4th International Conference on Video and Image Processing* (2020), pp. 179–185
33. W. Gao, S. Kwong, Q. Jiang, C.-K. Fong, P.H. Wong, W.Y. Yuen, Data-driven rate control for rate-distortion optimization in hevc based on simplified effective initial qp learning. IEEE Trans. Broadcast. **65**(1), 94–108 (2018)
34. W. Gao, A multi-objective optimization perspective for joint consideration of video coding quality, in *2019 Asia-Pacific Signal and Information Processing Association Annual Summit and Conference (APSIPA ASC)* (IEEE, New York, 2019), pp. 986–991

35. W. Gao, S. Kwong, Y. Jia, Joint machine learning and game theory for rate control in high efficiency video coding. IEEE Trans. Image Process. **26**(12), 6074–6089 (2017)
36. W. Gao, S. Kwong, Y. Zhou, H. Yuan, SSIM-based game theory approach for rate-distortion optimized intra frame CTU-level bit allocation. IEEE Trans. Multimedia **18**(6), 988–999 (2016)
37. W. Gao, S. Kwong, H. Yuan, X. Wang, DCT coefficient distribution modeling and quality dependency analysis based frame-level bit allocation for HEVC. IEEE Trans. Circuits Syst. Video Technol. **26**(1), 139–153 (2015)
38. W. Gao, S. Kwong, Phase congruency based edge saliency detection and rate control for perceptual image and video coding, in *2016 IEEE International Conference on Systems, Man, Cybernetics (SMC)* (IEEE, New York, 2016), pp. 000264–000269
39. H. Yuan, W. Gao, Openfastvc: An open source library for video coding fast algorithm implementation, in *Proceedings of the 31st ACM International Conference on Multimedia* (2023), pp. 9660–9663
40. H. Yuan, W. Gao, S. Ma, Y. Yan, Divide-and-conquer-based RDO-free CU partitioning for 8K video compression. ACM Trans. Multimed. Comput. Commun. Appl. **20**(4), 1–20 (2024)
41. L. Tao, W. Gao, A hardware implementation of entropy encoder for 8K video coding, in *2022 IEEE International Conference on Multimedia and Expo (ICME)* (IEEE, New York, 2022), pp. 1–6
42. Y. Guo, W. Gao, S. Ma, G. Li, Accelerating transform algorithm implementation for efficient intra coding of 8K UHD videos. ACM Trans. Multimed. Comput. Commun. Appl. (TOMM) **18**(4), 1–20 (2022)
43. Z. Cai, W. Gao, Efficient fast algorithm and parallel hardware architecture for intra prediction of avs3, in *2021 IEEE International Symposium on Circuits and Systems (ISCAS)* (IEEE, New York, 2021), pp. 1–5
44. W. Gao, H. Yuan, Y. Guo, L. Tao, Z. Cai, G. Li, Openhardwarevc: an open source library for 8K UHD video coding hardware implementation, in *Proceedings of the 30th ACM International Conference on Multimedia* (2022), pp. 7339–7342
45. W. Gao, H. Yuan, G. Liao, Z. Guo, J. Chen, PP8K: a new dataset for 8K UHD video compression and processing. IEEE MultiMedia **30**(3), 100–109 (2023)
46. X. Zang, W. Gao, G. Li, H. Fang, C. Ban, Z. He, H. Sun, A baseline investigation: transformer-based cross-view baseline for text-based person search, in *Proceedings of the 31st ACM International Conference on Multimedia* (2023), pp. 7737–7746
47. G. Liao, W. Gao, G. Li, J. Wang, S. Kwong, Cross-collaborative fusion-encoder network for robust RGB-thermal salient object detection. IEEE Trans. Circuits Syst. Video Technol. **32**(11), 7646–7661 (2022)
48. W. Gao, G. Liao, S. Ma, G. Li, Y. Liang, W. Lin, Unified information fusion network for multi-modal RGB-D and RGB-T salient object detection. IEEE Trans. Circuits Syst. Video Technol. **32**(4), 2091–2106 (2021)
49. Y. Chen, S. Sun, G. Li, W. Gao, T.H. Li, Closing the gap between theory and practice during alternating optimization for gans, in *IEEE Transactions on Neural Networks and Learning Systems* (2023)
50. Y. Chen, C. Jin, G. Li, T.H. Li, W. Gao, Mitigating label noise in gans via enhanced spectral normalization, in *IEEE Transactions on Circuits and Systems for Video Technology* (2023)
51. X. Zang, G. Li, W. Gao, Multidirection and multiscale pyramid in transformer for video-based pedestrian retrieval. IEEE Trans. Industr. Inform. **18**(12), 8776–8785 (2022)
52. X. Zang, G. Li, W. Gao, X. Shu, Learning to disentangle scenes for person re-identification. Image Vis. Comput. **116**, 104330 (2021)
53. Z. Yue, G. Li, W. Gao, Cross-level guided attention for human-object interaction detection, in *2023 IEEE International Conference on Multimedia and Expo Workshops (ICMEW)* (IEEE, New York, 2023), pp. 284–289
54. Z. Yao, W. Gao, Iterative saliency aggregation and assignment network for efficient salient object detection in optical remote sensing images, in *IEEE Transactions on Geoscience and Remote Sensing* (2024)

55. Y. Sun, Z. Li, S. Wang, W. Gao, Depth-assisted calibration on learning-based factorization for a compressive light field display. Opt. Express **31**(4), 5399–5413 (2023)
56. X. Zang, G. Li, W. Gao, X. Shu, Exploiting robust unsupervised video person re-identification. IET Image Process. **16**(3), 729–741 (2022)
57. Y. Sun, Z. Li, L. Li, S. Wang, W. Gao, Optimization of compressive light field display in dual-guided learning, in *ICASSP 2022-2022 IEEE International Conference on Acoustics, Speech and Signal Processing (ICASSP)* (IEEE, New York, 2022), pp. 2075–2079
58. W. Gao, S. Fan, G. Li, W. Lin, A thorough benchmark and a new model for light field saliency detection, in *IEEE Transactions on Pattern Analysis and Machine Intelligence* (2023)
59. Z. Guo, W. Gao, H. Wang, J. Wang, S. Fan, No-reference deep quality assessment of compressed light field images, in *2021 IEEE International Conference on Multimedia and Expo (ICME)* (IEEE, New York, 2021), pp. 1–6
60. G. Liao, W. Gao, Rethinking feature mining for light field salient object detection, in *ACM Transactions on Multimedia Computing, Communications, and Applications* (2024)
61. S. Sun, J. Liu, T.H. Li, H. Li, G. Liu, W. Gao, Streamflow: streamlined multi-frame optical flow estimation for video sequences. arXiv preprint arXiv:2311.17099 (2023)
62. R. Liu, J. Huang, W. Gao, T.H. Li, G. Li, Mug-STAN: adapting image-language pretrained models for general video understanding. arXiv preprint arXiv:2311.15075 (2023)
63. C. Zhang, W. Gao, Learned rate control for frame-level adaptive neural video compression via dynamic neural network, in *European Conference on Computer Vision* (Springer, Berlin, 2024)
64. W. Gao, G. Li, H. Yuan, R. Hamzaoui, Z. Li, S. Liu, Apccpa'22: 1st international workshop on advances in point cloud compression, processing and analysis, in *Proceedings of the 30th ACM International Conference on Multimedia* (2022), pp. 7392–7393
65. S. Fan, W. Gao, G. Li, Salient object detection for point clouds, in *European Conference on Computer Vision* (2022), pp. 1–19
66. X. Lu, W. Gao, Attentivenet: detecting small objects for lidar point clouds by attending to important points, in *2023 IEEE International Conference on Visual Communications and Image Processing (VCIP)* (IEEE, New York, 2023), pp. 1–5
67. Z. Pan, N. Zhang, W. Gao, S. Liu, G. Li, Less is more: label recommendation for weakly supervised point cloud semantic segmentation, in *Proceedings of the AAAI Conference on Artificial Intelligence*, vol. 38(5) (2024), pp. 4397–4405
68. N. Zhang, Z. Pan, T.H. Li, W. Gao, G. Li, Improving graph representation for point cloud segmentation via attentive filtering, in *Proceedings of the IEEE/CVF conference on computer vision and pattern recognition* (2023), pp. 1244–1254
69. D. Yang, W. Gao, G. Li, H. Yuan, J. Hou, S. Kwong, Exploiting manifold feature representation for efficient classification of 3d point clouds. ACM Trans. Multimed. Comput. Commun. Appl. **19**(1s), 1–21 (2023)
70. T. Qin, G. Li, W. Gao, S. Liu, Multi-grained point cloud geometry compression via dual-model prediction with extended octree. ACM Trans. Multimed. Comput. Commun. Appl. **20**(9), 1–30 (2024)
71. Y. Shao, W. Gao, S. Liu, G. Li, Advanced patch-based affine motion estimation for dynamic point cloud geometry compression. Sensors **24**(10), 3142 (2024)
72. Y. Shao, F. Song, W. Gao, S. Liu, G. Li, Texture-guided graph transform optimization for point cloud attribute compression. Appl. Sci. **14**(10), 4094 (2024)
73. Y. Shao, X. Yang, W. Gao, S. Liu, G. Li, 3d point cloud attribute compression using diffusion-based texture-aware intra prediction. IEEE Trans. Circuits Syst. Video Technol. **34**(10), 9633–9646 (2024)
74. J. Zhang, Y. Chen, G. Liu, W. Gao, G. Li, Efficient point cloud attribute compression framework using attribute-guided graph fourier transform, in *ICASSP 2024-2024 IEEE International Conference on Acoustics, Speech and Signal Processing (ICASSP)* (IEEE, New York, 2024), pp. 8426–8430
75. W. Gao, H. Yuan, G. Li, Z. Li, H. Yuan, Low complexity coding unit decision for video-based point cloud compression. IEEE Trans. Image Process. **33**, 149–162 (2023)

76. Y. Shao, G. Li, Q. Zhang, W. Gao, S. Liu, Non-rigid registration-based progressive motion compensation for point cloud geometry compression. IEEE Trans. Geosci. Remote Sens. **61**, 1–14 (2023)
77. Y. An, Y. Shao, G. Li, W. Gao, S. Liu, A fast motion estimation method with hamming distance for lidar point cloud compression, in *2022 IEEE International Conference on Visual Communications and Image Processing (VCIP)* (IEEE, New York, 2022), pp. 1–5
78. H. Yuan, W. Gao, G. Li, Z. Li, Rate-distortion-guided learning approach with cross-projection information for v-pcc fast cu decision, in *Proceedings of the 30th ACM International Conference on Multimedia* (2022), pp. 3085–3093
79. F. Song, G. Li, W. Gao, T.H. Li, Rate-distortion optimized graph for point cloud attribute coding. IEEE Signal Process Lett. **29**, 922–926 (2022)
80. F. Song, G. Li, X. Yang, W. Gao, T.H. Li, Fine-grained correlation representation for graph-based point cloud attribute compression, in *2022 IEEE International Conference on Multimedia and Expo (ICME)* (IEEE, New York, 2022), pp. 1–6
81. F. Shen, W. Gao, A rate control algorithm for video-based point cloud compression, in *2021 International Conference on Visual Communications and Image Processing (VCIP)* (IEEE, New York, 2021), pp. 1–5
82. F. Song, Y. Shao, W. Gao, H. Wang, T. Li, Layer-wise geometry aggregation framework for lossless lidar point cloud compression. IEEE Trans. Circuits Syst. Video Technol. **31**(12), 4603–4616 (2021)
83. L. Xie, W. Gao, H. Zheng, , G. Li, Spcgc: scalable point cloud geometry compression for machine vision, in *Proceedings of IEEE International Conference on Robotics and Automation* (2024)
84. L. Xie, W. Gao, H. Zheng, H. Ye, Semantic-aware visual decomposition for point cloud geometry compression, in *2024 Data Compression Conference (DCC)* (IEEE, New York, 2024), pp. 595–595
85. Z. Qi, W. Gao, Variable-rate point cloud geometry compression based on feature adjustment and interpolation, in *2024 Data Compression Conference (DCC)* (IEEE, New York, 2024), pp. 63–72
86. Z. Yu, W. Gao, When dynamic neural network meets point cloud compression: computation-aware variable rate and checkerboard context, in *2024 Data Compression Conference (DCC)* (IEEE, New York, 2024), pp. 600–600
87. L. Xie, W. Gao, S. Fan, Z. Yao, Pdnet: parallel dual-branch network for point cloud geometry compression and analysis, in *2024 Data Compression Conference (DCC)* (IEEE, New York, 2024), pp. 596–596
88. L. Xie, W. Gao, H. Zheng, End-to-end point cloud geometry compression and analysis with sparse tensor, in *Proceedings of the 1st International Workshop on Advances in Point Cloud Compression, Processing and Analysis* (2022), pp. 27–32
89. C. Fu, G. Li, R. Song, W. Gao, S. Liu, OctAttention: octree-based large-scale contexts model for point cloud compression, in *AAAI Conference on Artificial Intelligence* (2022), pp. 625–633
90. H. Zheng, W. Gao, Z. Yu, T. Zhao, G. Li, Viewpcgc: view-guided learned point cloud geometry compression, in *Proceedings of the 32nd ACM International Conference on Multimedia* (2024)
91. L. Xie, W. Gao, H. Zheng, G. Li, Roi-guided point cloud geometry compression towards human and machine vision, in *Proceedings of the 32nd ACM International Conference on Multimedia* (2024)
92. C. Peng, W. Gao, Laplacian matrix learning for point cloud attribute compression with ternary search-based adaptive block partition, in *Proceedings of the 32nd ACM International Conference on Multimedia* (2024)
93. S. Luo, B. Qu, W. Gao, Learning robust 3d representation from clip via dual denoising. arXiv preprint arXiv:2407.00905 (2024)
94. G. Li, G. Wei, W. Gao, *Point Cloud Compression: Technologies and Standardization* (Springer Nature, Belin, 2024)

95. G. Li, W. Gao, W. Gao, Introduction, in *Point Cloud Compression: Technologies and Standardization* (Springer, Berlin, 2024), pp. 1–28
96. G. Li, W. Gao, W. Gao, Background knowledge, in *Point Cloud Compression: Technologies and Standardization* (Springer, Berlin, 2024), pp. 29–51
97. G. Li, W. Gao, W. Gao, Predictive coding, in *Point Cloud Compression: Technologies and Standardization* (Springer, Berlin, 2024), pp. 53–70
98. G. Li, W. Gao, W. Gao, Transform coding, in *Point Cloud Compression: Technologies and Standardization* (Springer, Berlin, 2024), pp. 71–96
99. G. Li, W. Gao, W. Gao, Quantization techniques, in *Point Cloud Compression: Technologies and Standardization* (Springer, Berlin, 2024), pp. 97–112
100. G. Li, W. Gao, W. Gao, Entropy coding, in *Point Cloud Compression: Technologies and Standardization* (Springer, Berlin, 2024), pp. 113–133
101. G. Li, W. Gao, W. Gao, MPEG geometry-based point cloud compression (G-PCC) standard, in *Point Cloud Compression: Technologies and Standardization* (Springer, Berlin, 2024), pp. 135–165
102. G. Li, W. Gao, W. Gao, AVS point cloud compression standard, in *Point Cloud Compression: Technologies and Standardization* (Springer, Berlin, 2024), pp. 167–197
103. G. Li, W. Gao, W. Gao, MPEG video-based point cloud compression (V-PCC) standard, in *Point Cloud Compression: Technologies and Standardization* (Springer, Berlin, 2024), pp. 199–218
104. G. Li, W. Gao, W. Gao, MPEG AI-based 3d graphics coding standard, in *Point Cloud Compression: Technologies and Standardization* (Springer, Berlin, 2024), pp. 219–241
105. G. Li, W. Gao, W. Gao, Future work, in *Point Cloud Compression: Technologies and Standardization* (Springer, Berlin, 2024), pp. 243–250
106. W. Liu, W. Gao, X. Mu, Fast inter-frame motion prediction for compressed dynamic point cloud attribute enhancement, in *Proceedings of the AAAI Conference on Artificial Intelligence*, vol. 38(4) (2024), pp. 3720–3728
107. Z. Yang, W. Gao, X. Lu, Danet: density-adaptive network for geometry-based point cloud compression artifacts removal, in *2023 IEEE International Conference on Visual Communications and Image Processing (VCIP)* (IEEE, New York, 2023), pp. 1–5
108. X. Fan, G. Li, D. Li, Y. Ren, W. Gao, T.H. Li, Deep geometry post-processing for decompressed point clouds, in *2022 IEEE International Conference on Multimedia and Expo (ICME)* (IEEE, New York, 2022), pp. 1–6
109. X. Zhang, G. Liao, W. Gao, G. Li, TDRNET: transformer-based dual-branch restoration network for geometry based point cloud compression artifacts, in *2022 IEEE International Conference on Multimedia and Expo (ICME)* (IEEE, New York, 2022), pp. 1–6
110. R. Zhang, W. Gao, G. Li, T.H. Li, Qinet: decision surface learning and adversarial enhancement for quasi-immune completion of diverse corrupted point clouds. IEEE Trans. Geosci. Remote Sens. **60**, 1–14 (2022)
111. R. Zhang, J. Chen, W. Gao, G. Li, T.H. Li, PointOT: interpretable geometry-inspired point cloud generative model via optimal transport. IEEE Trans. Circuits Syst. Video Technol. **32**(10), 6792–6806 (2022)
112. S. Fan, W. Gao, Screen-based 3d subjective experiment software, in *Proceedings of the 31st ACM International Conference on Multimedia* (2023), pp. 9672–9675
113. J. Wang, W. Gao, G. Li, Zoom to perceive better: no-reference point cloud quality assessment via exploring effective multiscale feature, in *IEEE Transactions on Circuits and Systems for Video Technology* (2024)
114. C.R. Qi, H. Su, K. Mo, L.J. Guibas, PointNet: deep learning on point sets for 3D classification and segmentation, in *IEEE Conference on Computer Vision and Pattern Recognition* (2017), pp. 77–85
115. M.-H. Guo, J.-X. Cai, Z.-N. Liu, T.-J. Mu, R.R. Martin, S.-M. Hu, PCT: point cloud transformer. Comput. Visual Media **7**(2), 187–199 (2021)

116. C.R. Qi, H. Su, K. Mo, L.J. Guibas, Pointnet: deep learning on point sets for 3D classification and segmentation, in *Proceedings of the IEEE Conference on Computer Vision and Pattern Recognition* (2017), pp. 652–660
117. H. Su, S. Maji, E. Kalogerakis, E. Learned-Miller, Multi-view convolutional neural networks for 3D shape recognition, in *Proceedings of the IEEE International Conference on Computer Vision* (2015), pp. 945–953
118. M. Yavartanoo, E.Y. Kim, K.M. Lee, SPNET: deep 3D object classification and retrieval using stereographic projection, in *Proceedings of the Asian Conference on Computer Vision* (2018), pp. 691–706
119. D. Maturana, S. Scherer, Voxnet: a 3d convolutional neural network for real-time object recognition, in *2015 IEEE/RSJ International Conference on Intelligent Robots and Systems* (2015), pp. 922–928
120. C.R. Qi, L. Yi, H. Su, L.J. Guibas, PointNet++: deep hierarchical feature learning on point sets in a metric space. Adv. Neural Inform. Process. Syst. **30**, 5099–5108 (2017)
121. H. Zhao, L. Jiang, J. Jia, P.H. Torr, V. Koltun, Point transformer, in *Proceedings of the IEEE/CVF International Conference on Computer Vision* (2021), pp. 16259–16268
122. A. Vaswani, N. Shazeer, N. Parmar, J. Uszkoreit, L. Jones, A.N. Gomez, Ł. Kaiser, I. Polosukhin, Attention is all you need. Adv. Neural Inform. Process. Syst. **30**, 6000–6010 (2017)
123. H. Zhao, J. Jia, V. Koltun, Exploring self-attention for image recognition, in *Proceedings of the IEEE/CVF Conference on Computer Vision and Pattern Recognition* (2020), pp. 10076–10085
124. Y. Wang, Y. Sun, Z. Liu, S.E. Sarma, M.M. Bronstein, J.M. Solomon, Dynamic graph CNN for learning on point clouds. ACM Trans. Graphics **38**(5), 146:1–146:12 (2019)
125. G. Li, M. Muller, A. Thabet, B. Ghanem, Deepgcns: Can gcns go as deep as cnns? in *Proceedings of the IEEE/CVF International Conference on Computer Vision* (2019), pp. 9267–9276
126. Z. Wu, S. Song, A. Khosla, F. Yu, L. Zhang, X. Tang, J. Xiao, 3D ShapeNets: a deep representation for volumetric shapes, in *IEEE Conference on Computer Vision and Pattern Recognition* (2015), pp. 1912–1920
127. A.X. Chang, T. Funkhouser, L. Guibas, P. Hanrahan, Q. Huang, Z. Li, S. Savarese, M. Savva, S. Song, H. Su, et al., Shapenet: an information-rich 3d model repository. arXiv preprint arXiv:1512.03012 (2015)
128. M.A. Uy, Q.-H. Pham, B.-S. Hua, T. Nguyen, S.-K. Yeung, Revisiting point cloud classification: a new benchmark dataset and classification model on real-world data, in *Proceedings of the IEEE/CVF International Conference on Computer Vision* (2019), pp. 1588–1597
129. I. Armeni, O. Sener, A.R. Zamir, H. Jiang, I. Brilakis, M. Fischer, S. Savarese, 3D semantic parsing of large-scale indoor spaces, in *IEEE Conference on Computer Vision and Pattern Recognition* (2016), pp. 1534–1543
130. A. Dai, A.X. Chang, M. Savva, M. Halber, T.A. Funkhouser, M. Nießner, ScanNet: Richly-annotated 3d reconstructions of indoor scenes, in *IEEE Conference on Computer Vision and Pattern Recognition* (IEEE Computer Society, New York, 2017), pp. 2432–2443
131. D. Yang, W. Gao, G. Li, H. Yuan, J. Hou, S. Kwong, Exploiting manifold feature representation for efficient classification of 3d point clouds, in *ACM Transactions on Multimedia Computing, Communications and Applications*, vol. 19(1s), 1–21 (2023)
132. Y. Zhou, O. Tuzel, Voxelnet: End-to-end learning for point cloud based 3d object detection, in *Proceedings of the IEEE Conference on Computer Vision and Pattern Recognition* (2018), pp. 4490–4499
133. S. Shi, X. Wang, H. Li, Pointrcnn: 3d object proposal generation and detection from point cloud, in *Proceedings of the IEEE/CVF Conference on Computer Vision and Pattern Recognition* (2019), pp. 770–779
134. W. Liu, D. Anguelov, D. Erhan, C. Szegedy, S. Reed, C.-Y. Fu, A.C. Berg, SSD: single shot multibox detector, in *European Conference on Computer Vision* (Springer, Berlin, 2016), pp. 21–37

135. T.-Y. Lin, P. Dollár, R. Girshick, K. He, B. Hariharan, S. Belongie, Feature pyramid networks for object detection, in *Proceedings of the IEEE Conference on Computer Vision and Pattern Recognition* (2017), pp. 2117–2125
136. Y. Yan, Y. Mao, B. Li, Second: sparsely embedded convolutional detection. Sensors **18**(10), 3337 (2018)
137. A.H. Lang, S. Vora, H. Caesar, L. Zhou, J. Yang, O. Beijbom, Pointpillars: fast encoders for object detection from point clouds, in *Proceedings of the IEEE/CVF Conference on Computer Vision and Pattern Recognition* (2019), pp. 12697–12705
138. S. Shi, C. Guo, L. Jiang, Z. Wang, J. Shi, X. Wang, H. Li, PV-RCNN: point-voxel feature set abstraction for 3d object detection, in *Proceedings of the IEEE/CVF Conference on Computer Vision and Pattern Recognition* (2020), pp. 10529–10538
139. A. Geiger, P. Lenz, C. Stiller, R. Urtasun, Vision meets robotics: the kitti dataset. Int. J. Rob. Res. **32**(11), 1231–1237 (2013)
140. H. Caesar, V. Bankiti, A.H. Lang, S. Vora, V.E. Liong, Q. Xu, A. Krishnan, Y. Pan, G. Baldan, O. Beijbom, nuscenes: A multimodal dataset for autonomous driving, in *Proceedings of the IEEE/CVF Conference on Computer Vision and Pattern Recognition* (2020), pp. 11621–11631
141. M. Schwall, T. Daniel, T. Victor, F. Favaro, H. Hohnhold, Waymo public road safety performance data. arXiv preprint arXiv:2011.00038 (2020)
142. S. Wang, Y. Sun, C. Liu, M. Liu, Pointtracknet: An end-to-end network for 3-d object detection and tracking from point clouds. IEEE Rob. Autom. Lett. **5**(2), 3206–3212 (2020)
143. S. Giancola, J. Zarzar, B. Ghanem, Leveraging shape completion for 3D siamese tracking, in *Proceedings of the IEEE/CVF Conference on Computer Vision and Pattern Recognition* (2019), pp. 1359–1368

Chapter 6
Deep-Learning-Based Point Cloud Analysis II

Abstract The emergence of advanced 3D sensing technologies, such as LiDAR, has significantly increased the availability of point cloud data, driving the need for robust analytics through deep learning. Point clouds, with their detailed spatiotemporal structures, are vital across numerous applications, requiring innovative approaches for effective interpretation and utilization. This chapter delves into the intersection of deep learning and point cloud analytics, covering essential tasks like point classification and semantic segmentation. It then explores place recognition, object retrieval, and registration, emphasizing their importance in interpreting dynamic environments. This chapter concludes with an examination of multimodal analysis, showcasing the synergistic potential of integrating point cloud data with other data modalities. Each section systematically unpacks the problems, general solution strategies, seminal contributions, and emerging trends, encapsulating the state-of-the-art in deep-learning-based point cloud analytics and paving the way for future advancements in the field.

Keywords Point cloud · Deep learning · Point cloud analysis · Feature extraction · Point cloud place recognition · Point cloud registration · Multimodal analysis · Spatial awareness · Extracting relevant data

6.1 Introduction

3D sensing technologies like LiDAR have provided us with vast point cloud data, necessitating robust analytics driven by deep learning. This data richness demands a transformative approach to interpretation and utilization, fostering a concerted effort in the research community to develop adept deep learning techniques for analyzing point clouds. The past years have witnessed the big success of image processing and analysis technologies [1–50], and the research for point cloud technologies also has achieved the same prosperity, which can be seen from the research on compression [51–89], enhancement [90–102], and analysis [103–110]. This chapter is dedicated to an in-depth examination of the intersection between deep learning

W. Gao, G. Li, *Deep Learning for 3D Point Clouds*,
https://doi.org/10.1007/978-981-97-9570-3_6

and point cloud analytics, focusing on essential tasks such as point classification, semantic segmentation, place recognition, object retrieval, and registration.

At the heart of this exploration is the recognition of the transformative potential of deep learning algorithms in parsing the complexities of point cloud data. Place recognition, for instance, is pivotal for spatial awareness, enabling systems to identify and navigate through environments with precision. This chapter delves into the mechanisms of place recognition, discussing how deep learning models can be trained to discern and categorize locations based on point cloud features. The discussion encompasses the problem formulation, process description, and the categorization of existing methods, highlighting the evolution from traditional techniques to end-to-end deep learning pipelines.

Object retrieval in point clouds is another critical area of focus, where the challenge lies in defining measures of similarity that can robustly identify objects within unstructured 3D data. The chapter examines the advancements in deep learning that have facilitated the development of novel architectures capable of processing unordered point sets, extracting features that are both discriminative and invariant to transformations such as translation, rotation, and scaling.

Point cloud registration, the process of spatial transformation estimation between two point clouds, is also explored in detail. This task is fundamental in applications like 3D reconstruction and pose estimation. The chapter discusses the evolution of registration techniques from traditional optimization-based methods to modern deep learning approaches, underscoring the improvements in robustness and efficiency.

The chapter further extends its scope to multimodal analysis, underlining the synergistic potential of integrating point cloud data with other data modalities. This approach is particularly relevant in real-world scenarios where multiple sensors are employed, offering complementary perspectives and information that can enhance the performance of learning models.

Throughout the chapter, each topic is systematically unpacked, beginning with a clear problem statement, followed by a discussion of general solution strategies, a review of seminal contributions, and an examination of emerging trends. The aim is to encapsulate the current state-of-the-art in deep-learning-based point cloud analytics, providing a comprehensive overview that sets the stage for future advancements in the field.

By exploring these themes, the chapter serves not only as a guide for researchers and practitioners but also as a testament to the burgeoning potential of deep learning to revolutionize the way we analyze and interact with 3D spatial data. The insights presented here are a call to action for the development of innovative approaches that can harness the full spectrum of information embedded within point clouds, paving the way for more intelligent, efficient, and reliable systems across various industries.

6.2 Point Cloud Place Recognition

3D place recognition based on point clouds aims to retrieve the place scene in the trajectory map according to the point cloud feature representation shown in Fig. 6.1, which is widely applied to autonomous and robotic driving navigation [111–114]. It can also identify whether the current scene is in the planned route and determine whether changes in the recognized frame have occurred. Since the point clouds are invariant to the seasonal changes and lighting compared with images [111], the increasing number of researchers pay much attention to this field. The core challenges focus on acquiring the lightweight and distance global feature.

6.2.1 Problem Formulation

3D place recognition based on point cloud should first construct a database denoted as M with a set of m point clouds. Given a query point cloud denoted as Q, the ultimate goal of the task is to search some point clouds in M that are similar to the Q via their features, which can be defined as:

$$\text{KNN}(F(Q), F(M)), \tag{6.1}$$

where KNN denotes the K-nearest-neighbor searching technique, $F(.)$ is the point feature extraction function.

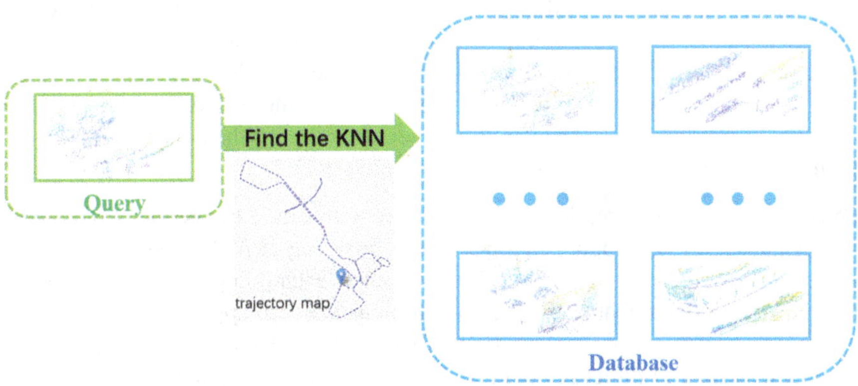

Fig. 6.1 Point cloud place recognition pipeline. Given a point cloud query, the recognition process involves finding the database's nearest neighbor (NN) (Source: Author)

6.2.2 Process Description

Traditional point cloud place recognition methods involve three parts in the process according to [115], namely feature extraction, feature encoding, and matching. Especially, feature extraction aims to obtain the all-rounded descriptors about the point cloud. Feature encoding focuses on aggregating the features in a global compact feature with less dimension. As for the matching, it finds the nearest neighbors of the current point cloud in the database. Recently, as the deep learning methods developed, more and more attention has been focused on training an end-to-end pipeline to fulfill the first two parts and then do the matching.

6.2.3 Categorization

In deep-learning-based methods, according to the existing point cloud place recognition methods [111–113, 116, 117], there exist two kinds of categories based on convolution type, PointNet-based or Minkowski-based. The former usually applies PointNet series network to extract features, while the latter adopts Minkowski convolutions to form the features. Two are involved if classified by the input: point cloud input and multimodal input. In the following, we will elaborate on them separately.

- **PointNetVLAD**

PointNetVLAD [111] is the pioneer in this field, which is a combination and modification of PointNet [118] and NetVLAD [111], allowing end-to-end training manner to extract the global feature from a given 3D point cloud. It is the PointNet-based method, and the input only contains point clouds. In addition, they propose the "lazy triplet and quadruplet" loss functions to achieve more distinct global features to tackle the retrieval task. The whole architecture contains three main components: PointNet, NetVLAD, and a fully connected network.

PointNet This section replicates the PointNet architecture before the max-pooling aggregation layer. The input is a point cloud consisting of N 3D points, denoted as $P = \{p_1, p_2, \ldots, p_N \mid p_n \in \mathbb{R}^3\}$. This part maps each point in the point cloud to a higher-dimensional feature space, transforming $P = \{p_1, p_2, \ldots, p_N \mid p_n \in \mathbb{R}^3\}$ to $P' = \{p'_1, p'_2, \ldots, p'_N \mid p'_n \in \mathbb{R}^D\}$, where $D \gg 3$. Here, PointNet serves as a module to extract D-dimensional local features for each point in the point cloud.

NetVLAD This part is used to aggregate the output of PointNet to a global feature denoted as the blue box in Fig. 6.2. The NetVLAD classifies K clusters as visual word, represented as $\{c_1, c_2, ..., c_K | k \in \mathbb{R}^D\}$, then outputs the vector $V(P')$ with $D \times K$ dimension. The $V(P')$ is defined as:

$$V(P') = \{V_1(P'), V_2(P'), ..., V_K(P')\}, V_k(P') \in \mathbb{R}^D, \tag{6.2}$$

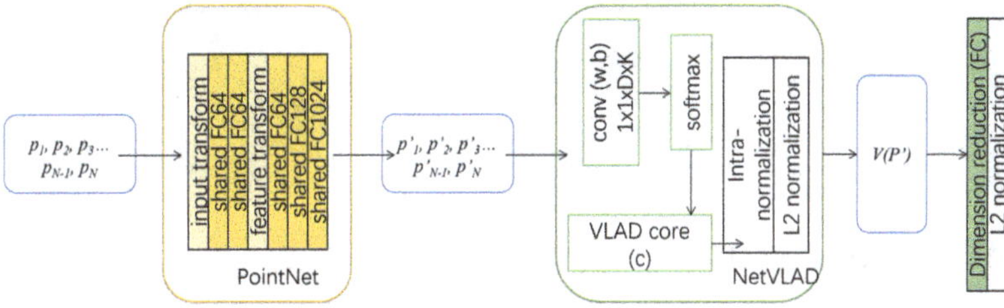

Fig. 6.2 The architecture of PointNetVLAD (©2018 IEEE. Reprinted, with permission, from ref [111])

$$V_k(P') = \sum_{i=1}^{n} \frac{e^{w_k^T p_i'} + b_k}{\sum_k' e^{w_{k'}^T p_i' + b_k'}} (p_i' - c_k), \tag{6.3}$$

where $\{w_k\}$ and $\{b_k\}$ are the corresponding weights and biases learned during training.

A Fully Connected Network This part is denoted as the green box in Fig. 6.2. The output of NetVLAD is $D \times K$ dimension and computationally expensive. To alleviate this problem, a fully connected layer is used to compress $D \times K$ into a compact feature vector, i.e., $O = 256$ dimension, which then uses L2-normalization to obtain the final global feature $f(P) \in \mathbb{R}^O$. This operation promotes the efficient retrieval of point clouds. As for the training strategy, PointNetVLAD proposes lazy quadruple defined as:

$$\begin{aligned} \mathcal{L}_{lazyQuad}(\mathcal{T}, P_{neg^*}) = &\max_j([\alpha + \sigma_{pos} - \sigma_{neg_j}]+) \\ &+ \max_k([\beta + \sigma_{pos} - \sigma_{neg_k^*}]+), \end{aligned} \tag{6.4}$$

where α and β are two constant parameters about the margin, [...]+ represents the hinge loss. d denotes the distance. $\sigma_{pos} = d(f(P_a), f(P_{pos}))$, $\sigma_{neg_j} = d(f(P_a), f(P_{neg_j}))$, $\sigma_{neg_k^*} = d(f(P_{neg^*}), f(P_{neg_k}))$, where P_a, P_{pos}, P_{neg} and P_{neg^*} denote an anchor point cloud, the positive point cloud, a set of negative point clouds to the anchor and randomly sampled negative point cloud from the training dataset, respectively.

- **MinkLoc3D**

MinkLoc3D [112] is the first point cloud-based place recognition method based on sparse 3D convolutions on voxelized point clouds inspired by Minkowski Engine [119], providing a generalizable and discriminative global feature of the point cloud. This method provides a simple and efficient architecture with better performance. The network is quite simple architecture as shown in Fig. 6.3. It consists

Fig. 6.3 The architecture of MinkLoc3D (©2021 IEEE. Reprinted, with permission, from ref [112])

of three parts: Sparse quantization, Local feature extraction, and Generalized-mean (GeM) pooling [120].

Sparse Quantization The input point cloud is denoted as $P = \{(x_i, y_i, z_i)\}$. Since the 3D sparse Minkowski convolution is based on 4 channels, this part quantizes the 3-channel input point cloud into a 4-channel sparse voxel tensor denoted as $\hat{P} = \{\hat{x}_i, \hat{y}_i.\hat{z}_i, 1\}$. The value of the fourth channel is fixed as 1 if it belongs to non-empty voxels. $\hat{x}_i$, $\hat{y}_i$ and $\hat{z}_i$ are quantized coordinates.

Local Feature Extraction Network Fed with the sparse tensors, this part aims to obtain a 3D sparse feature map:

$$\hat{F} = \{(\hat{x}_j, \hat{y}_j), \hat{z}_j, f_j^1, f_j^2, \ldots, f_j^c\}, \tag{6.5}$$

where the c denotes the feature dimension, i.e., 256 in this network, $f_j^1, f_j^2, ..., f_j^c$ represents the j-th feature map component. Motivated by MinkowkiNet sparse convolution architecture [119] and Feature Pyramid pattern [121], this part is designed with bottom-up and top-down parts. The whole network is shown in Fig. 6.3. The bottom-up part involves four convolutional blocks to produce 3D sparse feature maps with receptive field increased and spatial resolution decreased. The top-down part consists of a transposed convolution, which generates a feature map with unsampling. Then concatenate the upsampled feature in the top-down part with the skipped features from the bottom-up pass to produce the final 3D sparse feature map $\hat{F}$. This design aims to achieve a feature map with a large receptive field and relatively high spatial resolution. The detailed layers in each block are presented in Table 6.1.

GeM Once obtained the 3D sparse feature $\hat{F}$, this part pools $\hat{F}$ by a GeM layer [120], producing a global feature vector **g**. The GeM is defined as:

$$g(k) = \frac{1}{n} \sum_{j=1,\ldots,n} \left(f_j^{(k)}\right)^{p\,\frac{1}{p}}, \tag{6.6}$$

where $g(k)$ denotes the k-th component of the g, and n is the size of non-zero elements in $\hat{F}$. p is a learnable pooling parameter, which is set to 3 in experiments. The whole GeM can be seen as a generalization of a global average and max pooling

Table 6.1 Details of layers in local feature extraction network. Convolutions in bottom-up part Conv0,...,3 blocks are used batch norm and ReLu activation function. < ... > represents a residual block (Source: Author)

Block	Details
Conv0	$\mathbb{C}^{32}_{5_k1_s}$
Conv1	$\mathbb{C}^{32}_{2_k2_s}\left\langle \mathbb{C}^{32}_{3_k1_s}, \mathbb{C}^{32}_{3_k1_s} \right\rangle$
Conv2	$\mathbb{C}^{64}_{2_k2_s}\left\langle \mathbb{C}^{64}_{3_k1_s}, \mathbb{C}^{64}_{3_k1_s} \right\rangle$
Conv3	$\mathbb{C}^{64}_{2_k2_s}\left\langle \mathbb{C}^{64}_{3_k1_s}, \mathbb{C}^{64}_{3_k1_s} \right\rangle$
1×1×1Conv2, 3	$\mathbb{C}^{256}_{1_k1_s}$
1×1×1 Conv3	$\mathbb{C}^{256}_{1_k1_s}$
TConv3	${}_t\mathbb{C}^{256}_{2_k2_s}$

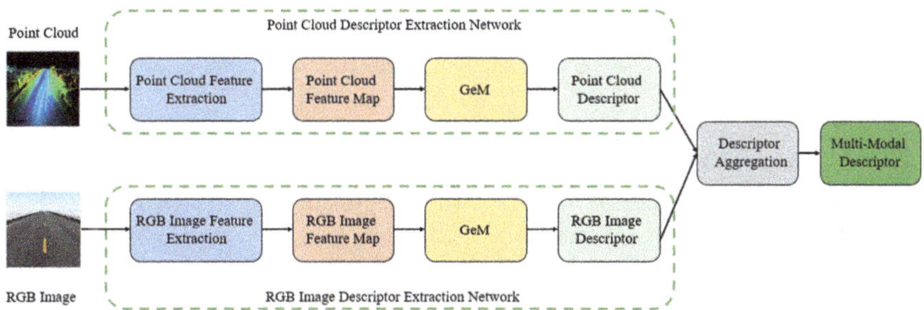

Fig. 6.4 The high-level architecture of MinkLoc++ (©2021 IEEE Reprinted, with permission, from ref [122])

operator. As for training strategy, MinkLoc3D uses a triplet margin loss defined as:

$$L(a_i, p_i, n_i) = \max\{d(a_i, p_i) - d(a_i, n_i) + m, 0\}, \tag{6.7}$$

where $d(x, y) = ||x - y||_2$ denotes Euclidean distance. a_i, p_i, and n_i represent the embeddings of an anchor, positive, and negative elements in i-th triplet. m is the margin parameter. This function is optimized by a stochastic gradient descent with an Adam optimizer.

- **MinkLoc++**

MinkLoc++ [122] is a multimodal input method that fuses point clouds from LiDAR and images from RGB cameras for place recognition. Each part is processed separately and aggregated in the final fusing part. The core challenge is how to avoid dominating modality when training a multimodal descriptor. The whole architecture is presented in Fig. 6.4. Two branches are involved with another fusion part.

Point Cloud Feature Extraction Network Branch This part computes a point cloud feature $D_{pc} \in \mathbb{R}^k$. k equals 128. This feature extraction part applies an

Table 6.2 Layers in point cloud feature extraction network branch. All convolutions in Conv0 . . . 3 blocks are followed by batch norm and ReLU non-linearity. C denotes a 3D convolution with a number of filters given as the top-right index, t decorator indicates a transposed convolution, lower k shows a filter size and lower s is a stride. $\mathbb{A}$ is ECA [123] channel attention and < ... > enclosures a residual block with a skip connection (Source: Author)

Block	Details
Conv0	$\mathbb{C}^{32}_{5_k 1_s}$
Conv1	$\mathbb{C}^{32}_{2_k 2_s} \left\langle \mathbb{C}^{32}_{3_k 1_s} \mathbb{C}^{32}_{3_k 1_s} \mathbb{A} \right\rangle$
Conv2	$\mathbb{C}^{64}_{2_k 2_s} \left\langle \mathbb{C}^{64}_{3_k 1_s} \mathbb{C}^{64}_{3_k 1_s} \mathbb{A} \right\rangle$
Conv3	$\mathbb{C}^{64}_{2_k 2_s} \left\langle \mathbb{C}^{64}_{3_k 1_s} \mathbb{C}^{64}_{3_k 1_s} \mathbb{A} \right\rangle$
1×1×1 Conv2, 3	$\mathbb{C}^{128}_{1_k 1_s}$
1×1×1 Conv3	$\mathbb{C}^{128}_{1_k 1_s}$
TConv3	${}_t\mathbb{C}^{128}_{2_k 2_s}$

improved version of MinkLoc3D [112], where an attention mechanism ECA [123] is adopted. The details of the feature extraction block are shown in Table 6.2.

RGB Image Feature Extraction Network Branch This part computes an RGB image feature $D_{RGB} \in \mathbb{R}^k$, k is 128. This feature extraction part uses the first four blocks of a pretrained ResNet18 to get a 256-channel 2D feature. Then this number of channels is reduced to k using a 1×1 filter convolution layer, then a GeM [120] pooling is also used to produce the final RGB image feature D_{RGB}.

Multi-modal Descriptor Aggregation The fusion part is processed after modalities are separately processed. This can be robust if one sensor fails and hold highly flexible. The aggregated point cloud feature D_{PC} and RGB image feature D_{RGB} are consented to make up the final $2k$-dimension multimodal feature.

Training Loss The loss function L is defined as a sum of three items: fused multimodal feature loss L_F, the point cloud feature loss L_{PC}, and the RGB feature loss L_{RGB}:

$$L = (1 - \alpha - \beta)L_F + \alpha L_{PC} + \beta L_{RGB}, \tag{6.8}$$

where α and β are weights. Each loss is a triplet margin loss defined as the same in Eq. (6.7).

6.2.4 Evaluation Metrics

Place recognition is an instance of point cloud retrieval. Similar to other point cloud-based place recognition tasks [111, 116, 117], average recall is used as the evaluation metric to assess the performance of all methods. Select a point cloud from the test dataset as a query and point clouds from different traversals that cover the same region from the database. The point cloud is successfully retrieved if at least one of the top N retrieved point clouds in the database is within $d = 25$ meters from the ground truth position of the query. $Recall@N$ is given by the percentage of correctly localized queries. Usually, the $Reacll@1$ and $Recall@1\%$ are reported.

6.2.5 Datasets

According to recent place recognition tasks based on LiDAR [111, 113, 116, 117], four large-scale datasets are usually applied as the benchmark, namely Oxford, Residential Area (R.A.), University Sector (U.S.), and Business District (B.D.). The first comes from the open source of [124], while the last three belong to in-house datasets. Table 6.3 presents the detailed split sub-maps of the benchmark datasets. As for Oxford, 21,711 training sub-maps are used to train, and 3030 testing sub-maps are used to test. Furthermore, the comparison of different methods of point cloud place recognition is presented in Table 6.4.

Table 6.3 Dataset split detail (Source: Author)

Dataset		Baseline		Refine	
		Train	Test	Train	Test
Oxford		21,711	3030	21,711	3030
In-house	U.S.	–	400[a]	}6671	80[a]
	B.A.	–	320[a]		75[a]
	B.D.	–	200[a]	–	200[a]

[a] Denotes the approximate number of sub-maps or runs, because the number of sub-maps differs slightly between each run

Table 6.4 Characteristic summary of the existing methods (Source: Author)

Name	Advantages	Disadvantages	Applicable scenarios
PointNetVLAD [111]	Easy to follow	Costly computation	Common scenes
MinkLoc3D [112]	Quickest speed	Hard to immigrate	Sparse point clouds scenes
MinkLoc++ [122]	Multi-feature fusion	A bit heavy	Multiple scenes

6.3 Point Cloud Registration

Point Cloud registration or alignment is a problem of spatial transformation estimation between two point clouds as shown in Fig. 6.5, which draws increasing attention and plays a unique role in lots of computer vision applications, i.e., 3D reconstruction, 3D localization, and pose estimation [125]. With the development of optimization-based methods and deep learning, point cloud registration robustness and efficiency have been improved. However, challenges still exist in this field, e.g., noise and outliers caused by the environment and sensors, partial overlap captured by different viewpoints, scale variation, and density difference in the cross-source domain, which need further exploration.

6.3.1 Problem Formulation

According to [125], given tow point clouds $X \in \mathbb{R}^{M\times 3}$ and $Y \in \mathbb{R}^{N\times 3}$. x_i^T and y_j^T can be seen as the i-th and j-th 3D coordinates in X and Y, respectively. Suppose that X and Y share K pairs of correspondences. The goal of point cloud registration is to find the transformation parameters g, which consists of rotation matrix $R \in SO(3)$ and translation vector $t \in \mathbb{R}^3$ to optimize and align the point X to Y as:

$$\underset{R\in SO(3),t\in\mathbb{R}^3}{\arg\max} \quad ||d(X, g(Y))||_2^2, \tag{6.9}$$

where $d(X, g(Y))$ denotes the projection error between X and $g(Y)$. In practice, it equals to $\sum_{k=1}^{K} ||x_k - (Ry_k + t)||_2$. This equation is a *chicken-and-egg* problem: on the one hand, the best transformation matrix can be obtained if the real correspondence is given; on the other hand, correspondences can be acquired if the best transformation matrix is presented. How to solve the joint problem is trivial.

Fig. 6.5 Point cloud registration (Source: Author)

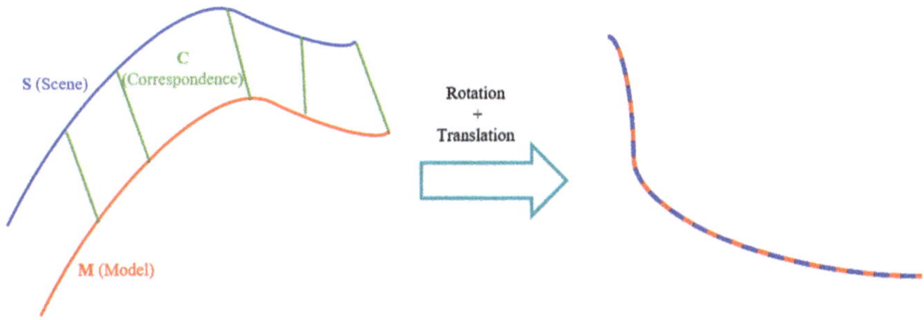

Fig. 6.6 Basic point cloud registration pipeline [126] (Source: Author)

6.3.2 *Process Description*

The classical traditional methods, i.e., Iterative Closest Point (ICP) [126], usually contains two steps to alternate optimization as shown in Fig. 6.6. The first step aims to search point correspondences, while the second step tries to use the point correspondence to estimate the transformation matrix that can minimize the Euclidean distance between the point correspondence.

6.3.3 *Categorization*

Point cloud registration can be loosely categorized into two types: same-source registration and cross-source registration. The former can be divided into three parts, including optimized-based registration approaches, feature-learning approaches, and end-to-end learning registrations. The latter category, cross-source registration, is a newly explored area that combines optimization-based and learning-based methods.

- **Optimization-based Methods in Same-Source**

These methods aim to use optimization strategies to estimate the final transformation matrix. Usually, the optimization-based architecture in the same-source domain is illustrated in Fig. 6.7. Given two point clouds, the optimization targets iteratively estimating the correspondences and transformation between two point clouds. Finally, the algorithm results in the optimal transformation solution $\mathbf{T}$.

Specifically, these methods [127–130] include two steps: search the correspondence and estimate the transformation. The first step is to search for the matched point in one point cloud corresponding to another point cloud, which can be seen in Fig. 6.8, which can be done by computing the difference between point coordinates or the features. This step is gradually accurate. The second step is to calculate the

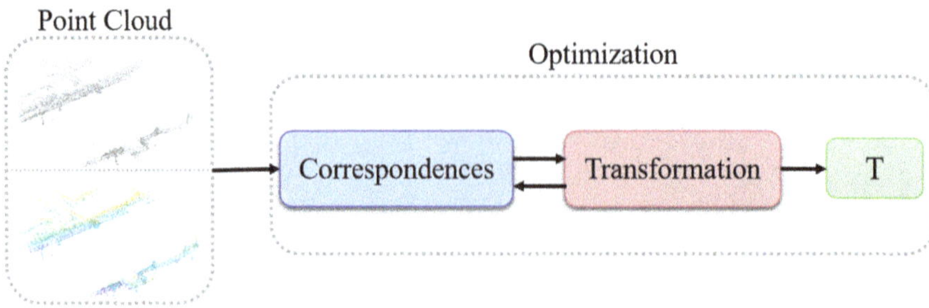

Fig. 6.7 The optimization-based architecture for point cloud registration in the same-source domain (Source: Author)

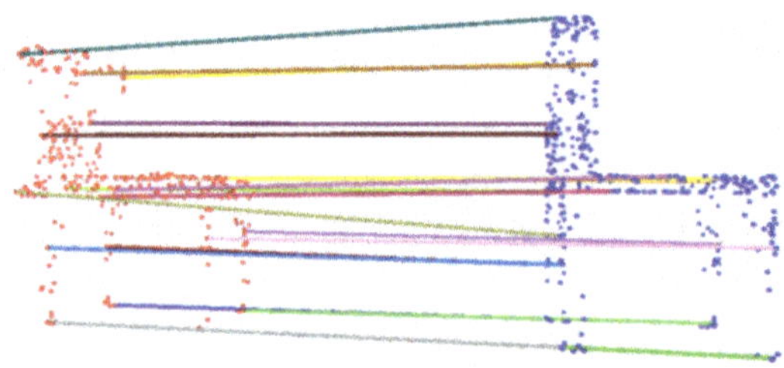

Fig. 6.8 Match the correspondence (Source: Author)

transformation matrix via the given correspondences. These two steps are conducted iteratively to output the final optimal transformation matrix.

Although the convergence of these methods could be guaranteed by the rigorous theories, no training data are required, and they have a good generalization performance in unknown scenes, they need many sophisticated strategies to overcome many problems, i.e., noise, outliers, density, and partial overlap, to be costly.

ICP [126] is the classical algorithm named iterative closest point, which works as follows. Define two point clouds $A = \{a_i\}$ and $B = \{b_i\}$. The goal is to find the transformation T that aligns these two point clouds best. T consists of 3D rotation and translation part, which is formulated as:

$$T = \arg\min_{T} \left\{ \sum_{i} ||Tb_i - m_i||^2 \right\}, \tag{6.10}$$

where m_i denotes the point cloud in A that is a nearest match with transformation T on b_i. If we have these point corresponding points (m_i, Tb_i), the optimal transformation can be obtained by these correspondences via singular value decomposition or a least square method. T_0 is obtained by a global alignment algorithm. A simple example of aligning two curves by ICP is shown in Fig. 6.6. It is the easiest method, but there is an assumption that the point correspondence is one-to-one in two point clouds, which may differ in real scenes.

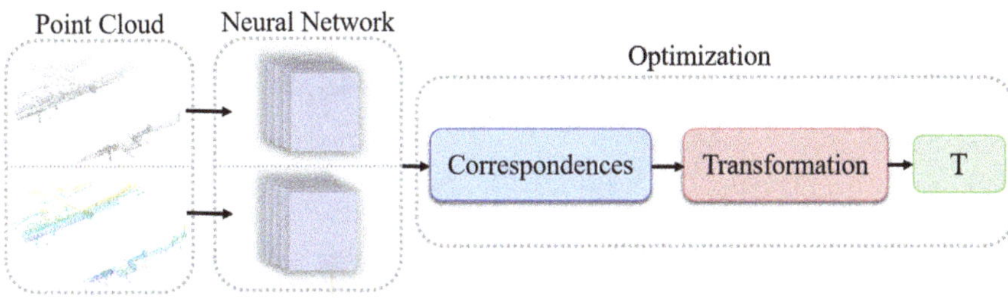

Fig. 6.9 The feature-learning architecture for point cloud registration in the same-source domain (Source: Author)

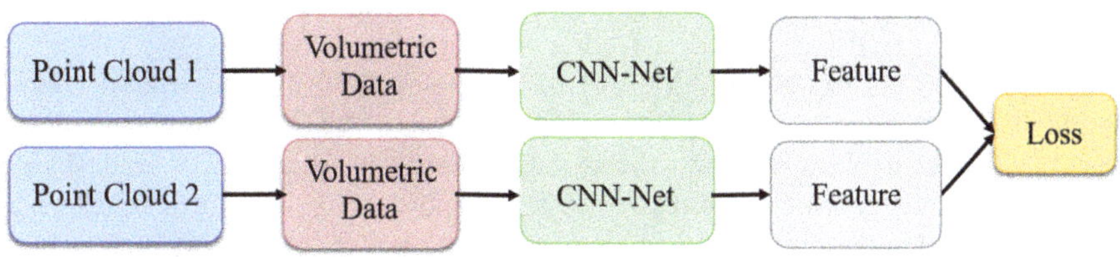

Fig. 6.10 The framework of 3DMatch (©2017 IEEE. Reprinted, with permission, from ref [133])

- **Feature-Learning Methods in Same-source**

The goal of this category concentrates on learning robust feature correspondence. The feature-learning architecture in the same-source domain is shown in Fig. 6.9. Given two-point clouds, two steps are involved. First, features are calculated using a deep neural network. Then, the final transformation matrix $\mathbf{T}$ is estimated by the algorithm (e.g. RANSAC) without iteration to get the correspondences and the transformation.

Specifically, all these methods [131–133] in first step use deep learning to extract features. The learned features can provide accurate and robust correspondence for transformation estimation without iteration. However, since the features are depended on large training data, the final performance dramatically drops in unseen scenes. Meanwhile, this stand-alone feature network requires point-to-point matching.

3DMatch [133] is a feature-learning methods trained on RGBD images, which extracts local features for point clouds via a parallel structure. The input is 3D volume data, while the output is a feature for a local patch with 512 dimension. The overall framework is shown in Fig. 6.10. the point clouds need to be transformed into 3D volume data and go through 3D CNN networks to obtain the feature.

- **End-to-End-Learning Methods in Same-Source**

The purpose of these methods is to deal with the point cloud registration problem in an end-to-end manner, which embeds the transformation estimation apart from feature learning. The original intention lies on transforming the basic registration

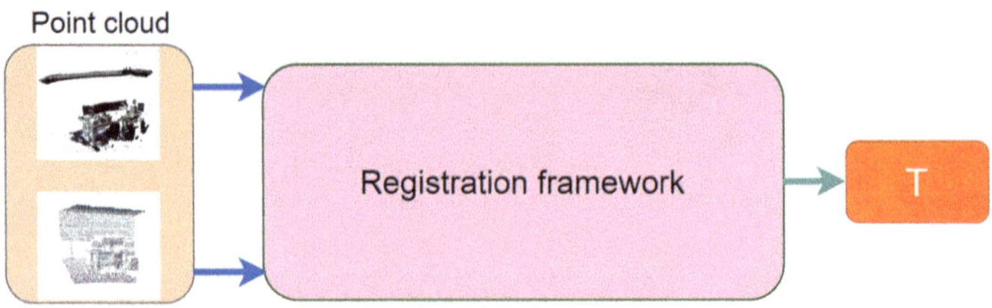

Fig. 6.11 The architecture for point cloud registration for cross-source domain (©2019 IEEE. Reprinted, with permission, from ref [135])

problem into a regression one. Various networks are proposed [134–136]. These methods are easy to operate since the network is end-to-end, but the regress process can be seen as a black box and the distance metric is usually coordinate-based Euclidean distance, which is sensitive to noise and density. The local structure is less considered at the meantime.

- **Cross-Source Methods**

This category aims to deal with point clouds from different types of sensors, which is more challenging because the uncontrollable conditions are more complex, i.e., noise, outlier, density difference, partial overlap, and scale difference. The architecture for cross-source domain is illustrated in Fig. 6.11. Given two point clouds from different sources, a registration network is designed to estimate the final solution **T**. Several algorithms [137–139] have tried complicated optimization strategies to solve these challenges. To overcome these challenges, these approaches all apply optimization strategies or the deep neural network to estimate the final transformation matrix.

These methods can benefit 3D vision tasks, i.e., augmented reality, and building construction. However, existing methods often face challenges in terms of accuracy and time complexity. This could also promote the development of combing sensor technology and cross-source registration.

FMR [140] is the pioneer to deal with cross-source domain point cloud registration, which converts the registration problem to minimize the feature difference by combining conventional optimization (Lucas–Kanade method) and deep learning. The whole framework is shown in Fig. 6.12, which consists of two parts, the encoder (orange box) and multitask semisupervised network, dubbed as MTSS (green box). The encoder aims to extract the features of two input point clouds P and Q. The MTSS focuses on solving the registration problem without correspondence. Task 1 corresponds to decoding the features by a decoder, which helps to train the encoder network in an unsupervised way. While Task 2 calculates the feature-metric projection error r via two input features F_P and F_Q. Then, the transformation increment $\nabla\theta$ is estimated via a nonlinear optimization algorithm and update the

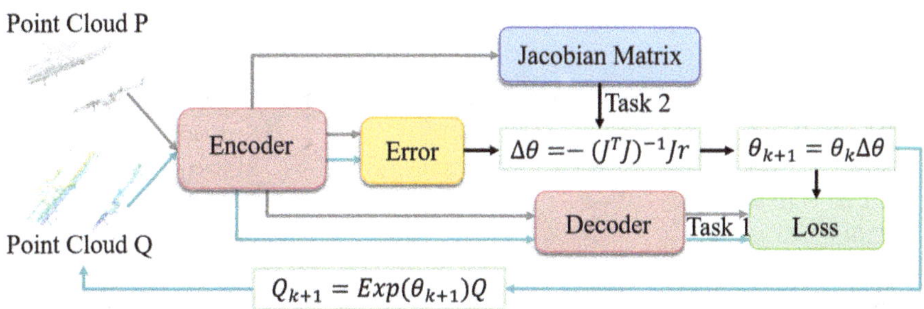

Fig. 6.12 The architecture of FMR (©2021 IEEE. Reprinted, with permission, from ref [140])

transformation parameters θ_{k+1}. Finally, the whole process runs iteratively by using these updated parameters θ_{k+1} and the input point cloud Q.

6.3.4 Evaluation Metrics

The following five metrics are usually considered.

Root Mean Square Error of Projection (rmseP) This metric is the average of point–point projection error after using the transformation.

Root Mean Square Error of Transformation (rmseT) This one evaluates the root-mean-square error between the estimated transformation g_{est} and the ground truth transformation g_{gt}.

The Rotation Error (RE) This evaluation calculates the Euclidean distance of rotation information between estimated r_{est} and ground truth r_{gt}. The rotation information is the angles on 3-axe.

The Translation Error (TE) This metric calculates the Euclidean distance of translation information between estimated t_{est} and the ground truth t_{gt}.

Recall The recall denotes the number of pairs that RE and TE are less than a threshold to the total pair number. Or, the rmseP is below the threshold.

6.3.5 Datasets and Results

As for same-source dataset, ModelNet40 [141], 3DMatch [133], KITTI [142], and ETHdata [125] are used. Toward to the corss-source benchmark, 3DCSR [125] is provided. The summary is shown in Table 6.5.

In detail, the ModelNet40 dataset consists of 3D CAD models with 40 categories and a total of 13,356 models. Each model contains several faces and nodes.

Table 6.5 Summary of the existing same-source and cross-source domain datasets (Source: Author)

Dataset	Sensor	SceneNum	Indoor	Outdoor	Dense	Sparse	Ground truth	xzy	Color
3DMatch	Depth	56	✓	×	✓	×	Synthetic	✓	✓
KITTI	LiDAR	8	×	✓	×	✓	Synthetic	✓	×
ETHdata	LiDAR	8	×	✓	×	✓	Synthetic	✓	✓
3DCSR	Indoor	21	✓	✓	✓	✓	Manual	✓	✓

Table 6.6 Summary of the existing same-source and cross-source domain methods (Source: Author)

Methods	Advantages	Disadvantages	Application scenes
ICP [126]	Rigorous theory	Sophisticated strategies	Traditional registration
	Quickest method		
	Generalized method		
3DMatch [133]	Feature-learning	Costly on 3D CNN	Volume data registration
		Point-to-point matching	
DeepVCP [135]	End-to-end	Sensitive to noise	Point cloud registration
	Global-feature-learning	Sensitive to density	
		Lack local structure	
FMR [140]	Tradition and deep learning	Low accuracy	Varying point clouds source
		High time complexity	

3DMatch contains over 200K RGB-D images of 62 different scenes. Each scene is divided into several fragments reconstructed from 50 depth frames using TSDF volumetric fusion. KITTI is the odometry dataset designed for stereo-matching performance evaluation, comprising 22 stereo sequences. ETH data are recorded with Laser, IMU, and GPS sensors, which contains eight scenes with each scene around 30 fragments. This dataset involves global aligned frames and local frames with ground truth transformation. 3DCSR has two types of cross-source data, the first is Kinect and Lidar, and the second is Kinect and 3D reconstruction. The former has 19 scenes with 165 pairs of cross-source point clouds using Kinect and Lidar. The latter involves 18 simple indoor objects and 19 multiple objects, with 37 pairs of cross-source point clouds obtained using Kinect and iPhone cameras. Furthermore, the comparison of different methods of point cloud registration is presented in Table 6.6.

6.4 Point Cloud Multimodal Analysis

The previous subsections have employed point cloud as a single input data type for training learning models in the context of given 3D tasks. However, in real-world scenarios, more than one type of sensor is usually involved in acquiring 3D information from the scenes. Therefore, a variety of data types can be utilized in conjunction with each other to achieve the given tasks. The incorporation of different data types can offer complementary perspectives and information to the learning model, thereby improving its performance. This learning way that relies on multiple data types is referred to as multimodal learning. Since multimodal learning methods are intrinsically tied to specific real-world applications, we present point cloud-based multimodal learning methods, with a focus on perception tasks in the field of autonomous driving as an illustrative example.

6.4.1 Research Tasks

Perception constitutes a crucial module for autonomous driving, encompassing various tasks such as 2D/3D object detection, semantic segmentation, and depth completion and prediction, among others [57, 143, 144]. Among these tasks, the first two occupy a fundamental position in perception and have been the subject of extensive research. They entail the detection of obstacles, traffic lights, traffic signs, as well as the segmentation of lanes or free space. Accordingly, our discussion on multimodal learning methods centers on these two tasks.

Despite the exciting results achieved by unimodal learning approaches in perception, there exist inherent drawbacks that can hamper the performance of the models [143, 145]. With respect to camera data, the view is limited [146], resulting in occlusions and deficiencies when confronted with complex scenes. From the perspective of LiDAR data, the resolution decreases as the distance increases due to the structural design of LiDAR [147]. Furthermore, the quality of LiDAR data can be disturbed in extreme weather conditions, such as fog and heavy rain [145]. Hence, in real-life scenarios, it becomes necessary and effective to utilize multimodal learning methods to compensate for the inherent data deficiencies in unimodal situations.

6.4.2 Categorization

The significant variability in form between camera data and LiDAR data makes it challenging for traditional learning methods to process them uniformly and fully exploit complementary information. However, recent advancements in deep learning have revolutionized the development of multimodal learning due to its powerful data-fitting capability. Neural networks can easily extract features of different types of data separately, which has led to significant progress in multimodal learning. The key to the effectiveness of multimodal learning methods lies in the fusion of different representations learned from different data types. Hence, we systematically introduce the existing techniques based on the classification of fusion methodology proposed in Huang et al. [148].

- **Strong-Fusion Category**

The strong-fusion category in multimodal learning can be further divided into four types, including early-fusion, deep-fusion, late-fusion, and asymmetry-fusion. These categories differ in terms of the stages at which the representations of LiDAR and camera data are combined. Figure 6.13 illustrates the distinctions and relationships between the different categories of strong-fusion. Notably, strong-fusion heavily relies on LiDAR data, with camera data serving as an auxiliary. In the following, we will describe each category in detail.

Early-Fusion Early-fusion refers to a data-level-fusion technique that differs from the traditional definition. In this technique, data are projected into the same modality by aligning it spatially at the original data. This process combines LiDAR data at the data-level with camera data at either the data-level or feature-level [149, 150].

Regarding the LiDAR branch discussed earlier, point clouds can be represented in multiple ways, including 3D points with reflectance, voxelized tensors, front-view/range-view/bird's eye view, and pseudo point clouds. These various representations of point clouds used for early-fusion can be directly visualized, as the data remain interpretable at this stage compared to embedding in feature space. In the case of the image path, early-fusion based on geometric relationships can fuse data as RGB or grayscale images and 2D features with positional attributes.

Deep-Fusion Methods Deep-fusion methods adopt a cascading approach to integrate features, which allows them to effectively utilize both raw and high-level semantic information, which is in contrast to other strong-fusion methods [145, 151, 152]. Deep fusion involves fusing the LiDAR branch at the feature level and the image branch either at the data level or the feature level, in a cross-modal manner.

Late-Fusion Methods Last-fusion, which is also known as object-level fusion, refers to a fusion technique that combines the results obtained from each branch where each branch's results are unimodally learned. It is important to ensure that the proposals for each branch are consistent with the final output format, although they may differ in terms of early-fusion precision. It is noteworthy that late-fusion can be considered a specific form of ensemble learning.

Asymmetry-Fusion Methods Asymmetric-fusion is a fusion technique that handles the information to be fused in each branch differently, by granting different privileges to each branch. Specifically, object-level information is fused from one branch, while data-level information or feature-level information is fused from other branches. Asymmetric-fusion is distinct from other robust fusion methods because the branches in asymmetric fusion have a clear priority, with non-object-

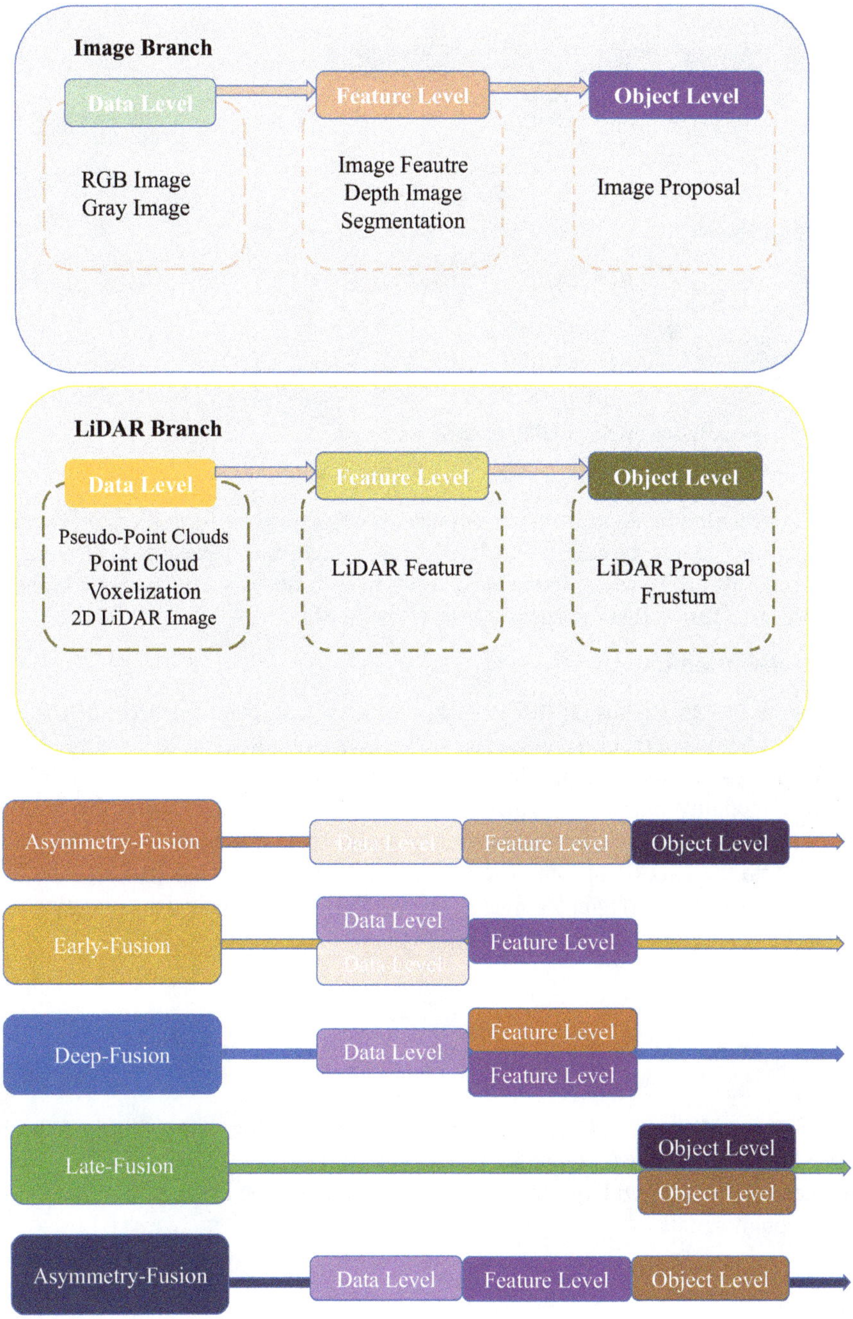

Fig. 6.13 Strong-fusion overview [148] (Source: Author)

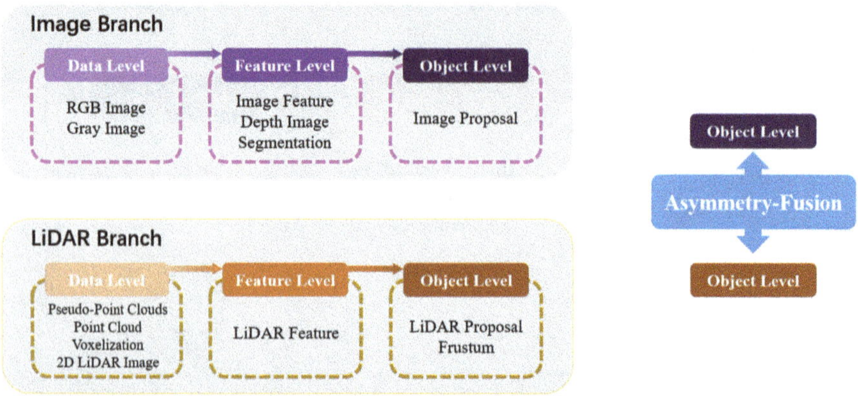

Fig. 6.14 Weak-fusion overview [148] (Source: Author)

level information being utilized to optimize the object-level information to generate the final prediction. In contrast to late-fusion, which may have identical features and proposals [153], asymmetric-fusion only fuses proposals from a single branch, whereas late-fusion fuses proposals from all branches.

- **Weak-Fusion Category**

In contrast to strong-fusion methods that directly fuse data, features, or objects from multimodal branches, weak-fusion-based techniques aim to leverage rules to extract a supervisory signal from one modality branch to guide the training of another modality branch. Specifically, weak-fusion involves utilizing the object-level proposal from the camera branch to correspond to a frustum in the raw point cloud from the LiDAR branch. The resultant frustum is then inputted into the 3D backbone network to obtain the final proposal [154]. A schematic demonstrating the weak-fusion approach is depicted in Fig. 6.14.

6.4.3 Datasets

More than a dozen datasets related to autonomous driving perception have been open-sourced. However, only three datasets (KITTI [143], Waymo [155], and nuScenes [156]) are widely used. Table 6.7 summarizes the characteristics of these three common datasets.

Table 6.7 Summary of the existing same-source and cross-source domain datasets (Source: Author)

Dataset	Year	LiDARs	Cameras	Annotated frames	3D Boxes	2D Boxes	Traffic scenario	Diversity
KITTI	2012	1 Velodyne HDL-64E	2 grayscale 2 color cameras	15k	80k	80k	Urban, suburban, highway	–
Waymo	2019	5 LiDARs	5 high-resolution pinhole cameras	230k	12M	9.9M	Urban, suburban	Locations
nuScenes	2019	1 Spinning 32-beams LiDAR	6 RGB cameras	40k	1.4M	–	Urban, suburban	Locations, weather

6.5 Summary

This chapter presents an in-depth exploration of various methodologies tailored to different scenarios in point cloud machine vision analysis. It systematically covers several critical topics, including point cloud place recognition, point cloud registration, and multimodal approaches to 3D point cloud analysis. Each section underscores the importance of these methods in the context of point cloud machine vision and elaborates on the specific implementation steps involved. In point cloud place recognition, the focus is on identifying and categorizing locations based on point cloud data, which is essential for applications like autonomous navigation and spatial mapping. The methodologies discussed provide robust frameworks for accurately recognizing and interpreting spatial environments. Point cloud registration is explored in detail, focusing on the techniques for aligning and integrating multiple point cloud datasets. This process is essential for creating cohesive and accurate representations from disparate data sources. Similarly, point cloud retrieval methods are discussed, illustrating the approaches for efficiently searching and extracting relevant point cloud data from large datasets. The chapter concludes with a discussion on multi-modal approaches, which combine point cloud data with other data modalities to enhance analysis capabilities. This section highlights the synergistic potential of integrating diverse data sources, leading to more robust and comprehensive machine vision systems. Overall, this chapter aims to provide readers with a thorough understanding of the various methods involved in point cloud machine vision analysis, emphasizing their significance and practical implementation steps. By systematically unpacking these topics, it offers a comprehensive overview that equips readers with the knowledge needed to apply these techniques effectively in their respective fields.

Exercises

1. How is point cloud tracking achieved in dynamic environments?
2. What are the advantages of using deep learning for point cloud semantic segmentation?
3. How is real-time processing achieved in point cloud tracking?
4. How does multimodal analysis enhance point cloud analytics?
5. Please explain the concept of "lazy triplet and quadruplet" loss functions as used in PointNetVLAD.
6. What are the typical evaluation metrics used for point cloud place recognition?
7. What datasets are commonly used for benchmarking point cloud place recognition, and what specific tasks are they used for?
8. Please discuss the advantages and disadvantages of MinkLoc3D compared to other point cloud place recognition methods.

9. How do the deep-learning-based methods improve upon traditional methods in point cloud place recognition?
10. What is the primary challenge of point cloud registration as described in the chapter, and how do deep learning methods address it?

References

1. B. Qu, X. Liang, S. Sun, W. Gao, Exploring aigc video quality: a focus on visual harmony, video-text consistency and domain distribution gap, in *Proceedings of the IEEE/CVF Conference on Computer Vision and Pattern Recognition Workshops* (2024)
2. B. Qu, H. Li, W. Gao, Bringing textual prompt to ai-generated image quality assessment, in *2024 IEEE International Conference on Multimedia and Expo (ICME)* (IEEE, Piscataway, 2024)
3. Y. Wu, L. Xie, S. Sun, W. Gao, Y. Yan, Adaptive intra period size for deep learning-based screen content video coding, in *2024 IEEE International Conference on Multimedia and Expo Workshops (ICMEW)* (IEEE, Piscataway, 2024)
4. H. Zheng, W. Gao, End-to-end RGB-D image compression via exploiting channel-modality redundancy. Proc. AAAI Conf. Artif. Intell. **38**(7), 7562–7570 (2024)
5. L. Tao, W. Gao, G. Li, C. Zhang, AdaNIC: towards practical neural image compression via dynamic transform routing, in *Proceedings of the IEEE/CVF International Conference on Computer Vision* (2023), pp. 16 879–16 888
6. Y. Wu, W. Gao, End-to-end lossless compression of high precision depth maps guided by pseudo-residual. Preprint. arXiv:2201.03195 (2022)
7. Y. Wu, Z. Qi, H. Zheng, L. Tao, W. Gao, Deep image compression with latent optimization and piece-wise quantization approximation, in *Proceedings of the IEEE/CVF Conference on Computer Vision and Pattern Recognition* (2021), pp. 1926–1930
8. W. Gao, L. Tao, L. Zhou, D. Yang, X. Zhang, Z. Guo, Low-rate image compression with super-resolution learning, in *Proceedings of the IEEE/CVF Conference on Computer Vision and Pattern Recognition Workshops* (2020), pp. 154–155
9. W. Gao, S. Sun, H. Zheng, Y. Wu, H. Ye, Y. Zhang, OpenDMC: an open-source library and performance evaluation for deep-learning-based multi-frame compression, in *Proceedings of the 31st ACM International Conference on Multimedia* (2023), pp. 9685–9688
10. Y. Guo, W. Gao, G. Li, Interpretable task-inspired adaptive filter pruning for neural networks under multiple constraints. Int. J. Comput. Vision **132**(6) 2060–2076 (2024)
11. W. Gao, Y. Guo, S. Ma, G. Li, S. Kwong, Efficient neural network compression inspired by compressive sensing. IEEE Trans. Neural Networks Learn. Syst. **35**(2), 1965–1979 (2022)
12. Y. Guo, W. Gao, Semantic-driven automatic filter pruning for neural networks, in *2022 IEEE International Conference on Multimedia and Expo (ICME)* (IEEE, Piscataway, 2022), pp. 1–6
13. L. Tao, W. Gao, Efficient channel pruning based on architecture alignment and probability model bypassing, in *2021 IEEE International Conference on Systems, Man, and Cybernetics (SMC)* (IEEE, Piscataway, 2021), pp. 3232–3237
14. Z. Yang, W. Gao, G. Li, Y. Yan, SUR-driven video coding rate control for jointly optimizing perceptual quality and buffer control. IEEE Trans. Image Proces. **32**, 5451–5464 (2023)
15. F. Shen, Z. Cai, W. Gao, An efficient rate control algorithm for intra frame coding in AVS3, in *2021 IEEE International Conference on Systems, Man, and Cybernetics (SMC)* (IEEE, Piscataway, 2021), pp. 3164–3169
16. H. Yuan, W. Gao, J. Wang, Dynamic computational resource allocation for fast inter frame coding in video conferencing applications, in *2021 IEEE International Conference on Multimedia and Expo (ICME)* (IEEE, Piscataway, 2021), pp. 1–6

17. W. Gao, Q. Jiang, R. Wang, S. Ma, G. Li, S. Kwong, Consistent quality oriented rate control in HEVC via balancing intra and inter frame coding. IEEE Trans. Ind. Inf. **18**(3), 1594–1604 (2021)
18. H. Yuan, W. Gao, A new coding unit partitioning mode for screen content video coding, in *Proceedings of the 2021 5th International Conference on Digital Signal Processing* (2021), pp. 66–72
19. W. Gao, On the performance evaluation of state-of-the-art rate control algorithms for practical video coding and transmission systems, in *Proceedings of the 2020 4th International Conference on Video and Image Processing* (2020), pp. 179–185
20. W. Gao, S. Kwong, Q. Jiang, C.-K. Fong, P.H. Wong, W.Y. Yuen, Data-driven rate control for rate-distortion optimization in HEVC based on simplified effective initial QP learning. IEEE Trans. Broadcast. **65**(1), 94–108 (2018)
21. W. Gao, A multi-objective optimization perspective for joint consideration of video coding quality, in *2019 Asia-Pacific Signal and Information Processing Association Annual Summit and Conference (APSIPA ASC)* (IEEE, Piscataway, 2019), pp. 986–991
22. W. Gao, S. Kwong, Y. Jia, Joint machine learning and game theory for rate control in high efficiency video coding. IEEE Trans. Image Proces. **26**(12), 6074–6089 (2017)
23. W. Gao, S. Kwong, Y. Zhou, H. Yuan, SSIM-based game theory approach for rate-distortion optimized intra frame CTU-level bit allocation. IEEE Trans. Multimedia **18**(6), 988–999 (2016)
24. W. Gao, S. Kwong, H. Yuan, X. Wang, DCT coefficient distribution modeling and quality dependency analysis based frame-level bit allocation for HEVC. IEEE Trans. Circuits Syst. Video Technol. **26**(1), 139–153 (2015)
25. W. Gao, S. Kwong, Phase congruency based edge saliency detection and rate control for perceptual image and video coding, in *2016 IEEE International Conference on Systems, Man, and Cybernetics (SMC)* (IEEE, Piscataway, 2016), pp. 000 264–000 269
26. H. Yuan, W. Gao, OpenFastVC: an open source library for video coding fast algorithm implementation, in *Proceedings of the 31st ACM International Conference on Multimedia* (2023), pp. 9660–9663
27. H. Yuan, W. Gao, S. Ma, Y. Yan, Divide-and-conquer-based RDO-free CU partitioning for 8K video compression. ACM Trans. Multimedia Comput. Commun. Appl. **20**(4), 1–20 (2024)
28. L. Tao, W. Gao, A hardware implementation of entropy encoder for 8k video coding, in *2022 IEEE International Conference on Multimedia and Expo (ICME)* (IEEE, Piscataway, 2022), pp. 1–6
29. Y. Guo, W. Gao, S. Ma, G. Li, Accelerating transform algorithm implementation for efficient intra coding of 8k UHD videos. ACM Trans. Multimedia Comput. Commun. Appl. **18**(4), 1–20 (2022)
30. Z. Cai, W. Gao, Efficient fast algorithm and parallel hardware architecture for intra prediction of AVS3, in *2021 IEEE International Symposium on Circuits and Systems (ISCAS)* (IEEE, Piscataway, 2021), pp. 1–5
31. W. Gao, H. Yuan, Y. Guo, L. Tao, Z. Cai, G. Li, OpenHardwareVC: an open source library for 8K UHD video coding hardware implementation, in *Proceedings of the 30th ACM International Conference on Multimedia* (2022), pp. 7339–7342
32. W. Gao, H. Yuan, G. Liao, Z. Guo, J. Chen, PP8K: a new dataset for 8K UHD video compression and processing. IEEE MultiMedia **30**(3), 100–109 (2023)
33. X. Zang, W. Gao, G. Li, H. Fang, C. Ban, Z. He, H. Sun, A baseline investigation: transformer-based cross-view baseline for text-based person search, in *Proceedings of the 31st ACM International Conference on Multimedia* (2023), pp. 7737–7746
34. G. Liao, W. Gao, G. Li, J. Wang, S. Kwong, Cross-collaborative fusion-encoder network for robust RGB-thermal salient object detection. IEEE Trans. Circuits Syst. Video Technol. **32**(11), 7646–7661 (2022)
35. W. Gao, G. Liao, S. Ma, G. Li, Y. Liang, W. Lin, Unified information fusion network for multi-modal RGB-D and RGB-T salient object detection. IEEE Trans. Circuits Syst. Video Technol. **32**(4), 2091–2106 (2021)

36. Y. Chen, S. Sun, G. Li, W. Gao, T.H. Li, Closing the gap between theory and practice during alternating optimization for gans. IEEE Trans. Neural Networks Learn. Syst. **35**(10), 14005–14017 (2024)
37. Y. Chen, C. Jin, G. Li, T.H. Li, W. Gao, Mitigating label noise in gans via enhanced spectral normalization. IEEE Trans. Circuits Syst. Video Technol. **33**(8), 3924–3934 (2023)
38. X. Zang, G. Li, W. Gao, Multidirection and multiscale pyramid in transformer for video-based pedestrian retrieval. IEEE Trans. Ind. Inf. **18**(12), 8776–8785 (2022)
39. X. Zang, G. Li, W. Gao, X. Shu, Learning to disentangle scenes for person re-identification. Image Vision Comput. **116**, 104330 (2021)
40. X. Zang, G. Li, W. Gao, X. Shu, Exploiting robust unsupervised video person re-identification. IET Image Proces. **16**(3), 729–741 (2022)
41. Z. Yue, G. Li, W. Gao, Cross-level guided attention for human-object interaction detection, in *2023 IEEE International Conference on Multimedia and Expo Workshops (ICMEW)* (IEEE, Piscataway, 2023), pp. 284–289
42. Z. Yao, W. Gao, Iterative saliency aggregation and assignment network for efficient salient object detection in optical remote sensing images. IEEE Trans. Geosci. Remote Sens. **62**, 1–13 (2024)
43. Y. Sun, Z. Li, S. Wang, W. Gao, Depth-assisted calibration on learning-based factorization for a compressive light field display. Opt. Exp. **31**(4), 5399–5413 (2023)
44. Y. Sun, Z. Li, L. Li, S. Wang, W. Gao, Optimization of compressive light field display in dual-guided learning, in *ICASSP 2022-2022 IEEE International Conference on Acoustics, Speech and Signal Processing (ICASSP)* (IEEE, Piscataway, 2022), pp. 2075–2079
45. W. Gao, S. Fan, G. Li, W. Lin, A thorough benchmark and a new model for light field saliency detection. IEEE Trans. Pattern Anal. Mach. Intell. **45**(7), 8003–8019 (2023)
46. Z. Guo, W. Gao, H. Wang, J. Wang, S. Fan, No-reference deep quality assessment of compressed light field images, in *2021 IEEE International Conference on Multimedia and Expo (ICME)* (IEEE, Piscataway, 2021), pp. 1–6
47. G. Liao, W. Gao, Rethinking feature mining for light field salient object detection. ACM Trans. Multimedia Comput. Commun. Appl. **20**(10), 1–24 (2024)
48. S. Sun, J. Liu, T.H. Li, H. Li, G. Liu, W. Gao, Streamflow: Streamlined multi-frame optical flow estimation for video sequences. Preprint. arXiv:2311.17099 (2023)
49. R. Liu, J. Huang, W. Gao, T.H. Li, G. Li, Mug-STAN: adapting image-language pretrained models for general video understanding. Preprint. arXiv:2311.15075 (2023)
50. C. Zhang, W. Gao, Learned rate control for frame-level adaptive neural video compression via dynamic neural network, in *European Conference on Computer Vision* (Springer, Berlin, 2024)
51. W. Gao, G. Li, H. Yuan, R. Hamzaoui, Z. Li, S. Liu, Apccpa'22: 1st international workshop on advances in point cloud compression, processing and analysis, in *Proceedings of the 30th ACM International Conference on Multimedia* (2022), pp. 7392–7393
52. T. Qin, G. Li, W. Gao, S. Liu, Multi-grained point cloud geometry compression via dual-model prediction with extended octree. ACM Trans. Multimedia Comput. Commun. Appl. **20**(9), 1–30 (2024)
53. Y. Shao, W. Gao, S. Liu, G. Li, Advanced patch-based affine motion estimation for dynamic point cloud geometry compression. Sensors **24**(10), 3142 (2024)
54. Y. Shao, F. Song, W. Gao, S. Liu, G. Li, Texture-guided graph transform optimization for point cloud attribute compression. Appl. Sci. **14**(10), 4094 (2024)
55. Y. Shao, X. Yang, W. Gao, S. Liu, G. Li, 3d point cloud attribute compression using diffusion-based texture-aware intra prediction. IEEE Trans. Circuits Syst. Video Technol. **34**(10), 9633–9646 (2024)
56. J. Zhang, Y. Chen, G. Liu, W. Gao, G. Li, Efficient point cloud attribute compression framework using attribute-guided graph fourier transform, in *ICASSP 2024-2024 IEEE International Conference on Acoustics, Speech and Signal Processing (ICASSP)* (IEEE, Piscataway, 2024), pp. 8426–8430

57. W. Gao, H. Yuan, G. Li, Z. Li, H. Yuan, Low complexity coding unit decision for video-based point cloud compression. IEEE Trans. Image Proces. **33**, 149–162 (2023)
58. Y. Shao, G. Li, Q. Zhang, W. Gao, S. Liu, Non-rigid registration-based progressive motion compensation for point cloud geometry compression. IEEE Trans. Geosci. Remote Sens. **61**, 1–14 (2023)
59. F. Song, G. Li, X. Yang, W. Gao, S. Liu, Block-adaptive point cloud attribute coding with region-aware optimized transform. IEEE Trans. Circuits Syst. Video Technol. **33**(8), 4294–4308 (2023)
60. Y. An, Y. Shao, G. Li, W. Gao, S. Liu, A fast motion estimation method with hamming distance for lidar point cloud compression, in *2022 IEEE International Conference on Visual Communications and Image Processing (VCIP)* (IEEE, Piscataway, 2022), pp. 1–5
61. H. Yuan, W. Gao, G. Li, Z. Li, Rate-distortion-guided learning approach with cross-projection information for V-PCC fast CU decision, in *Proceedings of the 30th ACM International Conference on Multimedia* (2022), pp. 3085–3093
62. F. Song, G. Li, W. Gao, T.H. Li, Rate-distortion optimized graph for point cloud attribute coding. IEEE Signal Proces. Lett. **29**, 922–926 (2022)
63. F. Song, G. Li, X. Yang, W. Gao, T.H. Li, Fine-grained correlation representation for graph-based point cloud attribute compression, in *2022 IEEE International Conference on Multimedia and Expo (ICME)* (IEEE, Piscataway, 2022), pp. 1–6
64. F. Shen, W. Gao, A rate control algorithm for video-based point cloud compression, in *2021 International Conference on Visual Communications and Image Processing (VCIP)* (IEEE, Piscataway, 2021), pp. 1–5
65. F. Song, Y. Shao, W. Gao, H. Wang, T. Li, Layer-wise geometry aggregation framework for lossless lidar point cloud compression. IEEE Trans. Circuits Syst. Video Technol. **31**(12), 4603–4616 (2021)
66. L. Xie, W. Gao, H. Zheng, G. Li, SPCGC: scalable point cloud geometry compression for machine vision, in *Proceedings of IEEE International Conference on Robotics and Automation* (2024)
67. L. Xie, W. Gao, H. Zheng, H. Ye, Semantic-aware visual decomposition for point cloud geometry compression, in *2024 Data Compression Conference (DCC)* (IEEE, Piscataway, 2024), pp. 595–595
68. Z. Qi, W. Gao, Variable-rate point cloud geometry compression based on feature adjustment and interpolation, in *2024 Data Compression Conference (DCC)* (IEEE, Piscataway, 2024), pp. 63–72
69. Z. Yu, W. Gao, When dynamic neural network meets point cloud compression: computation-aware variable rate and checkerboard context, in *2024 Data Compression Conference (DCC)* (IEEE, Piscataway, 2024), pp. 600–600
70. L. Xie, W. Gao, S. Fan, Z. Yao, PDNet: parallel dual-branch network for point cloud geometry compression and analysis, in *2024 Data Compression Conference (DCC)* (IEEE, Piscataway, 2024), pp. 596–596
71. L. Xie, W. Gao, H. Zheng, End-to-end point cloud geometry compression and analysis with sparse tensor, in *Proceedings of the 1st International Workshop on Advances in Point Cloud Compression, Processing and Analysis* (2022), pp. 27–32
72. C. Fu, G. Li, R. Song, W. Gao, S. Liu, OctAttention: octree-based large-scale contexts model for point cloud compression, in *AAAI Conference on Artificial Intelligence* (2022), pp. 625–633
73. H. Zheng, W. Gao, Z. Yu, T. Zhao, G. Li, ViewPCGC: view-guided learned point cloud geometry compression, in *Proceedings of the 32nd ACM International Conference on Multimedia* (2024)
74. L. Xie, W. Gao, H. Zheng, G. Li, ROI-guided point cloud geometry compression towards human and machine vision, in *Proceedings of the 32nd ACM International Conference on Multimedia* (2024)

75. C. Peng, W. Gao, Laplacian matrix learning for point cloud attribute compression with ternary search-based adaptive block partition, in *Proceedings of the 32nd ACM International Conference on Multimedia* (2024)
76. S. Luo, B. Qu, W. Gao, Learning robust 3d representation from clip via dual denoising. Preprint. arXiv:2407.00905 (2024)
77. G. Li, G. Wei, W. Gao, *Point Cloud Compression: Technologies and Standardization* (Springer Nature, Berlin, 2024)
78. G. Li, W. Gao, W. Gao, Introduction, in *Point Cloud Compression: Technologies and Standardization* (Springer, Berlin, 2024), pp. 1–28
79. G. Li, W. Gao, W. Gao, Background knowledge, in *Point Cloud Compression: Technologies and Standardization* (Springer, Berlin, 2024), pp. 29–51
80. G. Li, W. Gao, W. Gao, Predictive coding, in *Point Cloud Compression: Technologies and Standardization* (Springer, Berlin, 2024), pp. 53–70
81. G. Li, W. Gao, W. Gao, Transform coding, in *Point Cloud Compression: Technologies and Standardization* (Springer, Berlin, 2024), pp. 71–96
82. G. Li, W. Gao, W. Gao, Quantization techniques, in *Point Cloud Compression: Technologies and Standardization* (Springer, Berlin, 2024), pp. 97–112
83. G. Li, W. Gao, W. Gao, Entropy coding, in *Point Cloud Compression: Technologies and Standardization* (Springer, Berlin, 2024), pp. 113–133
84. G. Li, W. Gao, W. Gao, MPEG geometry-based point cloud compression (G-PCC) standard, in *Point Cloud Compression: Technologies and Standardization* (Springer, Berlin, 2024), pp. 135–165
85. G. Li, W. Gao, W. Gao, AVS point cloud compression standard, in *Point Cloud Compression: Technologies and Standardization* (Springer, Berlin, 2024), pp. 167–197
86. G. Li, W. Gao, W. Gao, MPEG video-based point cloud compression (V-PCC) standard, in *Point Cloud Compression: Technologies and Standardization* (Springer, Berlin, 2024), pp. 199–218
87. G. Li, W. Gao, W. Gao, MPEG AI-based 3d graphics coding standard, in *Point Cloud Compression: Technologies and Standardization* (Springer, Berlin, 2024), pp. 219–241
88. G. Li, W. Gao, W. Gao, Future work, in *Point Cloud Compression: Technologies and Standardization* (Springer, Berlin, 2024), pp. 243–250
89. W. Gao, H. Ye, G. Li, H. Zheng, Y. Wu, L. Xie, OpenPointCloud: an open-source algorithm library of deep learning based point cloud compression, in *ACM International Conference on Multimedia* (2022), pp. 7347–7350
90. W. Liu, W. Gao, X. Mu, Fast inter-frame motion prediction for compressed dynamic point cloud attribute enhancement. Proc. AAAI Conf. Artif. Intell. **38**(4), 3720–3728 (2024)
91. Z. Yang, W. Gao, X. Lu, DANet: density-adaptive network for geometry-based point cloud compression artifacts removal, in *2023 IEEE International Conference on Visual Communications and Image Processing (VCIP)* (IEEE, Piscataway, 2023), pp. 1–5
92. X. Fan, G. Li, D. Li, Y. Ren, W. Gao, T.H. Li, Deep geometry post-processing for decompressed point clouds, in *2022 IEEE International Conference on Multimedia and Expo (ICME)* (IEEE, Piscataway, 2022), pp. 1–6
93. X. Zhang, G. Liao, W. Gao, G. Li, TDRNet: transformer-based dual-branch restoration network for geometry based point cloud compression artifacts, in *2022 IEEE International Conference on Multimedia and Expo (ICME)* (IEEE, Piscataway, 2022), pp. 1–6
94. Z. Li, G. Li, T.H. Li, S. Liu, W. Gao, Semantic point cloud upsampling. IEEE Trans. Multimedia **25**, 3432–3442 (2023)
95. R. Zhang, W. Gao, G. Li, T.H. Li, QINet: decision surface learning and adversarial enhancement for quasi-immune completion of diverse corrupted point clouds. IEEE Trans. Geosci. Remote Sens. **60**, 1–14 (2022)
96. R. Bao, Y. Ren, G. Li, W. Gao, S. Liu, Flow-based point cloud completion network with adversarial refinement, in *ICASSP 2022-2022 IEEE International Conference on Acoustics, Speech and Signal Processing (ICASSP)* (IEEE, Piscataway, 2022), pp. 2559–2563

97. J. Chen, G. Li, R. Zhang, T.H. Li, W. Gao, PointIVAE: invertible variational autoencoder framework for 3d point cloud generation, in *2022 IEEE International Conference on Image Processing (ICIP)* (IEEE, Piscataway, 2022), pp. 3216–3220
98. R. Zhang, J. Chen, W. Gao, G. Li, T.H. Li, PointOT: interpretable geometry-inspired point cloud generative model via optimal transport. IEEE Trans. Circuits Syst. Video Technol. **32**(10), 6792–6806 (2022)
99. S. Fan, W. Gao, Screen-based 3d subjective experiment software, in *Proceedings of the 31st ACM International Conference on Multimedia* (2023), pp. 9672–9675
100. X. Mao, H. Yuan, X. Lu, R. Hamzaoui, W. Gao, PCAC-GAN: a sparse-tensor-based generative adversarial network for 3d point cloud attribute compression. Comput. Visual Media (2024)
101. J. Wang, W. Gao, G. Li, Applying collaborative adversarial learning to blind point cloud quality measurement. IEEE Trans. Instrum. Measure. **72**, 1–15 (2023)
102. Y. Zhang, W. Gao, G. Li, OpenPointCloud-V2: a deep learning based open-source algorithm library of point cloud processing, in *Proceedings of the 1st International Workshop on Advances in Point Cloud Compression, Processing and Analysis* (2022), pp. 51–55
103. S. Fan, W. Gao, G. Li, Salient object detection for point clouds, in *European Conference on Computer Vision* (2022), pp. 1–19
104. S. Luo, W. Gao, A general framework for rotation invariant point cloud analysis, in *ICASSP 2024-2024 IEEE International Conference on Acoustics, Speech and Signal Processing (ICASSP)* (IEEE, Piscataway, 2024), pp. 3665–3669
105. X. Lu, W. Gao, AttentiveNet: detecting small objects for lidar point clouds by attending to important points, in *2023 IEEE International Conference on Visual Communications and Image Processing (VCIP)* (IEEE, Piscataway, 2023), pp. 1–5
106. Z. Pan, N. Zhang, W. Gao, S. Liu, G. Li, Less is more: label recommendation for weakly supervised point cloud semantic segmentation. Proc. AAAI Conf. Artif. Intell. **38**(5) 4397–4405 (2024)
107. Z. Pan, G. Liu, W. Gao, T. Li, EPContrast: effective point-level contrastive learning for large-scale point cloud understanding, in *2024 IEEE International Conference on Multimedia and Expo (ICME)* (IEEE, Piscataway, 2024)
108. N. Zhang, Z. Pan, T.H. Li, W. Gao, G. Li, Improving graph representation for point cloud segmentation via attentive filtering, in *Proceedings of the IEEE/CVF conference on computer vision and pattern recognition* (2023), pp. 1244–1254
109. K. Wen, N. Zhang, G. Li, W. Gao, MPVNN: multi-resolution point-voxel non-parametric network for 3d point cloud processing, in *2024 IEEE International Conference on Multimedia and Expo (ICME)* (IEEE, Piscataway, 2024)
110. D. Yang, W. Gao, G. Li, H. Yuan, J. Hou, S. Kwong, Exploiting manifold feature representation for efficient classification of 3d point clouds. ACM Trans. Multimedia Comput. Commun. Appl. **19**(1s), 1–21 (2023)
111. M.A. Uy, G.H. Lee, PointNetVLAD: deep point cloud based retrieval for large-scale place recognition, in *IEEE Conference on Computer Vision and Pattern Recognition* (2018), pp. 4470–4479
112. J. Komorowski, MinkLoc3D: point cloud based large-scale place recognition, in *IEEE Winter Conference on Applications of Computer Vision* (2021), pp. 1789–1798
113. L. Hui, H. Yang, M. Cheng, J. Xie, J. Yang, Pyramid point cloud transformer for large-scale place recogition, in *IEEE Conference on Computer Vision and Pattern Recognition* (2021), pp. 6078–6087
114. R. Zhang, G. Li, W. Gao, T.H. Li, Compoint: can complex-valued representation benefit point cloud place recognition? IEEE Trans. Intell. Transport. Syst. **25**(7), 7494–7507 (2024)
115. S.B. Hegde, S. Gangisetty, An evaluation of feature encoding techniques for non-rigid and rigid 3d point cloud retrieval, in *British Machine Vision Conference* (2019), p. 47
116. W. Zhang, C. Xiao, PCAN: 3d attention map learning using contextual information for point cloud based retrieval, in *IEEE Conference on Computer Vision and Pattern Recognition* (2019), pp. 12 436–12 445

117. Q. Sun, H. Liu, J. He, Z. Fan, X. Du, DAGC: employing dual attention and graph convolution for point cloud based place recognition, in *International Conference on Multimedia Retrieval* (2020), pp. 224–232
118. C.R. Qi, H. Su, K. Mo, L.J. Guibas, PointNet: deep learning on point sets for 3D classification and segmentation, in *IEEE Conference on Computer Vision and Pattern Recognition* (2017), pp. 77–85
119. C. Choy, J. Gwak, S. Savarese, 4d spatio-temporal convnets: minkowski convolutional neural networks, in *IEEE Conference on Computer Vision and Pattern Recognition* (2019), pp. 3075–3084
120. F. Radenovic, G. Tolias, O. Chum, Fine-tuning CNN image retrieval with no human annotation. IEEE Trans. Pattern Anal. Mach. Intell. **41**(7), 1655–1668 (2019)
121. T. Lin, P. Dollár, R.B. Girshick, K. He, B. Hariharan, S.J. Belongie, Feature pyramid networks for object detection, in *IEEE Conference on Computer Vision and Pattern Recognition* (IEEE Computer Society, Washington, 2017), pp. 936–944
122. J. Komorowski, M. Wysoczanska, T. Trzcinski, Minkloc++: Lidar and monocular image fusion for place recognition, in *International Joint Conference on Neural Networks* (IEEE, Piscataway, 2021), pp. 1–8
123. Q. Wang, B. Wu, P. Zhu, P. Li, W. Zuo, Q. Hu, ECA-Net: efficient channel attention for deep convolutional neural networks, in *IEEE Conference on Computer Vision and Pattern Recognition* (2020), pp. 11 531–11 539
124. W. Maddern, G. Pascoe, C. Linegar, P. Newman, 1 year, 1000 km: the Oxford robotcar dataset. Int. J. Robot. Res. **36**(1), 3–15 (2017)
125. X. Huang, G. Mei, J. Zhang, R. Abbas, A comprehensive survey on point cloud registration. CoRR, vol. abs/2103.02690, 2021. [Online]. Available: https://arxiv.org/abs/2103.02690
126. P.J. Besl, N.D. McKay, A method for registration of 3-d shapes. IEEE Trans. Pattern Anal. Mach. Intell. **14**(2), 239–256 (1992)
127. L. Cheng, S. Chen, X. Liu, H. Xu, Y. Wu, M. Li, Y. Chen, Registration of laser scanning point clouds: a review. Sensors **18**(5), 1641 (2018)
128. H.M. Le, T. Do, T. Hoang, N. Cheung, SDRSAC: semidefinite-based randomized approach for robust point cloud registration without correspondences, in *IEEE Conference on Computer Vision and Pattern Recognition* (2019), pp. 124–133
129. F. Pomerleau, F. Colas, R. Siegwart, A review of point cloud registration algorithms for mobile robotics, Found. Trends Robot. **4**(1), 1–104 (2015)
130. H. Yang, L. Carlone, A polynomial-time solution for robust registration with extreme outlier rates, in *Robotics: Science and Systems XV, University of Freiburg, Freiburg im Breisgau, June 22–26, 2019*, ed. by A. Bicchi, H. Kress-Gazit, S. Hutchinson (2019)
131. H. Deng, T. Birdal, S. Ilic, PPFNet: Global context aware local features for robust 3d point matching, in *IEEE Conference on Computer Vision and Pattern Recognition* (2018), pp. 195–205
132. Z. Gojcic, C. Zhou, J.D. Wegner, A. Wieser, The perfect match: 3d point cloud matching with smoothed densities, in *IEEE Conference on Computer Vision and Pattern Recognition* (2019), pp. 5545–5554
133. A. Zeng, S. Song, M. Nießner, M. Fisher, J. Xiao, T.A. Funkhouser, 3DMatch: learning local geometric descriptors from RGB-D reconstructions, in *IEEE Conference on Computer Vision and Pattern Recognition* (2017), pp. 199–208
134. G. Elbaz, T. Avraham, A. Fischer, 3d point cloud registration for localization using a deep neural network auto-encoder, in *IEEE Conference on Computer Vision and Pattern Recognition* (2017), pp. 2472–2481
135. W. Lu, G. Wan, Y. Zhou, X. Fu, P. Yuan, S. Song, DeepVCP: an end-to-end deep neural network for point cloud registration, in *IEEE/CVF International Conference on Computer Vision* (IEEE, Piscataway, 2019), pp. 12–21
136. Z. Yang, J.Z. Pan, L. Luo, X. Zhou, K. Grauman, Q. Huang, Extreme relative pose estimation for RGB-D scans via scene completion, in *IEEE Conference on Computer Vision and Pattern Recognition* (2019), pp. 4531–4540

137. X. Huang, L. Fan, Q. Wu, J. Zhang, C. Yuan, Fast registration for cross-source point clouds by using weak regional affinity and pixel-wise refinement, in *IEEE International Conference on Multimedia and Expo* (2019), pp. 1552–1557
138. X. Huang, J. Zhang, L. Fan, Q. Wu, C. Yuan, A systematic approach for cross-source point cloud registration by preserving macro and micro structures. IEEE Trans. Image Proces. **26**(7), 3261–3276 (2017)
139. X. Huang, J. Zhang, Q. Wu, L. Fan, C. Yuan, A coarse-to-fine algorithm for registration in 3d street-view cross-source point clouds, in *International Conference on Digital Image Computing: Techniques and Applications* (2016), pp. 1–6
140. X. Huang, G. Mei, J. Zhang, Feature-metric registration: a fast semi-supervised approach for robust point cloud registration without correspondences, in *2020 IEEE/CVF Conference on Computer Vision and Pattern Recognition, CVPR 2020, Seattle, WA, June 13–19, 2020* (Computer Vision Foundation/IEEE, Piscataway, 2020), pp. 11 363–11 371
141. Z. Wu, S. Song, A. Khosla, F. Yu, L. Zhang, X. Tang, J. Xiao, 3D ShapeNets: a deep representation for volumetric shapes, in *IEEE Conference on Computer Vision and Pattern Recognition* (IEEE Computer Society, Washington, 2015), pp. 1912–1920
142. A. Geiger, P. Lenz, C. Stiller, R. Urtasun, Vision meets robotics: the KITTI dataset. Int. J. Robot. Res. **32**(11), 1231–1237 (2013)
143. A. Geiger, P. Lenz, R. Urtasun, Are we ready for autonomous driving? The KITTI vision benchmark suite, in *IEEE Conference on Computer Vision and Pattern Recognition* (2012), pp. 3354–3361
144. Y. Zhou, O. Tuzel, VoxelNet: end-to-end learning for point cloud based 3d object detection, in *Proceedings of the IEEE Conference on Computer Vision and Pattern Recognition* (2018), pp. 4490–4499
145. M. Bijelic, T. Gruber, F. Mannan, F. Kraus, W. Ritter, K. Dietmayer, F. Heide, Seeing through fog without seeing fog: deep multimodal sensor fusion in unseen adverse weather, in *Proceedings of the IEEE/CVF Conference on Computer Vision and Pattern Recognition* (2020), pp. 11 682–11 692
146. J.H. Yoo, Y. Kim, J. Kim, J.W. Choi, 3D-CVF: generating joint camera and lidar features using cross-view spatial feature fusion for 3d object detection, in *European Conference on Computer Vision* (2020), pp. 720–736
147. L. Xie, G. Xu, D. Cai, X. He, X-view: non-egocentric multi-view 3d object detector. IEEE Trans. Image Proces. **32**, 1488–1497 (2023)
148. K. Huang, B. Shi, X. Li, X. Li, S. Huang, Y. Li, Multi-modal sensor fusion for auto driving perception: a survey. Preprint. arXiv:2202.02703 (2022)
149. S. Vora, A. H. Lang, B. Helou, O. Beijbom, Pointpainting: sequential fusion for 3d object detection, in *Proceedings of the IEEE/CVF Conference on Computer Vision and Pattern Recognition* (2020), pp. 4604–4612
150. L. Xie, C. Xiang, Z. Yu, G. Xu, Z. Yang, D. Cai, X. He, PI-RCNN: an efficient multi-sensor 3d object detector with point-based attentive cont-conv fusion module. Proc. AAAI Conf. Artif. Intell. **34**(07), 12 460–12 467 (2020)
151. T. Huang, Z. Liu, X. Chen, X. Bai, EPNet: enhancing point features with image semantics for 3d object detection, in *European Conference on Computer Vision* (2020), pp. 35–52
152. M. Liang, B. Yang, S. Wang, R. Urtasun, Deep continuous fusion for multi-sensor 3d object detection, in *Proceedings of the European Conference on Computer Vision* (2018), pp. 641–656
153. S. Pang, D. Morris, H. Radha, CLOCs: camera-lidar object candidates fusion for 3d object detection, in *IEEE/RSJ International Conference on Intelligent Robots and Systems* (2020), pp. 10 386–10 393
154. C.R. Qi, W. Liu, C. Wu, H. Su, L.J. Guibas, Frustum pointnets for 3d object detection from RGB-D data, in *Proceedings of the IEEE Conference on Computer Vision and Pattern Recognition* (2018), pp. 918–927

155. P. Sun, H. Kretzschmar, X. Dotiwalla, A. Chouard, V. Patnaik, P. Tsui, J. Guo, Y. Zhou, Y. Chai, B. Caine, et al., Scalability in perception for autonomous driving: Waymo open dataset, in *Proceedings of the IEEE/CVF Conference on Computer Vision and Pattern Recognition* (2020), pp. 2446–2454
156. H. Caesar, V. Bankiti, A.H. Lang, S. Vora, V.E. Liong, Q. Xu, A. Krishnan, Y. Pan, G. Baldan, O. Beijbom, nuScenes: a multimodal dataset for autonomous driving, in *Proceedings of the IEEE/CVF Conference on Computer Vision and Pattern Recognition* (2020), pp. 11 621–11 631

Chapter 7
Point Cloud Pre-trained Models and Large Models

Abstract With advancements in deep learning, there has been a burgeoning interest in the exploration of pre-training techniques and the deployment of large models with billions of learning parameters. Self-supervised pre-training addresses the challenges associated with supervised learning, particularly the need for large amounts of labeled data, making it possible to leverage vast amounts of readily available data without annotations. Besides, it also catalyzes the emergence of large models that benefit from having more parameters to capture the variability and complexity of large-scale data. This chapter aims to provide a concise yet comprehensive overview of these domains, starting with an introduction to the emergences and foundational concepts of pre-training techniques and large models. Subsequently, we delve into the specific realm of point cloud data, demystifying the associated method designs related to pre-trained models and large models, which furnishes readers with a thorough understanding of these cutting-edge technologies.

Keywords Self-supervised pre-training · Large models · Point clouds · Pre-trained models · Contrastive learning · Auto-encoding · Auto-regressive · Multi-modality · Transformer

7.1 Introduction

The emergence of deep learning and the extensive use of point clouds have led to swift advancements in point cloud processing and analysis using deep learning techniques [1–57]. These methods have shown promise in performing complex vision tasks on point clouds, such as classification [57–60], object detection [52, 61, 62], and semantic parsing [53–55, 63], which are quite similar with the research for image and video processing [64–113]. However, developing high-performance models for these tasks requires labeling a substantial volume of point cloud data. Unlike traditional image labeling, annotating point clouds can be particularly challenging and time-intensive. This is mainly due to the inherent complexity of dealing with data in three dimensions, which adds layers of inconvenience and

W. Gao, G. Li, *Deep Learning for 3D Point Clouds*,
https://doi.org/10.1007/978-981-97-9570-3_7

complexity to the annotation process. Therefore, the lack of large-scale labeled point cloud data has become a restriction on the development of point cloud vision tasks.

Self-supervised learning, a groundbreaking technique in the unsupervised learning realm, harnesses the inherent learning capabilities of the data itself, eliminating the need for external annotations. This innovative approach leverages the underlying structures and patterns within datasets, empowering models to develop effective representations without relying on extensive, labeled data. By ingeniously crafting a range of meaningful pretext tasks, self-supervised algorithms are adept at distilling general features and insights from copious amounts of unlabeled data. This methodology significantly diminishes the reliance on costly and labor-intensive data labeling processes while simultaneously boosting the flexibility and adaptability of models across various fields. In disciplines ranging from natural language processing to computer vision, self-supervised learning has become an indispensable preliminary step in neural network pre-training, setting the stage for more specialized tasks. This evolution marks a pivotal shift, paving the way for more efficient, robust, and intuitive machine learning models.

Breakthroughs in self-supervised pre-training can be traced back to groundbreaking explorations in language models [114], such as BERT, and image processing [115, 116], exemplified by works like BEiT. These studies have been pivotal in establishing various innovative pretext tasks. Typically, models undergo an initial pre-training phase on these pretext tasks, followed by fine-tuning for specific downstream applications. It is important to note that the design of pretext tasks often bears a close relationship to these downstream applications, enabling the learning of knowledge that is beneficial for enhancing performance in these subsequent tasks. A landmark development occurred in 2018 with the advent of contrastive self-supervised learning, which revolutionized visual pre-training by favoring joint embedding methods as the premier approach. However, the dominance of this method has recently encountered a significant paradigm shift with the emergence of a novel generative approach. As shown in Fig. 7.1, this generative method commonly employs an encoder-decoder architecture, adeptly mapping inputs to latent representations and then reconstructing inputs from these representations. The ability of generative self-supervised pre-training to learn from context and unstructured data is particularly beneficial in areas where acquiring labeled data is challenging, making it a cornerstone for the next wave of advancements in machine learning. Apart from its outstanding performance, another reason for the high popularity of generative pre-training is its similar technical route to BERT-style pre-training in the language field. This cross-disciplinary synergy reduces the technical gap between linguistic and visual research, where insights and techniques from one area can catalyze innovations in another. The adaptability and transferability of these generative models point toward a future where artificial intelligence can seamlessly integrate knowledge from various domains, further blurring the lines between different areas of machine learning [46].

The swift progress in language and vision, driven by self-supervised pre-training, has sparked a surge of interest in the study of point clouds. This wave of enthusiasm has led to the development of a variety of innovative techniques, all rooted in self-

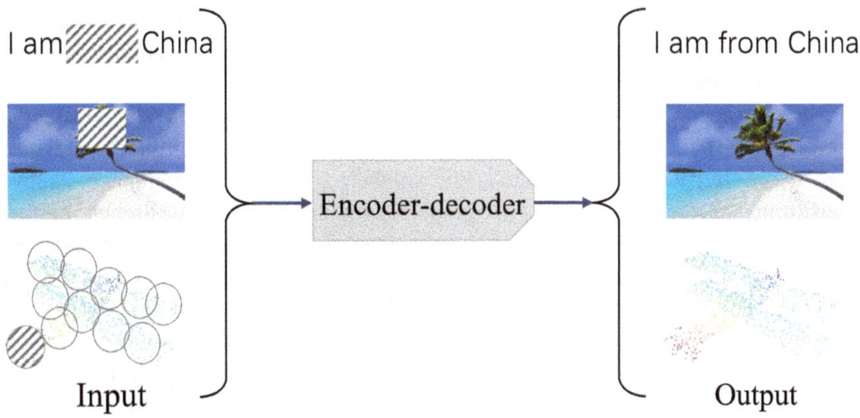

Fig. 7.1 Illustration of generative pre-training. This technique involves initially obscuring a segment of the input data. Following this, an autoencoder is employed to reconstruct the concealed portions using the original input data (Source: Author)

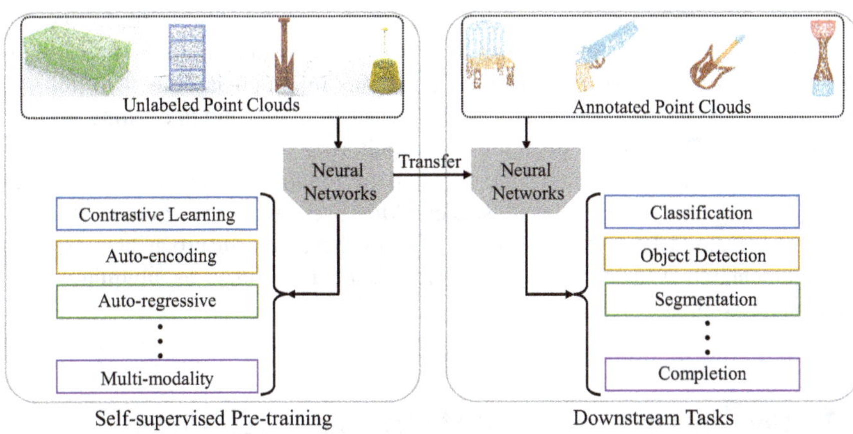

Fig. 7.2 The illustration of point cloud pre-training and its transfer to downstream tasks (Source: Author)

supervised pre-training principles, tailored to meet the unique challenges in point cloud research. As illustrated in Fig. 7.2, the latest methodologies in self-supervised pre-training for point clouds have been developed into various types in terms of their pretext tasks, such as contrastive learning, auto-encoding, auto-regressive, and multi-modality, to name a few. These groundbreaking strategies have transformed the field, enabling models to efficiently learn from unlabeled point cloud data, which is more abundant and readily available than labeled datasets. This advancement bypasses the need for expensive, labor-intensive data labeling. Moreover, pretext tasks in these methods endow models with a deep understanding of data priors and contextual nuances, leading to the development of robust, versatile feature representations [57]. These representations boast high levels of generalizability, equipping models to adapt seamlessly to a broad spectrum of tasks with minimal fine-tuning, a process emblematic of transfer learning.

The emergence of self-supervised pre-training has heralded a substantial paradigm shift in mitigating overfitting in models trained on limited-scale data due to the introduction of large-scale unlabeled data. This resilience against overfitting has opened the door to models with an increasingly higher number of parameters. These more substantial, parameter-rich models can capture a deeper and more nuanced understanding of the data, leading to more accurate and reliable predictions in numerous tasks. As a result, large models have surged to the forefront, becoming a new wave of development in the field. The advantages of large models are manifold. Firstly, their capacity to process and analyze vast quantities of data in a more efficient and effective manner is unparalleled. They exhibit a remarkable ability to uncover intricate patterns and relationships within the data, which might be invisible to smaller models. Additionally, these models bring robustness and versatility, making them suitable for a wide range of applications in point cloud processing, from 3D object recognition to scene understanding and beyond [117–119].

The applications of point cloud large models are vast and varied. In autonomous driving, they can process and understand complex urban environments to improve navigation and safety. In architecture and construction, they aid in creating detailed models from 3D scans for planning and monitoring. In the realm of virtual and augmented reality, they enable the creation of immersive, realistic experiences by accurately modeling physical spaces. Moreover, with the growth of smart cities, point cloud large models could play a crucial role in urban planning and management, showcasing a future where 3D data becomes as ubiquitous and analyzable as 2D images are today.

7.2 Concepts of Pre-trained Models and Large Models

This section provides an overview of fundamental concepts related to point cloud pre-trained models and large models. This foundational knowledge is designed to help readers grasp the technical details more easily before delving into the specifics of these models.

7.2.1 Difference Between Pre-trained Models and Large Models

Pre-trained models and large models represent two pivotal stages in the evolution of machine learning. Initially, researchers and practitioners primarily relied on pre-trained models. These models, trained on extensive datasets, encapsulate a broad spectrum of knowledge and patterns. They serve as a foundational bedrock, equipping subsequent models with a baseline understanding of diverse data characteristics, including those found in point cloud analysis. Pre-trained models are particularly advantageous in scenarios where data is scarce or the computational resources for training from scratch are limited. They provide a jumpstart in many machine learning tasks by offering a pre-established framework of learned patterns and relationships.

However, the field of artificial intelligence is witnessing a paradigm shift with the advent of large models. Large models were not just parameter or data scaled-up versions of pre-trained models; they represented a more profound transformation. Researchers discovered that as models are scaled in size, following what is referred to as the "scaling laws," they begin to exhibit behaviors distinct from their pre-trained origins. One of the most notable changes is in their context modeling capabilities. Large models demonstrate an enhanced ability to interpret and analyze data within its broader context, a crucial aspect in point cloud analysis where spatial relationships and environmental contexts play significant roles. This expanded capability allows for a more nuanced understanding and interpretation of the data, leading to more accurate and insightful analysis.

This leap in capability from pre-trained models to large models has altered the approach to developing and utilizing artificial intelligence algorithms. Unlike the relatively more straightforward implementation of pre-trained models, large models often transcend the capacities of conventional computational resources available to most researchers and organizations. As a result, accessing and leveraging these large models has predominantly shifted to API-based interactions. APIs provide a gateway to harness the power of these colossal models without the need for the end-user to possess the extensive computational infrastructure required to run them. This change signifies a move toward a more centralized model of AI resource utilization, where powerful AI capabilities are not hosted locally but accessed remotely [120].

The way research tasks are formatted and presented to these large models also differs markedly [21]. Given their expansive understanding and context-modeling abilities, large models require tasks to be structured in a manner that aligns with their advanced processing capabilities. This often involves a more sophisticated and nuanced framing of problems, allowing large models to apply their advanced understanding effectively. In the context of point cloud analysis, this could mean presenting data and queries in a way that capitalizes on the large model's ability to discern complex spatial relationships and patterns.

7.2.2 *Large Model Scaling Laws*

Predominantly, the development of contemporary large models is rooted in the transformer architecture [121]. These models are typically pre-trained on vast, large-scale datasets. A substantial body of experimental evidence has consistently demonstrated that scaling up either the volume of training data or the size of the model itself can lead to significant enhancements in model performance [122]. In order to thoroughly analyze the relationship between model performance and key factors such as model size or the volume of training data, with the aim of quantitatively describing the scaling effect, several researchers have embarked on in-depth studies. The KM Scaling Law [123] and the Chinchilla Scaling Law [124] law are two prominent examples of these efforts. They epitomize the scientific endeavor to encapsulate the intricate dynamics of model scaling in formulaic expressions, offering valuable insights into the optimal scaling strategies for achieving maximum efficiency and effectiveness.

KM Scaling Law A groundbreaking study by Kaplan et al. [123] from OpenAI introduces a novel conceptual framework, known as the KM Scaling Law. This law establishes the dependency between the performance of a model and three pivotal variables: the size of models (S), the volume of datasets (V), and the computational resources allocated for training (C). Under a fixed computational budget denoted as c, Kaplan et al. formulate three interrelated equations representing this scaling phenomenon, which can be expressed as:

$$L(S) = \left(\frac{S_c}{S}\right)^{\alpha_S}, \quad \alpha_S \sim 0.076, S_c \sim 8.8 \times 10^{13}, \tag{7.1}$$

$$L(V) = \left(\frac{V_c}{V}\right)^{\alpha_V}, \quad \alpha_V \sim 0.095, V_c \sim 5.4 \times 10^{13}, \tag{7.2}$$

$$L(C) = \left(\frac{C_c}{C}\right)^{\alpha_C}, \quad \alpha_C \sim 0.050, C_c \sim 3.1 \times 10^{8}. \tag{7.3}$$

In the above expressions, $L(\cdot)$ represents the cross-entropy loss in nats, and α is the scaling factor. These laws emerge from fitting performance metrics across varying the volume of datasets, the size of models, and training computational resources. This framework reveals a robust dependency of model performance on these three factors.

Chinchilla Scaling Law In a seminal contribution by Hoffmann et al. from Google DeepMind [124], an innovative perspective on scaling laws is introduced, providing guidelines for compute-efficient training of large models. Their extensive experimentation spanned a broad spectrum of model sizes and data volumes. This led to the formulation of a distinct scaling law with unique coefficients, articulated as follows:

$$L(S, V) = E + \frac{A}{S^{\alpha}} + \frac{B}{V^{\beta}}, \tag{7.4}$$

with defined constants $E = 1.69$, $A = 406.4$, and $B = 410.7$ and scaling factors $\alpha = 0.34$ and $\beta = 0.28$. By optimizing the loss $L(N, D)$ under the constraint

$C \approx 6ND$, their findings highlighted how optimal distribution of computational resources between model size and data size can be determined:

$$S_{opt}(C) = G\left(\frac{C}{6}\right)^{a}, \quad V_{opt}(C) = G^{-1}\left(\frac{C}{6}\right)^{b}, \tag{7.5}$$

In this context, $a = \frac{\alpha}{\alpha+\beta}$ and $b = \frac{\beta}{\alpha+\beta}$ represent proportional allocations of the compute budget to model size and data size, respectively, with G being a scaling coefficient derived from A, B, α, and β. As discussed by Hoffmann et al. [124], the KM scaling law shows the preference for a disproportionate increase in model size with the Chinchilla scaling law's recommendation for equal scaling of both model and data sizes, as indicated by the comparative values of a and b in Eq. (7.5).

Scaling laws in artificial intelligence are critical for understanding how model size impacts performance and efficiency. They guide the development of larger, more capable models, allowing for optimal resource allocation and performance optimization. These laws are crucial in advancing models that generalize better to new data, excel in transfer and few-shot learning, and potentially develop emergent abilities.

7.2.3 *Contrastive Learning*

Contrastive learning is a powerful technique in the field of machine learning, particularly within the realm of unsupervised and self-supervised learning [54]. Its primary goal is to learn useful representations by contrasting positive pairs (similar or related data points) against negative pairs (dissimilar or unrelated data points). This approach has gained significant traction due to its effectiveness in learning feature representations without requiring labeled data.

A critical component of modern contrastive learning methods is the Information Noise-Contrastive Estimation (InfoNCE) loss, which is first proposed by Oord et at. [125] to learn meaningful 2D image representations. This loss function is designed to pull together representations of positive pairs while pushing apart representations of negative pairs. The InfoNCE loss is formulated as:

$$L = -\sum_{i=1}^{N} \log \frac{\exp(\mathrm{sim}(z_i, z_{i^+})/\tau)}{\sum_{j=1}^{K} \exp(\mathrm{sim}(z_i, z_j)/\tau)}, \tag{7.6}$$

where z_i and z_{i^+} represent the feature vectors of a positive pair. $\mathrm{sim}(z_i, z_j)$ is a similarity measure between two vectors (often the dot product or cosine similarity). τ is a temperature parameter that scales the distribution of the similarities. The sum in the denominator runs over one positive and $K - 1$ negative samples for a given anchor z_i. N refers to the number of comparisons (or positive examples) used in the loss calculation, and K represents the number of total examples used to compute the softmax normalization for each anchor. The InfoNCE loss has a conceptual relationship with the cross-entropy loss, commonly used in supervised learning. Both aim to optimize the probability distribution of the predicted labels to match the true distribution. In the case of cross-entropy, this is done by comparing the predicted class probabilities with actual labels. In contrast, InfoNCE does this by comparing the similarities of representations in a way that the positive pairs get higher probabilities compared to negatives. Essentially, the InfoNCE loss can be seen as a form of cross-entropy loss where the classes are "positive" or "negative" pairings, and the model learns to discriminate between these two classes.

The introduction of contrastive learning has revolutionized self-supervised learning, especially in the pre-training of deep neural networks for images [126], such as MoCo [127] and SimCLR [128]. In self-supervised learning, where labels are not available, contrastive learning provides a way to leverage the inherent structure of the data to learn useful representations [125]. The key advantage of contrastive learning in self-supervised pre-training is its ability to learn rich, generalizable representations that capture underlying patterns in the data without the need for explicit labels. This not only reduces the dependency on large labeled datasets but also enables models to be more robust and versatile, adapting effectively to a variety of tasks. Recently, there are also some representative works introducing contrastive learning for point cloud pre-training and obtaining gratifying performance, such as Point-BERT [129] and POS-BERT [130].

7.3 Point Cloud Pre-trained Models

Self-supervised learning has been notably successful in the fields of language and image processing, as evidenced by models like BERT and various image pre-training techniques [56, 65]. Recently, researchers have adapted relative techniques to 3D point cloud data, developing various pretext tasks. Key among these methods are tasks like contrastive learning, auto-encoding, auto-regressive, and multi-modality, which have shown promising results in enhancing performance for various applications. This section delves into the specifics of Point-BERT [129], Point-MAE [131], Point-GPT [132], and Point-CLIP [133], showcasing their methodologies and contributions to the field.

7.3.1 Point-BERT

The primary aim of Point-BERT [129] is to adapt the pre-training approach, similar to that used in BERT, for point cloud Transformers. As shown in Fig. 7.3, this method consists of a specialized point cloud Tokenizer, built using a discrete Variational Autoencoder (dVAE)-based reconstruction technique [134]. This Tokenizer converts a point cloud sample into individual tokens following a learned

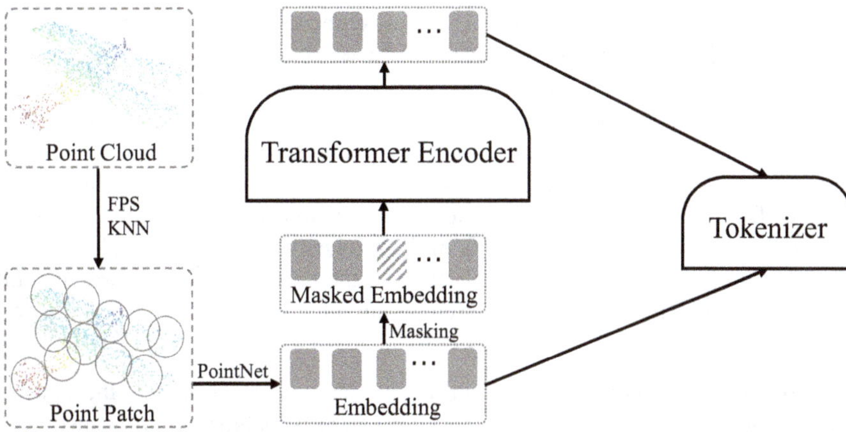

Fig. 7.3 Network architecture of Point-BERT. In the Point-BERT framework, the initial step involves segmenting the input point cloud into smaller clusters, known as point patches. Following this, a compact version of PointNet is employed to generate a series of point embeddings. A dVAE-based method is then used to develop a Tokenizer for converting the point cloud into discrete point tokens. This conversion is a key part of the pre-training phase, where some point embeddings are intentionally obscured with a mask token and processed through Transformers. The goal of the model is to accurately reconstruct the original point tokens. Additionally, Point-BERT incorporates an auxiliary contrastive learning task to enhance the Transformers' ability to understand complex semantic relationships within the data (©2022 IEEE. Reprinted, with permission, from ref. [129])

vocabulary. The aim is for these point tokens to represent local geometric patterns, with the vocabulary encompassing a diverse range of geometric shapes, enabling the representation of any point cloud, even those previously unseen. Additionally, a Masked Point Modeling (MPM) task is employed to pre-train Transformers. This task involves masking portions of the input point cloud and then learning to reconstruct the invisible token representations in these areas. The intention is for the model to deduce the geometric relationships across different point cloud patches within a sample, capturing essential geometric features vital for the understanding of point clouds.

Point Tokenization In the context of processing point clouds using Point-BERT, the approach starts by considering a given point cloud, denoted as $p \in \mathbb{R}^{N \times 3}$ and represented in a 3D space with N points. The method initially involves selecting g central points from the entire point cloud p using the farthest point sampling (FPS) technique. Subsequently, the k-nearest neighbor (kNN) algorithm is employed to identify n nearest neighbors for each of these central points. This process results in the formation of g local patches or sub-clouds, symbolized as $\{p_i\}_{i=1}^{g}$. The methodology then incorporates a mini-version of PointNet, referenced as mini-PointNet, to transform these sub-clouds into point embeddings. Drawing parallels from the use of the Transformer architecture in NLP and 2D vision tasks, the point cloud is represented as a point embedding sequence, denoted as $\{f_i\}_{i=1}^{g}$. A component known as the Point Tokenizer plays a pivotal role in processing point embeddings

$\{f_i\}_{i=1}^g$. Its primary function is to convert these embeddings into a series of discrete point tokens. These tokens are represented by $\mathbf{z} = [z_1, z_2, ..., z_g] \in \mathcal{V}$ and are part of a learned vocabulary $\mathcal{V}$, which encompasses a total of N distinct elements. In the experimental implementation of Point-BERT, the DGCNN [60] is employed as the Tokenizer network. The decoder within the framework is to process the input point tokens $\{z_i\}_{i=1}^g$, with the aim of reconstructing the associated sub-point clouds. Another DGCNN is employed to establish connections among neighboring point tokens, thereby bolstering the capacity of these tokens to represent a wide range of local structures with greater fidelity. Following the enhancement of representation through DGCNN, the FoldingNet is brought into play for the actual reconstruction of the sub-clouds.

Transformer Backbone In the experimental setup of Point-BERT, the authors adopt standard Transformers as the backbone, which includes multi-headed self-attention layers and feedforward neural network (FFN) blocks. The process begins with dividing each input point cloud into g local patches. These patches are centered around points $\{c_i\}_{i=1}^g$. The local patches are then transformed into point embeddings $\{f_i\}_{i=1}^g$ using a mini-PointNet. This version of PointNet is streamlined, consisting only of multilayer perceptrons (MLPs) and a global maxpool operation, which simplifies the model while retaining its essential features. Additionally, positional embeddings $\{pos_i\}$ for each patch are obtained by applying an MLP to their center points $\{c_i\}$. The input embeddings for the Transformer, denoted as $\{x_i\}_{i=1}^g$, are then formed by combining these point embeddings $\{f_i\}_{i=1}^g$ with the positional embeddings $\{pos_i\}_{i=1}^g$. The input embeddings are fed into the Transformer. In line with the approach outlined in the BERT paper, a class token denoted as $\mathbf{E}[\mathrm{s}]$ is concatenated with the input. Transformer is expressed as $H^0 = \left\{\mathbf{E}[\mathrm{s}], x_1, x_2, \cdots, x_g\right\}$. The Transformer comprises L layers, with the output of the final layer represented by $H^L = \left\{h_{\mathrm{s}}^L, h_1^L, \cdots, h_g^L\right\}$. This output encapsulates the global feature of the point cloud, along with the encoded representations of point patches.

Masked Point Modeling In their approach to pre-training the Point-BERT model, the authors utilize a novel strategy for masking point clouds, diverging from the random masking techniques used in BERT. They employ a block-wise masking strategy similar to that used in BEiT. This method involves selecting a center point c_i and its corresponding sub-point cloud p_i and then identifying m neighboring sub-point clouds to form a larger continuous local area. All local sub-point clouds within this area are masked to create the incomplete point cloud. The block-wise masking strategy is directly applied to the Transformer inputs. The positions of the masked patches are denoted as $\mathcal{M} \in \{1, \cdots, g\}^{\lfloor rg \rfloor}$, where r represents the mask ratio. The process involves replacing all masked point embeddings with the same learnable, pre-defined embeddings $\mathbf{E}[\mathrm{M}]$ while retaining their positional embeddings. The resulting corrupted inputs, denoted as $\mathrm{X}^{\mathcal{M}}$, are a combination of unmasked and masked elements and are fed into the Transformer encoder. The primary objective of the MPM task is to drive the model to learn the geometric structure of the masked parts based on visible ones. The pre-trained dVAE transform each local point patch into discrete tokens that represent geometric patterns. These tokens are then used as surrogate supervision signals for pre-training the Transformer backbone.

The pretext task of MPM aims to identify and recover point tokens that align with masked locations within the data. This process is framed as an optimization problem, where the primary objective is to maximize the log-likelihood of accurately predicting these point tokens, denoted as z_i, based on masked input embeddings, symbolized as $X^{\mathcal{M}}$. The mathematical expression of this objective can be formulated as:

$$\max \sum_{X} \mathbb{E}_{\mathcal{M}} \left[\sum_{i \in \mathcal{M}} \log \mathcal{P}\left(z_i \mid X^{\mathcal{M}}\right) \right]. \tag{7.7}$$

To promote the understanding of the more abstract point cloud semantics for Transformer architecture, the study integrates the MoCo, a contrastive learning method, to enhance the Transformer's ability to comprehend these high-level patterns. The use of a novel point patch mixing technique further refines this process. In this method, the model is trained to minimize the contrastive loss by aligning the features of artificially created mixed samples with those of the original samples. This approach is quantified as:

$$\mathcal{L}_q = -r \log \frac{\exp(q k_1^+ / \tau)}{\sum_{i=0}^{K} \exp(q k_i / \tau)} - (1 - r) \log \frac{\exp(q k_2^+ / \tau)}{\sum_{i=0}^{K} \exp(q k_i / \tau)}, \tag{7.8}$$

where q represents the feature of a mixed sample derived from two other samples with features k_1^+ and k_2^+ ($\{k_i\}$. The mixing ratio is denoted by r, and the contrastive loss is calculated based on this ratio, along with a temperature parameter τ and the size of the memory bank K. By combining the MPM objective with contrastive loss optimization, Point-BERT is effectively trained to simultaneously capture both the intricate geometric structures and the overarching semantic patterns present in point clouds. This dual focus is essential for robust and accurate point cloud representation learning.

Finally, the authors present their experimental findings related to various downstream applications. In addition to commonly recognized benchmarks, which encompass tasks like classification and segmentation, the research also delves into the capabilities of the model in scenarios involving few-shot learning and transfer learning. Experimental results reveal the effectiveness of Point-BERT.

7.3.2 *Point-MAE*

Though the recent advancement, Point-BERT, has been proposed to overcome the large data demand of Transformers backbone, this technique is noted for its

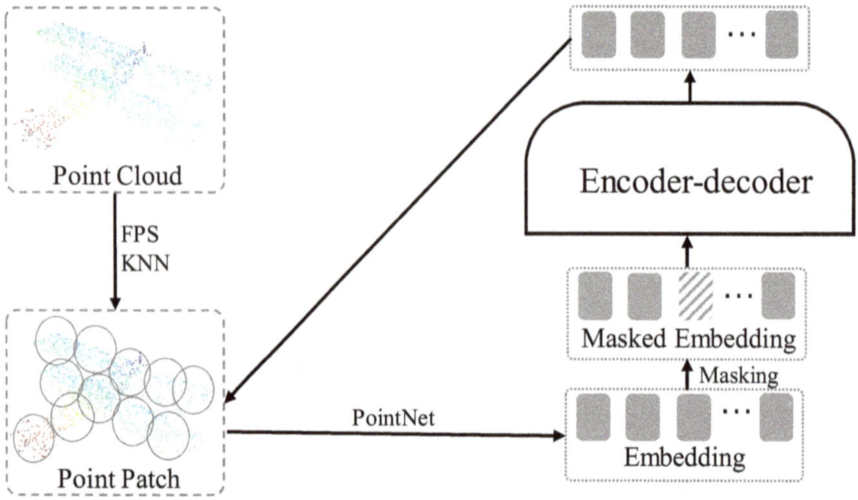

Fig. 7.4 Network architecture of Point-MAE [131]. Point-MAE contains a two-part process in its designs, where a point cloud is divided into patches, randomly masked, and then embedded. An autoencoder pre-trains, with the encoder processing only visible tokens, and the decoder reconstructing masked patches using added mask tokens (Source: Author)

complexity. Point-BERT necessitates pre-training a DGCNN-based dVAE [134] and heavily depends on both contrastive learning and data augmentation during this pre-training phase. Additionally, there's a mention of an inherent drawback: the invisible tokens in model inputs are processed by the encoder of Transformer during the pre-training phase. This can lead to premature location leakage of masked information and a significant demand on computational resources. Therefore, Point-MAE [131] (see Fig. 7.4) is devised to confront the drawback of Point-BERT. Unlike the more homogenized Transformer models in NLP and Vision Transformers in computer vision, Transformers for point clouds are diverse and less explored due to smaller datasets not meeting their extensive data needs. Point-MAE aims to establish a unified Transformer architecture for point clouds, diverging from prior methods like Point-BERT, which utilize additional models like DGCNN. Considering that providing location information to mask tokens in point clouds leads to information leakage, simplifying reconstruction tasks and impeding the learning of latent features, Point-MAE addresses this by shifting mask tokens to the decoder part, enhancing feature learning from unmasked point clouds.

Point Cloud Masking and Embedding In the approach inspired by Point-BERT, Point-MAE involves segmenting a point cloud sample into what are termed point patches, which are irregular and can overlap. This segmentation is achieved using a combination of the Farthest Point Sampling (FPS) and the K-nearest neighborhood (KNN) algorithms. Given a point cloud, designated as X^i, composed of p points and existing within a 3D space, the FPS method is employed to identify n central points (CT) within the point patches. These central points are essential for the subsequent steps in the process. Utilizing these center points as a reference, the KNN algorithm is then applied to select k points nearest to each center from the input point cloud. This selection forms the basis of the point patches P, which are mathematically represented as:

$$CT = FPS(X^i), \quad CT \in \mathbb{R}^{n\times 3}; \tag{7.9}$$

$$P = KNN(X^i, CT), \quad P \in \mathbb{R}^{n\times k\times 3}. \tag{7.10}$$

A crucial aspect of these point patches is the representation of each point. Points within a patch are denoted using coordinates normalized relative to the patch's center point. This normalization is pivotal for enhancing the convergence of the process.

Point-MAE addresses the issue of overlapping point patches by masking them individually. This ensures that each point patch retains complete information. They define a masking ratio, denoted as m, and the set of masked patches is represented as $P_{gt} \in \mathbb{R}^{mn\times k\times 3}$. These masked patches serve as the ground truth for calculating the reconstruction loss. For embedding the masked point patches, a shared-weight learnable mask token replaces each patch. The complete set of these mask tokens is denoted as $T_m \in \mathbb{R}^{mn\times C}$, where C represents the embedding dimension. In contrast, for visible point patches, the authors argue that a direct application of MLPs does not adhere to the permutation invariance principle and suggest a more suitable embedding approach. To address this, they employ a modified version of PointNet, which is primarily composed of MLP layers and max pooling operations. Consequently, the visible point patches $P_v \in \mathbb{R}^{(1-m)n\times k\times 3}$ are transformed into visible tokens T_v, as described by the equation:

$$T_v = PointNet(P_v), \quad T_v \in \mathbb{R}^{(1-m)n\times C}. \tag{7.11}$$

Because point patches are encoded from normalized coordinates, it is crucial to provide positional information to the embedding tokens. The authors propose a straightforward Position Embedding (PE) method by mapping the center coordinates to the embedding dimension using MLP layers.

Transformer Backbone The architecture of Point-MAE is an asymmetric encoder-decoder, where the encoder is built using conventional Transformer blocks and focuses exclusively on encoding visible tokens, symbolized as T_v, deliberately excluding mask tokens, represented as T_m. The outcome of this encoding process is expressed as T_e. Additionally, each Transformer block within the encoder is enhanced with positional embeddings, providing vital location information for the encoding process. Conversely, the decoder in this model, while mirroring the encoder in structure, comprises a reduced number of Transformer blocks. It processes both the encoded tokens T_e and the masks tokens T_m. In this stage, a comprehensive set of positional embeddings is incorporated into every Transformer block, ensuring that all tokens, including the mask tokens, receive location information. The decoder's primary function is to output the decoded mask tokens, denoted as H_m, which are then directed to a subsequent prediction head. The mathematical representation of this encoder-decoder structure is given by the following equations:

$$T_e = \text{Encoder}(T_v), \quad T_e \in \mathbb{R}^{(1-m)n \times C}; \tag{7.12}$$

$$H_m = \text{Decoder}(\text{concat}(T_e, T_m)), \quad H_m \in \mathbb{R}^{mn \times C}. \tag{7.13}$$

A key aspect of this model's design is the strategic placement of mask tokens in the less complex decoder, rather than processing them at the encoder's input. This approach yields two main benefits. Firstly, by using a high masking ratio and shifting the mask tokens to the decoder, the model effectively reduces the number of input tokens for the encoder. This leads to significant computational savings, especially considering the quadratic complexity characteristic of Transformers. Secondly, relocating the mask tokens to the decoder helps prevent premature exposure of location information to the encoder.

The prediction head functions as the final layer of the backbone, with its primary role being the reconstruction of masked point patches within the coordinate space. This crucial task is achieved through a straightforward design, utilizing a fully connected (FC) layer as the prediction head. The process begins with the prediction head receiving the output from the decoder, denoted as H_m. This output is then projected into a vector through the FC layer. The dimensionality of this vector is meticulously matched to the total number of coordinates present in a single point patch. Following this projection, the model implements a reshape operation. This operation is key to transforming the projected data into a structured format that effectively represents the predicted masked point patches, symbolized as P_{pre} in the framework:

$$P_{pre} = \text{Reshape}(FC(H_m)), \quad P_{pre} \in \mathbb{R}^{mn \times k \times 3}. \tag{7.14}$$

Reconstruction Target The objective of reconstruction is focused on accurately recovering the coordinates of points within each masked point patch. To evaluate the effectiveness of this reconstruction, Point-MAE employs a method of comparing the predicted point patches, denoted as P_{pre}, with the ground truth, referred to as P_{gt}. The metric used for this comparison is the l_2 Chamfer distance, which calculates a bidirectional distance between the predicted and ground-truth point sets. This calculation is formulated as follows:

$$L = \frac{1}{|P_{pre}|} \sum_{a \in P_{pre}} \min_{b \in P_{gt}} \|a - b\|_2^2 + \frac{1}{|P_{gt}|} \sum_{b \in P_{gt}} \min_{a \in P_{pre}} \|a - b\|_2^2. \tag{7.15}$$

Finally, Point-MAE is extensively tested and refined through a comprehensive set of experiments. Initially, the model is pre-trained using the ShapeNet training set. This foundational training is crucial for the model to learn a wide variety of shapes and structures. Following the pre-training, the model's performance is rigorously evaluated across several downstream tasks. These tasks include object classification, few-shot learning, and part segmentation, offering insights into the model's adaptability and efficiency in handling diverse data types and challenges.

7.3.3 PointGPT

As shown in Fig. 7.5, the authors of PointGPT probe the complex task of adapting the generative pre-training transformer (GPT) [136], commonly used in language processing, to the realm of point cloud understanding. However, this adaptation faces significant challenges due to the intrinsic differences between textual data and point clouds. Firstly, point clouds inherently lack the sequential arrangement found in language, posing a challenge for the sequential nature of GPT models. The authors address this by arranging point patches in a specific geometric sequence, namely, the Morton-order curve [137]. This method effectively imposes a sequential order on the point clouds, preserving their local structures and enabling the application of GPT-like models. Secondly, there's a stark contrast in information density between languages and point clouds. Languages are dense with information, requiring advanced understanding for effective auto-regressive prediction. Point clouds, however, tend to have considerable redundancy. To bridge this gap, the authors introduce a dual masking strategy. This approach masks additional tokens that a token attends to, reducing redundancy and creating a more challenging

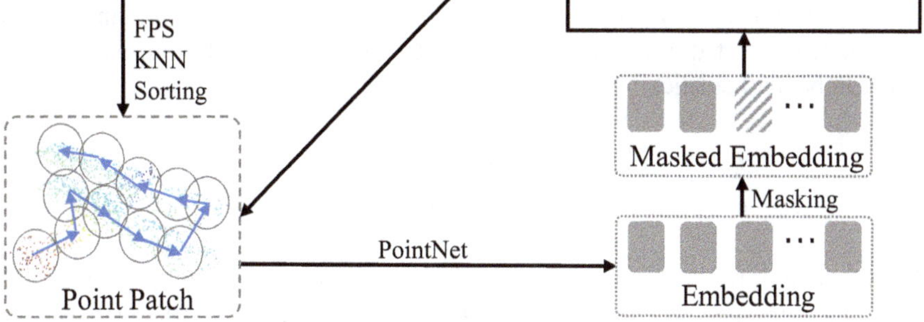

Fig. 7.5 Architecture of PointGPT [132]. It processes point clouds by dividing them into sorted patches. An extractor-generator transformer decoder [135], featuring a dual masking strategy, predicts point patches auto-regressively (Source: Author)

task that demands a comprehensive understanding of the data. Lastly, the authors recognize a disparity between the generation of individual points in point clouds and the requirements of downstream tasks, which often demand higher semantic understanding. The generation tasks tend to produce representations at a lower semantic level than what downstream tasks require [45]. To address this, they propose an extractor-generator architecture [135] within the transformer decoder. This architecture separates the generation task, handled by the generator, from the extraction of higher-level semantic representations, managed by the extractor. This division allows for more semantically rich latent representations, better suited for downstream applications.

Point Cloud Sequencer To adapt the GPT scheme to point clouds, PointGPT devise the point cloud sequencer to address the unique challenges posed by the sparse and unordered nature of point clouds, involving point patch partitioning, sorting, and embedding. Consider a point cloud denoted by X, which comprises M individual points. The procedure begins by selecting n center points, represented by C, from X through the farthest point sampling (FPS). This step is critical for establishing reference points within the point cloud. Subsequently, the K-nearest neighbors (KNN) algorithm plays a pivotal role in forming n distinct point patches, symbolized by P. This is achieved by identifying and grouping the k nearest points relative to each center point in C from the original point cloud X. The entire partitioning process is succinctly encapsulated by the following mathematical formulation:

$$\begin{aligned} C &= FPS(X), \quad C \in \mathbb{R}^{n\times 3}; \\ P &= \mathrm{KNN}(C, X), \quad P \in \mathbb{R}^{n\times k\times 3}. \end{aligned} \tag{7.16}$$

To effectively manage the disorder inherent in point clouds, a structured approach is adopted for organizing the extracted point patches. This is primarily achieved by arranging these patches into a sequential format based on their respective center points. The first step in this sequence involves encoding the coordinates of the center points into a one-dimensional Morton code. Once encoded, the center points are sorted to establish an order, denoted as O. The sorting process results in two key outcomes: the sorted array of center points $\boldsymbol{C}^s$ and the aligned point patches $\boldsymbol{P}^s$. This can be mathematically represented as follows:

$$\begin{aligned} &O = \mathrm{argmax}(\mathrm{MortonCode}(C)), \quad O \in \mathbb{R}^{n\times 1}; \\ &C^s, P^s = C[O], P[O], \quad C^s \in \mathbb{R}^{n\times 3}, P^s \in \mathbb{R}^{n\times k\times 3}. \end{aligned} \tag{7.17}$$

Similar to Point-MAE, a PointNet is adopted for processing point patches and extracting intricate geometric details from each point patch. To further enhance the model's performance and ensure smoother training convergence, a normalization technique is applied to the coordinates of each point in the patches. This normalization is relative to the center point of each patch, ensuring a consistent frame of reference and mitigating issues arising from variations in scale and position. The mathematical formulation of this transformation is as follows:

$$T = \text{PointNet}(P^s), \quad T \in \mathbb{R}^{n \times D}, \tag{7.18}$$

where T is a set of D-dimensional tokens. These tokens encapsulate the rich geometric information extracted by the PointNet network.

Transformer Decoder with a Dual Masking Strategy The application of a standard transformer decoder in an auto-regressive manner encounters severe challenges, particularly in capturing low-level semantics, which are attributed to the inherently limited information density in point clouds and the disconnect between the generative and downstream task objectives. To overcome these limitations and foster a more profound understanding of point clouds, a novel dual masking strategy is introduced. This innovative strategy builds upon the conventional approach by additionally masking a proportion of the attending preceding tokens for each token during the pre-training phase. This is not just a simple extension of existing masking techniques but a strategic enhancement to foster deeper learning. The self-attention mechanism is modified accordingly to incorporate this dual mask:

$$\text{SelfAttention}(T) = \text{softmax}\left(\frac{QK^T}{\sqrt{D}} - (1 - M^d) \cdot \infty\right) V. \tag{7.19}$$

In this formulation, Q, K, V are the query, key, and value matrices with D as channels, respectively, which are derived from the token T. The locations in M^d are set to 0 where masked and to 1 elsewhere.

The PointGPT extractor uses transformer decoder blocks and a dual masking strategy to create latent representations $\mathcal{T}$. Point patches, in normalized coordinates, are integrated with sinusoidal positional encodings (PE) [121] for mapping sorted center points C^s to the absolute positional encoding (APE). This process aids in grasping global structures essential for understanding point clouds. The generator, similar but simpler than the extractor, inputs extracted tokens $\mathcal{T}$ and outputs point tokens T^g. It addresses patch order ambiguities, a result of center point sampling, by providing relative direction prompts (RDPs). These RDPs, formulated as:

$$RDP_i = \text{PE}((C^s i + 1 - C^s i)/|C^s i + 1 - C^s i|_2), i \in 1, ..., n', \quad RDP \in \mathbb{R}^{n' \times D}, \tag{7.20}$$

assist in generating meaningful point cloud representations without revealing masked patch locations or overall shapes. As a result, the extractor-generator architecture can be expressed as:

$$\begin{aligned} \mathcal{T} &= \text{Extractor}(T + APE), \quad \mathcal{T} \in \mathbb{R}^{n \times D}; \\ T^g &= \text{Generator}(\mathcal{T}_{1:n'} + RDP), \quad T^g \in \mathbb{R}^{n' \times D}. \end{aligned} \tag{7.21}$$

The prediction head, comprising a two-layer MLP with fully connected (FC) layers and ReLU activation, is pivotal. It projects the generated tokens, $\boldsymbol{T}^g$, into vectors, aligning the output channels with the coordinates in a patch. These vectors are then reshaped into predicted point patches $\boldsymbol{P}^{pd}$, as described by:

$$\boldsymbol{P}^{pd} = \text{Reshape}(\text{MLP}(\boldsymbol{T}^g), \quad \boldsymbol{P}^{pd} \in \mathbb{R}^{n' \times k \times 3}. \tag{7.22}$$

This process effectively converts the tokenized representations into spatial point cloud predictions.

Generation Target The objective for generating each point patch is to predict coordinates for subsequent patches. The generation loss $\mathcal{L}^g$ is defined using predicted patches P^{pd} and ground-truth patches P^{gt}, the latter being the last n' sorted patches P^s. This loss uses both l_1 and l_2 forms of Chamfer distance (CD), represented as $\mathcal{L}_1^g$ and $\mathcal{L}_2^g$. The formula is $\mathcal{L}^g = \mathcal{L}_1^g + \mathcal{L}_2^g$. The l_n-form CD loss $\mathcal{L}_n^g$ is calculated by comparing each point in P^{pd} and P^{gt} using L_n distance.

Finally, the pre-trained extractor is evaluated on various downstream tasks, including object classification on a real-world dataset, object classification on a clean objects dataset, few-shot learning, and part segmentation. Extensive experiments show that PointGPT can outperform other counterparts visibly.

7.3.4 Point-CLIP

Unlike the more uniform structure of 2D images, 3D point clouds are characterized by their sparse and irregularly distributed nature [4]. This particular attribute poses a significant challenge in directly applying methods developed for the 2D domain to 3D point clouds. A critical issue arises with the frequent encounter of objects belonging to unseen categories. Such a situation often results in the failure of even the most advanced networks to correctly recognize these new objects. Continually re-training models to accommodate these unseen categories is not a feasible solution, highlighting the need for more adaptable approaches in handling 3D point cloud data. Inspired by Contrastive Vision-Language Pre-training (CLIP) [138] in the image domain, Point-CLIP [133] leverages the pre-trained knowledge of CLIP, a 2D image processing model, and adapts it for understanding 3D point clouds, as shown in Fig. 7.6. The primary challenge addressed by Point-CLIP is the modality gap between the unordered nature of point clouds and the structured image format that CLIP is designed to handle. To bridge this gap, Point-CLIP employs an online perspective projection technique, which does not require post-rendering. This method involves projecting each point of the cloud onto a set of predefined image planes, thereby creating scatter depth maps. Point-CLIP then utilizes the pre-trained CLIP visual encoder to process these multi-view features of inputs. For each view, it generates text-matched predictions independently using a zero-shot classifier. This classifier is crafted by embedding 3D category names into a template and using

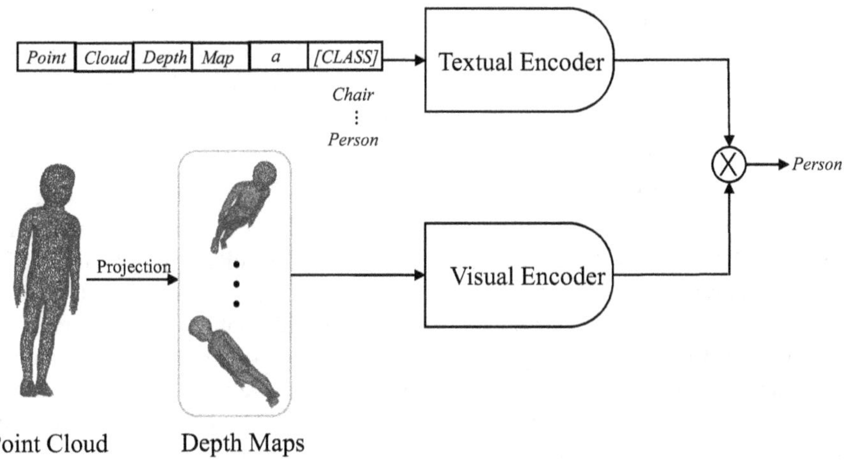

Fig. 7.6 Network pipeline of Point-CLIP. Point-CLIP adapts point clouds into multi-view depth maps for 3D recognition using CLIP [138], a 2D pre-trained model (©2022 IEEE. Reprinted, with permission, from ref. [133])

CLIP's textual encoder. Recognizing that different views contribute variably to the overall scene recognition [18], Point-CLIP achieves its final point cloud prediction through a weighted aggregation of these views. This methodology promises real-time prediction capabilities, crucial for applications like autonomous driving and indoor navigation.

Revisit of CLIP The CLIP model is designed for associating images with their respective linguistic descriptions, utilizing two distinct encoders for processing visual and textual information. Its training involves a batch of image-text pairs, from which it extracts features and aligns them in the feature space using contrastive learning. A significant aspect of CLIP is its large-scale training dataset comprising 400 million image-text pairs crawled from the Internet. This extensive dataset empowers CLIP to efficiently align images with a wide range of semantic concepts, facilitating zero-shot classification with an open vocabulary. In the context of a zero-shot classification task involving an unseen dataset with K classes, CLIP employs a unique approach. It generates textual inputs by incorporating all category names into a predetermined format, termed a prompt. The zero-shot classifier, represented as $W_t \in \mathbb{R}^{K \times C}$, is derived from the C-dimensional textual feature of these category prompts. Each row vector in W_t, totaling K, embodies the pre-trained category weights. Concurrently, the visual encoder of CLIP processes each test image's feature into $f_v \in \mathbb{R}^{1 \times C}$. The classification logits, logits $\in \mathbb{R}^{1 \times K}$, are calculated as follows:

$$\text{logits} = f_v W_t^T; \quad p_i = \text{softmax}_i(\text{logits}). \tag{7.23}$$

In this equation, $\text{softmax}_i(\cdot)$ refers to the softmax operation, and p_i represents the predicted probability for each category i. Notably, this process doesn't require any new training images. It relies solely on the pre-trained encoders, which remain unchanged, yet it still manages to achieve notable performance in zero-shot classification tasks.

Point Cloud Understanding by CLIP In the realm of 3D data processing, the unique nature of point clouds poses a significant challenge. Unlike the structured format of 2D images, point clouds consist of a disordered collection of points in a 3D space, each represented by coordinates (x, y, z). These points are characterized by their sparse and irregular distribution, which differs substantially from the grid-like arrangement found in 2D images. To bridge the gap between these two modalities and facilitate the application of CLIP to 3D point clouds, a novel approach is adopted by Point-CLIP. This method involves creating point-projected images from various perspectives. Specifically, by projecting a point cloud onto an image plane, each point's coordinates are transformed. For instance, using a bottom projection view, a point's location on the image plane is determined by its x and y coordinates divided by its z coordinate, resulting in a distorted or foreshortened image [10]. This effect mirrors the appearance of objects in real-life photographs, where objects appear smaller when farther away and larger when closer. Contrary to previous works where convolution layers are used to process depth maps, this new approach avoids any pre-convolutional processing. Instead, the pixel values in the generated images directly correspond to the z-coordinate of each point, replicated across all three color channels. This simplicity results in a process that is both time-efficient and computationally light.

Point-CLIP utilizes images projected from M different views, employing the CLIP model to extract visual features f_i for each view i, where i ranges from 1 to M. In parallel, the textual branch processes K category names by inserting them into a predefined template: "point cloud depth map of a [CLASS]." These names are encoded to form the textual features, shaping a zero-shot classifier $W_t \in \mathbb{R}^{K\times C}$. Classification logits logits_i for each view are calculated independently, and the final point cloud logits logits_p are obtained through a weighted summation:

$$\begin{aligned} \text{logits}_i &= f_i W_t^T, \text{ for } i = 1, \ldots, M, \\ \text{logits}_p &= \sum\nolimits_{i=1}^{M} \alpha_i \text{logits}_i. \end{aligned} \tag{7.24}$$

Here, α_i is a hyper-parameter that determines the significance of view i. Each view f_i captures a unique perspective of the point cloud, capable of performing independent zero-shot classification. The summation of these views synergizes different perspectives for a comprehensive understanding.

While Point-CLIP effectively enables zero-shot classification on point clouds, its performance is not on par with fully trained 3D neural networks such as PointNet. Point-CLIP introduces a three-layer Multi-layer Perceptron (MLP), termed as the inter-view adapter, for enhanced performance in few-shot settings. During training,

CLIP's visual and textual encoders are frozen, and the adapter is fine-tuned using cross-entropy loss. Specifically, Point-CLIP takes CLIP-encoded features from M views of a point cloud and concatenates them as $\text{Concate}(f_{1\sim M}) \in \mathbb{R}^{1\times MC}$. The first two layers of the inter-view adapter then process this to yield a compact global feature f_{global}:

$$f_{\text{global}} = \text{ReLU}(\text{Concate}(f_{1\sim M})W_1^T)W_2^T. \tag{7.25}$$

Here, $f_{\text{global}} \in \mathbb{R}^{1\times C}$, and W_1 and W_2 are the adapter's two-layer weights. This process aggregates multiple perspectives into a unified representation. Further, the adapted feature f_i^a is created from f_{global} and added to each view's original CLIP-encoded feature using a residual connection:

$$f_i^a = f_i + \text{ReLU}(f_{\text{global}}W_{3i}^T), \tag{7.26}$$

with $W_{3i} \in \mathbb{R}^{C\times C}$ and W_3^T incorporating all views. This integration enriches view-wise predictions and combines newly learned 3D knowledge with pre-trained 2D CLIP knowledge.

Finally, extensive experiments validate that Point-CLIP can accomplish cross-modality zero-shot and few-shot recognition by effectively transferring 2D pre-trained knowledge to 3D scenarios and obtain gratifying performance on 3D vision tasks.

7.4 Point Cloud Large Models

Recently, the scaling of pre-trained language models [140] has revolutionized natural language processing. Subsequent studies have adapted these advancements to 2D vision [141], demonstrating success in model and data scaling. Inspired by this, there's growing interest in extending these techniques to 3D representation [142, 143]. However, challenges remain in scaling beyond small-scale 3D models, and few works explore 3D large models. In this section, we take an early exploration, namely, Uni3D [139], as example to introduce relevant techniques. Uni3D stands out for its simplicity and adaptability, leveraging a plethora of pre-trained 2D models [144] for initialization. The framework systematically examines scalability and flexibility, varying from model scaling (6M to 1B parameters), 2D initialization techniques, to target models aligned with text-image (150M to 5B parameters). Notably, enhancements in performance are often observed with scaling in each facet under this unified framework.

Unified 3D Representation As shown in Fig. 7.7, Uni3D employs a structure akin to the 2D Vision Transformer (ViT) but uniquely tailored for 3D data. It differentiates itself by substituting ViT's patch embedding layer with a point tokenizer, aligning with the approach used in Point-BERT. This tokenizer group

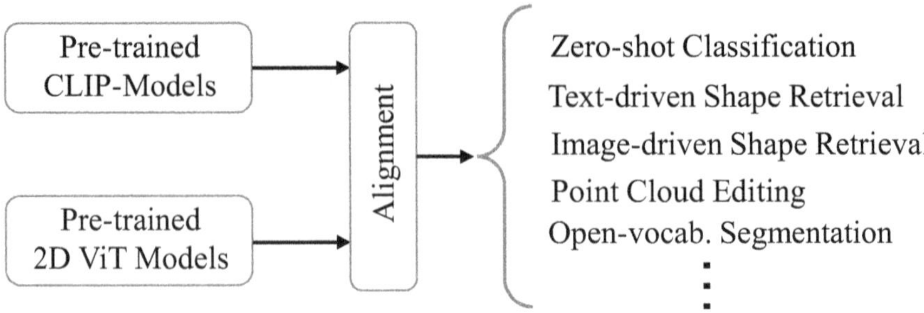

Fig. 7.7 Overall architecture of Uni3D. A robust 3D pre-training framework scales to one billion parameters, integrating a million 3D shapes with ten million images and 70 million texts. Utilizing a 2D ViT-based 3D encoder, initialized with the finest 2D priors from extensive pre-trained models, it aligns 3D point cloud features with image-text features from advanced CLIP models. This approach results in Uni3D outperforming existing benchmarks in large-scale 3D representation learning. Public domain open access image [139]

points into patches and extracts token embeddings with a compact PointNet, allowing for effective 3D embedding generation. The standard transformer then processes these tokens for 3D representation. In scaling up, Uni3D diverges from traditional models that focus on specific architectures for small datasets. Instead, it adopts a scaling approach similar to ViT, progressively enlarging the model from tiny to giant sizes. This method has been effective in improving performance within a unified framework, addressing the challenge of un-unified backbones and pre-training in 3D. A notable achievement of Uni3D is the development of a billion-scale 3D representation model, trained on a large-scale, multi-modal dataset. This model demonstrates exceptional transferability to various downstream tasks, marking a significant milestone in the field. To overcome the challenge of overfitting in larger models, Uni3D leverages pre-trained models from other modalities, like DINO and CLIP. These models provide a stable and rich foundation for learning large-scale 3D representations. The flexibility of Uni3D's design allows for the use of various Transformer-based pre-trained models, enhancing its performance and facilitating exploration in cross-modal pre-training.

Multi-Modal Alignment Uni3D is trained to understand the alignment between different modalities, including language, images, and point clouds. For dataset consistency and fair comparison with other counterparts, Uni3D utilizes the ensembled 3D dataset from OpenShape. This dataset includes Objaverse, ShapeNet, 3D-FUTURE, and ABO. Each 3D model in the dataset is processed to create a set of 10,000 points sampled from the model's surface, along with ten color images captured from various views. These point clouds and images, paired with corresponding textual descriptions, form the basis for training. The core objective of Uni3D is to align multi-modal data. The point encoder in Uni3D, denoted as f_P, is initialized using pre-trained 2D Vision Transformer (ViT) models. Meanwhile, the text and image encoders, f_T and f_I, are derived from CLIP models. The training focuses on teaching f_P to understand 3D representations by aligning them with the 2D and language representations of the CLIP models, effectively distilling knowledge across different modalities. In this setup, only f_P is learnable while other parts remain static due to their already optimized state. The training process involves handling batches of point cloud, image, and text triplets. For each triplet, normalized features are computed. The training employs a contrastive loss function to align point clouds with images and texts.

Uni3D marks a significant achievement by demonstrating a billion-scale 3D representation model, effectively adaptable to diverse downstream tasks. The model not only shows exceptional performance in zero-shot and few-shot 3D tasks but also matches some supervised methods in zero-shot classification accuracy on ModelNet [145]. Additionally, it achieves top-tier results in various 3D tasks, including open-world understanding and part segmentation. The study also highlights intriguing applications like point cloud painting and 3D shape retrieval based on text or image, using robust 3D representations developed by Uni3D.

7.5 Summary

In this chapter, we have delved into the transformative impact of self-supervised learning on point cloud processing. Self-supervised learning stands out for its ability to exploit the inherent structures within large volumes of unlabeled data. By creating innovative pretext tasks, these methods enable models to extract and learn valuable features autonomously, significantly reducing the dependence on labor-intensive and time-consuming data labeling processes. This shift is particularly vital in the context of point clouds, where annotating 3D data presents unique challenges. The chapter also highlights the historical development of self-supervised learning, tracing its roots from language models like BERT to visual pre-training methods. Then, several representative methods are discussed in detail, such as Point-BERT, Point-MAE, Point-GPT, and Point-CLIP. The impact of self-supervised learning on point cloud processing is profound. It enables the efficient learning from abundant unlabeled point cloud data, leading to the development of large, parameter-rich models. These models exhibit enhanced capabilities in capturing deeper insights from data, thus providing more accurate and reliable predictions in a variety of applications. The benefits of these large models are manifold, ranging from their ability to discern complex patterns to their adaptability in diverse applications like autonomous driving, architecture, virtual reality, and urban planning. In conclusion, the adoption of self-supervised learning in point cloud processing marks a significant milestone in the field. It not only addresses the challenges of data annotation and model training but also paves the way for more robust, versatile, and large-scale models. This paradigm shift promises to redefine the boundaries of what is achievable in point cloud analysis, opening up new frontiers in various applications and setting the stage for a future where 3D data analysis is as commonplace and efficient as 2D image processing.

Exercises

1. What types of pretext tasks have been developed in the field of self-supervised pre-training for point clouds?
2. Which two laws have been developed to analyze the relationship between model performance and key factors such as model size or the volume of training data and to quantitatively describe the scaling effect?
3. How is the InfoNCE loss formulated, and what are its key components?
4. What is the underlying technique used to construct the specialized tokenizer in Point-BERT for point cloud data?
5. How does Point-MAE segment an input point cloud into irregular point patches, and what algorithms does it use for this segmentation?
6. How does Point-MAE evaluate the effectiveness of point cloud reconstruction, and what specific metric and formula are used for this evaluation?
7. What challenges arise from adapting GPT models for point clouds due to the intrinsic differences between textual data and point clouds, and how do authors address these challenges?
8. How do authors of PointGPT address the disparity between the generation of individual points in point clouds and the requirements of downstream tasks that demand higher semantic understanding?
9. How does Point-CLIP enhance its performance in few-shot settings, and what training approach is used for this enhancement?
10. In the training process of Uni3D, which parameters are fixed and which are updated, and how does this contribute to its core objective?

References

1. T. Qin, G. Li, W. Gao, and S. Liu, Multi-grained point cloud geometry compression via dual-model prediction with extended octree. ACM Trans. Multimedia Comput. Commun. Appl. **20**(9), 1–30 (2024)
2. Y. Shao, W. Gao, S. Liu, and G. Li, Advanced patch-based affine motion estimation for dynamic point cloud geometry compression. Sensors **24**(10), 3142 (2024)
3. Y. Shao, F. Song, W. Gao, S. Liu, G. Li, Texture-guided graph transform optimization for point cloud attribute compression. Appl. Sci. **14**(10), 4094 (2024)
4. Y. Shao, X. Yang, W. Gao, S. Liu, G. Li, 3d point cloud attribute compression using diffusion-based texture-aware intra prediction. IEEE Trans. Circuits Syst. Video Technol. (2024)
5. J. Zhang, Y. Chen, G. Liu, W. Gao, G. Li, Efficient point cloud attribute compression framework using attribute-guided graph Fourier transform, in *ICASSP 2024-2024 IEEE International Conference on Acoustics, Speech and Signal Processing (ICASSP)* (IEEE, Piscataway, 2024), pp. 8426–8430
6. W. Gao, H. Yuan, G. Li, Z. Li, H. Yuan, Low complexity coding unit decision for video-based point cloud compression. IEEE Trans. Image Proces. **33**, 149–162 (2023)
7. Y. Shao, G. Li, Q. Zhang, W. Gao, S. Liu, Non-rigid registration-based progressive motion compensation for point cloud geometry compression. IEEE Trans. Geosci. Remote Sens. **61**, 1–14 (2023)

8. F. Song, G. Li, X. Yang, W. Gao, S. Liu, Block-adaptive point cloud attribute coding with region-aware optimized transform. IEEE Trans. Circuits Syst. Video Technol. **33**(8), 4294–4308 (2023)
9. Y. An, Y. Shao, G. Li, W. Gao, S. Liu, A fast motion estimation method with hamming distance for lidar point cloud compression, in *2022 IEEE International Conference on Visual Communications and Image Processing (VCIP)* (IEEE, Piscataway, 2022), pp. 1–5
10. H. Yuan, W. Gao, G. Li, and Z. Li, Rate-distortion-guided learning approach with cross-projection information for V-PCC fast CU decision, in *Proceedings of the 30th ACM International Conference on Multimedia* (2022), pp. 3085–3093
11. F. Song, G. Li, W. Gao, T.H. Li, Rate-distortion optimized graph for point cloud attribute coding. IEEE Sig. Proces. Lett. **29**, 922–926 (2022)
12. F. Song, G. Li, X. Yang, W. Gao, T.H. Li, Fine-grained correlation representation for graph-based point cloud attribute compression, in *2022 IEEE International Conference on Multimedia and Expo (ICME)* (IEEE, Piscataway, 2022), pp. 1–6
13. F. Shen, W. Gao, A rate control algorithm for video-based point cloud compression, in *2021 International Conference on Visual Communications and Image Processing (VCIP)* (IEEE, Piscataway, 2021), pp. 1–5
14. F. Song, Y. Shao, W. Gao, H. Wang, T. Li, Layer-wise geometry aggregation framework for lossless lidar point cloud compression. IEEE Trans. Circuits Syst. Video Technol. **31**(12), 4603–4616 (2021)
15. L. Xie, W. Gao, H. Zheng, G. Li, SPCGC: scalable point cloud geometry compression for machine vision, in *Proceedings of IEEE International Conference on Robotics and Automation* (2024)
16. L. Xie, W. Gao, H. Zheng, H. Ye, Semantic-aware visual decomposition for point cloud geometry compression, in *2024 Data Compression Conference (DCC)* (IEEE, Piscataway, 2024), pp. 595–595
17. Z. Qi, W. Gao, Variable-rate point cloud geometry compression based on feature adjustment and interpolation, in *2024 Data Compression Conference (DCC)* (IEEE, Piscataway, 2024), pp. 63–72
18. Z. Yu, W. Gao, When dynamic neural network meets point cloud compression: computation-aware variable rate and checkerboard context, in *2024 Data Compression Conference (DCC)* (IEEE, Piscataway, 2024), pp. 600–600
19. L. Xie, W. Gao, S. Fan, Z. Yao, PDNet: parallel dual-branch network for point cloud geometry compression and analysis, in *2024 Data Compression Conference (DCC)* (IEEE, Piscataway, 2024), pp. 596–596
20. L. Xie, W. Gao, H. Zheng, End-to-end point cloud geometry compression and analysis with sparse tensor, in *Proceedings of the 1st International Workshop on Advances in Point Cloud Compression, Processing and Analysis* (2022), pp. 27–32
21. C. Fu, G. Li, R. Song, W. Gao, S. Liu, Octattention: Octree-based large-scale contexts model for point cloud compression. Proc. AAAI Conf. Artif. Intel. **36**, no. 1, 2022, pp. 625–633.
22. H. Zheng, W. Gao, Z. Yu, T. Zhao, G. Li, ViewPCGC: view-guided learned point cloud geometry compression, in *Proceedings of the 32nd ACM International Conference on Multimedia* (2024)
23. L. Xie, W. Gao, H. Zheng, G. Li, ROI-guided point cloud geometry compression towards human and machine vision, in *Proceedings of the 32nd ACM International Conference on Multimedia* (2024).
24. C. Peng, W. Gao, Laplacian matrix learning for point cloud attribute compression with ternary search-based adaptive block partition, in *Proceedings of the 32nd ACM International Conference on Multimedia* (2024)
25. S. Luo, B. Qu, W. Gao, Learning robust 3d representation from clip via dual denoising. Preprint. arXiv:2407.00905 (2024)
26. G. Li, G. Wei, W. Gao, *Point Cloud Compression: Technologies and Standardization* (Springer Nature, Berlin, 2024)
27. G. Li, W. Gao, W. Gao, Introduction, in *Point Cloud Compression: Technologies and Standardization* (Springer, Berlin, 2024), pp. 1–28

28. G. Li, W. Gao, W. Gao, Background knowledge, in *Point Cloud Compression: Technologies and Standardization* (Springer, Berlin, 2024), pp. 29–51
29. G. Li, W. Gao, W. Gao, Predictive coding, in *Point Cloud Compression: Technologies and Standardization* (Springer, Berlin, 2024), pp. 53–70
30. G. Li, W. Gao, W. Gao, Transform coding, in *Point Cloud Compression: Technologies and Standardization* (Springer, Berlin, 2024), pp. 71–96
31. G. Li, W. Gao, W. Gao, Quantization techniques, in *Point Cloud Compression: Technologies and Standardization* (Springer, Berlin, 2024), pp. 97–112
32. G. Li, W. Gao, W. Gao, Entropy coding, in *Point Cloud Compression: Technologies and Standardization* (Springer, Berlin, 2024), pp. 113–133
33. G. Li, W. Gao, W. Gao, MPEG geometry-based point cloud compression (G-PCC) standard, in *Point Cloud Compression: Technologies and Standardization* (Springer, Berlin, 2024), pp. 135–165
34. G. Li, W. Gao, W. Gao, AVS point cloud compression standard, in *Point Cloud Compression: Technologies and Standardization* (Springer, Berlin, 2024), pp. 167–197
35. G. Li, W. Gao, W. Gao, MPEG video-based point cloud compression (V-PCC) standard, in *Point Cloud Compression: Technologies and Standardization* (Springer, Berlin, 2024), pp. 199–218.
36. G. Li, W. Gao, W. Gao, MPEG AI-based 3d graphics coding standard, in *Point Cloud Compression: Technologies and Standardization* (Springer, Berlin, 2024), pp. 219–241
37. G. Li, W. Gao, W. Gao, Future work, in *Point Cloud Compression: Technologies and Standardization*. (Springer, Berlin, 2024), pp. 243–250
38. W. Liu, W. Gao, X. Mu, Fast inter-frame motion prediction for compressed dynamic point cloud attribute enhancement. Proc. AAAI Conf. Artif. Intel. **38**(4), 3720–3728 (2024)
39. Z. Yang, W. Gao, X. Lu, DANet: density-adaptive network for geometry-based point cloud compression artifacts removal, in *2023 IEEE International Conference on Visual Communications and Image Processing (VCIP)* (IEEE, Piscataway, 2023), pp. 1–5
40. X. Fan, G. Li, D. Li, Y. Ren, W. Gao, T.H. Li, Deep geometry post-processing for decompressed point clouds, in *2022 IEEE International Conference on Multimedia and Expo (ICME)* (IEEE, Piscataway, 2022), pp. 1–6
41. X. Zhang, G. Liao, W. Gao, G. Li, TDRNet: transformer-based dual-branch restoration network for geometry based point cloud compression artifacts, in *2022 IEEE International Conference on Multimedia and Expo (ICME)* (IEEE, Piscataway, 2022), pp. 1–6
42. Z. Li, G. Li, T.H. Li, S. Liu, W. Gao, Semantic point cloud upsampling. IEEE Trans. Multimedia **25**, 3432–3442 (2023)
43. R. Zhang, W. Gao, G. Li, T. H. Li, QINet: decision surface learning and adversarial enhancement for quasi-immune completion of diverse corrupted point clouds. IEEE Trans. Geosci. Remote Sens. **60**, 1–14 (2022)
44. R. Bao, Y. Ren, G. Li, W. Gao, S. Liu, Flow-based point cloud completion network with adversarial refinement, in *ICASSP 2022-2022 IEEE International Conference on Acoustics, Speech and Signal Processing (ICASSP)* (IEEE, Piscataway, 2022), pp. 2559–2563
45. J. Chen, G. Li, R. Zhang, T.H. Li, W. Gao, PointIVAE: invertible variational autoencoder framework for 3d point cloud generation, in *2022 IEEE International Conference on Image Processing (ICIP)* (IEEE, Piscataway, 2022), pp. 3216–3220
46. R. Zhang, J. Chen, W. Gao, G. Li, T.H. Li, PointOT: interpretable geometry-inspired point cloud generative model via optimal transport. IEEE Trans. Circuits Syst. Video Technol. **32**(10), 6792–6806 (2022)
47. S. Fan, W. Gao, Screen-based 3d subjective experiment software, in *Proceedings of the 31st ACM International Conference on Multimedia* (2023), pp. 9672–9675
48. X. Mao, H. Yuan, X. Lu, R. Hamzaoui, W. Gao, PCAC-GAN: a sparse-tensor-based generative adversarial network for 3d point cloud attribute compression. Comput. Visual Media (2024)
49. J. Wang, W. Gao, G. Li, Applying collaborative adversarial learning to blind point cloud quality measurement. IEEE Trans. Instrum. Meas. (2023)

50. S. Fan, W. Gao, G. Li, Salient object detection for point clouds, in *European Conference on Computer Vision* (Springer, Berlin, 2022), pp. 1–19
51. S. Luo, W. Gao, A general framework for rotation invariant point cloud analysis, in *ICASSP 2024-2024 IEEE International Conference on Acoustics, Speech and Signal Processing (ICASSP)* (IEEE, Piscataway, 2024), pp. 3665–3669
52. X. Lu, W. Gao, AttentiveNet: detecting small objects for lidar point clouds by attending to important points, in *2023 IEEE International Conference on Visual Communications and Image Processing (VCIP)* (IEEE, Piscataway, 2023), pp. 1–5
53. Z. Pan, N. Zhang, W. Gao, S. Liu, G. Li, Less is more: label recommendation for weakly supervised point cloud semantic segmentation. Proc. AAAI Conf. Artif. Intel. **38**(5), 4397–4405 (2024)
54. Z. Pan, G. Liu, W. Gao, T. Li, EPContrast: effective point-level contrastive learning for large-scale point cloud understanding, in *2024 IEEE International Conference on Multimedia and Expo (ICME)* (IEEE, Piscataway, 2024)
55. N. Zhang, Z. Pan, T.H. Li, W. Gao, G. Li, Improving graph representation for point cloud segmentation via attentive filtering, in *Proceedings of the IEEE/CVF Conference on Computer Vision and Pattern Recognition* (2023), pp. 1244–1254
56. K. Wen, N. Zhang, G. Li, W. Gao, MPVNN: multi-resolution point-voxel non-parametric network for 3d point cloud processing, in *2024 IEEE International Conference on Multimedia and Expo (ICME)* (IEEE, Piscataway, 2024)
57. D. Yang, W. Gao, G. Li, H. Yuan, J. Hou, S. Kwong, Exploiting manifold feature representation for efficient classification of 3d point clouds. ACM Trans. Multimedia Comput. Commun. Appl. **19**(1s), 1–21 (2023)
58. C.R. Qi, H. Su, K. Mo, L.J. Guibas, PointNet: deep learning on point sets for 3d classification and segmentation, in *Proceedings of the IEEE/CVF Conference on Computer Vision and Pattern Recognition* (2017), pp. 652–660
59. C.R. Qi, L. Yi, H. Su, L.J. Guibas, PointNet++: deep hierarchical feature learning on point sets in a metric space. Adv. Neural Inf. Proces. Syst. **30**, 5099–5108 (2017)
60. Y. Wang, Y. Sun, Z. Liu, S.E. Sarma, M.M. Bronstein, J.M. Solomon, Dynamic graph CNN for learning on point clouds. ACM Trans. Graph. **38**(5), 1–12 (2019)
61. S. Shi, X. Wang, H. Li, PointRCNN: 3d object proposal generation and detection from point cloud, in *Proceedings of the IEEE/CVF Conference on Computer Vision and Pattern Recognition* (2019), pp. 770–779
62. Z. Yang, Y. Sun, S. Liu, J. Jia, 3DSSD: point-based 3d single stage object detector, in *Proceedings of the IEEE/CVF Conference on Computer Vision and Pattern Recognition* (2020), pp. 11 040–11 048
63. Q. Hu, B. Yang, L. Xie, S. Rosa, Y. Guo, Z. Wang, N. Trigoni, A. Markham, Learning semantic segmentation of large-scale point clouds with random sampling. IEEE Trans. Pattern Anal. Mach. Intel. **44**(11), 8338–8354 (2021)
64. B. Qu, X. Liang, S. Sun, W. Gao, Exploring AIGC video quality: a focus on visual harmony, video-text consistency and domain distribution gap, in *Proceedings of the IEEE/CVF Conference on Computer Vision and Pattern Recognition Workshops* (2024)
65. B. Qu, H. Li, W. Gao, Bringing textual prompt to ai-generated image quality assessment, in *2024 IEEE International Conference on Multimedia and Expo (ICME)* (IEEE, Piscataway, 2024)
66. Y. Wu, L. Xie, S. Sun, W. Gao, Y. Yan, Adaptive intra period size for deep learning-based screen content video coding, in *2024 IEEE International Conference on Multimedia and Expo Workshops (ICMEW)* (IEEE, Piscataway, 2024)
67. H. Zheng, W. Gao, End-to-end RGB-D image compression via exploiting channel-modality redundancy, in Proc. AAAI Conf. Artif. Intel. **38**(7), 7562–7570 (2024)
68. L. Tao, W. Gao, G. Li, C. Zhang, AdaNIC: towards practical neural image compression via dynamic transform routing, in *Proceedings of the IEEE/CVF International Conference on Computer Vision* (2023), pp. 16 879–16 888

69. Y. Wu, W. Gao, End-to-end lossless compression of high precision depth maps guided by pseudo-residual. Preprint. arXiv:2201.03195 (2022)
70. Y. Wu, Z. Qi, H. Zheng, L. Tao, W. Gao, Deep image compression with latent optimization and piece-wise quantization approximation, in *Proceedings of the IEEE/CVF Conference on Computer Vision and Pattern Recognition* (2021), pp. 1926–1930
71. W. Gao, L. Tao, L. Zhou, D. Yang, X. Zhang, Z. Guo, Low-rate image compression with super-resolution learning, in *Proceedings of the IEEE/CVF Conference on Computer Vision and Pattern Recognition Workshops* (2020), pp. 154–155
72. W. Gao, S. Sun, H. Zheng, Y. Wu, H. Ye, Y. Zhang, OpenDMC: an open-source library and performance evaluation for deep-learning-based multi-frame compression, in *Proceedings of the 31st ACM International Conference on Multimedia* (2023), pp. 9685–9688
73. Y. Guo, W. Gao, G. Li, Interpretable task-inspired adaptive filter pruning for neural networks under multiple constraints. Int. J. Comput. Vision **132**(6), 2060–2076 (2024)
74. W. Gao, Y. Guo, S. Ma, G. Li, S. Kwong, Efficient neural network compression inspired by compressive sensing. IEEE Trans. Neural Networks Learn. Syst. **35**(2), 1965–1979 (2024)
75. Y. Guo, W. Gao, Semantic-driven automatic filter pruning for neural networks, in *2022 IEEE International Conference on Multimedia and Expo (ICME)* (IEEE, Piscataway, 2022), pp. 1–6
76. L. Tao, W. Gao, Efficient channel pruning based on architecture alignment and probability model bypassing, in *2021 IEEE International Conference on Systems, Man, and Cybernetics (SMC)* (IEEE, Piscataway, 2021), pp. 3232–3237
77. Z. Yang, W. Gao, G. Li, Y. Yan, Sur-driven video coding rate control for jointly optimizing perceptual quality and buffer control. IEEE Trans. Image Proces. **32**, 5451–5464 (2023)
78. F. Shen, Z. Cai, W. Gao, An efficient rate control algorithm for intra frame coding in AVS3, in *2021 IEEE International Conference on Systems, Man, and Cybernetics (SMC)* (IEEE, Piscataway, 2021), pp. 3164–3169
79. H. Yuan, W. Gao, J. Wang, Dynamic computational resource allocation for fast inter frame coding in video conferencing applications, in *2021 IEEE International Conference on Multimedia and Expo (ICME)* (IEEE, Piscataway, 2021), pp. 1–6
80. W. Gao, Q. Jiang, R. Wang, S. Ma, G. Li, S. Kwong, Consistent quality oriented rate control in HEVC via balancing intra and inter frame coding. IEEE Trans. Ind. Inf. **18**(3), 1594–1604 (2021)
81. H. Yuan, W. Gao, A new coding unit partitioning mode for screen content video coding, in *Proceedings of the 2021 5th International Conference on Digital Signal Processing* (2021), pp. 66–72
82. W. Gao, On the performance evaluation of state-of-the-art rate control algorithms for practical video coding and transmission systems, in *Proceedings of the 2020 4th International Conference on Video and Image Processing* (2020), pp. 179–185
83. W. Gao, S. Kwong, Q. Jiang, C.-K. Fong, P.H. Wong, W.Y. Yuen, Data-driven rate control for rate-distortion optimization in HEVC based on simplified effective initial QP learning. IEEE Trans. Broadcast. **65**(1), 94–108 (2018)
84. W. Gao, A multi-objective optimization perspective for joint consideration of video coding quality, in *2019 Asia-Pacific Signal and Information Processing Association Annual Summit and Conference (APSIPA ASC)* (IEEE, Piscataway, 2019), pp. 986–991
85. W. Gao, S. Kwong, Y. Jia, Joint machine learning and game theory for rate control in high efficiency video coding. IEEE Trans. Image Proces. **26**(12), 6074–6089 (2017)
86. W. Gao, S. Kwong, Y. Zhou, H. Yuan, SSIM-based game theory approach for rate-distortion optimized intra frame CTU-level bit allocation. IEEE Trans. Multimedia **18**(6), 988–999 (2016)
87. W. Gao, S. Kwong, H. Yuan, X. Wang, DCT coefficient distribution modeling and quality dependency analysis based frame-level bit allocation for HEVC. IEEE Trans. Circuits Syst. Video Technol. **26**(1), 139–153 (2015)
88. W. Gao, S. Kwong, Phase congruency based edge saliency detection and rate control for perceptual image and video coding, in *2016 IEEE International Conference on Systems, Man, and Cybernetics (SMC)* (IEEE, Piscataway, 2016), pp. 000 264–000 269

89. H. Yuan, W. Gao, OpenFastVC: an open source library for video coding fast algorithm implementation, in *Proceedings of the 31st ACM International Conference on Multimedia* (2023), pp. 9660–9663
90. H. Yuan, W. Gao, S. Ma, Y. Yan, Divide-and-conquer-based RDO-free CU partitioning for 8K video compression. ACM Trans. Multimedia Comput. Commun. Appl. **20**(4), 1–20 (2024)
91. L. Tao, W. Gao, A hardware implementation of entropy encoder for 8K video coding, in *2022 IEEE International Conference on Multimedia and Expo (ICME)* (IEEE, Piscataway, 2022), pp. 1–6
92. Y. Guo, W. Gao, S. Ma, G. Li, Accelerating transform algorithm implementation for efficient intra coding of 8K UHD videos. ACM Trans. Multimedia Comput. Commun. Appl. **18**(4), 1–20 (2022)
93. Z. Cai, W. Gao, Efficient fast algorithm and parallel hardware architecture for intra prediction of AVS3, in *2021 IEEE International Symposium on Circuits and Systems (ISCAS)* (IEEE, Piscataway, 2021), pp. 1–5
94. W. Gao, H. Yuan, Y. Guo, L. Tao, Z. Cai, G. Li, OpenHardwareVC: an open source library for 8K UHD video coding hardware implementation, in *Proceedings of the 30th ACM International Conference on Multimedia* (2022), pp. 7339–7342
95. W. Gao, H. Yuan, G. Liao, Z. Guo, J. Chen, Pp8k: a new dataset for 8k UHD video compression and processing. IEEE MultiMedia **30**(3), 100–109 (2023)
96. X. Zang, W. Gao, G. Li, H. Fang, C. Ban, Z. He, H. Sun, A baseline investigation: transformer-based cross-view baseline for text-based person search, in *Proceedings of the 31st ACM International Conference on Multimedia* (2023), pp. 7737–7746
97. G. Liao, W. Gao, G. Li, J. Wang, S. Kwong, Cross-collaborative fusion-encoder network for robust RGB-thermal salient object detection. IEEE Trans. Circuits Syst. Video Technol. **32**(11), 7646–7661 (2022)
98. W. Gao, G. Liao, S. Ma, G. Li, Y. Liang, W. Lin, Unified information fusion network for multi-modal RGB-d and RGB-t salient object detection. IEEE Trans. Circuits Syst. Video Technol. **32**(4), 2091–2106 (2021)
99. Y. Chen, S. Sun, G. Li, W. Gao, T.H. Li, Closing the gap between theory and practice during alternating optimization for GANs. IEEE Trans. Neural Networks Learn. Syst. **35**(10), 14005–14017 (2024)
100. Y. Chen, C. Jin, G. Li, T.H. Li, W. Gao, Mitigating label noise in GANs via enhanced spectral normalization. IEEE Trans. Circuits Syst. Video Technol. **33**(8), 3924–3934 (2023)
101. X. Zang, G. Li, W. Gao, Multidirection and multiscale pyramid in transformer for video-based pedestrian retrieval. IEEE Trans. Ind. Inf. **18**(12), 8776–8785 (2022)
102. X. Zang, G. Li, W. Gao, X. Shu, Learning to disentangle scenes for person re-identification. Image Vision Comput. **116**, 104330 (2021)
103. X. Zang, G. Li, W. Gao, X. Shu, Exploiting robust unsupervised video person re-identification. IET Image Proces. **16**(3), 729–741 (2022)
104. Z. Yue, G. Li, W. Gao, Cross-level guided attention for human-object interaction detection, in *2023 IEEE International Conference on Multimedia and Expo Workshops (ICMEW)* (IEEE, Piscataway, 2023), pp. 284–289
105. Z. Yao, W. Gao, Iterative saliency aggregation and assignment network for efficient salient object detection in optical remote sensing images. IEEE Trans. Geosci. Remote Sens. **62**, 1–13 (2024)
106. Y. Sun, Z. Li, S. Wang, W. Gao, Depth-assisted calibration on learning-based factorization for a compressive light field display. Opt. Exp. **31**(4), 5399–5413 (2023)
107. Y. Sun, Z. Li, L. Li, S. Wang, W. Gao, Optimization of compressive light field display in dual-guided learning, in *ICASSP 2022-2022 IEEE International Conference on Acoustics, Speech and Signal Processing (ICASSP)* (IEEE, Piscataway, 2022), pp. 2075–2079
108. W. Gao, S. Fan, G. Li, W. Lin, A thorough benchmark and a new model for light field saliency detection. IEEE Trans. Pattern Anal. Mach. Intel. **45**(7), 8003–8019 (2023)
109. Z. Guo, W. Gao, H. Wang, J. Wang, S. Fan, No-reference deep quality assessment of compressed light field images, in *2021 IEEE International Conference on Multimedia and Expo (ICME)* (IEEE, Piscataway, 2021), pp. 1–6

110. G. Liao, W. Gao, Rethinking feature mining for light field salient object detection. ACM Trans. Multimedia Comput. Commun. Appl. **20**(10), 1–24 (2024)
111. S. Sun, J. Liu, T.H. Li, H. Li, G. Liu, W. Gao, Streamflow: streamlined multi-frame optical flow estimation for video sequences. Preprint. arXiv:2311.17099 (2023)
112. R. Liu, J. Huang, W. Gao, T.H. Li, G. Li, Mug-STAN: adapting image-language pretrained models for general video understanding. Preprint. arXiv:2311.15075 (2023)
113. C. Zhang, W. Gao, Learned rate control for frame-level adaptive neural video compression via dynamic neural network, in *European Conference on Computer Vision* (Springer, Berlin, 2024)
114. J.D.M.-W.C. Kenton, L.K. Toutanova, Bert: pre-training of deep bidirectional transformers for language understanding, in *Proceedings of NAACL-HLT* (2019), pp. 4171–4186
115. H. Bao, L. Dong, S. Piao, F. Wei, Beit: bert pre-training of image transformers, in *International Conference on Learning Representations* (2021)
116. K. He, X. Chen, S. Xie, Y. Li, P. Dollár, R. Girshick, Masked autoencoders are scalable vision learners, in *Proceedings of the IEEE/CVF Conference on Computer Vision and Pattern Recognition* (2022), pp. 16 000–16 009
117. W. Gao, H. Ye, G. Li, H. Zheng, Y. Wu, L. Xie, OpenPointCloud: an open-source algorithm library of deep learning based point cloud compression, in *Proceedings of the 30th ACM International Conference on Multimedia* (2022), pp. 7347–7350
118. Y. Zhang, W. Gao, G. Li, OpenPointCloud-v2: a deep learning based open-source algorithm library of point cloud processing, in *Proceedings of the 1st International Workshop on Advances in Point Cloud Compression, Processing and Analysis* (2022), pp. 51–55
119. W. Gao, G. Li, H. Yuan, R. Hamzaoui, Z. Li, S. Liu, Apccpa'22: 1st international workshop on advances in point cloud compression, processing and analysis, in *Proceedings of the 30th ACM International Conference on Multimedia* (2022), pp. 7392–7393
120. J.-X. Zhuang, X. Huang, Y. Yang, J. Chen, Y. Yu, W. Gao, G. Li, J. Chen, T. Zhang, Open-Media: open-source medical image analysis toolbox and benchmark under heterogeneous ai computing platforms, in *Chinese Conference on Pattern Recognition and Computer Vision (PRCV)* (Springer, Berlin, 2022), pp. 356–367
121. A. Vaswani, N. Shazeer, N. Parmar, J. Uszkoreit, L. Jones, A.N. Gomez, Ł. Kaiser, I. Polosukhin, Attention is all you need. Adv. Neural Inf. Proces. Syst. **30**, 5998–6008 (2017)
122. J. Xing, H. Yuan, C. Chen, W. Gao, Wiener filter-based color attribute quality enhancement for geometry-based point cloud compression, in *2022 Asia-Pacific Signal and Information Processing Association Annual Summit and Conference (APSIPA ASC)* (IEEE, Piscataway, 2022), pp. 1208–1212
123. J. Kaplan, S. McCandlish, T. Henighan, T.B. Brown, B. Chess, R. Child, S. Gray, A. Radford, J. Wu, D. Amodei, Scaling laws for neural language models. CoRR. vol. arXiv. Preprint. arXiv:2001.08361 (2020)
124. J. Hoffmann, S. Borgeaud, A. Mensch, E. Buchatskaya, T. Cai, E. Rutherford, D. de Las Casas, L.A. Hendricks, J. Welbl, A. Clark, T. Hennigan, E. Noland, K. Millican, G. van den Driessche, B. Damoc, A. Guy, S. Osindero, K. Simonyan, E. Elsen, J.W. Rae, O. Vinyals, L. Sifre, Training compute-optimal large language models. Preprint. arXiv:2203.15556 (2022)
125. A.v.d. Oord, Y. Li, O. Vinyals, Representation learning with contrastive predictive coding. Preprint. arXiv:1807.03748 (2018)
126. W. Gao, S. Kwong, Y. Zhou, Y. Jia, J. Zhang, W. Wu, Multiscale phase congruency analysis for image edge visual saliency detection, in *2016 International Conference on Machine Learning and Cybernetics (ICMLC)*, vol. 1 (IEEE, Piscataway, 2016), pp. 75–80
127. K. He, H. Fan, Y. Wu, S. Xie, R. Girshick, Momentum contrast for unsupervised visual representation learning, in *Proceedings of the IEEE/CVF Conference on Computer Vision and Pattern Recognition* (2020), pp. 9729–9738
128. T. Chen, S. Kornblith, M. Norouzi, G. Hinton, A simple framework for contrastive learning of visual representations, in *Proceedings of the International Conference on Machine Learning* (2020), pp. 1597–1607

129. X. Yu, L. Tang, Y. Rao, T. Huang, J. Zhou, J. Lu, Point-bert: pre-training 3d point cloud transformers with masked point modeling, in *Proceedings of the IEEE/CVF Conference on Computer Vision and Pattern Recognition* (2022), pp. 19 313–19 322
130. K. Fu, P. Gao, S. Liu, L. Qu, L. Gao, M. Wang, POS-BERT: point cloud one-stage bert pre-training. Expert Syst. Appl. **240**, 122563 (2023)
131. Y. Pang, W. Wang, F.E. Tay, W. Liu, Y. Tian, L. Yuan, Masked autoencoders for point cloud self-supervised learning, in *Proceedings of the European Conference on Computer Vision* (2022), pp. 604–621
132. G. Chen, M. Wang, Y. Yang, K. Yu, L. Yuan, Y. Yue, PointGPT: auto-regressively generative pre-training from point clouds. Adv. Neural Inf. Proces. Syst. **36** (2024)
133. R. Zhang, Z. Guo, W. Zhang, K. Li, X. Miao, B. Cui, Y. Qiao, P. Gao, H. Li, Pointclip: point cloud understanding by clip, in *Proceedings of the IEEE/CVF Conference on Computer Vision and Pattern Recognition* (2022), pp. 8552–8562
134. J.T. Rolfe, Discrete variational autoencoders, in *International Conference on Learning Representations* (2016)
135. P.J. Liu, M. Saleh, E. Pot, B. Goodrich, R. Sepassi, L. Kaiser, N. Shazeer, Generating Wikipedia by summarizing long sequences, in *International Conference on Learning Representations* (2018)
136. A. Radford, K. Narasimhan, T. Salimans, I. Sutskever, et al., Improving language understanding by generative pre-training (2018)
137. G.M. Morton, A computer oriented geodetic data base and a new technique in file sequencing (1966)
138. A. Radford, J.W. Kim, C. Hallacy, A. Ramesh, G. Goh, S. Agarwal, G. Sastry, A. Askell, P. Mishkin, J. Clark, et al., Learning transferable visual models from natural language supervision, in *Proceedings of International Conference on Machine Learning* (2021), pp. 8748–8763
139. J. Zhou, J. Wang, B. Ma, Y.-S. Liu, T. Huang, X. Wang, Uni3d: exploring unified 3d representation at scale. Preprint. arXiv:2310.06773 (2023)
140. Y. Liu, M. Ott, N. Goyal, J. Du, M. Joshi, D. Chen, O. Levy, M. Lewis, L. Zettlemoyer, V. Stoyanov, Roberta: a robustly optimized bert pretraining approach. Preprint. arXiv:1907.11692 (2019)
141. A. Dosovitskiy, L. Beyer, A. Kolesnikov, D. Weissenborn, X. Zhai, T. Unterthiner, M. Dehghani, M. Minderer, G. Heigold, S. Gelly, et al., An image is worth 16x16 words: transformers for image recognition at scale (2020), pp. 7598–7610
142. L. Xue, M. Gao, C. Xing, R. Martín-Martín, J. Wu, C. Xiong, R. Xu, J.C. Niebles, S. Savarese, ULIP: learning a unified representation of language, images, and point clouds for 3d understanding, in *Proceedings of the IEEE/CVF Conference on Computer Vision and Pattern Recognition* (2023), pp. 1179–1189
143. M. Liu, R. Shi, K. Kuang, Y. Zhu, X. Li, S. Han, H. Cai, F. Porikli, H. Su, OpenShape: scaling up 3d shape representation towards open-world understanding. Adv. Neural Inf. Proces. Syst. **36** (2024)
144. Y. Fang, W. Wang, B. Xie, Q. Sun, L. Wu, X. Wang, T. Huang, X. Wang, Y. Cao, Eva: exploring the limits of masked visual representation learning at scale, in *Proceedings of the IEEE/CVF Conference on Computer Vision and Pattern Recognition* (2023), pp. 19 358–19 369
145. W. Zhao, X. Liu, Z. Zhong, J. Jiang, W. Gao, G. Li, X. Ji, Self-supervised arbitrary-scale point clouds upsampling via implicit neural representation, in *Proceedings of the IEEE/CVF Conference on Computer Vision and Pattern Recognition* (2022), pp. 1999–2007

Chapter 8
Point Cloud-Language Multi-modal Learning

Abstract This chapter explores the evolution and applications of large language models (LLMs) in natural language processing, detailing their architecture, training methodologies, and usage in tasks like information retrieval and text generation. It then examines 2D visual language models (2D VLMs), which integrate visual and textual data for applications such as image captioning and visual question-answering, with insights into models like CLIP and BLIP. The chapter progresses to 2D multi-modal large language models (2D MLLMs), highlighting their enhanced contextual understanding, with examples like Flamingo, BLIP-2, and LLaVA. It further delves into 3D MLLMs, which process 3D data to understand and interact with 3D scenes and objects. Additionally, the concept of embodied AI is introduced, demonstrating the integration of perception, cognition, and action for complex tasks, exemplified by Google's PaLM-E and DeepMind's RT-2. The chapter concludes by anticipating future advancements in AI, particularly in robotics and advanced task automation, driven by the ongoing development of 3D MLLMs and embodied AI.

Keywords Large-scale language models · Modality alignment · 3D Multi-modal · Attention mask · Pre-training · Supervised fine-tuning · Prompt engineering

8.1 Introduction

In recent years, the research fields of multimedia computing and 2D/3D computer vision have achieved significant progress in diverse aspects [1–110]. Notably, large-scale language models [111–114] also have made significant progress, achieved by increasing the scale of data and models. These models possess astonishing generative capabilities [99]. While in most natural language processing (NLP) tasks, these large language models (LLMs) exhibit surprisingly strong zero/few-shot reasoning performance [115], they have inherent limitations in the visual domain as they can only understand discrete text and cannot process visual information. Meanwhile, large-scale visual base models [116–119] have made rapid progress in perception, with a particular focus on modality alignment and task unification

W. Gao, G. Li, *Deep Learning for 3D Point Clouds*,
https://doi.org/10.1007/978-981-97-9570-3_8

between traditional text and visual information [35, 120], but their development in reasoning has been relatively slow. Considering this complementarity, single-modal large language models (LLMs) and visual models are evolving in the direction of each other, ultimately giving rise to a new field, known as multi-modal large language models (MLLMs). Multi-modal large language models [121–130] (MLLMs) have emerged as a new research hotspot in recent years, leveraging powerful large language models as the brain to perform multi-modal tasks. Large language models (LLMs) and 2D visual language models (VLMs) [131–133] have been proven to excel in various tasks, such as common-sense reasoning. Despite their impressive capabilities, they are not grounded in a 3D physical world, which involves richer concepts like spatial relationships, physics, layout, and more. As a result, there is also research focused on the 3D multi-modal large model direction [134–137], attempting to inject the 3D world into large language models. This chapter will introduce 2D multi-modal visual language models and 3D multi-modal visual language models, building on large language models and visual models as their foundation.

8.2 Large Language Modeling in Natural Language Processing

Large language models (LLMs) represent a revolutionary technology in the field of artificial intelligence. They are capable of understanding and generating natural language texts through deep learning and extensive data training. These models are typically built on the Transformer architecture as auto-regressive models [86].

Based on the differences in attention masks used during feature extraction, language models can be categorized into three types, including Encoder-only (e.g., BERT), Encoder-Decoder (e.g., UniLM, T5), and Decoder-only (e.g., GPT, LLaMA). Existing LLMs are mainly divided into two architectures: Encoder-Decoder and Decoder-only. Attention masks of these three are shown in Fig. 8.1.

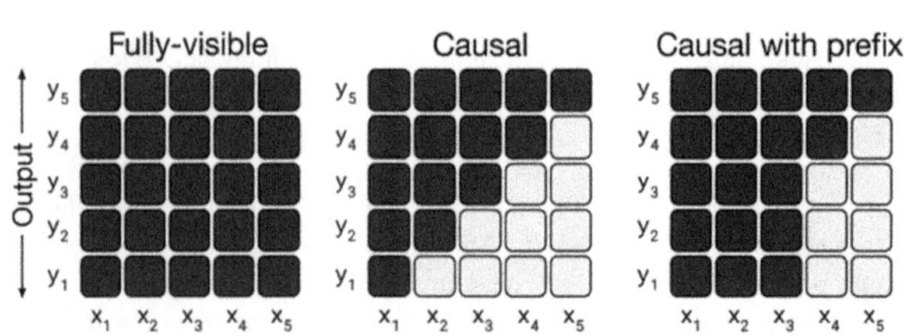

Fig. 8.1 Attention masks of the three types of language models (Source: Author)

8.2.1 Encoder-Decoder Architecture

Language models with an Encoder-Decoder architecture typically use the Encoder part to process the input and the Decoder part to autoregressively generate the output [34, 90]. The Encoder is primarily responsible for feature extraction of the input, while the Decoder is utilized for understanding the entire information and generating output. Notable implementations of the Encoder-Decoder structure include Microsoft's UniLM, Google's T5/FlanT5, and Tsinghua University's GLM.

8.2.2 Decoder-Only Architecture

In Decoder-only structured models, the attention mask is a strictly causal autoregressive form, meaning the model predicts the next word based on the current one in a next-token prediction language modeling. The Decoder-only structure is considered a unified architecture, integrating feature extraction and output generation within a single model framework. Famous series like GPT and LLaMA utilize the Decoder-only architecture. This structure is also the most widely used scheme in most current LLMs. Experiments indicate that, given the same amount of parameters, Decoder-only architecture models tend to perform better than those with Encoder-Decoder architectures [138].

8.2.3 Training Period and Inference Period of LLMs

Figure 8.2 shows the training and inference process of large language models (LLMs). It can be broadly divided into the following four parts:

- **Pre-training (Pre-train):** This stage involves language modeling using the next-token prediction method. The model undergoes pre-training with a vast corpus of data (on the scale of several terabytes of tokens), akin to reading extensively. The model post pre-training possesses basic text continuation capabilities.
- **Supervised Fine-Tuning (SFT):** At this stage, extensive supervised data are used to form question-answer pairs. The question (i.e., the instruction) is input into the LLM, and the answer is what the model predicts. This fine-tuning allows the model to generate better answers to the questions rather than merely continuing the text.
- **Reinforcement Learning via Human Feedback (RLHF):** This stage employs reinforcement learning [139, 140] to better align the language model's output with human understanding and expression. The typical process of RLHF is as follows: Having the language model generate N different answers for a question and then having humans score and rank these answers. A Reward Model is

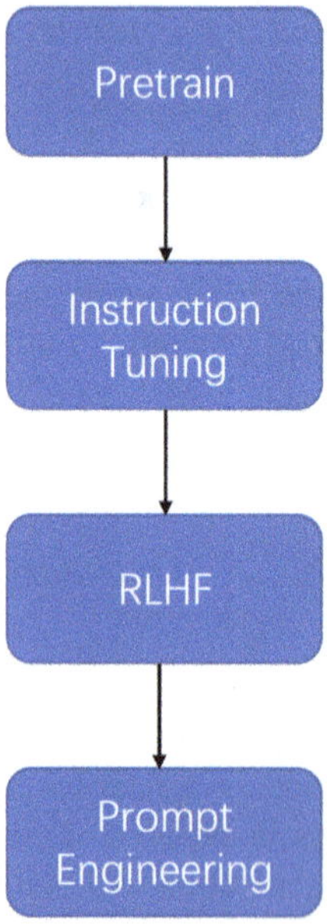

Fig. 8.2 Training and inference process of LLMs (Source: Author)

designed to learn from these ranking results. This Reward Model then guides further learning of the LLM.

- **Prompt Engineering:** For inference process, we interact with large language models (LLMs) through a conversational format. Specifically, a user poses a question, and the LLM, trained through the aforementioned stages, provides a corresponding answer. Sometimes, some degree of prompt engineering is also required to assist in eliciting more accurate or contextually relevant responses from the model. This engineering might involve crafting the question in a certain way or providing additional context or instructions to guide the model toward the desired type of answer. For different tasks, specific prompts are designed to achieve better performance. This process allows models to be directly deployed for various tasks without the need for further fine-tuning on downstream tasks.

8.2.4 The Most Influential Open-Source LLM-LLaMA

LLaMA, released by Meta AI in February 2023, stands out as one of the most influential open-source large language models in the field. As part of a commitment to open community and the practical application of artificial intelligence, LLaMA is designed to be more efficient and less resource-intensive than other models. This efficiency is achieved by training smaller models on more tokens, which means they require less computational power and resources for training and operation, as well as less memory and bandwidth for storage and transmission.

Table 8.1 Dataset specifications for LLaMA model training (Source: Author)

Dataset	Sampling prop.	Epochs	Disk size
CommonCrawl	67.0%	1.10	3.3 TB
C4	15.0%	1.06	783 GB
Github	4.5%	0.64	328 GB
Wikipedia	4.5%	2.45	83 GB
Books	4.5%	2.23	85 GB
ArXiv	2.5%	1.06	92 GB
StackExchange	2.0%	1.03	78 GB

For instance, LLaMA 13B outperforms GPT-3 175B in most benchmarks while using only about 7% of the parameters. This characteristic makes it feasible for individuals to deploy LLaMA, enhancing accessibility and personalization for researchers and enabling the exploration of new use cases and applications. LLaMA comes in four sizes of parameters: 7, 13, 33, and 65 billion. Even the smallest version can be run on a graphics card with 24G of memory. The seven-billion parameter LLaMA was trained on 1 trillion tokens, while the largest model utilized 1.4 trillion tokens. All training data comes from publicly available datasets, and the performance of LLaMA is comparable to that of GPT-3, which has 175 billion parameters.

Like the GPT series, the LLaMA model also employs a Decoder-only architecture. To enhance training stability, it normalizes the input of each Transformer sublayer instead of the output. It introduces the SwiGLU activation function, replacing the traditional ReLU non-linearity, and removes absolute position embeddings, adding rotary position embeddings to every layer of the network instead. LLaMA utilizes seven types of datasets for training, as shown in Table 8.1.

These diverse data sources contribute to LLaMA's comprehensive understanding and generation capabilities across a wide range of subjects and formats. The inclusion of recent data, such as the updated Wikipedia entries and public domain books, ensures the model's relevance and ability to produce informed and contextually accurate responses. The strategic alterations in architecture, such as the adoption of SwiGLU and rotary position embeddings, aim to enhance the model's performance and efficiency, making it a powerful tool for a wide array of AI applications.

8.3 2D Vision-Language Models

Before delving into 3D multi-modal large language models (MLLMs), it is important to have an understanding of 2D vision-language models (VLMs). These models integrate visual data with textual data, enabling the understanding and generation of content that combines both visual and linguistic elements. In order to have a global understanding of the entire visual-language multi-modal model, we will introduce several VLMs.

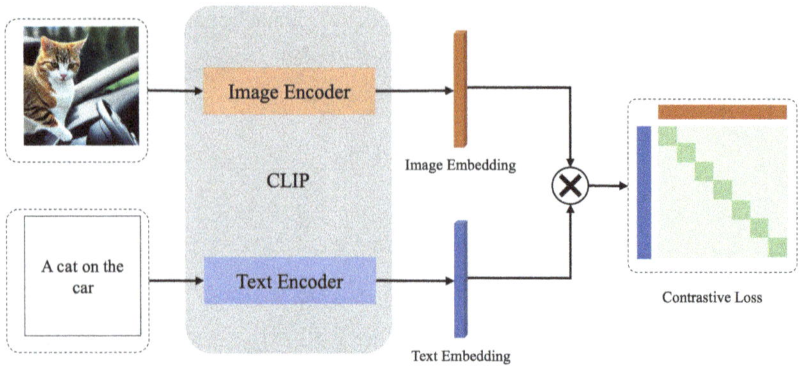

Fig. 8.3 CLIP architecture [131] (Source: Author)

8.3.1 CLIP

CLIP [131] is short for Contrastive Language-Image Pre-training, which is proposed by OpenAI. CLIP model has learned the relationship between a complete sentence and the image it describes. During its training, the model is given an input sentence, and it learns to extract the most relevant image to accompany it. This means it is trained on complete sentences rather than on discrete categories like "car" or "dog," which is crucial for its application. By training on complete phrases, the model can learn more and recognize patterns between photos and texts. When trained on a sufficiently large dataset of photos and corresponding sentences, the model can function as a open-vocabulary classifier.

Given an image I and its corresponding textual prompt T, let $f_{\theta_{\text{img}}}(I)$ represent the embedding produced by the image encoder with parameters θ_{img}, and let $h_{\theta_{\text{txt}}}(T)$ represent the embedding produced by the text encoder with parameters θ_{txt}. Additionally, we utilize the embedding of *[eot]* (end the text) token to represent the entire sentence. The architecture is shown in Fig. 8.3.

CLIP can be applied in the following areas:

Zero-Shot Detection CLIP can be used for target detection tasks to achieve zero-shot detection, i.e., detecting categories not included in the training dataset [95]. For example, Google's ViLD project implemented open-vocabulary object detection based on CLIP.

Image Retrieval Using text to search for images is a direct application of CLIP, which also serves as the ranking model for DALL-E, selecting images with high relevance to the text from generated images [141].

Video Understanding Although originally designed for text-image pairs, CLIP can be extended to text-video pairs. For instance, the VideoCLIP project applies CLIP in the video domain for some zero-shot video understanding tasks [38].

Image Editing CLIP can be used to guide image-editing tasks [142].

Image Generation CLIP is also applicable in image generation, such as the StyleCLIP project, which uses CLIP for text-guided StyleGAN image creation.

Self-supervised Learning Recent work by Huawei, like the MVP project, uses CLIP for visual self-supervised training [138].

VL Tasks As a multi-modal model, CLIP is also suitable for image-text multi-modal tasks, such as image captioning and visual question-answering (VQA).

8.3.2 BLIP

BLIP [132] is short for Bootstrapping Language-Image Pre-training. Most current VLMs excel in tasks based on either understanding or generation, but few models demonstrate excellence in both areas. BLIP is applicable for a unified framework of visual-language understanding and generation. It is a novel vision-language pre-training framework, offering wider applicability to downstream tasks compared to existing methods. BLIP introduces a multi-modal mixture of encoder-decoder architecture, which is highly versatile, serving as either a unimodal encoder or an image-based text encoder or decoder. BLIP is jointly trained with three visual-language objectives: contrastive learning between images and texts (ITC), image-text matching (ITM), and image-conditioned language modeling (LM), as shown in Fig. 8.4. During its pre-training phase, BLIP optimizes three key objectives: two aimed at enhancing understanding and one for generation tasks.

Image-Text Contrastive Loss (ITC) ITC primarily targets the visual and textual encoders, with the core objective of synchronizing the feature spaces of visuals and texts. It achieves this by increasing the similarity of positive image-text pairs and decreasing that of negative pairs.

Image-Text Matching Loss (ITM) ITM impacts both the visual encoder and the visual-text encoder, aiming to learn an integrated representation of images and texts to accurately capture the fine-grained alignment between visuals and language. ITM is a binary classification task that uses a classifier to determine whether an image-text pair is positive or negative, employing hard negative sampling techniques.

Language Modeling Loss (LM) BLIP includes a decoder specifically for generation tasks. This necessitates the introduction of a language modeling objective tailored to generation tasks. LM functions on both the visual encoder and the visual-text encoder, with the goal of auto-regressively generating textual descriptions based on given images. Compared to the widely used masked language modeling (MLM) loss, LM enables the model to transform visual information into coherent textual descriptions.

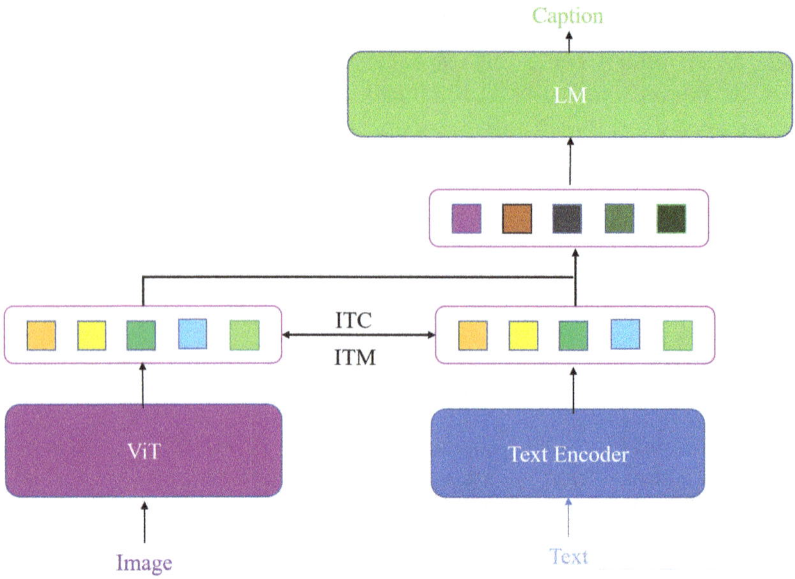

Fig. 8.4 BLIP architecture [132] (Source: Author)

8.4 2D Vision-Language Multi-modal Large Language Models

After introducing 2D vision-language models (VLMs), we will delve further into 2D multi-modal large language models (MLLMs). 2D MLLMs serve as a crucial reference for 3D point cloud MLLMs, as 2D data can be considered a perspective projection of 3D data. Many 3D MLLMs are structurally similar to 2D MLLMs and may even process 3D point clouds by projecting them into multi-view 2D images.

8.4.1 Flamingo

Flamingo [122], developed by DeepMind, is an advanced multi-modal large language model with a unique structure. It merges the textual features of LLM with the visual features of Vision Transformer (ViT) through the integration of specially designed cross-attention blocks within each LLM block, enabling the model to process multi-modal information concurrently. Drawing on the in-context learning capabilities inherent in LLMs, Flamingo utilizes interleaved image-text pairs for in-context training. This method allows Flamingo to demonstrate exceptional few-shot capabilities in numerous downstream tasks, efficiently learning and adapting even with limited data.

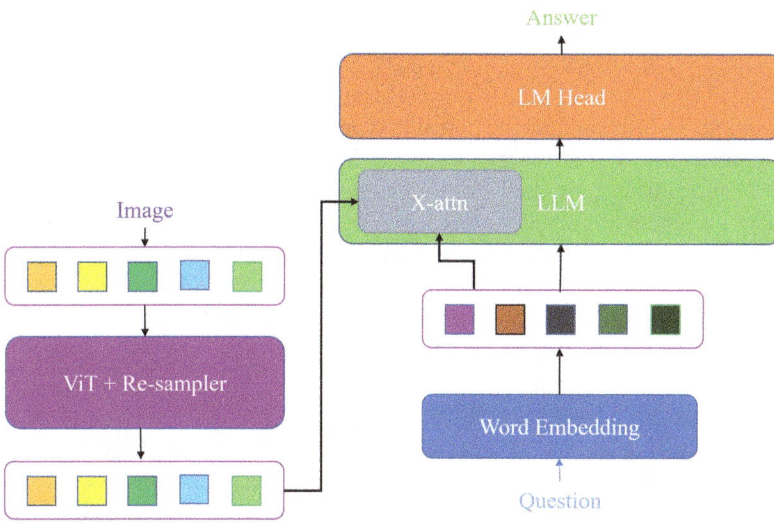

Fig. 8.5 Flamingo architecture [122] (Source: Author)

The network structure is illustrated in Fig. 8.5. For the input of interleaved image-text data, the image part first passes through a visual encoder and then is processed by a custom-designed perceptual reinvigorator. The text part is fed into a composite model that integrates a Gated XATTN-DENSE module with an LM. Here, the cross-attention mechanism of the Gated XATTN-DENSE module is responsible for the effective fusion of image and text features. The visual encoder is the NFNet-F6, a design original to the authors, and the perceptual reinvigorator is also independently designed. The language model is based on the Chinchilla model. During training, parameters of the visual encoder and language model are fixed, with only the perceptual reinvigorator and Gated XATTN-DENSE module being trainable. In the fine-tuning phase, the visual encoder is unfrozen and fine-tuned together with the perceptual reinvigorator and Gated XATTN-DENSE module.

The training loss for the model is based on the standard language modeling (LM) loss, which predicts the probability of the next generated token based on the given text and image inputs. The model training utilized several datasets: the M3W dataset, a large-scale image-text dataset collected from the Internet by the authors; the LTIP dataset, derived from the ALIGN dataset, containing 312 million high-quality image-text pairs; and the VTP dataset, comprising 27 million short videos and their textual descriptions. Training resources were TPUv4. The largest version of the model contains 80 billion parameters, deployed across 16 devices, utilizing a total of 1536 TPU chips, with a training duration of 15 days.

8.4.2 BLIP-2

BLIP-2 [121] is a 2D MLLM, whose full name is Bootstrapping Language-Image Pre-training. To fully harness the potential of large language models (LLMs), BLIP-2 incorporates LLM as the core of its vision-language encoder-decoder framework. BLIP-2 innovatively optimizes the vision-and-language pre-training (VLP) tasks, focusing on modal alignment and efficient training. In terms of modal alignment, BLIP-2 introduces a lightweight architecture, QFormer (querying transformer), specifically designed to establish connections between images and texts. For efficient multi-modal training, BLIP-2, in conjunction with QFormer, proposes a novel two-stage pre-training approach that effectively integrates the existing visual backbone with LLM models.

BLIP-2 is mainly used for zero-shot image-text generation. The network structure is shown in Fig. 8.6. The input image goes through an encoding module to generate image features and then enters the Q-Former module for fusion and alignment with text. After passing through a fully connected mapping, it finally inputs into the LLM Decoder to output result text. Here, the Image Encoder module comes from ViT, and the LLM Decoder module comes from FlanT5 or OPT model; only the Q-Former module is self-designed. During training, parameters of the Image Encoder and LLM Decoder modules are frozen, only the Q-Former module parameters can be trained, and when finetuning for some specific tasks, the Image Encoder can be unfrozen to update together with Q-Former. The detailed Q-Former network structure is shown in Fig. 8.7, implementing the fusion and alignment of image and text features in three ways. The training of the model is divided into two stages. The first stage is to train the Q-Former based on a frozen image encoder, making the output visual representations more relevant to the input text. The corresponding losses are three: (1) Image-Text Contrastive Learning (ITC), aligning image representations and text representations to maximize their mutual information and similarity; (2) Image-grounded Text Generation (ITG), which trains the Q-

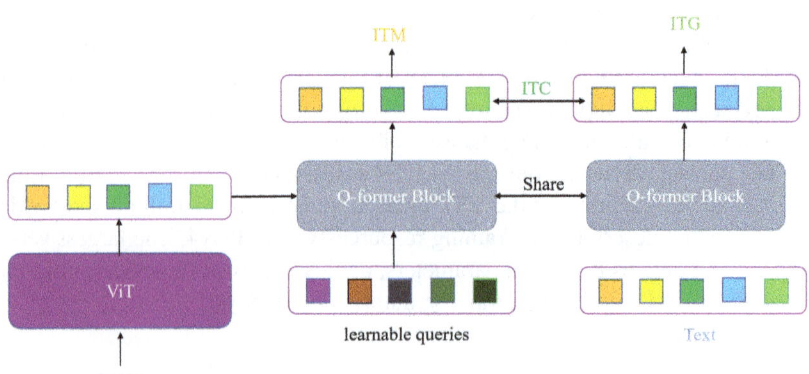

Fig. 8.6 BLIP-2 Q-former pre-training [121] (Source: Author)

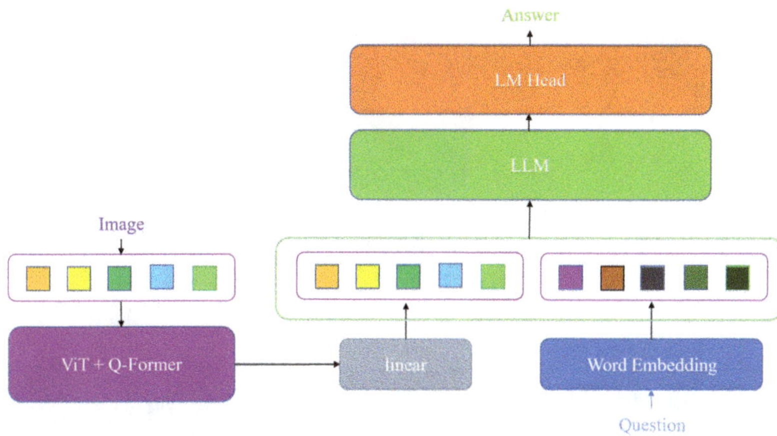

Fig. 8.7 BLIP-2 architecture [121] (Source: Author)

Former module to generate text based on input images; (3) Image-Text Matching (ITM), which aims to learn the fine-grained alignment between image features and text features. The second stage is to train the Q-Former based on a frozen LLM to make its output features generate the expected answers after entering the LLM, with the corresponding loss being the standard language model loss. Image datasets used for training include 129M images from COCO, Visual Genome, CC3M, CC12M, and SBU, and 115M images from the LAION400M dataset, while also using the CapFilt method to generate captions for network images.

In its visual component, BLIP-2 employs the EVA-ViT-G model, which boasts one billion parameters. For the Q-former section, the model utilizes the BERT language model for initialization, comprising 12 Transformer Blocks. In terms of language modeling, BLIP-2 uses large language models such as FLANT5-XXL (with 11 billion parameters) and OPT-13B. Training resources include a system with 16 A100 (40G) GPUs. For the largest parameter combination involving ViT-G and FlanT5-XXL, the total training time required is approximately 9 days.

8.4.3 LLaVA

To achieve open-end multi-modal visual question-answering (VQA), relying solely on surface-level text-image information is insufficient. Models need to delve into the deeper complexities of images and enhance their ability to understand the relationship between text and image. Microsoft's LLaVA [123] model, through Visual Instruction Tuning, endows the pure large language model LLaMA with multi-modal capabilities. LLaVA's structure is remarkably simple: it processes the visual tokens outputted by ViT through a linear layer or MLP and then concatenates them with language tokens for input into the LLM. Here, ViT is CLIP-ViT-L, while

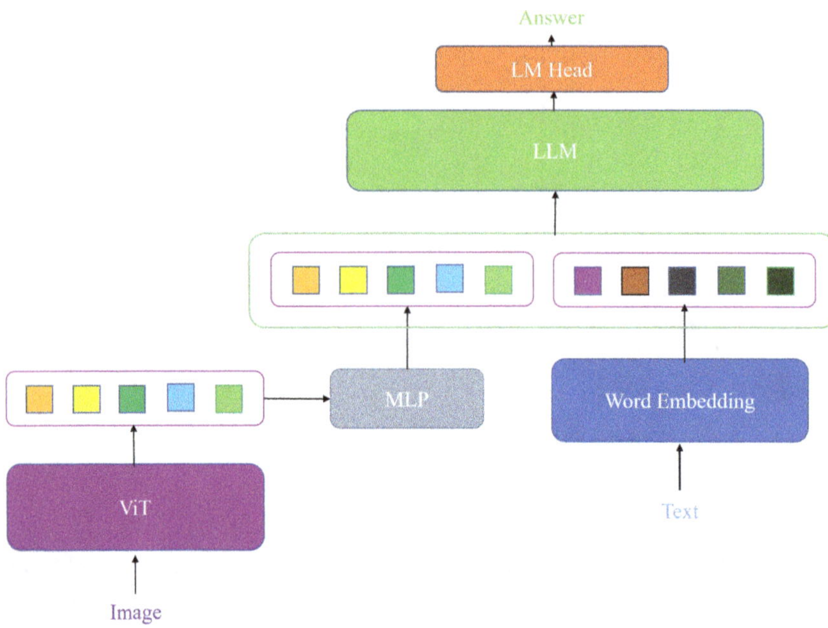

Fig. 8.8 LLaVA architecture [123] (Source: Author)

the language model is either LLaMA-7B or Vicuna-7B. The whole architecture is shown in Fig. 8.8.

At the initial stage of the processing pipeline, the image X_v is fed into the vision encoder $g()$, which transforms it into the corresponding visual features Z_v. These visual features are then transformed by the weight matrix W, producing a feature representation H_v akin to word embedding. Furthermore, these features, in conjunction with the token embeddings of the vocabulary expression X_q, are input into the language model LLaMA. Subsequently, the language model generates the textual output X_a via an autoregressive mechanism.

$$H_v = W \cdot Z_v, \text{ with } Z_v = g(\mathbf{X}_v)$$

LLaVA's training consists of two stages. The first stage focuses on early text-image alignment, training only the intermediate linear projection layer on a vast array of Internet-based text-image data. The second stage employs high-quality images, instructions, and answer data generated by GPT-4 for detailed instruction fine-tuning. During this stage, both the linear projection layer and the entire LLM are trained, while the ViT remains unchanged throughout both stages. LLaVA-1.5 represents an expansion of its predecessor, LLaVA, in several key aspects: image resolution has been enhanced from 224 to 336, the size of the language model has grown from 7 billion to 13 billion parameters, and there has been a significant increase in the scale of the instruction-tuning dataset. These improvements have enabled LLaVA-1.5 to achieve better performance across a variety of multi-modal tasks.

8.4.4 Kosmos-2

Kosmos-2 [126], developed by Microsoft, is a 2D multi-modal large language model (MLLM) capable of visual positioning and 2D question-answering. It processes input images through a Vision Transformer (ViT) to generate visual tokens, which are then concatenated with text tokens. These combined tokens are fed into a roughly two-billion-parameter large language model (LLM), from which the model produces textual outcomes. Notably, all parameters of the model are trained from scratch. The training loss is that of a standard language model, predicting the probability of the next token based on existing text and image inputs, with probabilities assigned by a softmax classifier across a vocabulary.

An important distinction of Kosmos-2, as compared to the previously mentioned MLLMs, is its ability to provide bounding box outputs. Specifically, Kosmos-2 divides an image into 1000 grids and utilizes 1000 special tokens to represent them. In terms of output format, Kosmos-2 employs a markup language similar to Markdown for its outputs, following the format of "[Text of the target](bounding box)." This approach, compared to the more global image captioning methods, enables a finer-grained interaction between text and images, supporting visual grounding and dense captioning. It allows the MLLM to better understand user inputs concerning images and instructions at a more granular level.

The training dataset utilized is GRIT, which is a large-scale, location-based image-text pairing dataset derived from the COYO-700M and LAION-2B datasets. GRIT comprises approximately 91 million images, 137 million object bounding boxes, and 115 million text sequences. The training is conducted on 256 V100 GPUs and typically requires about one day. The performance of the Kosmos-2 model is detailed in Table 8.2. When compared to models like Kosmos-1, Flamingo-3B, and Flamingo-9B, Kosmos-2's capabilities are evaluated using the Flickr30k test set for captioning and the VQAv2 test set for 2D question-answering accuracy. The

Table 8.2 Performance of Kosmos-2 (Source: Author)

	Flickr30k	VQA v2
Model	CIDEr	VQA acc.
FewVLM	31.0	–
METALM	43.4	41.1
Flamingo-3B	60.6	49.2
Flamingo-9B	61.5	51.8
KOSMOS-1	65.2	46.7
KOSMOS-2	66.7	45.6

results indicate that Kosmos-2 excels in captioning but is slightly outperformed by Flamingo in 2D question-answering.

8.5 3D Point Cloud Multi-modal Large Language Model

In everyday life and on the Internet, the abundance of image-text pairings provides ample training data for 2D multi-modal large language models (MLLMs), making them excel in multi-modal understanding. These models are adept at interpreting images and their relationship with associated texts, achieving notable success in fields like image captioning and visual question-answering. However, human perception of the world is 3D, while 2D images offer only limited perspectives and information. This limitation results in imprecise descriptions of positional information and inadequate representation of 3D shapes and textures. For instance, it is challenging to accurately grasp the depth, relative positioning, or 3D structure of objects through 2D images. This issue is particularly evident in areas requiring deep spatial understanding, such as autonomous driving, robot navigation, and embodied AI. Therefore, the development of 3D multi-modal large language models is crucial. These models can interpret not only the content of 2D images but also accurately identify and describe objects in 3D space. This capability is key for understanding complex 3D scenes, like urban streetscapes and indoor environments.

In the realm of autonomous driving, 3D MLLMs can more accurately interpret the environment around vehicles, enhancing decision-making accuracy and safety. In robotics, these models aid in more effective navigation and interaction with the environment. For embodied AI, 3D MLLMs provide richer environmental information, assisting intelligent agents in learning and performing tasks better in 3D spaces.

In summary, while 2D MLLMs have made significant strides in multi-modal understanding, 3D MLLMs reveal greater potential in handling more complex and realistic 3D world challenges. By integrating more spatial information, 3D MLLMs can understand and interpret the 3D world more profoundly, thus playing a larger role in various applications.

8.5.1 Point-LLM

Point-LLM [136] utilizes a robust large language model (LLM) with a powerful point cloud encoder to effectively fuse geometric, appearance, and language information, as shown in Fig. 8.9. It introduces an automatic data generation technique leveraging the large-scale point cloud captioning dataset, Cap3D, with the assistance of GPT-4. Additionally, a new dataset comprising 660K simple point-text pairs and 70K complex point-text instruction pairs was collected. This approach employs a

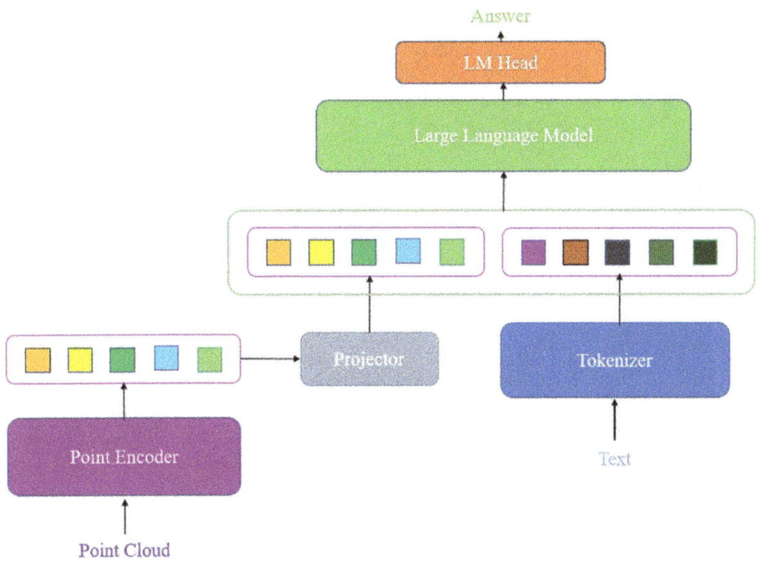

Fig. 8.9 Point-LLM architecture [136]. Public domain open access image [136]

two-stage training strategy, first aligning the latent spaces and then fine-tuning the unified model with instructions.

Point-LLM is a generative model designed to generate multi-modal sentences containing both point clouds and text. The model consists of three key components: a pre-trained point cloud encoder, a linear projector, and a large pre-trained language model (LLM). For various modal transformations and fusions, the pre-trained point cloud encoder encodes point clouds into tokens, extracting features from input point clouds and mapping them into the latent space of the LLM model. The LLM model processes sequences of point cloud tokens and text tokens, generating predicted tokens as output. Training is conducted using cross-entropy loss, computed only on tokens corresponding to the model's responses.

Point-LLM introduces an innovative dataset, Cap3D, which is a large-scale 3D object captioning dataset built on the foundation of Objaverse. It leverages the advanced inferencing capabilities of GPT-4 to guide the model in generating a variety of instruction tracking data based on the context provided by captions. Specifically, the dataset encompasses a vast collection of point cloud text instructions, including 660,000 concise descriptive instructions for 660,000 target point clouds and 70,000 more complex instructions for 15,000 target point clouds. In terms of computational resources, the training of the dataset was conducted on eight A100 GPUs, utilizing a cross-entropy loss function.

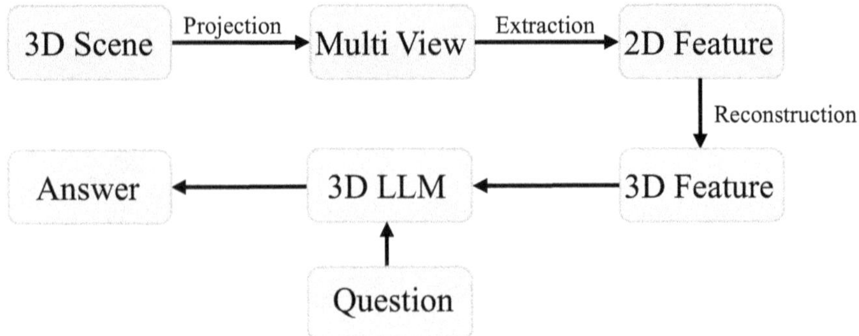

Fig. 8.10 3D LLM architecture [137] (Source: Author)

8.5.2 3D LLM

3D-LLM [137] is a system that integrates 3D visual capabilities into a large language model, specifically designed for various 3D tasks. The network structure, as shown in Fig. 8.10, processes 3D scene point clouds to generate 3D features, which, along with question text, are fed into 3D-LLM to obtain answers to queries. This model incorporates technologies from 2D vision-language models (VLMs), such as BLIP-2 and Flamingo. During training, language model parameters are fixed, focusing on training components like the QFormer, input/output embeddings, perceiver, and cross-attention layers. The model's loss function is based on the standard loss function for language modeling, i.e., next-token prediction.

Given the scarcity of large-scale 3D scene point clouds and their corresponding textual data, and the impracticality of manual annotation, the project's approach converts 3D scenes into 2D image data. This involves capturing multiple 2D images from different angles of 3D scene point clouds and using 2D VLMs like ChatCaptioner and BLIP to obtain textual data corresponding to these images. These 2D images are then converted back into 3D data to form a large-scale 3D-text paired dataset. The primary sources for the training dataset are Objaverse and Scannet. Regarding the hardware required for training, using BLIP-2 as the backbone necessitates 64 V100 GPUs, while using Flamingo as the backbone requires 8 A100 GPUs.

8.6 3D Embodied Intelligence

8.6.1 PaLM-E

PaLM-E [135] is a multi-modal language model capable of processing various types of inputs, including text and images. The model incorporates a pre-trained image

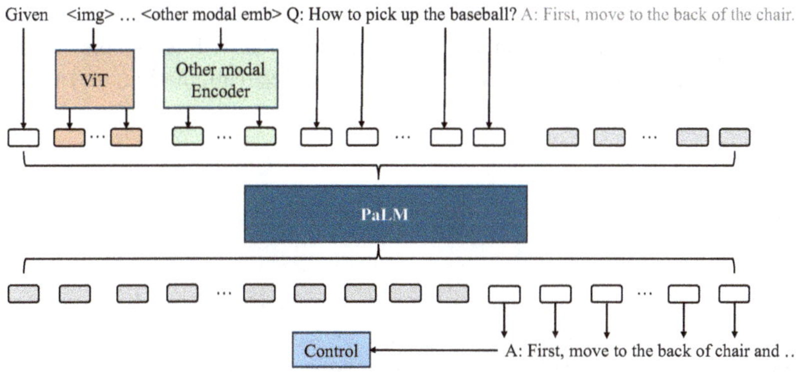

Fig. 8.11 PaLM-E architecture [135]. Public domain open access image [135]

embedder and a pre-trained encoder for embedding multi-modal information. These embedded vectors, along with text information, are fed into the language model to generate the desired output.

Regarding its network architecture, PaLM-E employs a decoder-only transformer structure similar to GPT-4, known as a Prefix-decoder structure. The fundamental architectural concept of PaLM-E is to integrate continuous, embodied observations (such as images, state estimations, or other sensor modalities) into the linguistic embedding space of the pre-trained language model. This integration is achieved by encoding continuous observations into a series of vectors that share the same dimensionality as the embeddings of linguistic tokens, allowing the continuous information to be infused into the language model in a manner akin to linguistic tokens. PaLM-E's input includes text and one or more continuous observations. Multi-modal tokens corresponding to these observations are interspersed with text to form multi-modal sentences. An example of such a multi-modal sentence might be the question, "What happened between $[img_1]$ and $[img_2]$," where "$[img_i]$" represents an image embedding. The output generated by PaLM-E is text produced autoregressively, which may be the answer to a question or a series of decisions to be executed by a robot, generated in text form. When PaLM-E is responsible for decision-making or planning, it is assumed that a lower-level strategy or planner can transform these decisions into concrete actions. To facilitate the conversion and fusion between different modalities, PaLM-E includes a Projector module, which maps the various dimensions of the original encoder output to a uniform dimension. The network structure of PaLM-E is illustrated in Fig. 8.11.

PaLM-E was trained and tested in three robotic environments: Task and Motion Planning (TAMP) domain, a desktop pushing environment, and a mobile manipulation domain. In the TAMP domain, robots are required to perform manipulation actions, such as grasping and stacking objects. In each environment, PaLM-E is trained using expert data specific to that domain. The model's text input consists of a prefix part and indices, formed by multi-modal sentences, while the prediction target includes only textual tokens. Consequently, the loss function employed is the average cross-entropy loss calculated over all non-prefix tokens, with the evaluation metric being the accuracy of each task action. Overall, PaLM-E is capable of solving tasks including robotic desktop manipulation, mobile manipulation, and task and motion planning.

8.6.2 RT-2

RT-2 [134] is an embodied AI agent trained by Google DeepMind. It is a promotion version of RT-1 model on vision-language understanding and action. The RT-1 model, trained on 130,000 robot teleoperation data entries, demonstrates its capability to handle diverse tasks and remarkable generalization ability. However, its universality is still limited by the size of the dataset. Given the impracticality of collecting hundreds of millions of robot data entries in the short term, to develop a large-scale robotic model that reflects the capabilities of current large language models (LLMs), this chapter proposes a novel approach. This involves utilizing vision-language models (VLMs), renowned for their robust image understanding and inference capabilities, in conjunction with robot data from the RT1 dataset and existing data. By co-fine-tuning the VLMs, they are transformed into a vision-language-action (VLA) model, capable of directly outputting robotic control instructions for real-time closed-loop control.

RT-2 studies how vision-language models trained on Internet-scale data can be incorporated directly into end-to-end robotic control to boost generalization and enable emergent semantic reasoning. In order to fit both natural language responses and robotic actions into the same format, RT-2 expresses actions as text tokens and incorporates them directly into the training set of the model in the same way as natural language tokens. RT-2 adapts two previously proposed VLMs to act as VLA models: PaLI-X and PaLM-E. RT-2 refers to vision-language-action versions of these models as RT-2-PaLI-X and RT-2-PaLM-E. As for robot-action fine-tuning, RT-2 takes a direct approach to this problem, representing actions as tokens in the model's output, which are treated in the same way as language tokens. RT-2 bases its action encoding on the discretization proposed by the RT-1 model. The action space consists of 6-DoF positional and rotational displacement of the robot end-effector, as well as the level of extension of the robot gripper and a special discrete command for terminating the episode, which should be triggered by the policy to signal successful completion. The whole pipeline is shown in Fig. 8.12.

In each prediction of the RT2 model, it first generates a natural language instruction description for an action, followed by the action itself. This approach significantly enhances RT2's ability to tackle more complex problems. This observation suggests that high-level task planning and low-level motion planning might now be addressable by a single vision-language-action (VLA) model.

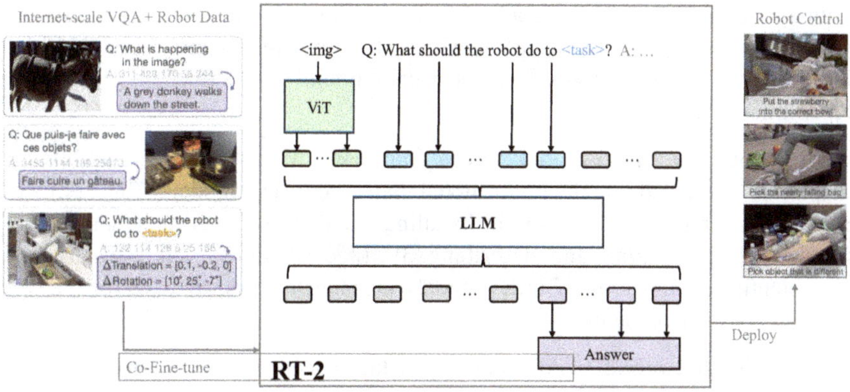

Fig. 8.12 RT-2 architecture [134]. Public domain open access image [134]

8.7 Summary

In this chapter, we begin by examining large language models (LLMs) in the field of natural language processing (NLP) and then move on to introduce 2D visual language models (2D VLMs) and 2D multi-modal large language models (2D MLLMs). Subsequently, we expand our focus to 3D multi-modal large language models (3D MLLMs), with a special emphasis on the significant role of multi-modal large language models in a key application area—embodied artificial intelligence (embodied AI).

Introduction to Large Language Models (LLMs) This section primarily explores the fundamental aspects of large language models (LLMs), encompassing their architecture, training methodologies, and various applications. It highlights the capabilities of LLMs in understanding and generating natural language, detailing their widespread use in areas such as information retrieval, text generation, and natural language understanding [38].

Exploring 2D Visual Language Models (2D VLMs) This part delves deeply into the world of 2D visual language models (2D VLMs), discussing how these models process and comprehend the interplay between image content and textual information [2, 33]. It covers their application in image captioning, visual question-answering, and their advantages in multi-modal data processing [101]. This includes an in-depth look at influential works like CLIP and BLIP in 2D VLMs, offering insights into their multi-modal understanding and generative capabilities.

Introducing 2D Multi-modal Large Language Models (2D MLLMs) This section focuses on 2D multi-modal large language models (2D MLLMs), discussing their unique features and capabilities in integrating text and image information. It emphasizes the importance of 2D MLLMs in providing richer contextual understanding and enhancing the interaction between language models and visual data.

With a focus on open dialogues and Q and A abilities, the section introduces works like Flamingo, BLIP-2, and LLaVA, which align text and image at a global level, and Kosmos-2, which aligns them at a finer granularity, showcasing the potent capabilities of 2D MLLMs.

Delving into 3D Multi-modal Large Language Models (3D MLLMs) This chapter is dedicated to 3D multi-modal large language models (3D MLLMs), exploring their unique strengths in handling 3D data, such as understanding 3D scenes and recognizing and describing 3D objects [41, 97]. It also discusses the potential applications of these models in understanding and interacting with complex 3D environments.

Introduction to Embodied AI Focusing on the concept and evolution of embodied AI, this part discusses how it integrates perception, cognition, and action to handle complex tasks [81, 105]. Applications in robotics, virtual assistants, and more are explored. It introduces Google's PaLM-E and DeepMind's RT-2 as examples of using 2D or 3D MLLMs in embodied intelligence. MLLMs aid in enabling embodied AI robots to perceive and understand the real world and make decisions based on worldly knowledge, highlighting embodied AI as a significant application domain for MLLMs.

Summary and Outlook Beginning with the basic concepts of LLMs, the book progressively moves into the realms of 2D and 3D multi-modal language models, culminating in a discussion on the application and development of embodied AI. This developmental trajectory illustrates the evolution from purely text-based processing to integrating visual information and onto understanding 3D data. Looking ahead, 3D MLLMs and embodied AI are expected to further push the boundaries of AI technology, especially in understanding and interacting with the 3D world, robotics and advanced task automation. With ongoing technological advancements and dataset expansions, we can anticipate these models demonstrating greater potential and value in a wide range of practical applications.

Exercises

1. What are the different forms of language model architecture?
2. What are the architectural structures of BERT, T5, LLaMA, and GPT models, respectively?
3. What type of loss function is used in CLIP?
4. What type of loss function is used in BLIP?
5. How does Kosmos-2 model the bounding boxes of objects?
6. How does Point LLM integrate with point cloud modality?
7. Which two large language models/multi-modal large language models is the RT-2 model based on?
8. Please list two famous open-source LLMs.

9. Please list two commercial LLMs of good performance?
10. How does BLIP-2 integrate the visual modality?

References

1. B. Qu, X. Liang, S. Sun, W. Gao, Exploring AIGC video quality: a focus on visual harmony, video-text consistency and domain distribution gap, in *Proceedings of the IEEE/CVF Conference on Computer Vision and Pattern Recognition Workshops* (2024)
2. B. Qu, H. Li, W. Gao, Bringing textual prompt to ai-generated image quality assessment, in *2024 IEEE International Conference on Multimedia and Expo (ICME)* (IEEE, Piscataway, 2024)
3. Y. Wu, L. Xie, S. Sun, W. Gao, Y. Yan, Adaptive intra period size for deep learning-based screen content video coding, in *2024 IEEE International Conference on Multimedia and Expo Workshops (ICMEW)* (IEEE, Piscataway, 2024)
4. H. Zheng, W. Gao, End-to-end RGB-D image compression via exploiting channel-modality redundancy. Proc. AAAI Conf. Artif. Intel. **38**(7), 7562–7570 (2024)
5. L. Tao, W. Gao, G. Li, C. Zhang, AdaNIC: towards practical neural image compression via dynamic transform routing, in *Proceedings of the IEEE/CVF International Conference on Computer Vision* (2023), pp. 16 879–16 888
6. Y. Wu, W. Gao, End-to-end lossless compression of high precision depth maps guided by pseudo-residual. Preprint. arXiv:2201.03195 (2022)
7. Y. Wu, Z. Qi, H. Zheng, L. Tao, W. Gao, Deep image compression with latent optimization and piece-wise quantization approximation, in *Proceedings of the IEEE/CVF Conference on Computer Vision and Pattern Recognition* (2021), pp. 1926–1930
8. W. Gao, L. Tao, L. Zhou, D. Yang, X. Zhang, Z. Guo, Low-rate image compression with super-resolution learning, in *Proceedings of the IEEE/CVF Conference on Computer Vision and Pattern Recognition Workshops* (2020), pp. 154–155
9. W. Gao, S. Sun, H. Zheng, Y. Wu, H. Ye, Y. Zhang, OpenDMC: an open-source library and performance evaluation for deep-learning-based multi-frame compression, in *Proceedings of the 31st ACM International Conference on Multimedia* (2023), pp. 9685–9688
10. Y. Guo, W. Gao, G. Li, Interpretable task-inspired adaptive filter pruning for neural networks under multiple constraints. Int. J. Comput. Vision, **132**(6), 2060–2076 (2024)
11. W. Gao, Y. Guo, S. Ma, G. Li, S. Kwong, Efficient neural network compression inspired by compressive sensing. IEEE Trans. Neural Networks Learn. Syst. **35**(2), 1965–1979 (2024)
12. Y. Guo, W. Gao, Semantic-driven automatic filter pruning for neural networks, in *2022 IEEE International Conference on Multimedia and Expo (ICME)* (IEEE, Piscataway, 2022), pp. 1–6
13. L. Tao, W. Gao, Efficient channel pruning based on architecture alignment and probability model bypassing, in *2021 IEEE International Conference on Systems, Man, and Cybernetics (SMC)* (IEEE, Piscataway, 2021), pp. 3232–3237
14. Z. Yang, W. Gao, G. Li, Y. Yan, SUR-driven video coding rate control for jointly optimizing perceptual quality and buffer control. IEEE Trans. Image Proces. **32**, 5451–5464 (2023)
15. F. Shen, Z. Cai, W. Gao, An efficient rate control algorithm for intra frame coding in AVS3, in *2021 IEEE International Conference on Systems, Man, and Cybernetics (SMC)* (IEEE, Piscataway, 2021), pp. 3164–3169
16. H. Yuan, W. Gao, J. Wang, Dynamic computational resource allocation for fast inter frame coding in video conferencing applications, in *2021 IEEE International Conference on Multimedia and Expo (ICME)* (IEEE, Piscataway, 2021), pp. 1–6
17. W. Gao, Q. Jiang, R. Wang, S. Ma, G. Li, S. Kwong, Consistent quality oriented rate control in HEVC via balancing intra and inter frame coding. IEEE Trans. Ind. Inf. **18**(3), 1594–1604 (2021)

18. H. Yuan, W. Gao, A new coding unit partitioning mode for screen content video coding, in *Proceedings of the 2021 5th International Conference on Digital Signal Processing* (2021), pp. 66–72
19. W. Gao, On the performance evaluation of state-of-the-art rate control algorithms for practical video coding and transmission systems, in *Proceedings of the 2020 4th International Conference on Video and Image Processing* (2020), pp. 179–185
20. W. Gao, S. Kwong, Q. Jiang, C.-K. Fong, P.H. Wong, W.Y. Yuen, Data-driven rate control for rate-distortion optimization in HEVC based on simplified effective initial QP learning, IEEE Trans. Broadcast. **65**(1), 94–108 (2018)
21. W. Gao, A multi-objective optimization perspective for joint consideration of video coding quality, in *2019 Asia-Pacific Signal and Information Processing Association Annual Summit and Conference (APSIPA ASC)* (IEEE, Piscataway, 2019), pp. 986–991
22. W. Gao, S. Kwong, Y. Jia, Joint machine learning and game theory for rate control in high efficiency video coding. IEEE Trans. Image Proces. **26**(12), 6074–6089 (2017)
23. W. Gao, S. Kwong, Y. Zhou, H. Yuan, SSIM-based game theory approach for rate-distortion optimized intra frame CTU-level bit allocation. IEEE Trans. Multimedia **18**(6), 988–999 (2016)
24. W. Gao, S. Kwong, H. Yuan, X. Wang, DCT coefficient distribution modeling and quality dependency analysis based frame-level bit allocation for HEVC. IEEE Trans. Circuits Syst. Video Technol. **26**(1), 139–153 (2015)
25. W. Gao, S. Kwong, Phase congruency based edge saliency detection and rate control for perceptual image and video coding, in *2016 IEEE International Conference on Systems, Man, and Cybernetics (SMC)* (IEEE, Piscataway, 2016), pp. 000 264–000 269
26. H. Yuan, W. Gao, OpenFastVC: an open source library for video coding fast algorithm implementation, in *Proceedings of the 31st ACM International Conference on Multimedia* (2023), pp. 9660–9663
27. H. Yuan, W. Gao, S. Ma, Y. Yan, Divide-and-conquer-based RDO-free CU partitioning for 8K video compression. ACM Trans. Multimedia Comput. Commun. Appl. **20**(4), 1–20 (2024)
28. L. Tao, W. Gao, A hardware implementation of entropy encoder for 8K video coding, in *2022 IEEE International Conference on Multimedia and Expo (ICME)* (IEEE, Piscataway, 2022), pp. 1–6
29. Y. Guo, W. Gao, S. Ma, G. Li, Accelerating transform algorithm implementation for efficient intra coding of 8K UHD videos. ACM Trans. Multimedia Comput. Commun. Appl. **18**(4), 1–20 (2022)
30. Z. Cai, W. Gao, Efficient fast algorithm and parallel hardware architecture for intra prediction of AVS3, in *2021 IEEE International Symposium on Circuits and Systems (ISCAS)* (IEEE, Piscataway, 2021), pp. 1–5
31. W. Gao, H. Yuan, Y. Guo, L. Tao, Z. Cai, G. Li, OpenHardwareVC: an open source library for 8K UHD video coding hardware implementation, in *Proceedings of the 30th ACM International Conference on Multimedia* (2022), pp. 7339–7342
32. W. Gao, H. Yuan, G. Liao, Z. Guo, J. Chen, Pp8k: a new dataset for 8K UHD video compression and processing. IEEE MultiMedia **30**(3), 100–109 (2023)
33. X. Zang, W. Gao, G. Li, H. Fang, C. Ban, Z. He, H. Sun, A baseline investigation: transformer-based cross-view baseline for text-based person search, in *Proceedings of the 31st ACM International Conference on Multimedia* (2023), pp. 7737–7746
34. G. Liao, W. Gao, G. Li, J. Wang, S. Kwong, Cross-collaborative fusion-encoder network for robust RGB-thermal salient object detection. IEEE Trans. Circuits Syst. Video Technol. **32**(11), 7646–7661 (2022)
35. W. Gao, G. Liao, S. Ma, G. Li, Y. Liang, W. Lin, Unified information fusion network for multi-modal RGB-D and RGB-T salient object detection. IEEE Trans. Circuits Syst. Video Technol. **32**(4), 2091–2106 (2021)
36. Y. Chen, S. Sun, G. Li, W. Gao, T.H. Li, Closing the gap between theory and practice during alternating optimization for GANs. IEEE Trans. Neural Networks Learn. Syst. **35**(10), 14005–14017 (2023)

37. Y. Chen, C. Jin, G. Li, T.H. Li, W. Gao, Mitigating label noise in GANs via enhanced spectral normalization. IEEE Trans. Circuits Syst. Video Technol. **33**(8), 3924–3934 (2023)
38. X. Zang, G. Li, W. Gao, Multidirection and multiscale pyramid in transformer for video-based pedestrian retrieval. IEEE Trans. Ind. Inf. **18**(12), 8776–8785 (2022)
39. X. Zang, G. Li, W. Gao, X. Shu, Learning to disentangle scenes for person re-identification. Image Vision Comput. **116**, 104330 (2021)
40. X. Zang, G. Li, W. Gao, X. Shu, Exploiting robust unsupervised video person re-identification. IET Image Proces. **16**(3), 729–741 (2022)
41. Z. Yue, G. Li, W. Gao, Cross-level guided attention for human-object interaction detection, in *2023 IEEE International Conference on Multimedia and Expo Workshops (ICMEW)* (IEEE, Piscataway, 2023), pp. 284–289
42. Z. Yao, W. Gao, Iterative saliency aggregation and assignment network for efficient salient object detection in optical remote sensing images. IEEE Trans. Geosci. Remote Sens. **62**, 1–13 (2024)
43. Y. Sun, Z. Li, S. Wang, W. Gao, Depth-assisted calibration on learning-based factorization for a compressive light field display. Opt. Exp. **31**(4), 5399–5413 (2023)
44. Y. Sun, Z. Li, L. Li, S. Wang, W. Gao, Optimization of compressive light field display in dual-guided learning, in *ICASSP 2022-2022 IEEE International Conference on Acoustics, Speech and Signal Processing (ICASSP)* (IEEE, Piscataway, 2022), pp. 2075–2079
45. W. Gao, S. Fan, G. Li, W. Lin, A thorough benchmark and a new model for light field saliency detection. IEEE Trans. Pattern Anal. Mach. Intell. **45**(7), 8003–8019 (2023)
46. T. Qin, G. Li, W. Gao, S. Liu, Multi-grained point cloud geometry compression via dual-model prediction with extended octree. ACM Trans. Multimedia Comput. Commun. Appl. **20**(9), 1–30 (2024)
47. Y. Shao, W. Gao, S. Liu, G. Li, Advanced patch-based affine motion estimation for dynamic point cloud geometry compression. Sensors **24**(10), 3142 (2024)
48. Y. Shao, F. Song, W. Gao, S. Liu, G. Li, Texture-guided graph transform optimization for point cloud attribute compression. Appl. Sci. **14**(10), 4094 (2024)
49. Y. Shao, X. Yang, W. Gao, S. Liu, G. Li, 3d point cloud attribute compression using diffusion-based texture-aware intra prediction. IEEE Trans. Circuits Syst. Video Technol. **34**(10), 9633–9646 (2024)
50. J. Zhang, Y. Chen, G. Liu, W. Gao, G. Li, Efficient point cloud attribute compression framework using attribute-guided graph Fourier transform, in *ICASSP 2024-2024 IEEE International Conference on Acoustics, Speech and Signal Processing (ICASSP)* (IEEE, Piscataway, 2024), pp. 8426–8430
51. W. Gao, H. Yuan, G. Li, Z. Li, H. Yuan, Low complexity coding unit decision for video-based point cloud compression. IEEE Trans. Image Proces. **33**, 149–162 (2023)
52. Y. Shao, G. Li, Q. Zhang, W. Gao, S. Liu, Non-rigid registration-based progressive motion compensation for point cloud geometry compression. IEEE Trans. Geosci. Remote Sens. **61**, 1–14 (2023)
53. F. Song, G. Li, X. Yang, W. Gao, S. Liu, Block-adaptive point cloud attribute coding with region-aware optimized transform. IEEE Trans. Circuits Syst. Video Technol. **33**(8), 4294–4308 (2023)
54. Y. An, Y. Shao, G. Li, W. Gao, S. Liu, A fast motion estimation method with hamming distance for lidar point cloud compression, in *2022 IEEE International Conference on Visual Communications and Image Processing (VCIP)* (IEEE, Piscataway, 2022), pp. 1–5
55. H. Yuan, W. Gao, G. Li, Z. Li, Rate-distortion-guided learning approach with cross-projection information for V-PCC fast cu decision, in *Proceedings of the 30th ACM International Conference on Multimedia* (2022), pp. 3085–3093
56. F. Song, G. Li, W. Gao, T.H. Li, Rate-distortion optimized graph for point cloud attribute coding. IEEE Signal Proces. Lett. **29**, 922–926 (2022)
57. F. Song, G. Li, X. Yang, W. Gao, T.H. Li, Fine-grained correlation representation for graph-based point cloud attribute compression, in *2022 IEEE International Conference on Multimedia and Expo (ICME)* (IEEE, Piscataway, 2022), pp. 1–6

58. F. Shen, W. Gao, A rate control algorithm for video-based point cloud compression, in *2021 International Conference on Visual Communications and Image Processing (VCIP)* (IEEE, Piscataway, 2021), pp. 1–5
59. F. Song, Y. Shao, W. Gao, H. Wang, T. Li, Layer-wise geometry aggregation framework for lossless lidar point cloud compression. IEEE Trans. Circuits Syst. Video Technol. **31**(12), 4603–4616 (2021)
60. L. Xie, W. Gao, H. Zheng, G. Li, SPCGC: scalable point cloud geometry compression for machine vision, in *Proceedings of IEEE International Conference on Robotics and Automation* (2024)
61. L. Xie, W. Gao, H. Zheng, H. Ye, Semantic-aware visual decomposition for point cloud geometry compression, in *2024 Data Compression Conference (DCC)* (IEEE, Piscataway, 2024), pp. 595–595
62. Z. Qi, W. Gao, Variable-rate point cloud geometry compression based on feature adjustment and interpolation, in *2024 Data Compression Conference (DCC)* (IEEE, Piscataway, 2024), pp. 63–72
63. Z. Yu, W. Gao, When dynamic neural network meets point cloud compression: computation-aware variable rate and checkerboard context, in *2024 Data Compression Conference (DCC)* (IEEE, Piscataway, 2024), pp. 600–600
64. L. Xie, W. Gao, S. Fan, Z. Yao, PDNet: parallel dual-branch network for point cloud geometry compression and analysis, in *2024 Data Compression Conference (DCC)* (IEEE, Piscataway, 2024), pp. 596–596
65. L. Xie, W. Gao, H. Zheng, End-to-end point cloud geometry compression and analysis with sparse tensor, in *Proceedings of the 1st International Workshop on Advances in Point Cloud Compression, Processing and Analysis* (2022), pp. 27–32
66. C. Fu, G. Li, R. Song, W. Gao, S. Liu, Octattention: octree-based large-scale contexts model for point cloud compression. Proc. AAAI Conf. Artif. Intell. **36**(1), 625–633 (2022)
67. H. Zheng, W. Gao, Z. Yu, T. Zhao, G. Li, ViewPCGC: view-guided learned point cloud geometry compression, in *Proceedings of the 32nd ACM International Conference on Multimedia* (2024)
68. L. Xie, W. Gao, H. Zheng, G. Li, ROI-guided point cloud geometry compression towards human and machine vision, in *Proceedings of the 32nd ACM International Conference on Multimedia* (2024)
69. C. Peng, W. Gao, Laplacian matrix learning for point cloud attribute compression with ternary search-based adaptive block partition, in *Proceedings of the 32nd ACM International Conference on Multimedia* (2024)
70. S. Luo, B. Qu, W. Gao, Learning robust 3d representation from clip via dual denoising. Preprint. arXiv:2407.00905 (2024)
71. G. Li, G. Wei, W. Gao, *Point Cloud Compression: Technologies and Standardization* (Springer Nature, Berlin, 2024)
72. G. Li, W. Gao, W. Gao, Introduction, in *Point Cloud Compression: Technologies and Standardization* (Springer, Berlin, 2024), pp. 1–28.
73. G. Li, W. Gao, W. Gao, Background knowledge, in *Point Cloud Compression: Technologies and Standardization* (Springer, Berlin, 2024), pp. 29–51
74. G. Li, W. Gao, W. Gao, Predictive coding, in *Point Cloud Compression: Technologies and Standardization* (Springer, Berlin, 2024), pp. 53–70
75. G. Li, W. Gao, W. Gao, Transform coding, in *Point Cloud Compression: Technologies and Standardization* (Springer, Berlin, 2024), pp. 71–96
76. G. Li, W. Gao, W. Gao, Quantization techniques, in *Point Cloud Compression: Technologies and Standardization* (Springer, Berlin, 2024), pp. 97–112
77. G. Li, W. Gao, W. Gao, Entropy coding, in *Point Cloud Compression: Technologies and Standardization* (Springer, Berlin, 2024), pp. 113–133
78. G. Li, W. Gao, W. Gao, MPEG geometry-based point cloud compression (G-PCC) standard, in *Point Cloud Compression: Technologies and Standardization* (Springer, Berlin, 2024), pp. 135–165

79. G. Li, W. Gao, W. Gao, AVS point cloud compression standard, in *Point Cloud Compression: Technologies and Standardization* (Springer, Berlin, 2024), pp. 167–197
80. G. Li, W. Gao, W. Gao, MPEG video-based point cloud compression (V-PCC) standard, in *Point Cloud Compression: Technologies and Standardization* (Springer, Berlin, 2024), pp. 199–218
81. G. Li, W. Gao, W. Gao, MPEG AI-based 3d graphics coding standard, in *Point Cloud Compression: Technologies and Standardization* (Springer, Berlin, 2024), pp. 219–241
82. G. Li, W. Gao, W. Gao, Future work, in *Point Cloud Compression: Technologies and Standardization* (Springer, Berlin, 2024), pp. 243–250
83. W. Liu, W. Gao, X. Mu, Fast inter-frame motion prediction for compressed dynamic point cloud attribute enhancement. Proc. AAAI Conf. Artif. Intell. **38**(4), 3720–3728 (2024)
84. Z. Yang, W. Gao, X. Lu, DANET: density-adaptive network for geometry-based point cloud compression artifacts removal, in *2023 IEEE International Conference on Visual Communications and Image Processing (VCIP)* (IEEE, Piscataway, 2023), pp. 1–5
85. X. Fan, G. Li, D. Li, Y. Ren, W. Gao, T.H. Li, Deep geometry post-processing for decompressed point clouds, in *2022 IEEE International Conference on Multimedia and Expo (ICME)* (IEEE, Piscataway, 2022), pp. 1–6
86. X. Zhang, G. Liao, W. Gao, G. Li, TDRNet: transformer-based dual-branch restoration network for geometry based point cloud compression artifacts, in *2022 IEEE International Conference on Multimedia and Expo (ICME)* (IEEE, Piscataway, 2022), pp. 1–6
87. Z. Li, G. Li, T.H. Li, S. Liu, W. Gao, Semantic point cloud upsampling. IEEE Trans. Multimedia **25**, 3432–3442 (2023)
88. R. Zhang, W. Gao, G. Li, T.H. Li, QINET: decision surface learning and adversarial enhancement for quasi-immune completion of diverse corrupted point clouds. IEEE Trans. Geosci. Remote Sens. **60**, 1–14 (2022)
89. R. Bao, Y. Ren, G. Li, W. Gao, S. Liu, Flow-based point cloud completion network with adversarial refinement, in *ICASSP 2022-2022 IEEE International Conference on Acoustics, Speech and Signal Processing (ICASSP)* (IEEE, Piscataway, 2022), pp. 2559–2563
90. J. Chen, G. Li, R. Zhang, T.H. Li, W. Gao, PointIVAE: invertible variational autoencoder framework for 3d point cloud generation, in *2022 IEEE International Conference on Image Processing (ICIP)* (IEEE, Piscataway, 2022), pp. 3216–3220
91. R. Zhang, J. Chen, W. Gao, G. Li, T.H. Li, PoinTOT: interpretable geometry-inspired point cloud generative model via optimal transport. IEEE Trans. Circuits Syst. Video Technol. **32**(10), 6792–6806 (2022)
92. S. Fan, W. Gao, Screen-based 3d subjective experiment software, in *Proceedings of the 31st ACM International Conference on Multimedia* (2023), pp. 9672–9675
93. X. Mao, H. Yuan, X. Lu, R. Hamzaoui, W. Gao, PCAC-GAN: a sparse-tensor-based generative adversarial network for 3d point cloud attribute compression. Comput. Visual Media (2024)
94. J. Wang, W. Gao, G. Li, Applying collaborative adversarial learning to blind point cloud quality measurement. IEEE Trans. Instrum. Measure. (2023)
95. S. Fan, W. Gao, G. Li, Salient object detection for point clouds, in *European Conference on Computer Vision* (Springer, Piscataway, 2022), pp. 1–19
96. S. Luo, W. Gao, A general framework for rotation invariant point cloud analysis, in *ICASSP 2024-2024 IEEE International Conference on Acoustics, Speech and Signal Processing (ICASSP)* (IEEE, Piscataway, 2024), pp. 3665–3669
97. X. Lu, W. Gao, AttentiveNet: detecting small objects for lidar point clouds by attending to important points, in *2023 IEEE International Conference on Visual Communications and Image Processing (VCIP)* (IEEE, Piscataway, 2023), pp. 1–5
98. Z. Pan, N. Zhang, W. Gao, S. Liu, G. Li, Less is more: label recommendation for weakly supervised point cloud semantic segmentation. Proc. AAAI Conf. Artif. Intell. **38**(5), 4397–4405 (2024)

99. Z. Pan, G. Liu, W. Gao, T. Li, EPContrast: effective point-level contrastive learning for large-scale point cloud understanding, in *2024 IEEE International Conference on Multimedia and Expo (ICME)* (IEEE, Piscataway, 2024)
100. N. Zhang, Z. Pan, T. H. Li, W. Gao, G. Li, Improving graph representation for point cloud segmentation via attentive filtering, in *Proceedings of the IEEE/CVF Conference on Computer Vision and Pattern Recognition* (2023), pp. 1244–1254
101. K. Wen, N. Zhang, G. Li, W. Gao, MPVNN: multi-resolution point-voxel non-parametric network for 3d point cloud processing, in *2024 IEEE International Conference on Multimedia and Expo (ICME)* (IEEE, Piscataway, 2024)
102. D. Yang, W. Gao, G. Li, H. Yuan, J. Hou, S. Kwong, Exploiting manifold feature representation for efficient classification of 3d point clouds. ACM Trans. Multimedia Comput. Commun. Appl. **19**(1s), 1–21 (2023)
103. W. Gao, G. Li, H. Yuan, R. Hamzaoui, Z. Li, S. Liu, Apccpa'22: 1st international workshop on advances in point cloud compression, processing and analysis, in *Proceedings of the 30th ACM International Conference on Multimedia* (2022), pp. 7392–7393
104. W. Gao, H. Ye, G. Li, H. Zheng, Y. Wu, L. Xie, OpenPointCloud: an open-source algorithm library of deep learning based point cloud compression, in *Proceedings of the 30th ACM International Conference on Multimedia* (2022), pp. 7347–7350
105. Y. Zhang, W. Gao, G. Li, OpenPointCloud-v2: a deep learning based open-source algorithm library of point cloud processing, in *Proceedings of the 1st International Workshop on Advances in Point Cloud Compression, Processing and Analysis* (2022), pp. 51–55
106. Z. Guo, W. Gao, H. Wang, J. Wang, S. Fan, No-reference deep quality assessment of compressed light field images, in *2021 IEEE International Conference on Multimedia and Expo (ICME)* (IEEE, Piscataway, 2021), pp. 1–6
107. G. Liao, W. Gao, Rethinking feature mining for light field salient object detection. ACM Trans. Multimedia Comput. Commun. Appl. **20**(10), 1–24 (2024)
108. S. Sun, J. Liu, T.H. Li, H. Li, G. Liu, W. Gao, Streamflow: streamlined multi-frame optical flow estimation for video sequences. Preprint. arXiv:2311.17099 (2023)
109. R. Liu, J. Huang, W. Gao, T.H. Li, G. Li, Mug-STAN: adapting image-language pretrained models for general video understanding. Preprint. arXiv:2311.15075 (2023)
110. C. Zhang, W. Gao, Learned rate control for frame-level adaptive neural video compression via dynamic neural network, in *European Conference on Computer Vision* (Springer, Berlin, 2024)
111. H. Touvron, T. Lavril, G. Izacard, X. Martinet, M.-A. Lachaux, T. Lacroix, B. Rozière, N. Goyal, E. Hambro, F. Azhar, et al., LLaMA: open and efficient foundation language models. Preprint. arXiv:2302.13971 (2023)
112. J. Achiam, S. Adler, S. Agarwal, L. Ahmad, I. Akkaya, F.L. Aleman, D. Almeida, J. Altenschmidt, S. Altman, S. Anadkat, et al., Gpt-4 technical report. Preprint. arXiv:2303.08774 (2023)
113. G. Team, R. Anil, S. Borgeaud, Y. Wu, J.-B. Alayrac, J. Yu, R. Soricut, J. Schalkwyk, A.M. Dai, A. Hauth, et al., Gemini: a family of highly capable multimodal models. Preprint. arXiv:2312.11805 (2023)
114. A. Chowdhery, S. Narang, J. Devlin, M. Bosma, G. Mishra, A. Roberts, P. Barham, H.W. Chung, C. Sutton, S. Gehrmann, et al., PaLM: scaling language modeling with pathways. J. Mach. Learn. Res. **24**(240), 1–113 (2023)
115. Y. Chen, X. Yu, S. Liu, W. Gao, G. Li, Zero-shot unsupervised image-to-image translation via exploiting semantic attributes. Image Vision Comput. **124**, 104489 (2022)
116. Q. Sun, Y. Fang, L. Wu, X. Wang, Y. Cao, Eva-clip: improved training techniques for clip at scale. Preprint. arXiv:2303.15389 (2023)
117. X. Wang, X. Zhang, Y. Cao, W. Wang, C. Shen, T. Huang, SegGPT: segmenting everything in context. Preprint. arXiv:2304.03284 (2023)
118. K. He, X. Chen, S. Xie, Y. Li, P. Dollár, R. Girshick, Masked autoencoders are scalable vision learners, in *Proceedings of the IEEE/CVF Conference on Computer Vision and Pattern Recognition* (2022), pp. 16 000–16 009

119. X. Chu, J. Su, B. Zhang, C. Shen, VisionLLaMA: a unified llama interface for vision tasks. Preprint. arXiv:2403.00522 (2024)
120. Y. Mao, Q. Jiang, R. Cong, W. Gao, F. Shao, S. Kwong, Cross-modality fusion and progressive integration network for saliency prediction on stereoscopic 3d images. IEEE Trans. Multimedia **24**, 2435–2448 (2021)
121. J. Li, D. Li, S. Savarese, S. Hoi, Blip-2: bootstrapping language-image pre-training with frozen image encoders and large language models, in *Proceedings of the International Conference on Machine Learning* (2023), pp. 19 730–19 742
122. J.-B. Alayrac, J. Donahue, P. Luc, A. Miech, I. Barr, Y. Hasson, K. Lenc, A. Mensch, K. Millican, M. Reynolds, et al., Flamingo: a visual language model for few-shot learning. Adv. Neural Inf. Proces. Syst. **35**, 23 716–23 736 (2022)
123. H. Liu, C. Li, Q. Wu, Y.J. Lee, Visual instruction tuning. Adv. Neural Inf. Proces. Syst. **36** (2024)
124. D. Zhu, J. Chen, X. Shen, X. Li, M. Elhoseiny, MiniGPT-4: enhancing vision-language understanding with advanced large language models. Preprint. arXiv:2304.10592 (2023)
125. J. Chen, D. Zhu, X. Shen, X. Li, Z. Liu, P. Zhang, R. Krishnamoorthi, V. Chandra, Y. Xiong, M. Elhoseiny, MiniGPT-V2: large language model as a unified interface for vision-language multi-task learning. Preprint. arXiv:2310.09478 (2023)
126. Z. Peng, W. Wang, L. Dong, Y. Hao, S. Huang, S. Ma, F. Wei, Kosmos-2: grounding multimodal large language models to the world. Preprint. arXiv:2306.14824 (2023)
127. T. Lv, Y. Huang, J. Chen, L. Cui, S. Ma, Y. Chang, S. Huang, W. Wang, L. Dong, W. Luo, et al., Kosmos-2.5: a multimodal literate model. Preprint. arXiv:2309.11419 (2023)
128. X. Chen, X. Wang, L. Beyer, A. Kolesnikov, J. Wu, P. Voigtlaender, B. Mustafa, S. Goodman, I. Alabdulmohsin, P. Padlewski, et al., PaLI-3 vision language models: smaller, faster, stronger. Preprint. arXiv:2310.09199 (2023)
129. X. Chen, J. Djolonga, P. Padlewski, B. Mustafa, S. Changpinyo, J. Wu, C.R. Ruiz, S. Goodman, X. Wang, Y. Tay, et al., PaLI-x: on scaling up a multilingual vision and language model. Preprint. arXiv:2305.18565 (2023)
130. X. Chen, X. Wang, S. Changpinyo, A. Piergiovanni, P. Padlewski, D. Salz, S. Goodman, A. Grycner, B. Mustafa, L. Beyer, et al., PaLI: a jointly-scaled multilingual language-image model. Preprint. arXiv:2209.06794 (2022)
131. A. Radford, J.W. Kim, C. Hallacy, A. Ramesh, G. Goh, S. Agarwal, G. Sastry, A. Askell, P. Mishkin, J. Clark, et al., Learning transferable visual models from natural language supervision, in *Proceedings of the International Conference on Machine Learning* (2021), pp. 8748–8763
132. J. Li, D. Li, C. Xiong, S. Hoi, BLIP: bootstrapping language-image pre-training for unified vision-language understanding and generation, in *Proceedings of the International Conference on Machine Learning* (2022), pp. 12 888–12 900
133. J. Li, R. Selvaraju, A. Gotmare, S. Joty, C. Xiong, S.C.H. Hoi, Align before fuse: vision and language representation learning with momentum distillation. Adv. Neural Inf. Proces. Syst. **34**, 9694–9705 (2021)
134. A. Brohan, N. Brown, J. Carbajal, Y. Chebotar, X. Chen, K. Choromanski, T. Ding, D. Driess, A. Dubey, C. Finn, et al., Rt-2: vision-language-action models transfer web knowledge to robotic control. Preprint. arXiv:2307.15818 (2023)
135. D. Driess, F. Xia, M.S. Sajjadi, C. Lynch, A. Chowdhery, B. Ichter, A. Wahid, J. Tompson, Q. Vuong, T. Yu, et al., Palm-e: an embodied multimodal language model. Preprint. arXiv:2303.03378 (2023)
136. R. Xu, X. Wang, T. Wang, Y. Chen, J. Pang, D. Lin, PointLLM: empowering large language models to understand point clouds. Preprint. arXiv:2308.16911 (2023)
137. Y. Hong, H. Zhen, P. Chen, S. Zheng, Y. Du, Z. Chen, C. Gan, 3D-LLM: injecting the 3d world into large language models. Adv. Neural Inf. Proces. Syst. **36**, 20 482–20 494 (2023)
138. W. Zhao, X. Liu, Z. Zhong, J. Jiang, W. Gao, G. Li, X. Ji, Self-supervised arbitrary-scale point clouds upsampling via implicit neural representation, in *Proceedings of the IEEE/CVF Conference on Computer Vision and Pattern Recognition* (2022), pp. 1999–2007

139. X. Zhang, W. Gao, HIRL: hybrid image restoration based on hierarchical deep reinforcement learning via two-step analysis, in *ICASSP 2022-2022 IEEE International Conference on Acoustics, Speech and Signal Processing (ICASSP)* (IEEE, Piscataway, 2022), pp. 2445–2449
140. X. Zhang, W. Gao, G. Li, Q. Jiang, R. Cong, Image quality assessment–driven reinforcement learning for mixed distorted image restoration. ACM Trans. Multimedia Comput. Commun. Appl. **19**(1s), 1–23 (2023)
141. J.-X. Zhuang, X. Huang, Y. Yang, J. Chen, Y. Yu, W. Gao, G. Li, J. Chen, T. Zhang, Open-media: open-source medical image analysis toolbox and benchmark under heterogeneous ai computing platforms, in *Chinese Conference on Pattern Recognition and Computer Vision (PRCV)* (Springer, Berlin, 2022), pp. 356–367
142. W. Gao, S. Kwong, Y. Zhou, Y. Jia, J. Zhang, W. Wu, Multiscale phase congruency analysis for image edge visual saliency detection, in *2016 International Conference on Machine Learning and Cybernetics (ICMLC)*, vol. 1 (IEEE, Piscataway, 2016), pp. 75–80

Chapter 9
Open-Source Projects for 3D Point Clouds

Abstract This chapter delves into the realm of point cloud technologies, emphasizing the significance of open-source projects and frameworks in advancing this field. The central focus is on the OpenPointCloud library, an open-source repository that encompasses a variety of deep learning methods for point cloud compression, processing, and analysis. This library utilizes popular deep learning frameworks such as TensorFlow, PyTorch, and MXNet, offering a robust platform for developers and researchers to engage in innovative point cloud applications. The evolution of point cloud technologies and its increasing relevance across various industries are also highlighted, driven by the growing availability of open-source tools and collaborative platforms that foster innovation and enhance research capabilities. The OpenPointCloud library serves as a pivotal resource, facilitating the development and testing of advanced algorithms and contributing significantly to the open-source community. This initiative not only enriches the diversity and availability of tools but also propels the forward momentum of research in point cloud technologies, underscoring the critical role of open-source projects in the technological landscape.

Keywords Open source · Point cloud technologies · OpenPointCloud · Point cloud processing · Algorithm benchmarking

9.1 Introduction

Point cloud technologies have flourished in recent years, including non-learning-based solutions [1–23] and learning-based solutions [24–46], for different kinds of processing tasks. These developments [47–58] have led to the rapid evolution of numerous open-source technologies and platforms focused on point cloud applications. This dynamic landscape highlights the increasing importance of this field with each passing day. An open-source algorithm library named OpenPointCloud [59, 60] has been developed to advance the progress and investigation of point cloud technology, particularly in the realm of deep learning. This library includes the representative algorithms for point cloud compression, processing, and analysis. The release of these open-source projects and test results is expected to

W. Gao, G. Li, *Deep Learning for 3D Point Clouds*,
https://doi.org/10.1007/978-981-97-9570-3_9

promote the development of point cloud research based on deep learning and to enrich the number and variety of algorithm libraries in the future, making valuable contributions to the point cloud open-source community. The increasing availability of open-source tools and resources is likely to foster innovation, collaboration, and further advancement in the field of point cloud technology. With the increasing availability of data and the continuous refinement of advanced algorithms, potential applications of point cloud technology are expected to expand significantly, opening up new opportunities for innovation and discovery in this exciting field.

The remainder of this chapter is structured as follows. We will first introduce the open-source concept and open-source community in Sect. 9.2. Then, open-source projects for point cloud processing (Sect. 9.3) are illustrated. Finally, we will summarize the content of this chapter in Sect. 9.4 and give some insights for future works.

9.2 Open-Source Culture and Open-Source Community

Open-source culture originated in the United States at the earliest. Since the 1960s, American open-source foundations and commercial companies have injected strong driving force into global industrial development through rapid technological evolution. The essence of open-source lies in openness, sharing, and collaboration. Open-source mode is a way to achieve continuous innovation by relying on the Internet platform and accumulating the wisdom of large groups through joint participation and collaboration. The open-source movement has gradually expanded from the early open-source projects focusing on Linux operating system, desktop office software and browser to databases, middleware, Internet of Things, microservices, big data, artificial intelligence, edge computing, cloud computing, and many other directions and fields. At the same time, the influence of open-source culture has begun to receive a lot of attention.

In recent years, with the wave of open source surging forward, the open-source movement is booming at home and abroad. For example, in June and November 2021, Huawei donated the core infrastructure of HarmonyOS and the open Euler operating system to the OpenAtom Open Source Foundation to jointly build and prosper the open-source ecosystem of domestic operating systems. In October 2021, Alibaba Pingtouge announced that it would open the source of the RISC-V series processors of Xuantie and open a series of tools and system software to promote the integration, development, and innovation of RISC-V software and hardware technologies. On January 31, 2022, the CentOS Linux community will officially stop updating and maintaining the CentOS Linux 8 operating system and will instead develop and maintain a new version of CentOS Stream to achieve a fully open-source model. In May 2022, Baidu announced its self-developed open-source platform for industrial in-depth learning, PaddlePaddle, which has gathered 4.77 million developers and served 180,000 enterprises and institutions. In July 2022, Xinhuazhang Technology officially announced to donate high-performance

Table 9.1 Comparisons of mainstream deep learning frameworks. Source: Author

Name	Supporter	Distribution	Mobile deployment	Programmatic interface	Framework type
TensorFlow	Google	✓	✓	Declarative programming	Static computation graph
PyTorch	Facebook	✓	✓	Imperative programming	Dynamic computation graph
MXNet	Amazon	✓	✓	Imperative programming	Dynamic/static computation graph

open-source digital emulator EpicSim to openDACS to promote the collaborative innovation of chip open-source technology.

With the development of deep learning technology, open-source frameworks for deep learning have also flourished [60–64]. Representative deep learning open-source frameworks include TensorFlow [65], PyTorch [66], and MXNet [67], as shown in Table 9.1. TensorFlow, a deep learning framework introduced by Google in 2015, initially supported only symbolic programming. Due to its early release and Google's significant influence in the deep learning domain, TensorFlow rapidly emerged as the most popular deep learning framework. TensorFlow has high flexibility and scalability, supports CPU and GPU acceleration, and provides rich APIs and tools such as TensorBoard and Keras. PyTorch is a deep learning framework built on the foundation of the original Torch framework, developed by Facebook and primarily using Python as the main programming language. Although PyTorch was only released in 2017, it has received widespread acclaim in the academic community due to its well-designed and compact interface. PyTorch adopts imperative programming, making it convenient to build and debug networks. PyTorch features dynamic computational graphs, supports GPU acceleration, and provides a wealth of community resources and tools such as pre-trained model libraries and visualization tools. MXNet is a deep learning framework developed by Amazon. It supports a hybrid programming approach of imperative and symbolic programming and has high flexibility and scalability. MXNet supports mixed programming models (imperative and declarative programming) and code in multiple programming languages (including Python, C++, R, Scala, Julia, MATLAB, and JavaScript). MXNet supports deep learning architectures such as convolutional neural networks (CNNs), recurrent neural networks (RNNs), and their variants such as long short-term memory (LSTM) networks. MXNet also provides features such as automatic mixed precision training and multi-GPU training, with excellent performance.

Before the OpenCloudOS community, OpenHarmony, OpenEuler, Dragon lizard, and other open-source communities were established. In particular, OpenEuler is positioned as an open-source operating system designed for digital infrastructure, supporting various application scenarios including servers, cloud computing, edge computing, and embedded systems. This positioning bears resemblance to that of OpenCloudOS. Understanding the relationship between the two entities and assessing the likelihood of collaboration necessitates a comprehensive analysis. At present, the open source in the field of point cloud mainly includes three modes, which are listed as follows:

- **General Programming Libraries for 3D Processing Technology**: These include PCL [68], Open3D [69], Cilantro [70], PDAL [71], and so on. Most of these libraries have defined their own data types and data structures. For tasks intended to be processed without deep learning methods, these libraries also provide abundant processing functions, like point cloud I/O, filters, geometric registration, visualization, etc.
- **Open-Source Point Cloud Datasets**: These include object and human point clouds and scenery point clouds. Examples of object point cloud datasets are 8i Voxelized Surface Light Field (8iVSLF) [72], ShapeNet [73], and ModelNet [74]. Examples of scenery point cloud datasets are S3DIS [75], ScanNet [76], Ford [77], and so on. Some dataset providers have built leaderboards to rate the performance of algorithms based on specific application tasks and test sets, such as KITTI [78], which is an object detection dataset on autonomous driving, and SemanticKITTI [79], a semantic segmentation dataset.
- **Open-Source Point Cloud Algorithm Library**: In this aspect, OpenPointCloud,[1] which is open source on OpenAI platform, serves as a typical exemplar. Under the background of the national implementation of the new generation of artificial intelligence development strategy, OpenAI is an open-source platform and community, organized, built, and shared by the New Generation of Artificial Intelligence Industrial Technology Innovation Strategic Alliance (AITISA). Based on Pengcheng Laboratory Cloud Brain scientific device and the software group developing method of Trustie,[2] it comprehensively promotes open source and collaborative innovation in the field of artificial intelligence. Under the principle of *open source and respect for innovation*, OpenAI gathers forces from academia, industry, and other sectors of society and strives to build an open-source platform and community of artificial intelligence with international impact.

OpenPointCloud is an open-source algorithm library for point cloud, jointly launched by Peking University Shenzhen Graduate School and Pengcheng Laboratory. It is oriented to three fields: point cloud compression, processing, and analysis. It collects the high-performance algorithms published in various top

[1] https://openi.pcl.ac.cn/OpenPointCloud

[2] Trustie, funded by the Ministry of Science and Technology, is an open-source platform and community jointly initiated and constructed by a number of well-known universities, scientific research institutions, and software enterprises around the clustering method of software development in the network era. Trustie is committed to systematically researching new software development methods and providing method guidance and practice guide for the construction of open source ecology. Website: https://www.trustie.net.

conferences and journals in recent years. Performances of algorithms are objectively and comprehensively tested and evaluated, and performances of similar algorithms are compared and analyzed. For deep learning algorithms, the code for multiple frameworks is also provided, encompassing the leading deep learning frameworks currently in use, such as PyTorch, TensorFlow, TensorLayer [80], etc. The emergence of OpenPointCloud can effectively address the issue of a continuous influx of various algorithms, which are often mixed with good and bad quality in the current era of information explosion. It can evaluate and screen algorithms objectively and effectively, which help promote the work of scholars and researchers in the field of point cloud. The code's support for multiple deep learning frameworks enhances research efficiency by eliminating the need for researchers to adapt to and transplant between different frameworks.

OpenPointCloud currently includes a total of 24 high-performance algorithms. In the field of point cloud compression, five geometric lossy compression algorithms, such as PCGCv1 [81], PCGCv2 [82], etc.; four geometric lossless compression algorithms, such as OctAttention [22], VoxelDNN [83], etc.; one attribute compression algorithm; and one compression post-processing algorithm are collected. The research [59] that summarizes the work of compression algorithms in OpenPointCloud has been included in ACM Multimedia Open Source Software 2022. In the field of point cloud processing, we have collected six point cloud sampling algorithms, such as PUNet [84] and SPU [85], and two point cloud completion algorithms, such as OPM [86]. In the field of point cloud analysis, we collected one point cloud salient object detection algorithm PCSOD [87] and four point cloud classification algorithms, such as PointNet [88].

9.3 Open-Source Project for Point Cloud Processing

Table 9.2 presents a collection of classical point cloud processing and analysis methods in the OpenPointCloud [59, 60]. These algorithms include point cloud upsampling, point cloud completion, point cloud salient object detection, point cloud classification, and segmentation. The library provides a range of tools for point cloud processing, enabling researchers to efficiently and accurately analyze and manipulate 3D point cloud data. The algorithms presented in this table represent a significant contribution to the field of point cloud processing and analysis, and they have been extensively used in various applications, from computer graphics to robotics.

Table 9.2 Basic information of point cloud processing and analysis. Source: Author

Algorithm	Publisher	Category
PUNet	2018 CVPR	Upsampling
PUGAN	2019 ICCV	Upsampling
PUGCN	2021 CVPR	Upsampling
SPU	2022 TMM	Upsampling
OPM	2020 ACM MM	Completion
PointNet	2017 CVPR	Classification and segmentation
PointNet++	2017 NIPS	Classification and segmentation

9.3.1 Point Cloud Enhancement Methods

9.3.1.1 Point Cloud Upsampling

The detail of PUNet is referred to [84]. It aims to enable more efficient and effective point cloud sampling by leveraging learned features to capture the important characteristics of the data. It utilizes a multi-branch convolution unit to extract features from the point cloud and subsequently decompose them into multiple components. The upsampling points are then reconstructed from these components.

In addition, PUGAN [89] introduces a generative adversarial network to the point cloud sampling and develops a GAN-based solution. By incorporating local features and composite loss functions, the proposed method obtains impressive performance in real-world scanning scenarios, specifically in the KITTI dataset, demonstrating strong generalization capabilities. This approach represents a significant advancement in point cloud upsampling, as it leverages the power of GANs to generate high-quality point cloud data while preserving the essential features of the original data. This study highlights the potential of using generative models in point cloud processing and analysis tasks, paving the way for future research in this area.

PUGCN [90] investigates the efficiency of the sampling pipeline in learning-based point cloud processing, highlighting the significance of the upsampling module and feature extractor utilized in the process. It introduces the innovative NodeShuffle model for the point upsampling module, which employs a graph convolution network (GCN) to encode local point information from neighboring points. Moreover, it features a newly developed multi-scale point feature extractor, Inception DenseGCN, for extracting features. PU-GCN delivers top-tier performance, achieving this with fewer parameters and enhanced computational efficiency, demonstrating the potential of utilizing GCN-based models in point cloud processing tasks, highlighting the benefits of incorporating local point information and multi-scale feature extraction for performance improvement.

Li et al. [85] propose a novel framework for improving the semantic representations of sparse point clouds. The proposed framework, named SPU, includes an upsampling network and a classification network. These two networks collaborate to enhance the semantic representations of the point cloud when upsampling. The upsampling network of SPU employs a method of graph aggregation convolution to establish hierarchical relationships among the points in the sparse point cloud. This network also incorporates point shuffling and pre-interpolation technologies to enhance stability and diversity during the point upsampling process. To further improve the upsampling quality, an attention mechanism is adopted to highlight the key positions of point cloud, leveraging semantic prior information derived from the sparse point cloud. The classification network is responsible for classifying the point cloud after upsampling. The proposed framework investigates various losses and conducts experiments on deep point networks to showcase its effectiveness. Overall, SPU addresses the challenge of information loss in sparse point clouds and provides a robust solution for point cloud upsampling.

9.3.1.2 Point Cloud Completion

Yan et al. [86] introduce Vaccine-Style-Net, a novel approach for creating detailed and high-resolution 3D models with fully smooth surfaces through point cloud completion. While contemporary techniques based on machine learning have demonstrated potential in filling gaps in point clouds, they typically output rough point clouds fixed in size. Vaccine-Style-Net approaches the task by operating within the function space of 3D surfaces, treating the surface as a continuous decision boundary function. This technique incorporates a reinforcement learning agent that reconstructs complete 3D structures from partial data. Distinct from conventional methods, the output from Vaccine-Style-Net can vary in resolution without requiring substantial memory resources. The method also enhances versatility and adaptability by incorporating two variations of free-form masks designed to mimic different types of degraded inputs and introduces a specialized mask dataset named onion-peeling-mask (OPM). This work also critiques the limitations of current metrics used to evaluate shape completion and suggests a new metric to improve assessment accuracy. Tests show that Vaccine-Style-Net delivers competitive outcomes in both visual and measurable terms. Furthermore, this approach can generate seamless 3D models at any desired resolution, marking a substantial advancement over prior techniques.

9.3.2 Point Cloud Analysis Methods

The field of point cloud analysis has seen significant contributions from PointNet [88] and PointNet++ [91], which develop improved feature extraction and sampling methods suitable for various point cloud tasks such as classification and segmentation.

Many researchers transform point cloud data into standard 3D voxel grids or sets of images, which results in voluminous data and causes issues. The pioneering work PointNet processes point clouds directly while retaining the permutation invariance of the input points. The network offers a consolidated framework for a variety of uses, including object classification, part segmentation, and scene semantic parsing. Despite its straightforward structure, PointNet is remarkably efficient and potent, delivering performance that equals or exceeds contemporary leading techniques. It offers a theoretical analysis for understanding what PointNet has learned and why it is robust regarding input perturbation and corruption. Empirically, PointNet demonstrates its strong performance through experimentation, showcasing its robustness and effectiveness. The proposed PointNet represents a valuable contribution to the field of point cloud analysis, providing a unified architecture for various applications and demonstrating strong performance.

PointNet++ [88] tackles the shortcomings of PointNet, which fails to detect local structural configurations inherent in the metric space inhabited by the points. This limitation restricts its capability to identify intricate patterns and adapt to detailed scene interpretations. To overcome this limitation, PointNet++ utilizes a hierarchical neural network that repeatedly implements PointNet across progressively smaller segments of the input point set. This approach, by leveraging distances within the metric space, enables the network to capture local details at progressively broader contexts. Point sets often feature inconsistent densities, which can degrade the performance of networks designed for uniform densities. To tackle this problem, it introduces innovative set learning layers that dynamically integrate features across various scales. The proposed PointNet++ represents a valuable contribution to the field of deep learning on point sets. By exploiting metric space distances and adapting to varying densities, PointNet++ can effectively capture local structures and generalize to complex scenes. These findings offer valuable insights into the development of more accurate and efficient point cloud analysis techniques.

9.3.3 *Performance Comparisons*

9.3.3.1 Algorithm Performance Evaluation for Point Cloud Processing

Regarding point cloud processing, performance comparisons of different deep learning frameworks are conducted. To evaluate the performance of various upsampling models, we design a set of unified comparative experiments on the same test set, using Chamfer Distance (CD) and Hausdorff Distance (HD) as evaluation metrics. The results of these experiments are presented in Table 9.3, providing valuable insights into strengths and weaknesses of each model and framework. This study represents a significant contribution to the field of point cloud processing, offering a comprehensive analysis of the performance of various models and frameworks under different conditions.

Table 9.3 Quantitative evaluation of PUNet, PUGAN, and PUGCN on a unified benchmark. Source: Author

Point clouds	PUNet [84]		PUGAN [89]		PUGCN [90]	
	CD (10^{-3})	HD (10^{-3})	CD (10^{-3})	HD (10^{-3})	CD (10^{-3})	HD (10^{-3})
a72-seated_jew_aligned	0.161	2.040	0.0178	0.305	0.0229	0.484
saint_lambert_aligned	0.135	2.387	0.0138	0.282	0.0198	0.993
madeleine_aligned	0.151	1.803	0.0145	0.584	0.0179	0.810
A9-vulcan_aligned	0.207	2.573	0.0161	0.451	0.0225	0.916
retheur-LowPoly_aligned	0.180	2.641	0.0212	0.383	0.0259	0.583
drunkard-CleanUp-LowPoly_aligned	0.182	1.957	0.0259	0.393	0.0354	0.877
cupid_aligned	0.219	2.610	0.0226	0.365	0.0304	0.911
cheval_terracotta-LowPoly-RealOne_aligned	0.173	2.695	0.0257	0.342	0.0332	0.937
Gramme_aligned	0.205	2.340	0.0258	0.432	0.0331	1.172
dame_assise-CleanUp-LowPoly_aligned	0.177	2.523	0.0209	0.271	0.0271	0.897
charite-CleanUp-LowPoly_aligned	0.185	2.085	0.0296	0.614	0.0406	1.431
baron_seutin_aligned	0.152	1.968	0.0185	0.265	0.0232	0.697
asklepios_aligned	0.186	2.222	0.0153	0.376	0.0222	0.693
Average	**0.178**	**2.296**	**0.0206**	**0.389**	**0.0272**	**0.877**

9.3.3.2 Algorithm Performance Evaluation for Point Cloud Analysis

Table 9.4 presents the results of segmentation performance on multiple categories for PointNet and PointNet++ in PyTorch framework, where the evaluation indicator is IOU (Intersection over Union). In summary, PointNet and PointNet++ have significantly advanced the field of point cloud analysis. Comparisons of different models and frameworks provide useful information for researchers seeking to develop more effective point cloud analysis methods.

Table 9.4 Quantitative evaluation of PointNet and PointNet++ in PyTorch. Source: Author

	Chair	Bag	Cap	Car	Guitar	Knife	Lamp	Laptop
PointNet	88.6	70.5	72.9	72.1	90.2	81.9	76.6	94.5
PointNet++	89.6	78.2	76.4	76.0	90.0	83.3	80.4	94.9

9.4 Summary

In this chapter, we outline open-source projects connected to point cloud technologies and unveil the premier open-source algorithm library for point clouds, namely, named OpenPointCloud [59, 60]. This library features essential algorithms for point cloud compression, processing, and analysis, each described comprehensively. The dissemination of these open-source projects and their testing findings is expected to foster advancements in point cloud research through deep learning methods and to augment the diversity and quantity of algorithm libraries moving forward, thus offering significant contributions to the point cloud open-source community. As algorithms and computing power continue to improve, the field of point cloud research based on open-source technology is expected to experience further development. The increasing availability of open-source tools and resources is likely to foster innovation and collaboration, driving the development of more efficient and effective point cloud processing and analysis techniques. Moreover, the growing interest in point cloud technology across a wide range of industries and applications is likely to fuel continued research and development in this field. With the increasing availability of data and the continuous refinement of advanced algorithms, potential applications of point cloud technology are poised to undergo significant expansion. This trend is anticipated to unlock new avenues for innovation and discovery across various domains. Overall, the future of point cloud research based on open-source technology is promising, with ample opportunities for growth and advancement. By continuing to invest in cutting-edge research and open-source initiatives, we can help unlock the full potential of this exciting technology, driving progress and innovation across a range of fields and applications. Moreover, we would like to mention other open-source projects, such as OpenAICoding [64],[3] OpenDatasets,[4] and others,[5,6,7,8] which can be found on the OpenAI website, and readers have interests in, since we have also make lots of efforts to conduct image- and video-related research works [61, 62, 64, 92–146].

---

[3] https://openi.pcl.ac.cn/OpenAICoding

[4] https://openi.pcl.ac.cn/OpenDatasets

[5] https://openi.pcl.ac.cn/OpenHardwareVC

[6] https://openi.pcl.ac.cn/OpenPCQA

[7] https://openi.pcl.ac.cn/OpenCompression

[8] https://openi.pcl.ac.cn/OpenVision

Exercises

1. What is the definition of the open source concept?
2. Please list three kinds of open-source community.
3. Please list four kinds of programming libraries for 3D processing technology.
4. Please describe the content of OpenPointCloud.
5. Please introduce the characteristic of PCGCv2.
6. What are the common tasks in point cloud processing?
7. Please introduce the characteristic of PUGAN.
8. What are the evaluation metrics for point cloud upsampling?
9. Please introduce the characteristic of VQA-PC.
10. Please introduce the characteristic of the ResSCNN.

References

1. W. Gao, G. Li, H. Yuan, R. Hamzaoui, Z. Li, S. Liu, Apccpa'22: 1st international workshop on advances in point cloud compression, processing and analysis, in *Proceedings of the 30th ACM International Conference on Multimedia* (2022), pp. 7392–7393
2. T. Qin, G. Li, W. Gao, S. Liu, Multi-grained point cloud geometry compression via dual-model prediction with extended octree, in *ACM Transactions on Multimedia Computing, Communications, and Applications* (2024)
3. Y. Shao, W. Gao, S. Liu, G. Li, Advanced patch-based affine motion estimation for dynamic point cloud geometry compression. Sensors **24**(10), 3142 (2024)
4. Y. Shao, F. Song, W. Gao, S. Liu, G. Li, Texture-guided graph transform optimization for point cloud attribute compression. Appl. Sci. **14**(10), 4094 (2024)
5. Y. Shao, X. Yang, W. Gao, S. Liu, G. Li, 3d point cloud attribute compression using diffusion-based texture-aware intra prediction, in *IEEE Transactions on Circuits and Systems for Video Technology* (2024)
6. J. Zhang, Y. Chen, G. Liu, W. Gao, G. Li, Efficient point cloud attribute compression framework using attribute-guided graph Fourier transform, in *ICASSP 2024-2024 IEEE International Conference on Acoustics, Speech and Signal Processing (ICASSP)* (IEEE, Piscataway, 2024), pp. 8426–8430
7. W. Gao, H. Yuan, G. Li, Z. Li, H. Yuan, Low complexity coding unit decision for video-based point cloud compression. IEEE Trans. Image Proc. **33**, 149–162 (2023)
8. Y. Shao, G. Li, Q. Zhang, W. Gao, S. Liu, Non-rigid registration-based progressive motion compensation for point cloud geometry compression. IEEE Trans. Geosci. Remote Sensing (2023)
9. F. Song, G. Li, X. Yang, W. Gao, S. Liu, Block-adaptive point cloud attribute coding with region-aware optimized transform. IEEE Trans. Circuits Syst. Video Technol. **33**, 4294–4308 (2023)
10. Y. An, Y. Shao, G. Li, W. Gao, S. Liu, A fast motion estimation method with hamming distance for LiDAR point cloud compression, in *2022 IEEE International Conference on Visual Communications and Image Processing (VCIP)* (IEEE, Piscataway, 2022), pp. 1–5
11. H. Yuan, W. Gao, G. Li, Z. Li, Rate-distortion-guided learning approach with cross-projection information for V-PCC fast CU decision, in *Proceedings of the 30th ACM International Conference on Multimedia* (2022), pp. 3085–3093
12. F. Song, G. Li, W. Gao, T.H. Li, Rate-distortion optimized graph for point cloud attribute coding. IEEE Signal Process. Lett. **29**, 922–926 (2022)

13. F. Song, G. Li, X. Yang, W. Gao, T.H. Li, Fine-grained correlation representation for graph-based point cloud attribute compression, in *2022 IEEE International Conference on Multimedia and Expo (ICME)* (IEEE, Piscataway, 2022), pp. 1–6
14. F. Shen, W. Gao, A rate control algorithm for video-based point cloud compression, in *2021 International Conference on Visual Communications and Image Processing (VCIP)* (IEEE, Piscataway, 2021), pp. 1–5
15. F. Song, Y. Shao, W. Gao, H. Wang, T. Li, Layer-wise geometry aggregation framework for lossless LiDAR point cloud compression. IEEE Trans. Circuits Syst. Video Technol. **31**(12), 4603–4616 (2021)
16. L. Xie, W. Gao, H. Zheng, G. Li, Spcgc: scalable point cloud geometry compression for machine vision, in *Proceedings of IEEE International Conference on Robotics and Automation* (2024)
17. L. Xie, W. Gao, H. Zheng, H. Ye, Semantic-aware visual decomposition for point cloud geometry compression, in *2024 Data Compression Conference (DCC)* (IEEE, Piscataway, 2024), pp. 595–595
18. Z. Qi, W. Gao, Variable-rate point cloud geometry compression based on feature adjustment and interpolation, in *2024 Data Compression Conference (DCC)* (IEEE, Piscataway, 2024), pp. 63–72
19. Z. Yu, W. Gao, When dynamic neural network meets point cloud compression: computation-aware variable rate and checkerboard context, in *2024 Data Compression Conference (DCC)* (IEEE, Piscataway, 2024), p. 600
20. L. Xie, W. Gao, S. Fan, Z. Yao, Pdnet: parallel dual-branch network for point cloud geometry compression and analysis, in *2024 Data Compression Conference (DCC)* (IEEE, Piscataway, 2024), p. 596
21. L. Xie, W. Gao, H. Zheng, End-to-end point cloud geometry compression and analysis with sparse tensor, in *Proceedings of the 1st International Workshop on Advances in Point Cloud Compression, Processing and Analysis* (2022), pp. 27–32
22. C. Fu, G. Li, R. Song, W. Gao, S. Liu, OctAttention: octree-based large-scale contexts model for point cloud compression, in *AAAI Conference on Artificial Intelligence* (2022), pp. 625–633
23. S. Fan, W. Gao, Screen-based 3d subjective experiment software, in *Proceedings of the 31st ACM International Conference on Multimedia* (2023), pp. 9672–9675
24. W. Liu, W. Gao, X. Mu, Fast inter-frame motion prediction for compressed dynamic point cloud attribute enhancement, in *Proceedings of the AAAI Conference on Artificial Intelligence*, vol. 38, no. 4 (2024), pp. 3720–3728
25. Z. Yang, W. Gao, X. Lu, Danet: density-adaptive network for geometry-based point cloud compression artifacts removal, in *2023 IEEE International Conference on Visual Communications and Image Processing (VCIP)* (IEEE, Piscataway, 2023), pp. 1–5
26. X. Fan, G. Li, D. Li, Y. Ren, W. Gao, T.H. Li, Deep geometry post-processing for decompressed point clouds, in *2022 IEEE International Conference on Multimedia and Expo (ICME)* (IEEE, Piscataway, 2022), pp. 1–6
27. X. Zhang, G. Liao, W. Gao, G. Li, Tdrnet: Transformer-based dual-branch restoration network for geometry based point cloud compression artifacts, in *2022 IEEE International Conference on Multimedia and Expo (ICME)* (IEEE, Piscataway, 2022), pp. 1–6
28. Z. Li, G. Li, T.H. Li, S. Liu, W. Gao, Semantic point cloud upsampling. IEEE Trans. Multimedia **25**, 3432–3442 (2022)
29. R. Zhang, W. Gao, G. Li, T.H. Li, Qinet: decision surface learning and adversarial enhancement for quasi-immune completion of diverse corrupted point clouds. IEEE Trans. Geosci. Remote Sensing **60**, 1–14 (2022)
30. R. Bao, Y. Ren, G. Li, W. Gao, S. Liu, Flow-based point cloud completion network with adversarial refinement, in *ICASSP 2022-2022 IEEE International Conference on Acoustics, Speech and Signal Processing (ICASSP)* (IEEE, Piscataway, 2022), pp. 2559–2563

31. J. Chen, G. Li, R. Zhang, T.H. Li, W. Gao, Pointivae: invertible variational autoencoder framework for 3d point cloud generation, in *2022 IEEE International Conference on Image Processing (ICIP)* (IEEE, Piscataway, 2022), pp. 3216–3220
32. R. Zhang, J. Chen, W. Gao, G. Li, T.H. Li, Pointot: interpretable geometry-inspired point cloud generative model via optimal transport. IEEE Trans. Circuits Syst. Video Technol. **32**(10), 6792–6806 (2022)
33. S. Fan, W. Gao, G. Li, Salient object detection for point clouds, in *European Conference on Computer Vision* (2022), pp. 1–19
34. S. Luo, W. Gao, A general framework for rotation invariant point cloud analysis, in *ICASSP 2024-2024 IEEE International Conference on Acoustics, Speech and Signal Processing (ICASSP)* (IEEE, Piscataway, 2024), pp. 3665–3669
35. X. Lu and W. Gao, Attentivenet: detecting small objects for LiDAR point clouds by attending to important points, in *2023 IEEE International Conference on Visual Communications and Image Processing (VCIP)* (IEEE, Piscataway, 2023), pp. 1–5
36. Z. Pan, N. Zhang, W. Gao, S. Liu, G. Li, Less is more: label recommendation for weakly supervised point cloud semantic segmentation, in *Proceedings of the AAAI Conference on Artificial Intelligence*, vol. 38, no. 5 (2024), pp. 4397–4405
37. Z. Pan, G. Liu, W. Gao, T. Li, Epcontrast: effective point-level contrastive learning for large-scale point cloud understanding, in *2024 IEEE International Conference on Multimedia and Expo (ICME)* (IEEE, Piscataway, 2024)
38. N. Zhang, Z. Pan, T.H. Li, W. Gao, G. Li, Improving graph representation for point cloud segmentation via attentive filtering, in *Proceedings of the IEEE/CVF Conference on Computer Vision and Pattern Recognition* (2023), pp. 1244–1254
39. K. Wen, N. Zhang, G. Li, W. Gao, MPVNN: multi-resolution point-voxel non-parametric network for 3d point cloud processing, in *2024 IEEE International Conference on Multimedia and Expo (ICME)* (IEEE, Piscataway, 2024)
40. X. Mao, H. Yuan, X. Lu, R. Hamzaoui, W. Gao, PCAC-GAN: a sparse-tensor-based generative adversarial network for 3d point cloud attribute compression. Computational Visual Media (2024)
41. J. Wang, W. Gao, G. Li, Applying collaborative adversarial learning to blind point cloud quality measurement. IEEE Trans. Instrument. Measur. (2023)
42. D. Yang, W. Gao, G. Li, H. Yuan, J. Hou, S. Kwong, Exploiting manifold feature representation for efficient classification of 3d point clouds. ACM Trans. Multimedia Comput. Commun. Appl. **19**(1s), 1–21 (2023)
43. H. Zheng, W. Gao, Z. Yu, T. Zhao, G. Li, Viewpcgc: view-guided learned point cloud geometry compression, in *Proceedings of the 32nd ACM International Conference on Multimedia* (2024)
44. L. Xie, W. Gao, H. Zheng, G. Li, Roi-guided point cloud geometry compression towards human and machine vision, in *Proceedings of the 32nd ACM International Conference on Multimedia* (2024)
45. C. Peng, W. Gao, Laplacian matrix learning for point cloud attribute compression with ternary search-based adaptive block partition, in *Proceedings of the 32nd ACM International Conference on Multimedia* (2024)
46. S. Luo, B. Qu, W. Gao, Learning robust 3d representation from clip via dual denoising (2024). arXiv preprint arXiv:2407.00905
47. G. Li, G. Wei, W. Gao, *Point Cloud Compression: Technologies and Standardization* (Springer, Berlin, 2024)
48. G. Li, W. Gao, W. Gao, Introduction, in *Point Cloud Compression: Technologies and Standardization* (Springer, Berlin, 2024), pp. 1–28
49. G. Li, W. Gao, W. Gao, Background knowledge, in *Point Cloud Compression: Technologies and Standardization* (Springer, Berlin, 2024), pp. 29–51
50. G. Li, W. Gao, W. Gao, Predictive coding, in *Point Cloud Compression: Technologies and Standardization* (Springer, Berlin, 2024), pp. 53–70

51. G. Li, W. Gao, W. Gao, Transform coding, in *Point Cloud Compression: Technologies and Standardization* (Springer, Berlin, 2024), pp. 71–96
52. G. Li, W. Gao, W. Gao, Quantization techniques, in *Point Cloud Compression: Technologies and Standardization* (Springer, Berlin, 2024), pp. 97–112
53. G. Li, W. Gao, W. Gao, Entropy coding, in *Point Cloud Compression: Technologies and Standardization* (Springer, Berlin, 2024), pp. 113–133
54. G. Li, W. Gao, W. Gao, MPEG geometry-based point cloud compression (G-PCC) standard, in *Point Cloud Compression: Technologies and Standardization* (Springer, Berlin, 2024), pp. 135–165
55. G. Li, W. Gao, W. Gao, AVS point cloud compression standard, in *Point Cloud Compression: Technologies and Standardization* (Springer, Berlin, 2024), pp. 167–197
56. G. Li, W. Gao, W. Gao, MPEG video-based point cloud compression (V-PCC) standard, in *Point Cloud Compression: Technologies and Standardization* (Springer, Berlin, 2024), pp. 199–218
57. G. Li, W. Gao, W. Gao, MPEG Ai-based 3d graphics coding standard, in *Point Cloud Compression: Technologies and Standardization* (Springer, Berlin, 2024), pp. 219–241
58. G. Li, W. Gao, W. Gao, Future work, in *Point Cloud Compression: Technologies and Standardization* (Springer, Berlin, 2024), pp. 243–250
59. W. Gao, H. Ye, G. Li, H. Zheng, Y. Wu, L. Xie, OpenPointCloud: an open-source algorithm library of deep learning based point cloud compression, in *ACM International Conference on Multimedia* (2022), pp. 7347–7350
60. Y. Zhang, W. Gao, G. Li, Openpointcloud-v2: a deep learning based open-source algorithm library of point cloud processing, in *Proceedings of the 1st International Workshop on Advances in Point Cloud Compression, Processing and Analysis* (2022), pp. 51–55
61. W. Gao, H. Yuan, Y. Guo, L. Tao, Z. Cai, G. Li, OpenHardwareVC: an open source library for 8k UHD video coding hardware implementation, in *Proceedings of the 30th ACM International Conference on Multimedia* (2022), pp. 7339–7342
62. H. Yuan, W. Gao, Openfastvc: an open source library for video coding fast algorithm implementation, in *Proceedings of the 31st ACM International Conference on Multimedia* (2023), pp. 9660–9663
63. J.-X. Zhuang, X. Huang, Y. Yang, J. Chen, Y. Yu, W. Gao, G. Li, J. Chen, T. Zhang, Open-media: open-source medical image analysis toolbox and benchmark under heterogeneous ai computing platforms, in *Chinese Conference on Pattern Recognition and Computer Vision (PRCV)* (Springer, Berlin, 2022), pp. 356–367
64. W. Gao, S. Sun, H. Zheng, Y. Wu, H. Ye, Y. Zhang, Opendmc: an open-source library and performance evaluation for deep-learning-based multi-frame compression, in *Proceedings of the 31st ACM International Conference on Multimedia* (2023), pp. 9685–9688
65. M. Abadi, A. Agarwal, P. Barham, E. Brevdo, Z. Chen, C. Citro, G.S. Corrado, A. Davis, J. Dean, M. Devin et al., Tensorflow: large-scale machine learning on heterogeneous distributed systems (2016). arXiv preprint arXiv:1603.04467
66. A. Paszke, S. Gross, F. Massa, A. Lerer, J. Bradbury, G. Chanan, T. Killeen, Z. Lin, N. Gimelshein, L. Antiga et al., Pytorch: an imperative style, high-performance deep learning library, in *Advances in Neural Information Processing Systems*, vol. 32 (2019), pp. 8026–8037
67. T. Chen, M. Li, Y. Li, M. Lin, N. Wang, M. Wang, T. Xiao, B. Xu, C. Zhang, Z. Zhang, Mxnet: a flexible and efficient machine learning library for heterogeneous distributed systems (2015). arXiv preprint arXiv:1512.01274
68. R.B. Rusu, S. Cousins, 3d is here: Point cloud library (PCL), in *2011 IEEE International Conference on Robotics and Automation* (2011), pp. 1–4
69. Q.-Y. Zhou, J. Park, V. Koltun, Open3D: a modern library for 3D data processing (2018). arXiv:1801.09847
70. K. Zampogiannis, C. Fermuller, Y. Aloimonos, Cilantro: a lean, versatile, and efficient library for point cloud data processing, in *Proceedings of the 26th ACM International Conference on Multimedia* (2018), pp. 1364–1367

71. H. Butler, B. Chambers, P. Hartzell, C. Glennie, PDAL: an open source library for the processing and analysis of point clouds. Comput. Geosci. **148**, 104680 (2021)
72. M. Krivokuca, P.A. Chou, P. Savill, 8i voxelized surface light field (8iVSLF) dataset. ISO/IEC JTC1/SC29/WG11 MPEG, input document m42914 (2018)
73. A.X. Chang, T. Funkhouser, L. Guibas, P. Hanrahan, Q. Huang, Z. Li, S. Savarese, M. Savva, S. Song, H. Su et al., Shapenet: an information-rich 3d model repository (2015). arXiv preprint arXiv:1512.03012
74. Z. Wu, S. Song, A. Khosla, F. Yu, L. Zhang, X. Tang, J. Xiao, 3D ShapeNets: a deep representation for volumetric shapes, in *IEEE Conference on Computer Vision and Pattern Recognition* (2015), pp. 1912–1920
75. I. Armeni, O. Sener, A.R. Zamir, H. Jiang, I. Brilakis, M. Fischer, S. Savarese, 3D semantic parsing of large-scale indoor spaces, in *IEEE Conference on Computer Vision and Pattern Recognition* (2016), pp. 1534–1543
76. A. Dai, A. X. Chang, M. Savva, M. Halber, T.A. Funkhouser, M. Nießner, ScanNet: richly-annotated 3d reconstructions of indoor scenes, in *Proceedings of IEEE Conference on Computer Vision and Pattern Recognition* (2017), pp. 2432–2443
77. S. Agarwal, A. Vora, G. Pandey, W. Williams, H. Kourous, J. McBride, Ford multi-AV seasonal dataset. Int. J. Robot. Res. **39**(12), 1367–1376 (2020)
78. A. Geiger, P. Lenz, R. Urtasun, Are we ready for autonomous driving? The KITTI vision benchmark suite, in *IEEE Conference on Computer Vision and Pattern Recognition* (2012), pp. 3354–3361
79. J. Behley, M. Garbade, A. Milioto, J. Quenzel, S. Behnke, C. Stachniss, J. Gall, SemanticKITTI: a dataset for semantic scene understanding of LiDAR sequences, in *IEEE/CVF International Conference on Computer Vision* (2019), pp. 9296–9306
80. C. Lai, J. Han, H. Dong, Tensorlayer 3.0: a deep learning library compatible with multiple backends, in *IEEE International Conference on Multimedia and Expo Workshops* (2021), pp. 1–3
81. J. Wang, H. Zhu, H. Liu, Z. Ma, Lossy point cloud geometry compression via end-to-end learning. IEEE Trans. Circuits Syst. Video Technol. **31**(12), 4909–4923 (2021)
82. J. Wang, D. Ding, Z. Li, Z. Ma, Multiscale point cloud geometry compression, in *Data Compression Conference* (2021), pp. 73–82
83. D.T. Nguyen, M. Quach, G. Valenzise, P. Duhamel, Learning-based lossless compression of 3d point cloud geometry, in *IEEE International Conference on Acoustics, Speech and Signal Processing* (2021), pp. 4220–4224
84. L. Yu, X. Li, C. Fu, D. Cohen-Or, P. Heng, PU-net: point cloud upsampling network, in *Proceedings of IEEE Conference on Computer Vision and Pattern Recognition* (2018), pp. 2790–2799
85. Z. Li, G. Li, T.H. Li, S. Liu, W. Gao, Semantic point cloud upsampling. IEEE Trans. Multimedia **25**, 3432–3442 (2023)
86. W. Yan, R. Zhang, J. Wang, S. Liu, T.H. Li, G. Li, Vaccine-style-net: point cloud completion in implicit continuous function space, in *Proceedings of the 28th ACM International Conference on Multimedia* (2020), pp. 2067–2075
87. S. Fan, W. Gao, G. Li, Salient object detection for point clouds, in *European Conference on Computer Vision* (2022), pp. 1–19
88. C.R. Qi, H. Su, K. Mo, L.J. Guibas, Pointnet: deep learning on point sets for 3d classification and segmentation, in *Proceedings of the IEEE Conference on Computer Vision and Pattern Recognition* (2017), pp. 652–660
89. R. Li, X. Li, C. Fu, D. Cohen-Or, P. Heng, PU-GAN: a point cloud upsampling adversarial network, in *Proceedings of the IEEE International Conference on Computer Vision* (2019), pp. 7202–7211
90. G. Qian, A. Abualshour, G. Li, A.K. Thabet, B. Ghanem, PU-GCN: point cloud upsampling using graph convolutional networks, in *Proceedings of the IEEE Conference on Computer Vision and Pattern Recognition* (2021), pp. 11683–11692

91. C.R. Qi, L. Yi, H. Su, L.J. Guibas, Pointnet++: deep hierarchical feature learning on point sets in a metric space. Adv. Neural Inform. Process. Syst. **30**, 5099–5108 (2017)
92. B. Qu, X. Liang, S. Sun, W. Gao, Exploring AIGC video quality: a focus on visual harmony, video-text consistency and domain distribution gap, in *Proceedings of the IEEE/CVF Conference on Computer Vision and Pattern Recognition Workshops* (2024)
93. B. Qu, H. Li, W. Gao, Bringing textual prompt to ai-generated image quality assessment, in *2024 IEEE International Conference on Multimedia and Expo (ICME)* (IEEE, Piscataway, 2024)
94. Y. Wu, L. Xie, S. Sun, W. Gao, Y. Yan, Adaptive intra period size for deep learning-based screen content video coding, in *2024 IEEE International Conference on Multimedia and Expo Workshops (ICMEW)* (IEEE, Piscataway, 2024)
95. H. Zheng, W. Gao, End-to-end RGB-D image compression via exploiting channel-modality redundancy, in *Proceedings of the AAAI Conference on Artificial Intelligence*, vol. 38, no. 7 (2024), pp. 7562–7570
96. L. Tao, W. Gao, G. Li, C. Zhang, Adanic: towards practical neural image compression via dynamic transform routing, in *Proceedings of the IEEE/CVF International Conference on Computer Vision* (2023), pp. 16879–16888
97. Y. Wu, W. Gao, End-to-end lossless compression of high precision depth maps guided by pseudo-residual (2022). arXiv preprint arXiv:2201.03195
98. Y. Wu, Z. Qi, H. Zheng, L. Tao, W. Gao, Deep image compression with latent optimization and piece-wise quantization approximation, in *Proceedings of the IEEE/CVF Conference on Computer Vision and Pattern Recognition* (2021), pp. 1926–1930
99. W. Gao, L. Tao, L. Zhou, D. Yang, X. Zhang, Z. Guo, Low-rate image compression with super-resolution learning, in *Proceedings of the IEEE/CVF Conference on Computer Vision and Pattern Recognition Workshops* (2020), pp. 154–155
100. Y. Guo, W. Gao, G. Li, Interpretable task-inspired adaptive filter pruning for neural networks under multiple constraints. Int. J. Comput. Vis. **132**, 2060–2076 (2024)
101. W. Gao, Y. Guo, S. Ma, G. Li, S. Kwong, Efficient neural network compression inspired by compressive sensing. IEEE Trans. Neural Netw. Learn. Syst. **35**(2), 1965–1979 (2024)
102. Y. Guo, W. Gao, Semantic-driven automatic filter pruning for neural networks, in *2022 IEEE International Conference on Multimedia and Expo (ICME)* (IEEE, Piscataway, 2022), pp. 1–6
103. L. Tao, W. Gao, Efficient channel pruning based on architecture alignment and probability model bypassing, in *2021 IEEE International Conference on Systems, Man, and Cybernetics (SMC)* (IEEE, Piscataway, 2021), pp. 3232–3237
104. Z. Yang, W. Gao, G. Li, Y. Yan, Sur-driven video coding rate control for jointly optimizing perceptual quality and buffer control. IEEE Trans. Image Process. **32**, 5451–5464 (2023)
105. F. Shen, Z. Cai, W. Gao, An efficient rate control algorithm for intra frame coding in avs3, in *2021 IEEE International Conference on Systems, Man, and Cybernetics (SMC)* (IEEE, Piscataway, 2021), pp. 3164–3169
106. H. Yuan, W. Gao, J. Wang, Dynamic computational resource allocation for fast inter frame coding in video conferencing applications, in *2021 IEEE International Conference on Multimedia and Expo (ICME)* (IEEE, Piscataway, 2021), pp. 1–6
107. W. Gao, Q. Jiang, R. Wang, S. Ma, G. Li, S. Kwong, Consistent quality oriented rate control in HEVC via balancing intra and inter frame coding. IEEE Trans. Ind. Inform. **18**(3), 1594–1604 (2021)
108. H. Yuan, W. Gao, A new coding unit partitioning mode for screen content video coding, in *Proceedings of the 2021 5th International Conference on Digital Signal Processing* (2021), pp. 66–72
109. W. Gao, On the performance evaluation of state-of-the-art rate control algorithms for practical video coding and transmission systems, in *Proceedings of the 2020 4th International Conference on Video and Image Processing* (2020), pp. 179–185
110. W. Gao, S. Kwong, Q. Jiang, C.-K. Fong, P.H. Wong, W.Y. Yuen, Data-driven rate control for rate-distortion optimization in HEVC based on simplified effective initial QP learning. IEEE Trans. Broadcasting **65**(1), 94–108 (2018)

111. W. Gao, A multi-objective optimization perspective for joint consideration of video coding quality, in *2019 Asia-Pacific Signal and Information Processing Association Annual Summit and Conference (APSIPA ASC)* (IEEE, Piscataway, 2019), pp. 986–991
112. W. Gao, S. Kwong, Y. Jia, Joint machine learning and game theory for rate control in high efficiency video coding. IEEE Trans. Image Process. **26**(12), 6074–6089 (2017)
113. W. Gao, S. Kwong, Y. Zhou, H. Yuan, SSIM-based game theory approach for rate-distortion optimized intra frame CTU-level bit allocation. IEEE Trans. Multimedia **18**(6), 988–999 (2016)
114. W. Gao, S. Kwong, H. Yuan, X. Wang, DCT coefficient distribution modeling and quality dependency analysis based frame-level bit allocation for HEVC. IEEE Trans. Circuits Syst. Video Technol. **26**(1), 139–153 (2015)
115. W. Gao, S. Kwong, Phase congruency based edge saliency detection and rate control for perceptual image and video coding, in *2016 IEEE International Conference on Systems, Man, and Cybernetics (SMC)* (IEEE, Piscataway, 2016), pp. 000264–000269
116. H. Yuan, W. Gao, S. Ma, Y. Yan, Divide-and-conquer-based RDO-free CU partitioning for 8k video compression. ACM Trans. Multimedia Comput. Commun. Appl. **20**(4), 1–20 (2024)
117. L. Tao, W. Gao, A hardware implementation of entropy encoder for 8k video coding, in *2022 IEEE International Conference on Multimedia and Expo (ICME)* (IEEE, Piscataway, 2022), pp. 1–6
118. Y. Guo, W. Gao, S. Ma, G. Li, Accelerating transform algorithm implementation for efficient intra coding of 8k UHD videos. ACM Trans. Multimedia Comput. Commun. Appl. **18**(4), 1–20 (2022)
119. Z. Cai, W. Gao, Efficient fast algorithm and parallel hardware architecture for intra prediction of AVS3, in *2021 IEEE International Symposium on Circuits and Systems (ISCAS)* (IEEE, Piscataway, 2021), pp. 1–5
120. W. Gao, H. Yuan, G. Liao, Z. Guo, J. Chen, Pp8k: a new dataset for 8k UHD video compression and processing. IEEE MultiMedia **30**(3), 100–109 (2023)
121. W. Liu, W. Gao, G. Li, S. Ma, T. Zhao, H. Yuan, Enlarged motion-aware and frequency-aware network for compressed video artifact reduction. IEEE Trans. Circuits Syst. Video Technol. **34**(10), 10339–10352 (2024)
122. X. Zang, W. Gao, G. Li, H. Fang, C. Ban, Z. He, H. Sun, A baseline investigation: transformer-based cross-view baseline for text-based person search, in *Proceedings of the 31st ACM International Conference on Multimedia* (2023), pp. 7737–7746
123. G. Liao, W. Gao, G. Li, J. Wang, S. Kwong, Cross-collaborative fusion-encoder network for robust RGB-thermal salient object detection. IEEE Trans. Circuits Syst. Video Technol. **32**(11), 7646–7661 (2022)
124. W. Gao, G. Liao, S. Ma, G. Li, Y. Liang, W. Lin, Unified information fusion network for multi-modal RGB-D and RGB-T salient object detection. IEEE Trans. Circuits Syst. Video Technol. **32**(4), 2091–2106 (2021)
125. Y. Chen, S. Sun, G. Li, W. Gao, T.H. Li, Closing the gap between theory and practice during alternating optimization for GANs. IEEE Trans. Neural Netw. Learn. Syst. **34**(10), 14005–14017 (2024)
126. Y. Chen, C. Jin, G. Li, T.H. Li, W. Gao, Mitigating label noise in GANs via enhanced spectral normalization. IEEE Trans. Circuits Syst. Video Technol. **33**(8), 3924–3934 (2023)
127. X. Zang, G. Li, W. Gao, Multidirection and multiscale pyramid in transformer for video-based pedestrian retrieval. IEEE Trans. Ind. Inform. **18**(12), 8776–8785 (2022)
128. X. Zang, G. Li, W. Gao, X. Shu, Learning to disentangle scenes for person re-identification. Image Vis. Comput. **116**, 104330 (2021)
129. X. Zang, G. Li, W. Gao, X. Shu, Exploiting robust unsupervised video person re-identification. IET Image Process. **16**(3), 729–741 (2022)
130. Z. Yue, G. Li, W. Gao, Cross-level guided attention for human-object interaction detection, in *2023 IEEE International Conference on Multimedia and Expo Workshops (ICMEW)* (IEEE, Piscataway, 2023), pp. 284–289

131. Z. Yao, W. Gao, Iterative saliency aggregation and assignment network for efficient salient object detection in optical remote sensing images. IEEE Trans. Geosci. Remote Sensing (2024)
132. Y. Sun, Z. Li, S. Wang, W. Gao, Depth-assisted calibration on learning-based factorization for a compressive light field display. Opt. Express **31**(4), 5399–5413 (2023)
133. Y. Sun, Z. Li, L. Li, S. Wang, W. Gao, Optimization of compressive light field display in dual-guided learning, in *ICASSP 2022-2022 IEEE International Conference on Acoustics, Speech and Signal Processing (ICASSP)* (IEEE, Piscataway, 2022), pp. 2075–2079
134. W. Gao, S. Fan, G. Li, W. Lin, A thorough benchmark and a new model for light field saliency detection. IEEE Trans. Pattern Anal. Mach. Intell. **45**(7), 8003–8019 (2023)
135. Z. Li, G. Li, T. Li, S. Liu, W. Gao, Information-growth attention network for image super-resolution, in *Proceedings of the 29th ACM International Conference on Multimedia* (2021), pp. 544–552
136. L. Zhou, W. Gao, G. Li, H. Yuan, T. Zhao, G. Yue, Disentangled feature distillation for light field super-resolution with degradations, in *2023 IEEE International Conference on Multimedia and Expo Workshops (ICMEW)* (IEEE, Piscataway, 2023), pp. 116–121
137. L. Zhou, W. Gao, G. Li, End-to-end spatial-angular light field super-resolution using parallax structure preservation strategy, in *2022 IEEE International Conference on Image Processing (ICIP)* (IEEE, Piscataway, 2022), pp. 3396–3400
138. W. Gao, L. Zhou, L. Tao, A fast view synthesis implementation method for light field applications. ACM Trans. Multimedia Comput. Commun. Appl. **17**(4), 1–20 (2021)
139. X. Zhang, W. Gao, G. Li, Q. Jiang, R. Cong, Image quality assessment–driven reinforcement learning for mixed distorted image restoration. ACM Trans. Multimedia Comput. Commun. Appl. **19**(1s), 1–23 (2023)
140. X. Zhang, W. Gao, H. Yuan, G. Li, JE^{2}NET: joint exploitation and exploration in reinforcement learning based image restoration, in *ICASSP 2022-2022 IEEE International Conference on Acoustics, Speech and Signal Processing (ICASSP)* (IEEE, Piscataway, 2022), pp. 2090–2094
141. X. Zhang, W. Gao, HIRL: hybrid image restoration based on hierarchical deep reinforcement learning via two-step analysis, in *ICASSP 2022-2022 IEEE International Conference on Acoustics, Speech and Signal Processing (ICASSP)* (IEEE, Piscataway, 2022), pp. 2445–2449
142. Z. Guo, W. Gao, H. Wang, J. Wang, S. Fan, No-reference deep quality assessment of compressed light field images, in *2021 IEEE International Conference on Multimedia and Expo (ICME)* (IEEE, Piscataway, 2021), pp. 1–6
143. G. Liao and W. Gao, Rethinking feature mining for light field salient object detection. ACM Trans. Multimedia Comput. Commun. Appl. (2024)
144. S. Sun, J. Liu, T.H. Li, H. Li, G. Liu, W. Gao, Streamflow: streamlined multi-frame optical flow estimation for video sequences (2023). arXiv preprint arXiv:2311.17099
145. R. Liu, J. Huang, W. Gao, T.H. Li, G. Li, Mug-STAN: adapting image-language pretrained models for general video understanding (2023). arXiv preprint arXiv:2311.15075
146. C. Zhang, W. Gao, Learned rate control for frame-level adaptive neural video compression via dynamic neural network, in *European Conference on Computer Vision* (Springer, Berlin, 2024)

Chapter 10
Typical Engineering Applications of 3D Point Clouds

Abstract Due to the limitation of traditional images in expressing 3D space, point clouds have been applied in many practical industrial production fields, including autonomous driving, reverse engineering, digital twin city, topography mapping, robotics, medical analysis, digital museums, etc. The introduction of point clouds in these fields not only improves production efficiency but also saves a lot of production costs. In autonomous driving, point clouds enable real-time environmental perception and precise mapping, improving vehicle navigation and decision-making. Reverse engineering uses point clouds for accurate object modelling and simplification. Robotics benefits from enhanced scene recognition and task execution. Additionally, point clouds are also widely used in the digital twin city, topography mapping, and digital museum fields, where point clouds facilitate high-resolution terrain mapping, urban infrastructure monitoring, and detailed medical modelling. In this chapter, we discuss in detail the engineering applications of 3D point clouds.

Keywords Point cloud applications · Autonomous driving · Reverse engineering · Robots · Topography mapping · Digital twin city · Medical analysis · Digital museum

10.1 Introduction

With the rapid development of point cloud acquisition technology [1–4], point cloud sensors are becoming more available and affordable [5–7]. The point cloud data acquired by these sensors can provide a wealth of geometry, shape, and scale information. Similar to the fast developments and research results for image and video technologies [2–4, 8–62], related point cloud processing technologies have achieved significant progress, including compression [5, 6, 63–97], enhancement [7, 98–105], analysis [106–113], quality assessment [114–116], and open-source projects [117, 118]. Therefore, point cloud technology has found widespread applications in numerous fields, e.g., autonomous driving, reverse engineering, robots, topography mapping, digital twin city, medical analysis, and digital museum. In the next

W. Gao, G. Li, *Deep Learning for 3D Point Clouds*,
https://doi.org/10.1007/978-981-97-9570-3_10

sections, the book will introduce their applications and the role point cloud play in the corresponding application [108, 119].

In the realm of autonomous driving, point cloud technology plays a pivotal role in enabling vehicles to perceive their surroundings and recognizing position [120]. On one hand, unmanned cars are always equipped with Light Laser Detection and Ranging (LiDAR), which provides reliable, large-scale, and real-time information of environment and position [47]. On the other hand, constructing a point cloud-based high-definition map contributes to building detailed road information and helping downstream modules in speed and decision. Through the utilization of point cloud, reverse engineering practitioners can capture intricate details of physical objects, denoise them, simplify them, and recreate accurate digital representations [111, 113]. By leveraging point cloud data, robots can recognize current scenes, create detailed maps, localize themselves, and perform tasks with enhanced precision and adaptability, e.g., path planning and mimics certain motor functions of the human hand and arm. The application of point cloud technology in terrain mapping has expedited the creation of high-resolution elevation models, helping extract useful geometric information. Point clouds become instrumental in the construction of digital twin city, enabling urban road traffic safety service, infrastructure health monitoring, natural disaster situational awareness, ecological resources quantitative survey, and ecological resources quantitative survey. In the medical analysis field, point clouds can provide accurate modelling and help cross-modal registration and remote surgical assistance. When building the digital museum, using point clouds to model, store, and visualize cultural heritage improves cultural heritage management [121].

10.2 Autonomous Driving

In this section, we first have a brief explanation of automatic driving. Subsequently, we introduce the application of point clouds in the automatic driving system. Autonomous driving, also known as unmanned driving, describes the technology that intelligentizes existing vehicles so that they can drive autonomously without relying on humans. These intelligent vehicles are realized by adding software and hardware modules of artificial intelligence on the basis of traditional vehicles. The intelligent software and hardware modules of the autonomous driving system mainly include three parts, i.e., perception module, decision module, and control module. The perception module first accurately perceives the current environment of the vehicle through various sensors, such as location, external vehicles and pedestrians, and traffic signals. Subsequently, the decision module processes the information collected by the perception module in multiple steps and calculates an optimal driving strategy. Ultimately, the control module translates the driving strategy specified by the decision module into actual operations of the vehicle components. Consequently, drivers can be freed from traditional tedious driving tasks. Due to its huge scientific research and application value, autonomous

Table 10.1 Classification of automatic driving level. Source: Author

Level	Motion control	Incident response	Dynamic takeover	Operational restriction
L0	Driver	Driver & System	Driver	Limited
L1	Driver & System	Driver & System	Driver	Limited
L2	System	Driver & System	Driver	Limited
L3	System	System	Driver & System	Limited
L4	System	System	System	Limited
L5	System	System	System	Unlimited

driving has attracted widespread attention and achieved rapid development. Many companies have carried out research work on autonomous driving, and relatively well-known companies include Apple, Aptiv, Argo AI, Aurora, Baidu, GM Cruise, Didi, Lyft, Pony.ai, Tesla, Zoox, etc.

From the perspective of automatic driving levels, autonomous driving systems can generally be categorized into six levels, from L0 to L5. Table 10.1 shows the comparison of different automatic driving levels. As can be seen, automatic driving levels from L0 to L3 require more or less human involvement, while levels of L4 and L5 can already perform all driving operations without the intervention of drivers at all, and drivers can focus on other work or have a rest. At present, most of the autonomous driving systems we can see are controlled at the L2 level, and some higher-end models can reach the L3 level. However, it is still relatively difficult to reach L4 and L5 levels with existing technologies.

To ensure that an autonomous driving vehicle can drive safely and reliably in different environments, the vehicle needs to comprehensively perceive the information on the road. As the eyes of an autonomous driving system, the perception module is made up of various sensors, e.g., camera, radar, GPS antenna, LiDAR, and so on. These sensors work together to collect external information from different aspects. Among all these sensors, LiDAR plays an important role in capturing the point cloud representation of the external environment and building the basic map with positioning. Compared with alternative approaches, point clouds have advantages of all-weather, fast collection, large amounts, high precision, and strong anti-interference ability.

Since knowing the traffic rules in real time is very difficult, especially when choosing the right road at an intersection, constructing a point cloud-based high-definition map (HD map) as the prior of other modules is very effective [122]. An HD map is a very precise map adopted in autonomous driving, covering many details absent from traditional maps, such as road shapes, traffic signs, and buildings. Generally, an HD map contains two levels of maps, i.e., point cloud map and traffic map, which simplifies the designs of multiple modules in autonomous systems:

- During the driving process of the vehicle, the HD map can provide some position calibration information, which can be used to register the current attitude and position.

- According to the prior information from the HD map, the perception module can preprocess the collected data and significantly reduce the computational load of downstream modules.
- The decision module relies on the information provided by the HD map to make optimal decisions. For example, information such as traffic lines and road signs in 3D roads can guide the next movement of the vehicle.

The purpose of locating the vehicle is to find the position of the vehicle in the HD map, which involves real-time point cloud registration to get the initial pose and needs to fuse the information of the HD map with the information of other sensors (such as GPS). Besides, in order to ensure very high safety, positioning in autonomous driving technology is often required. The translation error should be at the centimeter level, and the rotation angle error should be at the microradian level. The standard approach to fuse information from multiple sensors is to use Bayesian filters, such as Kalman filtering, extended Kalman filtering, or Particle filtering. Bayesian filters have two iterative steps, i.e., prediction and correction. The prediction step is to use Bayesian filters to predict the states of sensor models before reading physical sensors, while the calibration step is to correct corresponding sensor models based on the received physical sensor readings.

Given the HD map and real-time inputs from various sensors, the autonomous driving system needs to analyze and understand the current environment, such as identifying nearby pedestrians and vehicles [18, 102]. 3D object detection and semantic segmentation based on point clouds are popular research directions at present, and the accuracy of those algorithms has been significantly improved [42, 106]. According to the order of information fusion of multiple sensors and information analysis, there exist two technical routes: (1) fusion and analysis and (2) analysis and fusion. The latter technical route is more mature, while the former technical route is believed to have greater potential as it can mutually enhance multiple perceptual modalities in a high-dimensional feature space, especially based on deep learning [52, 53].

In recent years, many well-known companies have launched fierce competition in the field of autonomous driving, such as Waymo, Cruise, AutoX, Pony.AI, and Argo AI. Table 10.2 shows the comparison of autonomous driving companies in their test miles and miles per disengagement. Furthermore, several autonomous driving datasets have been launched, for example, Waymo [123], nuScenes [124],

Table 10.2 Comparison of test miles and miles per disengagement (Dec 2019–Nov 2020). Source: Author

Company name	Country	Miles	Miles per disengagement
Waymo	America	628,839	29,945
Crurise	America	770,049	28,520
AutoX	China	40,734	20367
Pony.AI	China	225,409	10,738
Argo.AI	America	21,037	10,519

ONCE [125], and KITTI [126]. Based on sensors including Lidar, camera, and Radar, various works [127] use these datasets. With the gradual maturity of point cloud technology, autonomous driving vehicles will become smarter and safer, completely changing the way people travel.

10.3 Reverse Engineering

In this section, we will discuss the role of reverse engineering in manufacturing, clarify the application of point clouds in reverse engineering, and detail how to reproduce a mechanical part by reverse engineering. With the development of 3D LiDAR scanning technology, the accuracy of collecting the surface of objects gets increasing promotion, which also facilitates the application of reverse engineering [70, 128]. The technology of reverse engineering is to infer the production process of an object, involving surveying, mechanical engineering, computer graphics, and many other disciplines [75]. It has been widely adopted in model processing, aerospace, digital models, etc. Different from the traditional forward design that analyzes and designs the drawings step by step according to the demands and finally manufactures corresponding products, reverse engineering first starts by digitizing existing products and then upgrades and iterates products based on digital ones, which can save a lot of manpower and material resources. The technical route of reverse engineering can shorten the product development cycle and speed up product iteration. Especially for those hard-to-reach products, their geometric information can be easily captured using LiDAR, reducing the difficulty and risk of developing new products [64, 76, 77].

As illustrated in Fig. 10.1, the whole process of reverse engineering includes four key nodes, i.e., data collection, data processing, model refactoring, and rapid production. The data collection phase means the scanning process by employing 3D scanners (often various LiDAR devices) where the 3D point cloud representation of a product can be obtained. Due to factors such as noise and occlusion, collected point clouds may contain a little noise or holes where information is lost. Several typical processing algorithms (such as denoising and simplification) are adopted in the data processing phase to enhance the raw point clouds. In the model refactoring, the processed point clouds are converted into the digital surface representation of the product. Finally, the rapid production phase can use the technologies of digital lathes or 3D printing to produce the corresponding product following the digital one.

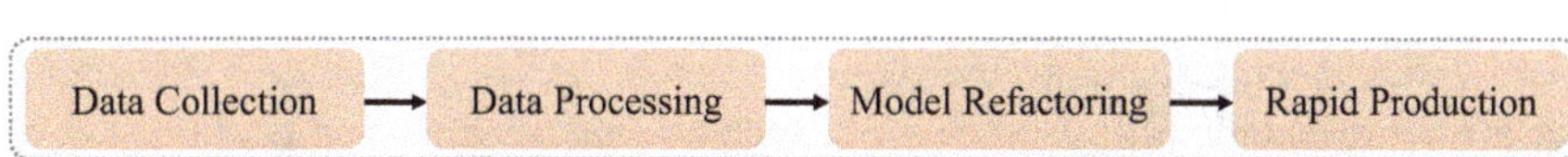

Fig. 10.1 Pipeline of reverse engineering. Source: Author

Point cloud has been applied in many steps of reverse engineering, such as point cloud denoising, point cloud simplification, and surface reconstruction [129]. In the process of scanning point clouds, many factors can affect the quality of point cloud acquisition, such as equipment accuracy, environment change, and object properties. These influential factors may incur noisy points or outliers. To obtain accurate point cloud representations, denoising algorithms need to be introduced to remove unreasonable noise and enhance the scanned point clouds. Unlike the regular grid topology of images, point clouds have the properties of unordered and irregularity. Therefore, traditional methods for image denoising cannot be applied in point cloud processing, and developing tailored algorithms for point clouds attracts wide participation from academia and industry. Previous point cloud denoising algorithms include isotropic denoising, anisotropic denoising, bilateral filtering denoising, and tensor voting denoising. At present, practical applications often choose different algorithms according to the distribution of point clouds. For instance, average filtering and Laplacian filtering [130] are used for point clouds with regular distribution and irregular distribution, respectively.

Although the development of the electronics industry has made the processing speed of computing equipment rapidly improved, the improvement of computing speed still lags far behind the growth of data scale. Directly using the raw point clouds containing a large number of points to reconstruct 3D surfaces not only consumes a lot of computational resources but also takes many noise points into account, which decreases the quality of reconstructed surfaces. Point cloud simplification is to reduce the number of points without losing the geometric details of original point clouds as much as possible, which can not only save a lot of computing and storage resources but also further reduce the impact of noise points on subsequent processing. The existing point cloud simplification algorithms can be roughly divided into two categories, i.e., uniform simplification and feature simplification. Uniform simplification simplifies point clouds uniformly based on the distance among points and ignores the geometric features of point clouds, such as curvature, thus being efficient. Uniform simplification is suitable for point clouds with simple geometric features, and related main algorithms include grid simplification and bounding box simplification. Feature simplification fully considers the distribution of points, and the feature-rich area contains as many points as possible to retain the original details of point clouds. Typical feature simplification methods have non-uniform grid simplification and curvature-based simplification.

The actual surface of a product tends to consist of many irregular and complex surfaces, which are difficult to express mathematically. Therefore, surface reconstruction, as the key of model refactoring, is to approximate the surface of a product using multiple mathematically expressible forms and obtain a digital representation while meeting the requirements of accuracy. Based on the digital surface representation, post-processing, such as analysis and modification, can be easily implemented. In terms of reconstructed surface types, surface reconstruction can be categorized into two classes, i.e., parametric reconstruction and algebraic reconstruction. Due to the limitation of algebraic reconstruction in expressing

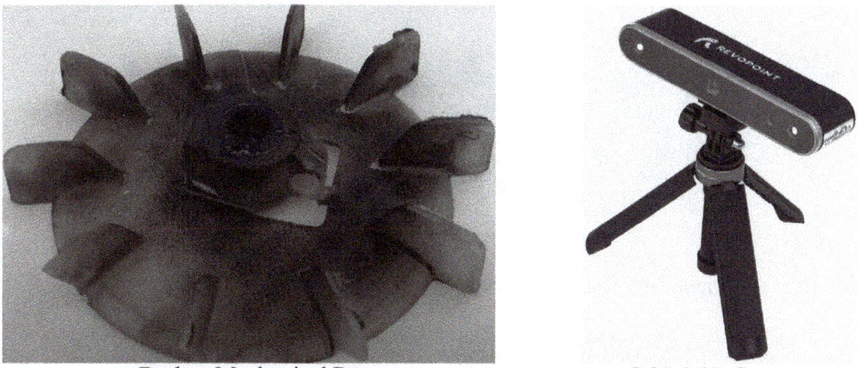

Broken Mechanical Part POP 2 3D Scanner

Fig. 10.2 Utilizing reverse engineering to reproduce a mechanical part. Source: Author

Scanning Process Window of Revo Scan

Fig. 10.3 Point cloud data collection on the mechanical part. Source: Author

complex surfaces, we often use parametric reconstruction in reverse engineering, where common mathematically expressible surfaces contain Bezier Surface, B-Spline Surface, NURBS Surface, and Triangular Bezierqu Surface.

Next, we explain the practical operation of reverse engineering using the example of reproducing a broken mechanical part. The hardware includes a PC, a 3D printer, and a POP 2 3D scanner (see Fig. 10.2). The software involves Revo Scan, Revo Studio, and Geomagic Design X. The POP 2 3D scanner combines the functions of a handheld 3D scanner and a desktop 3D scanner. The cores of a POP 2 3D scanner apply the principles of binocular and micro-structured light and enable a convenient acquisition of high-accuracy (up to 0.05mm) 3D point clouds. As depicted in Fig. 10.3, with the official software Revo Scan, the 3D scanner is utilized to scan the mechanical part two times from different views. Given the digital model, we can use 3D printing technology to automatically print a physical model according to the digital model. As shown in Fig. 10.6, although we have no drawing of the

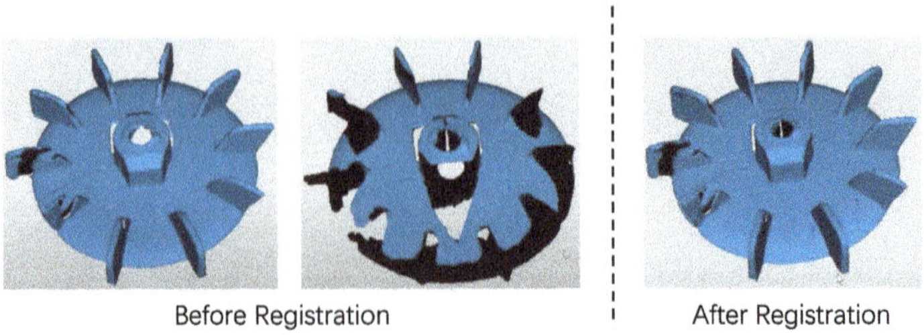

Fig. 10.4 Registration of point clouds in two times of scans. Source: Author

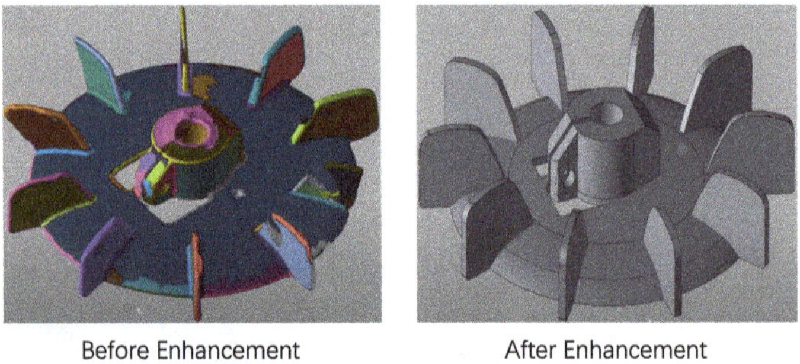

Fig. 10.5 Enhancement of digital surfaces by Geomagic Design X. Source: Author

broken mechanical part, an identical replacement can be easily made by reverse engineering.

As illustrated in Fig. 10.4, Revo Studio provides functions of one-key registration and surface reconstruction. We can easily convert the point clouds from two scans into a mesh representation. The initially reconstructed surfaces (see Fig. 10.4) are not only unsmooth but also contain many holes with missing information, which does not exactly match the original mechanical part. Geomagic Design X provides powerful tools for analyzing and refactoring the initially reconstructed surfaces. As demonstrated in Fig. 10.5, surfaces by enhanced Geomagic Design X have visible quality improvement. Figure 10.6 shows the comparisons of the reproduced mechanical part and the original one.

The introduction of point clouds in reverse engineering eases the collection of object shapes, especially inaccessible ones. Collected objects enable us to reproduce objects without knowing their composition, which effectively improves production efficiency. With the development of the electronics industry, the quality of captured point clouds may be higher for containing less noise. The process of human participation in reverse engineering will be significantly reduced, and reverse engineering is expected to be a fully automated process from data acquisition to object reproduction.

Fig. 10.6 Comparison of the reproduced mechanical part and the original one. Source: Author

10.4 Robots

This section introduces the main applications of point cloud in robots and summarizes the critical role of point clouds in intelligent robots. Robots are essential production and service equipment for industrial and non-industrial sectors and automation equipment for advanced manufacturing technologies. Robots can replace or assist humans in various tasks, including tedious, dangerous, toxic, or harmful work. In addition to the manufacturing industry, robots are also used in numerous fields, such as resource exploration and development, disaster relief and rescue, medical services, home entertainment, military, and aerospace.

Compared with traditional industrial robots, intelligent robots integrate a variety of sensors. They can make real-time judgments and responses to different environmental changes, thus meeting the use of more diverse and complex application scenarios. With the improvement of sensor accuracy and the development of efficient algorithms, application fields of intelligent robots have gradually expanded to include warehousing and logistics, surgical and medical rehabilitation, professional cleaning of complex environments and particular objects, urban emergency security, energy, mineral collection, etc. Intelligent robots are gradually shifting from sensing-based to interactive or even autonomous robots. The key to this breakthrough is the ability to accurately capture and perceive the 3D environment in which it is placed, with point clouds playing an irreplaceable role as a significant representation of 3D scenes. With the development of sensors, especially LiDAR, and multi-view stereo devices, point clouds are captured more efficiently and accurately, enhancing the reliability of algorithms for intelligent robots. In addition, the miniaturization of sensors has simplified the complex design structure of intelligent robots, allowing intelligent robots to enter various fields. Sweeping robots are gradually being accepted by millions of families, bringing great convenience to our home life. A simple word can "command" the sweeping robot to complete the sweeping and mopping work. The sweeper is small, but many technological innovations are integrated into it, involving mechanical, electronic, control, and other disciplines. Various technological synergies are adopted to complete the seemingly simple cleaning work.

The robot is equipped with various rangefinders and sensors to obtain high-quality point cloud modelling of indoor scenes, which is the basis for the robot to sense the external environment and make optimal decisions promptly. Ultrasonic sensors can continuously transmit ultrasonic signals outward, and the receiver uses the signals reflected when encountering obstacles to determine the size and distance of obstacles ahead [131]. An infrared range sensor emits an infrared signal, and using the strength of the reflected infrared signal can also determine the distance of the obstacle [132]. The photoelectric switch can achieve the anti-collision sensor in time to react after the collision. The anti-fall sensor is generally placed below the sweeping robot, mainly using ultrasonic distance measurement to sense the height of the ground in front to prevent falls on the stairs.

Another key technology in the sweeping robot is its path-planning technology. Path planning determines the efficiency of the work of the sweeping robot. Reasonable selection of a variety of path-cleaning programs is the primary function of the sweeping robot [133]. The earliest sweeping robots used the random collision mode, based on their equipped sensors, through multiple collisions to select the appropriate path. Obviously, this way is less efficient. With the development of Simultaneous Localization and Mapping (SLAM) with point clouds [134], a more accurate and efficient path-planning mode emerged.

Laser-ranging navigation uses a rotatable laser emitter on the top of the robot to generate a map of the room and to figure out the location of the walls and furniture based on which the path is planned. The image-based measurement and navigation system first uses the camera on the top to cruise and scan the whole house, combined with infrared sensors to accurately model the house environment, based on which navigation and path planning are performed. We need to establish a fixed-point signal transmitter in the house, through which the robot can locate the reference point, and then establish the indoor map utilizing collision to facilitate cleaning.

In recent years, with the development of robotics, applying robot structures with high speed, high accuracy, and high load capacity has received attention in industry and aerospace. Robotic arms are usually programmable and have similar functions to a human arm; the arm may be the sum of an entire mechanism or part of a more complex robot. Links of such robotic arms are connected by joints that allow rotational motion (e.g., in an articulated robot) or translational (linear) displacement. The links of a robotic arm can be considered to form a kinematic chain. The end of the robot arm kinematic chain is called the end-effector, similar to a human arm.

The core problem in the current robot arm operation contains two aspects. One is to find a suitable gripping point (or adsorption point), and the other is to plan the motion of the robot arm based on that gripping point and the target placement point. Both aspects are inseparable from the visual perception system to perceive the objects on the operated platform. In finding the gripping point, the target object needs to be visually identified, and its suitable gripping position needs to be analyzed. In the motion planning process, avoiding obstacles on the planned route in real time is necessary, which also requires the simultaneous participation of the visual perception system.

The robotic arm needs a visual servo system to determine the object's position, which can be divided into eye-to-hand and eye-in-hand systems according to the relative position of the end-effector (hand) and the vision sensor (eye). Eye-to-hand has a separated distribution with a fixed field of view, and if the calibration accuracy of the camera is high, the higher the accuracy of vision positioning for grasping. Eye-in-hand, on the other hand, fixes the robot arm and vision sensor together, and the field of view changes with the movement of the robot arm. The closer the sensor is, the higher the accuracy, but the target may be out of the field of view when it is too close. Traditional vision servo systems [135] rely primarily on 2D data from images or videos, which increases the burden of analyzing object depth information. With the research of point cloud acquisition devices and point cloud intelligence algorithms, the vision servo system on the robotic arm can perceive depth, dramatically improving the accuracy of identifying scenes and objects and facilitating the robotic arm's subsequent operation in 3D space. Some work in this area has been proposed, such as [136].

Sewer systems are an essential part of urban infrastructure, which can effectively prevent urban flooding, protecting social assets and lives. However, sewer systems inevitably age and damage during years of use, leading to impaired function or even failure. Therefore, timely maintenance and retrofitting are essential while saving costs for subsequent repairs. Manual maintenance of sewer systems is very subjective, tedious, labor-intensive, and unsuitable for large-scale maintenance of urban sewer systems. Therefore, the development and use of sewer inspection robots can effectively solve this task. A simple sewer inspection robot is shown in Fig. 10.7.

Like sweeping robots, sewer inspection robots require visual perception systems to plan routes and detect multiple sewer deterioration and damage. However, unlike sweeping robots, sewer inspection robots have more stringent requirements for vision sensors. Because they operate inside pipes and lighting conditions are usually point sources mounted on robots, conventionally captured 2D data cannot meet the identification requirements. Point cloud capture devices are widely used in

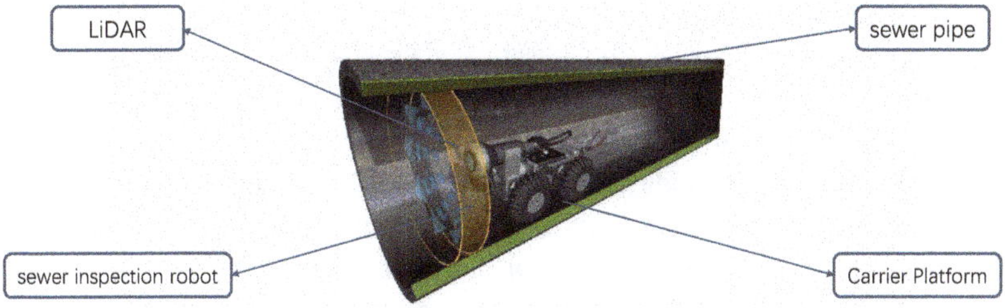

Fig. 10.7 A sewer inspection robot. The image shown is introduced with MPEG open access (OA) work under CC BY Licence (Copyright ©1988–2024, www.mpeg.org) [137]

sewer inspection robot research because of their low requirements for illumination conditions and ability to perceive 3D accurately [138]. They have shown great potential for sewer inspection robots.

The miniaturization and ubiquitous use of LiDAR sensors have enabled the acquisition of the ability to handle 3D objects in intelligent robots. By processing and analyzing the point clouds captured by the sensor, the intelligent robot recognizes the current 3D scene through its intelligent processing unit and reacts accordingly and simultaneously. It can be said that the point cloud has significantly improved the process of robot intelligence, making automatic cruising, obstacle avoidance, and other vital technologies' breakthrough development. In the future, how to efficiently combine data from multiple sensors to further enhance intelligence will be an important research direction.

10.5 Topography Mapping

In this section, we will discuss the application of point clouds in terrain mapping and explain in detail how to use 3D point cloud data for mapping, generating topographic maps, etc. The topographic map production process is shown in Fig. 10.8. With the development of UAVs, companies such as DJI and Pegasus have rapidly changed the concept of operation, operation methods, and operation efficiency of mapping nowadays with an attitude of changing the industry. The airborne LiDAR is mainly used in basic mapping, urban 3D modelling and forestry applications, railroad, electric power, etc. In the past decade, it has gained wide recognition as a tool for accurate and rapid acquisition of ground 3D data.

Currently, low-cost UAVs + airborne LiDAR create exponential reduction in the cost of high-precision mapping. Although there are relatively mature commercial systems for airborne LiDAR, the LiDAR data processing system is still relatively immature today, and the main software used now is Terrasolid from Finland, in addition to the software provided by various hardware companies. Terrasolid mainly includes TerraModelerTM, TerraScanTM, TerraPhotoTM, and so on. Among the software provided by hardware manufacturers, the main ones are DJI's Zenith L1 supporting DJI SmartMap software and Pegasus' RIEGL mini210 LiDAR supporting UAV Manager Pro.

The point cloud data is generally mainly in LAS format. LAS files are collections of LiDAR point cloud points, each with horizontal coordinates (X and Y) and vertical elevation (Z) values. In addition to the elevation values, LAS files provide a common format to store additional information such as laser intensity, scan angle, return information, etc. Some of this additional information (e.g., intensity) is very useful for visualization. The accuracy of the laser point cloud, on the other hand, plays an important role in the accuracy of terrain mapping.

The airborne LiDAR system uses the flight platform as a carrier and uses differential GPS for real-time positioning, i.e., the ground reference station and the airborne GPS receiver, which simultaneously receive the navigation and positioning

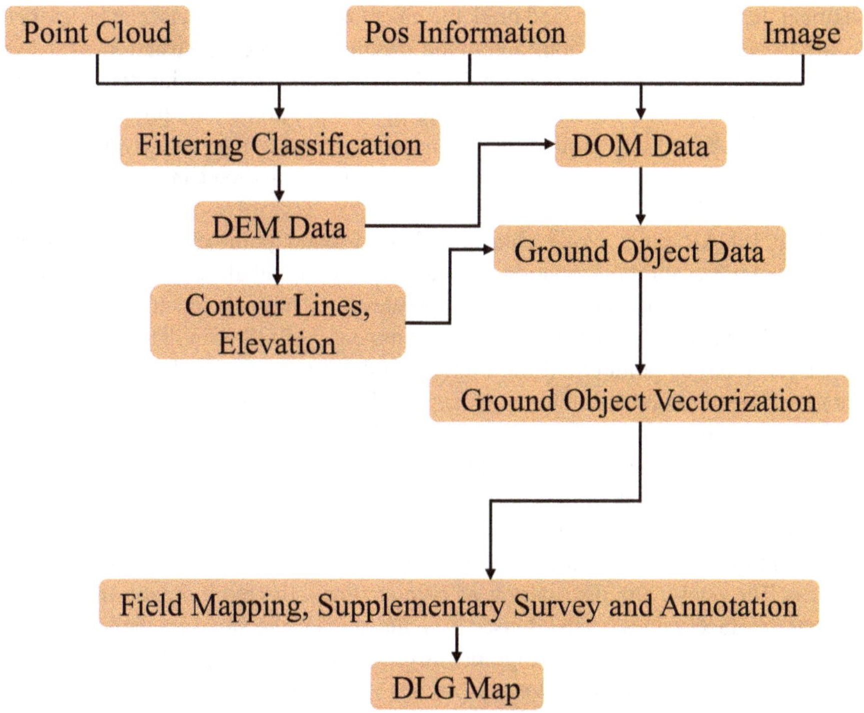

Fig. 10.8 Topographic map production process. Source: Author

signals from the same satellites, as a way to correct the real-time positioning values. The inertial navigation system receives the correction parameters of DGPS and obtains the Euler angle parameters of the projection center in real time to accurately locate the spot position of the laser ranging unit's organ beam irradiating on the object. The laser has strong penetrating ability, which can effectively overcome the influence of vegetation and accurately obtain the 3D data of the terrain ground and combine with the high-resolution influence data to generate the topographic map with the help of specialized software. In the actual operation process, the airborne LiDAR system plans the route according to the survey area, obtains 3D point cloud data and high-definition images, carries out air three encryption, draws digital elevation model (DEM) and digital orthophoto (DOM) with point cloud data, generates contour lines, extracts elevation points, collects geomorphological data by interpreting ground objects, generates DLG sketch map, and carries out field mapping, supplementary survey and annotation, map checking, and finishing. The map is checked and decorated.

The 3D world we live in consists of a rich variety of object objects, such as houses, bridges, trees, cars, etc. Different objects have different appearances forms and functions. Point clouds are dots of different heights and colors in the eyes of machines. The use of deep learning technology to automatically and accurately segment the point cloud data, and mark the names of different objects, can be applied to urban physical examination, automatic driving, and the construction of a live 3D Earth. The most common one in GIS is automatic ground point detection and classification. After successfully extracting the ground points, the point cloud data set can be classified into ground points and non-ground points, and given different colors to distinguish them, the points of a certain classification can be revealed and hidden separately.

When LiDAR point cloud data completes ground point extraction, accurate ground point elevation information is obtained. The digital elevation model (DEM, Digital Elevation Model) generated by these elevation values is much more accurate than the DEM data produced by other means, e.g., ALOS-12m. The accuracy of DEM generated by point cloud can even reach the centimeter level (the point cloud data itself needs to be accurate enough). The TIF topographic (DEM) data results are generated in a common format by constructing an irregular triangulated network (TIN) surface from the extracted non-ground points.

Contour lines are one of the common methods of representing surfaces on maps. Contour lines are smooth curves that connect adjacent points of equal value. The distribution of contour lines reflects the change of elevation values on the raster surface. The denser the distribution of contour lines, the more drastic the change of raster surface values is; the denser it is, the steeper the slope is; the sparser the distribution, the smaller the change of raster surface values is, and the gentler the slope is. By extracting contour lines, locations with the same elevation values can be found, while the distribution of contour lines can also show steep and gentle areas of change. After high precision terrain is generated by point cloud, high precision contour lines are then extracted based on the terrain. Finally, the topographic map is obtained by exporting the high-precision terrain (DEM) and contour data extracted from the point cloud data.

3D laser scanning measurement system can quickly and densely obtain the "point cloud" data of the solid surface, which can quickly and accurately establish a detailed terrain scene model expressed in the "point cloud" in the computer, and then in the virtual "point cloud" terrain scene model for topographic mapping. With the emergence of various modern instruments for rapid acquisition of spatial information and the rapid development of computer technology, the rapid and high-resolution acquisition of spatial information in the field, and then in the virtual environment of the computer to extract the user's concern and useful geographic information, is the future direction of the development of mapping technology, but also point cloud data is one of the important application directions.

10.6 Digital Twin City

This section will discuss the application of point clouds in digital twin cities. The digital twin city is a very macro concept, and there are numerous applications. Therefore, this section will lay out the role of point clouds in the construction of digital twin cities. The digital twin city [139] is a mapping of the city in virtual space using digital twin technology and a complex integrated technology system and integration of virtual cities in the physical dimension and virtual cities in the information dimension to support the construction of new smart cities. An important point in building a digital twin city is a high-precision city model, which requires not only a high-precision building model but also the location relationship between buildings, greenery, roads, and underground corridors. If we use traditional methods to obtain parameters for modelling, the labor and material resources spent are huge, but using 3D laser scanning technology to collect 3D point cloud data and then modelling can largely reduce the labor and material resources invested.

3D laser point cloud data can accurately obtain a variety of parameters, precision control in the millimeter level, and at the same time obtain parameter values of all surrounding features within a certain range, only one person can complete the past 2–3 people can complete the work, and the work time has been significantly reduced. In the subsequent modelling process, the accuracy of modelling relying on point cloud data is also much higher than that of traditional methods. Therefore, the use of point cloud data modelling in the construction process of digital twin cities can achieve a huge improvement in accuracy and efficiency, saving costs and improving quality.

The subsection will elaborate on applications of the point cloud in five directions of digital twin city, including urban road traffic safety service, urban infrastructure health monitoring, urban natural disaster situational awareness, urban ecological resources quantitative survey, and urban cultural heritage digital management. Aiming at large-scale, multi-density, and highly dynamic road scenes, point cloud scene cognition can efficiently and accurately acquire high-precision semantic maps containing geometric structure, semantic information, topological connectivity, and dynamic updates through recognition, pickup, association, and other processing modules. It realizes intelligent perception and multi-dimensional monitoring of the traffic road network and provides accurate, timely, and intuitive safe traffic strategies for drivers and autonomous vehicles in transit.

For the needs of service status monitoring and fine operation and maintenance of major infrastructure, point cloud scene cognition can obtain structural geometry information with high accuracy, reconstruct surface texture details at multiple levels, and characterize health status indicators in multiple dimensions, providing a fast and effective perception mode for quality control of large building construction, health inspection of key elements of urban roads [140], and dynamic assessment of bridge health [141] and strongly supporting infrastructure scientific diagnosis of health status and whole life cycle protection.

In natural disaster situational awareness, point cloud scene cognition can efficiently, accurately, and timely obtain 3D models of bad geological bodies, calculate deformation and displacement data of bad geological bodies based on multi-temporal 3D models, analyze the evolution law of bad geological bodies, and then reveal the natural disaster triggering mechanism, which provides key support for rapid localization, rescue and relief, risk assessment, and key support for rapid localization, rescue, risk assessment, and disaster warning [142]. For example, rapid

3D modelling of collapsed buildings using images from unmanned aerial vehicles (UAVs) can greatly aid USaR's operations and improve disaster response [143].

Point cloud scene cognition realizes all-round, multi-level, refined, and intelligent state cognition of ecological resources through point cloud coupled observation, accurate acquisition of 3D structure information, quantitative inversion of ecological parameters, and dynamic evolution analysis of spatial patterns, which greatly improves the efficiency of a quantitative survey of natural resources and provides scientific support for the formulation of sustainable development policies to protect ecological natural resources. It provides scientific support for the formulation of sustainable development policies to protect ecological and natural resources. For example, living vegetation volume can be easily calculated with the help of T-LiDAR point cloud [144].

The construction of digital twin cities cannot be separated from the real-time follow-up of 3D data, which is accurate and can meet more functional requirements, while the new technology of mobile measurement can improve operational efficiency, reduce the intensity of field labor, and provide multi-view, multi-resolution, and multi-scene spatial information, which has become a necessary means for the construction of digital twin cities. Point cloud cognition has been widely used in many major projects and typical fields in the construction of digital twin cities. In the future, with increasing complexity, uncertainty, and dynamic evolution of application scenes, cognitive processing algorithms of point cloud scenes still need to strengthen the research on the fusion, extraction, association, and learning of multi-category, multi-level, and multi-dimensional point cloud features.

10.7 Medical Analysis

This section will lay out the role of point clouds in medicine and summarize applications of point clouds in medical analysis. Medical analysis is the process of examining and interpreting medical data, such as clinical observations, laboratory tests, medical images, and patient records, to extract meaningful information and derive insights for medical diagnosis, treatment planning, and research purposes. Medical analysis involves applying various analytical techniques and tools to understand and interpret complex medical data. Nowadays, people use big data and deep learning (DL) techniques to analyze medical signals that cannot be seen by human doctors [145]. DL tasks such as segmentation, classification, and registration of focal areas based on medical point clouds can provide important information for medical processes such as disease diagnosis, surgical guidance, and treatment planning [146]. For example, [147] helps diagnose early pancreatic cancer by analyzing color contrast and parameter variability issues in pancreatic tumors.

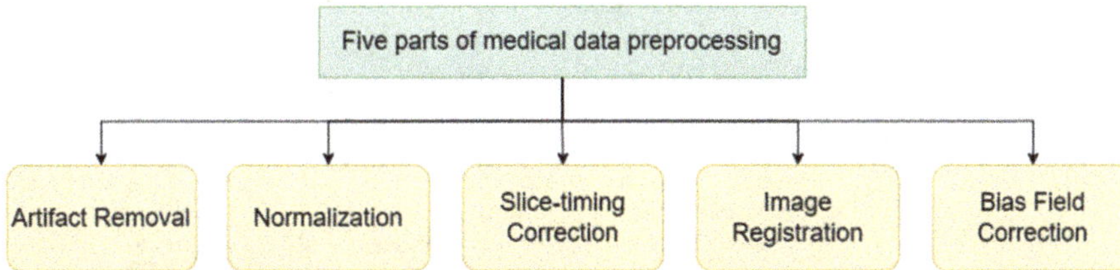

Fig. 10.9 Point clouds used for disease detection. Source: Author

According to the dimension of data, medical data can be divided into three categories. The first one is one-dimensional data. It contains many biosignals such as electronic signals produced by the human heart (ECG) and encephalogram (EEG), phonocardiogram (PCG), and spectroscopy signals. The second one is 2D data, including all static images produced by X-ray, ultrasound, and MRI, which plays a crucial role in modern medical diagnosis. The third one is 3D data, e.g., computed axial tomography, Doppler ultrasonography, and sequential images. 3D data can be reconstructed from several images taken from different angles or from Lidar scans. Figure 10.9 shows the five parts of medical data preprocessing.

In medical scenarios, point clouds offer several advantages over images in terms of data type. Point clouds provide accurate and intuitive modelling of organs and tissues, which greatly benefits disease detection and postoperative simulation. For instance, 3D CT data has been utilized to segment voxel levels of constructed pulmonary nodules, aiding in the identification of disease foci. Point cloud-based 3D face data is commonly employed in medical cosmetic surgery and postoperative simulation [148]. Laser scanning and reverse engineering have gradually replaced dental plaster models with digital point cloud tooth models [149] or other issues [150], providing guidance for orthodontic programs.

Furthermore, point clouds play a crucial role in cross-modal registration and remote surgical assistance [151]. The use of point cloud characterization learning enables the construction of registrations from 3D CT images to 2D X-ray images, assisting in the evaluation of minimally invasive surgery outcomes. Moreover, point clouds facilitate the reconstruction of 3D shapes from images, enhancing the intuitiveness of remote surgical procedures [152].

The utilization of point clouds offers significant advantages in medical applications. Point clouds provide accurate modelling of organs and tissues, aiding in disease detection and postoperative simulation. Additionally, they contribute to cross-modal registration and remote surgical assistance, enhancing surgical evaluation and improving the intuitiveness of remote procedures. As point cloud technology continues to advance, it holds great potential for further advancements and innovations in the medical field. Figure 10.10 shows the details of point clouds in medical treatment.

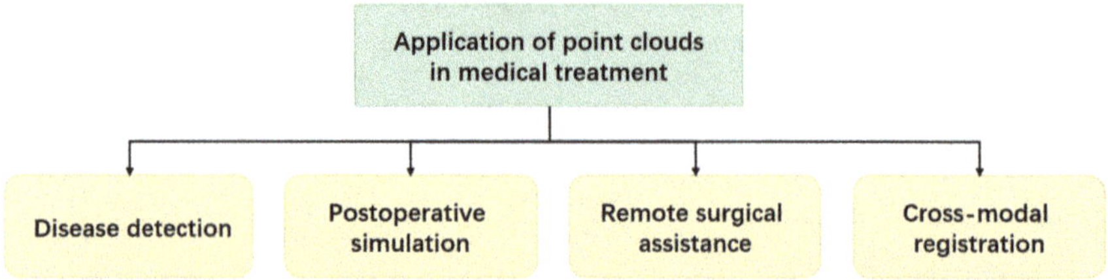

Fig. 10.10 The application of point clouds in medical treatment. Source: Author

10.8 Digital Museum

This section will lay out the role of point clouds in digital museum. Museums are centralized exhibition places for historical and cultural artefacts, carrying the responsibility of managing, preserving, and showcasing treasures. They serve educational, entertainment, and research purposes. With the development of information technology, digital museums have emerged as a prominent trend. A digital museum is established in the digital space, focusing on collecting, processing, and presenting data. This can be achieved through photography, but more recently, many digital museums have been created in 3D format, allowing visitors to explore different routes and observe exhibits from various angles. By establishing digital museums, it becomes possible to document the current state of artefacts, expand the research capabilities of museums, and continue their educational functions. Digital museums employ various technologies to accurately record and preserve information about the shape, texture, and materials of artefacts. This data remains unaffected by environmental factors and the passage of time, providing scholars with comprehensive research materials.

Digital museums also extend the display capabilities of traditional museums. Due to the fragility and preciousness of artefacts, physical exhibits in traditional museums are often protected and inaccessible to close examination due to a large number of visitors. However, through precise and detailed recording and presentation, visitors can observe the intricate details, textures, and materials of artefacts, gaining a deeper understanding of them. Furthermore, digital museums excel in fulfilling the educational function of museums by providing a more flexible and interactive means of presentation and dissemination. Online exhibitions of artefacts offer a unique visiting experience to a wider audience, fostering their understanding of historical and cultural aspects while promoting and preserving local cultural traditions.

Point cloud scene cognition can provide reliable, complete, and accurate data and information resources for high-precision 3D modelling, digital storage, virtualization restoration, visualization display, and network dissemination of cultural heritage through actual data collection, processing, and reconstruction. It significantly improves the efficiency and quality of cultural heritage management and provides valuable resources for cultural heritage restoration, reconstruction, and subsequent research work. By scanning objects with a 3D scanner, a dense point cloud of data is obtained, which provides a highly detailed digital representation of the scanned object. For complex objects, multiple scans from different angles are usually required. 3D scanners are usually divided into two types based on the measuring distance. Long-range 3D scanners, which typically use the laser pulse time-of-flight ranging principle, are often used for the digital information acquisition of large cultural relics. The corresponding surveying instruments may include total stations, real-time kinematic, levels, etc. Short-range 3D scanning has multiple technical implementations, which can be roughly divided into three types, line laser 3D scanning, structured-light 3D scanning, and close-range photogrammetry, all of which are based on the principle of triangulation.

At present, more and more museums around the world are establishing their own online exhibition areas, and it is foreseeable that digital museums supported by the point cloud will provide more benefits for the conservation, research, and display of cultural relics.

10.9 Summary

Point clouds are an essential tool in various industries such as autonomous driving, reverse engineering, robots, topography mapping, and digital twin city. In autonomous driving, point clouds can represent the environment of the vehicle in terms of 3D points, allowing the vehicle's sensors to perceive its surroundings accurately. In reverse engineering, the point cloud technology plays an important role in point cloud denoising, point cloud simplification, and surface reconstruction. Point clouds are also useful for robots to navigate through an environment by providing a 3D representation of objects and obstacles. Topography mapping is another significant use of point clouds, where they can create an accurate representation of an area's land surface, including buildings, vegetation, and other natural or artificial features. Finally, point clouds are instrumental in creating a digital twin city, where a virtual replication of a city can be used to make informed decisions about its physical infrastructure and its future growth. Therefore, point clouds are incredibly beneficial in providing accurate, high-resolution data for a variety of applications. With the development of technology, point clouds will be used more in various fields, making life more convenient.

Exercises

1. Please list several applications of point clouds in practical production.
2. What modules can the automatic driving system be divided into? Please briefly explain the function of each module.
3. Please briefly describe the composition of the high-definition map for an autonomous driving system and the role of the high-definition map.

4. What are the stages involved in reverse engineering? Please briefly introduce the role of each stage.
5. What are the two main types of surface reconstruction in reverse engineering?
6. Please list several types of robots that apply the point cloud technology.
7. Please list several key steps that use point cloud technology in the field of topography mapping.
8. Please give examples of several key applications of point cloud technology in the digital twin city.
9. Please give examples of the main sources of medical point clouds.
10. Please explain the commonly used 3D scanner and its principle in cultural relic scanning.

References

1. W. Gao, G. Li, H. Yuan, R. Hamzaoui, Z. Li, S. Liu, Apccpa'22: 1st international workshop on advances in point cloud compression, processing and analysis, in *Proceedings of the 30th ACM International Conference on Multimedia* (2022), pp. 7392–7393
2. Y. Sun, Z. Li, S. Wang, W. Gao, Depth-assisted calibration on learning-based factorization for a compressive light field display. Opt. Express **31**(4), 5399–5413 (2023)
3. Y. Sun, Z. Li, L. Li, S. Wang, W. Gao, Optimization of compressive light field display in dual-guided learning, in *ICASSP 2022-2022 IEEE International Conference on Acoustics, Speech and Signal Processing (ICASSP)* (IEEE, Piscataway, 2022), pp. 2075–2079
4. W. Gao, S. Fan, G. Li, W. Lin, A thorough benchmark and a new model for light field saliency detection. IEEE Trans. Pattern Anal. Mach. Intell. (2023).
5. L. Xie, W. Gao, S. Fan, Z. Yao, Pdnet: parallel dual-branch network for point cloud geometry compression and analysis, in *2024 Data Compression Conference (DCC)* (IEEE, Piscataway, 2024), pp. 596–596
6. Y. Shao, G. Li, Q. Zhang, W. Gao, S. Liu, Non-rigid registration-based progressive motion compensation for point cloud geometry compression. IEEE Trans. Geosci. Remote Sensing (2023)
7. Z. Yang, W. Gao, X. Lu, Danet: density-adaptive network for geometry-based point cloud compression artifacts removal, in *2023 IEEE International Conference on Visual Communications and Image Processing (VCIP)* (IEEE, Piscataway, 2023), pp. 1–5
8. B. Qu, X. Liang, S. Sun, W. Gao, Exploring AIGC video quality: a focus on visual harmony, video-text consistency and domain distribution gap, in *Proceedings of the IEEE/CVF Conference on Computer Vision and Pattern Recognition Workshops* (2024)
9. B. Qu, H. Li, W. Gao, Bringing textual prompt to ai-generated image quality assessment, in *2024 IEEE International Conference on Multimedia and Expo (ICME)* (IEEE, Piscataway, 2024)
10. Y. Wu, L. Xie, S. Sun, W. Gao, Y. Yan, Adaptive intra period size for deep learning-based screen content video coding, in *2024 IEEE International Conference on Multimedia and Expo Workshops (ICMEW)* (IEEE, Piscataway, 2024)
11. H. Zheng, W. Gao, End-to-end RGB-D image compression via exploiting channel-modality redundancy, in *Proceedings of the AAAI Conference on Artificial Intelligence*, vol. 38, no. 7 (2024), pp. 7562–7570
12. L. Tao, W. Gao, G. Li, C. Zhang, Adanic: towards practical neural image compression via dynamic transform routing, in *Proceedings of the IEEE/CVF International Conference on Computer Vision* (2023), pp. 16879–16888

13. Y. Wu, W. Gao, End-to-end lossless compression of high precision depth maps guided by pseudo-residual (2022). arXiv preprint arXiv:2201.03195
14. Y. Wu, Z. Qi, H. Zheng, L. Tao, W. Gao, Deep image compression with latent optimization and piece-wise quantization approximation, in *Proceedings of the IEEE/CVF Conference on Computer Vision and Pattern Recognition* (2021), pp. 1926–1930
15. W. Gao, L. Tao, L. Zhou, D. Yang, X. Zhang, Z. Guo, Low-rate image compression with super-resolution learning, in *Proceedings of the IEEE/CVF Conference on Computer Vision and Pattern Recognition Workshops* (2020), pp. 154–155
16. W. Gao, S. Sun, H. Zheng, Y. Wu, H. Ye, Y. Zhang, Opendmc: an open-source library and performance evaluation for deep-learning-based multi-frame compression, in *Proceedings of the 31st ACM International Conference on Multimedia* (2023), pp. 9685–9688
17. Y. Guo, W. Gao, G. Li, Interpretable task-inspired adaptive filter pruning for neural networks under multiple constraints. Int. J. Comput. Vis. **132**(6), 2060–2076 (2024)
18. W. Gao, Y. Guo, S. Ma, G. Li, S. Kwong, Efficient neural network compression inspired by compressive sensing. IEEE Trans. Neural Netw. Learn. Syst. **35**(2), 1965–1979 (2024)
19. Y. Guo, W. Gao, Semantic-driven automatic filter pruning for neural networks, in *2022 IEEE international conference on multimedia and expo (ICME)* (IEEE, Piscataway, 2022), pp. 1–6
20. L. Tao, W. Gao, Efficient channel pruning based on architecture alignment and probability model bypassing, in *2021 IEEE International Conference on Systems, Man, and Cybernetics (SMC)* (IEEE, Piscataway, 2021), pp. 3232–3237
21. Z. Yang, W. Gao, G. Li, Y. Yan, Sur-driven video coding rate control for jointly optimizing perceptual quality and buffer control. IEEE Trans. Image Process. **32**, 5451–5464 (2023)
22. F. Shen, Z. Cai, W. Gao, An efficient rate control algorithm for intra frame coding in AVS3, in *2021 IEEE International Conference on Systems, Man, and Cybernetics (SMC)* (IEEE, Piscataway, 2021), pp. 3164–3169
23. H. Yuan, W. Gao, J. Wang, Dynamic computational resource allocation for fast inter frame coding in video conferencing applications, in *2021 IEEE International Conference on Multimedia and Expo (ICME)* (IEEE, Piscataway, 2021), pp. 1–6
24. W. Gao, Q. Jiang, R. Wang, S. Ma, G. Li, S. Kwong, Consistent quality oriented rate control in hevc via balancing intra and inter frame coding. IEEE Trans. Ind. Inform. **18**(3), 1594–1604 (2021)
25. H. Yuan, W. Gao, A new coding unit partitioning mode for screen content video coding, in *Proceedings of the 2021 5th International Conference on Digital Signal Processing* (2021), pp. 66–72
26. W. Gao, On the performance evaluation of state-of-the-art rate control algorithms for practical video coding and transmission systems, in *Proceedings of the 2020 4th International Conference on Video and Image Processing* (2020), pp. 179–185
27. W. Gao, S. Kwong, Q. Jiang, C.-K. Fong, P.H. Wong, W. Y. Yuen, Data-driven rate control for rate-distortion optimization in HEVC based on simplified effective initial QP learning. IEEE Trans. Broadcasting **65**(1), 94–108 (2018)
28. W. Gao, A multi-objective optimization perspective for joint consideration of video coding quality, in *2019 Asia-Pacific Signal and Information Processing Association Annual Summit and Conference (APSIPA ASC)* (IEEE, Piscataway, 2019), pp. 986–991
29. W. Gao, S. Kwong, Y. Jia, Joint machine learning and game theory for rate control in high efficiency video coding. IEEE Trans. Image Process. **26**(12), 6074–6089 (2017)
30. W. Gao, S. Kwong, Y. Zhou, H. Yuan, Ssim-based game theory approach for rate-distortion optimized intra frame CTU-level bit allocation. IEEE Trans. Multimedia **18**(6), 988–999 (2016)
31. W. Gao, S. Kwong, H. Yuan, X. Wang, DCT coefficient distribution modeling and quality dependency analysis based frame-level bit allocation for HEVC. IEEE Trans. Circuits Syst. Video Technol. **26**(1), 139–153 (2015)
32. W. Gao, S. Kwong, Phase congruency based edge saliency detection and rate control for perceptual image and video coding, in *2016 IEEE International Conference on Systems, Man, and Cybernetics (SMC)* (IEEE, Piscataway, 2016), pp. 000264–000269

33. H. Yuan, W. Gao, Openfastvc: an open source library for video coding fast algorithm implementation, in *Proceedings of the 31st ACM International Conference on Multimedia* (2023), pp. 9660–9663
34. H. Yuan, W. Gao, S. Ma, Y. Yan, Divide-and-conquer-based RDO-free CU partitioning for 8k video compression. ACM Trans. Multimedia Comput. Commun. Appl. **20**(4), 1–20 (2024)
35. L. Tao, W. Gao, A hardware implementation of entropy encoder for 8k video coding, in *2022 IEEE International Conference on Multimedia and Expo (ICME)* (IEEE, Piscataway, 2022), pp. 1–6
36. Y. Guo, W. Gao, S. Ma, G. Li, Accelerating transform algorithm implementation for efficient intra coding of 8k UHD videos. ACM Trans. Multimedia Comput. Commun. Appl. **18**(4), 1–20 (2022)
37. Z. Cai, W. Gao, Efficient fast algorithm and parallel hardware architecture for intra prediction of AVS3, in *2021 IEEE International Symposium on Circuits and Systems (ISCAS)* (IEEE, Piscataway, 2021), pp. 1–5
38. W. Gao, H. Yuan, Y. Guo, L. Tao, Z. Cai, G. Li, Openhardwarevc: an open source library for 8k UHD video coding hardware implementation, in *Proceedings of the 30th ACM International Conference on Multimedia* (2022), pp. 7339–7342
39. W. Gao, H. Yuan, G. Liao, Z. Guo, J. Chen, Pp8k: a new dataset for 8k UHD video compression and processing. *IEEE MultiMedia* **30**(3), 100–109 (2023)
40. W. Liu, W. Gao, G. Li, S. Ma, T. Zhao, H. Yuan, Enlarged motion-aware and frequency-aware network for compressed video artifact reduction. IEEE Trans. Circuits Syst. Video Technol. **34**(10), 10339–10352 (2024)
41. X. Zang, W. Gao, G. Li, H. Fang, C. Ban, Z. He, H. Sun, A baseline investigation: transformer-based cross-view baseline for text-based person search, in *Proceedings of the 31st ACM International Conference on Multimedia* (2023), pp. 7737–7746
42. G. Liao, W. Gao, G. Li, J. Wang, S. Kwong, Cross-collaborative fusion-encoder network for robust RGB-thermal salient object detection. IEEE Trans. Circuits Syst. Video Technol. **32**(11), 7646–7661 (2022)
43. W. Gao, G. Liao, S. Ma, G. Li, Y. Liang, W. Lin, Unified information fusion network for multi-modal RGB-D and RGB-T salient object detection. IEEE Trans. Circuits Syst. Video Technol. **32**(4), 2091–2106 (2021)
44. Y. Chen, S. Sun, G. Li, W. Gao, T.H. Li, Closing the gap between theory and practice during alternating optimization for GANs. IEEE Trans. Neural Netw. Learn. Syst. **35**(10), 14005–14017 (2023)
45. Y. Chen, C. Jin, G. Li, T.H. Li, W. Gao, Mitigating label noise in GANs via enhanced spectral normalization. IEEE Trans. Circuits Syst. Video Technol. **33**(8), 3924–3934 (2023)
46. X. Zang, G. Li, W. Gao, Multidirection and multiscale pyramid in transformer for video-based pedestrian retrieval. IEEE Trans. Ind. Inform. **18**(12), 8776–8785 (2022)
47. X. Zang, G. Li, W. Gao, X. Shu, Learning to disentangle scenes for person re-identification. Image Vis. Comput. **116**, 104330 (2021)
48. X. Zang, G. Li, W. Gao, X. Shu, Exploiting robust unsupervised video person re-identification. IET Image Process. **16**(3), 729–741 (2022)
49. Z. Yue, G. Li, W. Gao, Cross-level guided attention for human-object interaction detection, in *2023 IEEE International Conference on Multimedia and Expo Workshops (ICMEW)* (IEEE, Piscataway, 2023), pp. 284–289
50. Z. Yao, W. Gao, Iterative saliency aggregation and assignment network for efficient salient object detection in optical remote sensing images. IEEE Trans. Geosci. Remote Sensing (2024)
51. Z. Li, G. Li, T. Li, S. Liu, W. Gao, Information-growth attention network for image super-resolution, in *Proceedings of the 29th ACM International Conference on Multimedia* (2021), pp. 544–552
52. L. Zhou, W. Gao, G. Li, H. Yuan, T. Zhao, G. Yue, Disentangled feature distillation for light field super-resolution with degradations, in *2023 IEEE International Conference on Multimedia and Expo Workshops (ICMEW)* (IEEE, Piscataway, 2023), pp. 116–121

53. L. Zhou, W. Gao, G. Li, End-to-end spatial-angular light field super-resolution using parallax structure preservation strategy, in *2022 IEEE International Conference on Image Processing (ICIP)* (IEEE, Piscataway, 2023), pp. 3396–3400
54. W. Gao, L. Zhou, L. Tao, A fast view synthesis implementation method for light field applications. ACM Trans. Multimedia Comput. Commun. Appl. **17**(4), 1–20 (2021)
55. X. Zhang, W. Gao, G. Li, Q. Jiang, R. Cong, Image quality assessment–driven reinforcement learning for mixed distorted image restoration. ACM Trans. Multimedia Comput. Commun. Appl. **19**(1s), 1–23 (2023)
56. X. Zhang, W. Gao, H. Yuan, G. Li, Je 2 net: joint exploitation and exploration in reinforcement learning based image restoration, in *ICASSP 2022-2022 IEEE International Conference on Acoustics, Speech and Signal Processing (ICASSP)* (IEEE, Piscataway, 2022), pp. 2090–2094
57. X. Zhang, W. Gao, Hirl: hybrid image restoration based on hierarchical deep reinforcement learning via two-step analysis, in *ICASSP 2022-2022 IEEE International Conference on Acoustics, Speech and Signal Processing (ICASSP)* (IEEE, Piscataway, 2022), pp. 2445–2449
58. Z. Guo, W. Gao, H. Wang, J. Wang, S. Fan, No-reference deep quality assessment of compressed light field images, in *2021 IEEE International Conference on Multimedia and Expo (ICME)* (IEEE, Piscataway, 2021), pp. 1–6
59. G. Liao, W. Gao, Rethinking feature mining for light field salient object detection. ACM Trans. Multimedia Comput. Commun. Appl. (2024)
60. S. Sun, J. Liu, T.H. Li, H. Li, G. Liu, W. Gao, Streamflow: streamlined multi-frame optical flow estimation for video sequences (2023). arXiv preprint arXiv:2311.17099
61. R. Liu, J. Huang, W. Gao, T.H. Li, G. Li, Mug-stan: adapting image-language pretrained models for general video understanding (2023). arXiv preprint arXiv:2311.15075
62. C. Zhang, W. Gao, Learned rate control for frame-level adaptive neural video compression via dynamic neural network, in *European Conference on Computer Vision* (Springer, Berlin, 2024)
63. T. Qin, G. Li, W. Gao, S. Liu, Multi-grained point cloud geometry compression via dual-model prediction with extended octree. ACM Trans. Multimedia Comput. Commun. Appl. (2024)
64. Y. Shao, W. Gao, S. Liu, G. Li, Advanced patch-based affine motion estimation for dynamic point cloud geometry compression. Sensors **24**(10), 3142 (2024)
65. Y. Shao, F. Song, W. Gao, S. Liu, G. Li, Texture-guided graph transform optimization for point cloud attribute compression. Appl. Sci. **14**(10), 4094 (2024)
66. Y. Shao, X. Yang, W. Gao, S. Liu, G. Li, 3d point cloud attribute compression using diffusion-based texture-aware intra prediction, in *IEEE Transactions on Circuits and Systems for Video Technology* (2024)
67. J. Zhang, Y. Chen, G. Liu, W. Gao, G. Li, Efficient point cloud attribute compression framework using attribute-guided graph Fourier transform, in *ICASSP 2024-2024 IEEE International Conference on Acoustics, Speech and Signal Processing (ICASSP)* (IEEE, Piscataway, 2024), pp. 8426–8430
68. W. Gao, H. Yuan, G. Li, Z. Li, H. Yuan, Low complexity coding unit decision for video-based point cloud compression. IEEE Trans. Image Proc. **33**, 149–162 (2023)
69. F. Song, G. Li, X. Yang, W. Gao, S. Liu, Block-adaptive point cloud attribute coding with region-aware optimized transform. IEEE Trans. Circuits Syst. Video Technol. **33**, 4294–4308 (2023)
70. Y. An, Y. Shao, G. Li, W. Gao, S. Liu, A fast motion estimation method with hamming distance for LiDAR point cloud compression, in *2022 IEEE International Conference on Visual Communications and Image Processing (VCIP)* (IEEE, Piscataway, 2022), pp. 1–5
71. H. Yuan, W. Gao, G. Li, Z. Li, Rate-distortion-guided learning approach with cross-projection information for V-PCC fast CU decision, in *Proceedings of the 30th ACM International Conference on Multimedia* (2022), pp. 3085–3093
72. F. Song, G. Li, W. Gao, T.H. Li, Rate-distortion optimized graph for point cloud attribute coding. IEEE Signal Process. Lett. **29**, 922–926 (2022)

73. F. Song, G. Li, X. Yang, W. Gao, T.H. Li, Fine-grained correlation representation for graph-based point cloud attribute compression, in *2022 IEEE International Conference on Multimedia and Expo (ICME)* (IEEE, Piscataway, 2022), pp. 1–6
74. F. Shen, W. Gao, A rate control algorithm for video-based point cloud compression, in *2021 International Conference on Visual Communications and Image Processing (VCIP)* (IEEE, Piscataway, 2021), pp. 1–5
75. F. Song, Y. Shao, W. Gao, H. Wang, T. Li, Layer-wise geometry aggregation framework for lossless LiDAR point cloud compression. IEEE Trans. Circuits Syst. Video Technol. **31**(12), 4603–4616 (2021)
76. L. Xie, W. Gao, H. Zheng, G. Li, Spcgc: scalable point cloud geometry compression for machine vision, in *Proceedings of IEEE International Conference on Robotics and Automation* (2024)
77. L. Xie, W. Gao, H. Zheng, H. Ye, Semantic-aware visual decomposition for point cloud geometry compression, in *2024 Data Compression Conference (DCC)* (IEEE, Piscataway, 2024), pp. 595–595
78. Z. Qi, W. Gao, Variable-rate point cloud geometry compression based on feature adjustment and interpolation, in *2024 Data Compression Conference (DCC)* (IEEE, Piscataway, 2024), pp. 63–72
79. Z. Yu, W. Gao, When dynamic neural network meets point cloud compression: computation-aware variable rate and checkerboard context, in *2024 Data Compression Conference (DCC)* (IEEE, Piscataway, 2024), p. 600
80. L. Xie, W. Gao, H. Zheng, End-to-end point cloud geometry compression and analysis with sparse tensor, in *Proceedings of the 1st International Workshop on Advances in Point Cloud Compression, Processing and Analysis* (2022), pp. 27–32
81. C. Fu, G. Li, R. Song, W. Gao, S. Liu, OctAttention: octree-based large-scale contexts model for point cloud compression, in *AAAI Conference on Artificial Intelligence* (2022), pp. 625–633
82. H. Zheng, W. Gao, Z. Yu, T. Zhao, G. Li, Viewpcgc: view-guided learned point cloud geometry compression, in *Proceedings of the 32nd ACM International Conference on Multimedia* (2024)
83. L. Xie, W. Gao, H. Zheng, G. Li, Roi-guided point cloud geometry compression towards human and machine vision, in *Proceedings of the 32nd ACM International Conference on Multimedia* (2024)
84. C. Peng, W. Gao, Laplacian matrix learning for point cloud attribute compression with ternary search-based adaptive block partition, in *Proceedings of the 32nd ACM International Conference on Multimedia* (2024)
85. S. Luo, B. Qu, W. Gao, Learning robust 3d representation from clip via dual denoising (2024). arXiv preprint arXiv:2407.00905
86. G. Li, G. Wei, W. Gao, *Point Cloud Compression: Technologies and Standardization* (Springer, Berlin, 2024)
87. G. Li, W. Gao, W. Gao, Introduction, in *Point Cloud Compression: Technologies and Standardization* (Springer, Berlin, 2024), pp. 1–28
88. G. Li, W. Gao, W. Gao, Background knowledge, in *Point Cloud Compression: Technologies and Standardization* (Springer, Berlin, 2024), pp. 29–51
89. G. Li, W. Gao, W. Gao, Predictive coding, in *Point Cloud Compression: Technologies and Standardization* (Springer, Berlin, 2024), pp. 53–70
90. G. Li, W. Gao, W. Gao, Transform coding, in *Point Cloud Compression: Technologies and Standardization* (Springer, Berlin, 2024), pp. 71–96
91. G. Li, W. Gao, W. Gao, Quantization techniques, in *Point Cloud Compression: Technologies and Standardization* (Springer, Berlin, 2024), pp. 97–112
92. G. Li, W. Gao, W. Gao, Entropy coding, in *Point Cloud Compression: Technologies and Standardization* (Springer, Berlin, 2024), pp. 113–133
93. G. Li, W. Gao, W. Gao, MPEG geometry-based point cloud compression (G-PCC) standard, in *Point Cloud Compression: Technologies and Standardization* (Springer, Berlin, 2024), pp. 135–165

94. G. Li, W. Gao, W. Gao, AVS point cloud compression standard, in *Point Cloud Compression: Technologies and Standardization* (Springer, Berlin, 2024), pp. 167–197
95. G. Li, W. Gao, W. Gao, MPEG video-based point cloud compression (V-PCC) standard, in *Point Cloud Compression: Technologies and Standardization* (Springer, Berlin, 2024), pp. 199–218
96. G. Li, W. Gao, W. Gao, MPEG Ai-based 3d graphics coding standard, in *Point Cloud Compression: Technologies and Standardization* (Springer, Berlin, 2024), pp. 219–241
97. G. Li, W. Gao, W. Gao, Future work, in *Point Cloud Compression: Technologies and Standardization* (Springer, Berlin, 2024), pp. 243–250
98. W. Liu, W. Gao, X. Mu, Fast inter-frame motion prediction for compressed dynamic point cloud attribute enhancement, in *Proceedings of the AAAI Conference on Artificial Intelligence*, vol. 38, no. 4 (2024), pp. 3720–3728
99. X. Fan, G. Li, D. Li, Y. Ren, W. Gao, T.H. Li, Deep geometry post-processing for decompressed point clouds, in *2022 IEEE International Conference on Multimedia and Expo (ICME)* (IEEE, Piscataway, 2022), pp. 1–6
100. X. Zhang, G. Liao, W. Gao, G. Li, Tdrnet: Transformer-based dual-branch restoration network for geometry based point cloud compression artifacts, in *2022 IEEE International Conference on Multimedia and Expo (ICME)* (IEEE, Piscataway, 2022), pp. 1–6
101. Z. Li, G. Li, T.H. Li, S. Liu, W. Gao, Semantic point cloud upsampling. IEEE Trans. Multimedia **25**, 3432–3442 (2022)
102. R. Zhang, W. Gao, G. Li, T.H. Li, Qinet: decision surface learning and adversarial enhancement for quasi-immune completion of diverse corrupted point clouds. IEEE Trans. Geosci. Remote Sensing **60**, 1–14 (2022)
103. R. Bao, Y. Ren, G. Li, W. Gao, S. Liu, Flow-based point cloud completion network with adversarial refinement, in *ICASSP 2022-2022 IEEE International Conference on Acoustics, Speech and Signal Processing (ICASSP)* (IEEE, Piscataway, 2022), pp. 2559–2563
104. J. Chen, G. Li, R. Zhang, T.H. Li, W. Gao, Pointivae: invertible variational autoencoder framework for 3d point cloud generation, in *2022 IEEE International Conference on Image Processing (ICIP)* (IEEE, Piscataway, 2022), pp. 3216–3220
105. R. Zhang, J. Chen, W. Gao, G. Li, T.H. Li, Pointot: interpretable geometry-inspired point cloud generative model via optimal transport. IEEE Trans. Circuits Syst. Video Technol. **32**(10), 6792–6806 (2022)
106. S. Fan, W. Gao, G. Li, Salient object detection for point clouds, in *European Conference on Computer Vision* (2022), pp. 1–19
107. S. Luo, W. Gao, A general framework for rotation invariant point cloud analysis, in *ICASSP 2024-2024 IEEE International Conference on Acoustics, Speech and Signal Processing (ICASSP)* (IEEE, Piscataway, 2024), pp. 3665–3669
108. X. Lu and W. Gao, Attentivenet: detecting small objects for LiDAR point clouds by attending to important points, in *2023 IEEE International Conference on Visual Communications and Image Processing (VCIP)* (IEEE, Piscataway, 2023), pp. 1–5
109. Z. Pan, N. Zhang, W. Gao, S. Liu, G. Li, Less is more: label recommendation for weakly supervised point cloud semantic segmentation, in *Proceedings of the AAAI Conference on Artificial Intelligence*, vol. 38, no. 5 (2024), pp. 4397–4405
110. Z. Pan, G. Liu, W. Gao, T. Li, Epcontrast: effective point-level contrastive learning for large-scale point cloud understanding, in *2024 IEEE International Conference on Multimedia and Expo (ICME)* (IEEE, Piscataway, 2024)
111. N. Zhang, Z. Pan, T.H. Li, W. Gao, G. Li, Improving graph representation for point cloud segmentation via attentive filtering, in *Proceedings of the IEEE/CVF Conference on Computer Vision and Pattern Recognition* (2023), pp. 1244–1254
112. K. Wen, N. Zhang, G. Li, W. Gao, MPVNN: multi-resolution point-voxel non-parametric network for 3d point cloud processing, in *2024 IEEE International Conference on Multimedia and Expo (ICME)* (IEEE, Piscataway, 2024)
113. D. Yang, W. Gao, G. Li, H. Yuan, J. Hou, S. Kwong, Exploiting manifold feature representation for efficient classification of 3d point clouds. ACM Trans. Multimedia Comput. Commun. Appl. **19**(1s), 1–21 (2023)

114. S. Fan, W. Gao, Screen-based 3d subjective experiment software, in *Proceedings of the 31st ACM International Conference on Multimedia* (2023), pp. 9672–9675
115. X. Mao, H. Yuan, X. Lu, R. Hamzaoui, W. Gao, PCAC-GAN: a sparse-tensor-based generative adversarial network for 3d point cloud attribute compression. Computational Visual Media (2024)
116. J. Wang, W. Gao, G. Li, Applying collaborative adversarial learning to blind point cloud quality measurement. IEEE Trans. Instrument. Measur. (2023)
117. W. Gao, H. Ye, G. Li, H. Zheng, Y. Wu, L. Xie, OpenPointCloud: an open-source algorithm library of deep learning based point cloud compression, in *ACM International Conference on Multimedia* (2022), pp. 7347–7350
118. Y. Zhang, W. Gao, G. Li, Openpointcloud-v2: a deep learning based open-source algorithm library of point cloud processing, in *Proceedings of the 1st International Workshop on Advances in Point Cloud Compression, Processing and Analysis* (2022), pp. 51–55
119. Y. Wang, W. Gao, X. Mu, H. Yuan, Rate control optimization for joint geometry and attribute coding of LiDAR point clouds, in *2023 IEEE International Conference on Visual Communications and Image Processing (VCIP)* (IEEE, Piscataway, 2023), pp. 1–5
120. R. Zhang, G. Li, W. Gao, T.H. Li, Compoint: can complex-valued representation benefit point cloud place recognition? IEEE Trans. Intell. Transp. Syst. **25**(7), 7494–7507 (2024)
121. J.-X. Zhuang, X. Huang, Y. Yang, J. Chen, Y. Yu, W. Gao, G. Li, J. Chen, T. Zhang, Open-media: open-source medical image analysis toolbox and benchmark under heterogeneous ai computing platforms, in *Chinese Conference on Pattern Recognition and Computer Vision (PRCV)* (Springer, Berlin, 2022), pp. 356–367
122. H.G. Seif, X. Hu, Autonomous driving in the iCITY–HD maps as a key challenge of the automotive industry. Engineering **2**(2), 159–162 (2016)
123. P. Sun, H. Kretzschmar, X. Dotiwalla, A. Chouard, V. Patnaik, P. Tsui, J. Guo, Y. Zhou, Y. Chai, B. Caine et al., Scalability in perception for autonomous driving: Waymo open dataset, in *Proceedings of the IEEE/CVF Conference on Computer Vision and Pattern Recognition* (2020), pp. 2446–2454
124. H. Caesar, V. Bankiti, A.H. Lang, S. Vora, V.E. Liong, Q. Xu, A. Krishnan, Y. Pan, G. Baldan, O. Beijbom, nuscenes: a multimodal dataset for autonomous driving, in *Proceedings of the IEEE/CVF Conference on Computer Vision and Pattern Recognition* (2020), pp. 11621–11631
125. J. Mao, M. Niu, C. Jiang, H. Liang, J. Chen, X. Liang, Y. Li, C. Ye, W. Zhang, Z. Li et al., One million scenes for autonomous driving: once dataset (2021). arXiv preprint arXiv:2106.11037
126. A. Geiger, P. Lenz, R. Urtasun, Are we ready for autonomous driving? The KITTI vision benchmark suite, in *IEEE Conference on Computer Vision and Pattern Recognition* (2012), pp. 3354–3361
127. S. Chen, B. Liu, C. Feng, C. Vallespi-Gonzalez, C. Wellington, 3D point cloud processing and learning for autonomous driving: impacting map creation, localization, and perception. IEEE Signal Process. Mag. **38**(1), 68–86 (2021)
128. T. Varady, R.R. Martin, J. Cox, Reverse engineering of geometric models–an introduction. Comput-aided Design **29**(4), 255–268 (1997)
129. Y. Zhou, S. Kwong, W. Gao, X. Zhang, X. Wang, Complexity reduction in multi-dictionary based single-image superresolution reconstruction via phase congruency, in *2015 International Conference on Wavelet Analysis and Pattern Recognition (ICWAPR)* (IEEE, Piscataway, 2015), pp. 146–151
130. J. Zeng, G. Cheung, M. Ng, J. Pang, C. Yang, 3d point cloud denoising using graph Laplacian regularization of a low dimensional manifold model. IEEE Trans. Image Processing **29**, 3474–3489 (2019)
131. J. Borenstein, Y. Koren, Obstacle avoidance with ultrasonic sensors. IEEE J. Robot. Autom. **4**(2), 213–218 (1988)
132. E.M. Gorostiza, J.L. Lázaro Galilea, F.J. Meca Meca, D. Salido Monzú, F. Espinosa Zapata, L. Pallarés Puerto, Infrared sensor system for mobile-robot positioning in intelligent spaces. Sensors **11**(5), 5416–5438 (2011)

133. P.K. Mohanty, A.K. Singh, A. Kumar, M.K. Mahto, S. Kundu, Path planning techniques for mobile robots: a review, in *Proceedings of the International Conference on Soft Computing and Pattern Recognition* (2021), pp. 657–667
134. P. Kim, J. Chen, Y.K. Cho, Slam-driven robotic mapping and registration of 3d point clouds. Autom. Construct. **89**, 38–48 (2018)
135. L.E. Weiss, A.C. Sanderson, C.P. Neuman, Dynamic visual servo control of robots: an adaptive image-based approach, in *Proceedings of the IEEE International Conference on Robotics and Automation*, vol. 2 (1985), pp. 662–668
136. C. Kingkan, S. Ito, S. Arai, T. Nammoto, K. Hashimoto, Model-based virtual visual servoing with point cloud data, in *Proceedings of the IEEE/RSJ International Conference on Intelligent Robots and Systems* (2016), pp. 5549–5555
137. A. Bulgakov, D. Sayfeddine, Air conditioning ducts inspection and cleaning using telerobotics. Proc. Eng. **164**, 121–126 (2016)
138. C.H. Bahnsen, A.S. Johansen, M.P. Philipsen, J.W. Henriksen, K. Nasrollahi, T.B. Moeslund, 3d sensors for sewer inspection: a quantitative review and analysis. Sensors **21**(7), 2553 (2021)
139. T. Deng, K. Zhang, Z.-J.M. Shen, A systematic review of a digital twin city: a new pattern of urban governance toward smart cities. J. Manag. Sci. Eng. **6**(2), 125–134 (2021)
140. S.I. El-Halawany, D.D. Lichti, Detection of road poles from mobile terrestrial laser scanner point cloud, in *Proceedings of the International Workshop on Multi-Platform/Multi-Sensor Remote Sensing and Mapping* (2011), pp. 1–6
141. H. Kim, J. Yoon, S.-H. Sim, Automated bridge component recognition from point clouds using deep learning. Struct. Control Health Monitor. **27**(9), e2591 (2020)
142. T. Kedia, J. Ratcliff, M. O'Connor, S. Oluic, M. Rose, J. Freeman, K. Rainwater-Lovett, Technologies enabling situational awareness during disaster response: a systematic review. Disaster Med. Public Health Preparedness **16**(1), 341–359 (2022)
143. S. Verykokou, A. Doulamis, G. Athanasiou, C. Ioannidis, A. Amditis, Uav-based 3d modelling of disaster scenes for urban search and rescue, in *Proceedings of the IEEE International Conference on Imaging Systems and Techniques (IST)* (2016), pp. 106–111
144. L. Li, C. Liu, A new approach for estimating living vegetation volume based on terrestrial point cloud data. PLOS One **14**(8), e0221734 (2019)
145. F. Piccialli, V. Di Somma, F. Giampaolo, S. Cuomo, G. Fortino, A survey on deep learning in medicine: why, how and when? Inform. Fusion **66**, 111–137 (2021)
146. M. Li, Z. Yu, X. Liu, R. Yan, Y. Yu, D. Wang, J. Chen, J. Lu, P. Qi, J. Wang et al., Progress of point cloud algorithm in medical field. J. Image Graph. **25**(10), 2013–2023 (2020)
147. T. Boers, Y. Hu, E. Gibson, D. Barratt, E. Bonmati, J. Krdzalic, F. van der Heijden, J. Hermans, H. Huisman, Interactive 3d u-net for the segmentation of the pancreas in computed tomography scans. Phys. Med. Biol. **65**(6), 065002 (2020)
148. Z. Rao, S. Sun, M. Li, X. Ji, J. Huang, 3d facial plastic surgery simulation: based on the structured light. Appl. Sci. **13**(1), 659 (2023)
149. T. Ma, Y. Li, Z. Li, A survey of three-dimensional reconstruction methods for tooth models, in *Proceedings of the IEEE International Conference on Signal Processing, Communications and Computing* (2018), pp. 1–6
150. W. Li, Y.-J. Zhang, Y. Hu, Q. Chen, W. Tang, H. Wang, Combination of laser-point cloud and reverse engineering to rapidly establish a three-dimensional soft tissue model in cosmetic surgery. Chin. J. Tissue Eng. Res. **19**(15), 2346 (2015)
151. X. Chen, Z. Song, M. Wang, Automated global optimization surface-matching registration method for image-to-patient spatial registration in an image-guided neurosurgery system. J. Med. Imaging Health Inform.**4**(6), 942–947 (2014)
152. R. Schaffert, J. Wang, P. Fischer, A. Borsdorf, A. Maier, Metric-driven learning of correspondence weighting for 2-d/3-d image registration, in *Proceedings of the German Conference on Pattern Recognition* (2018), pp. 140–152

Chapter 11
Future Work on Deep Learning-Based Point Cloud Technologies

Abstract Although deep learning-based point cloud technologies have achieved significant progress during the past decade, lots of further investigations are still needed due to opportunities given by recent remarkable advances in deep learning and artificial intelligence. In this chapter, we discuss future works in the relevant research fields, including point cloud enhancement, point cloud analysis, pre-trained model and large model, generative model, multi-modal large model and embodied intelligence, open-source project for point cloud technologies, and point cloud engineering applications.

Keywords Point cloud technologies · Deep learning · Point cloud enhancement · Point cloud analysis · Large model and multi-modal large model · Open-source project and engineering applications

11.1 Introduction

Besides image and video technologies [1–58], point cloud technologies have become vital in various fields, such as computer vision, robotics, and autonomous systems. However, ongoing developments of deep learning-based point cloud processing present new opportunities for continued research [59, 60].

First, a central area of future research is point cloud quality enhancement. Point cloud data can witness various degradation situations, such as compression, noise, part missing, spatial and temporal downsampling, etc. Therefore, technologies of quality enhancement, including compression artifacts removal [61–64], denoising, completion [65, 66], upsampling [67], and frame interpolation, become very importance for the practical use of point cloud data. More accurate and coherent point cloud data can bring better human and machine perceptions.

Second, another critical aspect for future exploration is deep learning-based point cloud analysis with advanced modeling techniques. This includes developing more sophisticated object detection [68], classification [69], and segmentation [70–73] methods for performance improvements in autonomous driving, robotics, augmented reality, etc. Future work on pre-trained and large-scale models can

W. Gao, G. Li, *Deep Learning for 3D Point Clouds*,
https://doi.org/10.1007/978-981-97-9570-3_11

enhance transfer learning and generalization across different point cloud tasks. Meanwhile, recent advances in generative models, multi-modal large models, and embodied intelligence can offer a new path for point cloud data generation, multi-modal integration, and AI interaction with the physical world.

Finally, open-source projects [9, 26, 74, 75] and point cloud engineering applications require much more attention. Open-source collaboration facilitates development and sharing of tools, datasets, and algorithms, which can efficiently accelerates technological innovations. Future work on point cloud engineering applications could refine current use cases and uncover new ones, thereby expanding the benefits of point cloud technologies to human society. By addressing these various aspects, researchers can continue to advance the field of deep learning-based point cloud processing, leading to broader adoptions and innovative applications.

Next, we will provide a detailed explanation for future research directions in point cloud technologies.

11.2 Future Work on Point Cloud Enhancement

Quality enhancement is always one of the key research problems for visual media [33, 47–53]. Similarly, point cloud enhancement will undertake processing tasks in various point cloud-based systems. Although point cloud compression task is also highly related to the quality [54, 76–78], which is similar to point cloud enhancement, we will discuss neither non-learning-based compression methods [79–92] nor learning-based compression methods [93–99]. According to the applications, there are three trends for the research of point cloud enhancement technologies.

The first trend is how to improve robustness. Because noise and distortion inevitably exist in data collection and transmission in the real world, pre-processing and post-processing have to face a certain number of "unseen" point clouds. However, due to limited training samples, existing learning-based methods tend to overfit some specific distributions. If a model is trained in an online mode that constantly updates parameters according to the new data, it easily causes catastrophic forgetting problem that the model will achieve declined performance in the original data. An appropriate consideration is combining deep learning model and optimization method, and making the output of the model depends on the current data distribution.

The second trend is how to build connections with compression tasks. Compression is an indispensable task in practical multimedia systems, including image and video coding [3–9, 14–31, 31] and point cloud compression [79–115]. Point cloud enhancement can be deemed a pre-processing or post-processing task for compression. The processing is not only unilaterally serving the compression, but also compression can give feedback to pre-processing tasks or provide guidance with prior knowledge to the post-processing tasks. For example, if the downsampling algorithm knows what point clouds are suitable for compression, it will indirectly improve compression efficiency. While for the point cloud upsampling, it also needs to learn the distribution of compressed point clouds or makes sure that the frequency information after transformation in compression is used to guide which areas to focus. Hence, the training of compression, upsampling, and other downstream tasks should be jointly conducted, and the loss functions with its optimizing strategy should also be combined in an end-to-end manner.

The last trend is to regard the image enhancement task as a generative task, although this involves the quality evaluation problem of Artificial Intelligence–generated content (AIGC) [1, 2, 77, 78]. The large model technology equipped with Pretrain-Prompt-Predict Paradigm has been widely used in speech processing, text prediction, and image and video generation tasks. One approach is to design a unified point cloud generation [116, 117] framework to simultaneously process low-quality degraded point clouds based on prompt words or descriptions of degradation methods related to specific enhancement tasks. Another approach is to use self-supervised learning technology, which enables a large language model to predict certain properties or transformations of point cloud data. In this way, the model can learn the representation of point cloud data and generate outputs similar to the enhanced data.

11.3 Future Work on Point Cloud Analysis

Point cloud analysis, a critical aspect of 3D computer vision, is rapidly evolving with advancements in deep learning and 3D scanning technologies. The potential future work in this domain can be broadly categorized into the following areas.

The first work is the investigation of point cloud object retrieval. Point cloud object retrieval is gaining prominence, especially for applications requiring identification and extraction of objects from large-scale spatial datasets. Unlike 2D data systems, point cloud systems must effectively handle unstructured 3D data, encapsulating geometric and topological information. The future work can focus on developing more sophisticated similarity measures to deal with irregularities inherent in point cloud data, such as varying point densities, occlusions, and noise from 3D scanning devices.

The second work is improving robustness and efficiency in point cloud registration. Point cloud registration, which is vital for 3D reconstruction, localization, and pose estimation, faces challenges like noise, outliers, partial overlaps, scale variation, and density differences. Future research can explore optimization-based methods and deep learning methods to enhance the robustness and efficiency of point cloud registration, especially in complex and noisy environments. Moreover, there is a growing interest in end-to-end learning methods for point cloud registration. These methods, which integrate transformation estimation with feature learning, can be further developed to handle complex registration scenarios more efficiently. The integration of point clouds from different sensor types introduces additional complexities such as varying noise levels, density differences, and scale variations. Future work can include developing advanced algorithms to estimate the final transformation in cross-source registration tasks. Other point cloud analysis tasks have similar robustness problems to handle [68, 118].

The last work is overcoming limitations of LiDAR Data. The efficacy of LiDAR data, often affected by environmental conditions such as fog and heavy rain, can be enhanced. Future work can explore methods to compensate for data deficiencies inherent in unimodal LiDAR situations, potentially through the integration of multi-modal data sources. Multi-modal learning, which combines data from different sensor types, is becoming increasingly relevant in real-world scenarios. Future research can focus on leveraging multiple data types to provide complementary information, thereby improving performance of learning models in diverse applications like autonomous driving and urban planning.

11.4 Future Work on Point Cloud-Based Pre-trained Model and Large Model

Self-supervised pre-training has shown great potential for pre-training point cloud data. However, several challenges remain because of complex structures and diverse tasks of point clouds. Each of these elements plays a crucial role in enhancing effectiveness and efficiency of 3D data processing.

The first element is the unified backbone network design. The concept of a unified backbone network in point cloud models is pivotal for future advancements. The current landscape of point cloud processing involves a diverse array of architectures tailored for specific tasks like segmentation, classification, or detection. However, a unified backbone network aims to establish a versatile, scalable, and efficient architecture that can handle multiple tasks without the need for significant modifications or separate models. This approach is inspired by the success of unified networks in 2D image processing, such as convolutional neural networks (CNNs) that have been effectively adapted for various tasks. In the context of point cloud models, a unified backbone would facilitate easier transfer learning, reduce computational costs, and streamline model development. Future research might focus on developing such networks that can inherently process point cloud data while being adaptable to a range of applications, from autonomous driving to augmented reality.

The second element is higher-quality training dataset. The quality of training datasets is paramount in the development of more advanced point cloud models. Currently, one of the challenges in point cloud processing is the limited availability of large-scale, high-quality, annotated datasets. Unlike 2D images, 3D point cloud data requires more complex and detailed annotations, which are resource-intensive to produce. Future research and development are expected to focus on creating richer datasets that not only have a higher volume of points but also contain more diverse and complex annotations. This includes datasets that cover a wider range of scenarios, environments, and objects, as well as those that provide more detailed annotations, such as finer object boundaries and more comprehensive class labels. Enhanced datasets will significantly improve the training of point cloud models, leading to better performance and generalizability.

The last element is inheriting multi-modal information [34–36]. Integrating multi-modal information is another crucial direction for future research. Point cloud data, when used in isolation, can be limited in terms of the information it provides. However, when combined with other data modalities such as images, videos, or sensor data, it can offer a much richer context for analysis and interpretation. The challenge lies in effectively merging these different types of data in a way that enhances, rather than complicates, the learning process. Future models may focus on developing more sophisticated methods for multi-modal data fusion, enabling models to leverage strengths of each data type. This can involve creating new neural network architectures that are specifically designed for multi-modal data or developing better techniques for aligning and integrating data from different sources.

11.5 Future Work on Point Cloud-Based Generative Model, Multi-modal Large Model, and Embodied Intelligence

As we progress in the field of artificial intelligence, the next frontier involves profound enhancements across generative models [37, 37, 38, 38], multi-modal large models, and . These areas are not only expanding in scope but also becoming more interconnected, reflecting the complexity and integrative potential of future AI systems.

Generative models, which have already revolutionized tasks ranging from automated content creation to drug discovery, are poised for further breakthroughs. The primary focus will be on refining these models to generate outputs that are not only more accurate but also more diverse. This involves addressing and mitigating biases presented in training data, which can often skew model outputs in undesirable ways. Furthermore, enhancing the efficiency of these models is critical, particularly for applications requiring real-time processing. Another significant area of development will be improving the interpretability of these models. As AI systems are increasingly deployed in sensitive areas, it is crucial to understand how and why certain decisions or outputs are generated. This transparency will help build trust and facilitate broader adoption in critical sectors such as healthcare, law, and public policy.

Multi-modal large models represent another exciting area of AI developments. These models process and integrate multiple types of data, including text, images, audios, and more, to make accurate decisions. The challenge here is to improve the interaction between different modalities so that AI can provide a more seamless and effective response. Future research will explore new architectures that allow for better data fusion techniques, which could reduce computational demands of these systems while boosting their performances.

Embodied intelligence, where AI is integrated into physical entities, allows for direct interaction with the physical world. The future in this domain involves creating more autonomous systems capable of sophisticated decision-making and interactions in dynamic environments. Advances in sensor technology, motion planning, and algorithms for environment manipulation will be essential. Moreover, integrating emotional intelligence into these systems could revolutionize various industries, including robotics, where machines that can perceive and react to human emotional states will provide more natural and effective interactions.

The integration of these three domains, i.e., generative models, multi-modal systems, and embodied intelligence, can lead to the development of highly advanced, efficient, and responsive AI systems. However, this technological advancement must be matched with rigorous ethical considerations. As AI becomes more capable and widespread, ensuring that these systems are developed and deployed responsibly becomes paramount. This includes establishing strong regulatory frameworks and ethical guidelines to prevent misuse and ensure that AI advancements benefit society as a whole.

In conclusion, the journey ahead for AI research and application is filled with opportunities to fundamentally reshape our interaction with technology. By advancing generative models, multi-modal large models, and embodied intelligence, we can create more intelligent, efficient, and empathetic systems. However, the success of these endeavors will largely depend on our ability to navigate the ethical landscapes, ensuring that AI serves the common good and enhances rather than undermines human dignity and agency.

11.6 Future Work on Open-Source Projects for Point Cloud Technologies

We have established a typical open-source project named OpenPointCloud [74, 75]. From the perspective of open source, the future research work of point cloud open-source projects can focus on the following aspects:

Community Participation and Development We encourage more developers and researchers to participate in the point cloud open-source community to jointly promote the development of point cloud technologies. Through the interaction and collaboration of open-source community, knowledge sharing and technological exchanges can be promoted, driving the continuous innovation and improvement of point cloud technologies.

Open-Source Tool and Framework Development We can develop and promote more point cloud processing tools and frameworks, including tools for point cloud data acquisition, pre-processing, feature extraction, semantic understanding, etc. By providing easy-to-use open-source tools and frameworks, the threshold of point cloud processing can be lowered, accelerating the popularization and application of technologies.

Open-Source Dataset Creation and Maintenance It is important to establish and maintain public point cloud datasets to promote the development of data-driven point cloud technologies. Through sharing and use of open-source datasets, the optimization of point cloud algorithms and application innovations can be promoted.

Cross Platform and Scalability We can optimize existing point cloud open-source projects to enable cross-platform operation and scalability. By achieving cross-platform support and scalability, the needs of different users and application scenarios can be satisfied, promoting widespread application of point cloud technologies. We have implemented this for OpenPointCloud [74, 75] and OpenAICoding (i.e., OpenDMC [9]).

Diversification of Open-Source Licenses With the popularity of open source, the diversification of open-source licenses will become a trend. Different open-source licenses will be selected based on the characteristics and needs of the projects, which will help protect the rights and interests of developers while promoting the sharing and communication of projects.

Security and Privacy Protection Under the premise of open source, ensure the security and privacy protection of point cloud data to prevent data leakage and misuse. By adopting secure programming practices and encryption technology, the privacy of users and the security of data can be guaranteed.

Sustainability and Long-Term Maintenance We can ensure the sustainability and long-term maintenance of point cloud open-source projects. By establishing a sustainable maintenance and update mechanism, the stability and long-term development of the projects can be ensured.

Open-Source Projects for Large Models As data increases and models become more complex, privacy and security issues will become important considerations for open-source projects for large models. Developers will need to pay more attention to data protection and model encryption to ensure the security and reliability of the projects.

11.7 Future Work on Point Cloud-Based Engineering Applications

Point cloud is an essential tool for 3D modeling in various industries, such as autonomous driving, reverse engineering, robotics, topography mapping, digital twin city, medical analysis and digital museum, etc. Due to the limitations of current sensing technologies and the needs of practical applications, there is still much work to be done.

In autonomous driving, point clouds can represent the environment of the vehicle in terms of 3D points, allowing vehicle sensors to perceive its surroundings accurately. The development of autonomous technologies based on point cloud should develop in these ways. First, future works should improve robustness. In order to ensure safety, the autonomous driving algorithm that can be put into use needs to have a good performance of corner case. Second, autonomous driving algorithm should consider the speed. Driving scenarios require efficient reasoning processes.

In reverse engineering, point cloud technologies play an important role in point cloud denoising, point cloud simplification, and surface reconstruction. Information like geometric regularities and dimensions could allow a more effective reconstruction.

Point clouds are also useful for robots to navigate through an environment by providing a 3D representation of objects and obstacles. This may benefit the development of embodied AI, which can interact with the environment to make decision and plan. Some novel works have made some efforts in this aspect and find that point clouds can provide richer information than images for learning obstacle avoidance. However, there are still some problems to be solved, e.g., limitation of capacity, multi-task learning, and robustness.

Topography mapping is another significant use case of point clouds, where they can create an accurate representation of the land surface, including buildings, vegetation, and other natural or artificial features. However, most methods use unmanned aerial vehicle (UAVs) as sensor. Compared with other methods like GPS point survey and laser scanner, the level of details given by UAVs is less accurate, sparser, and slower. Besides, slope crests, water reflection, and even suspended dust may decrease the quality of point clouds. To solve the problem, users need to shoot more points and use post-processing algorithms. Figuring out a suitable method to gain accurate point data will save time and effort.

Point clouds are instrumental in creating a digital twin city, where a virtual replication of a city can be used to make informed decisions about its physical infrastructure and its future growth. However, data management is still a problem, where how to balance accuracy and data capacity should be considered carefully. The large scale of urban scenes makes point cloud processing and modeling time-consuming, which calls for efficient algorithm solutions.

Medical analysis is another important use case of point clouds. It helps disease diagnosis, postoperative simulation, auxiliary diagnosis, targeted therapy, and remote surgery. In the field of medical field, research is limited by the difficulty of data collection and annotation. Compared with the natural scene point cloud, the medical point cloud has characteristics of complex surface and internal structure, and thus, mainstream point cloud characterization methods cannot model it well.

Digital museums employ various technologies to accurately record and preserve information about the shape, texture, and materials of artifacts. It require optimal 3D preparation of digital exhibits, which may be difficult for some immovable and fragile exhibits. Therefore, specific algorithms should be designed to gain efficient data of culture heritages.

Therefore, point clouds are incredibly beneficial in providing accurate and high-resolution data for a variety of applications. However, depending on the scenarios, many challenges of point cloud processing algorithms need to be better solved. Additionally, model compression and acceleration methods [10–13] are expected to be developed better to cater for data distribution characteristics, task requirements, and involved networks of point clouds.

11.8 Summary

This chapter explores future works in deep learning-based point cloud processing. It covers several critical areas where advancements are anticipated. Point cloud enhancement remains a priority, focusing on noise reduction and efficient integration with compression tasks. Deep learning-based point cloud analysis opens opportunities for improving object retrieval, registration, and multi-modal learning, with advancements in cross-source data processing. Research on pre-trained models and large models stresses the need for a unified backbone network and higher-quality training datasets. Potentials for generative models, multi-modal large models, and embodied intelligence are also noted, with implications for synthetic data generation and AI interaction with the physical world. Open-source projects play a crucial role in promoting the adoption of point cloud technologies, suggesting that future work should prioritize community engagement, cross-platform compatibility, and data security. Finally, typical point cloud applications are discussed, from autonomous driving and reverse engineering to medical analysis and digital museums. While point clouds are highly beneficial for various applications, many challenges of point cloud processing algorithms still require further research efforts.

References

1. B. Qu, X. Liang, S. Sun, W. Gao, Exploring AIGC video quality: a focus on visual harmony, video-text consistency and domain distribution gap, in *Proceedings of the IEEE/CVF Conference on Computer Vision and Pattern Recognition Workshops* (2024)
2. B. Qu, H. Li, W. Gao, Bringing textual prompt to ai-generated image quality assessment, in *2024 IEEE International Conference on Multimedia and Expo (ICME)* (IEEE, Piscataway, 2024)
3. Y. Wu, L. Xie, S. Sun, W. Gao, Y. Yan, Adaptive intra period size for deep learning-based screen content video coding, in *2024 IEEE International Conference on Multimedia and Expo Workshops (ICMEW)* (IEEE, Piscataway, 2024)
4. H. Zheng, W. Gao, End-to-end RGB-D image compression via exploiting channel-modality redundancy, in *Proceedings of the AAAI Conference on Artificial Intelligence*, vol. 38, no. 7 (2024), pp. 7562–7570

5. L. Tao, W. Gao, G. Li, C. Zhang, Adanic: towards practical neural image compression via dynamic transform routing, in *Proceedings of the IEEE/CVF International Conference on Computer Vision* (2023), pp. 16879–16888
6. Y. Wu, W. Gao, End-to-end lossless compression of high precision depth maps guided by pseudo-residual (2022). arXiv preprint arXiv:2201.03195
7. Y. Wu, Z. Qi, H. Zheng, L. Tao, W. Gao, Deep image compression with latent optimization and piece-wise quantization approximation, in *Proceedings of the IEEE/CVF Conference on Computer Vision and Pattern Recognition* (2021), pp. 1926–1930
8. W. Gao, L. Tao, L. Zhou, D. Yang, X. Zhang, Z. Guo, Low-rate image compression with super-resolution learning, in *Proceedings of the IEEE/CVF Conference on Computer Vision and Pattern Recognition Workshops* (2020), pp. 154–155
9. W. Gao, S. Sun, H. Zheng, Y. Wu, H. Ye, Y. Zhang, Opendmc: an open-source library and performance evaluation for deep-learning-based multi-frame compression, in *Proceedings of the 31st ACM International Conference on Multimedia* (2023), pp. 9685–9688
10. Y. Guo, W. Gao, G. Li, Interpretable task-inspired adaptive filter pruning for neural networks under multiple constraints. Int. J. Comput. Vis. **132**(6), 2060–2076 (2024)
11. W. Gao, Y. Guo, S. Ma, G. Li, S. Kwong, Efficient neural network compression inspired by compressive sensing. IEEE Trans. Neural Netw. Learn. Syst. **35**(2), 1965–1979 (2024)
12. Y. Guo, W. Gao, Semantic-driven automatic filter pruning for neural networks, in *2022 IEEE international conference on multimedia and expo (ICME)* (IEEE, Piscataway, 2022), pp. 1–6
13. L. Tao, W. Gao, Efficient channel pruning based on architecture alignment and probability model bypassing, in *2021 IEEE International Conference on Systems, Man, and Cybernetics (SMC)* (IEEE, Piscataway, 2021), pp. 3232–3237
14. Z. Yang, W. Gao, G. Li, Y. Yan, Sur-driven video coding rate control for jointly optimizing perceptual quality and buffer control. IEEE Trans. Image Process. **32**, 5451–5464 (2023)
15. F. Shen, Z. Cai, W. Gao, An efficient rate control algorithm for intra frame coding in AVS3, in *2021 IEEE International Conference on Systems, Man, and Cybernetics (SMC)* (IEEE, Piscataway, 2021), pp. 3164–3169
16. H. Yuan, W. Gao, J. Wang, Dynamic computational resource allocation for fast inter frame coding in video conferencing applications, in *2021 IEEE International Conference on Multimedia and Expo (ICME)* (IEEE, Piscataway, 2021), pp. 1–6
17. W. Gao, Q. Jiang, R. Wang, S. Ma, G. Li, S. Kwong, Consistent quality oriented rate control in hevc via balancing intra and inter frame coding. IEEE Trans. Ind. Inform. **18**(3), 1594–1604 (2021)
18. H. Yuan, W. Gao, A new coding unit partitioning mode for screen content video coding, in *Proceedings of the 2021 5th International Conference on Digital Signal Processing* (2021), pp. 66–72
19. W. Gao, On the performance evaluation of state-of-the-art rate control algorithms for practical video coding and transmission systems, in *Proceedings of the 2020 4th International Conference on Video and Image Processing* (2020), pp. 179–185
20. W. Gao, S. Kwong, Q. Jiang, C.-K. Fong, P.H. Wong, W. Y. Yuen, Data-driven rate control for rate-distortion optimization in HEVC based on simplified effective initial QP learning. IEEE Trans. Broadcasting **65**(1), 94–108 (2018)
21. W. Gao, A multi-objective optimization perspective for joint consideration of video coding quality, in *2019 Asia-Pacific Signal and Information Processing Association Annual Summit and Conference (APSIPA ASC)* (IEEE, Piscataway, 2019), pp. 986–991
22. W. Gao, S. Kwong, Y. Jia, Joint machine learning and game theory for rate control in high efficiency video coding. IEEE Trans. Image Process. **26**(12), 6074–6089 (2017)
23. W. Gao, S. Kwong, Y. Zhou, H. Yuan, Ssim-based game theory approach for rate-distortion optimized intra frame CTU-level bit allocation. IEEE Trans. Multimedia **18**(6), 988–999 (2016)
24. W. Gao, S. Kwong, H. Yuan, X. Wang, DCT coefficient distribution modeling and quality dependency analysis based frame-level bit allocation for HEVC. IEEE Trans. Circuits Syst. Video Technol. **26**(1), 139–153 (2015)

25. W. Gao, S. Kwong, Phase congruency based edge saliency detection and rate control for perceptual image and video coding, in *2016 IEEE International Conference on Systems, Man, and Cybernetics (SMC)* (IEEE, Piscataway, 2016), pp. 000264–000269
26. H. Yuan, W. Gao, Openfastvc: an open source library for video coding fast algorithm implementation, in *Proceedings of the 31st ACM International Conference on Multimedia* (2023), pp. 9660–9663
27. H. Yuan, W. Gao, S. Ma, Y. Yan, Divide-and-conquer-based RDO-free CU partitioning for 8k video compression. ACM Trans. Multimedia Comput. Commun. Appl. **20**(4), 1–20 (2024)
28. L. Tao, W. Gao, A hardware implementation of entropy encoder for 8k video coding, in *2022 IEEE International Conference on Multimedia and Expo (ICME)* (IEEE, Piscataway, 2022), pp. 1–6
29. Y. Guo, W. Gao, S. Ma, G. Li, Accelerating transform algorithm implementation for efficient intra coding of 8k UHD videos. ACM Trans. Multimedia Comput. Commun. Appl. **18**(4), 1–20 (2022)
30. Z. Cai, W. Gao, Efficient fast algorithm and parallel hardware architecture for intra prediction of AVS3, in *2021 IEEE International Symposium on Circuits and Systems (ISCAS)* (IEEE, Piscataway, 2021), pp. 1–5
31. W. Gao, H. Yuan, Y. Guo, L. Tao, Z. Cai, G. Li, Openhardwarevc: an open source library for 8k UHD video coding hardware implementation, in *Proceedings of the 30th ACM International Conference on Multimedia* (2022), pp. 7339–7342
32. W. Gao, H. Yuan, G. Liao, Z. Guo, J. Chen, Pp8k: a new dataset for 8k UHD video compression and processing. *IEEE MultiMedia* **30**(3), 100–109 (2023)
33. W. Liu, W. Gao, G. Li, S. Ma, T. Zhao, H. Yuan, Enlarged motion-aware and frequency-aware network for compressed video artifact reduction. IEEE Trans. Circuits Syst. Video Technol. **34**(10), 10339–10352 (2024)
34. X. Zang, W. Gao, G. Li, H. Fang, C. Ban, Z. He, H. Sun, A baseline investigation: transformer-based cross-view baseline for text-based person search, in *Proceedings of the 31st ACM International Conference on Multimedia* (2023), pp. 7737–7746
35. G. Liao, W. Gao, G. Li, J. Wang, S. Kwong, Cross-collaborative fusion-encoder network for robust RGB-thermal salient object detection. IEEE Trans. Circuits Syst. Video Technol. **32**(11), 7646–7661 (2022)
36. W. Gao, G. Liao, S. Ma, G. Li, Y. Liang, W. Lin, Unified information fusion network for multi-modal RGB-D and RGB-T salient object detection. IEEE Trans. Circuits Syst. Video Technol. **32**(4), 2091–2106 (2021)
37. Y. Chen, S. Sun, G. Li, W. Gao, T.H. Li, Closing the gap between theory and practice during alternating optimization for GANs. IEEE Trans. Neural Netw. Learn. Syst. **35**(10), 14005–14017 (2023)
38. Y. Chen, C. Jin, G. Li, T.H. Li, W. Gao, Mitigating label noise in GANs via enhanced spectral normalization. IEEE Trans. Circuits Syst. Video Technol. **33**(8), 3924–3934 (2023)
39. X. Zang, G. Li, W. Gao, Multidirection and multiscale pyramid in transformer for video-based pedestrian retrieval. IEEE Trans. Ind. Inform. **18**(12), 8776–8785 (2022)
40. X. Zang, G. Li, W. Gao, X. Shu, Learning to disentangle scenes for person re-identification. Image Vis. Comput. **116**, 104330 (2021)
41. X. Zang, G. Li, W. Gao, X. Shu, Exploiting robust unsupervised video person re-identification. IET Image Process. **16**(3), 729–741 (2022)
42. Z. Yue, G. Li, W. Gao, Cross-level guided attention for human-object interaction detection, in *2023 IEEE International Conference on Multimedia and Expo Workshops (ICMEW)* (IEEE, Piscataway, 2023), pp. 284–289
43. Z. Yao, W. Gao, Iterative saliency aggregation and assignment network for efficient salient object detection in optical remote sensing images. IEEE Trans. Geosci. Remote Sensing (2024)
44. Y. Sun, Z. Li, S. Wang, W. Gao, Depth-assisted calibration on learning-based factorization for a compressive light field display. Opt. Express **31**(4), 5399–5413 (2023)

45. Y. Sun, Z. Li, L. Li, S. Wang, W. Gao, Optimization of compressive light field display in dual-guided learning, in *ICASSP 2022-2022 IEEE International Conference on Acoustics, Speech and Signal Processing (ICASSP)* (IEEE, Piscataway, 2022), pp. 2075–2079
46. W. Gao, S. Fan, G. Li, W. Lin, A thorough benchmark and a new model for light field saliency detection. IEEE Trans. Pattern Anal. Mach. Intell. (2023).
47. Z. Li, G. Li, T. Li, S. Liu, W. Gao, Information-growth attention network for image super-resolution, in *Proceedings of the 29th ACM International Conference on Multimedia* (2021), pp. 544–552
48. L. Zhou, W. Gao, G. Li, H. Yuan, T. Zhao, G. Yue, Disentangled feature distillation for light field super-resolution with degradations, in *2023 IEEE International Conference on Multimedia and Expo Workshops (ICMEW)* (IEEE, Piscataway, 2023), pp. 116–121
49. L. Zhou, W. Gao, G. Li, End-to-end spatial-angular light field super-resolution using parallax structure preservation strategy, in *2022 IEEE International Conference on Image Processing (ICIP)* (IEEE, Piscataway, 2023), pp. 3396–3400
50. W. Gao, L. Zhou, L. Tao, A fast view synthesis implementation method for light field applications. ACM Trans. Multimedia Comput. Commun. Appl. **17**(4), 1–20 (2021)
51. X. Zhang, W. Gao, G. Li, Q. Jiang, R. Cong, Image quality assessment–driven reinforcement learning for mixed distorted image restoration. ACM Trans. Multimedia Comput. Commun. Appl. **19**(1s), 1–23 (2023)
52. X. Zhang, W. Gao, H. Yuan, G. Li, Je 2 net: joint exploitation and exploration in reinforcement learning based image restoration, in *ICASSP 2022-2022 IEEE International Conference on Acoustics, Speech and Signal Processing (ICASSP)* (IEEE, Piscataway, 2022), pp. 2090–2094
53. X. Zhang, W. Gao, Hirl: hybrid image restoration based on hierarchical deep reinforcement learning via two-step analysis, in *ICASSP 2022-2022 IEEE International Conference on Acoustics, Speech and Signal Processing (ICASSP)* (IEEE, Piscataway, 2022), pp. 2445–2449
54. Z. Guo, W. Gao, H. Wang, J. Wang, S. Fan, No-reference deep quality assessment of compressed light field images, in *2021 IEEE International Conference on Multimedia and Expo (ICME)* (IEEE, Piscataway, 2021), pp. 1–6
55. G. Liao, W. Gao, Rethinking feature mining for light field salient object detection. ACM Trans. Multimedia Comput. Commun. Appl. (2024)
56. S. Sun, J. Liu, T.H. Li, H. Li, G. Liu, W. Gao, Streamflow: streamlined multi-frame optical flow estimation for video sequences (2023). arXiv preprint arXiv:2311.17099
57. R. Liu, J. Huang, W. Gao, T.H. Li, G. Li, Mug-stan: adapting image-language pretrained models for general video understanding (2023). arXiv preprint arXiv:2311.15075
58. C. Zhang, W. Gao, Learned rate control for frame-level adaptive neural video compression via dynamic neural network, in *European Conference on Computer Vision* (Springer, Berlin, 2024)
59. W. Gao, G. Li, H. Yuan, R. Hamzaoui, Z. Li, S. Liu, Apccpa'22: 1st international workshop on advances in point cloud compression, processing and analysis, in *Proceedings of the 30th ACM International Conference on Multimedia* (2022), pp. 7392–7393
60. K. Wen, N. Zhang, G. Li, W. Gao, MPVNN: multi-resolution point-voxel non-parametric network for 3d point cloud processing, in *2024 IEEE International Conference on Multimedia and Expo (ICME)* (IEEE, Piscataway, 2024)
61. W. Liu, W. Gao, X. Mu, Fast inter-frame motion prediction for compressed dynamic point cloud attribute enhancement, in *Proceedings of the AAAI Conference on Artificial Intelligence*, vol. 38, no. 4 (2024), pp. 3720–3728
62. Z. Yang, W. Gao, X. Lu, Danet: density-adaptive network for geometry-based point cloud compression artifacts removal, in *2023 IEEE International Conference on Visual Communications and Image Processing (VCIP)* (IEEE, Piscataway, 2023), pp. 1–5
63. X. Fan, G. Li, D. Li, Y. Ren, W. Gao, T.H. Li, Deep geometry post-processing for decompressed point clouds, in *2022 IEEE International Conference on Multimedia and Expo (ICME)* (IEEE, Piscataway, 2022), pp. 1–6

64. X. Zhang, G. Liao, W. Gao, G. Li, Tdrnet: Transformer-based dual-branch restoration network for geometry based point cloud compression artifacts, in *2022 IEEE International Conference on Multimedia and Expo (ICME)* (IEEE, Piscataway, 2022), pp. 1–6
65. R. Zhang, W. Gao, G. Li, T.H. Li, Qinet: decision surface learning and adversarial enhancement for quasi-immune completion of diverse corrupted point clouds. IEEE Trans. Geosci. Remote Sensing **60**, 1–14 (2022)
66. R. Bao, Y. Ren, G. Li, W. Gao, S. Liu, Flow-based point cloud completion network with adversarial refinement, in *ICASSP 2022-2022 IEEE International Conference on Acoustics, Speech and Signal Processing (ICASSP)* (IEEE, Piscataway, 2022), pp. 2559–2563
67. Z. Li, G. Li, T.H. Li, S. Liu, W. Gao, Semantic point cloud upsampling. IEEE Trans. Multimedia **25**, 3432–3442 (2022)
68. X. Lu and W. Gao, Attentivenet: detecting small objects for LiDAR point clouds by attending to important points, in *2023 IEEE International Conference on Visual Communications and Image Processing (VCIP)* (IEEE, Piscataway, 2023), pp. 1–5
69. D. Yang, W. Gao, G. Li, H. Yuan, J. Hou, S. Kwong, Exploiting manifold feature representation for efficient classification of 3d point clouds. ACM Trans. Multimedia Comput. Commun. Appl. **19**(1s), 1–21 (2023)
70. Z. Pan, N. Zhang, W. Gao, S. Liu, G. Li, Less is more: label recommendation for weakly supervised point cloud semantic segmentation, in *Proceedings of the AAAI Conference on Artificial Intelligence*, vol. 38, no. 5 (2024), pp. 4397–4405
71. Z. Pan, G. Liu, W. Gao, T. Li, Epcontrast: effective point-level contrastive learning for large-scale point cloud understanding, in *2024 IEEE International Conference on Multimedia and Expo (ICME)* (IEEE, Piscataway, 2024)
72. N. Zhang, Z. Pan, T.H. Li, W. Gao, G. Li, Improving graph representation for point cloud segmentation via attentive filtering, in *Proceedings of the IEEE/CVF Conference on Computer Vision and Pattern Recognition* (2023), pp. 1244–1254
73. S. Fan, W. Gao, G. Li, Salient object detection for point clouds, in *European Conference on Computer Vision* (2022), pp. 1–19
74. W. Gao, H. Ye, G. Li, H. Zheng, Y. Wu, L. Xie, OpenPointCloud: an open-source algorithm library of deep learning based point cloud compression, in *ACM International Conference on Multimedia* (2022), pp. 7347–7350
75. Y. Zhang, W. Gao, G. Li, Openpointcloud-v2: a deep learning based open-source algorithm library of point cloud processing, in *Proceedings of the 1st International Workshop on Advances in Point Cloud Compression, Processing and Analysis* (2022), pp. 51–55
76. S. Fan, W. Gao, Screen-based 3d subjective experiment software, in *Proceedings of the 31st ACM International Conference on Multimedia* (2023), pp. 9672–9675
77. X. Mao, H. Yuan, X. Lu, R. Hamzaoui, W. Gao, PCAC-GAN: a sparse-tensor-based generative adversarial network for 3d point cloud attribute compression. Comput. Visual Media (2024)
78. J. Wang, W. Gao, G. Li, Applying collaborative adversarial learning to blind point cloud quality measurement. IEEE Trans. Instrument. Measur. (2023)
79. T. Qin, G. Li, W. Gao, S. Liu, Multi-grained point cloud geometry compression via dual-model prediction with extended octree. ACM Trans. Multimedia Comput. Commun. Appl. (2024)
80. Y. Shao, W. Gao, S. Liu, G. Li, Advanced patch-based affine motion estimation for dynamic point cloud geometry compression. Sensors **24**(10), 3142 (2024)
81. Y. Shao, F. Song, W. Gao, S. Liu, G. Li, Texture-guided graph transform optimization for point cloud attribute compression. Appl. Sci. **14**(10), 4094 (2024)
82. Y. Shao, X. Yang, W. Gao, S. Liu, G. Li, 3d point cloud attribute compression using diffusion-based texture-aware intra prediction, in *IEEE Transactions on Circuits and Systems for Video Technology* (2024)

83. J. Zhang, Y. Chen, G. Liu, W. Gao, G. Li, Efficient point cloud attribute compression framework using attribute-guided graph Fourier transform, in *ICASSP 2024-2024 IEEE International Conference on Acoustics, Speech and Signal Processing (ICASSP)* (IEEE, Piscataway, 2024), pp. 8426–8430
84. W. Gao, H. Yuan, G. Li, Z. Li, H. Yuan, Low complexity coding unit decision for video-based point cloud compression. IEEE Trans. Image Proc. **33**, 149–162 (2023)
85. Y. Shao, G. Li, Q. Zhang, W. Gao, S. Liu, Non-rigid registration-based progressive motion compensation for point cloud geometry compression. IEEE Trans. Geosci. Remote Sensing (2023)
86. F. Song, G. Li, X. Yang, W. Gao, S. Liu, Block-adaptive point cloud attribute coding with region-aware optimized transform. IEEE Trans. Circuits Syst. Video Technol. **33**, 4294–4308 (2023)
87. Y. An, Y. Shao, G. Li, W. Gao, S. Liu, A fast motion estimation method with hamming distance for LiDAR point cloud compression, in *2022 IEEE International Conference on Visual Communications and Image Processing (VCIP)* (IEEE, Piscataway, 2022), pp. 1–5
88. H. Yuan, W. Gao, G. Li, Z. Li, Rate-distortion-guided learning approach with cross-projection information for V-PCC fast CU decision, in *Proceedings of the 30th ACM International Conference on Multimedia* (2022), pp. 3085–3093
89. F. Song, G. Li, W. Gao, T.H. Li, Rate-distortion optimized graph for point cloud attribute coding. IEEE Signal Process. Lett. **29**, 922–926 (2022)
90. F. Song, G. Li, X. Yang, W. Gao, T.H. Li, Fine-grained correlation representation for graph-based point cloud attribute compression, in *2022 IEEE International Conference on Multimedia and Expo (ICME)* (IEEE, Piscataway, 2022), pp. 1–6
91. F. Shen, W. Gao, A rate control algorithm for video-based point cloud compression, in *2021 International Conference on Visual Communications and Image Processing (VCIP)* (IEEE, Piscataway, 2021), pp. 1–5
92. F. Song, Y. Shao, W. Gao, H. Wang, T. Li, Layer-wise geometry aggregation framework for lossless LiDAR point cloud compression. IEEE Trans. Circuits Syst. Video Technol. **31**(12), 4603–4616 (2021)
93. L. Xie, W. Gao, H. Zheng, G. Li, Spcgc: scalable point cloud geometry compression for machine vision, in *Proceedings of IEEE International Conference on Robotics and Automation* (2024)
94. L. Xie, W. Gao, H. Zheng, H. Ye, Semantic-aware visual decomposition for point cloud geometry compression, in *2024 Data Compression Conference (DCC)* (IEEE, Piscataway, 2024), pp. 595–595
95. Z. Qi, W. Gao, Variable-rate point cloud geometry compression based on feature adjustment and interpolation, in *2024 Data Compression Conference (DCC)* (IEEE, Piscataway, 2024), pp. 63–72
96. Z. Yu, W. Gao, When dynamic neural network meets point cloud compression: computation-aware variable rate and checkerboard context, in *2024 Data Compression Conference (DCC)* (IEEE, Piscataway, 2024), p. 600
97. L. Xie, W. Gao, S. Fan, Z. Yao, Pdnet: parallel dual-branch network for point cloud geometry compression and analysis, in *2024 Data Compression Conference (DCC)* (IEEE, Piscataway, 2024), pp. 596–596
98. L. Xie, W. Gao, H. Zheng, End-to-end point cloud geometry compression and analysis with sparse tensor, in *Proceedings of the 1st International Workshop on Advances in Point Cloud Compression, Processing and Analysis* (2022), pp. 27–32
99. C. Fu, G. Li, R. Song, W. Gao, S. Liu, OctAttention: octree-based large-scale contexts model for point cloud compression, in *AAAI Conference on Artificial Intelligence* (2022), pp. 625–633
100. H. Zheng, W. Gao, Z. Yu, T. Zhao, G. Li, Viewpcgc: view-guided learned point cloud geometry compression, in *Proceedings of the 32nd ACM International Conference on Multimedia* (2024)

101. L. Xie, W. Gao, H. Zheng, G. Li, Roi-guided point cloud geometry compression towards human and machine vision, in *Proceedings of the 32nd ACM International Conference on Multimedia* (2024)
102. C. Peng, W. Gao, Laplacian matrix learning for point cloud attribute compression with ternary search-based adaptive block partition, in *Proceedings of the 32nd ACM International Conference on Multimedia* (2024)
103. S. Luo, B. Qu, W. Gao, Learning robust 3d representation from clip via dual denoising (2024). arXiv preprint arXiv:2407.00905
104. G. Li, G. Wei, W. Gao, *Point Cloud Compression: Technologies and Standardization* (Springer, Berlin, 2024)
105. G. Li, W. Gao, W. Gao, Introduction, in *Point Cloud Compression: Technologies and Standardization* (Springer, Berlin, 2024), pp. 1–28
106. G. Li, W. Gao, W. Gao, Background knowledge, in *Point Cloud Compression: Technologies and Standardization* (Springer, Berlin, 2024), pp. 29–51
107. G. Li, W. Gao, W. Gao, Predictive coding, in *Point Cloud Compression: Technologies and Standardization* (Springer, Berlin, 2024), pp. 53–70
108. G. Li, W. Gao, W. Gao, Transform coding, in *Point Cloud Compression: Technologies and Standardization* (Springer, Berlin, 2024), pp. 71–96
109. G. Li, W. Gao, W. Gao, Quantization techniques, in *Point Cloud Compression: Technologies and Standardization* (Springer, Berlin, 2024), pp. 97–112
110. G. Li, W. Gao, W. Gao, Entropy coding, in *Point Cloud Compression: Technologies and Standardization* (Springer, Berlin, 2024), pp. 113–133
111. G. Li, W. Gao, W. Gao, MPEG geometry-based point cloud compression (G-PCC) standard, in *Point Cloud Compression: Technologies and Standardization* (Springer, Berlin, 2024), pp. 135–165
112. G. Li, W. Gao, W. Gao, AVS point cloud compression standard, in *Point Cloud Compression: Technologies and Standardization* (Springer, Berlin, 2024), pp. 167–197
113. G. Li, W. Gao, W. Gao, MPEG video-based point cloud compression (V-PCC) standard, in *Point Cloud Compression: Technologies and Standardization* (Springer, Berlin, 2024), pp. 199–218
114. G. Li, W. Gao, W. Gao, MPEG Ai-based 3d graphics coding standard, in *Point Cloud Compression: Technologies and Standardization* (Springer, Berlin, 2024), pp. 219–241
115. G. Li, W. Gao, W. Gao, Future work, in *Point Cloud Compression: Technologies and Standardization* (Springer, Berlin, 2024), pp. 243–250
116. J. Chen, G. Li, R. Zhang, T.H. Li, W. Gao, Pointivae: invertible variational autoencoder framework for 3d point cloud generation, in *2022 IEEE International Conference on Image Processing (ICIP)* (IEEE, Piscataway, 2022), pp. 3216–3220
117. R. Zhang, J. Chen, W. Gao, G. Li, T.H. Li, Pointot: interpretable geometry-inspired point cloud generative model via optimal transport. IEEE Trans. Circuits Syst. Video Technol. **32**(10), 6792–6806 (2022)
118. S. Luo, W. Gao, A general framework for rotation invariant point cloud analysis, in *ICASSP 2024-2024 IEEE International Conference on Acoustics, Speech and Signal Processing (ICASSP)* (IEEE, Piscataway, 2024), pp. 3665–3669

Index

W. Gao, G. Li, *Deep Learning for 3D Point Clouds*,
https://doi.org/10.1007/978-981-97-9570-3

www.ingramcontent.com/pod-product-compliance
Lightning Source LLC
Chambersburg PA
CBHW050812231224
19414CB00011B/8

9 789819 795697